# Python

## ALL-IN-ONE

by John Shovic and Alan Simpson

A Wiley Brand

## Python All-in-One For Dummies®

Published by: **John Wiley & Sons, Inc.**, 111 River Street, Hoboken, NJ 07030-5774, www.wiley.com

Copyright © 2019 by John Wiley & Sons, Inc., Hoboken, New Jersey

Published simultaneously in Canada

For general information on our other products and services, please contact our Customer Care Department within the U.S. at 877-762-2974, outside the U.S. at 317-572-3993, or fax 317-572-4002. For technical support, please visit https://hub.wiley.com/community/support/dummies.

Wiley publishes in a variety of print and electronic formats and by print-on-demand. Some material included with standard print versions of this book may not be included in e-books or in print-on-demand. If this book refers to media such as a CD or DVD that is not included in the version you purchased, you may download this material at http://booksupport.wiley.com. For more information about Wiley products, visit www.wiley.com.

Library of Congress Control Number: 2019937504

ISBN 978-1-119-55759-3 (pbk); ISBN 978-1-119-55767-8 (ebk); ISBN 978-1-119-55761-6 (ebk)

Manufactured in the United States of America

C10009343_041019

# Contents at a Glance

# Table of Contents

# Introduction

The power of Python. The Python language is becoming more and more popular, and in 2017 it became the most popular language in the world according to IEEE Spectrum. The power of Python is real.

Why is Python the number one language? Because it is incredibly easy to learn and use. Part of it is its simplified syntax and its natural-language flow, but a lot of it has to do with the amazing user community and the breadth of applications available.

## About This Book

This book is a reference manual to guide you through the process of learning Python and how to use it in modern computer applications, such as data science, artificial intelligence, physical computing, and robotics. If you are looking to learn a little about a lot of exciting things, then this is the book for you. It gives you an introduction to the topics that you will need to go deeper into any of these areas of technology.

This book guides you through the Python language and then it takes you on a tour through some really cool libraries and technologies (the Raspberry Pi, robotics, AI, data science, and so on) all revolving around the Python language. When you work on new projects and new technologies, Python is there for you with an incredibly diverse number of libraries just waiting for you to use.

This is a hands-on book. There are examples and code all throughout the book. You are expected to take the code, run it, and then modify it to do what you want. You don't just buy a robot, you build it so you can understand all the pieces and can make sense of the way Python works with the robot to control all the motors and sensors. Artificial intelligence is complicated, but Python helps make a significant part of it accessible. Data science is complicated, but Python helps you do data science more easily. Robotics is complicated, but Python gives you the code that controls the robot. And Python even allows us to tie these pieces together and use, say, AI in robotics.

In this book, we take you through the basics of the Python language in small, easy-to-understand steps. After we have introduced you to the language, then we step into the world of Python and artificial intelligence, exploring programming in machine learning and neural networks using Python and TensorFlow and actually working on real problems and real software, not just toy applications.

After that, we're off to the exciting world of Big Data and data science with Python. We look at big public data sets such as medical and environmental data all using Python.

Finally, you get to experience the magic of what I call "physical computing." Using the small, inexpensive Raspberry Pi computer (it's small, but incredibly popular) we show you how to use Python to control motors and read sensors. This is a lead-up to our final book, "Python and Robotics." Here you learn how to build a robot and how to control that robot with Python and your own programs, even using artificial intelligence.

This is not your mother's RC car.

Python data science, robotics, AI, and fun all in the same book.

This book won't make you understand everything about these fields, but it will give you a great introduction to the terminology and the power of Python in all these fields. Enjoy the book and go forth and learn more afterwards.

## Foolish Assumptions

We assume you know how to use a computer in a very basic way. If you can turn on the computer and use a mouse, you're ready for this book. We assume you don't know how to program yet, although you will have some skills in programming by the end of the book. If we're wrong and you do already know Python (or some other computer language), jump ahead to minibook 4 and dig right into learning something new. Our intent is to guide you through the language of Python and then through some of the amazing technologies and devices that use Python. We provide complete examples. If you get stuck on something, look it up on the web, read a tutorial, and then come back to it.

## Icons Used in This Book

What's a *For Dummies* book without icons pointing you in the direction of truly helpful information that's sure to speed you along your way? Here we briefly describe each icon we use in this book.

TIP

The Tip icon points out helpful information that's likely to make your job easier.

REMEMBER

This icon marks a generally interesting and useful fact — something you may want to remember for later use.

WARNING

The Warning icon highlights lurking danger. When we use this icon, we're telling you to pay attention and proceed with caution.

TECHNICAL
STUFF

When you see this icon, you know that there's techie-type material nearby. If you're not feeling technical-minded, you can skip this information.

# Beyond the Book

In addition to the material in the print or ebook you're reading right now, this product also comes with some access-anywhere goodies on the web. No matter how well you understand Python concepts, you'll likely come across a few questions where you don't have a clue. To get this material, simply go to www.dummies. com and search for "*Python All-in-One For Dummies* Cheat Sheet" in the Search box.

# Where to Go from Here

*Python All-in-One For Dummies* is designed so that you can read a chapter or section out of order, depending on what subjects you're most interested in. Where you go from here is entirely up to you!

Book 1 is a great place to start reading if you've never used Python before. Discovering the basics and common terminology can be quite helpful for later chapters that use the terms and commands regularly!

Occasionally, we have updates to our technology books. If this book does have any technical updates, they'll be posted at www.dummies.com/go/pythonaiofdupdates.

# 1

# Getting Started with Python

# Contents at a Glance

# Chapter **1**

# Starting with Python

The fact that you're reading this implies you know that Python is a great thing to know if you're looking for a good job in programming. It's also good to know if you're looking to expand your existing programming skills into exciting cutting-edge technologies like artificial intelligence (AI), machine learning (ML), data science, or robotics, or even if you're just building apps in general. So we're not going to try to sell you on Python. It sells itself.

Our approach, especially in this book, leans heavily toward the hands-on. A common failure in many tutorials is that they already assume you're a professional programmer in Python or some other language, and they skip over things they assume you already know.

This book is different in that we *don't* assume you're already programming in Python or some other language. We assume you can use a computer and understand basics like files and folders. But that's about it for assumptions.

We also assume you're not up for settling down in an easy chair in front of the fireplace to read page after page of theoretical stuff "about" Python, like some kind of novel. You don't have that much free time to kill. So we're going to get right into it and focus on *doing*, hands-on, because that's the only way most of us learn. Personally, we've never seen anybody read a book "about" Python and then sit at a computer and write Python like a pro. Human brains don't work that way. We learn through practice and repetition, and that requires hands-on.

# Why Python Is Hot

We promised we weren't going to spend a bunch of time trying to "sell" you on Python, and that's not our intent here. Python is hot — that's probably why you want to learn it, and that's good. But we would like to talk briefly about *why* it's so hot.

Python is hot primarily because it has all the right stuff for the kind of software development that's really driving the whole software development world these days. Machine learning, robotics, artificial intelligence, and data science are the leading technologies today and for the foreseeable future. Python is popular mainly because it already has lots of capabilities in those areas, while many older languages lag behind in these technologies.

If you're not familiar with programming languages like C and Java, feel free to skip to the next section, "Python versions," as this information is only for people who wonder about differences among the languages. But in case you're wondering, just as there are different brands of toothpaste, shampoo, cars, and just about every other product you can buy, there are different "brands" of programming languages with names like Java, C, C++ (*pronounced C plus plus*), and C# (*pronounced C sharp*). They're all programming languages, just like all brands of toothpaste are toothpaste. The main reasons cited for Python's current popularity are

>> Python is relatively easy to learn.

>> Everything you need to learn (and do) Python is free.

>> Python offers more readymade tools for current hot technologies like data science, machine learning, artificial intelligence, and robotics than most other languages.

## HTML, CSS, AND JavaScript

Some of you may have heard of languages like HTML, CSS and JavaScript. Those aren't traditional programming languages for developing apps or other generic software. HTML and CSS are specialized for developing Web pages. JavaScript is a programming language; however, it too is heavily geared to Website development and isn't quite in the same category of general programming languages like Python and Java.

Another way to look at it is, you wouldn't learn HTML, CSS, and JavaScript instead of Python, as there is too little overlap to justify it. If you specifically want to design and create websites, you have to learn HTML, CSS, and JavaScript whether you're already familiar with Python or some other programming language.

Figure 1-1 shows Google search trends over the last five years. As you can see, Python has been gaining in popularity (as indicated by the upward slope of the trend) whereas other languages have stayed about the same or declined. This certainly supports the notion that Python is the language people want to learn right now and for the future. Most people would agree that given trends in modern computing, learning Python gives you the best opportunity for getting a secure, high-paying job in the world of information technology.

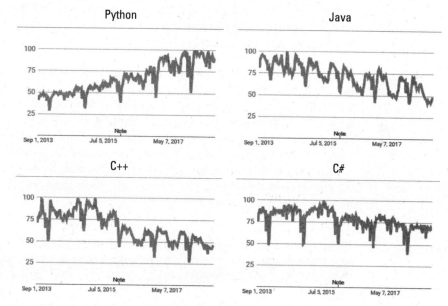

**FIGURE 1-1:**
Google search trends for the last five years or so.

**TIP** You can do your own Google trend searches at `https://trends.google.com`.

# Choosing the Right Python

There are different *versions* of Python out roaming the world, prompting many a beginner to wonder things like

>> Why are there different versions?

>> How are they different?

>> Which one should I learn?

All good questions, and we'll start with the first. A version is kind of like a car year. You can go out a buy a 1968 Ford Mustang or a 1990 Ford Mustang or a 2000 Ford Mustangs, and a 2019 Ford Mustang, They're all Ford Mustangs. The only difference is that the one with the highest year number is the most "current" Ford Mustang. That Mustang is different from the older models in that it has some improvements based on experience with earlier models, as well as features that are current with the times.

Programming languages (and most other software products) work the same way. But as a rule we don't ascribe year numbers to them, because they're not released on a yearly basis. They're released whenever they're released. But the principle is the same. The version with the highest number us the newest, most recent "model," sporting improvements based on experience with earlier versions, as well as features that are relevant to the current times.

Just as we use a decimal point with money to separate dollars from cents, we use decimal points with version numbers to indicate "how much it's changed." When there's a significant change, the whole version number is usually changed. More minor changes are expressed as decimal points. You can see how the version number increases along with the year in Table 1-1, which shows the release dates of various Python versions. We've skipped a few releases here because there is little reason to know or understand the differences between all the versions. We only present the table so you can see how newer versions have higher version numbers; that's all that matters.

**TABLE 1-1**　　## Examples of Python Versions and Release Dates

| Version | When Released |
| --- | --- |
| Python 3.7 | June 2018 |
| Python 3.6 | December 2016. |
| Python 3.5 | September 2015 |
| Python 3.4 | March 2014 |
| Python 3.3 | September 2012 |
| Python 3.2 | February 2011 |
| Python 3.1 | September 2012 |
| Python 3.0 | December 2008 |
| Python 2.7 | July 2010 |
| Python 2.6 | October 2008 |
| Python 2.0 | October 2000. |
| Python 1.6 | September 2000. |
| Python 1.5 | February 1998 |
| Python 1.0 | January 1994 |

If you paid close attention you may notice that Version 3.0 starts in December 2008, but Version 2.7 extends into 2010. So if versions are like car years, why the overlap?

The car years analogy is just an analogy indicating that the larger the number, the more recent the version. But in Python it's the most recent within the main Python version. When the first number changes, that's usually a change that's so significant, software written in prior versions may not even work in that version. If you happen to be a software company with a product, written in Python 2, on the market, and have millions of dollars invested in that product, you may not be too thrilled to have to start over from scratch to go with the current version. So "older versions" often continue to be supported and evolve, independent of the most recent version, to support developers and businesses that are already heavily invested in the previous version.

The biggest question on most beginners minds is "what version should I learn?" The answer to that is simple . . . whatever is the most current version. You'll know what that is because when you go to the Python.org website to download Python, they will tell you what the most current stable build (version) is. That's the one they'll recommend, and that's the one you should use.

The only reason to learn something like Version 2 or 2.7 or something else older would be if you've already been hired to work on some project, and that company requires you to learn and use a specific version. That sort of thing is rare, because as a beginner you're not likely to already have a full-time job as a programmer. But in the messy real world there are companies heavily invested in some earlier version of a product, so when hiring, they'll be looking for people with knowledge of that version.

In this book, we focus on versions of Python that are current in late 2018 and early 2019, from Python 3.7 and above. Don't worry about version differences after the first and second digits. Version 3.7.2 is similar enough go version 3.7.1 that it's not important, especially to a beginner. Likewise, Version 3.8 isn't that big a jump from 3.7. So don't worry about these miner version differences when first learning. Most of what's in Python is the across all versions. So you need not worry about investing time in learning a version that's obsolete or soon will be — unless you happen to be learning from a very old book.

# Tools for Success

Now, we need to start getting your computer set up so you *can* learn, and do, Python hands-on. For one, you'll need a good Python interpreter and editor. The editor lets you type the code, the interpreter lets you run that code. When you run (or execute) code, you're telling the computer to "do whatever my code tells you to do."

**TECHNICAL STUFF**

The term *code* refers to anything written in a programming language to provide instructions to a computer. The term *coding* is often used to describe the act or writing code. A code editor is an app that lets you type code, in much the same way an app like Word or Pages helps you type regular plain-English text.

Just as there are many brands of toothpaste, soap, and shampoo in the worlds, there are many "brands" of code editors that work well with Python. There isn't a right one or wrong one, a good one or bad one, a best one or worst one. Just a lot of different products that basically do the same thing but vary slightly in their approach and what that editor's creators thing is "good."

If you already started learning Python on your own before this book, and are happy with whatever you've been using, you're welcome to continue using that and ignore our suggestions. If you're just getting started with this stuff, we suggest you use VS Code, because it is . . .

## An excellent, free learning environment

The editor we recommend, and will be using in this book, is called Visual Studio Code, officially. But most often you hear is spoken or written as **VS Code**. The main reasons it's our own favorite are as follows:

>> It is an excellent editor for learning coding.

>> It is an excellent editor for writing code professionally, and is in fact used by millions or professional programmers and developers.

>> It's relatively easy to learn and use.

>> It works pretty much the same on Windows, Mac, and Linux.

>> It's free.

The editor is an important part of learning and doing Python code. But you also need the Python interpreter. Chances are, you're also going to want some Python packages, too. The packages are simply code already written by someone else to do common tasks so that you don't have to start from scratch and reinvent the wheel every time you want to perform one of those tasks.

**TIP**

Python packages are not a "crutch" for beginners. They are major components of the entire Python development environment and are used by seasoned professionals as much as they are used by beginners.

Historically, managing Python, the packages, and the editor was a somewhat laborious task involving typing cryptic commands at a command prompt. Although that's not a particularly "bad" thing, it certainly isn't the most efficient way to do things, especially when you're first getting started. You end up spending most of your time upfront trying to learn and type awkward commands just to get Python to work on your computer, rather than actually learning Python itself.

An excellent alternative to the old command-line driven ways of doing thing is to use a more complete Python development environment with a more intuitive and more easily managed graphic user interface, as on a Mac or Windows or any phone or tablet. The one we recommend is called Anaconda. It is free, and it is excellent. If you've never heard of it and aren't so sure about downloading something you've never heard of, you can explore what it's all about at the Anaconda website at https://www.anaconda.com/.

Anaconda is often referred to as a data science platform because many of the packages that come with it are data-science–oriented. But don't let that worry you if you're interested in doing other things with Python. Anaconda is excellent for learning and doing all kinds of things with Python. And it also comes with VS Code, our personal favorite coding editor, as well as Jupyter Notebook, which provides another excellent means of coding with Python. And best of all, it's 100 percent free, so it's well worth the effort of downloading and installing it.

We can't really take you step-by-step through every part of downloading and installing Anaconda because it's distributed from the a website, and people change their websites whenever they feel like it. But we can certainly give you the broad strokes. You should be able to follow along, using Mac, Windows, or Linux. You just have to keep an eye on your screen as you go along, and follow any onscreen instructions as they arise, while following the steps.

## Installing Anaconda and VS Code

To download and install Anaconda, and VS Code you'll need to connect to the Internet and use a web browser. Any Web browser should do, be in Google Chrome, Firefox, Safari, Edge, Internet Explorer, or whatever. Fire up whatever browser you normally use to browse the Web, then follow these steps:

1. **Browse to** https://www.anaconda.com/download/ **to get to a page that looks something like this (don't worry about version numbers or dates, just download whatever they recommend when you get there).**

2. **Scroll down a little and you should see some download options that look something like the example shown in Figure 1-2.**

   We used a Windows computer for that screenshot, but Mac and Linux users will see something similar.

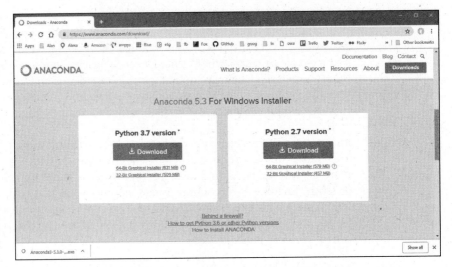

**FIGURE 1-2:**
Click Download
under the largest
version number.

3. **Click Download under whichever version number is the highest on your screen.**

   For me, right now, it's version 3.7 but a higher-numbered version may be available when you get there. Don't worry about that.

   **TIP**

   Jot down the Python version number you're downloading for future reference a little later in this chapter. You can also click How to Install ANACONDA on the download page if you'd like to see the instructions from the Anaconda team.

4. **If prompted for your email address, either provide it or click the X in the pop-up window's upper-right corner to close the prompt without entering your email address.**

5. **If you see Keep/Discard options in the lower-left corner of your screen, click Keep.**

6. **When the download is complete, open your Downloads folder (or whichever folder to which you downloaded the file).**

7. **If you're using Mac or Linux, double-click the file you downloaded. If you're using Windows, right-click that file and choose Run as Administrator, as shown in Figure 1-3.**

   **TECHNICAL STUFF**

   The Run-As-Administrator business in Windows ensures that you can install everything. If that option isn't available to you, double-clicking the file's icon should be sufficient.

8. **Click Next, Continue, Agree, or I Agree on the first installation pages until you get to one of the pages shown in Figures 1-4 (Mac will be on the one on the left, Windows the one on the right).**

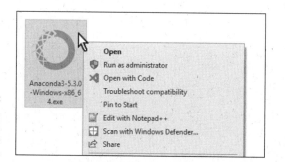

FIGURE 1-3:
In Windows,
right-click and
choose Run As
Administrator.

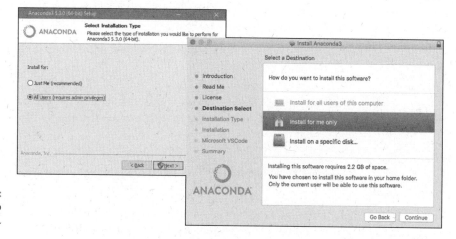

FIGURE 1-4:
Choose how to
install Anaconda.

9. Choose whichever option makes sense to you. Or, if in double, choose Install on a specific disk (for Mac), and then Macintosh HD, or choose Install for All Users (if on Windows using Administrator privileges. If the option we suggested isn't available to you, click the one closest to it.

10. Click Continue or Next and follow the onscreen instructions. If you're unsure about what options to choose on any page, don't choose any. Just accept the default suggestions.

11. It may take several minutes, but eventually you'll come to a page where it asks if you want to installed Microsoft VS Code. Click Install Microsoft VS Code (or whatever option on your screen indicates that you want to install VS Code).

TIP

If VS Code is already installed on your computer, no worries. The Anaconda installer will just tell you that, or perhaps update your version to the more current version.

12. Continue to follow any onscreen instructions, click Continue or Next to proceed through the installation steps, then click Close or Finish on the last page.

You may be prompted to sign up with Anaconda Cloud. Doing so is free, but not required. So you can decide for yourself if that's something you want to do.

## Opening Anaconda (Mac)

After it's installed on your Mac, you can open Anaconda as you would any other app. Use whichever of the following methods appeals to you:

>> Open Launchpad and open Anaconda Navigator.

>> Or click the Spotlight magnifying glass, start typing **Anaconda**, and then double-click Anaconda Navigator.

>> Or open Finder and your Applications folder and double-click the Anaconda-Navigator icon there.

After Anaconda Navigator opens, right-click its icon in the Dock and choose Keep in Dock to keep its icon visible in the Dock at all times so it's easy to find when you need it.

## Opening Anaconda (Windows)

After Anaconda is installed in Windows, you can start it as you would any other app. Although there are some differences among different versions of Windows, you should be able to use just about any of these options:

>> Click the Start button then click Anaconda Navigator on the Start menu.

>> Or click the Start button, start typing **Anaconda**, then click Anaconda-Navigator on the Start menu once you see it there.

On the Start menu you can right-click Anaconda-Navigator and choose Pin to Start or right-click and choose More⇨Pin to Taskbar to make the icon easy to find in the future.

## Using Anaconda Navigator

Anaconda Navigator, as the name implies, is the component of the Anaconda environment that lets you navigate around through different features of the app and choose what you want to run. When you first start it, it open to the Anaconda Navigator home page, which should look something like Figure 1-5.

**TIP**

If you see a prompt for getting an updated version when you open Anaconda, it's okay to install the update. It won't cost anything or affect your ability to follow along in this book.

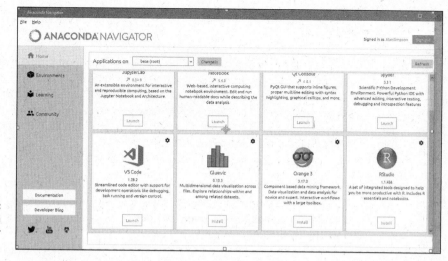

**FIGURE 1-5:**
Anaconda
Navigator
Home page.

Down the left side of the Anaconda Navigator home page you see options like Home, Environments, Learning, Community, Documentation, and Developer Blog. You're welcome to explore these on your own. However, they're not directly related to learning and doing Python, so we'll let you choose which of those, if any, you're interested in exploring.

# Writing Python in VS Code

Most of the Python coding we do here, we'll do in VS Code. Whenever you want to use VS Code to write Python, we suggest that you open VS Code from Anaconda Navigator, rather than from the Start menu or Launch Pad. That way VS Code will already be "pointing to" to version of Python that comes with Anaconda, which is easier than trying to figure out all of that yourself. So the steps are

1. If you haven't already done so, open Anaconda Navigator.

2. If necessary, scroll down a little until you see the Launch button under VS Code, then click the Launch button.

The very first time you open VS Code you may be prompted to make some decisions. None of the suggested are required, so you can just click the X in the upper-right corner of the each one. Note, however, the one that mentions Git will keep popping up at you unless you click Don't Show Again.

When you're finished, the VS Code window will look something like Figure 1-6. If you don't see quite that many options on your screen, choose Help⇨Welcome from the menu bar.

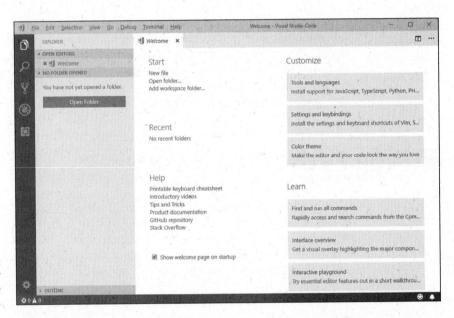

**FIGURE 1-6:** VS Code editor with welcome screen.

Your screen will likely be black with white and colored text. In this book, we show everything as white with black text because it's easier to read on paper that way. You can keep the dark background if you like. If you would rather have a light background, on a Mac click Code on the menu and choose Preferences⇨Color Theme. In Windows, choose File⇨Preferences⇨Color Theme. Then choose a lighter color theme, like Light (Visual Studio) and your VS Code screens will look more like the ones in this book.

To make sure you're ready to do Python coding, click the Extensions icons in the left pane (it looks like a puzzle piece). You should see at least three extensions listed, Anaconda Extension Pack, Python, and YAML, as shown in Figure 1-7.

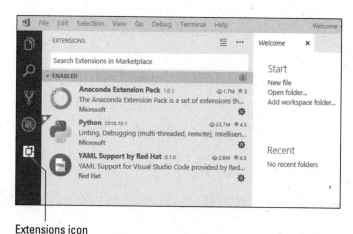

**FIGURE 1-7:**
VS Code extensions for Python.

Extensions icon

# Choosing your Python interpreter

Before you start doing any Python coding in VS Code, you want to make sure you're using the correct Python interpreter. Do to so, follow these steps:

1. **Choose View⇨Command Palette from VS Code's menu.**

2. **Type** python **and then click Python: Select Interpreter.**

   Choose the Python version number that matches your download (the one you jotted down while first downloading Anaconda). If you have multiple options with the same version number, choose the one that includes the names *base* and *conda*, as in Figure 1-8.

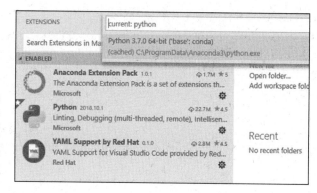

**FIGURE 1-8:**
Choose your Python interpreter (usually the highest version number).

# Writing some Python code

To test everything to make sure it's going to work, follow these steps:

1. **In VS Code, choose View⇨Terminal from the VS Code menu.**

   You should see a pane along the bottom-right that looks like one of those shown in Figure 1-9.

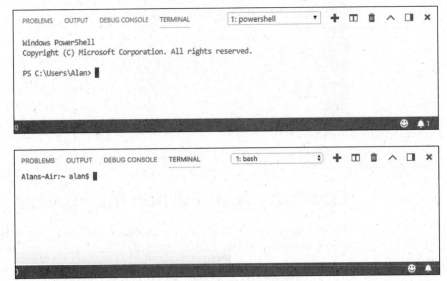

**FIGURE 1-9:** Terminal in VS Code (Windows and Mac).

2. **In the Terminal, type** python **and press Enter.**

   You should see some information about Python followed by a >>> prompt. That >>> prompt is your Python interpreter; if you type Python code there and press Enter, the code will execute.

3. **Type** 1+1 **and press Enter.**

   You should now see 2 (the sum of one plus one), followed by another Python prompt, as shown in Figure 1-10.

```
(base) C:\Users\Alan\OneDrive\AIO Python>python
Python 3.7.0 (default, Jun 28 2018, 08:04:48) [MSC v.1912 64 bit (AMD64)] :: Anaconda, Inc. on win32
Type "help", "copyright", "credits" or "license" for more information.
>>> 1+1
2
>>>
```

**FIGURE 1-10:** Python shows the sum of one plus one.

The 1+1 exercise is about as simple an exercise as you can do. However, all we care about right now is that you saw the 2, because that means your Python development environment is all set up and ready to go. You won't have to repeat any of these steps in the future. Now let me show you how to exit out of Python and VS Code. Here are the steps:

1. **In the VS Code Terminal pane, press CTRL+D or type** exit() **and press Enter. The last prompt at the bottom of the terminal window should now be whatever it was before you went to the Python prompt, indicating that you're no longer in the Interpreter.**

2. **To close VS Code in Windows, click the Close (X) button in the upper-right corner or choose View ⇨ Exit from the menu. On a Mac, click the round red dot in the upper-left corner, or choose Code ⇨ Quit Visual Studio Code from the menu.**

3. **You can also close Anaconda Navigator using similar techniques: click the X in the upper-right corner or choose File ⇨ Quit from the menu bar in Windows. Or click the red dot or go to Anaconda Navigator in the menu and choose Quit Anaconda-Navigator.**

## Getting back to VS Code Python

In the future, any time you want to work in Python in VS Code, we suggest you open Anaconda Navigator and then Launch VS Code from there. You'll be ready to roll and do any of the hands-on exercises presented in future chapters.

# Using Jupyter Notebook for Coding

Jupyter Notebook is another popular tool for writing Python code. The name Jupyter comes from the fact that it supports writing code in three popular languages:

**Ju**lia

**Pyt**hon

**R**

Julia and R are popular for data science, Python is of course, a more generic programming language that happens to be popular in data science as well, though Python is good for all kinds of development, not just data science.

People often use Jupyter to share code on the Internet. It's free, and comes with Anaconda. So if you're installed Anaconda, you already have it and can open it at any time by following these simple steps:

1. **Open Anaconda as discussed earlier in this chapter**

2. **Click Launch under Jupyter Notebook (shown in Figure 1-11).**

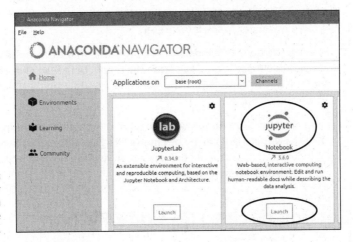

**FIGURE 1-11:**
Launch Jupyter
Notebook from
Anaconda's home
page.

Jupyter notebooks are web-based, meaning that when Jupyter opens, it does so in your default Web browser, which may be Safari, Google Chrome, Edge, or Internet Explorer. At first, it doesn't look like it has much to do with coding, because it just shows an alphabetized list of folder (directory) names to which it has access, as shown in Figure 1-12. (Of course, the names you see may different from those in the figure, because those folder names are from my computer, not yours.)

3. **Click a folder name of your choosing (the Desktop is fine, we're not making any commitment here).**

4. **Click New, and then choose Python 3 under Notebook, as shown in Figure 1-13.**

A new, empty notebook named Untitled opens. You should see a rectangle with In [ ]: at the left side. That's called a *cell*, and a cell can contain either code (words written in the Python language) or just regular text and pictures. If you want to write Code, make sure the drop-down menu in the toolbar shows the word Code. You can change that to Markdown if you want to write regular text rather than Python code.

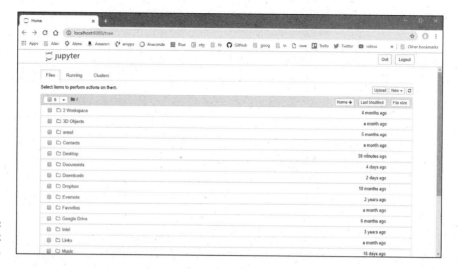

**FIGURE 1-12:**
Jupyter Notebook opening page.

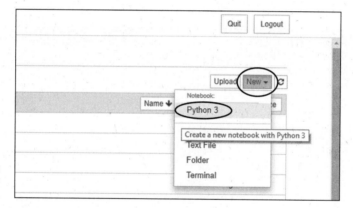

**FIGURE 1-13:**
Creating a new Jupyter notebook.

**TECHNICAL STUFF**

*Markdown* is a language for writing text that uses fonts, pictures, and such. We'll talk more about that in the next chapter. For now, let's just stay focused on Python code, since that what this book is all about.

A cell is not like the Python interpreter, where your code executes immediately. You have to type some code first (any amount), and then run that code using the Run button in the toolbar. To see for yourself, follow these steps:

1. **Click inside the code cell.**

2. **Type** 1+1.

3. **Press Enter.**

   You see the 1+1 in the cell, but not result, 2. To get the result, click Run in the toolbar or put the mouse pointer into the cell and click the Run icon at the left side of the cell, as shown in Figure 1-14.

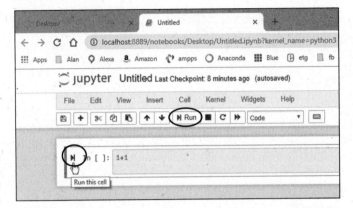

**FIGURE 1-14:**
Two ways to run code in a Jupyter cell.

You'll see the number 2 to the right of Out[1], as in Figure 1-15. The Out indicates that you're seeing the output from executing the code in the cell, which of course is 2 because one plus one is two.

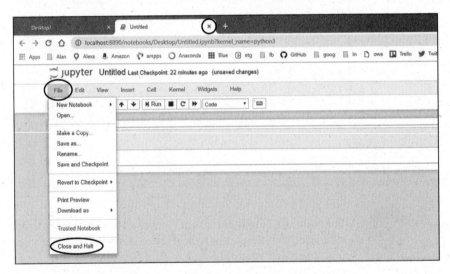

**FIGURE 1-15:**
Result of running code in a Jupyter Notebook cell.

To close a notebook, you can used either of these methods:

» Close the tab in the browser that's showing the cell.

» Or, choose File ⇨ Close and Halt from the toolbar above the cells.

Figure 1-15 shows an example using Chrome as the browser. Your tabs may look different if you're using a different browser. You may be prompted to save your work. For now, you don't need to save because we're just focused on the absolute basics . . . the thing you may be doing every time you want to run some Python code.

Even if you don't specifically save a notebook, you will see an icon for it in the folder in which you created the notebook. Its name will be Untitled, and if you have filename extensions visible, you'll see a .ipynb filename extension. The *pynb* part is short for Python notebook. The *i* in that extension, in case you're wondering, comes from iPython, which is the name of the app from which Jupyter Notebook was created, and is short for "interactive."

You can delete a notebook file if you are just practicing and don't want to keep it. Just make sure you close the notebook in the web browser (or just close the whole browser first) — otherwise, you may get an error message stating that you can't delete the file while it's open.

So now you are ready to go. You have great set of tools set up for learning Python. The simple skills you've learned in this chapter will serve you well through your learning process, as well as you professional programming after you've mastered the basics. Come on over to Chapter 2 in this minibook now and we'll get a bit deeper into Python and using the tools you now have available on your computer.

IN THIS CHAPTER

» Using the Python interactive mode

» Creating a Python development
workspace

» Create a folder for your Python code

» Typing, editing, and debugging
Python code

» Writing code in a Jupyter notebook

Chapter **2**

# Interactive Mode, Getting Help, Writing Apps

Now that you have Anaconda and VS Code installed, you're ready to start digging deeper into writing Python code. In this chapter we take you briefly through the interactive, help, and code editing features of VS Code and Jupyter Notebook to build on what you've learned so far. Most of you are probably anxious to get started on more advanced topics like data science, artificial intelligence, robotics, or whatever. But learning that will be easier if you have a good understand of the many tools available to you, and the skills to use them.

## Using Python Interactive Mode

Many teachers and authors will suggest you try things hands-on at the Python prompt, and assume you already know how to get there. We've seen many frustrated beginners complain that trying activities recommended in some tutorial never work for them. The frustration often steps from the fact that they're typing and executing the code in the wrong place. With Anaconda, the Terminal in VS Code is a great place to type Python code. So in this chapter we'll start with that.

## Opening Terminal

To use Python interactively with Anaconda, we suggest you follow these steps:

1. **Open Anaconda Navigator, then open VS Code by clicking its Launch button on the Anaconda home page.**

2. **If you don't see the Terminal pane at the bottom of the VS Code window, choose View ⇨ Terminal from the VS Code menu bar.**

3. **If the words Terminal isn't highlighted at the top of the pane, click Terminal (circled in Figure 2-1).**

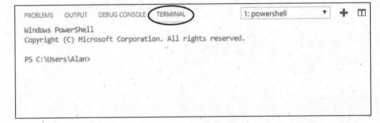

**FIGURE 2-1:**
Terminal pane
in VS Code.

The very first prompt you see is typically for your computer's operating system, and likely shows the user name of the account you're in. For example, on a Mac it may look like `Alans-Air:~ alan$` but with the name of your computer in place of `Alans-Air`. In Windows it would likely be `C:\Users\Alan>` with your user name in place of `Alan`, and possibly a path that's different from `C:\Users`.

## Getting your Python version

At the operating system command prompt, you can type this and press Enter to see what version of Python you're using. Note that there is a space before the first hyphen, and no other spaces.

```
python --version
```

# COLORS AND ICONS IN VS CODE

By default, the VS Code terminal displays white text against a black background. We will be reversing those colors in this book, just because we think the dark against light works better for print like this. You're welcome to use any color scheme you like. If you just want to switch to black on white, as shown in this book, use either of these methods:

On a Mac choose Code ⇨ Preferences ⇨ Color Theme ⇨ Light (Visual Studio).

In Windows choose File ⇨ Preferences ⇨ Color Theme ⇨ Light (Visual Studio).

If you want your icons in VS Code to match the ones we're using, you'll need to download and install the Material Icon Theme. You may also want to download the Material color theme and try it out. We won't be using it for the book because it doesn't play well when printed on paper. But you may want to take it for a spin. Follow these steps:

1. **Click Extensions in the left pane.**

2. **Type** material, **look for Material Icon Theme, and click its Install option.**

3. **Click Reload on any selected extension to install both extensions. If you see a prompt at bottom right asking if you want to activate the icons, click Activate.**

4. **Choose File (in Windows) or Code (on a Mac) then Preferences ⇨ File Icon Theme then click Material Icon Theme.**

5. **If you'd like to try out the color theme, open File (in Windows) or Code (on a Mac) and then choose Preferences ⇨ Color Theme and click Material Icon Theme.**

If at any time you change your mind about the color theme, repeat step 5 above and choose something other than Material Icon Theme.

You should see something like Python 3.x.x (where the x's are numbers representing the version of Python you're using. If instead you see an error message, you're not quite where you need to be. You want to make sure you start VS Code from within Anaconda, not just from Launchpad or your Start menu. Type **python --version** in the VS Code Terminal pane, and press Enter again. If it still doesn't work, choose View ⇨ Command Palette from the VS Code menu bar, type **python**, choose Python: Select Interpreter, and then choose the Python interpreter you downloaded with Anaconda.

# Going into the Python Interpreter

When you're able to enter `python --version` and not get an error, you know you're ready to work with Python in VS Code. From there you can get into the Python interpreter by entering the command

```
python
```

**REMEMBER**

When we, or anyone else, says "enter the command," that means you have to type the command and then press Enter. Nothing happens until you press Enter. So if you just type the command and wait for something to happen, you will be waiting for a long, long time.

You should see some information about the Python version you're using, and the ⟩⟩⟩ prompt, which represents the Python interpreter.

## Entering commands

Entering commands in the Python interpreter is the same as typing the anywhere else. You must type the command correctly, and then press Enter. If you spell something wrong in the command, you will likely see an error message, which is just the interpreter telling you it doesn't understand what you mean. But don't worry, you can't break anything. For example if you enter the command

```
howdy
```

## A NOTE ABOUT PyLint

PyLint is a feature of Anacaona that helps you find and avoid errors in your code. It's usually turned on by default. Though in the past we've gotten different results with different VS Code versions. It's possible that the first time you try to use Python you'll see some messages in the lower-right corner of VS Code. Don't be alarmed if you don't see them. If you do see any, however, here is how you can respond:

If you see a message about Python Language Server, click Try It Now and then click Reload.

If you see a message that Linter PyLint Is Not Installed, click Install.

If you see Select Python Environment near the lower-left corner of VS Code's window, click that and choose the Anaconda option from the menu that drops down near the top center. If you see multiple Anaconda options, choose the one with the largest version number.

After you press Enter, you see some techie gibberish on the screen that is trying to tell you that it doesn't know what "howdy" means, so it can't do that. But again, nothing has broken. You're just back to another ››› prompt where you can try again, as shown in Figure 2-2.

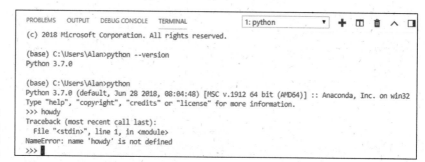

Interactive Mode, Getting Help, Writing Apps

**FIGURE 2-2:**
Python doesn't know what *howdy* means.

```
PROBLEMS    OUTPUT    DEBUG CONSOLE    TERMINAL           1: python          ▼  ✚  ▭  🗑  ∧  ▢
(c) 2018 Microsoft Corporation. All rights reserved.

(base) C:\Users\Alan>python --version
Python 3.7.0

(base) C:\Users\Alan>python
Python 3.7.0 (default, Jun 28 2018, 08:04:48) [MSC v.1912 64 bit (AMD64)] :: Anaconda, Inc. on win32
Type "help", "copyright", "credits" or "license" for more information.
>>> howdy
Traceback (most recent call last):
  File "<stdin>", line 1, in <module>
NameError: name 'howdy' is not defined
>>> █
```

## Using Python's built-in help

On of the prompts on your screen mentioned that you can type help as a comment in the Python interpreter. Note that you don't type the quotation marks, just the word help (and then press Enter, as always). This time you see

```
Type help() for interactive help, or help(object) for help about object.
```

Note that this time they're telling you to type **help** followed by an empty pair of parentheses, or help with a specific word in parentheses (object is the example given). Even though they use the word "type" at the start of the sentence, they mean to enter the command. . .type it and press Enter. Go ahead and enter

```
help()
```

Note that there are no spaces in the line. After you press Enter the screen provides some information about using Python's interactive help, as shown in Figure 2-3.

Seeing help› at the bottom of the window tells you that you're no longer in the operating system shell or the Python interpreter (which always shows ›››) but are now in a new area that provides help. Any commands you type here should be ones that the help recognizes. As a beginner you're not likely to know those. But for future reference know you can use this help prompt for reminders about different parts of Python.

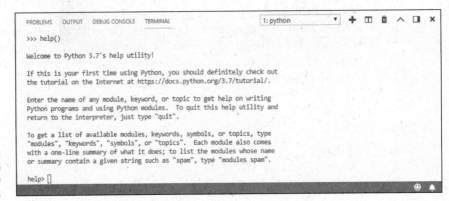

**FIGURE 2-3:**
Python's interactive help utility.

For example, Python uses certain keywords, which have special meaning in the language. You get a list of those, just type

```
keywords
```

at the `help>` prompt and press Enter, and you'll see a list of keywords, as in Figure 2-4.

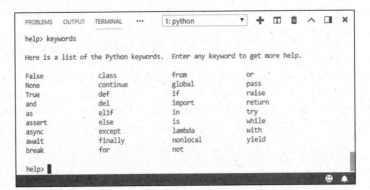

**FIGURE 2-4:**
Keyword help.

Above the list of keywords it tells you that you can type any keyword at the `help>` prompt for more information about that keyword. For example, entering the keyword `class` provides information about Python classes, as shown in Figure 2-5. These are not the kind of classes you attend at school; rather, they're the kind you create in Python (after you've learned the basics and are ready to move onto more advanced topics).

Needless to say, all the technical jargon in the help text is going to leave the average beginner totally flummoxed. But the point here is that, for future reference, as you learn about things in Python, you can use the Python interactive help for reminders on those concepts as needed.

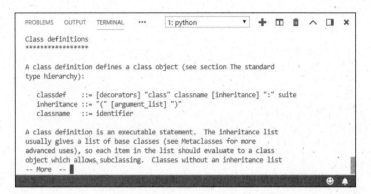

FIGURE 2-5:
Python class help.

The --More-- at the bottom of the text isn't a prompt where you type commands. Instead, it's just letting you know that there is more text to come. Press the Space-bar. There may be several pages of information. Every time you see -- More --, you can press Enter to get to the next page. Eventually you'll get back to the help> prompt, and that's when you know you've reached the end of that help.

## Exiting interactive help

To get out of interactive help and return to the Python prompt, type the letter **q** (for quit) or press Ctrl+Z, then press Enter. You should be back to the >>> prompt. At the >>> prompt you can type exit() or python.

To leave the Python prompt and get back to the operating system, type **exit()** and press Enter. Note that if you make a mistake, such as leaving off the parentheses, you'll get some help on the screen. For example, if you enter exit and press Enter you see

```
Use exit() or Ctrl-Z plus Return to exit.
```

Thist tells you that in order to exit the Python prompt you should type **exit()** (with the parentheses, no spaces), or press Ctrl+Z, then press Enter. You'll know you've exited the Python interpreter when you see the operating system prompt rather than >>> at the end of the Terminal window, as in Figure 2-6.

## Searching for specific help topics online

Python's built-in help is somewhat archaic, but it can help you when you just need a quick reminder about some Python keyword you've forgotten. But if you're online, you're probably better off just searching the Web for help. You may want to start at https://www.youtube.com/ if you're specifically looking for videos, and if not, https://stackoverflow.com/ is a good place to ask questions and search for help. And of course there's always Google, Bing, and other search engines.

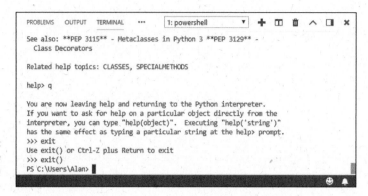

**FIGURE 2-6:**
Back to the operating system prompt.

```
PROBLEMS   OUTPUT   TERMINAL   ...        1: powershell        ▼  +  ⊡  🗑  ∧  ⬜  ✕

See also: **PEP 3115** - Metaclasses in Python 3 **PEP 3129** -
   Class Decorators

Related help topics: CLASSES, SPECIALMETHODS

help> q

You are now leaving help and returning to the Python interpreter.
If you want to ask for help on a particular object directly from the
interpreter, you can type "help(object)".  Executing "help('string')"
has the same effect as typing a particular string at the help> prompt.
>>> exit
Use exit() or Ctrl-Z plus Return to exit
>>> exit()
PS C:\Users\Alan>
```

Regardless of what you use to search, remember to start your search with the word *python* or *python 3*. A lot of programming languages out there share similar concepts and keywords, so if you don't specify the Python language in your search request, there's no telling what kinds of results you may get.

## Lots of free cheat sheets

Another good resource for learners are the countless cheat sheets available online for free. Whenever you start to feel overwhelmed by all the possibilities of a language like Python, a cheat sheet summarizing things down to a single page or so can really help bring things down to a more manageable (and less intimidating) size.

Of course, you're not really "cheating" with a cheat sheet, unless you us it while taking a test that you're supposed to answer from memory. But writing code in real life is much different from answering multiple-choice questions. So what we often call a *cheat sheet* in the tech world is really just another tool to help you learn. There are many of them out there, and exactly what appeals to you depends on your own learning style. To see what's available, just head out to Google or Bing or any search engine you like and search for *free python 3 cheat sheet*. Most are in a format you can download, print, and keep handy as you learn the seemingly infinite possibilities of writing code in Python.

# Creating a Python Development Workspace

Although interactive modes and online help and the rest are certainly decent support tools, most people want to use Python to create apps. Personally, we've found this easiest to do if you set up a VS Code development environment specifically for learning and doing Python. You can set up other development environments for other types of coding, such as HTML, CSS, and JavaScript for the Web, fine-tuning each as you go along to best support whatever language you're working in.

We often switch between Mac and Windows computers, and so we actually have one dev environment for each. Alan keep his in a OneDrive folder so he can get to them from anywhere. Although this is certainly not a requirement, it sure comes in handy. But if you'll be working strictly from one computer, you can put your environment on your computer's hard drive rather than out on a cloud drive.

In VS Code, they use the term *workspace* to define what we call a development environment. It's basically the specific Python interpreter you're using plus any additional extensions you gather along to the way to make learning and doing easier.

To make it easy to get to these workspaces from any Internet-connected computer in the world, Alan has a folder on a cloud drive (OneDrive) named VS Code Workspaces. However, you can store your workspaces anyplace you like — even on your own computer, if you don't have or don't want to use a cloud drive. But if you do want to create a folder for storing workspaces, do so now, before proceeding with the following steps. Then

1. **If VS Code isn't already open, open launch it from Anaconda.**

2. **Choose File ⇨ Save Workspace As.**

3. **Navigate to the folder in which you want to save the workspace settings.**

4. **Type a name for the workspace. Alan uses** Python 3 **followed by** Mac **or** Windows **depending on which type of machine he's on, as shown in Figure 2-7.**

   ● On a Mac, choose Code ⇨ Preferences ⇨ Settings.

   ● In Windows, choose File ⇨ Preferences ⇨ Settings.

5. **If you see a page like the one in Figure 2-7, click the three dots near the top-right corner and choose Open Settings.json, as shown in Figure 2-8.**

6. **In the next window, select the entire line of code that starts with** python. pythonpath **(this tells VS Code where to find the Python interpreter on your computer). You can also select any other command lines that you'd like to make part of the workspace, but don't select the curly braces.**

7. **Click Workspace Settings above the code you just selected.**

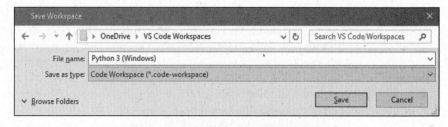

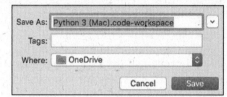

**FIGURE 2-7:**
Saving current
settings as
workspace
settings.

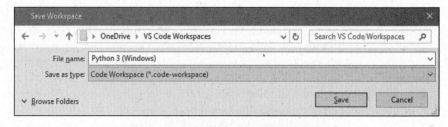

Commonly Used

**Files: Auto Save**
Controls auto save of dirty files. Read more about autosave here.

afterDelay

**Files: Auto Save Delay**
Controls the delay in ms after which a dirty file is saved automatically. Only applies when Files: Auto Save is set to afterDelay.

1000

**FIGURE 2-8:**
VS Code Settings.

8. **Click between the setting's curly braces and paste in the lines of code there, as shown in Figure 2-9. Keep in mind that your python path may not look like the one in the image.**

**FIGURE 2-9:**
Python path
moved to
workspace
settings.

```
USER SETTINGS    WORKSPACE SETTINGS

        Place your settings here to overwrite the User Settings.
1   {
2       "folders": [],
3       "settings": {
4           "python.pythonPath": "C:\\ProgramData\\Anaconda3",
5           "workbench.colorTheme": "Visual Studio Light"
6       }
7   }
```

9. Choose File ⇨ Save from the VS Code menu.

10. Close the Settings and User Settings tabs by clicking the X on the right side of each tab.

11. Close VS Code.

12. Close Anaconda.

You'll see how to take advantage of the new workspace settings in a moment. But first, you'd be wise to create a directory (folder) to store all the code you'll be writing in this book so it's easy to find when you want to review.

# Creating a Folder for your Python Code

Next, we create a folder in which to store all the Python code that you write in this book, so it's all together in one place and easy to find when you need it. You can put this folder anywhere you like. Alan again will use a cloud drive (OneDrive) so he can get to it from any computer. But you can put yours wherever you like. He'll name his folder *AIO Python* (for All-In-One Python), but you can name yours whatever you like.

The steps are the same as for any other folder, there's nothing special about the folder. In Windows you can navigate to the folder which will contain the new folder (Alan would use OneDrive, but you can use your Desktop, Documents, or any other folder). On a Mac, right-click some empty place in the folder and choose New Folder. In Windows, right-click an empty spot in the folder and choose New ⇨ Folder. Type the folder name (*AIO Python*, in our example) and press Enter.

Last but not least, you want to associate the code folder you just created with the VS Code workspace you just created, so that any time you work in the AIO Python folder you're using the correct Python interpreter and other Python-related settings you choose over time with the files in the code folder. Here's how:

1. Open Anaconda and launch VS Code from there.

2. From the VS Code menu choose File ⇨ Open Workspace.

3. Navigate to the folder where you saved your workspace and open the workspace from there.

4. Choose File ⇨ Add Folder to Workspace.

5. Navigate to the folder in which you created the AIO Python folder, click that folder's icon, and choose Add.

The Explorer bar in VS Code shows that you have the workspace open, and under that you can see you also have that folder open, as shown in Figure 2-10. If you see something entirely different in the left pane, click the Explorer icon at the top-left (near the arrow in the Figure) to make sure you're viewing that pane.

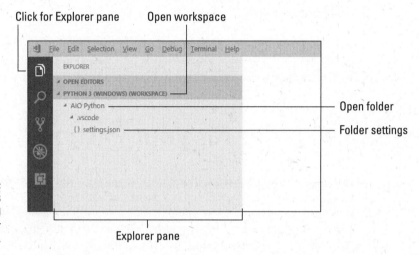

FIGURE 2-10:
Python 3
workspace and
AIO Python folder
open in VS Code.

The Open Editors bar lists files that are currently open (over to the right). For example, if you see Welcome there, that means you're viewing the Welcome page. To close that page, click the X next to its name in the Explorer pane or tab. Any time you want to reopen that Welcome page, choose Help ➪ Welcome from the VS Code menu bar.

The .vscode icon is just a subfolder that stores your settings for this workspace, and settings.json is the file in that folder that contains those settings. The triangle next to each name allows you to expand or collapse that list. So if something is hidden, click the triangle next to an item to expand that item and see what it contains.

TIP

If you see a symbol other than a triangle, or no symbol at all, next to folder names, you maybe be using an icon theme that's different from the default. No worries, just click to the left of any folder to expand/collapse it even if there's no symbol there at all.

The beauty of this approach now is that any time you want to work with Python in VS Code, all you have to do is follow these steps:

1. **If you've closed VS Code, launch it from Anaconda Navigator.**

2. **Choose File ⇨ Open Workspace from the VS Code menu.**

3. **Open your workspace.**

   The workspace and any folders you've associated with that workspace open up, and you're ready to go.

# Typing, Editing, and Debugging Python Code

Most likely, the vast majority of code you write you'll write in and editor. This will be a plain text file with a .py filename extension. For this book, we suggest you keep any files you create in that AIO Python folder which you should be able to see any time you have VS Code and your Python 3 workspace open. So to create a .py file at any time, follow these steps:

1. **If you haven't already done so, open VS Code on your Python 3 workspace.**

2. **If the Explorer pane isn't open, click the Explorer icon near the top-left of VS Code.**

3. **To create a new file in your AIO Python folder, right-click AIO Python and choose New File (Figure 2-11).**

4. **Type the filename with the .py extension (hello.py for this first one) and press ENTER.**

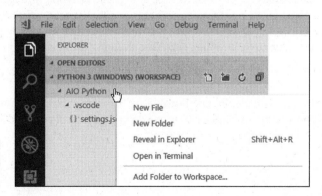

**FIGURE 2-11:**
Right-click a folder name and choose New File.

The new file opens and you can see its name on top of the tab to the right. That larger area is where you'll type your Python code. You'll also see hello.py under Open Editors. That's just a convenience so that when you have many open files you can pick one to bring to the forefront just by clicking its name there. The filename also appears under the AUO Python folder name in the Explorer pane, because that's where it's stored, as shown in Figure 2-12.

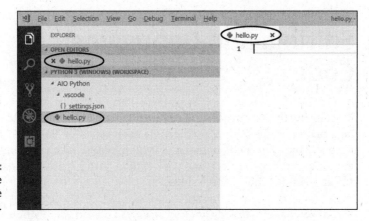

**FIGURE 2-12:**
New hello.py file open in VS Code for editing.

# Writing Python code

Now that you have a py file open, you can use it to write some Python code. As it typical when learning a new programming language you'll start by typing a simple Hello World program. Here are the steps:

1. **Click next to the 1 in the editing area.**

2. **Type (exactly)** print("Hello World"), **and as you're typing you may notice text appearing on the screen. That is** *intellisense* **text, which detects what you're typing and shows you some information about that keyword. You don't have to do anything with that though, just keep typing.**

3. **Press Enter after you've typed the line.**

The new line of code shows, but doesn't execute. That's because you typically don't type and run one line of code at a time. You may also notice a couple of other changes, as shown in Figure 2-13:

>> The Explorer icon shows a circled 1, indicating that you current have one unsaved change.

>> The hello.py name in the tab and Open Editors areas show a dot, indicating that you have unsaved changes in the file.

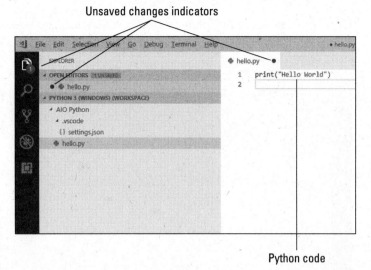

Unsaved changes indicators

Python code

## Saving your code

Code you type in VS Code is saved automatically. There are a couple of ways to deal with that. One is to try to remember to save any time you make a change that's worth saving. The easiest way to do that is to choose File⇨Save from VS Code's menu bar, or press Ctrl + S in Windows or Command+S on a Mac.

Personally, we prefer to use AutoSave, which automatically saves changes you make, so that you don't have to remember. To enable Auto Save, just choose File⇨Auto Save from VS Code's menu bar. When you see a checkmark next to Auto Save on the File menu, that means Auto Save is turned on, so you don't have to remember to save every change. If you decide you no longer want to use Auto Save at any time in the future, just choose File⇨Auto Save again from the menu bar to remove the checkmark and turn Auto Save off.

## Running Python in VS Code

To test your Python code in VS Code, you need to run it. The easiest way to do that in VS Code is probably to right-click the file's name (hello.py in this example) and choose Run Python File in Terminal as shown in Figure 2-14.

The Terminal pane opens along the bottom of the VS Code window. You'll see a command prompt followed by a comment to run the code in the Python interpreter (python.exe). And below that, you'll see the output of the program: the words *Hello World*, in this example, and then another prompt, as in Figure 2-15. This is not the most exciting app in the world, but at least now you know how to write, save, and execute Python programs in VS Code, and that's a skill you'll be using often as you continue through this book and through your Python programming career.

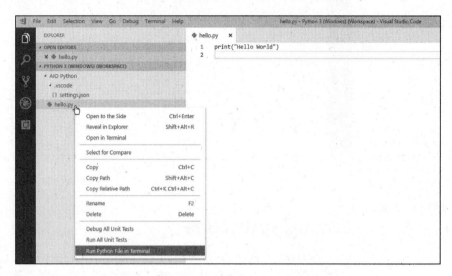

**FIGURE 2-14:**
Run hello.py.

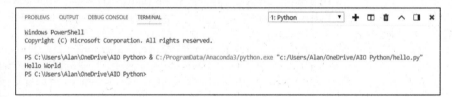

**FIGURE 2-15:**
Output from
hello.py.

**TECHNICAL
STUFF**

If you are using PowerShell in the Terminal window you may see a message about switching to the Command Prompt. Unless you happen to be a PowerShell expert and really need it (for whatever reason), you might as well click Use Command Prompt if you see that option so that prompt won't keep pestering you in the future.

## Simple debugging

When you're first learning to write code, you're bound to make a lot of mistakes. The good news is that they're no big deal. You won't break or destroy anything. The code just won't work as expected.

Before you even attempt to run some code, you may see several indicators on the screen indicating that there is an error in your code:

>> The name of the folder and file that contain the error will be red in the Explorer pane.

>> The number of errors in the file will show in red next to the filename in the Explorer bar.

>> The total number of errors will show next to the circled X at the bottom left corner of the CS Code window.

>> The bad code will likely have a wave red underline beneath it.

Figure 2-16 shows an example where we typed PRINT in all uppercase, which is not allowed in Python. Python is case sensitive, so when we show a command to type in lowercase, that means you have to type it in lowercase, too.

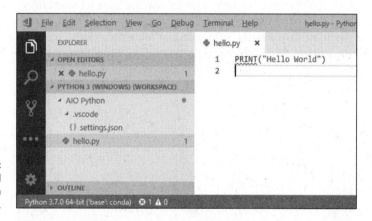

FIGURE 2-16: PRINT is typed incorrectly in hello.py.

To run the file in Terminal, you'll have to fix the error. Touching the mouse pointer to the word with the red wavy line below will give you a brief (though highly technical) description of the problem. In the example shown in the image, we just typed *PRINT* (uppercase) rather than *print* (lowercase). So, to fix the error we would just replace *PRINT* with *print* and then save the change (unless you've turned on Auto Save). Then you can right-click and choose Run Python File in Terminal to run the corrected code.

## The VS Code Python debugger

VS Code also has a built-in debugger that can help when working with more complex programs and also provides another means of running Python programs in

VS Code. We won't be doing anything super complex right now. But there certainly is no harm in getting the debugger set up and ready as part of your Python development workspace. Follow these steps to do so now:

1. **Click the Debug icon to the left of the Explorer pane.**

2. **Next to No Configurations near the top of the pane click the Gear icon (which is probably showing a red dot right now, because you haven't specified a debugger yet). A new file named launch.json opens to the right.**

3. **Click open the drop-down menu at the top of the pane and choose Python: Current File (Integrated Terminal) (AIO Python), as shown in Figure 2-17.**

4. **Close launch.json by clicking the X on its tab.**

From now on, as an alternative to using the right-click method to run Python code, you can use the Debug pane. But first, you have to know which file will run. For now that's easy because hello.py is the only one we have. In the future, when you may have several open, you can tell which one is open because it appears in the editing area to the right of the explore pane. To run it, from the Debug pane, click the Start Debugging arrow near the top of the Debug pane, which shows as a green triangle.

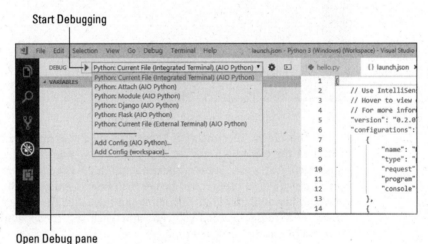

**FIGURE 2-17:**
VS Code
Debug pane.

When you click Start Debugging, the Python code will run as it did when you chose Run Python File in Terminal. However, it will take a little longer, and there will be more text output on the screen in Terminal. However, so long as there aren't any actual errors, you should see the output under all of that (Hello World) followed by the command prompt for your operating system.

If that seems like a lot to remember, for now all you have to do is remember that whenever you want to run the some Python code in VS Code, you can do either of the following, whichever is most convenient for you at the moment:

» Right-click the .py file's name and choose Run File in Terminal.

» Click the .py file's name in the Explorer bar to select that file, click Debug, and then click Start Debugging at the top of the Debug pane.

If you can remember those two things, you're well on your way to learning Python, and you have a good environment in which to work.

# Writing Code in a Jupyter Notebook

In Chapter 1 you learned about Jupyter notebooks as another way to write and run Python code. In this chapter, we'd like to build on what you learned there by showing you how to create, save, and open Jupyter notebooks. You can, of course, save your Jupyter notebooks wherever you want using any filenames you want. For our working example here we'll create subfolder named Jupyter Notebooks inside your AIO Python folder just to keep everything together.

## Creating a folder for Jupyter Notebook

A Jupyter Notebooks folder is no different from any other, so you can create it using whatever method you normally use in your operating system. We'll put ours in the AIO Python folder we created, again just to keep all the files for this book in one place. The steps to do this are as follows:

1. **Open your AIO Python folder in Finder (Mac) or Explorer (Windows).**

2. **Right-click an empty spot in that folder and choose New ⇨ Folder (in Windows) or New Folder on a Mac.**

3. **Type** Jupyter Notebooks **as the folder name and press Enter.**

Now that you have a folder in which to save Jupyter notebooks, you can create a notebook, as discussed next.

# Creating and saving a Jupyter notebook

To create a Jupyter notebook and save it in a folder, follow these steps:

1. **Open Anaconda (if it isn't already open) and launch Jupyter Notebooks from there.**

2. **On the first page, navigate to the Jupyter Notebooks folder you created in the previous section. You should see something like *The notebook list is empty* because the folder is empty.**

3. **Click New and choose Python 3.**

4. **Near the top of the new notebook that opened click Untitled, type in the new name** 01 Notebook, **and click Rename.**

That's it, the notebook is created and saved in your AIO Python folder as shown in Figure 2-18.

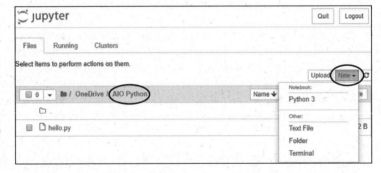

**FIGURE 2-18:**
01 Notebook
created in Jupyter
Notebook.

# Typing and running code in a notebook

When your notebook is open, you can type Python code into any Code cell and text into any Markdown cell. When you see the word Code in the drop-down menu in the toolbar below the menu bar, the active cell is for typing code. To take it for a spin, follow these steps:

1. **Click in the Code cell (to the right of In [ ]: and type** print("Hello World") **and don't forget to use lowercase letters for the word *print*.**

2. **To run the code, hold down the Alt key (in Windows) or the Option key (on a Mac) and press Enter, or click the Play triangle to the left of the word *In*.**

    The output from the code appears below the cell, and another cell opens below.

# Adding some Markdown text

As mentioned, you can add text (and actually pictures and video) to Jupyter notebooks. You don't need to use any special coding for typing regular text. If you want to do some formatting or add pictures and videos, you'll need to use Markdown code. Markdown is a popular markup language, something like a greatly simplified HTML. Although w can't go into a lengthy tutorial on Markdown here in a Python book, we can tell you that it's probably actually easier to type up the Markdown content in VS Code and then copy/paste it over into a Markdown cell than it is to type directly in the Markdown cell in Jupyter. Just make sure that when you're working with Markdown, you choose Markdown from the drop-down menu in the toolbar.

Figure 2-19 shows where we added some Markdown and text to a Markdown cell in Jupyter.

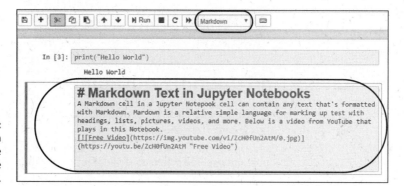

**FIGURE 2-19:**
A Markdown cell with some Markdown code and text in it.

TIP

Alan has some free video tutorials in his online school at `https://alansimpson.thinkific.com/courses/easy-markdown-with-vs-code` if you'd be interested in learning more about Markdown.

To run a cell that contains Markdown, click the cell then click Run in the toolbar. The code is rendered into text and any other content you've put in the cell, as in Figure 2-20.

To change code in a Code cell, just click the cell and type your code normally. To change the content of a Markdown cell, first double-click some text or the empty space inside the cell so you can see the code again, then make your changes.

After making changes, click Run again. Note that only the cell that contains the cursor will run again. If you want to run all of the cells in a notebook, use the double triangle button a little to the right of the Run button.

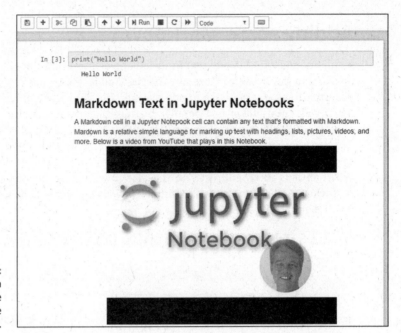

In [3]: `print("Hello World")`

Hello World

## Markdown Text in Jupyter Notebooks

A Markdown cell in a Jupyter Notepook cell can contain any text that's formatted with Markdown. Mardown is a relative simple language for marking up test with headings, lists, pictures, videos, and more. Below is a video from YouTube that plays in this Notebook.

**FIGURE 2-20:** A Markdown cell with some Markdown code and text in it.

## Saving and opening notebooks

To save a Jupyter notebook, click the Save button on the toolbar, or choose File⇨Save and Checkpoint from the menu.

To close a notebook, choose File⇨Save and Halt from the menu.

Any time that you want to reopen a notebook in the future, open Anaconda and launch Jupyter Notebook from there. Then, navigate to the file you saved and click its filename. The filename will probably show a .ipynb filename extension, as that's standard for Jupyter notebooks.

It's worth noting that when you open the AIO Python folder in VS Code, you'll see the new Jupyter Notebooks folder in the Explorer pane. Keep in mind that we put that folder there just to keep files from this book organized. There wouldn't really be any reason to open that folder in VS Code. The folder is named Jupyter Notebooks because it's just for files you create and manage in the Jupyter Notebook app.

Okay, so we've dug a little deeper in VS Code and Jupyter Notebook here, mostly so that you can save and open Python files and Jupyter Notebooks whenever you want in future chapters. All of these skills will prove useful when you start getting deeper into writing Python code. See you there!

# Chapter **3**

# Python Elements and Syntax

M any programming languages focus on things that the computer does and how it does them rather than on the way humans think and work. This one simple fact makes most programming languages difficult for most people to learn. Python is different in that's is based on the philosophy that a programming language should be geared more toward how humans think, work, and communicate than what happens inside the computer. The Zen of Python is the perfect example of that human orientation, so we start this chapter with that.

## The Zen of Python

The Zen of Python is a list of guiding principles for the design of the Python language. (See Figure 3-1.) These principles are actually hidden in an *Easter egg* (a slang term for something in a programming language or app that's not easy to find and that serves as a bit of an inside joke to people who have learned enough Python to be able to find it). To get to the Easter egg, follow these steps:

1. **Launch VS Code from Anaconda Navigator and open your Python 3 workspace.**

2. **If the Terminal pane isn't open, choose View ⇨ Terminal from the VS Code menu bar.**

**3.** **Type** python **and press Enter to get to the Python prompt (>>>).**

**WARNING**

If you get an error message after you enter the python command, don't panic. You just need to remind VS Code which Python interpreter you're using. Choose View ⇨ Command Palette from the menu, type **python**, and then click Python: Select Interpreter and choose the Python 3 version that came with Anaconda.

**4.** **Type** import this **and press Enter.**

The list of 19 aphorisms appears. You may have to scroll up and down or make the Terminal pane taller to see them all. But as you can see, the aphorisms are somewhat tongue-and-cheek in their philosophical rhetoric. But the general idea they express is always to try to make the code more human-readable than machine-readable.

```
PROBLEMS    OUTPUT    DEBUG CONSOLE    TERMINAL

The Zen of Python, by Tim Peters

Beautiful is better than ugly.
Explicit is better than implicit.
Simple is better than complex.
Complex is better than complicated.
Flat is better than nested.
Sparse is better than dense.
Readability counts.
Special cases aren't special enough to break the rules.
Although practicality beats purity.
Errors should never pass silently.
Unless explicitly silenced.
In the face of ambiguity, refuse the temptation to guess.
There should be one-- and preferably only one --obvious way to do it.
Although that way may not be obvious at first unless you're Dutch.
Now is better than never.
Although never is often better than *right* now.
If the implementation is hard to explain, it's a bad idea.
If the implementation is easy to explain, it may be a good idea.
Namespaces are one honking great idea -- let's do more of those!
>>> █
```

**FIGURE 3-1:**
The Zen of
Python.

The Zen is sometimes referred to as *PEP 20*, where *PEP* is an acronym for *Python enhancement proposals*. The 20 perhaps refers to the 20 Zen of Python principles, only 19 of which have been written down. We all get to wonder about, or make up our own, final principle. But it's all in fun, so don't worry about the twentieth (nonexistent) Zen . . . it won't be on any tests.

There are many other PEPs, all of which you can find on the Python.org website at https://www.python.org/dev/peps/. The one you're likely to hear about the most is PEP 8, which is the Style Guide for Python code. The guiding principle for these guidelines is "readability counts" — and what they mean is readable by *humans*. Admittedly, when you're first learning Python code, most other peoples' code will seem like some gibberish scribbled down by aliens, and you may not have any idea what it means or does. But as you gain experience with the language, the style consistency will become more apparent, and you'll find it easier and easier to read and understand other peoples' code, which is an excellent way to learn coding yourself.

We'll fill you in on Python coding style as we go along in this book. Trying to read about it before actually working on it is sure to bore you to tears. So for now, any time you hear mention of PEP, or especially PEP 8, remember that it's a reference to the Python Coding Style Guidelines from the Python.org website, and you can find it any time you like just by googling *pep 8*.

Truthfully, this PEP 8 business can be a kind of double-edged sword for learners. On one hand, you don't want to learn a bunch of bad habits only to discover you have to unlearn them later. On the other hand, the formatting demands of PEP 8 are so strict many learners get frustrated just trying to get the stuff to work without having to worry about blank spaces, upper-/lowercase letters, and other details.

To deal with all of this, we will be following and explaining PEP 8 conventions as we go along. You can take it a step further, if you like, by configuring PyLint to help you along. *PyLint* is a tool that comes with Anaconda that makes suggestions about your code as you're typing. Follow these steps to turn on Pylint and PEP 8 now if you'd like to take it for a spin:

1. **On the Mac menu, click Code; in Windows, click File on the menu.**

2. **Choose Preferences ⇨ Settings.**

3. **Click Workspace Settings.**

4. **Click the three dots near the top-right of the settings and choose Open Settings.json.**

5. **Click Workspace Settings.**

6. **In the Search Settings box, type** pylint.

7. **Touch the mouse pointer to python.linting.enabled, and if that option isn't enabled, click it and select True to enable linting.**

8. **Scroll down and touch the mouse pointer to python.linting.pep8Enabled, click the little pencil icon that shows, and click True.**

   You'll see a couple of lines added to your Workspace Settings, each starting with *python.linting*, as shown in Figure 3-2.

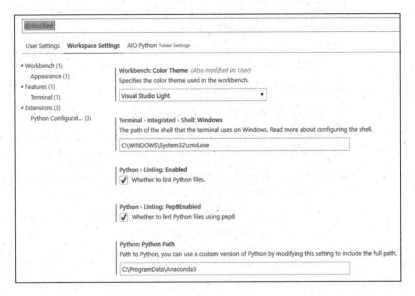

```
USER SETTINGS    WORKSPACE SETTINGS    AIO PYTHON Folder Settings
         Place your settings here to overwrite the User Settings.
1  {
2      "folders": [
3          {
4              "path": "C:\\Users\\Alan\\OneDrive\\AIO Python"
5          }
6      ],
7      "settings": {
8          "python.pythonPath": "C:\\ProgramData\\Anaconda3",
9          "terminal.integrated.shell.windows": "C:\\WINDOWS\\System32\\cmd.exe",
10         "workbench.colorTheme": "Visual Studio Light",
11         "python.linting.enabled": true,
12         "python.linting.pep8Enabled": true,
13
14
15     }
16 }
```

FIGURE 3-2:
Workspace
settings with
Pylint and
PEP 8 enabled.

When you're done, choose File ➪ Save All. Then you can close the settings pages by clicking the X in their tabs. If at any time in the future you feel that the linting is just too much and is actually making it harder for you to learn, you can turn those features off by following these steps:

1. **Choose Code ➪ Preferences ➪ Settings (on a Mac) or File ➪ Preferences ➪ Settings (in Windows).**

2. **Click Workspace Settings, and then click the three dots and choose Show Modified Settings.**

   You will see Workspace settings in the non-code format shown in Figure 3-3.

FIGURE 3-3:
A different view
of Workspace
Settings.

3. **If you want to disable just PEP 8 (which is the one that drives most beginners a little crazy), click the checkmark for Python ⇨ Linting: Pep8Enabled.**

Try things with PEP 8 disabled. If the linting still feels like it's too much, you can repeat the steps and clear the checkmark next to Python ⇨ Linting:Enabled.

# Object-Oriented Programming

At the risk of getting too technical/computer science-y, we should mention that there are different kinds of languages and different approaches to designing languages. Perhaps the most successful and widely used model is what's called object-oriented programming, or OOP for short. It's a design philosophy that tries to mimic the real world in the sense that it consists of objects, with properties, and methods (actions) that those objects perform.

Take a car, for example. Any one car is an object. Not all cars are exactly the same. Different cars have different properties, such as make, model, year, color, size, and so forth that make them different from one another. And yet, they all serve the same basic purpose . . . to get us from point A to point B without having to walk or use some other mode of transportation.

All cars have certain methods (things they can do) in common. We can drive them, steer them, speed them up, slow them down, control the inside temperature, and more using *controls* within the car that we can manipulate with our hands.

An object in an object-oriented programming language isn't a physical thing, like a car, because it exists only inside a computer. However, you can have a class (which you can think as an object creator, such as a car factory) that can produce many different kinds of objects (cars) for varying purposes (sporty, off-road, sedan). All these objects can be controlled through the controls that all have in common, much as all cars are controlled by the steering wheel, brakes, accelerator, and gearshift.

Python is very much an object-oriented language. This may not be readily apparent when you first start learning because the core language consists of "controls" (in the form of words) that allow you to control all different kinds of objects. You need to learn the core language first so that when you're ready to start using other peoples' objects, you know how to do so. This is sort of like, once you know how to drive one car, you pretty much know how to drive them all. You don't have to worry about renting a car only to discover that the accelerator is on the roof, the steering wheel on the floor, and you have to use voice commands rather than a brake to slow it down. The basic skill of "driving" applies to all cars.

# Indentations Count, Big Time

In terms of the basic style of writing code, the one thing that really makes Python different from other languages is that it uses indentations rather than parentheses and curly braces and such, to indicate "blocks" or "chunks" of code. In this book, we don't assume you're familiar with other languages, so don't worry if that means nothing to you. But if you do happen to have some familiarity with a language like JavaScript, you know that there's quite a bit of wrangling with parentheses and such to control "what's inside of what." For example, here's some JavaScript code. If you're familiar with the Magic 8 Ball toy, you may have a sense of what this program is doing. But that's not what's important. Just notice that there are a lot of parentheses, curly braces, and semicolons in there:

```javascript
document.addEventListener("DOMContentLoaded", function () {var question =
    prompt("Ask magic 8 ball a question");var answer = Math.floor(Math.random()
    * 8) + 1; if (answer == 1) {alert("It is certain");} else if (answer == 2)
    {alert("Outlook good");} else if (answer == 3) {alert("You may rely on
    it");} else if (answer == 4) {alert("Ask again later");} else if (answer ==
    5) {alert("Concentrate and ask again");} else if (answer == 6) {alert
    ("Reply  hazy, try again");} else if (answer == 7) {alert("My reply is
    no");} else if (answer == 8) {alert("My sources say no")} else {alert
    ("That's not a question");}alert("The end");})
```

That code is a mess and not fun to read. We can make reading it a little easier by breaking it into multiple lines and indenting some of those lines. Doing so isn't required in JavaScript, but it can be done to make the code a little easier for a human to read, as shown below:

```javascript
document.addEventListener("DOMContentLoaded", function () {
    var question = prompt("Ask magic 8 ball a question");
    var answer = Math.floor(Math.random() * 8) + 1;
    if (answer == 1) {
        alert("It is certain");
    } else if (answer == 2) {
        alert("Outlook good");
    } else if (answer == 3) {
        alert("You may rely on it");
    } else if (answer == 4) {
        alert("Ask again later");
    } else if (answer == 5) {
        alert("Concentrate and ask again");
    } else if (answer == 6) {
        alert("Reply hazy, try again");
    } else if (answer == 7) {
        alert("My reply is no");
```

```
    } else if (answer == 8) {
        alert("My sources say no")
    } else {
        alert("That's not a question");}
    alert("The end");
})
```

In JavaScript, all the parentheses and curly braces are required because they identify where chunks of code begin and end. The indentations for readability are
optional.

Things are quite the opposite in Python because Python doesn't use curly braces
or any other special characters to mark the beginnings and ends of blocks of
code. The indentations themselves mark those. So those indentations aren't at all
optional — they are in fact required, and they have a considerable impact on how
the code runs. But the upside is, when you read the code, (as a human, not as a
computer), it's relatively easy to see what's going on, and you're not distracted
by a ton of extra quotation marks. Here is that JavaScript code written in Python:

```
import random
question = input("Ask magic 8 ball a question")
answer = random.randint(1,8)
if answer == 1:
    print("It is certain")
elif answer == 2:
    print("Outlook good")
elif answer == 3:
    print("You may rely on it")
elif answer == 4:
    print("Ask again later")
elif answer == 5:
    print("Concentrate and ask again")
elif answer == 6:
    print("Reply hazy, try again")
elif answer == 7:
    print ("My reply is no")
elif answer == 8:
    print ("My sources say no")
else:
    print("That's not a question")
print ("The end")
```

You may notice at the top of the Python code there is a line that starts with the
word import. Those are very common in Python, and you'll see why in the next
section.

# Using Python Modules

One of the secrets to Python's success is that it's comprised of a relatively simple, clean, core language. That's the part you really need to learn first. In addition to that core language, there are many, many modules out there that you can grab for free and access from your own code. These modules are also written in the core language, but you don't really need to see that or even know it, because you can access all the power of the modules from the basic core language.

Most modules are for some kind of specific application like science or numbers or artificial intelligence or working with dates and time or . . . whatever. The beauty of it is that somebody else (probably a lot of people) spent a lot of time creating, testing, and fine-tuning that module so you don't have to. You just have to import whichever modules you want into your own .py file, and use the modules' capabilities as instructed in the documentation that's available for each module.

The preceding sample Magic 8 Ball program starts with this line:

```
import random
```

As it turns out, the core Python language has nothing built into it to generate a random number. Although we could probably figure out some way to make one, there's no need to because somebody else has already figured out how to do this and made the code freely available. Starting our program with `import random` tells the program we want to use the capabilities of that module to generate a random number. Then, later in the program, we generate a random number between 1 and 8 with this specific line of code:

```
answer = random.randint(1,8)
```

Using the existing module saves me from having to reinvent the wheel trying to figure out how to make a random number from the core language. And there are literally hundreds of free modules for Python, which means you pretty much never have to reinvent any wheels. You just need to know which module to import into your program.

Now, you may be wondering where all the modules are located and where you can get them. Well, truthfully, they're all over the place online. But chances are, you will never need to go and download one because you already have all the most widely used modules in the world. You have them because they came along with Anaconda when you downloaded and installed that. To see for yourself, follow these steps:

1. **Open Anaconda in the usual manner on your computer.**

2. **Click Environments in the left column.**

Those things you see to the right are actually Python modules that are already installed on your computer and ready for you to import and use as needed. (See Figure 3-4.) As you scroll down through the names, you'll see that you already have a ton of them. In the right column, you even get to see which version of the module you have.

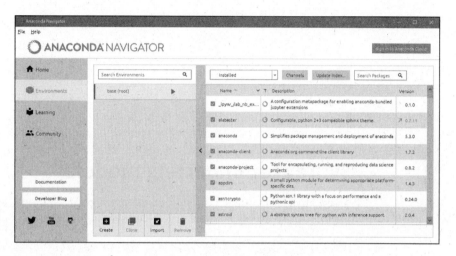

**FIGURE 3-4:**
Installed
modules.

You may also notice that some of the version numbers in the right column are colored and have an arrow showing. These represent modules that may have a more recent version available for you to download. As with programming languages, modules evolve over time and version as their authors improve things and add new capabilities. You're not required to always have the latest version, though. If the version you have is working, you can stick with that.

One of many nice things about Anaconda is that in order to get the latest version, you don't have to do any weird `pip` commands, as many older Python tutorials tell you to do. Instead, just click the arrow or version number of the module you want to download. In fact, you can click as many as you want. Then click Apply at the bottom-right. Anaconda does all the dirty work of finding the current module, determining whether there actually is a newer version available, and then downloading that version, if it's available.

When all the downloads are done, you'll see a dialog box like the one shown in Figure 3-5. If no names are listed, then that means all the selected modules are actually up-to-date so you can just click Cancel and then click Home in the left pane to return to Anaconda's home page. If, on the other hand, you do see some names listed under The Following Packages Will Be Modified, click Apply to install the latest versions.

Python Elements and Syntax

**FIGURE 3-5:**
All our packages
are installed and
up-to-date.

## Syntax for importing modules

As we already mentioned, in your own Python code, you must import a module before you can access its capabilities. The syntax for doing so is

```
import modulename [as alias]
```

When you see such a chart, always remember four things:

>> The code is case-sensitive, meaning you must type import and as using all lowercase letters, as shown. It won't work if you use uppercase letters.

>> Anything in italics is a placeholder for specific information that you'll supply in your own code. For example, there are dozens of modules available to you. In your code, you must replace *modulename* with the exact name of the module you want to import.

>> Anything in square brackets is optional, meaning you can type the command with or without that part.

>> You never type the square brackets in your code because they are not part of the Python language. They are used only to indicate optional parts in the syntax.

You can type the import any place you type Python code: the Python command prompt (>>>), in a .py file, or in a Jupyter notebook. In a .py file you should always put the import statements first, so their capabilities are available to the rest of the code.

# Using an alias with modules

As mentioned in the previous section, you can assign an alias, a "nickname," to any module you import just by following the module name with a space, the word as, and then a name of your own choosing. This is usually a short name that's easy to type and remember, so you don't have to type the long name every time you want to access the module's capabilities.

For example, instead of typing `import random` to import that module, we could import it and give it a nickname like `rnd`, which is shorter:

```
import random as rnd
```

Then, in subsequent code, you wouldn't use the full name, `random`, to refer to the module. Instead, you'd use the short name, `rnd`, as in the example below:

```
answer = rnd.randint(1,8)
```

It may not seem like a big deal in this short example. But you may come across some modules that have lengthy names, and your code requires referring to that module in many different places. Having the alias name available lets you type just that short name, you don't need to type the full name.

In previous chapters, we promised lots of hands-on in this book. Telling you all these facts without a lot of guided hands-on practice amounts may seem like cheating, then. We've done so, however, because these bits of background knowledge will help you make sense of things as you learn Python, and should help with seeing the big picture and remembering things. But now, without any further ado, it's time to really apply all you've learned so far and start getting your hands dirty with some real Python code. See you in the next chapter.

IN THIS CHAPTER

» **Open the Python app file**

» **Typing and using Python comments**

» **Understanding Python data types**

» **Doing work with Python operators**

» **Creating and using variables**

» **What syntax is and why it matters**

» **Putting code together**

# Chapter **4**

# Building Your First Python Application

So you want to build an application in Python, huh? Whether you want to code a website, analyze data, or create a script for automating something, this chapter gives you all the basics you need to get started on your journey. Most people use programming languages like Python to create application programs, which are often referred to as just applications or just programs or even apps for short. To create apps, you need to know how to write code inside a code editor. You also need to start learning the language (Python, in this book) in which you'll be creating those apps.

Like any language, you need to understand the individual words so that you can start building sentences and, finally, the blocks of code that will enable your app to work. First, we walk you through creating an app file in which you create your code. You then learn all about the various data types, operators, and variables that are the words of the Python language, and then Python syntax. Along the way, you see how to save your app, catch mistakes with linting, and even how to comment your code so that you and others can understand how you built it and why.

Are you ready?

# Open the Python App File

As we mentioned in the preceding chapters, we'll be using the ever-popular Visual Studio Code (VS Code) editor in this book to learn Python and to create Python apps. Here we assume you've already set up your learning/development environment as described in this chapter, and know how to open the main tools, Anaconda Navigator and VS Code. To follow along hands-on in this chapter, start with these steps:

1. **Open Anaconda Navigator and launch VS Code from there.**

2. **If your Python 3 workspace doesn't open automatically, choose File ⇨ Open Workspace from the VS Code menu and open the Python 3 workspace you created in Chapter 2.**

3. **Click the `hello.py` file you created in the previous chapter.**

4. **Select all the text on the first line and delete it, so we can start from scratch here.**

At this point, you should have `hello.py` open in the editor as shown in Figure 4-1. If you still have any other tabs open from before, close those now by clicking the X in each.

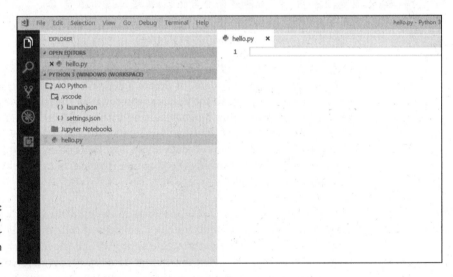

**FIGURE 4-1:**
The `hello.py` file, open for editing in VS Code.

# Typing and Using Python Comments

Before you type any code, let's start with a *programmer's comment*. A programmer's comment (usually called a *comment* for short) is text in the program that does nothing. Which brings up the question . . ." If it doesn't *do* anything, then why type it in?" As a learner, you can use comments in your code as notes to yourself about what the code is doing. These can help a lot when you're first learning.

Comments in code aren't strictly for beginners. When working in teams, professionals often use comments to explain to team members what their code is doing. Developers will also put comments in their code as notes to themselves, so that if they review the code in the future, they can refer to their own notes for reminders on why they did something in the code. Because a comment isn't code, your wording can be anything you want. However, to be identified as a comment, the text must

» Start with a pound sign

» Or be enclosed in triple quotation marks

If it's a short comment (if it doesn't extend to two or more lines), the leading pound sign is sufficient. Often you'll see that pound sign followed by a space, as in the example below, but that space is optional:

```
# This is a Python comment
```

To type a Python comment into your own code

**1.** **Click next to the 1 in VS Code under the hello.py tab and type** # This is a Python comment in my first Python app.

**2.** **Press Enter.**

The comment you typed appears on line 1 as in Figure 4-2. The comment text will be green if you're using the default color theme. You'll notice that the blinking cursor is now on line 2.

Although you won't use multiline comments just yet, be aware that you can type longer multiline comments in Python by enclosing them in triple quotation marks. These larger comments are sometimes called *docstrings* and often appear at the top of a Python module, function class, or method definition, which are app building blocks you will learn about a little later in this book. It isn't necessary to type one right now, but here's an example of what one may look like in Python code:

```
"""This is a multiline comment in Python
This type of comment is sometimes called a docstring.
A docstring starts with three double-quotation marks (""") and also ends with
    three double quotation marks.
```

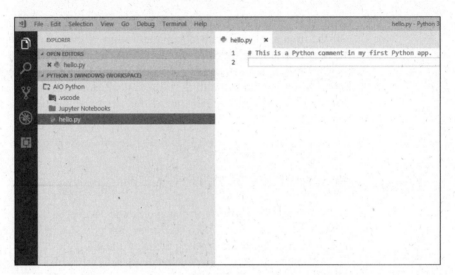

FIGURE 4-2:
A comment in
hello.py.

In VS Code, comments are usually colored differently than code. Short comments that start with # are green, whereas docstrings are brown, to help them stand out from the actual Python code that runs when you run the app.

In case you're wondering, there is no limit to how many comments you can put in your code. If you're waiting for something to happen after you type a comment . . . don't. When you're working in an editor like this, code doesn't do anything until you run it. Right now, all we have is a comment, so even if we did run this code, nothing would happen because code is for human readers, not computers. Before you go hands-on and start typing actual code, we need to start with the absolute basics, which would be . . .

# Understanding Python Data Types

You deal with written information all the time and probably don't think about the difference between numbers and text (that is, letters and words). But there's a big difference between numbers and text in a computer because with numbers, you can do arithmetic (add, subtract, multiple, divide). For example, everybody knows that 1+1 = 2. The same doesn't apply to letters and words. The expression A+A doesn't necessary equal B or AA or anything else because unlike numbers, letters and words aren't quantities. You can buy *12 apples* at the store, because 12 is a quantity, a number — a *scalar value* in programming jargon. You can't really buy a *snorkel apples* because a snorkel is a thing, it's not a quantity, number, or scalar value.

# Numbers

Numbers in Python must start with a number digit, (0–9); a dot (period), which is a decimal point; or a hyphen (–) used as a negative sign for negative numbers. A number can contain only one decimal point. It should contain no letters, spaces, dollar signs, or anything else that isn't part of a normal number. Table 4-1 shows example of good and bad Python numbers.

**TABLE 4-1**    ## Examples of Good and Bad Python Numbers

| Number | Okay? | Reason |
|---|---|---|
| 1 | Good | A whole number (integer) |
| 1.1 | Good | A number with a decimal point |
| 1234567.89 | Good | A large number with a decimal point and no commas |
| -2 | Good | A negative number, as indicated by the starting hyphen |
| .99 | Good | A number that starts with a decimal point because it's less than one. |
| $1.99 | Bad | Contains a $ |
| 12,345.67 | Bad | Contains a comma |
| 1101 3232 | Bad | Contains a space |
| 91740-3384 | Bad | Contains a hyphen |
| 123-45-6789 | Bad | Contains two hyphens |
| 123 Oak Tree Lane | Bad | Contains spaces and words |
| (267)555-1234 | Bad | Contain parentheses and hyphens |
| 127.0.0.1 | Bad | Only one decimal point is allowed |

**TIP**

If you're worried that the number rules won't let you work with dollar amounts, zip codes, addresses or anything else, stop worrying. You can store and work with *all* kinds of information, as you'll see shortly.

The vast majority of numbers you use will probably match one of the first four examples of good numbers. However, if you happen to be looking at code used for more advanced scientific or mathematical applications, you may occasionally see numbers that contain the letter *e* or the letter *j*. That's because Python actually supports three different types of numbers, as discussed in the sections that follow.

## Integers

An *integer* is any whole number, positive or negative. There is no limit to its size. Numbers like 0, -1, and 999999999999999 are all perfectly valid integers. From your perspective, an integer is just any valid number that doesn't contain a decimal point.

## Floats

A *floating point number*, often called a *float* for short, is just any valid number that contains a decimal point. Again, there is no size limit, 1.1 and -1.1 and 123456.789012345 are all perfectly valid floats.

If you happen to work with very large scientific numbers, you can put an *e* in a number to indicate the power of 10. For example, 234e1000 is a valid number, and will be treated as a float even if there's no decimal point. If you're familiar with scientific notation, you know 234e3 is 234,000 (replace the *e3* with 3 zeroes). If you're not familiar with scientific notation, don't worry about it. If you're not using it in your day-to-day work now, chances are you'll never need it in Python either.

## Complex numbers

Just about any kind of number can be expressed as an integer or float, so being familiar with those is sufficient for just about everyone. Though in the interest of being accurate we should point out that Python also supports *complex numbers*. These bizarre little charmers always end with the letter *j*, which is the *imaginary* part of the number. If you have absolutely no idea what we're talking about, then you're a normal person because only people who are really "out there" in math land care about these. If you've never heard of them before now, chances are you won't be using them in your computer work or Python programming.

# Words (strings)

Strings are sort of the opposite of numbers. With numbers, you can add, subtract, multiply, and divide because the numbers represent quantities. Strings are for just about everything else. Names, addresses, and all other kinds of text you see every day would be a *string* in Python (and for computers in general). It's called a *string* because it's a string of characters (letters, spaces, punctuation marks, maybe some numbers). To us, a string usually has some meaning, like a person's name or address, but computers don't have eyes to see with or brains to think with or any awareness that humans even exist, so if it's not something on which you can do arithmetic, it's just a string of characters.

Unlike numbers, a string must always be enclosed in quotation marks. You can use either double quotation marks (") or singles ('). All the following are valid strings:

```
"Hi there, I am a string"
'Hello world'
"123 Oak Tree Lane"
"(267)555-1234"
"18901-3384"
```

Notice that it's perfectly fine to use numeric characters (0–9) as well as hyphens and dots in strings. Each is still a string because it's enclosed in quotation marks.

A word of caution. If a string contains an apostrophe (single quote), then the whole string should be enclosed in double quotation marks like this:

```
"Mary's dog said Woof"
```

The double quotation marks are necessary because there's no confusion about where the string starts and ends. If you instead used single quotes, like this:

```
'Mary's dog said Woof'
```

. . . the computer would be too dumb to get that right. It would see the first single quote as the start of the string, the second one (after Mary) as the end of the string, and then it wouldn't know what to do with the rest of the stuff, and your app wouldn't run correctly.

Similarly, if the string contains double-quotation makes, then the whole thing should be enclosed in single quotation marks to avoid confusion. For example:

```
'The dog of Mary said "Woof".'
```

So the first single quotation mark starts the string, the second one ends it, and the double quotation marks cause no confusion because they're inside that string.

So what if we have a string that contains both single and double quotation marks, like this?:

```
Mary's dog said "Woof".
```

This deserves a resounding *hmm*. Fortunately, the creators of Python realized this sort of thing can happen, so they came up with an escape. In fact, the things you use are called *escape characters* because, in a sense, they allow you to escape (avoid) the "special meaning" of a character like a single or double quotation mark. To escape a character, just precede it with a backslash (\). Make sure you use a backslash (the one that leans back toward the previous character, like this \) or it won't work right.

Using that last example, we could enclose the whole thing in single quotation marks, and then escape the apostrophe (which is the same character) by preceding it with a backslash, like this:

```
'Mary\'s dog said "Woof".'
```

Or, we could enclose the whole thing in double quotation marks, and escape the quotation marks embedded with the string, like this:

```
"Mary's dog said \"Woof\"."
```

Another common use of the backslash is to add a line break to end a line, on the screen where a user is viewing it (the *user* being anybody who uses some app you wrote). For example, this string

```
"The old pond\nA frog jumped in,\nKerplunk!"
```

. . . would look like this when displayed to a user:

```
The old pond
A frog jumped in,
Kerplunk!
```

. . . because each \n would be converted to a line break, ending the line there:

# True/false Booleans

There is a third data type in Python that isn't exactly a number, or a string. It's called a *Boolean* (named after a mathematician named George Boole), and it can be one of two values: either True or False. It may seem a little odd to have a data type for something that can only be True or False. However, because of the way computers do their work, it's actually efficient to make True/False its own data type. A single bit, which is the smallest unit of storage in a computer, is all that's required to store a value that can only be True or False.

In Python code, people store True or False values in *variables* (placeholders in code that we discuss later in this chapter) using a format similar to this:

```
x = True
```

. . . or perhaps this:

```
X = False
```

You know `True` and `False` are Boolean here because they're not enclosed in quotation marks (as a string would be), and they're not numbers. Also, the *initial cap* is required. In other words, the first letter has to be capitalized and all the remaining letters after that have to be lowercase.

# Doing Work with Python Operators

You use computers in a couple of ways. One way is to simply *store* information, like a file cabinet but without any paper. As we discussed in the previous section, with Python and for computers in general it helps to think of information as being one of the following data types: number, string, or Boolean. You also use computers to *operate* on that information, meaning to do any necessary math or comparisons or searches or whatever to help you find information and organize it in a way that makes sense to you.

Python offers many different *operators* for working with and comparing types of information. Here we just summarize them all for future reference, without going into great detail. Whether you use an operator in your own work depends on the types of apps you develop. For now, it's sufficient just to be aware that they're available.

## Arithmetic operators

As the name implies, arithmetic operators are for doing arithmetic; addition, subtraction, multiplication, division, and others. Table 4-2 lists Python's arithmetic operators.

**TABLE 4-2**  **Python's Arithmetic Operators**

| Operator | Description | Example |
|----------|-------------|---------|
| + | Addition | 1 + 1 = 2 |
| - | Subtraction | 10 - 1 = 9 |
| * | Multiplication | 3 * 5 = 15 |
| / | Division | 10 / 5 = 2 |
| % | Modulus (remainder after division) | 11 % 5 = 1 |
| ** | Exponent | 3**2 = 9 |
| // | Floor division | 11 // 5 = 2 |

The first four items in the table are the same as you learned in elementary school. The last three are a little more advanced so we'll explain them here:

» The *modulus* is the remainder after division. So, for example, 11 % 5 is 1 because if you divide 11 by 2 you get 5 remainder 1. That 1 is the modulus (sometimes called the *modulo*).

» The *exponent* is ** because you can't type a small raised number in code. But it just means "raised to the power of" in the sense that 3**2 is $3^2$ or 3 squared, which is 3*3 or 9. And of course 3**4 would be 3*3*3*3 or 81.

» *Floor division*, indicated by //, is integer division in that anything after the decimal point is truncated (ignored). The term *truncated* in this sense means "cut off," without any rounding. For example, in regular division 9/5 is 1.8. But 9//5 is just 1 because the .8 is just chopped off, it doesn't even round up the 1 to a 2.

## Comparison operators

Computers can make decisions as part of doing their work. But these decisions are not "judgement call" decisions or anything "human" like that. They are decisions based on absolute facts based on comparisons. The operators Python offers to help you write code that makes decisions are listed in Table 4-3.

The first few are self-explanatory, so we won't go into detail there. The last two are tricky because they concern Python *objects*, which we haven't talked about yet. Talking about Python objects right now would be a big digression, so if you're at all confused about any operators right now, don't worry about it. For now, we just want to show them so that in case you're ever looking at other people's code, you'll have some sense of what they mean.

**TABLE 4-3**

## Python Comparison Operators

| Operator | Meaning |
|----------|---------|
| < | Less than |
| <= | Less than or equal to |
| > | Greater than |
| >= | Greater than or equal to |
| == | Equal to |
| != | Not equal to |
| is | Object identity |
| is not | Negated object identity |

# Boolean operators

The Boolean operators work with Boolean values (True or False) and are used to determine if one or more things is True or False. Table 4-4 summarizes the Boolean operators.

**TABLE 4-4**

## Python Boolean Operators

| Operator | Code Example | What It Determines |
|----------|--------------|--------------------|
| or | x or y | Either x or y is true |
| and | x and y | Both x and y are true |
| not | not x | x is not full |

Python style guide recommends always putting whitespace around operators. In other words, you want to use the spacebar on the keyboard to put a space before the operator, then type the operator, then add another space before continuing the line of code. Here is a somewhat simple example. We know you're not familiar with coding just yet so don't worry too much about the exact meaning of the code. Instead, notice the spaces around the = and > (greater than) operators.

```
num = 10
if num > 0:
    print("Positive number")
else:
    print("Negative number")
```

The first line stores the number 10 in a variable named num. Then the if checks to see whether num is greater than (>) 0. If it is, the program prints Positive number. Otherwise, it prints Negative number. So, let's say you change the first line of the program to this:

```
num = -1
```

If you make that change and run the program again, it prints Negative number because -1 is a negative number.

We used num as a sample variable name in this example so we could show you some operators with space around them. Of course, we haven't told you what variables are, so that part of the example may have left you scratching your head. We'll clear up that part of this business next.

# Creating and Using Variables

Variables are a big part of Python and all computer programming languages. A *variable* is simply a placeholder for information that may vary (change). For example, when you browse Amazon today, you can see your name and "member since" date appear on their home page, as shown in Figure 4-3.

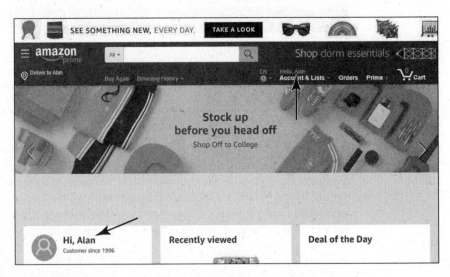

FIGURE 4-3:
The user's name and "Member since" date on Amazon's home page.

Certainly not everyone who goes to Amazon that day is named Alan and has been a member since 1996. Other people must be seeing other stuff there. But Amazon certainly can't make a custom home page for every one of its millions of users. So most of what's on that page is probably *literal* — meaning everybody who views the page sees the same stuff. Only the information that changes depending on who is viewing the page is stored as a variable (that is, only the information that is variable). A variable, in Python, is simply a storage place for information that can change at any time. But in your code it's represented by a variable *name* rather than a place.

Here is another way to think of it. Anytime you buy one or more of some product, the extended price is the unit price times the number of items you bought. In other words

*Quantity * Unit Price = Extended Price*

You can consider Quantity and Unit Price to be variables, because no matter what numbers you plug in for Quantity and Unit Price, you get the correct extended price. For example, if you buy 3 turtle doves for $1.00 apiece, your extended price is $3.00 (3 * $1.00). If you buy two dozen roses for $1.50 apiece, the extended price is $36 because 1.5 * 24 is 36.

So, if you consider Quantity and Unit Price to be *variables* in which you can store numbers, you get the correct extended price when you multiple those two numbers no matter what numbers you use to replace Quantity and Unit Price.

## Creating valid variable names

In our explanation of what a variable *is* we used names like Quantity and Unit Price, and this is certainly fine for a general example. Those are names we just made up. In Python, you can also make up your own variable names. But the rules are more stringent than when making them up in plain English. Python variable names have to conform to certain rules to be recognized as variable names. The rules are

>> The variable name must start with a letter or underscore (_).

>> After the first letter you can use letters, numbers, or underscores.

>> Variable names are case-sensitive, so once you make up a name, any other reference to that variable must use the same uppercase and lowercase letters as the name you originally made up.

>> Variable names cannot be enclosed in, or contain, single or double quotation marks.

>> PEP 8 style conventions recommend using only lowercase letters in variable names, use an underscore to separate multiple words in the variable name.

PEP 8, which we mentioned in previous chapters, is a style guide for writing code, rather than strict must-follow rules. So you often see variable names that don't conform to that last style. *Camel caps* formatting — whereby the first letter is made lowercase and new words are capitalized instead of separated by spaces — is pretty common, even in Python. For example, `extendedPrice` or `unitPrice` are Camel caps terms that are both technically valid and will not make your program fail. But experienced Python purists sometimes get that "disgusted" look on their face when they see names like these in you code. They would prefer you stick with the PEP 8 style guidelines, which recommend using `extended_price` and `unit_price` as your variable names, on the grounds that the PEP 8 syntax is more readable for human programmers.

## Creating variables in code

To create a variable, you use the syntax (order of things) as follows:

```
variablename = value
```

As mentioned, the *variablename* is the name you make up. You can use *x* or *y*, like people often do in math, but in larger programs, it's a good idea to give your variables more meaningful names, like `quantity` or `unit_price` or `sales_tax` or `user_name`, so that you can always remember what you're storing in the variable.

The *value* is whatever you want to store in the variable. It can be a number, a string, or a Boolean True or False value.

The = sign in the *assignment operator* is so named because it assigns the value (on the right) to the variable (on the left). For example, here . . .

```
x = 10
```

. . . we are storing the number 10 in a variable named *x*. Or, in other words, we're assigning the value 10 to the variable named *x*.

Here . . .

```
user_name = "Alan"
```

We're putting the string `Alan` in a variable named `username`.

# Manipulating variables

Much of computer programming revolves around storing values in variables and manipulating that information with operators. Let's go hands-on and try some simple examples just to get the hang of it. If you still have VS Code open with that one comment showing, follow these steps in the VS Code editor:

1. **Under the line that reads *# This is a Python comment in my first Python app.*, type this comment #** This variable contains an integer.

2. **Press Enter, type** quantity = 10 **(don't forget to put a space before and after the = sign), and press Enter.**

3. **Type #** This variable contains a float **and press Enter again.**

4. **Type** unit_price = 1.99 **and press Enter again (don't type a dollar sign!).**

5. **Type #** This variable contains the result of multiplying quantity times unit price **and press Enter.**

6. **Type** extended_price = quantity * unit_price **(again with spaces around the operators) and press Enter.**

7. **Type #** Show the results **and press Enter.**

8. **Type** print(extended_price) **and press Enter.**

Your Python app creates some variables, stores some value in them, and even calculates a new value, extended_price, based on the contents of the quantity and unit_price variables. The very last line displays the contents of the extended-price variable on the screen. Remember, the comments don't actually *do* anything in the program as it's running. The comments are just notes to yourself about what's going on in the program.

Figure 4-4 shows how things should look now. If you made any errors, you may see some red wavy lines near where there is an error, or possibly green wavy lines if it's just a stylistic error such as an extra space or an omitted Enter at the end of a line. If yours does have errors, make sure that you understand that when typing code, you *have to* be accurate. You can't type something that looks sorta like what you were supposed to type. When texting to humans, you can make all kinds of typographical errors and your human recipient can usually figure out what you meant based on the context of the message. But computers don't have eyes or brains or any concept of "context," and so they will generally just not work properly if there are errors in your code.

In other words, if the code is wrong, it won't work when you run it. It's as simple as that, no exception.

```
hello.py    ×

1    # This is a Python comment in my first Python app.
2    # This variable contains an integer
3    quantity = 10
4    # This variable contains a float
5    unit_price = 1.99
6    # This variable contains the result of multiplying quantity times unit price
7    extended_price = quantity * unit_price
8    # Show the results
9    print(extended_price)
10   |
```

**FIGURE 4-4:**
Your first
Python app
typed into
VS Code.

## Saving your work

Typing code is like typing other documents on a computer. If you don't save your work, you may not have it the next time you sit down at your computer and go looking for it. So if you haven't enabled Auto Save on the File menu, as discussed in previous chapters, choose File, then choose Save.

## Running your Python app in VS Code

Now we can run the app and see if it works. And an easy way to do that is to right-click the `hello.py` filename in the Explorer bar and choose Running a Python app in VS Code is easy. Just right-click the file's name (`hello.py`, in this example) and choose Run Python File in Terminal as shown in Figure 4-5.

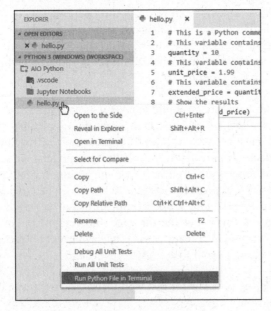

**FIGURE 4-5:**
Right-click a .py
file and choose
Run Python File
in Terminal.

If your code is typed correctly, you should see the result, 19.9, in the Terminal, as shown in Figure 4-6.

FIGURE 4-6:
The 19.9 is
the output
from print
(extended
price) in
the code.

```
PROBLEMS    OUTPUT    DEBUG CONSOLE    TERMINAL

(base) C:\Users\Alan\OneDrive\AIO Python>C:/ProgramData/Anaconda3/python.exe "c:/Users/Alan/OneDrive/AIO Python/hello.py"
19.9

(base) C:\Users\Alan\OneDrive\AIO Python>
```

The result of running the app appears down in the Terminal window. It certainly doesn't look like a typical phone, Mac, or Windows app. That's because you're just getting started and so need to keep things simple. The only indication that the app ran at all is the number 19.9 in the results. This is the output from print(extendedprice) in the code, and it's 19.9 because the quantity (10) times the unit price (1.99) is 19.9.

Suppose your app must calculate the cost of 14 items going for $26.99 each. Can you think of how to make that happen? You certainly wouldn't need to write a whole new app. Instead, in the code you're working with now, change the value of the quantity variable from 10 to 14. Change the value of the unitprice variable to 26.99 (remember, no dollars in your number). Here's how the code looks with those changes:

```python
# This is a Python comment in my first Python app.
# This variable contains an integer
quantity = 14
# This variable contains a float
unit_price = 26.99
# This variable contains the the result of multiplying quantity times unit price
extended_price = quantity * unit_price
# Show some results on the screen.
print(extended_price)
```

Save your work (unless you already turned on AutoSave as mentioned earlier in this chapter). Then run that app with the changes by right-clicking and choosing Run Python File in Terminal once again . . . just like the first time. The results are again quite a bit of gobbledygook. But you should see the correct answer, 377.85999999999996, in the Terminal near the bottom of the VS Code window. It doesn't round to pennies and it doesn't even look like a dollar amount. But you need to learn to crawl before you can learn to pole vault, so for now let's just be happy with getting our apps to run.

# What Syntax Is and Why It Matters

If you look up the word *syntax* in the dictionary, you'll probably see it defined as something like "the arrangement of words and phrases to create well-formed sentences in a language." In programming languages like Python, there really is no such thing as a well-formed sentence. With code, we generally refer to each line of code a *statement* or a *line* (of code). But the order of words is important, and there are "words" in the sense that you need a space between each word, just as you do when typing regular text like this.

Syntax is important in human languages because the order contributes much to the meaning. For example, compare these three short sentences:

Mary kissed John.

John kissed Mary.

Kissed Mary John.

All three sentences contain the same exact words. But the meanings are very different. The first two make it clear who kissed whom, and the last one is a little hard to interpret. Even though they all contain exactly the same words.

Proper syntax in programming languages is every bit as important as it is in human languages — even more so, in some ways, because when you make a mistake speaking or writing to someone, that other person can usually figure out what you meant by the context of your words. But computers aren't nearly that smart. Computers don't have brains, can't "guess your actual meaning" based on context, and in fact the whole concept of "context" doesn't even exist for computers. So syntax matters even more when writing code to tell a computer what to do than it does for human languages.

Looking back at our earliest code, notice that all the lines of actual code (not the comments, which start with #) follow the syntax . . .

```
variablename = value
```

. . . where `variablename` is some name we made up, and `value` is something we are storing in that variable. It works because it's the proper syntax. If you try to do it like this . . .

```
value = variablename
```

. . . it won't work. For example, this is the correct way to store the value 10 in a variable named x:

```
x = 10
```

It may seem you could also do it this way . . .

```
10 = x
```

. . . but that won't work in Python. If you run the app with that line in it, nothing terrible will happen . . . you won't break anything. But you will get an error message that looks something like this:

```
File ".../AIO Python/hello.py", line 10
    10=x
     ^
SyntaxError: can't assign to literal
```

The SyntaxError part tells you that Python doesn't know what to do with that line of code because you didn't follow the proper syntax. To fix the error, just rewrite the line as

```
x = 10
```

The Python language consists of lines of code, each one ending with a line break or semicolon. In other words, this is three lines of Python code:

```
first_name="Alan"
last_name="Simpson"
print(first_name,last_name)
```

It would also be perfectly acceptable to us a semicolon wherever instead of a line break, as below.

```
first_name="Alan"; last_name="Simpson"
print(first_name,last_name)
```

Or, if you prefer:

```
first_name="Alan"; last_name="Simpson"; print(first_name,last_name)
```

Note that there is no advantage or disadvantage to doing so in terms of how the code runs. The code runs exactly the same either way. The semicolons are just an alternative to line breaks that you can use if, for whatever reason, you want to put a lot of code alone one physical line in your editor.

Note how our variables' names are all lowercase, and the words are separated by an underscore:

```
first_name
last_name
```

This is a *naming convention* used in Python — to use all lowercase letters for variable names with words separated by underscores. But note that a *convention* is not the same as a *syntax rule*. You could name the variables as

```
FirstName
LastName
```

This is perfectly okay in Python and doesn't break any syntax rules. The naming *convention* is just there to try to get programmers to follow some basic stylistic rules that make the code more readable to other programs, which is especially important when working in programming teams or groups.

So far we're looked at lines of code. There are also blocks of code or code *blocks* where two or more lines of code work together in some manner. Here is an example:

```
x = 10
if x == 0:
    print("x is zero")
else:
    print("x is ",x)
print("All done")
```

The == (two equal signs) means "is equal to" in Python and is used to compare values to one another to see if they're equal. That's different from just = (one equal sign), which is the assignment operator for assigning variables.

The first line, x=10, is just a line of code. Next, the if x == 0 tests to see whether the x variable contains the number zero. If x *does* contain zero, then the indented line (print("x is zero")) executes and that's what you see on the screen. However, if x does not contain zero, then that indented line is skipped over and the else: statement executes. The indented line under else: print("x is ",x) executes, but *only* if the x doesn't contain zero. The last line, print("All done!"), executes no matter what, since it's not indented.

So, in other words, indentations matter a lot in Python, since only one of the indented lines above will execute depending on the value in x. We'll get into the specifics of using indentations in your code as we progress through the book. For now, just try to remember that syntax, and indentations are important in Python, so you must type carefully when writing code.

Next time you run the app, it will run and you won't get a syntax error for that line.

If you have linting and PEP 8 enabled in your Workspace settings, as described in Chapter 3, then you may see red wavy underlines or green wavy underlines on code that appears to be perfectly okay. Touching the mouse pointer to such an underline will usually show a message at the mouse pointer indicating what the problem is, as in Figure 4-7.

FIGURE 4-7:
Touched the
mouse pointer
to a red wavy
underline.

```
hello.p
1        [pep8] missing whitespace around operator
2        quantity: int                            ion app.
3        quantity=14
4        # This variable contains a float
5        unit price = 26.99
```

The first part of the message reads:

```
[pep8] missing whitespace around operator
```

That's telling you that this particular error is related to Pep 8 syntax, which says you should put whitespace around operators.

The second part just tells you that the variable named quantity contains an integer (int), a whole number. That's not an error, just information.

To fix the error, put whitespace around the = sign. In other words, us the spacebar on your keyboard to put a space before the = sign, and then another space after the = sign.

Now let's suppose you fix that spacing issue but still see a green wavy underline under the 14. What's up with that? Well, to find out, simply click the green wavy underline and leave the mouse pointer sitting right there until you see an explanation, as in Figure 4-8.

```
hello.py      ✕
1   # This is a       [pep8] trailing whitespace
2   # This vari  14: int
3   quantity = 14
4   # This variable contains a float
5   unit_price = 26.99
6   # This variable contains the result of
7   extended_price = quantity * unit_price
8   # Show the results
9   print(extended_price)
```

FIGURE 4-8:
Touching the
mouse pointer
to a green wavy
underline.

Building Your First
Python Application

This time, the top message shows *[pep8] trailing whitespace* on top, and *14: int* on the bottom. Again, the bottom part is just informational, telling you that the 14 is stored as an integer. The error is the trailing whitespace. What this means is that, for whatever reason, there happens to be a blank space after the 14 on that line. You can't see it, because it's just a space. But if you click the end of that line and press Backspace until the cursor is right up to the 4 in 14, then you will have eliminated any trailing spaces, and that should clear that error.

Keep in mind that not all red errors are the same and not all green errors are the same. So don't make any assumptions. In general, red errors are likely to prevent the app from running correctly, while green errors are just stylistic errors. But you won't know, specifically, what the error is unless you click the wavy underline and leave the mouse pointer there until you see the message. And the error won't go away until you take whatever action is required to fix that error.

**TIP**

If the PeP 8 errors really drive you nuts when trying to learn, remember you can go into the VS Code Workspace Settings and turn off the Python ⇨ Linting: Pep8Enabled setting so it doesn't check your code so aggressively.

# Putting Code Together

The exercises you've just completed explain how to type, save, run, change, and save again, run an app again after making your changes. All those different things define what you'll be doing with any kind of software development in any language. So you want to practice them often until they become second nature to you. But don't worry, that doesn't mean you have to do this one chapter over and over again to get the hang of it. You'll be using all these same skills throughout this book as you work your way from absolute beginner to hot-shot twenty-first century Python developer.

# 2

# Understanding Python Building Blocks

# Contents at a Glance

IN THIS CHAPTER

» **Mastering whole numbers**

» **Juggling numbers with decimal points**

» **Simplifying strings**

» **Conquering Boolean true/false**

» **Uncovering dates and times**

# Chapter **1**

# Working with Numbers, Text, and Dates

Computers in general, and certainly Python, deal with information in ways that are different from what you may be used to in your everyday life. This takes some getting used to. In the computer world, *numbers* are numbers you can add, subtract, multiply, and divide. Python also differentiates between whole numbers (called *integers*) and numbers that contain a decimal point (called *floats*). Words (textual information like names and addresses) are stored as *strings*, which is short for "a string of characters."

In addition to numbers and strings, there are Boolean values, which can be either True or False, but nothing else. In real life, we also have to deal with dates and times, which are yet another type of information. Python doesn't actually have any built-in data type for dates and times, but thankfully, a free module you can import any time works with such information. This chapter is all about taking full advantage of the various Python data types.

# Calculating Numbers with Functions

A *function* in Python is similar to a function on a calculator, in that you pass something into the function, and the function passes something back. For example, most calculators and programming languages have a square root function: You give it a number, and it gives back the square root of that number.

Python functions generally have the syntax:

*variablename = functioname(param,[param])*

Because most functions return some value, you typically start by defining a variable to store what the function returns. Follow that with an = sign and the function name, followed by a pair of parentheses. Inside the parentheses you may pass one or more values (called *parameters* or *arguments*) to the function.

For example, the abs() function accepts one number and returns the absolute value of that number. If you're not a math nerd, this just means if you pass it a negative number, it returns that same number as a positive number. If you pass it a positive number, it returns exactly the same number you passed it. In other words, the abs() function simply converts negative numbers to positive numbers.

As an example, in Figure 1-1 (which you can try out for yourself hands-on in a Jupyter notebook, the Python prompt, or a .py file in VS Code), I created a variable named x and assigned it the value -4. Then I create a variable named y and assigned it the absolute value of x using the abs() function. Printing x then shows its value, -4, which hasn't changed. Printing y shows 4, the absolute value of x as returned by the abs() function.

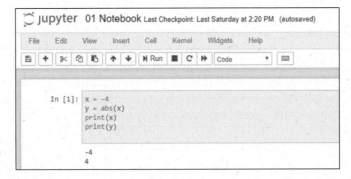

**FIGURE 1-1:**
Trying out the
abs() function.

Even though a function always returns one value, there are some that accept two or more values. For example, the round() function takes one number as its first argument. The second value is the number of decimal places to which you want to round that number, for example, 2 for two decimal places. In the example in

Figure 1-2, we created a variable, x, with a whole lot of numbers after the decimal point. Then we created a variable named y to return that same number rounded to two decimal places. Then we printed both results.

**FIGURE 1-2:**
Trying out
the round()
function.

```
In [2]: x = 1.234567890987654321000000000000000000000001
        y = round(x,2)
        print(x)
        print(y)

        1.2345678909876543
        1.23
```

Python has many built-in functions for working with numbers, as shown in Table 1-1. Some of them may not mean much to you if you're not into math in a big way, but don't let that intimidate you. If you don't understand what a function does, chances are it's not doing something that's relevant to the kind of work you do. But if you're curious, you can always google the word *python* followed by the function name for more information. For a more extensive list, google *python 3 built-in functions*.

**TABLE 1-1** **Some Built-In Python Functions for Numbers**

| Built-In Function | Purpose |
|---|---|
| abs($x$) | Returns the absolute value of number $x$ (converts negative numbers to positive) |
| bin(x) | Returns a string representing the value of $x$ converted to binary. |
| float($x$) | Converts a string or number $x$ to a the float data type |
| format(x,y) | Returns $x$ formatted as directed by format string $y$. In modern Python you're more likely to use f-strings, as described later in this chapter |
| hex(x) | Returns a string containing $x$ converted to hexadecimal, prefixed with 0x. |
| int(x) | Converts $x$ to the integer data type by truncating (not rounding) the decimal point and any digits after it. |
| max(x,y,z ...) | Takes any number of numeric arguments and returns whichever one is the largest. |
| min(x,y,z ...) | Takes any number of numeric arguments and returns whichever one is the smallest. |
| oct(x) | Converts $x$ to an octal number, prefixed with 0o to indicate octal. |
| round($x, y$) | Rounds the number $x$ to $y$ number of decimal places. |
| str(x) | Converts number $x$ to the string data type. |
| type(x) | Returns a string indicating the data type of $x$. |

Figure 1-3 shows examples of proper Python syntax for using the built-in math functions.

```
pi=3.14159265358979
x=128
y=-345.67890987
z=-999.9999
print(abs(z))
print(int(z))
print(int(abs(z)))
print(round(pi,4))
print(bin(x))
print(hex(x))
print(oct(x))
print(max(pi,x,y,z))
print(min(pi,x,y,z))
print(type(pi))
print(type(x))
print(type(str(y)))

999.9999
-999
999
3.1416
0b10000000
0x80
0o200
128
-999.9999
<class 'float'>
<class 'int'>
<class 'str'>
```

**FIGURE 1-3:**
Playing around with built-in math functions at the Python prompt.

You can also "nest" functions — meaning you can put functions inside of functions. For example, when $z = -999.9999$, the expression `print(int(abs(z)))` prints the integer portion of the absolute value of z, which is 999 (the original number converted to positive, and then the decimal point and everything to its right chopped off).

# Still More Math Functions

The built-in math functions are handy, but there are still others you can import from the math module. If you need them in an app, put `import math` near the top of the .py file or Jupyter cell to make those functions available to the rest of the code. At the command prompt, you can just enter the command `import math` before using those functions at the command prompt.

One of the functions of the math module is the `sqrt()` function that gets the square root of a number. Because it's part of the math module, you cannot use it without importing the module first. For example, if you enter this:

```
print(sqrt(81))
```

. . . you'll get an error because `sqrt()` isn't a built-in function. Even if you do two commands like this:

```
import math
print(sqrt(81))
```

. . . you still get an error because you're treating `sqrt()` as a built-in function.

To use a function from a module, you have to import the module *and* precede the function name with the module name and a dot. So let's say you have some value, x, and you want the square root. You have to import the `math` module and use `math.sqrt(x)` to get the correct answer, as shown in Figure 1-4.

**FIGURE 1-4:**
Using the `sqrt()`
function from the
math module.

```
In [11]:  import math
          z = 81
          print(math.sqrt(81))

          9.0
```

Entering that command shows 9.0 as the result, which is indeed the square root of 81.

The `math` module offers a lot trigonometric and hyperbolic functions, powers and logarithms, angular conversions, constants like `pi` and `e`. We won't delve into all of them since advanced math isn't all that relevant to most people. You can check them all out at any time by googling *python 3 math module functions*. Table 1-2 offers a handful of examples, some of which may prove useful in your own work.

**TABLE 1-2**  ### Some Functions from the Python Math Module

| Built-In Function | Purpose |
|---|---|
| `math.acos(x)` | Returns the arc cosine of x in radians. |
| `math.atan(x)` | Returns the arc tangent of x, in radians. |
| `math.atan2(y, x)` | Returns atan(y / x), in radians. |
| `math.ceil(x)` | Returns the ceiling of x, the smallest integer greater than or equal to x. |
| `math.cos(x)` | Returns the cosine of x radians. |
| `math.degrees(x)` | Converts angle x from radians to degrees. |
| `math.e` | Returns the mathematical constant e (2.718281 . . .). |

*(continued)*

**TABLE 1-2** *(continued)*

| Built-In Function | Purpose |
|---|---|
| `math.exp(x)` | Returns *e* raised to the power *x*, where *e* is the base of natural logarithms. |
| `math.factorial(x)` | Returns the factorial of *x*. |
| `math.floor()` | Returns the floor of *x*, the largest integer less than or equal to *x*. |
| `math.isnan(x)` | Returns True if *x* is not a number, otherwise returns False. |
| `math.log(x,y)` | Returns the natural logarithm of *x* to base *y*. |
| `math.log2(x)` | Returns the base-2 logarithm of *x*. |
| `math.pi` | Returns the mathematical constant pi (3.141592 . . .). |
| `math.pow(x, y)` | Returns *x* raised to the power *y*. |
| `math.radians(x)` | Converts angle *x* from degrees to radians. |
| `math.sin(x)` | Returns the arc sine of *x*, in radians. |
| `math.sqrt(x)` | Takes any number of numeric arguments and returns whichever one is the smallest. |
| `math.tan(x)` | Returns the tangent of *x* radians. |
| `math.tau()` | Returns the mathematical constant tau (6.283185 . . .). |

The constants `pi`, `e`, and `tau` are unusual for functions in that you don't use any parentheses. As with any function, you can use those functions in expressions (calculations) or assign their values to variables. Figure 1-5 shows some examples of using functions from the `math` module.

```
In [22]:  import math
          pi = math.pi
          e = math.e
          tau = math.tau
          x = 81
          y = 7
          z = -23234.5454
          print(pi)
          print(e)
          print(tau)
          print(math.sqrt(x))
          print(math.factorial(y))
          print(math.floor(z))
          print(math.degrees(y))
          print(math.radians(45))

          3.141592653589793
          2.718281828459045
          6.283185307179586
          9.0
          5040
          -23235
          401.07045659157626
          0.7853981633974483
```

**FIGURE 1-5:**
More playing around with built-in math functions at the Python prompt.

# Formatting Numbers

Over the years Python has offered different methods for getting numbers to display in formats that are familiar to us humans. For example, we may prefer it display $1,234.56 rather than 1234.56006595069540569405959. As of version 3.6 of Python, f-strings seem to the fastest, easiest, and most preferred method of achieving this.

## Formatting with f-strings

F-string formatting is relatively simple to do. All you need is a lowercase or uppercase *f* followed immediately by some text or expressions enclosed in quotation marks. Something along these lines:

```
f"Hello {username}"
```

The f before the first quotation mark tells Python that what follows is a format string (f-string). Inside the quotation marks, the text, called the *literal part*, is displayed literally (exactly as typed in the f-string). Anything in curly braces is the *expression* part of the f-string. The expression part is a placeholder for what's actually going to show there when the code executes. Inside the curly braces you can have an *expression* (a formula to perform some calculation, a variable name, or a combination of the two). Here is an example:

```
username = "Alan"
print(f"Hello {username}")
```

When you run this code, the print function displays the word Hello, followed by a space, followed by the contents of a variable named username, as in Figure 1-6.

**FIGURE 1-6:**
A super simple
f-string for
formatting.

```
In [24]: username = "Alan"
         print(f"Hello {username}")

         Hello Alan
```

Here is another example where we have an expression — the formula quantity times unit_price — inside the curly braces.

```
unit_price = 49.99
quantity = 30
print(f"Subtotal: ${quantity * unit_price}")
```

The output from that, when executed, is:

```
Subtotal: $1499.7
```

That $1499.7 isn't really an ideal way to show dollar amounts. Typically we like to use commas in the thousands places, and two digits for the pennies, as in the example below:

```
Subtotal: $1,499.70
```

Fortunately, f-strings provide you with the means to do this, as you learn next.

## Showing dollar amounts

To get a comma to show in the dollar amount and the pennies to be two digits, you can use a *format string* inside the curly braces of an expression in an f-string. The format string starts with a colon and needs to be placed inside the closing curly brace, right up against the variable name or the value being shown.

To show commas in thousands places, use a comma in your format string right after the colon, like this:

```
:,
```

Using our current example, this would be:

```
print(f"Subtotal: ${quantity * unit_price:,}")
```

Executing this statement produced this output:

```
Subtotal: $1,499.7
```

To get the pennies to show as two digits, follow the comma with

```
.2f
```

The .2f means "two decimal places, fixed" (never any more or less than two decimal places). So here's how the code looks to show the number with commas and two decimal places:

```
print(f"Subtotal: ${quantity * unit_price:,.2f}")
```

Here is how this code looks when executed:

```
Subtotal: $1,499.70
```

Perfect! That's exactly the format we want. So any time you want to show a number with commas in the thousands places and exactly two digits after the decimal point, use an f-string with the format string `,.2f`.

## Formatting percent numbers

Now, suppose your app applies sales tax. This app needs to know the sales tax rate, which should be expressed as a decimal number. So if the sales tax rate is 6.5 percent, then it has to be written as 0.065 (or .065, if you prefer) in your code, like this:

```
sales_tax_rate = 0.065
```

It's the same amount with or without the leading zero, so just use whichever format works for you.

This number format is ideal for Python, and you wouldn't want to mess with that. But if you want to show that number to a human, simply displaying it with a `print()` function shows it exactly as Python stores it:

```
sales_tax_rate = 0.065
print(f"Sales Tax Rate {sales_tax_rate}")

Sales Tax Rate 0.065
```

When displaying the sales tax rate for people to read, you'll probably want to use the more familiar 6.5% format rather than .065. You can use the same idea as with fixed numbers (`.2f`); however, don't use the f for "fixed numbers." Instead replace that with a % sign, like this:

```
print(f"Sales Tax Rate {sales_tax_rate:.2%}")
```

Running this code multiples the sales tax rate by 100 and follows it with a % sign, as you can see in Figure 1-7.

In both of the preceding examples, we used 2 for the number of digits. But of course you can display any number of digits you want, from zero (none) to whatever level of precision you need. For example, using 1.%, as in the following:

```
print(f"Sales Tax Rate {sales_tax_rate:.1%}")
```

FIGURE 1-7:
Formatting a
percentage
number
with .2%.

```
In [36]: sales_tax_rate = 0.065
         print(f"Sales Tax Rate {sales_tax_rate:.2%}")

         Sales Tax Rate 6.50%
```

. . . shows this output when executed:

```
Sales Tax Rate 6.5%
```

Replacing that 1 with a 9, like this

```
print(f"Sales Tax Rate {sales_tax_rate:.9%}")
```

. . . displays the percentage with nine digits after the decimal point.

```
Sales Tax Rate 6.500000000%
```

Your format string doesn't have to be one short thing inside the parentheses of a print() function. You can store it to a variable too, then print the variable. The format string itself is like any other string in that it must be enclosed in single, double, or triple quotation marks. It doesn't matter which you use as the outermost quotation marks on the format string, the output is the same regardless, as you can see in the example shown in Figure 1-8.

```
: sales_tax_rate = 0.065
  sample1 = f'Sales Tax Rate {sales_tax_rate:.2%}'
  sample2 = f"Sales Tax Rate {sales_tax_rate:.2%}"
  sample3 = f"""Sales Tax Rate {sales_tax_rate:.2%}"""
  sample4 = f'''Sales Tax Rate {sales_tax_rate:.2%}'''

  print(sample1)
  print(sample2)
  print(sample3)
  print(sample4)

  Sales Tax Rate 6.50%
  Sales Tax Rate 6.50%
  Sales Tax Rate 6.50%
  Sales Tax Rate 6.50%
```

FIGURE 1-8:
An f-string can be
encased in single,
double, or triple
quotation marks.

TIP

For single and double quotation marks, use the ones on the keyboard key that shows both kinds of quotation marks. For triple quotation marks, you can use three of either. Make sure you end the string with exactly the same characters you used to start the string. For example, all the strings in Figure 1-8 are perfectly valid code, and they will all be treated the same.

# Making multiline format strings

If you want to have line breaks in your format strings for multiline output, you have a couple of choices:

» **Use /n:** You can use a single-line format string with \n any place you want a line break. Just make sure you put the \n in the literal portion of the format string, not inside any curly braces. For example:

```
user1 = "Alberto"
user2 = "Babs"
user3 = "Carlos"
output=f"{user1} \n{user2} \n{user3}"
print(output)
```

When executed, this code displays:

```
Alberto
Babs
Carlos
```

» **Use triple quotation marks:** If you use triple quotation marks around your format string, then you don't need to use \n. You can just break the line in the format string wherever you want it to break in the output. For example, look at the code in Figure 1-9. The format string is in triple quotation marks and contains multiple line breaks. The output from running the code has line breaks in all the same places.

As you can see, the output honors the line breaks and even the blank spaces in the format string. Unfortunately it's not perfect — in real life, we would right-align all the numbers so all the decimal points line up. All is not lost, though, because with format strings you can also control the width and alignments of your output.

**FIGURE 1-9:**
A multiline
f-string
enclosed in
triple
quotation
marks.

```
unit_price = 49.95
quantity = 32
sales_tax_rate = 0.065
subtotal = quantity * unit_price
sales_tax = sales_tax_rate * subtotal
total = subtotal + sales_tax
output=f"""
Subtotal:  ${subtotal:,.2f}
Sales Tax: ${sales_tax:,.2f}
Total:     ${total:,.2f}
"""
print(output)
```

```
Subtotal:  $1,598.40
Sales Tax: $103.90
Total:     $1,702.30
```

# Formatting width and alignment

You can also control the width of your output (and the alignment of content within that width) by following the colon in your f-string with < (for left-aligned), ^ (for centered), or > (for right-aligned). Put any of these characters right after the colon in your format string. For example

```
:>20
```

. . . says "make this output 20 characters wide, with the content right-aligned."

In the last example in the previous section, we were able to get all the dollar amounts left-aligned in the output by making then left-aligned in the format string. But because the numbers aren't all the same width, they're not right-aligned. To get around that, in Figure 1-10 we used > to make each of the dollar amounts right-align a width of 9. The printed output shows the numbers are correctly right-aligned.

```python
unit_price = 49.95
quantity = 32
sales_tax_rate = 0.065
subtotal = quantity * unit_price
sales_tax = sales_tax_rate * subtotal
total = subtotal + sales_tax
output=f"""
Subtotal:   ${subtotal:>9,.2f}
Sales Tax: ${sales_tax:>9,.2f}
Total:      ${total:>9,.2f}
"""

print(output)


Subtotal:  $ 1,598.40
Sales Tax: $   103.90
Total:     $ 1,702.30
```

**FIGURE 1-10:** All dollar amounts are right-aligned within a width of 9 characters (>9).

You may look at Figure 1-10 and wonder why the dollar signs are lined up the way they are. Why aren't they aligned right next to their numbers? This is because the dollar signs are part of the literal string, outside the curly braces. So they aren't affected by the >9 inside the curly braces.

Getting around this issue is a little more complicated than you may imagine, because you can only use the , .2f formatting on a number. You can't attach a $ to the front of a number unless you change the number to a string . . . but then it won't be a number anymore so the , .2f won't work. Complicated, however, doesn't mean impossible; it just means inconvenient. We can convert each dollar amount to a string in the current format, stick the dollar sign on that string, and then format the width and alignment on this string. For example, here is how we could do the subtotal variable:

```
s_subtotal = "$" + f"{subtotal:,.2f}"
```

The subtotal is a number calculated by multiplying the quantity times the unit_price. The s"{subtotal:,2f}" formats that number in the fixed two-decimal-places format with commas in the thousands places, like this:

```
1,598.40
```

This is a string rather than a number, because an f-string always produces a string. The app sticks a dollar sign on the front of that string using "$"+. So you end up with a string that looks like $1,598.40. We put this in a new variable named s_subtotal. (We added the leading s_ to remind us that this is the string equivalent of the subtotal number, not the original number.) Later in the format string we just give this a width and right-align it to that width using >9, like this:

```
Subtotal:  {s_subtotal:>9}
```

**REMEMBER**

When you use + with strings you *concatenate* (join together) the two strings. The + only does addition with numbers, not strings.

Figure 1-11 shows the whole kit-and-caboodle, including the output from running the code. All the numbers are right-aligned with the dollar signs in the usual place.

```
# Numerical values
unit_price = 49.95
quantity = 32
sales_tax_rate = 0.065
subtotal = quantity * unit_price
sales_tax = sales_tax_rate * subtotal
total = subtotal + sales_tax

# Format amounts to show as string with leading dollar sign
s_subtotal = "$" + f"{subtotal:,.2f}"
s_sales_tax = "$" + f"{sales_tax:,.2f}"
s_total = "$" + f"{total:,.2f}"

# Output the string with dollar sign already attached
output=f"""
Subtotal:  {s_subtotal:>9}
Sales Tax: {s_sales_tax:>9}
Subtotal:  {s_total:>9}
"""
print(output)


Subtotal:  $1,598.40
Sales Tax:   $103.90
Subtotal:  $1,702.30
```

**FIGURE 1-11:**
All the dollar amounts neatly aligned.

# Grappling with Weirder Numbers

Most of us deal with simple numbers like quantities and dollar amounts all the time. If your work requires you to deal with bases other than 10, or with imaginary numbers, Python has the stuff you need to get the job done. But keep in mind that you don't need to learn these things to use Python or any other language. You would only use these if your actual work (or perhaps homework) requires it. We'll start with binary, octal, and hex numbers, which are used frequently in computer science.

## Binary, octal, and hexadecimal numbers

If your work requires dealing with base 2, base 8, or base 16 numbers, you're in luck with Python because it has symbols for writing these as well as functions for converting among them. Table 1-3 shows the three non-decimal bases and the digits used by each.

**TABLE 1-3**      **Python for Base 2, 8, and 16 Numbers**

| System | Also Called | Digits Used | Symbol | Function |
|---|---|---|---|---|
| Base 2 | Binary | 0,1 | 0b | bin( ) |
| Base 8 | Octal | 0,1,2,3,4,5,6,7 | 0o | oct( ) |
| Base 16 | Hexadecimal or Hex | 0,1,2,3,4,5,6,7,8,9, A,B,C,D,E,F | 0x | hex( ) |

In all honesty, most people never have to work with binary, octal, or hexadecimal numbers. So if all of this is giving you the heebie-jeebies, don't sweat it. If you never heard of them before, chances are you'll never hear of them again after you've completed this section.

**TIP**

If you want more information about the various numbering systems, you can go to your favorite search engine and search for *binary number* or *octal*, or *decimal*, or *hexadecimal*.

If you do need to work in other numbering systems for computer science homework or whatever, you can use the various functions to convert between numbering systems. You can do so right at the Python prompt, of course, as well as in an apps you create. At the prompt, just use the print( ) function with the conversion function inside the parentheses, and the number you want to convert inside the innermost parentheses. For example, this gets you the hexadecimal equivalent of the number 255:

```
print(hex(255))
```

The result is 0xff, where the 0x is there just to indicate that the number that follows is expressed in hex, and ff is the hexadecimal equivalent of 255.

To convert from binary, octal, or hex to decimal, you don't need to use a function. Just use print() with the number you want to convert inside the parentheses. For example, print(0xff) displays 255, the decimal equivalent of hex ff. Figure 1-12 shows some more examples you can try at the Python prompt.

```
x=255
# Convert decimal to other number systems
print(bin(x))
print(oct(x))
print(hex(x))

# Show number in decimal number system (no conversion required)
print(0b11111111)
print(0o377)
print(0xff)

0b11111111
0o377
0xff
255
255
255
```

**FIGURE 1-12:**
Messing about with binary, octal, and hex.

**TECHNICAL STUFF**

In case you're wondering about the print("\n") in Figure 1-12, it displays a line break, which produces the blank line you see in the output.

## Complex numbers

Complex numbers are another one of those weird numbering things you may never have to deal with unless you happen to be into electrical engineering, higher math, or a branch of science that uses them. A *complex number* is one that can be expressed as *a+bi* where *a* and *b* are real numbers, and *i* represents the imaginary number satisfied by the equation $x^2=-1$. There is no number *x* whose square equals −1, so that's why it's called an *imaginary number*.

Some branches of math actually use the lowercase letter *i* to indicate an imaginary number. But Python uses *j*, as does electrical engineering, where *i* is used to indicate current. Anyway, if your application requires working with complex numbers, you can use the `complex()` function to generate an imaginary number, using the syntax:

```
complex(real,imaginary)
```

Replace *real* with the real part of the complex number, replace *imaginary* with the imaginary number. For example, in code or the command prompt try this:

```
z = complex(2,-3)
```

The variable z gets the imaginary number 2-3j. Using a `print()` function to display the contents of z, like this:

```
print(z)
```

. . . displays the imaginary number (2-3j).

You can tack .real or .imag into an imaginary number to get the real or imaginary part. For example,

```
print(z.real)
```

. . . produces 2.0, which is the real part of the number z, and

```
print(z.imag)
```

. . . returns -3.0, which is the imaginary part of z.

Once again, if none this makes any sense to you, don't worry about it. It's not required for learning or doing Python. Python simply offers complex numbers and those functions for people who happen to require the use of such numbers.

**TECHNICAL STUFF**

If your work requires working with complex numbers, google *python cmath* to learn about Python's cmath module, which provides functions for complex numbers.

# Manipulating Strings

In Python and other programming languages, we refer to words and chunks of text as strings, short for "a string of characters," which has no numeric meaning or value. (We discuss the basics of strings in Book 1, Chapter 4.)

# Concatenating strings

You can join strings together using a + sign. This is commonly called *string concat-enation* in nerd-o-rama world. One thing that often catches beginners off-guard is the fact that the computer doesn't know a "word" from a bologna sandwich. So when you join strings together, it doesn't automatically put spaces where you'd expect them. For example, in the following code, the full_name is a concatenation of the first three strings.

```
first_name = "Alan"
middle_init = "C"
last_name = "Simpson"
full_name = first_name+middle_init+last_name
print(full_name)
```

Running this code to print the contents of the full_name variable reveals that Python did indeed join them together in one long string:

```
AlanCSimpson
```

There is nothing "wrong" with this output, per se, except that we usually put spaces between words and between parts of a person's name.

Because Python won't automatically put in spaces where you think they should go, you'll have to put them in yourself. The easiest way to represent a single space is by using a pair of quotation marks with one space between them, like this:

```
" "
```

If you forget to put the space between the quotation marks, like this:

```
""
```

. . . you won't get a space in your string either. You can, of course, put multiple spaces between the quotation marks if you want multiple spaces in your out-put, but typically one space is enough. In the following example we put a space between first_name and last_name. We also stuck a period and space after mid-dle_init. When we display the contents of that full_name variable, it looks more like the kind of name we're used to seeing.

```
first_name = "Alan"
middle_init = "C"
last_name = "Simpson"
full_name = first_name + " " + middle_init + ". " + last_name
print(full_name)
```

The output of that code is:

```
Alan C. Simpson
```

# Getting the length of a string

To determine how many characters are in a string, use the built-in `len()` function (short for *length*). The length includes spaces because spaces are characters, each one having a length of one. An empty string — that is, a string with nothing in it, not even a space — has a length of zero.

Here are some examples. In the first line we define a variable named s1 and put an empty string in it (a pair of quotation marks with nothing in between). The s2 variable gets a space (a pair of quotation marks with a space between). The s3 variable gets a string with some letters and spaces. Then, three `print()` functions display the length of each string:

```
s1 = ""
s2 = " "
s3 = "A B C"

print(len(s1))
print(len(s2))
print(len(s3))
```

Here is the output from that code, when executed, which makes perfect sense when you understand how `len()` measures the length of strings as the number of characters (including spaces) contained within the string:

```
0
1
5
```

# Working with common string operators

Python offers several operators for working with sequences of data. One weird thing about strings in Python (and in most other programming languages) is that when you're counting characters, the first character counts as zero, not one. This makes no sense to us humans. But the reasons for doing it that way have to do with what's most efficient for the way computers work. So even though the string in Figure 1-13 is five characters long, the last character in that string is the number 4, because the first character is number 0. Go figure.

```
ABCDE
01234
```

Table 1-4 summarizes the Python 3 operators for working with strings. Figure 1-14 shows examples of trying things out, just playing around with them in Jupyter Notebook.

**TABLE 1-4**     ## Python Sequence Operators That Work with Strings

| Operator | Purpose |
| --- | --- |
| x in s | Returns True if x exists somewhere in string s. |
| x not in s | Returns True if x is not contained within string s. |
| s * n or n * s | Repeats string s n times. |
| s[i] | The i th item of string s where the first character is 0. |
| s[i:j] | A slice from string x beginning with the character at position i through to the character at position j. |
| s[i:j:k] | A slice of s from i to j with step k. |
| min(s) | The smallest (lowest) item of string s. |
| max(s) | The largest (highest) item of string s. |
| s.index(x[, i[, j]]) | The numeric position of the first occurrence of x in string s. The optional i and j let you limit the search to the characters from i to j. |
| s.count(x) | The total number of times string x appears in larger string s. |

Figure 1-14 shows examples or using the string operators. When the output of a print() function doesn't look right, keep in mind two very important facts about strings in Python:

» The first character is always number 0.

» Every space counts as one character, so don't skip over spaces when counting.

```
: s = "Abracadabra Hocus Pocus you're a turtle dove"
  # Is there a lowercase letter t is contained in S?
  print("t" in s)
  # Is there an uppercase letter t is contained in S?
  print("T" in s)
  # Is there no uppercase T in s?S
  print("T" not in s)
  # Print 15 hyphens in a row
  print("-" * 15)
  # Print first character in string X
  print(s[0])
  # Print characters 33 - 39 from string x
  print(s[33:39])
  #Print every third character in s starting at zero
  print(s[0:44:3])
  #Print lowest character is s (a space is lower than the letter a)
  print(min(s))
  #Print the highest character is s
  print(max(s))
  # Where is the first uppercase P?
  print(s.index("P"))
  # Where is the first lowercase o in the latter half of string s
  # Note that the returned value still starts counting from zero
  print(s.index("o",22,44))
  # How many lowercase letters a are in string s?
  print(s.count("a"))

  True
  False
  True
  ---------------
  A
  turtle
  AadrHuPuy' tt v

  y
  18
  25
  5
```

FIGURE 1-14:
Playing around
with string
operators
in Jupyter
Notebook.

You may also notice that `min(s)` returns a blank space, meaning that the blank space character is the lowest character in that string. But what exactly makes the space "lower" than the letter *A* or the letter *a*? The simple answer is the letter's *ASCII number*. Every character you can type at your keyboard, and many additional characters, have a number assigned by the American Standard Code for Information Interchange (ASCII).

Figure 1-15 shows a chart with ASICC numbers for many common characters. Spaces and punctuation characters are "lower" than *A* because they have smaller ASCII numbers. Uppercase letters are "lower" than lowercase letters because they have smaller ASCII numbers. Are you wondering what happened to the characters assigned to numbers 0–31? These numbers have characters too, but they are "control characters" and they are essentially invisible, like when you hold down the Ctrl key and press another key.

Python offers two functions for working with ASCII. The `ord()` function takes a character as input and returns the ASCII number of that character. For example, `print(ord("A"))` returns 65, because an uppercase *A* is character 65 in the ASCII chart. The `chr()` function does the opposite. You give it a number, and it returns the ASCII character for that number. For example, `print(chr(65))` returns A because *A* is character 65 in the ASCII chart.

| Number | Character | Number | Character | Number | Character |
|--------|-----------|--------|-----------|--------|-----------|
| 32 | [space] | 65 | A | 97 | a |
| 33 | ! | 66 | B | 98 | b |
| 34 | " | 67 | C | 99 | c |
| 35 | # | 68 | D | 100 | d |
| 36 | $ | 69 | E | 101 | e |
| 37 | % | 70 | F | 102 | f |
| 38 | & | 71 | G | 103 | g |
| 39 | ' | 72 | H | 104 | h |
| 40 | ( | 73 | I | 105 | i |
| 41 | ) | 74 | J | 106 | j |
| 42 | * | 75 | K | 107 | k |
| 43 | + | 76 | L | 108 | l |
| 44 | , | 77 | M | 109 | m |
| 45 | - | 78 | N | 110 | n |
| 46 | . | 79 | O | 111 | o |
| 47 | / | 80 | P | 112 | p |
| 48 | 0 | 81 | Q | 113 | q |
| 49 | 1 | 82 | R | 114 | r |
| 50 | 2 | 83 | S | 115 | s |
| 51 | 3 | 84 | T | 116 | t |
| 52 | 4 | 85 | U | 117 | u |
| 53 | 5 | 86 | V | 118 | v |
| 54 | 6 | 87 | W | 119 | w |
| 55 | 7 | 88 | X | 120 | x |
| 56 | 8 | 89 | Y | 121 | y |
| 57 | 9 | 90 | Z | 122 | z |
| 58 | : | 91 | [ | 123 | { |
| 59 | ; | 92 | \ | 124 | \| |
| 60 | < | 93 | ] | 125 | } |
| 61 | = | 94 | ^ | 126 | ~ |
| 62 | > | 95 | _ | 127 | □ |
| 63 | ? | 96 | ` | 128 | € |
| 64 | @ | | | | |

**FIGURE 1-15:** ASCII numbers for common characters.

# Manipulating strings with methods

Every string in Python 3 is considered a *str object*. Yes, that's pronounced like *string object*; the *str* is there to distinguish it as the current, new way of doing things, as opposed to the older method called the *string object*. It's just another of those crazy things that seem deliberately confusing. Just remember that in Python 3, str is all about strings of characters.

The str methods (also called *string methods*) are different from functions in that the syntax is:

```
string.methodname(params)
```

where *string* is the string you're analyzing, *methodname* is the name of a method from Table 1-5, and *params* refers to any parameters (if required) that you need to pass to the method. The leading *s* in the first column of Table 1-5 means "any string," be it a literal string enclosed in quotation marks or the name of a variable that contains a string.

**TABLE 1-5**     **Built-In Methods for Python 3 Strings**

| Method | Purpose |
|---|---|
| s.capitalize() | Returns a string with the first letter capitalized, the rest lowercase. |
| s.count(*x*, [*y.z*]) | Returns the number of times string *x* appears in string s. Optionally you can add *y* as a starting point and *z* as an ending point to search only a portion of the string. |
| s.find(*x*, [*y.z*]) | Returns a number indicating the first position at which string *x* can be found in string s. Optional *y* and *z* parameters allow you to limit the search to a portion of the string. Returns –1 if none found. |
| s.index(*x*, [*y.z*]) | Similar to find but returns a "substring not found" error if string *x* can't be found in string *y*. |
| s.isalpha() | Returns True if s is at least one character long and contains only letters (A-Z or a-z). |
| s.isdecimal() | Returns True if s is at least one character long and contains only numeric characters (0-9). |
| s.islower() | Returns True if s contains letters and all those letters are lowercase. |
| s.isnumeric() | Returns True if s is at least one character long and contains only numeric characters (0-9). |
| s.isprintable() | Returns True if string s contains only printable characters. |
| s.istitle() | Returns True if string s contains letters and the first letter of each word is uppercase followed by lowercase letters. |
| s.isupper() | Returns True if all letters in the string are uppercase. |
| s.lower() | Returns s with all letters converted to lowercase. |
| s.lstrip() | Returns s with any leading spaces removed. |
| s.replace(*x*,*y*) | Returns a copy of string s with all characters *x* replaced by character *y*. |
| s.rfind(*x*, [*y,z*]) | Similar to find but searches backwards from the start of the string. If *y* and *z* are provided, searches backwards from position *z* to position *y*. Returns –1 if string *x* not found. |
| s.rindex() | Same as .rfind but returns an error if the substring isn't found. |
| s.rstrip() | Returns string *x* with any trailing spaces removed. |
| s.strip() | Returns string *x* with leading and trailing spaces removed. |
| s.swapcase() | Returns string s with uppercase letters converted to lowercase and lowercase letters converted to uppercase. |
| s.title() | Returns string s with the first letter of every word capitalized and all other letters lowercase. |
| s.upper() | Returns string s with all letters converted to uppercase. |

You can certainly play around with these methods in a Jupyter Notebook, the Python prompt, or a .py file. Figure 1-16 shows some examples in a Jupyter Notebook using three variables named s1, s2, and s3 as strings to experiment with. The result of running the code appears below the code.

**REMEMBER**

Don't bother trying to memorize or even make sense of every string method. Remember instead that if you need to operate on a string in Python, you can google *python 3 string methods* to find out what's available.

```
s1 = "There is no such word as schmeedledorp"
s2="   a b c   "
s3="ABC"
# Captialize first letter, the rest lowercase
print(s3.capitalize())
# Count the number of spaces in s1
print(s1.count(" "))
# Find the dot in s4
print(s4.find("."))
# Is s2 all lowercase letters?
print(s2.islower())
# Convert s3 to all lowercase
print(s3.lower())
# String leading characters from s2
print(s2.lstrip())
# String leading and trailing characters from s2
print(s2.strip())
# Swap the case of letters in s1
print(s1.swapcase())
# Show s1 in title case (initial caps)
print(s1.title())
# Show s1 uppercase
print(s1.upper())
```

```
Abc
6
3
True
abc
a b c
a b c
tHERE IS NO SUCH WORD AS SCHMEEDLEDORP
There Is No Such Word As Schmeedledorp
THERE IS NO SUCH WORD AS SCHMEEDLEDORP
```

**FIGURE 1-16:**
Playing around with Python 3 string functions.

# Uncovering Dates and Times

In the world of computers, we often use dates and times for scheduling, or for calculating when something is due or how many days it's past due. We sometimes use *timestamps* to record exactly when some user did something or when some event occurred. There are lots of reasons for using dates and times in Python, but perhaps surprisingly, no built-in data type for them exists like the ones for strings and numbers.

To work with dates and times, you typically need to use the `datetime` module. Like any module, you need to import it before you can use it. You can do that using `import datetime`. As with any import, you can add an alias (nickname) that's easier to type, if you like. For example, `import datetime as dt` will work too. You just have to remember to type `dt` rather than `datetime` in your code when calling upon the capabilities of that module.

The `datetime` module is actually an abstract base class, which is kind of a fancy way of saying it offers new data types to the language. For dates and times those data types are as follows:

>> **`datetime.date`:** A date consisting of month, day, and year (no time information).

>> **`datetime.time`:** A time consisting of hour, minute, second, microsecond, and optionally time zone information if needed (but no date).

>> **`datetime.datetime`:** A single item of data that includes date, time, and optionally time zone information.

We preceded each type with the full word `datetime` in the preceding examples, but if you use an alias, like `dt`, then you can use that in your code instead. We talk about each of these data types separately in the sections that follow.

## Working with dates

`Datetime.date` is ideal for working with dates when time isn't an issue. There are two ways to create a date object: You can use the `today()` method, which gets today's date from the computer's internal clock using the `today()` method. Or you can specify a year, month, and day (in that order) inside parentheses.

**REMEMBER**

When specifying the month or day, never use a leading zero for `datetime.date()`. For example, April 1 2020 has to be expressed as `2020,4,1` — if you type `2020,04,01`, it won't work.

For example, after importing the `datetime` module, you can use `date.today()` to get the current date from the computer's internal clock. Or use `date(year, month, day)` syntax to create a date object for some other date:

```
# Import the datetime module, nickname dt
import datetime as dt
# Store today's date in a variable named today.
```

```
today = dt.date.today()
# Store some other date in a variable called last_of_teens
last_of_teens = dt.date(2019,12,31)
```

If you want to try it for yourself, type the code in a Jupyter notebook, Python prompt, or .py file. Use the `print()` function to see what's in each variable as in Figure 1-17. Your `today` variable won't be the same as in the figure; it will be today's date for whenever you try this.

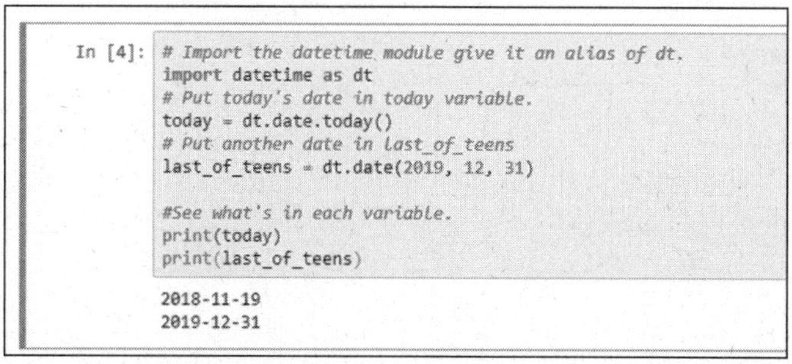

**FIGURE 1-17:**
Experiments with
datetime.date
objects in a
Jupyter notebook.

```
In [4]:  # Import the datetime module give it an alias of dt.
         import datetime as dt
         # Put today's date in today variable.
         today = dt.date.today()
         # Put another date in last_of_teens
         last_of_teens = dt.date(2019, 12, 31)

         #See what's in each variable.
         print(today)
         print(last_of_teens)

         2018-11-19
         2019-12-31
```

You can isolate any part of a date object using .month, .day, or .year. For example, in the same Jupyter cell or Python prompt, executing this code:

```
print(last_of_teens.month)
print(last_of_teens.day)
print(last_of_teens.year)
```

. . . produces each of the three components of that date on a separate line, like this:

```
12
31
2019
```

As you saw on the first printout, the default date display is *yyyy-mm-dd*, but you can format dates and times however you want. Use f-strings, which we discuss earlier in this chapter, along with the directives shown in Table 1-6 (which includes the format for dates as well as for times, as we discuss later in this chapter).

**TABLE 1-6**    **Formatting Strings for Dates and Times**

| Directive | Description | Example |
|---|---|---|
| %a | Weekday, abbreviated | Sun |
| %A | Weekday, full | Sunday |
| %w | Weekday number 0-6, where 0 is Sunday | 0 |
| %d | Number day of the month 01-31 | 31 |
| %b | Month name abbreviated | Jan |
| %B | Month name full | January |
| %m | Month number 01-12 | 01 |
| %y | Year without century | 19 |
| %Y | Year with century | 2019 |
| %H | Hour 00-23 | 23 |
| %I | Hour 00-12 | 11 |
| %p | AM/PM | PM |
| %M | Minute 00-59 | 01 |
| %S | Second 00-59 | 01 |
| %f | Microsecond 000000-999999 | 495846 |
| %z | UTC offset | −0500 |
| %Z | Time zone | EST |
| %j | Day number of year 001-366 | 300 |
| %U | Week number of year, Sunday as the first day of week, 00-53 | 50 |
| %W | Week number of year, Monday as the first day of week, 00-53 | 50 |
| %c | Local version of date and time | Tue Dec 31 23:59:59 2018 |
| %x | Local version of date | 12/31/18 |
| %X | Local version of time | 23:59:59 |
| %% | A % character | % |

**TECHNICAL STUFF**

Some tutorials tell you to use `strftime` rather than f-strings for formatting dates and times, and that's certainly a valid way to do it. We're sticking with the newer f-strings here, however, because we think they'll be preferred over `strftime` in the future.

When using format strings, make sure you put spaces, slashes, and anything else you want between directives where you want those to appear in the output. For example, this line:

```
print(f"{last_of_teens:%A, %B %d, %Y}")
```

. . . when executed, shows this:

```
Tuesday, December 31, 2019
```

To show the date in the *mm/dd/yyyy* format, use `%m/%d/%Y`, like this:

```
todays_date = f"{today:%m/%d/%Y}"
```

The output will be the current date for you when you try it, but the format should be like this:

```
11/19/2018
```

Table 1-7 shows a few more examples you can try out with different dates.

**TABLE 1-7**

## Sample Date Format Strings

| Format String | Example |
| --- | --- |
| %a, %b %d %Y | Sat, Jun 01 2019 |
| %x | 06/01/19 |
| %m-%d-%y | 06-01-19 |
| This %A %B %d | This Saturday June 01 |
| %A %B %d is day number %j of %Y | Saturday June 01 is day number 152 of 2019 |

## Working with times

If you want to work strictly with time data, use the `datetime.time` class. The basic syntax for defining a time object using the `time` class is

```
variable = datetime.time([hour,[minute,[second,[microsecond]]]])
```

Notice how all the arguments are optional. For example, using no arguments like this:

```
midnight = dt.time()
print(midnight)
```

. . . stores the time as 00:00:00, which is exactly midnight. To verify that it's really a time, entering `print(type(midnight))` shows

```
00:00:00
<class 'datetime.time'>
```

That second line tells you that the 00:00:00 number is a `time` object from the `datetime` class.

The fourth optional value you can pass to `time()` is `microseconds` (millionths of a second). For example, the following code puts a time that's a millionth of a second before midnight in a variable named `almost_midnight` and then displays that time onscreen with a `print()` function.

```
almost_midnight = dt.time(23,59,59,999999)
print(almost_midnight)
23:59:59.999999
```

You can use format strings with the time directives from Table 1-6 to control the format of the time. Table 1-8 shows some examples using 23:59:59:999999 as the sample time.

**TABLE 1-8**

## Sample Date Format Strings

| Format String | Example |
|---|---|
| %I:%M %p | 11:59 PM |
| %H:%M:%S and %f microseconds | 23:59:59 and 999999 microseconds |
| %X | 23:59:59 |

Sometimes you want to just work with dates, and sometimes you want to just work with times. Often you want to pinpoint a moment in time using both date and time. For that, use the datetime class of the datetime module. This class supports a now() method that can grab the current date and time from the computer clock, as follows:

```
import datetime as dt
right_now = dt.datetime.now()
print(right_now)
```

Exactly what you see on the screen from the print() function depends on when you execute this code. But the format of the datetime value will be like this:

```
2019-11-19 14:03:07.525975
```

This means November 19, 2019 at 2:03 PM (with 7.525975 seconds tacked on).

You can also define a datetime using any the parameters shown below. The month, day, and year are required. The rest are optional and set to zero in the time if you omit them.

```
datetime(year, month, day, hour, [minute, [second, [microsecond]]])
```

Here is an example using 11:59 PM on December 31 2019:

```
import datetime as dt
new_years_eve = dt.datetime(2019,12,31,23,59)
print(new_years_eve)
```

Here is the output of that print() statement with no formatting:

```
2019-12-31 23:59:00
```

Table 1-9 shows examples of formatting the datetime using directives shown back in Table 1-6.

TABLE 1-9

## Sample Datetime Format Strings

| Format String | Example |
|---|---|
| %A, %B %d at %I:%M%p | Tuesday, December 31 at 11:59PM |
| %m/%d/%y at %H:%M%p | 12/31/19 at 23:59 |
| %I:%M %p on %b %d | 11:59 PM on Dec 31 |
| %x | 12/31/19 |
| %c | Tue Dec 31 23:59:00 2019 |
| %m/%d/%y at %I:%M %p | 12/31/19 at 11:59 PM |
| %I:%M %p on %m/%d/%y | 1:59 PM on 12/31/2019 |

# Calculating timespans

Sometimes just knowing the date or time isn't enough. Sometimes you need to know the duration or *timespan* as it's typically called in the computer world. In other words, not the date, not the o'clock, but the "how long" in terms of years, months, weeks, days, hours, minutes, or whatever. For timespans, the Python datetime module includes the datetime.timedelta class.

A timedelta object is created automatically whenever you subtract two dates, times, or datetimes to determine the duration between them. For example, suppose you create a couple of variables to store dates, perhaps one for New Year's Day, another for Memorial Day. Then you create a third variable named days_between and put in it the difference you get by subtracting the earlier date from the later date, as follows:

```
import datetime as dt
new_years_day = dt.date(2019,1,1)
memorial_day = dt.date(2019,5,27)
days_between = memorial_day - new_years_day
```

So what exactly is days_between in terms of a data type? If you print its value, you get 146 days, 0:00:00. In other words, there is 146 days between those dates; the 0:00:00 is time but because we didn't specify a time of day in either date, these are all just set to zero. If you use the Python type() function to determine the data type of days_between, you see it's a timedelta object from the datetime class, as follows:

```
146 days, 0:00:00
<class 'datetime.timedelta'>
```

The timedelta happens automatically when you subtract one date from another to get the time between. You can also define any timedelta (duration) using this syntax:

```
datetime.timedelta(days=, seconds=, microseconds=, milliseconds=, minutes=,
    hours=, weeks=)
```

If you provide an argument, you must include a number after the = sign. If you omit an argument, its value is set to zero.

To get an understanding of how this works, try out the following code. After importing the datetime module, create a date using .date(). Then create a timedelta using .timedelta. If you add the date and timedelta, you get a new date — in this case, a date that's 146 days after 1/1/2019.

```
import datetime as dt
new_years_day = dt.date(2019,1,1)
duration = dt.timedelta(days=146)
print(new_years_day + duration)

2019-05-27
```

Of course, you can subtract too. For example, if you start off with a date of 5/27/2019 and subtract 146 days, you get 1/1/2019, as shown here:

```
import datetime as dt
memorial_day = dt.date(2019,5,27)
duration = dt.timedelta(days=146)
print(memorial_day - duration)

2019-01-01
```

It works with datetimes too. If you're looking for a duration that's less than a day, just give both times the same date. For example, consider the following code and the results of the subtraction:

```
import datetime as dt
start_time = dt.datetime(2019, 3, 31, 8, 0, 0)
finish_time = dt.datetime(2019, 3, 31, 14, 34, 45)
time_between = finish_time - start_time
print(time_between)
print(type(time_between))
```

```
6:34:45
<class 'datetime.timedelta'>
```

We know that 6:34:45 is a time duration of 6 hours 34 minutes and 45 seconds because, for one thing, it's the result of subtracting one moment of time from another. Also, printing the type() of that data type tells us it's a timedelta (a duration), not an o'clock time.

Here is another example using datetimes with different dates, one being the current datetime, the other being a date of birth with the time down to the minute (March 31 1995 at 8:26 AM). To calculate age, subtract the birthdate from the now time:

```
import datetime as dt
now = dt.datetime.now()
birthdatetime = dt.datetime(1995, 3, 31, 8, 26)
age = now - birthdatetime
print(age)
print(type(age))
8634 days, 7:55:07.739804
<class 'datetime.timedelta'>
```

The result is expressed as 8634 days, 7 hours, 52 minutes, and 1.967031 seconds (the tiny seconds value stems from the fact that datetime.now grabs the date and time from the computer's clock down to the microsecond).

You don't always need microseconds or even seconds in your timedelta. For example, say you're trying to determine somebody's age. You could start by creating two dates, one named today for today's date and another named birthdate that contains the birthdate. The following example uses the birthdate of Jan 31, 2000:

```
import datetime as dt
today = dt.date.today()
birthdate = dt.date(2000, 12, 31)
delta_age = (today - birthdate)
print(delta_age)
```

The last two lines create a variable named delta_age and prints what's in the variable. If you actually run this code yourself, you'll see something like the following output (but it won't be exactly that because your "today" date will be whatever today's date is when you run the app).

```
6533 days, 0:00:00
```

Let's say what we really want is the age in years. You can convert the timedelta to a number of days by tacking .days onto the timedelta. You can put that in another variable called days_old. Printing days_old and its type shows you that days_old is an int, a regular old integer you can do math with:

```
delta_age = (today - birthdate)
days_old = delta_age.days
print(days_old, type(days_old))

6533 <class 'int'>
```

To get the number of years, divide the number of days by 365. If you want just the number of years as an integer, use the floor division operator (//) rather than regular division (/). Put that in a variable named years_old and print that value, as follows:

```
years_old = days_old // 365
print(years_old)

18
```

So there you have the age, in years, as 18. If you want the number of months too, you can ballpark that just by taking the remainder of dividing the days by 365 to get the number of days left over. Then floor divide that value by 30 (because on average each month has about 30 days) to get a good approximation of the number of months. Use % for division rather than / to get just the remainder after the division. Figure 1-18 shows the whole sequence of events in a Jupyter notebook, with comments to explain what's going on.

```
import datetime as dt
# Today's date according to your computer
today = dt.date.today()

# Any birthdate expressed as year, month, day
birthdate = dt.date(2000, 1, 31)

# Duration between the dates as a timedelta
delta_age = (today - birthdate)

# Duration between the dates as a number (of days)
days_old = delta_age.days

# Floor divide days by 365 to get the number of years
years = days_old // 365

# Days left over is remainder of days_old divided by 365.
# Floor divide that remainder by 30 for approximate months.
months = (days_old % 365) // 30

# Print in a format to your liking
print(f"You are {years} years and {months} months old.")

You are 18 years and 9 months old.
```

**FIGURE 1-18:**
Calculating age
in years and
months from a
timedelta.

# Accounting for Time Zones

As you may know, just because it's noon, or whatever, in your neighborhood doesn't mean its noon everywhere. This is because the earth is divided into time zones so that "noon" means roughly "middle of the day" no matter where you happen to be on earth.

Figure 1-19 shows a map of all the time zones. It's not easy to see in this book, but you can easily find a larger version just by googling *time zone map* if you want a closer look.

**FIGURE 1-19:**
Time zones
(larger maps
available online).

Figure 1-19 shows how at any given moment, it's a different day and time of day depending on where you happen to be on the globe. There is a universal time, called the Coordinated Universal Time or Universal Time Coordinated (UTC). You may have heard of Greenwich Mean Time (GMT) or Zulu time used by the military, which is the same idea. It's the time at the Prime Meridian on Earth, or 0 degrees longitude, smack dab in the middle of the time zone map in Figure 1-19.

These days, most people rely on the Olson Database as the primary source of information about time zones. It lists all the current time zones and locations. Feel free to Google *Olson database* or *tz database* if you're interested in all the details. There are too many time zone names to list here, but Table 1-10 shows some examples of American time zones. The left column is the "official name" from the database. The second column shows the more familiar name. The last two columns show the offset from UTC for standard time and daylight savings time.

**TABLE 1-10**   ## Sample Time Zones from the Olson Database

| Time Zone | Common Name | UTC Offset | UTC DST Offset |
| --- | --- | --- | --- |
| Etc/UCT | UCT | +00:00 | +00:00 |
| Etc/UTC | Universal | +00:00 | +00:00 |
| America/Anchorage | US/Alaska | -09:00 | -08:00 |
| America/Adak | US/Aleutian | -10:00 | -09:00 |
| America/Phoenix | US/Arizona | -07:00 | -07:00 |
| America/Chicago | US/Central | -06:00 | -05:00 |
| America/New_York | US/Eastern | -05:00 | -04:00 |
| America/Indiana/Indianapolis | US/East-Indiana | -05:00 | -04:00 |
| Pacific/Honolulu | US/Hawaii | -10:00 | -10:00 |
| America/Indiana/Knox | US/Indiana-Starke | -06:00 | -05:00 |
| America/Detroit | US/Michigan | -05:00 | -04:00 |
| America/Denver | US/Mountain | -07:00 | -06:00 |
| America/Los_Angeles | US/Pacific | -08:00 | -07:00 |
| Pacific/Pago_Pago | US/Samoa | -11:00 | -11:00 |
| Etc/UTC | UTC | +00:00 | +00:00 |
| Etc/UTC | Zulu | +00:00 | +00:00 |

So why are we telling you all this? It's because Python lets you work with two different types of datetimes:

» **Naïve:** Any datetime that does not include information that relates it to a specific time zone is called a *naïve datetime*.

» **Aware:** A datetime that includes time zone information is considered an *aware datetime*.

Timedeltas and dates that you define with .date() are always naïve. Any time or datetime you create as time() or datetime() objects will also by naïve, by default. But with those two you have the option of including time zone information if it's useful in your work, such as when you're showing event dates to an audience that spans multiple time zones.

# Working with Time Zones

When you get the time from your computer's system clock, it will be for your time zone. There just isn't any indication of what that time zone that *is*. But you can tell the difference by comparing .now() for your location to .utc_now(), which is UTC time, and then subtracting the difference, as in Figure 1-20.

```
# Get the dateime module and give it an alias
import datetime as dt

# Get the time from computer clock
here_now = dt.datetime.now()

# Get the UTC datetime right now
utc_now = dt.datetime.utcnow()

# Subtract to see difference
time_difference = (utc_now - here_now)

# Show results
print(f"My time   : {here_now:%I:%M %p}")
print(f"UTC time  : {utc_now:%I:%M %p}")
print(f"Difference: {time_difference}")
```

```
My time   : 01:02 PM
UTC time  : 06:02 PM
Difference: 5:00:00
```

**FIGURE 1-20:**
Time zones
(larger maps
available online).

When we ran that code, the current time was 1:02PM and the UTC time was 6:02PM. The difference is 5:00:00, which means five hours (no minutes or seconds). Our time is earlier, so our time zone is really UTC – 5 hours.

Not that if you subtract the earlier time from the later time you get a negative number, which can be misleading, as follows:

```
time_difference = (here_now - utc_now)
Difference: -1 day, 19:00:00
```

That's still five hours, really, because if you subtract 1 day and 19 hours from 24 hours (one day), you still get 5 hours. Tricky business. But keep in mind the left side of the time zone map is east, and the sun rises in the east in each time zone. So when it's rising in your time zone, it's already risen in time zones to the right, and hasn't yet risen in time zones to your left.

If you want to work directly with time zone names, you'll need to import some dateutils. In particular, you need gettz (short for *get timezone*) from the tz class of dateutil. So in your code, right after the line where you import datetime, use from dateutil.tz import gettz like this:

```
# import datetime and dateutil tz
import datetime as dt
from dateutil.tz import gettz
```

Afterwards, you can use gettz('*name*') to get time zone information for any time zone. Replace *name* with the name of the time zone from the Olson database. For example, America/New_York for USA Eastern Time, or Etc_UTC for UTC Time.

Figure 1-21 shows an example where we get the current date and time using datetime.now() with five different time zones — UTC and four USA time zones.

All the USA times are standard time because nobody in the USA is on daylight savings time (DST) in November. Let's see if it's smart enough to figure out daylight savings time if we schedule an event for some time in July, when the USA is on back on daylight savings time.

In this code (see Figure 1-22), we import datetime and gettx from dateutil, as we did in the previous example. But we're not concerned about the current time. We're concerned about an event scheduled for date and time of July 4, 2020 at 7:00 PM in our local time zone. So we define that using the following:

```
event = dt.datetime(2020,7,4,19,0,0)
```

```
# import datetime, give it an alias
import datetime as dt
# import timezone helpers from dateutil
from dateutil.tz import gettz

# UTC time right now.
utc=dt.datetime.now(gettz('Etc/UTC'))
print(f"{utc:%A %D %I:%M %p %Z}")

# USA Eastern time.
est = dt.datetime.now(gettz('America/New_York'))
print(f"{est:%A %D %I:%M %p %Z}")

# USA Central time
cst=dt.datetime.now(gettz('America/Chicago'))
print(f"{cst:%A %D %I:%M %p %Z}")

# USA Mountain time
mst=dt.datetime.now(gettz('America/Boise'))
print(f"{mst:%A %D %I:%M %p %Z}")

pst=dt.datetime.now(gettz('America/Los_Angeles'))
print(f"{pst:%A %D %I:%M %p %Z}")
```

```
Friday 11/23/18 06:37 PM UTC
Friday 11/23/18 01:37 PM EST
Friday 11/23/18 12:37 PM CST
Friday 11/23/18 11:37 AM MST
Friday 11/23/18 10:37 AM PST
```

**FIGURE 1-21:**
The current date and time for five different time zones.

We didn't say anything about time zone in that date time, so it will automatically be for our time zone. That datetime is stored in a variable named event.

```
# import datetime and dateutil tz
import datetime as dt
from dateutil.tz import gettz

# July 4 Event, 7:00 local time (no specific time zone).
event = dt.datetime(2020,7,4,19,0,0)
# Show local date and time
print("Local: " + f"{event:%D %I:%M %p %Z}" + "\n")

event_eastern = event.astimezone(gettz("America/New_York"))
print(f"{event_eastern:%D %I:%M %p %Z}")

event_central = event.astimezone(gettz("America/Chicago"))
print(f"{event_central:%D %I:%M %p %Z}")

event_mountain = event.astimezone(gettz("America/Denver"))
print(f"{event_mountain:%D %I:%M %p %Z}")

event_pacific = event.astimezone(gettz("America/Los_Angeles"))
print(f"{event_pacific:%D %I:%M %p %Z}")

event_utc = event.astimezone(gettz("Etc/UTC"))
print(f"{event_utc:%D %I:%M %p %Z}")
```

```
  Local: 07/04/20 07:00 PM

  07/04/20 07:00 PM EDT
  07/04/20 06:00 PM CDT
  07/04/20 05:00 PM MDT
  07/04/20 04:00 PM PDT
  07/04/20 11:00 PM UTC
```

**FIGURE 1-22:**
Date and time for a scheduled event in multiple time zones.

This line of code shows the date and time, again local, since we didn't say anything about time zone. We added the word `"Local:"` to the start of the text, and put a line break at the end with `\n` to visually separate it a little from the rest of the output:

```
# Show local date and time
print("Local: " + f"{event:%D %I:%M %p %Z}" + "\n")
```

When the app runs, it displays this output based on the datetime and our format string:

```
Local: 07/04/20 07:00 PM
```

The remaining code calculates the correct datetime for each of five time zones using this code:

```
name = event.astimezone(gettz("tzname"))
```

The first *name* is just a variable name we made up, and it could be any valid variable name. In `event.astimezone()`, the name `event` refers to the initial event time defined in a previous line. The `astimezone()` is a built-in `dateutil` function that uses the following syntax:

```
.astimezone(gettz("tzname"))
```

In each line of code that calculates the date and time for a time zone, we replace *tzname* with the name of the time zone from the Olson database. As you can see in the output, the datetime of the event for five different time zones is displayed. Note that the USA time zones are daylight savings time (such as EDT). Because we happen to be on the USA east coast, and because the event in question is in July, the correct local time zone is Eastern Daylight Time. When you look at the output of the dates, the first one matches our time zone, as it should, and the times for the remaining dates are adjusted for different time zones.

If you're thinking "Eek, what a complicated mess," you won't get any argument from us. None of this strikes us as intuitive, easy, or in even in the general ballpark of "fun." But if you're in a pinch and really need some time zone information for your data, this shows you how to get it.

**TECHNICAL STUFF**

If you research Python time zones online, you'll probably find that many people recommend using the `arrow` module rather than the `dateutil` module to make everything easier. We won't get into all of that here, because `arrow` isn't part of your initial Python installation and this book is hefty enough. (If we tried to cover literally everything, you'd need a wheelbarrow to carry it around.)

IN THIS CHAPTER

» Making decisions with `if`

» Repeating a process with `for`

» Looping with `while`

» Protecting your users from errors

» Understanding contextual coding

# Chapter **2**

# Controlling the Action

S o far in this book we've talked a lot about storing information in computers, mostly in variables that Python and your computer can work with. Having the information there in a form that the computer can work with is certainly critical to getting a computer to do anything. Think of this as the "having" part — having some information with which to work. But now we need to turn our attention to the "doing" part . . . actually working with that information to create something useful or entertaining. In this chapter, we cover the most important and the most commonly used operations for making the computer *do* stuff. We start with something that computers do well, do quickly, and do a lot — make decisions.

## Main Operators for Controlling the Action

You control what your program (and the computer) does by making decisions, which often involves making comparisons. We use operators, such as those in Table 2-1 to make comparisons. These are often referred to as *relational operators* or *comparison operators* because by comparing items the computer is determining how two items are related.

TABLE 2-1

## Python Comparison Operators for Decision-Making

| Operator | Meaning |
| --- | --- |
| == | is equal to |
| != | is not equal to |
| < | is less than |
| > | is greater than |
| <= | is less than or equal to |
| >= | is greater than or equal to |

Python also offers three *logical operators*, also called *Boolean operators* that can allow you assess multiple comparisons before making a final decision. Those operators use the English word for, well, basically what they mean, as shown in Table 2-2.

TABLE 2-2

## Python Logical Operators

| Operator | Meaning |
| --- | --- |
| and | both are true |
| or | one or the other is true |
| not | is not true |

**TECHNICAL STUFF**

In case you're wondering about that *Boolean* word, it's a reference to a guy named George Boole who, in the mid–1800s, helped establish the algebra of logic, which pretty much laid the foundation for today's computers. Feel free to google his name to learn more if you're interested.

All these operators are often used in conjunction with if ... then ... else **type** decisions to control exactly what an app or program does. To make such decisions, you use the Python *if statements*.

# Making Decisions with if

The word *if* is used a lot in all apps and computer programs to make decisions. The simplest syntax for *if* is:

```
if condition: do this
do this no matter what
```

So the first do this line is executed only if the condition is true. If the condition is false, that first do this is ignored. Regardless of what the condition turns out to be, the second line is executed next. Notice that neither line is indented. This means a lot in Python, as you'll see shortly. But first, let's do a couple of simple examples with this simple syntax. You can try it for yourself in a Jupyter notebook or .py file if you want to follow along.

Figure 2-1 shows a simple example where the variable named sun receives the string "down." Then an if statement checks to see whether the variable sun contains the word down and, if it does, prints "Good night!" Then it just continues on normally to print I am here. You can see in the output that the result is that both lines are displayed.

**FIGURE 2-1:**
The result of a simple if when the condition proves true.

```
sun = "down"
if sun == "down": print("Good night!")
print("I am here")

Good night!
I am here
```

**WARNING**

Make sure you always use two equal signs with no space between (==) to test equality. It's easy to forget that. If you type it wrong, it won't work as expected.

If you run the same code with some word other than down in the sun variable, then the first print is ignored, but the next line is still executed normally because it's not dependent on the condition being true, as shown in Figure 2-2.

**FIGURE 2-2:**
Result of simple "if" when the condition proves false.

```
sun = "up"
if sun == "down": print("Good night!")
print("I am here")

I am here
```

In the second example, it's not true that the variable named sun contains True, therefore the rest of that line is ignored and only the next line is executed.

That syntax, where the code to be executed when the condition proves true is on the same line as the if works, but often you want to do more than one thing when the condition proves true. For that, you'll need to indent each line to be executed only if the condition proves true. And code that's not indented below the if is executed whether the condition proves true or not. The recommendation is to indent by four spaces, but that's not a hard and fast rule. You just have to remember that each line has to be indented the same amount.

Also, you can use the "indented" syntax even if only one line of code is to be executed should the condition prove true. In fact, that's the most common way to write an if in Python because most people agree it makes the code more "readable" from a human perspective. So really the syntax is

```
if condition:
    do this

    ...
do this no matter what
```

So if the condition proves true, the do this line is executed as are any other lines that are indented equally to that one. The first un-indented line under the if is executed no matter what. So you could write the simple sun example like this:

```
sun = "down"
if sun == "down":
    print("Good night!")
print("I am here")
```

As you can see in Figure 2-3, the code works exactly the same as putting the code on one line. If sun is down, then Good night! prints before the second print is executed. If sun doesn't contain down, then the print statement for Good night! is skipped over and ignored.

```
sun = "down"
if sun == "down":
    print("Good night!")
print("I am here")

    Good night!
    I am here

sun = "up"
if sun == "down":
    print("Good night!")
print("I am here")

    I am here
```

**FIGURE 2-3:** Result of simple if when the condition proves false.

If you're wondering which method is better, it depends on what you mean by *better*. If you mean *better* in terms of which method executes the fastest, then neither. You won't be able to see any speed difference when executing the code. If by *better* you mean "easier for a human programmer to read." then most people would probably lean toward the second method with the code indented under the if statement.

Remember, you can indent any number of lines under the if, and those indented lines execute only if the condition proves true. If the condition proves false, none of the indented lines are executed. The code under the indented lines is always executed because it's not dependent on the condition. Here is an example where we have four lines of code that execute only if the condition proves true:

```python
total = 100
sales_tax_rate = 0.065
taxable = True
if taxable:
    print(f"Subtotal : ${total:.2f}")
    sales_tax = total * sales_tax_rate
    print(f"Sales Tax: ${sales_tax:.2f}")
    total = total + sales_tax
print(f"Total    : ${total:.2f}")
```

You must spell True and False with an initial capital letter and the rest lowercase. If you type it any other way, Python won't recognize it as a Boolean True or False and your code won't run as expected.

Notice that in the if statement we used

```python
if taxable:
```

This is perfectly okay because we made taxable a Boolean that can only be True or False. You may see other people type it as

```python
if taxable == True:
```

That's okay too, and it won't have any negative effect on the code. The == True is just unnecessary because, by itself, taxable is already either True or not False.

Anyway, as you can see, we start off with a total, a sales_tax_rate, and a taxable variable. When taxable is True, then all four lines under the if are executed and you end up with the output shown in Figure 2-4.

```
total = 100
sales_tax_rate = 0.065
taxable = True
if taxable:
    print(f"Subtotal : ${total:.2f}")
    sales_tax = total * sales_tax_rate
    print(f"Sales Tax: ${sales_tax:.2f}")
    total = total + sales_tax
print(f"Total    : ${total:.2f}")

    Subtotal : $100.00
    Sales Tax: $6.50
    Total    : $106.50
```

**FIGURE 2-4:**
When taxable is
True, sales_tax
is added to the
total.

When `taxable` is set to `False`, all the indented lines are skipped over, and the total shown is the original total without any sales tax added in, as shown in Figure 2-5.

```
total = 100
sales_tax_rate = 0.065
taxable = False
if taxable:
    print(f"Subtotal : ${total:.2f}")
    sales_tax = total * sales_tax_rate
    print(f"Sales Tax: ${sales_tax:.2f}")
    total = total + sales_tax
print(f"Total    : ${total:.2f}")

    Total    : $100.00
```

**FIGURE 2-5:**
When taxable
is False,
sales_tax
is not added
into the total.

**TECHNICAL
STUFF**

The curly braces and .2f stuff in Figures 2-4 and 2-5 are just for formatting, as we discuss in Book 2, Chapter 1, and have nothing to do with the `if` logic of the code.

## Adding else to your if login

So far we've looked at code examples in which some code is executed if some condition proves true. If the condition proves false, then that code is ignored. Sometimes, you may have a situation where you want one chunk of code to execute *if* a condition proves true, *otherwise* (*else*) if it doesn't prove true, you want some other chunk of code to be execute. In that case, you can add an `else:` to your `if`. Any lines of code undented under the `else:` are executed only if the condition did not prove true. Here is the logic and syntax:

```
if condition:
    do indented lines here
    ...
```

```
else:
    do indented lines here
    ...
do remaining un-indented lines no matter what.
```

Figure 2-6 shows a simple example where we grab the current time from the computer clock using `datetime.now()`. If the hour of that time is less than 12, then the program shows `Good morning!` Otherwise, it shows `Good afternoon!` Regardless of the hour, it prints `I hope you are doing well`. So if you write such a program and run it in the morning, you get the appropriate greeting followed by `I hope you are doing well!`, as in Figure 2-6.

**FIGURE 2-6:**
Print an initial greeting based on time of day.

```
import datetime as dt
# Get the current date and time
now = dt.datetime.now()
# Make a decision based on hour
if now.hour < 12:
    print("Good morning")
else:
    print("Good afternoon")
print("I hope you are doing well!")

Good morning
I hope you are doing well!
```

**FIGURE 2-6:** Print an initial greeting based on time of day.

Now you may look at that and say "Wow, that's really impressive, Einstein. But what if it's 11:00 at night? Do you really want to say "Good afternoon"? Yet another question deserving of a resounding *Hmm*. What we need is an `if...else` where there are multiple `else`'s possible. That's where the `elif` statement comes into play.

## Handling multiple else's with elif

When `if...else` isn't enough to handle all the possibilities, there's `elif` (which, as you may have guessed, is a word made up from `else if`. An if statement can include any number of `elif` conditions. You can include or not include a final `else` statement that executes only if the `if` and all the previous `elif`s prove false. In its simplest form, the syntax for an `if` with `elif` and `else` is

```
if condition:
    do these indented lines of code
    ...
elif condition
    do these indented lines of code
    ...
do these un-indented lines of code no matter what.
```

Controlling the Action

Given that structure, it is possible that none of the indented code executes. Take a look at this example:

```python
light_color = "green"
if light_color == "green":
    print("Go")
elif light_color == "red":
    print("Stop")
print("This code executes no matter what")
```

Executing that code results in:

```
Go
This code executes no matter what
```

If you change the light color to red, like this:

```python
light_color = "red"
if light_color == "green":
    print("Go")
elif light_color == "red":
    print("Stop")
print("This code executes no matter what")
```

. . . then the result is

```
Stop
This code executes no matter what
```

Suppose you change the light color to anything other than red or green, as follows:

```python
light_color = "yellow"
if light_color == "green":
    print("Go")
elif light_color == "red":
    print("Stop")
print("This code executes no matter what")
```

Executing this code produces the following output, because neither color=="green" or color=="red" proved true, so none of the indented code was executed:

```
This code executes no matter what
```

You can add an else option that happens only if the previous conditions all prove false, like this:

```
light_color = "yellow"
if light_color == "green":
    print("Go")
elif light_color == "red":
    print("Stop")
else:
    print("Proceed with caution")
print("This code executes no matter what")
```

The output is:

```
Proceed with caution
This code executes no matter what
```

The fact that the `light_color` is yellow prevents the first two if conditions from proving true, so only the `else` code is executed. And that's true for *anything* you put into the `light_color` variable because the else isn't looking for a specific condition. It's just playing an "if all else fails, do this" kind of role in the logic.

# Ternary operations

In this book, we don't assume you're familiar with other programming languages, but we need to mention this for those readers who are familiar with other languages. Many languages have a shorthand way of doing `if ... else` all on one line of code. For example, consider the following JavaScript code:

```
//JavaScript code example, won't work in Python
age=14;
beverage = (age > 20) ? "beer" : "milk";
alert("Have a " + beverage);
```

The third line is a shorthand way of saying "Put into the `beverage` variable *beer* or *milk* depending on the contents of the `age` variable" In Python you may write that as something like this:

```
age = 31
if age < 21:
    beverage = "milk"
elif age >= 21 and age < 80:
    beverage = "beer"
else:
    beverage = "prune juice"

print("Have a " + beverage)
```

The code is longer and more wordy, but easier to understand. Adding comments, which is always an option, helps a lot too, as follows:

```
age = 31

if age < 21:
    # If under 21, no alcohol
    beverage = "milk"

elif age >= 21 and age < 80:
    # Ages 21 - 79, suggest beer
    beverage = "beer"

else:
    # If 80 or older, prune juice might be a good choice.
    beverage = "prune juice"

print("Have a " + beverage)
```

If you're wondering what the rule is for indenting comments, there is no rule. Comments are just notes to yourself, they are not executable code. So they are never executed like code, no matter what their level indentation.

# Repeating a Process with for

Decision-making is a big part of writing all kinds of apps, be it games, artificial intelligence, robotics . . . whatever. But there are also cases where you need to count or perform some task over and over. A *for loop* is one way to do that. It allows you to repeat a line of code, or several lines of code, as many times as you like.

## Looping through numbers in a range

If you know how many times you want a loop to repeat, using this syntax may be easiest:

```
for x in range(y):
    do this
    do this
    ...
un-indented code is executed after the loop
```

Replace *x* with any variable name of your choosing. Replace *y* with any number or range of numbers. If you specify one number, the range will be from zero to one less than the final number. For example, run this code in a Jupyter notebook or .py file:

```
for x in range(7):
    print(x)
print("All done")
```

The output is the result of executing `print(x)` once for each pass through the loop, with x starting at zero. The final line, which isn't indented, executes after the loop has finished looping. So the output is:

```
0
1
2
3
4
5
6
All done
```

If you find this a bit annoying because the loop doesn't do what you meant, you can put two numbers, separated by a comma, as the range. The first number is where the counting for the loop starts. The second number is one greater than where the loop stops (which is unfortunate for readability but such is life). For example, here is a for loop with two numbers in the range:

```
for x in range(1, 10):
    print(x)
print("All done")
```

When you run that code, the counter starts at 1, and as indicated, it stops short of the last number:

```
1
2
3
4
5
6
7
8
9
All done
```

If you really want the loop to count from 1 to 10, the range will have to be 1,11. This won't make your brain cells any happier, but at least it gets the desired goal of 1 to 10, as shown in Figure 2-7.

```
for x in range(1, 11):
    print(x)
print("All done")

1
2
3
4
5
6
7
8
9
10
All done
```

FIGURE 2-7:
A loop that counts from 1 to 10.

## Looping through a string

Using `range()` in a `for` loop is optional. You can replace `range` with a string, and the loop repeats once for each character in the string. The variable x (or whatever you name the variable) contains one character from the string with each pass through the loop, going from left to right. The syntax here is:

```
for x in string
    do this
    do this
    . . .
Do this when the loop is done
```

As usual, replace *x* with any variable name you like. The string should be text enclosed in quotation marks, or it should be the name of a variable that contains a string. For example, type this code into a Jupyter notebook or .py file:

```
for x in "snorkel":
    print(x)
print("Done")
```

When you run this code, you get the following output. The loop printed one letter from the word "snorkel" with each pass through the loop. When the looping was finished, execution fell to the first un-indented line outside the loop.

```
s
n
o
r
k
e
l
Done
```

The string doesn't have to be a literal string. It can be the name of any variable that contains a string. For example, try this code:

```
my_word = "snorkel"
for x in my_word:
    print(x)
print("Done")
```

The result is exactly the same. The only difference is we used a variable name rather than a string in the for loop. But it "knew" that you meant the content of my_word, because my_word isn't enclosed in quotation marks.

```
s
n
o
r
k
e
l
Done
```

## Looping through a list

A list, in Python, is basically any group of items, separated by commas, inside square brackets. You can loop through such a list either directly in the for loop or through a variable that contains the list. Here is an example of looping through the list with no variable:

```
for x in ["The", "rain", "in", "Spain"]:
    print(x)
print("Done")
```

This kind of loop repeats once for each item in the list. The variable (x in the preceding example) gets its value from one item in the list, going from left to right. So, running the preceding code produces the output you see in Figure 2-8.

```
for x in ["The", "rain", "in", "Spain"]:
    print(x)
print("Done")

The
rain
in
Spain
Done
```

FIGURE 2-8:
Looping
through a list.

You can assign the list to a variable too, and then use the variable name in the for loop rather than the list. Figure 2-9 shows an example where the variable seven_dwarves is assigned a list of seven names. Again, notice how the list is contained within square brackets. These are what make Python treat it as a list. The *for* loop then loops through the list, printing the name of one dwarf (one item in the list) with each pass through the loop. We used the variable name dwarf rather than x, but that name can be any valid name you like. We could have used x or little_person or name_of_fictional_entity or goober_wocky or anything else, so long as the name in the first line matches the name used in the for loop.

```
seven_dwarves = ["Happy", "Grumpy", "Sleepy", "Bashful", "Sneezy", "Doc", "Dopey"]
for dwarf in seven_dwarves:
    print(dwarf)
print("And Snow White too")

Happy
Grumpy
Sleepy
Bashful
Sneezy
Doc
Dopey
And Snow White too
```

FIGURE 2-9:
Looping through
a list.

## Bailing out of a loop

Typically, you want a loop to go through an entire list or range of items, but you can also force a loop to stop early if some condition is met. Use the break statement inside an if statement to force the loop to stop early. The syntax is:

```
for x in items:
    if condition:
        [do this ... ]
        break
    do this
do this when loop is finished
```

We put the [do this ... ] in square brackets because putting code above the `continue` is optional, not required. So let's say someone took an exam and we want to loop through their answers. But we have a rule that says if they leave an answer empty, then we mark it Incomplete and ignore the rest of the items in the list. Here is one where all items are answered (no blanks):

```
answers = ["A", "C", "B", "D"]
for answer in answers:
    if answer == "":
        print("Incomplete")
        break
    print(answer)
print("Loop is done")
```

In the result, all four answers are printed:

```
A
C
B
D
Loop is done
```

Here is the same code, but the third item in the list is blank, as indicated by the empty string "".

```
answers = ["A", "C", "", "D"]
for answer in answers:
    if answer == "":
        print("Incomplete")
        break
    print(answer)
print("Loop is done")
```

Here is the output of running that code:

```
A
C
Incomplete
Loop is done
```

So the logic is, as long as there is some answer provided, the `if` code is not executed and the loop runs to completion. However, if the loop encounters a blank answer, it prints Incomplete and also "breaks" the loop, jumping down to the first statement outside the loop (the final un-indented code), which says Loop is done.

## Looping with continue

You can also use a `continue` statement in a loop, which is kind of the opposite of `break`. Whereas `break` makes code execution jump past the end of the loop and stop looping, `continue` makes it jump back to the top of the loop and continue with the next item (that is, after the item that triggered the `continue`). So here is the same code as the previous example, but instead of executing a `break` when it hits a blank answer, it continues with the next item in the list:

```python
answers = ["A", "C", "", "D"]
for answer in answers:
    if answer == "":
        print("Incomplete")
        continue
    print(answer)
print("Loop is done")
```

The output of that code is as follows. It doesn't print the blank answer, it prints Incomplete, but then it goes back and continues looping through the rest of the items:

```
A
C
Incomplete
D
Loop is done
```

## Nesting loops

It's perfectly okay to *nest* loops . . . that is, to put loops inside of loops. Just make sure you get your indentations right because only the indentations determine which loop, if any, a line of code is located within. For example, in Figure 1-10 an outer loop loops through the words First, Second, and Third. With each pass through the loop, it prints a word, then it prints the numbers 1–3 (by looping through a range and adding 1 to each range value).

So you can see, the loops work because we see each word in the outer list followed by the numbers 1–3. The end of the loop is the first un-indented line at the bottom, which doesn't print until the outer loop has completed its process.

```
# Outer Loop
for outer in ["First", "Second", "Third"]:
    print(outer)
    # Inner Loop
    for inner in range(3):
        print(inner + 1)

print("Both loops are done")
#Out of both Loops here
```

```
First
1
2
3
Second
1
2
3
Third
1
2
3
Both loops are done
```

**FIGURE 2-10:**
Nested loops.

# Looping with while

As an alternative to looping with for, you can loop with while. The difference is subtle. With for, you generally get a fixed number of loops, one for each item in a range or one for each item in a list. With a while loop, the loop keeps going *as long as* (while) some condition is true. Here is the basic syntax:

```
while condition
    do this ...
    do this ...
do this when loop is done
```

With while loops, you have to make sure that the *condition* that makes the loop stop happens eventually. Otherwise, you get an infinite loop that just keeps going and going and going until some error causes it to fail, or until you force it to stop by closing the app, shutting down the computer, or doing some other awkward thing.

Here is an example where the while condition runs for a finite number of times because of three things:

>> We create a variable named counter and give it a starting value (65).

>> We say to run the loop *while* counter is less than 91.

>> Inside the loop, we increase counter by 1 (counter += 1). This eventually increases counter to more than 91, which ends the loop.

The chr() function inside the loop just displays the ASCII character for whatever the number in counter. Going from 65 to 90 is enough to print all the uppercase letters in the alphabet, as in you see in Figure 2-11.

```
counter = 65
while counter < 91:
    print(str(counter) + "=" + chr(counter))
    counter += 1
print("all done")
```
```
65=A
66=B
67=C
68=D
69=E
70=F
71=G
72=H
73=I
74=J
75=K
76=L
77=M
78=N
79=O
80=P
81=Q
82=R
83=S
84=T
85=U
86=V
87=W
88=X
89=Y
90=Z
all done
```

**FIGURE 2-11:** Looping while counter is less than 91.

The easy and common mistake to make with this kind of loop is to forget to increment the counter so that it grows with each pass through the loop and eventually makes the while condition false and stops the loop. In Figure 2-12, we intentionally removed counter += 1 to cause that error. As you can see, it keeps printing A. It keeps going longer after what you see in the figure; you would have to scroll down to see how many it's done so far at any time.

If this happens to you in a Jupyter notebook, don't panic. Just hit the square Stop button to the right of Run (it shows Interrupt the kernel, which is nerd=speak for stop" when you touch the mouse pointer to it). This gets all code execution to stop in the notebook. Then you can click the curved arrow to the right of the Stop button to restart the kernel and get back to square one. Then you can fix the error in your code and try again.

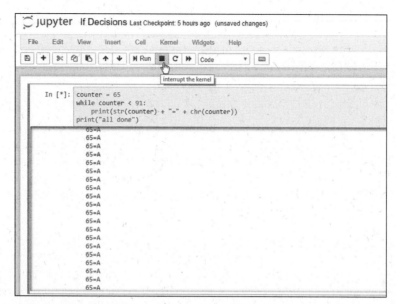

**FIGURE 2-12:**
In an infinite loop.

## Starting while loops over with continue

You can use if and continue in a while loop to skip back to the top of the loop just as you can with for loops. Take a look at the code in Figure 2-13 for an example.

```
import random
print("Odd numbers")
counter = 0
while counter < 10:
    # Get a random number
    number = random.randint(1,999)
    if int(number / 2) == number /2:
        # If it's an even number, don't print it.
        continue
    #Otherwise, if it's odd, print it and increment the couter.
    print(number)
    # Increment the Loop counter.
    counter += 1
print("Loop is done")
```

```
Odd numbers
697
449
91
567
949
333
591
699
895
837
Loop is done
```

**FIGURE 2-13:**
A while loop
with continue.

A `while` loop keeps going while a variable named `counter` is less than 10. Inside the loop, the variable named number gets a random number in the range of 1 to 999 assigned to it. Then this statement:

```
if int(number / 2) == number / 2:
```

. . . checks to see if the number is even. Remember, the `int()` function returns only the whole portion of a number. So let's say the random number that gets generated is 5. Dividing this number by 2 gets you 2.5. Then `int(number)` is 2 because the `int()` of a number drops everything after the decimal point. 2 does not equal 2.5, so the code skips over the `continue`, prints that odd number, increments the counter, and keeps going.

If the next random number is, say, 12; well, 12 divided by 2 is 6 and `int(6)` does equal 6 (since neither number has a decimal point). That causes the `continue` to execute, skipping over the `print(number)` statement and the `counter` increment, so it just tries another random number and continues on its merry way. Eventually, it finds 10 odd numbers, at which point the loop stops and the final line of code displays `"Loop is done."`

## Breaking while loops with break

You can also break a `while` loop using `break`, just as you can with a `for` loop. When you break a `while` loop, you force execution to continue with the first line of code that's under and outside the loop, thereby stopping the loop but continuing the flow with the rest of the action after the loop.

Another way to think of a `break` is as something that allows you to stop a `while` loop before the `while` condition proves false. So it allows you to literally break out of the loop before its time. Truthfully, however, we can't even remember a situation where breaking out of a loop before its time was a good solution to the problem, so it's hard to come up with a practical example. In lieu of that, then, we'll just show you the syntax and provide a generic example. The syntax is like this:

```
while condition1:
    do this.
    ...
    if condition2
break
do this code when loop is done
```

So basically there are two things that can stop this loop. Either *condition1* proves False, or *condition2* proves True. Regardless of which of those two things happen, code execution resumes at the first line of code outside the loop, the line that reads do this code when loop is done in the sample syntax.

Here is an example where the program prints *up to* ten numbers that are evenly divisible by five. It may print fewer than that, though, because when it hits a random number that's evenly divisible by five, it bails out of the loop. So the only thing you can predict about it is that it will print between zero and ten numbers that are evenly divisible by five. You can't predict how many it will print on any given run, because there's no way to tell if or when it will get a random number that's evenly divisible by five during the ten tries it's allowed:

```
import random
print("Numbers that aren't evenly divisible by 5")
counter = 0
while counter < 10:
    # Get a random number
    number = random.randint(1,999)
    if int(number / 5) == number / 5:
        # If it's evenly divisible by 5, bail out.
        break
    # Otherwise, print it and keep going for a while.
    print(number)
    # Increment the loop counter.
    counter += 1
print("Loop is done")
```



So the first time you run that app, your output may look something like Figure 2-14. The second time you may get something like Figure 2-15. There's just no way to predict because the random number is indeed random and not predictable (which is an important concept in many games).

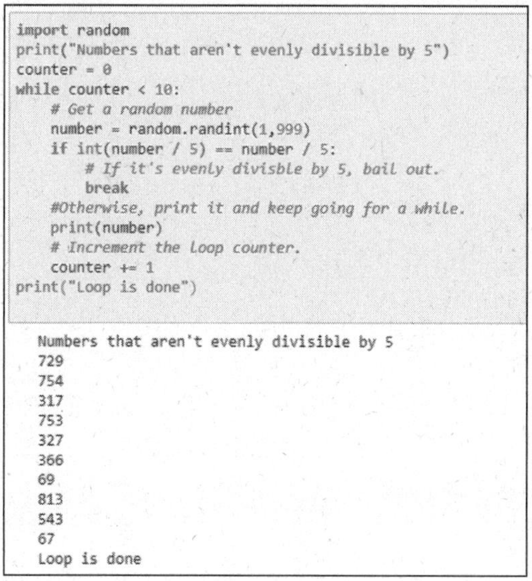

```
import random
print("Numbers that aren't evenly divisible by 5")
counter = 0
while counter < 10:
    # Get a random number
    number = random.randint(1,999)
    if int(number / 5) == number / 5:
        # If it's evenly divisble by 5, bail out.
        break
    #Otherwise, print it and keep going for a while.
    print(number)
    # Increment the loop counter.
    counter += 1
print("Loop is done")
```

```
Numbers that aren't evenly divisible by 5
729
754
317
753
327
366
69
813
543
67
Loop is done
```

**FIGURE 2-14:** A `while` loop with `break`.

```
import random
print("Numbers that aren't evenly divisible by 5")
counter = 0
while counter < 10:
    # Get a random number
    number = random.randint(1,999)
    if int(number / 5) == number / 5:
        # If it's evenly divisble by 5, bail out.
        break
    #Otherwise, print it and keep going for a while.
    print(number)
    # Increment the loop counter.
    counter += 1
print("Loop is done")
```

```
Numbers that aren't evenly divisible by 5
866
377
197
Loop is done
```

Chapter **3**

# Speeding Along with Lists and Tuples

S ometimes in code you work with one item of data at a time, such as a person's name or a unit price or a username. There are also plenty of times where you work with larger sets of data, like a list of people's names or a list of products and their prices. These sets of data are often referred to as *lists* or *arrays* in most programming languages.

Python has lots of really great ways for dealing with all kinds of data collections in easy, fast, and efficient ways. You learn about those in this chapter. As always, I encourage you to follow along hands-on in a Jupyter notebook or .py file as you read this chapter. The "doing" really helps with the "understanding" part, and helps it all to sink in better.

## Defining and Using Lists

The simplest data collection in Python is a list. We provided examples of these in the previous chapter. A *list* is any list of data items, separated by commas, inside square brackets. Typically, you assign a name to the list using an = sign, just as you would with variables. If the list contains numbers, then don't use quotation marks around them. For example, here is a list of test scores:

```
scores = [88, 92, 78, 90, 98, 84]
```

If the list contains strings then, as always, those strings should be enclosed in single or double quotation marks, as in this example:

```
students = ["Mark", "Amber", "Todd", "Anita", "Sandy"]
```

To display the contents of a list on the screen, you can print it just as you would print any regular variable. For example, executing `print(students)` in your code after defining that list shows this on the screen.

```
['Mark', 'Amber', 'Todd', 'Anita', 'Sandy']
```

This may not be exactly what you had in mind. But don't worry, Python offers lots of great ways to access data in lists and display it however you like.

## Referencing list items by position

Each item in a list has a position number, starting with zero, even though you don't see any numbers. You can refer to any item in the list by its number using the name for the list followed by a number in square brackets. In other words, use this syntax:

```
listname[x]
```

### REALLY, REALLY LONG LISTS

All the lists in this chapter are short to make the examples easy and manageable. In real life, however, you may have lists containing hundreds or even thousands of items that change frequently. These kinds of lists you wouldn't type into the code directly because doing so makes the code difficult to work with. You'll more likely store such lists in an external file or external database where everything is easier to manage.

All the techniques you learn in this chapter apply to lists that are stored in external files. The only difference is that you have to write code to pull the data into the list first. This is a lot easier than trying to type every list directly into the code. But before you start tackling those really huge lists, you need to know all the techniques for working with them. So stick with this chapter before you try moving on to managing external data. You'll be glad you did.

Replace *listname* with the name of the list you're accessing and replace *x* with the position number of item you want. Remember, the first item is always number zero, not one. For example, in the first line below, I define a list named `students`, and then print item number zero from that list. The result, when executing the code, is that the name `Mark` is displayed.

```
students = ["Mark", "Amber", "Todd", "Anita", "Sandy"]
print(students[0])
Mark
```

**TECHNICAL STUFF**

When reading access list items, professionals use the word *sub* before the number. For example, *students[0]* would be spoken as *students sub zero*.

This next example shows a list named `scores`. The `print()` function prints the position number of the last score in the list, which is 4 (because the first one is always zero).

```
scores = [88, 92, 78, 90, 84]
print(scores[4])


84
```

If you try to access a list item that doesn't exist, you get an "index out of range" error. The *index* part is a reference to the number inside the square brackets. For example, Figure 3-1 shows a little experiment in a Jupyter notebook where we created a list of scores and then tried to print `score[5]`. It failed and generated an error because there is no `scores[5]`. There's only `scores[0]`, `scores[1]`, `scores[2]`, `scores[3]`, and `scores[4]` because the counting always starts at zero with the first one on the list.

```
#Define a list of numbers.
scores = [88, 92, 78, 90, 84]

print(scores[5])

---------------------------------------------------------------------------
IndexError                                Traceback (most recent call last)
<ipython-input-9-240d3b4f5443> in <module>()
      5
      6 #Experiment with the lists
----> 7 print(scores[5])

IndexError: list index out of range
```

**FIGURE 3-1:** Index out of range error because there is no `scores[5]`.

# Looping through a list

To access each item in a list, just use a `for` loop with this syntax:

```
for x in list:
```

Replace *x* with a variable name of your choosing. Replace *list* with the name of the list. An easy way to make the code readable is to always use a plural for the list name (such as `students`, `scores`). Then you can use the singular name (`student`, `score`) for the variable name. You don't need to use subscript numbers (numbers in square brackets) with this approach either. For example, the following code prints each score in the scores list:

```
for score in scores:
    print(score)
```

Remember to always indent the code that's to be executed within the loop. Figure 3-2 shows a more complete example where you can see the result of running the code in a Jupyter notebook.

```
#Define a list of numbers.
scores = [88, 92, 78, 90, 84]
for score in scores:
    print(score)
print("Done")

88
92
78
90
84
Done
```

**FIGURE 3-2:**
Looping through a list.

# Seeing whether a list contains an item

If you want your code to check the contents of a list to see whether it already contains some item, use `in listname` in an `if` statement or a variable assignment. For example, the code in Figure 3-3 creates a list of names. Then, two variables store the results of searching the list for the names *Anita* and me *Bob*. Printing the contents of each variable shows True for the one where the name (Anita) is in the list. The test to see whether Bob is in the list proves False.

```
students = ["Mark", "Amber", "Todd", "Anita", "Sandy"]

# Is Anita in the list?
has_anita = "Anita" in students
print(has_anita)

#Is Bob in the list?
has_bob = "Bob" in students
print(has_bob)

True
False
```

**FIGURE 3-3:**
Seeing whether
an item is in a list.

## Getting the length of a list

To determine how many items are in a list, use the `len()` function (short for *length*). Put the name of the list inside the parentheses. For example, type the following code into a Jupyter notebook or Python prompt or whatever:

```
students = ["Mark", "Amber", "Todd", "Anita", "Sandy"]
print(len(students))
```

Running that code produces this output:

```
5
```

There are indeed five items in the list, though the last one is always one less than the number because Python starts counting at zero. So the last one, Sandy, actually refers to `students[4]` and not `students[5]`.

## Adding an item to the end of a list

When you want your code to add a new item to the end of a list, use the `.append()` method with the value you want to add inside the parentheses. You can use either a variable name or a literal value inside the quotation marks. For instance, in Figure 3-4 the line that reads `students.append("Goober")` adds the name Goober to the list. The line that reads `students.append(new_student)` adds whatever name is stored in the variable named `new_student` to the list. The `.append()` method always adds to the end of the list. So when you print the list you see those two new names at the end.

FIGURE 3-4:
Appending two
new names to the
end of the list.

```
#Create a list of strings (names)
students = ["Mark", "Amber", "Todd", "Anita", "Sandy"]

#Add the name Goober to the list
students.append("Goober")

new_student = "Amanda"
#Add whatever name is in new_student to the list.
students.append(new_student)

#Print the entire list
print(students)

['Mark', 'Amber', 'Todd', 'Anita', 'Sandy', 'Goober', 'Amanda']
```

You can use a test to see whether an item is in a list and then append it only when the item isn't already there. For example, the code below won't add the name Amber to the list because that name is already in the list:

```
student_name = "Amanda"

#Add student_name but only if not already in the list.
if student_name in students:
    print (student_name + " already in the list")
else:
    students.append(student_name)
    print (student_name + " added to the list")
```

## Inserting an item into a list

Although the append() method allows you to add an item to the end of a list, the insert() method allows you to add an item to the list in any position. The syntax for insert() is

```
listname.insert(position, item)
```

Replace *listname* with the name of the list, *position* with the position at which you want to insert the item (for example, 0 to make it the first item, 1 to make it the second item, and so forth). Replace *item* with the value, or the name of a variable that contains the value, that you want to put into the list.

For example, the following code makes Lupe the first item in the list:

```
#Create a list of strings (names).
students = ["Mark", "Amber", "Todd", "Anita", "Sandy"]
```

```
student_name = "Lupe"
# Add student name to front of the list.
students.insert(0,student_name)

#Show me the new list.
print(students)
```

If you run the code, `print(students)` will show the list after the new name has been inserted, as follows:

```
['Lupe', 'Mark', 'Amber', 'Todd', 'Anita', 'Sandy']
```

## Changing an item in a list

You can change an item in a list using the = assignment operator just like you do with variables. Just make sure you include the index number in square brackets of the item you want to change. The syntax is:

```
listname[index]=newvalue
```

Replace *listname* with the name of the list; replace *index* with the subscript (index number) of the item you want to change; and replace *newvalue* with whatever you want to put in the list item. For example, take a look at this code:

```
#Create a list of strings (names).
students = ["Mark", "Amber", "Todd", "Anita", "Sandy"]
students[3] = "Hobart"
print(students)
```

When you run this code, the output is as follows, because Anita's name has been changed to Hobart.

```
['Mark', 'Amber', 'Todd', 'Hobart', 'Sandy']
```

## Combining lists

If you have two lists that you want to combine into a single list, use the `extend()` function with the syntax:

```
original_list.extend(additional_items_list)
```

In your code, replace *original_list* with the name of the list to which you'll be adding new list items. Replace *additional_items_list* with the name of the list that contains the items you want to add to the first list. Here is a simple example using lists named list1 and list2. After executing list1.extend(list2), the first list contains the items from both lists, as you can see in the output of the print() statement at the end.

```
# Create two lists of Names.
list1 = ["Zara", "Lupe", "Hong", "Alberto", "Jake"]
list2 = ["Huey", "Dewey", "Louie", "Nader", "Bubba"]

# Add list2 names to list1.
list1.extend(list2)

# Print list 1.
print(list1)

['Zara', 'Lupe', 'Hong', 'Alberto', 'Jake', 'Huey', 'Dewey', 'Louie', 'Nader',
    'Bubba']
```

Easy Parcheesi, no?

## Removing list items

Python offers a remove() method so you can remove any value from the list. If the item is in the list multiple times, only the first occurrence is removed. For example, the following code shows a list of letters with the letter *C* repeated a few times. Then the code uses letters.remove("C") to remove the letter *C* from the list:

```
#Create a list of strings.
letters = ["A", "B", "C", "D", "C", "E", "C"]

# Remove "C" from the list.
letters.remove("C")

#Show me the new list.
print(letters)
```

When you actually execute this code and then print the list, you'll see that only the first letter *C* has been removed:

```
['A', 'B', 'D', 'C', 'E', 'C']
```

If you need to remove all of an item, you can use a `while` loop to repeat the `.remove` as long as the item still remains in the list. For example, this code repeats the .remove as long as the "C" is still in the list.

```
#Create a list of strings.
letters = ["A", "B", "C", "D", "C", "E", "C"]
```

If you want to remove an item based on its position in the list, use pop( ) with an index number rather than remove( ) with a value. If you want to remove the last item from the list, use pop( ) without an index number. For example, the following code creates a list, one line removes the first item (0), and another removes the last item (pop( ) with nothing in the parentheses). Printing the list shows those two items have been removed:

```
#Create a list of strings.
letters = ["A", "B", "C", "D", "E", "F", "G"]

#Remove the first item.
letters.pop(0)
#Remove the last item.
letters.pop()

#Show me the new list.
print(letters)
```

Running the code shows that the popping the first and last items did, indeed, work:

```
['B', 'C', 'D', 'E', 'F']
```

When you pop( ) an item off the list, you can store a copy of that value in some variable. For example Figure 3-5 shows the same code as above. However, it stores copies of what's been removed in variables named `first_removed` and `last_removed`. At the end it prints the list, and also shows which letters were removed.

```
# Create a list of strings.
letters = ["A", "B", "C", "D", "E", "F", "G"]

# Make a copy of first list item then remove it from the list.
first_removed = letters.pop(0)
# Make a copy of last list item then remove it from the list.
last_removed = letters.pop()

# Show the new list.
print(letters)
# Show what's been removed.
print(first_removed + " and " + last_removed + " were removed from the list.")

['B', 'C', 'D', 'E', 'F']
A and G were removed from the list.
```

**FIGURE 3-5:**
Removing
list items
with pop( ).

Python also offers a del (short for *delete*) command that deletes any item from a list based on its index number (position). But again, you have to remember that the first item is zero. So, let's say you run the following code to delete item number 2 from the list:

```
# Create a list of strings.
letters = ["A", "B", "C", "D", "E", "F", "G"]

# Remove item sub 2.
del letters[2]

print(letters)
```

Running that code shows the list again, as follows. The letter *C* has been deleted, which is the correct item to delete because letters are numbered 0, 1, 2, 3, and so forth.

```
['A', 'B', 'D', 'E', 'F', 'G']
```

You can also use del to delete an entire list. Just don't use the square brackets and the index number. For example, the code in Figure 3-6 creates a list then deletes it. Trying to print the list after the deletion causes an error, because the list no longer exists when the print() statement is executed.

```
# Create a list of strings.
letters = ["A", "B", "C", "D", "E", "F", "G"]

# Delete the entire list.
del letters

# Show me the new list.
print(letters)
-------------------------------------------------------------------
NameError                             Traceback (most recent call last)
<ipython-input-28-dbf55f0c2da1> in <module>()
      6
      7 # Show me the new list.
----> 8 print(letters)

NameError: name 'letters' is not defined
```

FIGURE 3-6:
Deleting a
list and then
trying to print it
causes an error.

## Clearing out a list

If you want to delete the contents of a list but not the list itself, use .clear(). The list still exists; however, it contains no items. In other words, it's an empty list. The following code shows how you could test this. Running the code displays [] at the end, which lets you know the list is empty:

```
# Create a list of strings.
letters = ["A", "B", "C", "D", "E", "F", "G"]

# Clear the list of all entries.
letters.clear()

# Show me the new list.
print(letters)

[]
```

# Counting how many times an item appears in a list

You can use the Python count() method to count how many times an item appears in a list. As with other list methods, the syntax is simple:

```
listname.count(x)
```

Replace *listname* with the name of your list, and *x* with the value you're looking for (or the name of a variable that contains that value).

The code in Figure 3-7 counts how many times the letter *B* appears in the list, using a literal B inside the parentheses of .count(). This same code also counts the number of *C* grades, but we stored that value in a variable just to show the difference in syntax. Both counts worked, as you can see in the output of the program at the bottom. We also added one to count the *F*'s, not using any variables. We just counted the *F*'s right in the code that displays the message. There are no *F* grades, so this returns zero, as you can see in the output.

```
# Create a List of strings.
grades = ["C", "B", "A", "D", "C", "B", "C"]

# Count the B's
b_grades = grades.count("B")

# Use a variable for value to count.
look_for = "C"
c_grades = grades.count(look_for)

print("There are " + str(b_grades) + " B grades in the list.")
print("There are " + str(c_grades) + " " + look_for + " grades in the list.")

#Count Fs too.
print("There are " + str(grades.count("F")) + " F grades in the list.")
```
```
There are 2 B grades in the list.
There are 3 C grades in the list.
There are 0 F grades in the list.
```

**FIGURE 3-7:** Counting items in a list.

**REMEMBER**

When trying to combine numbers and strings to form a message, remember you have to convert the numbers to strings using the `str()` function. Otherwise, you get an error that reads something like `can only concatenate str (not "int")` to `str`. In that message, `int` is short for *integer*, and `str` is short for *string*.

## Finding an list item's index

Python offers an `.index()` method that returns a number indicating the position, based on index number, of an item in a list. The syntax is:

```
listname.index(x)
```

As always, replace *listname* with name of the list you want to search. Replace *x* what whatever you're looking for (either as a literal or as a variable name, as always). Of course, there's no guarantee that the item is in the list, and even if it is, there's no guarantee that the item is in the list only once. If the item isn't in the list, then an error occurs. If the item is in the list multiple times, then the index of the first matching item is returned.

Figure 3-8 shows an example where the program crashes at the line `f_index = grades.index(look_for)` because there is no *F* in the list.

```
# Create a list of strings.
grades = ["C", "B", "A", "D", "C", "B", "C"]

# Find the index for "B"
b_index = grades.index("B")

#Find the index for F
look_for = "F"
f_index = grades.index(look_for)

# Show the results.
print("The first B is index " + str(b_index))
print("There first "+ look_for + " is at " + str(f_index))
-----------------------------------------------------------------
ValueError                             Traceback (most recent call last)
<ipython-input-38-ee447e55d5c6> in <module>()
      7 #Find the index for F
      8 look_for = "F"
----> 9 f_index = grades.index(look_for)
     10
     11 # Show the results.

ValueError: 'F' is not in list
```

**FIGURE 3-8:**
Program fails when trying to find index of a nonexistent list item.

An easy way to get around that problem is to use an `if` statement to see whether an item is in the list before you try to get its index number. If the item isn't in the list, display a message saying so. Otherwise, get the index number and show it in a message. That code is as follows:

```
# Create a list of strings.
grades = ["C", "B", "A", "D", "C", "B", "C"]


# Decide what to look for
look_for = "F"
# See if the item is in the list.
if look_for in grades:
    # If it's in the list, get and show the index.
    print(str(look_for) + " is at index " + str(grades.index(look_for)))
else:
    # If not in the list, don't even try for index number.
    print(str(look_for) + " isn't in the list.")
```

# Alphabetizing and sorting lists

Python offers a sort() method for sorting lists. In its simplest form, it alphabet-izes the items in the list (if they're strings). If the list contains numbers, they're sorted smallest to largest. For a simple sort like that, just use sort() with empty parentheses:

```
listname.sort()
```

Replace *listname* with the name of your list. Figure 3-9 shows an example using a list of strings and a list of numbers. We created a new list for each of them simply by assigning each sorted list to a new list name. Then the code prints the contents of each sorted list.

```
# Create a list of strings.
names = ["Zara", "Lupe", "Hong", "Alberto", "Jake", "Tyler"]
# Create a list of numbers
numbers = [14, 0, 56, -4, 99, 56, 11.23]

# Sort the names list.
names.sort()
# Sort the numbers list.
numbers.sort()

# Show the results
print(names)
print(numbers)

['Alberto', 'Hong', 'Jake', 'Lupe', 'Tyler', 'Zara']
[-4, 0, 11.23, 14, 56, 56, 99]
```

**FIGURE 3-9:**
Sorting strings
and numbers.

**TIP**

If your list contains strings with a mixture of uppercase and lowercase let-ters, and if the results of the sort don't look right, try replacing .sort() with .sort(key=lambda s:s.lower()) and then running the code again. See Book 2, Chapter 5 if you're curious about the details of this.

Dates are a little trickier because you can't just type them in as strings, like "12/31/2020". They have to be the date data type to sort correctly. This means using the datetime module and the date() method to define each date. You can add the dates to the list as you would any other list. For example, in the following line, the code creates a list of four dates, and the code is perfectly fine.

```
dates = [dt.date(2020,12,31), dt.date(2019,1,31), dt.date(2018,2,28),
    dt.date(2020,1,1)]
```

The computer certainly won't mind if you create the list this way. But if you want to make the code more readable to yourself or other developers, you may want to create and append each date, one at a time, so just so it's a little easier to see what's going on and so you don't have to deal with so many commas in one line of code. Figure 3-10 shows an example where we created an empty list named datelist:

```
datelist = []
```

Then we appended one date at a time to the list using the dt.date(*year*, *month*, *day*) syntax, as shown in Figure 3-10.

```
: # Need this modules for the dates.
  import datetime as dt

  # Create a list of dates, empty for starters
  datelist = []
  # Append dates one at time so code is easier to read.
  datelist.append(dt.date(2020,12,31))
  datelist.append(dt.date(2019,1,31))
  datelist.append(dt.date(2018,2,28))
  datelist.append(dt.date(2020,1,1))

  # Sort the dates (earliest to latest) and show formatted.
  datelist.sort()
  for date in datelist:
      print(f"{date:%m/%d/%Y}")

  02/28/2018
  01/31/2019
  01/01/2020
  12/31/2020
```

**FIGURE 3-10:**
Sorting and displaying dates in a nice format.

After the list is created, the code uses datelist.sort() to sort them into chronological order (earliest to latest). We didn't use print(datelist) in that code because that method displays the dates with the data type information included, like this:

```
[datetime.date(2018, 2, 28), datetime.date(2019, 1, 31), datetime.date
    (2020, 1, 1), datetime.date(2020, 12, 31)]
```

Not the easiest list to read. So, rather than print the whole list with one `print()` statement, we looped through each date in the list, and printed each one formatted with the f-string %m/%d/%Y. This displays each date on its own line in *mm/dd/yyyy* format, as you can see at the bottom of Figure 3-10.

If you want to sort items in reverse order, put `reverse=True` inside the sort() parentheses (and don't forget to make the first letter uppercase). Figure 3-11 shows examples of sorting all three lists in descending (reverse) order using reverse=True.

```
# Need this modules for the dates.
import datetime as dt

# Create a list of strings.
names = ["Zara", "Lupe", "Hong", "Alberto", "Jake", "Tyler"]

# Create a list of numbers.
numbers = [14, 0, 56, -4, 99, 56, 11.23]

# Create a list of dates, empty for starters because code is long.
datelist = []
datelist.append(dt.date(2020,12,31))
datelist.append(dt.date(2019,1,31))
datelist.append(dt.date(2018,2,28))
datelist.append(dt.date(2020,1,1))

# Sort strings in reverse order (Z to A) and show.
names.sort(reverse=True)
print(names)
print() # This just adds a blank line to the output.

#Sort numbers in reverse order (largest to smallest) and show.
numbers.sort(reverse=True)
print(numbers)
print() # This just adds a blank line to the output.

# Sort the dates in reverse order (latest to earliest) and show formatted.
datelist.sort(reverse = True)
for date in datelist:
    print(f"{date:%m/%d/%Y}")


['Zara', 'Tyler', 'Lupe', 'Jake', 'Hong', 'Alberto']

[99, 56, 56, 14, 11.23, 0, -4]

12/31/2020
01/01/2020
01/31/2019
02/28/2018
```

**FIGURE 3-11:** Sorting strings, numbers, and dates in reverse order.

# Reversing a list

You can also reverse the order of items in a list using the `.reverse` method. This is not the same as sorting in reverse, because when you sort in reverse, you still actually sort: Z–A for strings, largest to smallest for numbers, latest to earliest for dates. When you reverse a list, you simply reverse the items in the list, no matter their order, without trying to sort them in any way. The following code shows an example in which we reverse the order of the names in the list and then print the list. The output shows the list items reversed from their original order:

```
# Create a list of strings.
names = ["Zara", "Lupe", "Hong", "Alberto", "Jake"]
# Reverse the list
names.reverse()
# Print the list
print(names)

['Jake', 'Alberto', 'Hong', 'Lupe', 'Zara']
```

## Copying a list

If you ever need to work with a copy of a list, use the .copy() method so as not to alter the original list,. For example, the following code is similar to the preceding code, except that instead of reversing the order of the original list, we make a copy of the list and reverse that one. Printing the contents of each list shows how the first list is still in the original order whereas the second one is reversed:

```
# Create a list of strings.
names = ["Zara", "Lupe", "Hong", "Alberto", "Jake"]

# Make a copy of the list
backward_names = names.copy()
# Reverse the copy
backward_names.reverse()

# Print the list
print(names)
print(backward_names)

['Zara', 'Lupe', 'Hong', 'Alberto', 'Jake']
['Jake', 'Alberto', 'Hong', 'Lupe', 'Zara']
```

For future references, Table 3-1 summarizes the methods you've learned about so far in this chapter. As you will see in upcoming chapters, those same methods with other kinds of *iterables* (a fancy name that means any list or list-like thing that you can go through one at a time).

**TABLE 3-1**

## Methods for Working with Lists

| Method | What it Does |
|---|---|
| append() | Adds an item to the end of the list. |
| clear() | Removes all items from the list, leaving it empty. |
| copy() | Makes a copy of a list. |
| count() | Counts how many times an element appears in a list. |
| extend() | Appends the items from one list to the end of another list. |
| index() | Returns the index number (position) of an element within a list. |
| insert() | Inserts an item into the list at a specific position. |
| pop() | Removes an element from the list, and provides a copy of that item that you can store in a variable. |
| remove() | Removes one item from the list. |
| reverse() | Reverses the order of items in the list. |
| sort() | Sorts the list in ascending order. Put reverse=True inside the parentheses to sort in descending order. |

# What's a Tuple and Who Cares?

In addition to lists, Python supports a data structure known as a *tuple*. Some people pronounce that like *two*-pull. Some people pronounce it like *tupple* (rhymes with *couple*). But it's not spelled *tupple* or *touple* so our best guess is that it's pronounced like *two-pull*. (Heck, for all we know, there may not even be a "correct" way to pronounce it. This probably doesn't stop people from arguing about the "correct" pronunciation at length, though.)

Anyway, despite the oddball name, a tuple is just an immutable list (like that tells you a lot). In other words, a tuple is a list, but after it's defined you can't change it. So why would you want to put immutable, unchangeable data in an app? Consider Amazon. If we could all go into Amazon and change things at will, everything would cost a penny and we'd all have housefuls of Amazon stuff that cost a penny, rather than housefuls of Amazon stuff that cost more than a penny.

The syntax for creating a tuple is the same as the syntax for creating a list, except you don't use square brackets. You have to use parentheses, like this:

```
prices = (29.95, 9.98, 4.95, 79.98, 2.95)
```

Most of the techniques and methods that you learned for using lists back in Table 3-1 *don't* work with tuples because they are used to modify something in a list, and a tuple can't be modified. However, you can get the length of a tuple using len, like this:

```
print(len(prices))
```

You can use .count() to see how many time an item appears within the tuple. For example:

```
print(prices.count(4.95))
```

You can use in to see whether a value exists in a tuple, as in the following sample code:

```
print(4.95 in prices)
```

This returns True of the tuple contains 4.95. It returns False if it doesn't contain that.

If an item exists within the tuple, you can get its index number. You'll get an error, though, if the item doesn't exist in the list. You can use in first to see whether the item exists before checking for its index number, and then you can return some nonsense value like −1 if it doesn't exist, as in this code:

```
look_for = 12345
if look_for in prices:
    position = prices.index(look_for)
else:
    position=-1
print(position)
```

You can loop through the items in a tuple and display them in any format you want using format strings. For example, this code displays each item with a leading dollar sign and two digits for the pennies:

```
#Loop through and display each item in the tuple.
for price in prices:
    print(f"${price:.2f}")
```

The output from running this code with the sample tuple is as follows:

```
$29.95
$9.98
$4.95
$79.98
$2.95
```

You cannot change the value of an item in a tuple using this kind of syntax:

```
prices[1] = 234.56
```

If you try that, you'll get an error message that reads TypeError: 'tuple' object does not support item assignment. This is telling you that you can't use the assignment operator, =, to change the value of an item in a tuple because a tuple is immutable, meaning its content cannot be changed.

Any of the methods that alter data, or even just copy data, from a list cause an error when you try them with a tuple. This incudes .append(), .clear(), .copy(), .extend(), .insert(), .pop(), .remove(), .reverse(), and .sort(). In short, a tuple makes sense if you want to *show* data to users without giving them any means to *change* any of the information.

# Working with Sets

Python also offers *sets* as a means of organizing data. The difference between a set and a list is that the items in set have no specific order. Even though you may define the set with the items in a certain order, none of the items get index numbers to identify their positions.

To define a set, use curly braces where you would have used square brackets for a list and parentheses for a tuple. For example, here's a set with some numbers in it:

```
sample_set = {1.98, 98.9, 74.95, 2.5, 1, 16.3}
```

Sets are similar to lists and tuples in a few ways. You can use len() to determine how many items are in a set. Use in to determine whether an item is in a set. But you cannot get an item in a set based on its index number. Nor can you change an item that is already in the set.

You can't change the order of items in a set either. So you cannot use .sort() to sort the set or .reverse() to reverse its order.

You can add a single new item to a set using .add(), as in the following example:

```
sample_set.add(11.23)
```

You can also add multiple items to a set using .update(). But the items you're adding should be defined as a list in square brackets, as in the following example:

```
sample_set.update([88, 123.45, 2.98])
```

You can copy a set. However, because the set has no defined order, when you display the copy, its items may not be in the same order as the original set, as shown in this code and its output:

```
# Define a set named sample_set.
sample_set = {1.98, 98.9, 74.95, 2.5, 1, 16.3}
# Show the whole set
print(sample_set)
# Make a copy and shoe the copy.
ss2 = sample_set.copy()
print(ss2)

{1.98, 98.9, 2.5, 1, 74.95, 16.3}
{16.3, 1.98, 98.9, 2.5, 1, 74.95}
```

You can loop through a set and display its contents formatted with f-strings. The last couple of code lines in Figure 3-12 show a loop that uses >6.2f to format all the prices right-aligned within a width of six characters. The output from that code is shown at the bottom of the figure. You can see the output from the first few print statements. The list at the end is output from the loop that prints each value right-aligned.

Lists and tuples are two of the most commonly-used Python data structures. Sets don't seem to get as much play as the other two, but it's good to know about them. A fourth, and very widely-used Python data structure is the data dictionary, which you will learn about in the next chapter.

```
# Define a set named sample_set.
sample_set = {1.98, 98.9, 74.95, 2.5, 1, 16.3}
# Show the whole set
print(sample_set)

# Use len to get the length of a set.
print(len(sample_set))

# Use in to determine if the set contains a value
print(74.95 in sample_set)

# Use add() to add one item to a set.
sample_set.add(11.23)

# Use update() to add a [list] to a set.
sample_set.update([88, 123.45, 2.98])

print("\nSample set after .add() and .update()")
print(sample_set)

# Loop through the set and print each item right-aligned and formatted.
print("\nLoop through set and print each item formatted.")
for price in sample_set:
    print(f"{price:>6.2f}")
```

```
{1.98, 98.9, 2.5, 1, 74.95, 16.3}
6
True

Sample set after .add() and .update()
{1.98, 98.9, 2.5, 1, 2.98, 74.95, 11.23, 16.3, 88, 123.45}

Loop through set and print each item formatted.
  1.98
 98.90
  2.50
  1.00
  2.98
 74.95
 11.23
 16.30
 88.00
123.45
```

**FIGURE 3-12:**
Playing about
with Python sets.

# Chapter **4**

# Cruising Massive Data with Dictionaries

> **D**ata dictionaries, also called *associative arrays* in some languages, are kind of like lists, which we discuss in Chapter 3. But instead of each item in the list being identified by its position in the list, each item is uniquely identified by a *key*. You can define the key, which can be a string or a number, yourself. All that matters is that it be unique to each item in the dictionary.

To understand why uniqueness matters, think about phone numbers, email addresses, and Social Security numbers. If two or more people had the same phone number, then whenever someone called that number, all those people would get the call. If two or more people had the same email address, then all those people would get the same email messages. If two or more people had the same Social Security number, and one of those people was a million dollars behind in their taxes, you better hope you can convince the tax folks you're not the one who owes a million dollars, even though your Social Security number is on the past-due bill.

The key in a dictionary represents one unique thing, and you can associate a *value* with that key. The value can be a number, string, list, tuple — just about anything, really. So you can think of a data dictionary as being kind of like a table where the first column contains a single item of information that's unique to that item and the second column, the value, contains information that's relevant to, and perhaps unique to, that key. In the example in Figure 4-1, the left column contains a key that's unique to each row. The second column is the value assigned to each key.

| Key | | Value |
|-----|---|-------|
| "htanaka" | = | "Haru Tanaka" |
| "ppatel" | = | "Priya Patel" |
| "bagarcia" | = | "Benjamin Alberto Garcia" |
| "zmin" | = | "Zhang Min" |
| "farooqi" | = | "Ayesha Farooqi" |
| "hajackson" | = | "Hanna Jackson" |
| "papatel" | = | "Pratyush Aarav Patel" |
| "hrjackson" | = | "Henry Jackson" |

FIGURE 4-1: A data dictionary with keys in the left column, values in the right.

The left column shows an abbreviation for a person's name. Some businesses use names like these to give user accounts and email addresses to their employees.

The value for the key doesn't have to be a string or an integer. It can be a list, tuple, or set. For example, in the dictionary in Figure 4-2, the value of each key includes a name, a year (perhaps the year of hire or birth year), a number (which may be number of dependents the person claims for taxes), and a Boolean True or False value (which may have indicate whether they have a company cellphone). For now, it doesn't matter what each item of data represents. What matters is that for each key you have a list (enclosed in square brackets) that contains four pieces of information about each key.

| Key | | Value |
|-----|---|-------|
| "htanaka" | = | ["Haru Tanaka", 2000, 0, True] |
| "ppatel" | = | ["Priya Patel", 2015, 1, False] |
| "bagarcia" | = | ["Benjamin Alberto Garcia", 1999, 2, True] |
| "zmin" | = | ["Zhang Min", 2017, 0, False] |
| "farooqi" | = | ["Ayesha Farooqi", 2001, 1, True] |
| "hajackson" | = | ["Hanna Jackson", 1998, 0, False] |
| "papatel" | = | ["Pratyush Aarav Patel", 2011, 2, True] |
| "hrjackson" | = | ["Henry Jackson", 2016, 0, False] |

FIGURE 4-2: A data dictionary with lists as values.

A dictionary may also consist of several different keys, each representing a piece of data. For example, rather than have a row for each item with a unique key, you may make each employee their own little dictionary, Then you can assign a key name to each unit of information. The dictionary for htanaka, then, may look like Figure 4-3.

| 'htanaka'= | 'full_name' | = | 'Haru Tanaka' |
|------------|-------------|---|---------------|
| | 'year_hired' | = | 2000 |
| | 'dependents' | = | 0 |
| | 'has_company_cell' | = | True |

FIGURE 4-3: A data dictionary for one employee.

The dictionary for another employee may have all the same key names, full_name, year_hired, dependents, and has_company_cell, but a different value for each of those keys. (See Figure 4-4.)

FIGURE 4-4:
A data
dictionary
for another
employee.

| 'ppatel' = | 'full_name' | = | 'Priya Patel' |
| | 'year_hired' | = | 2015 |
| | 'dependents' | = | 1 |
| | 'has_company_cell' | = | False |

Each dictionary having multiple keys is common in Python, because the language makes it easy to isolate the specific item of data you want using *object.key* syntax, like this:

```
ppatel.full_name = 'Priya Patel'
ppatel.year_hired= 2015
ppatel,dependents = 1
ppatel.has_company_cell=True
```

The key name is more descriptive that using an index that's based on position, as you can see in the following example.

```
ppatel[0] = 'Priya Patel'
ppatel[1]= 2015
ppatel[2] = 1
ppatel[3]=True
```

# Creating a Data Dictionary

The code for creating a data dictionary follows the basic syntax:

```
name = {key:value, key:value, key:value, key:value, ...}
```

The *name* is a name you make up and generally describes to whom or what the key-value pairs refer. The *key:value* pairs are enclosed in curly braces. The *key* values are usually strings enclosed in quotation marks, but you can use integers instead if you like. Each colon (:) separates the key name from the value assigned to it. The *value* is whatever you want to store for that key name, and can be a number, string, list . . . pretty much anything. The ellipsis ( . . . ) just means that you can have as many key-value pairs as you want. Just remember to separate the key-value pairs with commas, as shown in the syntax example.

To make the code more readable, developers often place each key-value pair on a separate line. But the syntax is still the same. The only difference is that there is a line break after each comma, as in the following:

```
name = {
    key:value,
    key:value,
    key:value,
    key:value,
    ...
}
```

If you want to try it out hands-on, open up a Jupyter notebook, a .py file, or a Python prompt, and type in the following code. Notice we created a dictionary named people. It contains multiple key-value pairs, each separated by a comma. The keys and values are strings so they're enclosed in quotation marks, and each key is separated from its value with a colon. It's important to keep all of that straight, otherwise the code won't work — yes, even just one missing or misplaced or mistyped quotation mark, colon, comma, or curly brace can mess the whole thing up.

```
people = {
    'htanaka': 'Haru Tanaka',
    'ppatel': 'Priya Patel',
    'bagarcia': 'Benjamin Alberto Garcia',
    'zmin': 'Zhang Min',
    'afarooqi': 'Ayesha Farooqi',
    'hajackson': 'Hanna Jackson',
    'papatel': 'Pratyush Aarav Patel',
    'hrjackson': 'Henry Jackson'
}
```

## Accessing dictionary data

After you have added the data in, you can work with it in a number of ways. Using print(people) — that is, a print() function with the name of the dictionary in the parentheses — you get a copy of the whole dictionary, as follows:

```
print(people)
{'htanaka': 'Haru Tanaka', 'ppatel': 'Priya Patel', 'bagarcia': 'Benjamin
    Alberto Garcia', 'zmin': 'Zhang Min', 'afarooqi': 'Ayesha Farooqi',
    'hajackson': 'Hanna Jackson', 'papatel': 'Pratyush Aarav Patel',
    'hrjackson': 'Henry Jackson'}
```

Typically this is not what you want. More often, you're looking for one specific item in the dictionary. In that case, use this syntax:

```
dictionaryname[key]
```

where *dictionaryname* is the name of the dictionary, and *key* is the key value for which you're searching. For example, if you want to know the value of the zmin key, you would enter

```
print(people['zmin'])
```

Think of this line as saying *print people sub zmin* where *sub* just means *the specific key*. When you do that, Python returns the value for that one person . . . the full name for zmin, in this example. Figure 4-5 shows that output after running the code in a Jupyter notebook cell.

```
# Make a data dictionary named people
people = {
    'htanaka': 'Haru Tanaka',
    'ppatel': 'Priya Patel',
    'bagarcia': 'Benjamin Alberto Garcia',
    'zmin': 'Zhang Min',
    'afarooqi': 'Ayesha Farooqi',
    'hajackson': 'Hanna Jackson',
    'papatel': 'Pratyush Aarav Patel',
    'hrjackson': 'Henry Jackson'
    }

print(people['zmin'])

Zhang Min
```

Notice that in the code, zmin is in quotation marks. Those are required because zmin is a string. You can use a variable name instead, so long as that variable contains a string. For example, consider the following two lines of code. The first one creates a variable named person and puts the string 'zmin' into that variable. The next line, print(people[person]) (print people sub person) requires no quotation makes because person is a variable name.

```
person = 'zmin'
print(people[person])
```

So what do you think would happen if you executed the following code?

```
person = 'hrjackson'
print(people[person])
```

You would, of course, see `Henry Jackson`, the name (value) that goes with the key `'hrjackson'`.

How about if you ran this bit of code?

```
person = 'schmeedledorp'
print(people[person])
```

Figure 4-6 shows what would happen. You get an error because nothing in the `people` dictionary has the key value `'schmeedledorp'`.

```
# Make a data dictionary named people
people = {
    'htanaka': 'Haru Tanaka',
    'ppatel': 'Priya Patel',
    'bagarcia': 'Benjamin Alberto Garcia',
    'zmin': 'Zhang Min',
    'afarooqi': 'Ayesha Farooqi',
    'hajackson': 'Hanna Jackson',
    'papatel': 'Pratyush Aarav Patel',
    'hrjackson': 'Henry Jackson'
    }

# Look for a person.
person = 'schmeedledorp'
print(people[person])
```

```
-------------------------------------------------------------
KeyError                              Traceback (most recent call last)
<ipython-input-16-3e728d397aa2> in <module>()
     13 # Look for a person.
     14 person = 'schmeedledorp'
---> 15 print(people[person])

KeyError: 'schmeedledorp'
```

**FIGURE 4-6:**
Python's way of
saying there is no
*schmeedledorp*.

## Getting the length of a dictionary

The number of items in a dictionary is considered its *length*. As with lists, you can use the `len()` statement to determine a dictionary's length. The syntax is:

```
len(dictionaryname)
```

As always, replace *dictionaryname* with the name of the dictionary you're check-ing. For example, the following code creates a dictionary, then stores its length in a variable named `howmany`:

```
people = {
    'htanaka': 'Haru Tanaka',
    'ppatel': 'Priya Patel',
    'bagarcia': 'Benjamin Alberto Garcia',
```

```
    'zmin': 'Zhang Min',
    'afarooqi': 'Ayesha Farooqi',
    'hajackson': 'Hanna Jackson',
    'papatel': 'Pratyush Aarav Patel',
    'hrjackson': 'Henry Jackson'
    }
# Count the number of key:value pairs and put in a variable.
howmany = len(people)
# Show how many.
print(howmany)
```

When executed, the print statement shows 8, the value of the hominy variable, as determined by the number of key-value pairs in the dictionary.

TIP

As you may have guessed, an empty dictionary that contains no key-value pairs has a length of zero.

## Seeing whether a key exists in a dictionary

You can use the in keyword to see whether a key exists. If the key exists, then in returns True. If the key does not exist, in returns False. Figure 4-7 shows a simple example with two print() statements. The first one checks to see whether hajackson exists in the dictionary. The second checks to see whether schmeedledorp exists in the dictionary.

```
# Make a data dictionary named people
people = {
    'htanaka': 'Haru Tanaka',
    'ppatel': 'Priya Patel',
    'bagarcia': 'Benjamin Alberto Garcia',
    'zmin': 'Zhang Min',
    'afarooqi': 'Ayesha Farooqi',
    'hajackson': 'Hanna Jackson',
    'papatel': 'Pratyush Aarav Patel',
    'hrjackson': 'Henry Jackson'
    }

# Is there an hajackson in the people dictionary?
print('hajackson' in people)

# Is there an schmeedledorp in the people dictionary?
print('schmeedledorp' in people)

    True
    False
```

**FIGURE 4-7:**
Seeing if a key exists in a dictionary.

As you can see, the first print() statement shows True because hajackson is in the dictionary. The second one returns False because schmeedledorp isn't in the dictionary.

# Getting dictionary data with get()

Having the program kind of crash and burn when you look for something that isn't in the dictionary is a little harsh. A more elegant way to handle that is to use the .get() method of a data dictionary. The syntax is:

```
dictionaryname.get(key)
```

Replace *dictionaryname* with the name of the dictionary you're searching. Replace *key* with the thing you're looking for. Notice that get() uses parentheses, not square brackets. If you look for something that *is* in the dictionary, such as this:

```
# Look for a person.
person = 'bagarcia'
print(people.get(person))
```

. . . you get the same result as you would using square brackets.

What makes .get() different is what happens when you search for a non-existent name. You don't get an error, and the program doesn't just crash and burn. Instead, get() just gracefully returns the word None to let you know that no person named schmeedledorp is in the people dictionary. Figure 4-8 shows an example.

```
# Make a data dictionary named people
people = {
    'htanaka': 'Haru Tanaka',
    'ppatel': 'Priya Patel',
    'bagarcia': 'Benjamin Alberto Garcia',
    'zmin': 'Zhang Min',
    'afarooqi': 'Ayesha Farooqi',
    'hajackson': 'Hanna Jackson',
    'papatel': 'Pratyush Aarav Patel',
    'hrjackson': 'Henry Jackson'
}

# Look for a person.
person = 'schmeedledorp'
print(people.get(person))

None
```

**FIGURE 4-8:**
Python's way of saying there is no schmeedledorp.

You can actually pass two values to get(), the second one being what you want it to return if the get fails to find what you're looking for. For instance, in the following line of code we search for schmeedledorp again, but this time if it doesn't find that person it doesn't display the word None. Instead, it displays the rather more pompous message Unbeknownst to this dictionary.

```
print(people.get('schmeedledorp','Unbeknownst to this dictionary'))
```

# Changing the value of a key

Dictionaries are mutable, which means you can change the contents of the dictionary from code (not that you can make the dictionary shut up). The syntax is simply:

```
dictionaryname[key] = newvalue
```

Replace *dictionaryname* with the name of the dictionary, *key* with the key that identifies that item, and *newvalue* with whatever you want the new value to be.

For example, supposed Hanna Jackson gets married and changes her name to Hanna Jackson-Smith. You want to keep the same key, just change the value. The line that reads people['hajackson'] = "Hanna Jackson-Smith" actually makes the change. The print() statement below that line shows the value of hajackson after executing that line of code. As you can see, that name has indeed been changed to Hana Jackson-Smith. See Figure 4-9.

```
# Print hajackson's current value.
print(people['hajackson'])

# Change the value of the hajackson key.
people['hajackson'] = "Hanna Jackson-Smith"

#Print the hajackson key to verify that the value has changed.
print(people['hajackson'])


Hanna Jackson
Hanna Jackson-Smith
```

**FIGURE 4-9:** Changing the value associated with a key in dictionary.

**TECHNICAL STUFF**

In real life, the data in the dictionary would probably also be stored in some kind of external file so it's permanent. Additional code would be required to save the dictionary changes to that external file. But you need to learn these basics before you get into all of that. So let's just forge ahead with dictionaries for now.

# Adding or changing dictionary data

You can use the dictionary update() method to add a new item to a dictionary, or to change the value of a current key. The syntax is

```
dictionaryname.update(key, value)
```

Replace *dictionaryname* with the name of the dictionary. Replace *key* with the key of the item you want to add or change. If the key you specify doesn't already exist with the dictionary, it will be added as a new item with the *value* you specify. If the *key* you specify does exist, then nothing will be added. The value of the key will be changed to whatever you specify as the *value*.

For example, consider the following Python code that creates a data dictionary named people and put two peoples' names into it:

```
# Make a data dictionary named people.
people = {
    'papatel': 'Pratyush Aarav Patel',
    'hrjackson': 'Henry Jackson'
    }

# Change the value of the hrjackson key.
people.update({'hrjackson':'Henrietta Jackson'})
print(people)

# Update the dictionary with a new property:value pair.
people.update({'wwiggins':'Wanda Wiggins'})
```

The first update line, shown below. . .

```
people.update({'hrjackson':'Henrietta Jackson'})
```

. . . changes the value for hrjackson from Henry Jackson to 'Henrietta Jackson. It changes the existing name because the key hrjackson already exists in the data dictionary.

The second update( ) reads as follows:

```
people.update({'wwiggins':'Wanda Wiggins'})
```

There is no key wwiggins in the dictionary. So update() can't change the name for wwiggins. So instead that line adds a new key-value pair to the dictionary with wwigins as the key and Wanda Wiggins as the value.

The code doesn't specify whether to change or add the value. It doesn't need to because the decision is made automatically. Each key in a dictionary must be unique; you can't have two or more rows with the same key. So when you do an update( ), it first checks to see whether the key already exists. If it does, then only the value of that key is modified; nothing new is added. If the key does not already exist in the dictionary, then there is nothing to modify so the whole new key-value is added to the dictionary. That's automatic, and the decision about which action to perform is simple:

>> If the key already exists in the dictionary, then its value is updated, because no two items in a dictionary are allowed to have the same key.

>> If the key does *not* already exist, then the key-value pair is added because there is nothing in the dictionary that already has that key, so the only choice is to add it.

After running the code above, the dictionary contains three items, `paptel`, `hrjackson` (with the new name), and `wwiggins`. Adding the following lines to the end of that code displays everything in the dictionary:

```
# Show what's in the data dictionary now.
for person in people.keys():
        print(person + "=" + people[person])
```

If you add that code and run it again, you get the output below, which shows the complete contents of the data dictionary at the end of that program:

```
papatel = Pratyush Aarav Patel
hrjackson = Henrietta Jackson
wwiggins = Wanda Wiggins
```

As you may have guessed, you can loop through a dictionary in much the same way you loop through lists, tuples, and sets. But there are some extra things you can do with dictionaries, so let's take a look at those next.

# Looping through a Dictionary

You can loop through each item in a dictionary in much the same way you can loop through lists and tuples. But you have some extra options. If you just specify the dictionary name in the `for` loop, you get all the keys, as follows:

```
for person in people:
    print(person)


htanaka
ppatel
bagarcia
zmin
afarooqi
hajackson
papatel
hrjackson
```

If you want to see the value of each item, keep the `for` loop the same, but print *dictionaryname*[*key*] where dictionary name is the name of the dictionary (`people` in our example) and *key* is whatever name you use right after the `for` in the loop (`person`, in the following example).

```
for person in people:
    print(people[person])
```

Running this code against the sample `people` dictionary lists all the names, as follows:

```
Haru Tanaka
Priya Patel
Benjamin Alberto Garcia
Zhang Min
Ayesha Farooqi
Hanna Jackson
Pratyush Aarav Patel
Henry Jackson
```

You can also get all the names just by using a slightly different syntax in the `for` loop: . . . add .`values()` to the dictionary name as in the following. Then you can just print the variable name (`person`), and you will still see the value before you're looping through the values.

```
for person in people.values():
    print(person)
```

Lastly, you can loop through the keys and values at the same time by using .`items()` after the dictionary name in the `for` loop. But you will need two variables after the `for` as well, one to reference the key, the other to reference the value. If you want so see both as you're looking through, then you'll need to use those same names inside the parentheses of the `print`.

For example, the loop in Figure 4-10 uses two variable names, `key` and `value` (although they could be x and y or anything else) to loop through `people.items()`. The `print` statement displays both the `key` and the `value` with each pass through the loop. In that example, the `print()` also has a literal equal sign (enclosed in quotation marks) to separate the key from the value. As you can see in the output, you get a list of all the keys followed by an equal sign and the value assigned to that key.

```
# Make a data dictionary named people
people = {
    'htanaka': 'Haru Tanaka',
    'ppatel': 'Priya Patel',
    'bagarcia': 'Benjamin Alberto Garcia',
    'zmin': 'Zhang Min',
    'afarooqi': 'Ayesha Farooqi',
    'hajackson': 'Hanna Jackson',
    'papatel': 'Pratyush Aarav Patel',
    'hrjackson': 'Henry Jackson'
    }

# Loop through .items to get the key and the value.
for key, value in people.items():
    # Show the key and value with = in between.
    print(key, "=", value)
```

```
htanaka = Haru Tanaka
ppatel = Priya Patel
bagarcia = Benjamin Alberto Garcia
zmin = Zhang Min
afarooqi = Ayesha Farooqi
hajackson = Hanna Jackson
papatel = Pratyush Aarav Patel
hrjackson = Henry Jackson
```

**FIGURE 4-10:**
Looping through
a dictionary with
items() and two
variable names.

# Data Dictionary Methods

If you've been diligently following along chapter to chapter, you may have noticed that some of the methods for data dictionaries look similar to those for lists, tuples, and sets. So maybe now would be a good time to list all the methods that dictionaries offer for future reference. (See Table 4-1.) You've already seen some put to use in this chapter. We get to the others a little later.

**TABLE 4-1**

## Data Dictionary Methods

| Method | What it Does |
|---|---|
| clear() | Empties the dictionary by remove all keys and values. |
| copy() | Returns a copy of the dictionary. |
| fromkeys() | Returns a new copy of the dictionary but with only specified keys and values. |
| get() | Returns the value of the specified key, or None if it doesn't exist. |
| items() | Returns a list of items as a tuple for each key-value pair. |
| keys() | Returns a list of all the keys in a dictionary. |
| pop() | Removes the item specified by the key from the dictionary, and stores it in a variable. |
| popitem() | Removes the last key-value pair. |

*(continued)*

TABLE 4-1 *(continued)*

| Method | What it Does |
|---|---|
| setdefault() | Returns the value of the specified key. If the key does not exist: insert the key, with the specified value. |
| update() | Updates the value of an existing key, or adds a new key-value pair if the specified key isn't already in the dictionary. |
| values() | Returns a list of all the values in the dictionary. |

# Copying a Dictionary

If you need to make a copy of a data dictionary to work with, use this syntax:

```
newdictionaryname = dictionaryname.copy()
```

Replace *newdictionaryname* with whatever you want to name the new dictionary. Replace *dictionaryname* with the name of the existing dictionary that you want to copy.

Figure 4-11 shows a simple example in which we created a dictionary named people. Then we create another dictionary named peeps2 as a copy of that people dictionary. Printing the contents of each dictionary shows that they are indeed identical.

```
# Define a dictionary named people.
people = {
    'htanaka': 'Haru Tanaka',
    'zmin': 'Zhang Min',
    'afarooqi': 'Ayesha Farooqi',
    }

# Make a copy of the people dictionary and put it in peeps 2.
peeps2 = people.copy()

#Show what's in both dictionaries
print(people)
print(peeps2)

{'htanaka': 'Haru Tanaka', 'zmin': 'Zhang Min', 'afarooqi': 'Ayesha Farooqi'}
{'htanaka': 'Haru Tanaka', 'zmin': 'Zhang Min', 'afarooqi': 'Ayesha Farooqi'}
```

FIGURE 4-11:
Copying a
dictionary.

# Deleting Dictionary Items

There are several ways to remove data from data dictionaries. The del keyword (short for *delete*) can remove any item based on its key. The syntax is as follows:

```
del dictionaryname[key]
```

For example, the following code creates a dictionary named `people`. Then it uses `del people["zmin"]` to remove the item that has `zmin` as its key. Printing the contents of the dictionary afterwards shows that `zmin` is no longer in that dictionary.

```
# Define a dictionary named people.
people = {
    'htanaka': 'Haru Tanaka',
    'zmin': 'Zhang Min',
    'afarooqi': 'Ayesha Farooqi',
    }

# Show original people dictionary.
print(people)

# Remove zmin from the dictionary.
del people["zmin"]

#Show what's in people now.
print(people)
```

Here is the output of that program:

```
{'htanaka': 'Haru Tanaka', 'zmin': 'Zhang Min', 'afarooqi': 'Ayesha Farooqi'}
{'htanaka': 'Haru Tanaka', 'afarooqi': 'Ayesha Farooqi'}
```

If you forget to include a specific key with the `del` keyword, and specify only the dictionary name, then the entire dictionary is deleted, even its name. For example, if you executed `del people` instead of using `del people["zmin"]` in the preceding code, the output of the second `print(people)` would be an error, as in the following, because after it's deleted the `people` dictionary no longer exists and its content cannot be displayed.

```
{'htanaka': 'Haru Tanaka', 'zmin': 'Zhang Min', 'afarooqi': 'Ayesha Farooqi'}
---------------------------------------------------------------
NameError                      Traceback (most recent call last)
<ipython-input-32-24401f5e8cf0> in <module>()
     13
     14 #Show what's in people now.
---> 15 print(people)

NameError: name 'people' is not defined
```

To remove all key-value pairs from a dictionary without deleting the entire dictionary, use the clear method with this syntax:

```
dictionaryname.clear()
```

The following code creates a dictionary named people, puts some key-value pairs in it, and then prints that dictionary so you can see its content. Then, people. clear() empties out all the data.

```
# Define a dictionary named people.
people = {
    'htanaka': 'Haru Tanaka',
    'zmin': 'Zhang Min',
    'afarooqi': 'Ayesha Farooqi',
    }

# Show original people dictionary.
print(people)

# Remove all data from the dictionary.
people.clear()

#Show what's in people now.
print(people)
```

The output of running this code shows that initially the people data dictionary contains three property:value pairs. After using people.clear() to wipe it clear, printing the people dictionary displays {}, which is Python's way of telling you that the dictionary is empty.

```
{'htanaka': 'Haru Tanaka', 'zmin': 'Zhang Min', 'afarooqi': 'Ayesha Farooqi'}
{}
```

## Using pop() with Data Dictionaries

The pop() method offers another way to remove data from a data dictionary. It actually does two things:

>> If you store the results of the pop() to a variable, that variable gets the value of the popped key.

>> Regardless of whether you store the result of the pop in a variable, the specified key is removed from the dictionary.

Figure 4-12 shows an example where in the output, you first see the entire dictionary. Then `adios = people.pop("zmin")` is executed, putting the value of the zmin **key into a variable named** adios. Printing the variable (adios) shows that the adios **variable does indeed contain** Zhang Min, the value of the zmin variable. Printing the entire people dictionary again proves that zmin has been removed from the dictionary.

```
# Define a dictionary named people.
people = {
    'htanaka': 'Haru Tanaka',
    'zmin': 'Zhang Min',
    'afarooqi': 'Ayesha Farooqi',
    }
# Show original people dictionary.
print(people)

# Pop zmin from the dictionary, store its value in adios variable.
adios = people.pop("zmin")

# Print the contents of adios and people.
print(adios)
print(people)
```

```
{'htanaka': 'Haru Tanaka', 'zmin': 'Zhang Min', 'afarooqi': 'Ayesha Farooqi'}
Zhang Min
{'htanaka': 'Haru Tanaka', 'afarooqi': 'Ayesha Farooqi'}
```

**FIGURE 4-12:**
Popping an item
from a dictionary.

Data dictionaries offer a variation on pop( ) that uses this syntax:

```
dictionaryname = popitem()
```

This one is tricky because in some earlier versions of Python it would remove some item at random. That's kind of weird unless you're writing a game or something and you do indeed want to remove things at random. But as of Python version 3.7 (the version used in this book), popitem() always removes the very last key-value pair.

If you store the results of popitem to a variable, you *don't* get that item's value, which is different from the way pop( ) works. Instead, you get both the key and its value. The dictionary no longer contains that key-value pair. So, in other words, if you replace adios = people.pop("zmin") in Figure 4-12 with adios = people.popitem(), the output is as follows:

```
{'htanaka': 'Haru Tanaka', 'zmin': 'Zhang Min', 'afarooqi': 'Ayesha Farooqi'}

('afarooqi', 'Ayesha Farooqi')

{'htanaka': 'Haru Tanaka', 'zmin': 'Zhang Min'}
```

# Fun with Multi-Key Dictionaries

So far you've worked with a dictionary that has one value (a person's name) for each key (an abbreviation of that person's name). But it's not at all unusual for a dictionary to have multiple key-value pairs for one item of data.

For example, suppose that just knowing the person's full name isn't enough. You want to also know the year they were hired, their date of birth, and whether or not that employee has been issued a company laptop. The dictionary for any one person may look more like this:

```
employee = {
    'name' : 'Haru Tanaka',
    'year_hired' : 2005,
    'dob' : '11/23/1987',
    'has_laptop' : False
}
```

Suppose you need a dictionary of products that you sell. For each product you want to know its name, its unit price, whether or not it's taxable, and how many you currently have in stock. The dictionary may look something like this (for one product):

```
product = {
    'name' : 'Ray-Ban Wayfarer Sunglasses',
    'unit_price' : 112.99,
    'taxable' : True,
    'in_stock' : 10
}
```

Notice that in each example, the key name is always enclosed in quotation marks. We even enclosed the date in dob (date of birth) in quotation marks. If you don't, it may be treated as a set of numbers, as in "11 divided by 23 divided by 1987" which isn't useful information. Booleans are either True or False (initial caps) with no quotation marks. Integers (2005, 10) and floats (112.99) are not enclosed in quotation marks either. It's important to make sure you always do these correctly, as shown in the examples above.

The value for a property can be a list, tuple, or set; it doesn't have to be a single value. For example, for the sunglasses product, maybe you offer two models (color), black and tortoise. You could add a colors or model key and list the items as a comma-separated list in square brackets like this:

```
product = {
    'name' : 'Ray-Ban Wayfarer Sunglasses',
    'unit_price' : 112.99,
    'taxable' : True,
    'in_stock' : 10,
    'models' : ['Black', 'Tortoise']
}
```

Next let's look at how you may display the dictionary data. You can use the simple *dictionaryname*[*key*] syntax to print just the value of each key. For example, using that last product example, the output of this code:

```
print(product['name'])
print(product['unit_price'])
print(product['taxable'])
print(product['in_stock'])
print(product['models'])
```

. . . would be:

```
Ray-Ban Wayfarer Sunglasses
112.99
True
10
['Black', 'Tortoise']
```

You could fancy it up by adding some descriptive text to each print statement, followed by a comma and the code. You could also loop through the list to print each model on a separate line. And you can use an f-string to format any data if you like. For example, here is a variation on the print() statements shown above:

```
product = {
    'name' : 'Ray-Ban Wayfarer Sunglasses',
    'unit_price' : 112.99,
    'taxable' : True,
    'in_stock' : 10,
    'models' : ['Black', 'Tortoise']
}
print('Name:     ', product['name'])
print('Price:    ',f"${product['unit_price']:.2f}")
print('Taxable: ',product['taxable'])
print('In Stock:',product['in_stock'])
print('Models:')
for model in product['models']:
    print(" " * 10 + model)
```

Here is the output of that code:

```
Name:     Ray-Ban Wayfarer Sunglasses
Price:    $112.99
Taxable:  True
In Stock: 10
Models:
          Black
          Tortoise
```

**WARNING**

The " " * 10 on the last line of code says *to print a space (" ") ten times*. In other words, indent ten spaces. If you don't put exactly one space between those quotation marks, you won't get 10 spaces. You'll get 10 of whatever is between the quotation marks, which also means you'll get nothing if you don't put anything between the quotation marks.

## Using the mysterious fromkeys and setdefault methods

Data dictionaries in Python offer two methods, named fromkeys() and setdefault(), which are the cause of much head-scratching among Python learners — and rightly so because it's not easy to find practical applications for their use. But we'll take a shot at it and at least show you exactly what to expect if you ever use these methods in your code.

The fromkeys() method uses this syntax:

```
newdictionaryname = dict(iterable[,value])
```

Replace *newdictionary* name with whatever you want to name the new dictionary. It doesn't have to be a generic name like *product*. It can be something that uniquely identifies the product, such as a UPC (Universal Product Code) or SKU (Stock Keeping Unit) that's specific to your own business.

Replace the *iterable* part with any iterable — meaning, something the code can loop through; a simple list will do. The *value* part is optional. If omitted, each key in the dictionary gets a value of None, which is simply Python's way of saying *no value has been assigned to this key in this dictionary yet*.

Here is an example in which we created a new dictionary DWC001 (pretend this is an SKU for some product in our inventory). We gave it a list of key names enclosed in square brackets and separated by commas, which makes it a properly defined list for Python. We provided nothing for *value*. The code then prints the new dictionary. As you can see, the last line of code prints the dictionary, which contains the specified key names with each key having a value of None.

```
DWC001 = dict.fromkeys(['name', 'unit_price', 'taxable', 'in_stock', 'models'])
print(DWC001)
{'name': None, 'unit_price': None, 'taxable': None, 'in_stock': None, 'models':
    None}
```

Now, let's say you don't want to type out all those key names. You just want to use the same keys you're using in other dictionaries. In that case, you can use *dictionary*.keys() for your iterable list of key names, so long as dictionary refers to another dictionary that already exists in the program. For example, in the following code, we created a dictionary named product that has some key names and nothing specific for the values. Then we used DWC001 = dict.fromkeys(product.keys()) to create a new dictionary with the specific name DWC001 that has the same keys as the generic product dictionary. We didn't specify any values in the dict.fromkeys(product.keys()) line, so each of those keys in the new dictionary will have values set to None.

```
# Create a generic dictionary for products name product.
product = {
    'name': '',
    'unit_price': 0,
    'taxable': True,
    'in_stock': 0,
    'models': []
}
# Create a dictionary names DWC001 that has the same keys as product.
DWC001 = dict.fromkeys(product.keys())

#Show what's in the new dictionary.
print(DWC001)
```

The final print() statement shows what's in the new dictionary. You can see it has all the same keys as the product dictionary, with each value set to None.

```
{'name': None, 'unit_price': None, 'taxable': None, 'in_stock': None, 'models':
    None}
```

The .setdefault() value lets you add a new key to a dictionary, with a predefined value. It only adds a new key and value, though. It will not alter the value for an existing key, even if that key's value is None. So it could come in handy after the fact if you defined dictionaries and then later wanted to add a another property:value pair, but only to dictionaries that don't already have that property in them.

Figure 4-13 shows an example in which we created the DWC001 dictionary using the same keys as the product dictionary. After the dictionary is created, setdefault('taxable',True) adds a key named taxable and sets its value to True — but only if that dictionary doesn't already have a key named taxable. It also adds a key named reorder_point and sets its value to 10, but again, only if that key doesn't already exist.

As you can see in the output from the code, after the fromkeys and setdefault operations, the new dictionary has all the same keys as the product dictionary plus a new key-value pair, reorder_point:10, which was added by the second setdefault. The taxable key in that output, though, is still None, because setdefault won't change the value of an existing key. It only adds a new key with the default value to a dictionary that doesn't already have that key.

```
# Create a generic dictionary for products name product.
product = {
    'name': '',
    'unit_price': 0,
    'taxable': True,
    'in_stock': 0,
    'models': []
}
# Create a dictionary for product SKU # DWC001
DWC001 = dict.fromkeys(product.keys())
DWC001.setdefault('taxable',True)
DWC001.setdefault('models',[])
DWC001.setdefault('reorder_point',100)

# Show what's in the new dictionary.
print("Dictionary after fromkeys() and setdefault()")
print(DWC001)

# Change the taxable field from None to True
print("\nDictionary after fromkeys() and setdefault()")
DWC001['taxable']=True

#Print the dictionary after changing taxable to True
print(DWC001)

Dictionary after fromkeys() and setdefault()
{'name': None, 'unit_price': None, 'taxable': None, 'in_stock': None, 'models': None, 'reorder_point': 100}

Dictionary after fromkeys() and setdefault()
{'name': None, 'unit_price': None, 'taxable': True, 'in_stock': None, 'models': None, 'reorder_point': 100}
```

**FIGURE 4-13:**
Experimenting
with fromkeys
and setdefault.

So what if you really did want to set the default of taxable to True, rather than none. The simple solution there would be to use the standard syntax, *dictionaryname [key]* = *newvalue* to change the value of the extant taxable key from None to True. The second output in Figure 4-13 proves that changing the value of the key in that manner did work.

# Nesting Dictionaries

By now it may have occurred to you that any given program you write may require several dictionaries, each with a unique name. But if you just define a bunch of dictionaries with names, how could you loop through the whole kit-and-caboodle without specifically accessing each dictionary by name? The answer is, make each of those dictionaries a key-value pair in some containing dictionary, where the key is the unique identifier for each dictionary (for example, a UPC or SKU for each product). The value for each key would then be a dictionary of all the key-value pairs for that dictionary. So the syntax would be:

```
containingdictionaryname = {
    key : {dictionary},
    key : {dictionary},
    key : {dictionary},
    ...
}
```

That's just the syntax for the dictionary of dictionaries. You have to replace all the italicized placeholder names as follows:

» *containingdictionaryname*: This is the name assigned to the dictionary as a whole. It can be any name you like, but should describe what the dictionary contains.

» *key*: Each key value must be unique, such as the UPC or SKU for a product, or the username for people, or even just some sequential number, so long as it's never repeated.

» *{dictionary}* Enclose all the key-value pairs for that one dictionary item in curly braces, and follow that whole thing with a comma if another dictionary follows.

Figure 4-14 shows an example in which we have a dictionary named products (plural, because it contains many products). This dictionary in turn contains four individual products. Each of those products has a unique key, like RB0011, DWC0317, and so forth, which are perhaps in-house SKU numbers that the business uses to manage its own inventory. Each of those four products in turn has name, price, and models keys.

FIGURE 4-14:
Multiple product
dictionaries
contained within
a larger products
dictionary.

```
# Create a generic dictionary to contain multiple product dictionaries.
products = {
    'RB00111':{'name':'Rayban Sunglasses', 'price':112.98, 'models':['black', 'tortoise']},
    'DWC0317':{'name':'Drone with Camera', 'price':72.95, 'models':['white', 'black']},
    'MTS0540':{'name':'T-Shirt', 'price':2.95, 'models':['small', 'medium', 'large']},
    'ECD2989':{'name':'Echo Dot', 'price':29.99, 'models':[]},
}
```

The complex syntax with all the curly braces, commas, and colons makes it hard to see what's really going on there (not to mention hard to type). But outside of

Python, where you don't have to do all the coding, the exact same data could be stored as a simple table named Products with the key names as column headings, like the one in Table 4-2.

TABLE 4-2

## A Table of Products

| ID (key) | Name | Price | Models |
|----------|------|-------|--------|
| RB00111 | Rayban Sunglasses | 112.98 | black, tortoise |
| DWC0317 | Drone with Camera | 72.95 | white, black |
| MTS0540 | T-Shirt | 2.95 | small, medium, large |
| ECD2989 | Echo Dot | 29.99 | |

Using a combination of f-strings and some loops, you could get Python to display that data from the data dictionaries in a neat, tabular format. Figure 4-15 shows an example of such code in a Jupyter notebook, with the output from that code right below it.

```python
# Create a generic dictionary to contain multiple product dictionaries.
products = {
    'RB00111':{'name':'Rayban Sunglasses', 'price':112.98, 'models':['black','tortoise']},
    'DWC0317':{'name':'Drone with Camera', 'price':72.95, 'models':['white', 'black']},
    'MTS0540':{'name':'T-Shirt', 'price':2.95, 'models':['small', 'medium', 'large']},
    'ECD2989':{'name':'Echo Dot', 'price':29.99, 'models':[]}
    }
print(f"{'ID':<6} {'Name':<17} {'Price':>8}  {'Models'}")
print('-' * 60)
# Loop through each dictionary in the products dictionary
for oneproduct in products.keys():
    # Get the id of one product.
    id = oneproduct
    # Get the name of one product.
    name = products[oneproduct]['name']
    # Get the unit price of one product and format with $
    unit_price = '$' + f"{products[oneproduct]['price']:,.2f}"
    # Create and empty string variable named models
    models = ''
    # Loop through the models list and tack onto models
    # one item from the list followed by a comma and a space.
    for m in products[oneproduct]['models']:
        models += m + ', '
    # If the models variable is more than two characters in length,
    # Peel off the last two characters (last comma and space)
    if len(models) > 2:
        models = models[:-2]
    else:
        models="<none>"
    # Print all the variables with a neat f-string.
    print(f"{id:<6} {name:<17} {unit_price:>8} {models}")


ID      Name              Price  Models
------------------------------------------------------------
RB00111 Rayban Sunglasses $112.98 black, tortoise
DWC0317 Drone with Camera  $72.95 white, black
MTS0540 T-Shirt             $2.95 small, medium, large
ECD2989 Echo Dot           $29.99 <none>
```

**FIGURE 4-15:** Printing data dictionaries formatted into rows and columns.

IN THIS CHAPTER

» Creating a function

» Commenting a function

» Passing information to a function

» Returning values from functions

» Unmasking anonymous functions

# Chapter **5**

# Wrangling Bigger Chunks of Code

I n this chapter you learn how to better manage larger code projects by creating your own functions. Functions provide a way to compartmentalize your code into small tasks that can be called from multiple places within an app. For example, if something you need to access throughout the app requires a dozen lines of code, chances are you don't want to repeat that code over and over again every time you need it. Doing so just makes the code larger than it needs to be. Also, if you want to change something, or if you have to fix an error in that code, you don't want to have to do it repeatedly in a bunch of different places. If all that code were contained in a function, you would just have to change or fix it in that one location.

To access the task that the function performs, you just *call* the function from your code. You do this in exactly the same way you call a built-in function like `print`: You just type the name into your code. You can make up your own function names too. So, think of functions as a way to personalize the Python language so its commands fit what you need in your application.

# Creating a Function

Creating a function is easy. In fact, feel free to follow along here in a Jupyter notebook cell or .py file if you want to get some hands-on experience. Going hands-on really helps with the understanding and remembering things.

To create a function, start a new line with `def` (short for *definition*) followed by a space, and then a name of your own choosing followed by a pair of parentheses with no spaces before or inside. Then put a colon at the end of that line. For example, to create a simple function named `hello()`, type:

```
def hello():
```

This is a function. However, it doesn't do anything. To make the function do something, you have to write the Python code that tells it what to do on subsequent lines. To ensure that the new code is "inside" the function, indent each of those lines.

**REMEMBER**

Indentations count big time in Python. There is no command that marks the end of a function. All indented lines below the `def` line are part of that function. The first un-indented line (indented as far out as the `def` line) is outside the function.

To make this function do something, you need to put an indented line of code under the `def`. We'll start easy by just having the function say `hello`. So, type `print('Hello')` indented under the `def` line. Now your code looks like this:

```
def hello():
    print('Hello')
```

If you run the code now, nothing will happen. That's okay. Nothing should happen because the code inside a function isn't executed until the functioned is *called*. You call your own functions the same way you call built-in functions, by writing code that calls the function by name, including the parentheses at the end.

For example, if you're following along, press Enter to add a blank line and then type `hello()` (no spaces in there) and make sure it's *not* indented. (You don't want this code to be indented because it's *calling* the function to execute its code; it's not *part of* the function.) So it looks like this:

```
def hello():
    print('Hello')

hello()
```

Still, nothing happens if you're in a Jupyter cell or a .py file because you've only typed in the code so far. For anything to happen, you have to run the code in the usual way in Jupyter or VS Code (if you're using a .py file in VS Code). When the code executes, you should see the output, which is just the word `Hello`, as shown in Figure 5-1.

FIGURE 5-1:
Writing, and calling, a simple function named hello().

```
def hello():
    print('Hello')

hello()

Hello
```

# Commenting a Function

Comments are always optional in code. But it's somewhat customary to make the first line under the `def` statement a docstring (text enclosed in triple quotation marks) that describes what the function does. It's also fairly common to put a comment, preceded by a # sign, to the right of the parentheses in the first line. Here's an example using the simple `hello()` function:

```
def hello():    # Practice function
    """ A docstring describing the function """
    print('Hello')
```

Because they're just comments, they don't have any effect on what the code does. Running the code again displays exactly the same results. This is because comments are just notes to yourself or to programming team members describing what the code is about.

As an added bonus for VS Code users, when you start typing the function name, VS Code's IntelliSense help shows the `def` statement for your custom function as well as the docstring you typed for it, as in Figure 5-2. So you get to create your own custom help for your own custom functions.

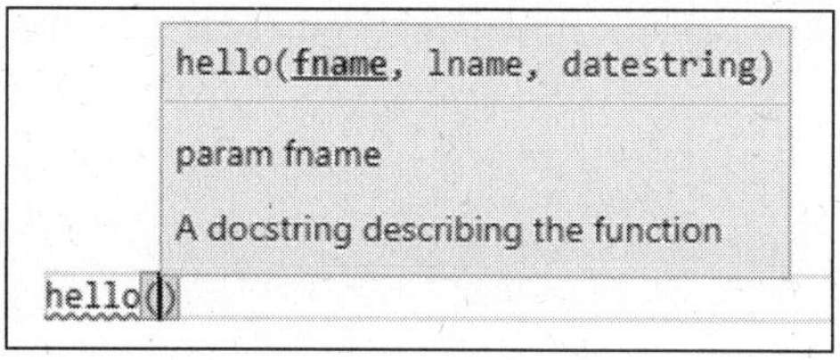

FIGURE 5-2:
The docstring comment for your functions appears in VS Code IntelliSense help.

```
hello(fname, lname, datestring)

param fname

A docstring describing the function

hello()
```

# Passing Information to a Function

You can pass information to functions for them to work on. To do so, enter a parameter name for each piece of information you'll be passing into the function. A parameter name is the same as a variable name. You can make it up yourself. Use lowercase letters, no spaces or punctuation. Ideally, the parameter should describe what's being passed in, for code readability, but you can use generic names like x and y, if you prefer.

Any name you provide as a parameter is local only to that function. For example, if you have a variable named x outside the function, and another variable named x that's inside the function, and changes you make to x inside the function won't affect the variable named x that's outside the function.

The technical term for the way variables work inside functions is *local scope*, meaning the scope of the variables' existence and influence stays inside the function and extends out no further. Variables that are created and modified inside a function literally cease to exist the moment the function stops running, and any variables that were defined outside to the function are unaffected by the goings-on inside the function. This is a good thing, because when you're writing a function, you don't have to worry about accidentally changing a variable outside the function that happens to have the same name.

A function can *return* a value, and that returned value *is* visible outside the function. More on how all that works in a moment.

As an example, let's say you want the hello function to say hello to whoever is using the app (and you have access to that information in some variable). To pass the information into the function and use it there:

>> Put a name inside the function's parentheses to act as a placeholder for the incoming information.

>> Inside the function, use that exact same name to work with the information that's passed in.

For example, suppose you want to pass a person's name into the hello function, and then use it in the print() statement. You could use any generic name for both, like this:

```
def hello(x):    # Practice function
    """ A docstring describing the function """
    print('Hello ' + x)
```

Generic names don't exactly help make your code easy to understand. So you'd probably be better off using a more descriptive name, such as name or even user_name, as in the following:

```
def hello(user_name):   # Practice function
    """ A docstring describing the function """
    print('Hello ' + user_name)
```

In the print() function, we added a space after the *o* in *Hello* so there'd be a space between Hello and the name in the output.

When a function has a parameter, you have to pass it a value when you call it or it won't work. For example, if you added the parameter to the def statement and still tried to call the function without the parameter, as in the code below, running the code would produce an error:

```
def hello(user_name):   # Practice function
    """ A docstring describing the function """
    print('Hello ' + user_name)

hello()
```

The exact error would read something like hello() missing 1 required positional argument: 'user_name', which is a major nerd-o-rama way of saying the hello function expected something to be passed into it.

For this particular function, a string needs to be passed. We know this because we concatenate whatever is passed into the variable to another string (the word hello followed by a space). If you try to concatenate a number to a string, you get an error.

The value you pass in can be a literal (the exact date you want to pass in), or it can be the name of a variable that contains that information. For example, when you run this code:

```
def hello(user_name):   # Practice function
    """ A docstring describing the function """
    print('Hello ' + user_name)

hello('Alan')
```

...the output is Hello Alan because you passed in Alan as a string in hello('Alan') so the name Alan is included in the output.

You can use a variable to pass in data too. For example, in the following code we store the string "Alan" in a variable named this_person. Then we call the function using that variable name. So running that code produces `Hello Alan`, as shown in Figure 5-3.

```
def hello(user_name):    # Practice function
    """ A docstring describing the function """
    print('Hello ' + user_name)

# Put a string in a variable named this_person.
this_person = 'Alan'
# Pass that variable name to the function.
hello(this_person)

Hello Alan
```

**FIGURE 5-3:** Passing data to a function via a variable.

## Defining optional parameters with defaults

In the previous section we mention that when you call a function that "expects" parameters without passing in those parameters, you get an error. That's was a little bit of a lie. You *can* write a function so that passing in a parameter is optional, but you have to tell it what to use if nothing gets passed in. The syntax for that is:

```
def functioname(paremetername = defaultvalue):
```

The only thing that's really different is the `= defaultvalue` part after the parameter name. For example, you could rewrite our sample `hello()` function with a default value, like this:

```
def hello(user_name = 'nobody'):    # Practice function
    """ A docstring describing the function """
    print('Hello ' + user_name)
```

Figure 5-4 shows the function after making that change. That code also called the function, both with a parameter and without. As you can see in the output, there's no error. The first call displays `hello` followed by the passed-in name. The empty `hello()` call to the functions executes the function with the default user name, nobody, so the output is `Hello nobody`.

```
def hello(user_name = 'nobody'):    # Practice function
    """ A docstring describing the function """
    print('Hello ' + user_name)

hello('Alan')
hello()

Hello Alan
Hello nobody
```

**FIGURE 5-4:** An optional parameter with a default value added to the `hello()` function.

# Passing multiple values to a function

So far in all our examples we've passed just one value to the function. But you can pass as many values as you want. Just provide a parameter name for each value, and separate the names with commas.

For example, suppose you want to pass the user's first name, last name, and maybe a date into the function. You could define those three parameters like this:

```
def hello(fname, lname, datestring):    # Practice function
    """ A docstring describing the function """
    print('Hello ' + fname + ' ' + lname)
    print('The date is ' + datestring)
```

Notice that none of the parameters is optional. So when calling the function, you need to pass in three values, like this:

```
hello('Alan', 'Simpson', '12/31/2019')
```

Figure 5-5 shows this code and the output from passing in three values.

**FIGURE 5-5:**
The hello
function
with three
parameters.

```
def hello(fname, lname, datestring):    # Practice function
    """ A docstring describing the function """
    msg = "Hello " + fname + " " + lname
    msg += " you mentioned " + datestring
    print(msg)

hello('Alan', 'Simpson', '12/31/2019')

Hello Alan Simpson you mentioned 12/31/2019
```

If you want to use some (but not all) optional parameters with multiple parameters, make sure the optional ones are the last ones entered. For example, consider the following, which would *not* work right:

```
def hello(fname, lname='unknown', datestring):
```

If you try to run this code with that arrangement, you get an error that reads something along the lines of SyntaxError: non-default argument follows default argument. This is trying to tell you that if you want to list both required parameters and optional parameters in a function, you have to put in all the required ones first (in any order). Then the optional parameters can be listed after that with their = signs (in any order). So this would work fine:

```
def hello(fname, lname, datestring=''):
    msg = 'Hello ' + fname + ' ' + lname
```

```
    if len(datestring) > 0:
        msg += ' you mentioned ' + datestring
    print(msg)
```

Logically the code inside the function says:

>> Create a variable named message and put in Hello and the first and last name.

>> If the datestring passed has a length greater than zero, add "you mentioned" and that datestring to that msg variable.

>> Print whatever is in the msg variable at this point.

Figure 5-6 shows two examples of calling that version of the function. The first call passes three values, and the second call passes only two. Both work because that third parameter is optional. The output from the first call is the full output including the date. The second one omits the part about the date in the output.

```
def hello(fname, lname, datestring=''):
    msg = 'Hello ' + fname + ' ' + lname
    if len(datestring) > 0:
        msg += ' you mentioned ' + datestring
    print(msg)

hello('Alan', 'Simpson', '12/31/2019')
hello('Sammy', 'Schmeedledorp')


Hello Alan Simpson you mentioned 12/31/2019
Hello Sammy Schmeedledorp
```

## Using keyword arguments (kwargs)

If you've ever looked at the official Python documentation at Python.org, you may have noticed they throw the term *kwargs* around a lot. That's short for *keyword arguments* and is yet another way to pass data to a function.

The term *argument* is the technical term for "the value you are passing to a function's parameters." So far we've used strictly positional arguments. For example, consider these three parameters:

```
def hello(fname, lname, datestring=''):
```

When you call the function like this:

```
hello("Alan", "Simpson")
```

Python "assumes" `"Alan"` is the first name, because it's the first argument passed and `fname` is the first parameter in the function. `"Simpson"`, the second argument, is assumed to be `lname` because `lname` is the second parameter in the `def` statement. The `datestring` is assumed to be empty because `datestring` is the third parameter in the `def` statement and nothing is being passed as a third parameter.

It doesn't have to be this way. If you like, you can tell the function what's what by using the syntax *parameter = value* in the code that's calling the function. For example, take a look at this call to `hello`:

```
hello(datestring='12/31/2019', lname='Simpson', fname='Alan')
```

When you run this code, it works fine even though the order of the arguments passed in doesn't match the order of the parameter names in the `def` statement. But the order doesn't matter here because the parameter that each argument goes with is included with the call. Clearly the `'Alan'` argument goes with the `fname` parameter because `fname` is the name of the parameter in the `def` statement.

It works if you pass in variables too. Again, the order doesn't matter. Here's another way to do this:

```
attpt_date = '12/30/2019'
last_name = 'Janda'
first_name = 'Kylie'
hello(datestring=apt_date, lname=last_name, fname=first_name)
```

Figure 5-7 shows the result of running the code both ways. As you can see, it all works fine because there's no ambiguity about which argument goes with which parameter, because the parameter name is specified in the calling code.

```
def hello(fname, lname, datestring):    # Practice function
    """ A docstring describing the function """
    msg = "Hello " + fname + " " + lname
    msg += " you mentioned " + datestring
    print(msg)

# Pass in in literal kwargs (identify each by parameter name)
hello(datestring='12/31/2019', lname='Simpson', fname='Alan')

# Pass in in kwargs from variables (identify each by parameter name)
appt_date = '12/30/2019'
last_name = 'Janda'
first_name = 'Kylie'
hello(datestring=appt_date, lname=last_name, fname=first_name)

Hello Alan Simpson you mentioned 12/31/2019
Hello Kylie Janda you mentioned 12/30/2019
```

**FIGURE 5-7:** Calling a function with keyword arguments (kwargs).

# Passing multiple values in a list

So far we've been passing one piece of data at a time. But you can also pass iterables to a function. Remember an iterable is anything that Python can loop through to get values. A list is a simple and perhaps the most commonly used literal. It's just a bunch of comma-separated values enclosed in square brackets.

The main trick to working with lists is that, if you want to alter the list contents in any way (for example, by sorting the list contents), you need to make a copy of the list within the function and make changes to that copy. This is because the function doesn't receive the original list in a mutable (changeable) format, it just receives a "pointer" to the list, which is basically a way of telling it where the list is so it can get its contents. It can certainly get those contents, but it can't change them in that original list.

It's not a huge problem because you can sort any list using the simple `sort()` method (or `sort(reverse=True)`, if you want to sort in descending order). For example, here is a new function named `alphabetize()` that takes one argument called `names`. Inside this function is assumed to be a list of values. So the function can alphabetize a list of any number of words or names:

```python
def alphabetize(original_list=[]):
    """ Pass any list in square brackets, displays a string with items
    sorted """
    # Inside the function make a working copy of the list passed in.
    sorted_list = original_list.copy()
    # Sort the working copy.
    sorted_list.sort()
    # Make a new empty string for output
    final_list = ''
    # Loop through sorted list and append name and comma and space.
    for name in sorted_list:
        final_list += name + ', '
    # Knock of last comma space if final list is long enough
    final_list = final_list[:-2]
    # Print the alphabetized list.
    print(final_list)
```

We'll walk you through this function to explain what's going on. The first line defines the function. You'll notice that for the parameter we put `original_list=[]`. The default value (`=[]`) is optional, but we put it there for two reasons. For one, so that if you accidentally call it without passing in a list, it doesn't "crash." It just returns an empty list. The docstring provides additional information. For example, when you start to type the function name in VS Code, you get both the `def` statement and the docstring as IntelliSense help to remind you how to use the function, as in Figure 5-8.

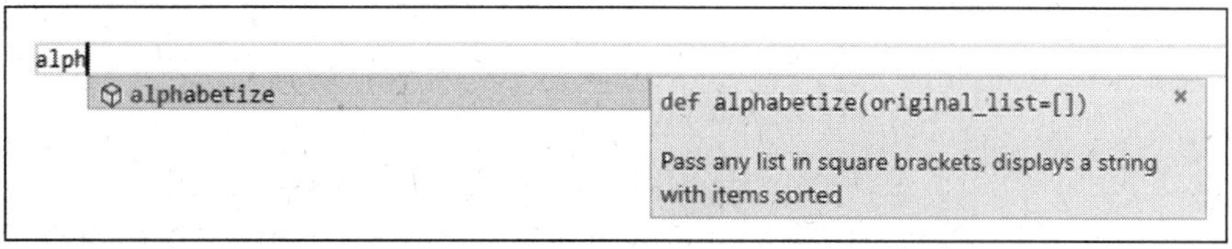

**FIGURE 5-8:**
Using the
alphabetize
function
in VS Code.

Because the function can't alter the list directly, it first makes a copy of the original list (the one that was passed in) in a new list called sorted_list, with this line of code:

```
sorted_list = original_list.copy()
```

At this point, the sorted_list isn't really sorted, it's still just a copy of the original. The next line of code does the actual sorting:

```
sorted_list.sort()
```

This function actually creates a string with the sorted items separated by commas. So this line creates a new variable name, final_list, and starts it off as an empty string after the = sign (that's two single quotation marks with no space in between).

```
final_list = ''
```

This loop loops through the sorted list and adds each item from the list, separated by a comma and a space, to that final_list string:

```
for name in sorted_list:
    final_list += name + ', '
```

When that's done, if anything was added to final_list at all, it will have an extra comma and a space at the end. So this statement removes those last two characters, assuming the list is at least two characters in length:

```
final_list = final_list[:-2]
```

The next statement just prints the final_list so you can see it.

To call the function, you can pass a list right inside the parentheses of the function, like this:

```
alphabetize(['Schrepfer', 'Maier', 'Santiago', 'Adams'])
```

As always, you can also pass in the name of a variable that already contains the list, as in this example.

```
names = ['Schrepfer', 'Maier', 'Santiago', 'Adams']
alphabetize(names)
```

Either way, the function shows those names in alphabetical order, as follows.

```
Adams, Maier, Santiago, Schrepfer
```

## Passing in an arbitrary number of arguments

A list provides one way of passing a lot of values into a function. You can also design the function so that it accepts any number of arguments. It's not particularly faster or better, so there's no "right time" or "wrong time" to use this method. Just use whichever seems easiest to you, or whichever seems to make the most sense at the moment. To pass in any number of arguments, use *args as the parameter name, like this:

```
def sorter(*args)
```

Whatever you pass in becomes a tuple named args inside the function. A tuple is an immutable list (a list you can't change). So again, if you want to change things, you need to copy the tuple to a list and then work on that copy. Here is an example where the code uses the simple statement newlist = list(args) (you can read that as *the variable named newlist is a list of all the things that are in the args tuple*). The next line, newlist.sort() sorts the list, and the print displays the contents of the list:

```
def sorter(*args):
    """ Pass in any number of arguments separated by commas
    Inside the function, they treated as a tuple named args """
    # The passed-in
    # Create a list from the passed-in tuple
    newlist = list(args)
    # Sort and show the list.
    newlist.sort()
    print(newlist)
```

Figure 5-9 shows an example of running this code with a series of numbers as arguments in a Jupyter cell. As you can see, the resulting list is in sorted order, as expected.

FIGURE 5-9:
A function
accepting any
number of
arguments
with *args.

```
def sorter(*args):
    """ Pass in any number of arguments separated by commas
    Inside the function, they treated as a tuple named args """
    # The passed-in
    # Create a list from the passed-in tuple
    newlist = list(args)
    # Sort and show the list.
    newlist.sort()
    print(newlist)

sorter(1, 0.001, 100000,-900,  2)
```

```
[-900, 0.001, 1, 2, 100000]
```

# Returning Values from Functions

So far, all our functions have just displayed some output on the screen so you can make sure the function works. In real life, it's more common for a function to *return* some value and put it in a variable that was specified in the calling code. This is typically the last line of the function followed by a space and the name of the variable (or some expression) that contains the value to be returned.

Here is a variation on the alphabetize function. It contains no print statement. Instead, at the end, it simply returns the final_list that the function created:

```
def alphabetize(original_list=[]):
    """ Pass any list in square brackets, displays a string with items
    sorted """
    # Inside the function make a working copy of the list passed in.
    sorted_list = original_list.copy()
    # Sort the working copy.
    sorted_list.sort()
    # Make a new empty string for output
    final_list = ''
    # Loop through sorted list and append name and comma and space.
    for name in sorted_list:
        final_list += name + ', '
    # Knock of last comma space if final list is long enough
    final_list = final_list[:-2]
    # Return the alphabetized list.
    return final_list
```

The most common way to use functions is to store whatever they return into some variable. For example, in the following code, the first line defines a variable called random_list, which is just a list containing names in no particular order, enclosed in square brackets (which is what tells Python it's a list). The second line creates a new variable named alpha_list by passing random_list to the `alphabetize()` function and storing whatever that function returns. The final `print` statement displays whatever is in the `alpha_list` variable:

```
random_list = ['McMullen', 'Keaser', 'Maier', 'Wilson', 'Yudt', 'Gallagher',
    'Jacobs']
alpha_list = alphabetize(random_list)
print(alpha_list)
```

Figure 5-10 shows the result of running the whole kit-and-caboodle in a Jupyter cell.

```
def alphabetize(original_list=[]):
    """ Pass any list in square brackets, displays a string with items sorted """
    # Inside the function make a working copy of the list passed in.
    sorted_list = original_list.copy()
    # Sort the working copy.
    sorted_list.sort()
    # Make a new empty string for output
    final_list = ''
    # Loop through sorted list and append name and comma and space.
    for name in sorted_list:
        final_list += name + ', '
    # Knock of last comma space if final list is long enough
    final_list = final_list[:-2]
    # Print the alphabetized list.
    print(final_list)

names = ['McMullen', 'Keaser', 'Maier', 'Wilson', 'Yudt', 'Gallagher', 'Jacobs']
alphabetize(names)

Gallagher, Jacobs, Keaser, Maier, McMullen, Wilson, Yudt
```

**FIGURE 5-10:** Printing a string returned by the `alphabetize()` function.

# Unmasking Anonymous Functions

Python supports the concept of *anonymous functions*, also called *lambda functions*. The *anonymous* part of the name is based on the fact that the function doesn't need to have a name (but *can* have one if you want it to). The *lambda* part is based on the use of the keyword *lambda* to define them in Python. *Lambda* is also the 11th letter of the Greek alphabet. But the main reason that the name is used in Python is because the term *lambda* is used to describe anonymous functions in calculus. Now that we've cleared that up, you can use this info to spark enthralling conversation at office parties.

The minimal syntax for defining a lambda expression (with no name) is:

```
Lambda arguments : expression
```

When using it:

>> Replace *arguments* with data being passed into the expression.

>> Replace *expression* with an expression (formula) that defines what you want the lambda to return.

A fairly common example of using that syntax is when you're trying to sort strings of text where some of the names start with uppercase letters and some start with lowercase letters, as in these names:

```
Adams, Ma, diMeola, Zandusky
```

Suppose you write the following code to put the names into a list, sort it, and then print the list, like this:

```
names = ['Adams', 'Ma', 'diMeola', 'Zandusky']
names.sort()
print(names)
```

That output from this is:

```
['Adams', 'Ma', 'Zandusky', 'diMeola']
```

Having diMeola come after Zandusky seems wrong to me, and probably to you. But computers don't always see things the way we do. (Actually, they don't "see" anything because they don't have eyes or brains . . . but that's beside the point.) The reason diMeola comes after Zandusky is because the sort is based on ASCII, which is a system in which each character is represented by a number. All the lowercase letters have numbers that are higher than uppercase numbers. So, when sorting, all the words starting with lowercase letters come after the words that start with an uppercase letter. If nothing else, it at least warrants a minor *hmm*.

To help with these matters, the Python sort() method lets you include a key= expression inside the parentheses, where you can tell it how to sort. The syntax is:

```
.sort(key = transform)
```

The *transform* part is some variation on the data being sorted. If you're lucky and one of the built-in functions like len (for *length*) will work for you, then you can just use that in place of *transform*, like this:

```
names.sort(key=len)
```

Unfortunately for us, the length of the string doesn't help with alphabetizing. So when you run that, the order turns out to be:

```
['Ma', 'Adams', 'diMeola', 'Zandusky']
```

The sort is going from the shortest string (the one with the fewest characters) to the longest string. Not helpful at the moment.

You can't write `key=lower` or `key=upper` to base the sort on all lowercase or all uppercase letters either, because `lower` and `upper` aren't built-in functions (which you can verify pretty quickly by googling *python 3.7 built-in functions*).

In lieu of a built-in function, you can use a custom function that you define your-self using `def`. For example, we can create a function named `lower()` that accepts a string and returns that string with all of its letters converted to lowercase. Here is the function:

```
def lower(anystring):
    """ Converts string to all lowercase """
    return anystring.lower()
```

The name `lower` is a name I made up, and *anystring* is a placeholder for whatever string you pass to it in the future. The `return anystring.lower()` returns that string converted to all lowercase using the `.lower()` method of the `str` (string) object.

You can't use `key=lower` in the `sort()` parentheses because `lower()` isn't a built-in function. It's a method . . . not the same. Kind of annoying with all these buzzwords, I know.

Suppose you write this function in a Jupyter cell or .py file. Then you call the function with something like `print(lowercaseof('Zandusky'))`. What you get as output is that string converted to all lowercase, as in Figure 5-11.

```
: def lowercaseof(anystring):
      """ Converts string to all lowercase """
      return anystring.lower()

print(lowercaseof('Zandusky'))

zandusky
```

**FIGURE 5-11:**
Putting a custom function named `lower()` to the test.

Okay, so now we have a custom function to convert any string to all lowercase letters. How do we use that as a sort key? Easy, use `key=transform` the same as before, but replace *transform* with your custom function name. Our function is named `lowercaseof`, so we'd use `.sort(key= lowercaseof)`, as shown in the following:

```
def lowercaseof(anystring):
    """ Converts string to all lowercase """
    return anystring.lower()


names = ['Adams', 'Ma', 'diMeola', 'Zandusky']
names.sort(key=lowercaseof)
```

Running this code to display the list of names puts them in the correct order, because it based the sort on strings that are all lowercase. The output is the same as before because only the sorting, which took place behind the scenes, used lowercase letters. The original data is still in its original uppercase and lowercase letters.

```
'Adams', 'diMeola', 'Ma', 'Zandusky'
```

If you're still awake and conscious after reading all of this you may be thinking, "Okay, you solved the sorting problem. But I thought we were talking about lambda functions here. Where's the lambda function?" There is no lambda function yet. But this is a perfect example of where you *could* use a lambda function, because the function you're calling, `lowercaseof()`, does all of its work with just one line of code: `return anystring.lower()`.

When your function can do its thing with a simple one-line expression like that, you can skip the `def` and the function name and just use this syntax:

```
lambda parameters : expression
```

Replace *parameters* with one or more parameter names that you make up yourself (the names inside the parentheses after `def` and the function name in a regular function). Replace *expression* with what you want the function to return without the word `return`. So in this example the key, using a lambda expression, would be:

```
lambda anystring : anystring.lower()
```

Now you can see why it's an anonymous function. The whole first line with function name `lowercaseof()` has been removed. So the advantage of using the lambda expression is that you don't even need the external custom function at all. You just need the parameter followed by a colon and an expression that tells it what to return.

Figure 5-12 shows the complete code and the result of running it. You get the proper sort order without the need for a customer external function like `lowercaseof()`. You just use `anystring : anystring.lower()` (after the word `lambda`) as the sort key.

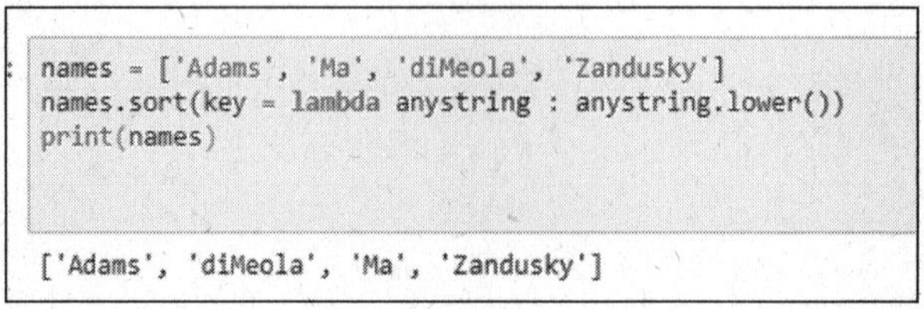

FIGURE 5-12:
Using a lambda
expression as a
sort key.

```
names = ['Adams', 'Ma', 'diMeola', 'Zandusky']
names.sort(key = lambda anystring : anystring.lower())
print(names)
```

```
['Adams', 'diMeola', 'Ma', 'Zandusky']
```

I may also add that *anystring* is a longer parameter name than most Pythonistas would use. Python folks are fond of short names, even single-letter names. For example, you could replace *anystring* with *s* (or any other letter), as in the following, and the code will work exactly the same:

```
names = ['Adams', 'Ma', 'diMeola', 'Zandusky']
names.sort(key=lambda s: s.lower())
print(names)
```

Way back at the beginning of this tirade I mentioned that a `lambda` function doesn't have to be anonymous. You can give them names and call them as you would other functions.

For example, here is a `lambda` function named `currency` that takes any number and returns a string in currency format (that is, with a leading dollar sign, commas between thousands, and two digits for pennies):

```
currency = lambda n : f"${n:,.2f}"
```

Here is one named `percent` that multiplies any number you send to it by 100 and shows it with two a percent sign at the end:

```
percent = lambda n : f"{n:.2%}"
```

Figure 5-13 shows examples of both functions defined at the top of a Jupyter cell. Then a few `print` statements call the functions by name and pass some sample data to them. Each `print()` statements displays the number in the desired format.

The reason you can define those as single-line lambdas is because you can do all the work in one line, `f"${n:,.2f}"` for the first one and `f"{n:.2%}"` for the second one. But just because you *can* do it that way, doesn't mean you *must*. You could use regular functions too, as follows:

```
# Show number in currency format.
def currency(n):
    return f"${n:,.2f}"
```

```
def percent(n):
    # Show number in percent format.
    return f"{n:.2%}"
```

```
# Show number in currency format.
currency = lambda n : f"${n:,.2f}"
# Show number in percent format.
percent = lambda n : f"{n:.2%}"

# Test currency function
print(currency(99))
print(currency(123456789.09876543))

# Test percent function
print(percent(0.065))
print(percent(.5))
```

**FIGURE 5-13:**
Two functions
for formatting
numbers.

```
$99.00
$123,456,789.10
6.50%
50.00%
```

With this longer syntax, you could pass in more information too. For example, you may default to a right-aligned format within a certain width (say 15 characters) so all numbers came out right-aligned to the same width. Figure 5-14 shows this variation on the two functions.

```
# Show number in currency format, specify width.
def currency(n, w=15):
    """ Show in currency format, width = 15 or width of your choosing """
    s = f"${n:,.2f}"
    # Pad left of output with spaces to width of w.
    return s.rjust(w)

# Show number in percent format, specify width.
def percent(n, w=15):
    """ Show in percent format, width = 15 or width of your choosing """
    # Show number in percent format.
    s = f"{n:.1%}"
    # Pad left of output with spaces to width of w.
    return s.rjust(w)
```

**FIGURE 5-14:**
Two functions
for formatting
numbers with
fixed width.

In Figure 5-14, the second parameter is optional and defaults to 15 if omitted. So if you call it like this:

```
print(currency(9999))
```

. . . you get $9,999.00 padding with enough spaces on the left to make it 15 characters wide. If you call it like this instead:

```
print(currency(9999,20)
```

. . . you still get $9,999.00 but padded with enough spaces on the left to make it 20 characters wide.

TIP

The .ljust() used in Figure 5-14 is a Python built-in string method that pads the left side of a string with sufficient spaces to make it the specified width. There's also an rjust() method to pad the right side. You can also specify a character other than a space. Google *python 3 ljust rjust* if you need more info.

So there you have it, the ability to create your own custom functions in Python. In real life, what you want to do is, any time you find that you need access to the same chunk of code — the same bit of login — over and over again in your app, don't simply copy/paste that chunk of code over and over again. Instead, put all that code in a function that you can call by name. That way, if you decide to change the code, you don't have to go digging through your app to find all the places that need changing. Just change it in the function where it's all defined in one place.

IN THIS CHAPTER

» **Mastering classes and objects**

» **Creating a class**

» **Initializing an object in a class**

» **Populating an object's attributes**

» **Giving a class methods**

» **Understanding class inheritance**

Chapter **6**

# Doing Python with Class

I n the previous chapter, we talk about functions, which allow you to compartmentalize chunks of code that do specific tasks. In this chapter, you learn about classes, which allow you to compartmentalize code *and* data. You discover all the wonder, majesty, and beauty of classes and objects (okay, maybe we oversold things a little there). But classes have become a defining characteristic of modern object-oriented programming languages like Python.

We're aware we threw a whole lot of techno jargon your way in the previous chapters. Don't worry. For the rest of this chapter we start off assuming that — like 99.9 percent of people in this world — you don't know a class from an object from a pastrami sandwich.

## Mastering Classes and Objects

Object-oriented programming (OOP) has been a major buzzword in the computer world for at least a couple decades now. The term *object* stems from the fact that the model resembles objects in the real word in that each object is a thing that has certain attributes and characteristics that make it unique. For example, a chair is an object. In the world, there are lots of different chairs that differ in size, shape, color, and material. But they're all still chairs.

How about cars? We all recognize a car when we see one. (Well, usually.) Even though cars aren't all exactly the same, they all have certain *attributes* (year, make, model, color) that make each unique. They have certain *methods* in common, where a method is an action or a thing the car can do. For example, cars all have go, stop, and turn actions you can control pretty much the same in each one.

Figure 6-1 shows the concept where all cars (although not identical) have certain attributes and methods in common. In this case, you can think of the class "cars" as being sort of a factory that creates all cars. After it's created, each car is an independent object. Changing one car has no effect on the other cars or the Car class.

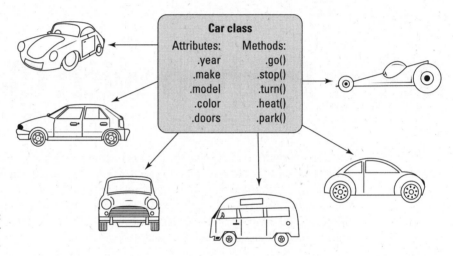

**FIGURE 6-1:** Different car objects.

If the factory idea doesn't work for you, think of a class as type of blueprint. For instance, take dogs. No, there is no physical blueprint for creating dogs. But there is some dog DNA that pretty much does the same thing. The dog DNA can be considered a type of blueprint (like a Python class) from which all dogs are created. Dogs vary in the attributes like breed, color, and size, but they share certain behaviors (methods) like "eat" and "sleep." Figure 6-2 shows an example where there is a class of animal called Dog from which all dogs originate.

Even people can easily be viewed as objects in this manner. In your code, you could create a Member class with which you manage your site members. Each member would have certain attributes, such as a username, full name, and so forth. You could also have methods such as .archive() to deactivate an account and .restore() to reactivate an account. The .archive() and .restore()

methods are behaviors that let you control membership, in much the same way the accelerator, brake, and steering wheel allow you to control a car. Figure 6-3 shows the concept.

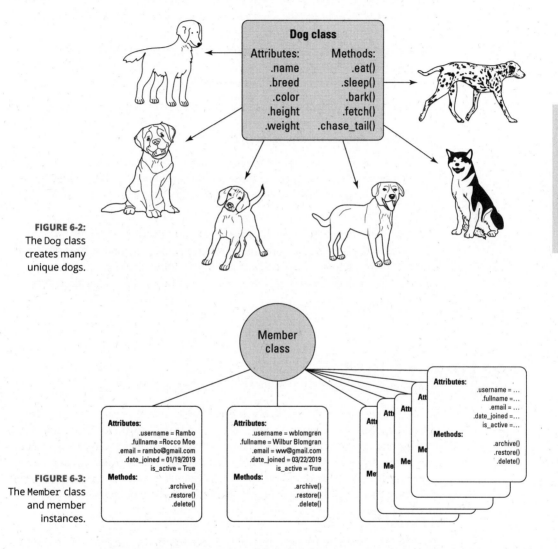

**FIGURE 6-2:**
The Dog class creates many unique dogs.

**FIGURE 6-3:**
The Member class and member instances.

The main point is that each instance of a class is its own independent object with which you can work. Changing one instance of a class has no effect on the class or on other instances, just as painting one car a different color has no effect on the car factory or on any other cars produced by that factory.

All this business of classes and instances stems from a type of programming called object-oriented programming (OOP for short). It's been a major concept in the biz for a few decades now. Python, like any significant, serious, modern programming language is object-oriented. The main buzzwords you need to get comfortable with are the ones I've harped on in the last few paragraphs:

>> **Class:** A piece of code from which you can generate a unique object, where each object is a single instance of the class. Think of it as a blueprint or factory from which you can create individual objects.

>> **Instance:** One unit of data plus code generated from a class as an instance of that class. Each instance of a class is also called an *object* just like all the different cars are objects, all created by some car factory (class).

>> **Attribute:** A characteristic of an object that contains information about the object. Also called a *property* of the object. An attribute name is preceded by dot, as in member.username which may contain the username for one site member.

>> **Method:** A Python function that's associated with the class. It defines an action that object can perform. In an object, you call a method by preceding the method name with a dot, and following it with a pair of parentheses. For example member.archive() may be a method that archives (deactivates) the member's account.

# Creating a Class

You create your own classes like you create your own functions. You are free to name the class whatever you want, so long as it's a legitimate name that starts with a letter and contains no spaces or punctuation. It's customary to start a class name with an uppercase letter to help distinguish classes from variables. To get started, all you need is the word class followed by a space, a class name of your choosing, and a colon. For example, to create a new class named Member, use class Member:

To make your code more descriptive, feel free to put a comment above the class definition. You can also put a docstring below the class line, which will show up whenever you type the class name in VS Code. For example, to add comments for your new Member class, you might type up the code like this:

```
# Define a new class name Member.
class Member:
    """ Create a new member. """
```

## EMPTY CLASSES

If you start a class with class *name*: and then run your code before finishing the class, you'll actually get an error. To get around that, you can tell Python that you're just not quite ready to finish writing the class by putting the keyword pass below the definition, as in the following code:

```
# Define a new class name Member.
class Member:
    pass
```

In essence, what you're doing there is telling Python "Hey I know this class doesn't really work yet, but just let it pass and don't throw an error message telling me about it."

That's it for defining a new class. However, it isn't useful until you specify what attributes you want each object that you create from this class to inherit from the class.

# How a Class Creates an Instance

To grant to your class the ability to create instances (objects) for you, you give the class an *init method*. The word *init* is short for *initialize*. As a method, it's really just a function that's defined inside of a class. But it must have the specific name __init__ — that's two underscores followed by init followed by two more underscores.

TIP

That __init__ is sometimes spoken as "*dunder init.*" The *dunder* part is short for *double underline.*

The syntax for creating an init method is:

```
def __init__(self[, suppliedprop1, suppliedprop2,...])
```

The def is short for *define*, and __init__ is the name of a built-in Python method that's capable of creating objects from within a class. The *self* part is just a variable name, and it is used to refer to the object being created at the moment. You can use the name of your own choosing instead of *self*. But *self* would be considered by most a good "best practice" since it's explanatory and customary.

This whole businesses of classes is easier to learn and understand if you start off simply. So, for a working example, let's create a class named Member, into which you will pass a username (uname) and full name (fname) whenever you want to create a member. As always, you can precede the code with a comment. You can also put a docstring (in triple quotation marks) under the first line both as a comment but also as an IntelliSense reminder when typing code in VS Code:

```
# Define a class named Member for making member objects.
class Member:
    """ Create a member from uname and fname """
    def __init__(self, uname, fname):
```

When that def __init__ line executes, you have an empty object, named self, inside of the class. The uname and fname parameters just hold whatever data you pass in, and you'll see how that works in a moment.

An empty object with no data doesn't do you much good. What makes an object useful is the information it contains that's unique to that object (its attributes). So, in your class, the next step is to assign a value to each of the object's attributes.

# Giving an Object Its Attributes

Now that you have a new, empty Member object, you can start giving it attributes and *populate* (store values in) those attributes. For example, let's say you want each member to have a .username attribute that contains the user's username (perhaps for logging in). You have a second attribute named fullname, which is the member's full name. To define and populate those attributes use

```
self.username = uname
self.fullname = fname
```

The first line creates an attribute named username for the new instance (self) and puts into it whatever was passed into the uname attribute when the class was called. The second line creates an attribute named fullname for the new self object, and puts into it whatever was passed in as the fname variable. Add in a comment and the whole class may look like this:

```
# Define a new class name Member.
class Member:
    """ Create a new member. """
    def __init__(self, uname, fname):
        # Define attributes and give them values.
```

Barnes & Noble Booksellers #2590
1701 E Empire
Bloomington, IL 61701
309-662-1506

STR:2590 REG:009 TRN:7999  CSHR:Jillian A

BARNES & NOBLE MEMBER      EXP: 12/31/2019

Python All-in-One For Dummies
  9781119557593        T1
  (1 @ 39.99) Member Card 10% (4.00)
  (1 @ 35.99)                       35.99

Subtotal                            35.99
Sales Tax T1 (8.750%)                3.15
TOTAL                               39.14
MASTERCARD DEBIT                    39.14
  Card#:  XXXXXXXXXXXXX3725

  Application Label: Debit
  AID: a0000000042203
  PIN Verified
  TVR: 8000048000
  TSI: 6800

MEMBER SAVINGS                       4.00

Connect with us on Social

Facebook-  @BNBloomingtonIL
Instagram- @barnesandnoblebloomingtonil
Twitter-   @BNBloomington

051.05C              08/28/2019  05:50PM

CUSTOMER COPY

---

= uname

fname

ppening there? The __init__ line creates a new empty
n the self.username = uname line adds an attribute
empty object, and puts into that attribute whatever was
the self.fullname = fname line does the same thing for
nd the fname value that was passed in.

ing things in classes suggests using an initial cap for the
tes should follow the standard for variables, being all
score to separate words within the name.

## nstance from a class

the class, you can create instances (objects) from it using

```
mber('uname', 'fname')
```

_name with a name of your own choosing (in much the
me a dog, who is an instance of the dog class). Replace
he username and full name you want to put into the object
ke sure you don't indent that code; otherwise, Python will
ll belongs to the class's code. It doesn't. It's new code to

mple, let's say you want to create a member named new_guy
mbo and the full name Rocco Moe. Here's the code for that:

```
bo','Rocco Moe')
```

nd don't get any error messages, then you know it at least
fan. But to make sure, you can print the object or its attributes. So to see what's
really in the new_guy instance of Members, you can print it as a whole. You can also
print just its attributes, new_guy.username and new_guy.fullname. You can also
print type(new_guy) to ask Python what "type" new_guy is. Here is that code:

```
print(new_guy)
print(new_guy.username)
print(new_guy.fullname)
print(type(new_guy))
```

Figure 6-4 shows all the code and the result of running it in a Jupyter cell.

Doing Python with Class

```
:  # Define a new class name Member.
   class Member:
       """ Create a new member. """
       def __init__(self, uname, fname):
           # Define attributes and give them values.
           self.username = uname
           self.fullname = fname

   # The class ends at the first un-indented line.

   # Create an instance of the Member class named new_guy
   new_guy = Member('Rambo','Rocco Moe')

   #See what's in the instance, as well as its individual properties.
   print(new_guy)
   print(new_guy.username)
   print(new_guy.fullname)
   print(type(new_guy))

   <__main__.Member object at 0x000002175EA2E160>
   Rambo
   Rocco Moe
   <class '__main__.Member'>
```

**FIGURE 6-4**
Creating a member from the Member class in a Jupyter cell.

In the figure you can see that the first line of output is this:

```
<__main__.Member object at 0x000002175EA2E160>
```

This is telling you that new_guy is an object created from the Member class. The number at the end is its location in memory, but don't worry about that; you won't need to know about those right now.

The next three lines of output are

```
Rambo
Rocco Moe
<class '__main__.Member'>
```

The Rambo line is new_guy's username (new_guy.username), the Rocco Moe is new_guy's full name (new_guy.fullname). The type is <class '__main__. Member'>, which again is just telling you that new_guy is an instance of the Member class.

**WARNING**

Much as we hate to put any more burden on your brain cells right now, the words *object* and *property* are synonymous with *instance* and *attribute*. The new_guy instance of the Member class can also be called an object, and the fullname and username attributes of new_guy are also properties of that object.

Admittedly it can be a little difficult to wrap your head around this at first, but it's really quite simple: An object is just a handy way to compartmentalize information about an item that's similar to other items (like all dogs are dogs and all cars are cars). What makes the item unique is its attributes, which won't necessarily all be the same as the attributes of other objects of the same type, in much the same way that not all dogs are the same breed and not all cars are the same color.

We intentionally used uname and fname as parameter names to distinguish them from the attribute names username and fullname. However, this isn't a requirement. In fact, if anything, people tend to use the same names for the parameters as they do for the attributes.

Instead of uname for the placeholder, you can use username (even though it's the same as the attribute name). Likewise, you can use fullname in place of fname. Doing so won't alter how the class behaves. You just have to remember that the same name is being used in two different ways, first as a placeholder for data being passed into the class, and then later as an actual attribute name that gets its value from that passed-in value.

Figure 6-5 shows the same code as Figure 6-4 with uname replaced with username and fname replaced with fullname. Running the code produces exactly the same output as before; using the same name for two different things didn't bother Python one bit.

```
# Define a new class name Member.
class Member:
    """ Create a new member. """
    def __init__(self, username, fullname):
        # Define attributes and give them values.
        self.username = username
        self.fullname = fullname

# The class ends at the first un-indented line.

# Create an instance of the Member class named new_guy
new_guy = Member('Rambo','Rocco Moe')

#See what's in the instance, as well as its individual properties.
print(new_guy)
print(new_guy.username)
print(new_guy.fullname)
print(type(new_guy))
```
```
<__main__.Member object at 0x000002175EA2E240>
Rambo
Rocco Moe
<class '__main__.Member'>
```

FIGURE 6-5:
The Member class
with username
and fullname for
parameters and
attributes.

After you type a class name and the opening parenthesis in VS Code, its IntelliSense shows you the syntax for parameters and the first docstring in the code, as shown in Figure 6-6. Naming things in a way that's meaningful to you and including a descriptive docstring in the class makes it easier for you to remember how to use the class in the future.

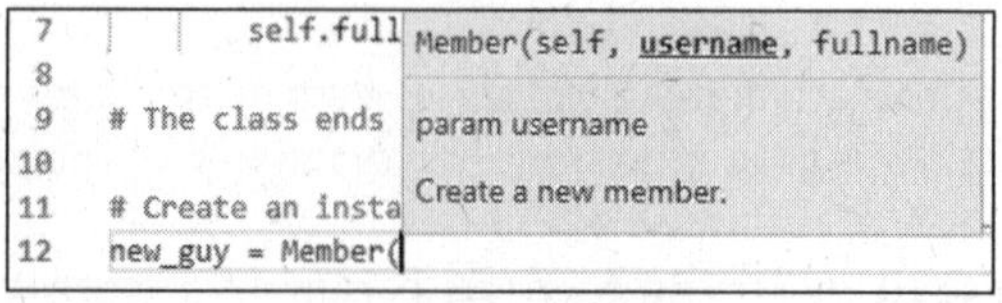

**FIGURE 6-6:**
VS Code displays
help when
accessing your
own custom
classes.

```
 7           self.full Member(self, username, fullname)
 8
 9    # The class ends  param username
10
11    # Create an insta  Create a new member.
12    new_guy = Member(
```

# Changing the value of an attribute

When working with tuples, you can define *key:value* pairs, much like the *attribute:value* pairs you see here with instances of a class. There is one major difference, though: Tuples are immutable, meaning that after they're defined, you code can't change anything about them. This is not true with objects. After you create an object, you can change the value of any attribute at any time using the following simple syntax:

```
objectname.attributename = value
```

Replace *objectname* with the name of the object (which you've already created via the class). Replace *attributename* with the name of the attribute whose value you want to change. Replace *value* with the new value.

Figure 6-7 shows an example in which, after initially creating the new_guy object, the following line of code executes:

```
new_guy.username = "Princess"
```

The lines of output under that show that new_guy's username has indeed been changed to Princess. His full name hasn't changed because you didn't do anything to that in your code.

# Defining attributes with default values

You don't have to pass in the value of every attribute for a new object. If you're always going to give those some default value at the moment the object is created, you can just use self.attributename = value, the same as before, in which attributename is some name of your own choosing. The value can be some value you just set, such as True or False for a Boolean, or today's date, or anything that can be calculated or determined by Python without your telling it the value.

For example, let's say that whenever you create a new membe, you want to track the date that you created that member in an attribute named date_joined. And you want the ability to activate and deactivate accounts to control user logins. So you create an attribute named is_active. Let's suppose that you want to start off a new member with that set to True.

```
# Define a new class name Member.
class Member:
    """ Create a new member. """
    def __init__(self, username, fullname):
        # Define attributes and give them values.
        self.username = username
        self.fullname = fullname

# The class ends at the first un-indented line.

# Create an instance of the Member class named new_guy
new_guy = Member('Rambo','Rocco Moe')

# See what's in the instance, as well as its individual properties.
print(new_guy.username)
print(new_guy.fullname)
print() #This just prints a blanks line.

# Change new_guy's user name then print both attributes again.
new_guy.username = "Princess"
print(new_guy.username)
print(new_guy.fullname)
```

```
Rambo
Rocco Moe

Princess
Rocco Moe
```

**FIGURE 6-7:**
Changing the value of an object's attribute.

If you're going to be doing anything with dates and times, you'll want to import the `datetime` module, so put that at the top of your file, even before the `class Member:` line. Then you can add these lines before or after the other lines that assign values to attributes within the class:

```
        self.date_joined  = dt.date.today()
        self.is_active = True
```

Here is how you could add the `import` and those two new attributes to the class:

```
import datetime as dt

# Define a new class name Member.
class Member:
    """ Create a new member. """
    def __init__(self, username, fullname):
        # Define attributes and give them values.
        self.username = username
        self.fullname = fullname

        # Default date_joined to today's date.
        self.date_joined =  dt.date.today()
        # Set is active to True initially.
        self.is_active = True
```

**WARNING**

If you forget to import `datetime` at the top of the code, you'll get an error message when you run the code telling you it doesn't know what `dt.date.today()` means. Just add the `import` line to the top of the code and try again.

There is no need to pass any new data into the class for the date_joined and is_active attributes, because those can be determined by the code.

Note that a default value is just that: It's a value that gets assigned automatically when you first create the object. But that doesn't mean it can't be changed. You can change those values the same as you would change any other attribute's value using the syntax

```
objectname.attributename = value
```

For example, suppose you use the is_active attribute to determine whether a user is active and can log into your site. If a member turns out to be an obnoxious troll and you don't want him logging in anymore, you could just change the is_active attribute to False like this:

```
newmember.is_active = False
```

# Giving a Class Methods

Any object you define can have any number of attributes, each given any name you like, in order to store information *about* the object, like a dog's breed and color or a car's make and model. You can also define you own methods for any object, which are more like behaviors than facts about the object. For example, a dog can eat, sleep, and bark. A car can go, stop, and turn. A method is really just a function, like you learned about in the previous chapter. What makes it a method is the fact that it's associated with a particular class and with each specific object you create from that class.

Method names are distinguished from attribute names for an object by the pair of parentheses that follow the name. To define what the methods will be in your class, use this syntax for each method:

```
def methodname(self[, param1, param2, ...])
```

Replace *methodname* with a name of your choosing (all lowercase, no spaces). Keep the word self in there as a reference to the object being defined by the class. You can also pass in parameters after self using commas, as with any other function, but this is entirely optional. Never type the square brackets ([ ]). They're shown here in the syntax only to indicate that parameter names after self are allowed but not required.

Let's create a method named .show_date_joined() that returns the user's name and date joined in a formatted string. Here is how you could write that code to define this method:

```
# Define methods as functions, use self for "this" object.
def show_datejoined(self):
    return f"{self.fullname} joined on {self.date_joined:%m/%d/%y}"
```

The name of the method is show_datejoined. The task of this method, when called, is to simply put together some nicely formatted text containing the display the member's full name and date joined. Make sure you indent the def at the same level as the first def, as these cannot be indented under attributes.

To call the method from your code, use this syntax:

```
objectname.methodname()
```

Replace *objectname* with the name of the object to which you're referring. Replace *methodname* with the name of the method you want to call. Include the parentheses (no spaces) and leave them empty if inside the class the only parameter between the parentheses is the self parameter. Figure 6-8 shows a complete example.

Notice in Figure 6-8 how the show_datejoined() method is defined within the class. Its def is indented to the same level of the first def. The code that the method executes is indented under that. Outside the class, new_guy = Member('romo', 'Rocco Moe') creates a new member named new_guy. Then new_guy.show_datejoined() executes the show_datejoined() method, which in turn displays Rocco Moe joined 12/06/18, the day I ran the code.

```
import datetime as dt

# Define a new class name Member.
class Member:
    """ Create a new member. """
    def __init__(self, username, fullname):
        # Define attributes and give them values.
        self.username = username
        self.fullname = fullname
        # Default date_joined to today's date.
        self.date_joined = dt.date.today()
        # Set is active to True initially.
        self.is_active = True

    # Methods for each instance created (instance methods)

    # A method to return a formatted string with showing date joined.
    def show_datejoined(self):
        return f"{self.fullname} joined on {self.date_joined:%m/%d/%y}"

# The class ends at the first un-indented line.

# Create an instance of the Member class named new_guy.
new_guy = Member('Rambo','Rocco Moe')

# Try out the date_joined method.
print(new_guy.show_datejoined())

Rocco Moe joined on 12/06/18
```

**FIGURE 6-8:**
Changing
the value of
an object's
attributes.

## Passing parameters to methods

You can pass data into methods in the same way you do functions, by using parameter names inside the parentheses. However, keep in mind that self always appears there first, and it never receives data from the outside. For example, let's say you want to create a method called .activate() and set it to True if the user is allowed to log in, False when the user isn't. Whatever you pass in is assigned to the .is_active attribute. Here is how to define that method in your code:

```
# Method to activate (True) or deactivate (False) account.
def activate(self, yesno):
    """ True for active, False to make inactive """
    self.is_active = yesno
```

The docstring we put in there is optional. But it does appear on the screen when you're typing relevant code in VS Code, so it serves as a good reminder about what you can pass in. When executed, this method doesn't show anything on the screen, it just changes the is_active attribute for that member to whatever you passed in as the yesno parameter.

**REMEMBER**

It helps to understand that a *method* is really just a *function*. What makes a method different from a generic function is the fact that a method is always associated with some class. So it's not as generic as a function.

Figure 6-9 shows the whole class followed by some code to test it. The line `new_guy = Member('romo', 'Rocco Moe')` creates a new member object named `new_guy`. Then, `print(new_guy.is_active)` displays the value of the `is_active` attribute, which is `True` because that's the default for all new members.

```python
import datetime as dt

# Define a new class name Member.
class Member:
    """ Create a new member. """
    def __init__(self, username, fullname):
        # Define attributes and give them values.
        self.username = username
        self.fullname = fullname
        # Default date_joined to today's date.
        self.date_joined = dt.date.today()
        # Set is_active to True initially.
        self.is_active = True

    # Methods for each instance created (instance methods)

    # A method to return a formatted string with showing date joined.
    def show_datejoined(self):
        return f"{self.fullname} joined on {self.date_joined:%m/%d/%y}"

    # Method to activate (True) or deactive (False) account.
    def activate(self, yesno):
        """ True for active, False to make inactive """
        self.is_active = yesno

# The class ends at the first un-indented line.

# Create an instance of the Member class named new_guy.
new_guy = Member('Rambo','Rocco Moe')

# Is new-guy active?
print(new_guy.is_active)

# Try out the activate method.
new_guy.activate(False)

# Is new-guy still active?
print(new_guy.is_active)
```
```
True
False
```

**FIGURE 6-9**
Adding and testing an `.activate()` method.

The line `new_guy.activate(False)` calls the `activate()` method for that object and passes to it a Boolean `False`. Then `print(new_guy.is_active)` proves that the call to activate did indeed change the `is_active` attribute for `new_guy` from `True` to `False`.

## Calling a class method by class name

As you've seen, you can call a class's method using the syntax

```
specificobject.method()
```

An alternative is to use the specific class name, which can help make the code a little easier to understand for a human. There's no right or wrong way, no best practice or worst practice, to do this. There's just two different ways to achieve a goal, and you can use whichever you prefer. Anyway, that alternative syntax is:

```
Classname.method(specificobject)
```

Replace *Classname* with the name of the class (which we typically define starting with a capital letter), followed by the method name, and then put the specific object (which you've presumably already created) inside the parentheses.

For example, suppose we create a new member named Wilbur using the Member class and this code:

```
wilbur = Member('wblomgren', 'Wilbur Blomgren')
```

Here, wilbur is the specific object we created from the Member class. We can call the show_datejoined() method on that object using the syntax you've already seen, like this:

```
print(wilbur.show_datejoined())
```

The alternative is to call the show_datejoined() method of the Member class and pass to it that specific object, wilbur, like this:

```
print(Member.show_datejoined(wilbur))
```

The output from both methods is exactly the same, as in the following (but with the date on which you ran the code):

```
Wilbur Blomgren joined on 12/06/18
```

Again, the latter method isn't faster, slower, better, worse, or anything like that. It's just an alternative syntax you can use, and some people prefer it because starting the line with Member makes it clear to which class the show_datejoined() method belongs. This in turn can make the code more readable by other programmers, or by yourself a year from now when you don't remember any of the things you originally wrote in this app.

## Using class variables

So far you've seen examples of attributes, which are sometimes called *instance variables*, because they're placeholders that contain information that varies from one instance of the class to another. For example, in a dog class, dog.breed may be Poodle for one dog, Schnauzer for another dog.

There is another type of variable you can use with classes, called a *class variable*, which is applied to all new instances of the class that haven't been created yet. Class variables inside a class don't have any tie-in to self, because the keyword self always refers to the specific object being created at the moment. To define a class variable, place the mouse pointer above the def __init__ line and define the variable using the standard syntax:

```
variablename = value
```

Replace *variablename* with a name of your own choosing, and replace *value* with the specific value to want to assign that variable. For example, let's say there is code in your member's application that grants people three months (90 days) of free access on sign-up. You're not sure if you want to commit to this forever, so rather than hardcode it into your app (so it's difficult to change), you can just make it a class variable that's automatically applied to all new objects, like this:

```
# Define a class named Member for making member objects.
class Member:
    """ Create a member object """
    free_days = 90

    def __init__(self, username, fullname):
```

That free_days variable is defined before the __init__ is defined, so it's not tied to any specific object in the code. Then, let's say, later in the code you want to store the date that the free trial expires. You could have attributes named date_joined and free_expires which represent today's date plus the number of days defined by free_days. Intuitively it may seem as though you could add free_days to the date using a simple syntax like this:

```
self.free_expires = dt.date.today() + dt.timedelta(days = free_days)
```

This wouldn't work. If you tried to run the code that way, you'd get an error saying Python doesn't recognize the free_days variable name (even though it's defined right at the top of the class). For this to work, you have to precede the variable name with the class name or self. For example, this would work:

```
self.free_expires = dt.date.today() + dt.timedelta(days = Member.free_days)
```

Figure 6-10 shows the bigger picture. We removed some of the code from the original class to trim it down and make it easier to focus on the new stuff. The free_days = 365 line near the top sets the value of the free_days variable to 365. Then, later in the code a method used Member.free_freedays to add that number of days to the current date. Running this code by creating a new member named wilbur and viewing his date_joined and free_expires attributes shows the current date (whatever that is where you're sitting when you run the code), and the date 365 days after that.

```
import datetime as dt
# Define a new class name Member.
class Member:
    # Default number of free days.
    free_days = 365

    """ Create a new member. """
    def __init__(self, username, fullname):
        self.date_joined =  dt.date.today()
        # Set an expiration date
        self.free_expires = dt.date.today() + dt.timedelta(days = Member.free_days)

# The class ends at the first un-indented line.

# Create an instance of the Member class named new_guy.
wilbur = Member('wblomgren', 'Wilbur Blomegren')

print(wilbur.date_joined)
print(wilbur.free_expires)
```

```
2018-12-06
2019-12-06
```

**FIGURE 6-10:**
The variable free_days is a class variable in this class.

So, what if later down the road you decide giving people 90 free days is plenty. You could just change that in the class directly, but since it's a variable, you can do it on-the-fly, like this, outside the class:

```
#Set a default for free days.
Member.free_days = 90
```

When you run this code, you still create a user named wilbur with date_joined and free_days variables. But this time, wilbur.free_expires will be 90 days after the datejoined, not 365 days

## Using class methods

Recall that a method is a function that's tied to a particular class. So far, the methods you've used, like .show_datejoined() and .activate() have been *instance methods*, because you always use them with a specific object . . . a specific instance of the class. With Python, you can also create *class methods*.

As the name implies, a class method is a method that is associated with the class as a whole, not specific instances of the class. In other words, class methods are similar in scope to class variables in that they apply to the whole class and not just individual instances of the class.

As with class variables, you don't need the `self` keyword with class methods, because that keyword always refers to the specific object being created at the moment, not to all objects created by the class. So for starters, if you want a method to do something to the class as a whole, don't use def *name*(`self`) because the `self` immediately ties the method to one object.

It would be nice if all you had to do to create class methods is exclude the word `self`, but unfortunately it doesn't work that way. To define a class method, you first need to type this into your code:

```
@classmethod
```

The `@` at the start of this defines it as a *decorator* — yep, yet another buzzword to add to your ever-growing list of nerd-o-rama buzzwords. A decorator is generally something that alters or extends the functionality of that to which it is applied.

Underneath that line, define your class method using this syntax:

```
def methodname(cls,x):
```

Replace *methodname* with whatever name you want to give you method. Leave the `cls` as-is because that's a reference to the class as a whole (because the `@classmethod` decorator defined it as such behind-the-scenes). After the `cls`, you can have commas and the names of parameters that you want to pass to the method, just as you can with regular instance methods.

For example, suppose you want to define a method that sets the number of free days just before you start creating objects, so all objects get that same `free_days` amount. The code below accomplishes that by first defining a class variable named `free_days` that has a given default value of zero (the default value can be anything).

Further down in the class is this class method:

```
# Class methods follow @classmethods and use cls rather then self.
@classmethod
def setfreedays(cls,days):
    cls.free_days = days
```

This code tells Python that when someone calls the `setfreedays()` method on this class, it should set the value of `cls.free_days` (the `free_days` class variable for this class) to whatever number of days they passed in. Figure 6-11 shows a complete example in a Jupyter cell (which you can certainly type in and try for yourself), and the results of running that code.

FIGURE 6-11:
The set
freedays()
method is a
class method
in this class.

```
import datetime as dt
# Define a new class name Member.
class Member:
    # Default number of free days.
    free_days = 365

    """ Create a new member. """
    def __init__(self, username, fullname):
        self.date_joined = dt.date.today()
        # Set an expiration date
        self.free_expires = dt.date.today() + dt.timedelta(days = Member.free_days)

    # Class methods follow @classmethod decorator and refer to cls rather then to self.
    @classmethod
    def setfreedays(cls,days):
        cls.free_days = days
```

So let's see what happens when you run this code. This line:

```
Member.setfreedays(30)
```

. . . tells Python to call the setfreedays() method of the Python class and to pass to it the number 30. So, inside the class, the free_days = 0 variable receives a new value of 30, overriding the original 0.

**REMEMBER**

It's easy to forget that upper- and lowercase letters matter a lot in Python, especially since it seems you're using lowercase 99.9 percent of the time. But as a rule, class names start with an initial cap, so any call to the class name must also start with an initial cap.

Next, the code creates a member named wilbur, and then prints the values of his date_joined and free_expires attributes:

```
wilbur = Member('wblomgren', 'Wilbur Blomgren')
print(wilbur.date_joined )
print(wilbur.free_expires)
```

The exact output of this depends on the date of the day when you run this code. But the first date should be today's date, whereas the free_expires date should be 30 days later (or whatever number of days you specified in the Member. setfreedays(30) line).

## Using static methods

Just when you thought you may finally be done learning about classes, it turns out there is another kind of method you can create in a Python class. It's called a *static method* and it starts with this decorator: @staticmethod.

So at least that part is easy. What makes a static method different from instance and class methods is that a static method doesn't relate specifically to an instance of an object, or even to the class as a whole. It really is generic function, and really the only reason to define it as part of a class would be that you wanted to use that same name elsewhere for something else in your code. In other words, it's strictly an organizational thing to keep together code that goes together so it's easy to find when you're looking through your code to change or embellish things.

Anyway, underneath that @staticmethod line you define your static method the same as any other method, but you don't use self and you don't use cls. Because a static method isn't strictly tied to a class or object, except to the extent you want to keep it there for organizing your code. Here's an example:

```
@staticmethod
def currenttime():
    now = dt.datetime.now()
    return f"{now:%I:%M %p}"
```

So we have a method called currenttime() that isn't expecting any data to be passed in, and doesn't even care about that object you're working with, or even the class; it just gets the current datetime using now = dt.datetime.now() and then returns that information in a nice 12:00 PM type format.

Figure 6-12 shows a complete example in which you can see the static method properly indented and typed near the end of the class. When code outside the class calls Member.currenttime(), it dutifully returns whatever the time is at the moment, even without your saying anything about a specific object from that class.

```
import datetime as dt

# Define a class named Member for making member objects.
class Member:
    # This is a class variable that's the same for all instances.
    free_days = 0

    """ Create a member object from username and fullname """
    def __init__(self, username, fullname):
        # Define properties and assign default values.
        self.datejoined = dt.date.today()
        self.free_expires = dt.date.today() + dt.timedelta(Member.free_days)

    # Class methods follow @classmethods and use cls rather then self.
    @classmethod
    def setfreedays(cls,days):
        cls.free_days = days

    @staticmethod
    def currenttime():
        now = dt.datetime.now()
        return f"{now:%I:%M %p}"

# Class definition ends at last indented line

# Try out the new static method (no object required)
print(Member.currenttime())

03:24 PM
```

**FIGURE 6-12:**
The Member class now has a static method named currenttime().

# Understanding Class Inheritance

People who are really into object-oriented programming live to talk about class inheritance and subclasses and so on, stuff that means little or nothing to the average Joe or Josephine on the street. Still, what they're talking about as a Python concept is actually something you see in real life all the time.

As mentioned earlier, if we consider dog DNA to be a kind of "factory" or Python class, we can lump all dogs together as members of class of animals we call dogs. Even though each dog is unique, all dogs are still dogs because they are members of the class we call dogs, and we can illustrate that, as in Figure 6-13.

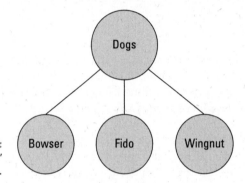

**FIGURE 6-13:**
Dogs as "objects"
of the class dogs.

So each dog is unique (although no other dog is as good as yours), but what makes dogs similar to each another are the characteristics that they *inherit* from the class of dogs.

The notions of class and class inheritance that Python and other object-oriented languages offer didn't materialize out of the clear blue sky just to make it harder and more annoying to learn this stuff. Much of the world's information can best be stored, categorized, and understood by using classes and subclasses and sub-subclasses, on down to individuals.

For example, you may have noticed that there are other dog-like creatures roaming the planet (although they're probably not the kind you'd like to keep around the house as pets). Wolves, coyotes, and jackals come to mind. They are similar to dogs in that they all *inherit* their dogginess from a higher level class we could call canines, as shown in Figure 6-14.

Using our dog analogy, we certainly don't need to stop at canines on the way up. We can put mammals above that, because all canines are mammals. We can put animals above that, because all mammals are animals. And we can put living things above that, because all animals are living things. So basically all the things that make a dog a dog stem from the fact that each one *inherits* certain characteristics from numerous "classes" or critters that preceded it.

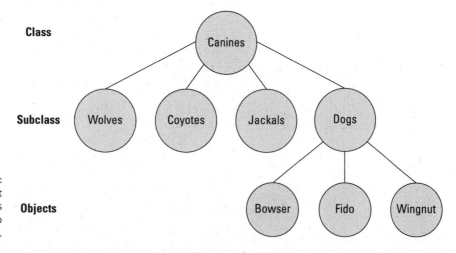

**Class**

Canines

**Subclass**  Wolves  Coyotes  Jackals  Dogs

**Objects**  Bowser  Fido  Wingnut

**FIGURE 6-14:**
Several different
kinds of animals
are similar to
dogs.

**TECHNICAL STUFF**

To the biology brainiacs out there, yes I know that Mammalia is a class, Canis is a genus, and below that are species. So you don't need to email or message me on that. I'm using *class* and *subclass* terms here just to relate the *concept* to classes, subclasses, and objects in Python.

Obviously the concept doesn't just apply to dogs. There are lots of different cats in the world too. There's cute little Bootsy, with whom you'd be happy to share your bed, and plenty of other felines, such as lions, tigers, and jaguars, with whom you probably wouldn't.

**TIP**

If you google *living things hierarchy* and click Images, you'll see just how many ways there are to classify all living things, and how inheritance works its way down from the general to the specific living thing.

Even our car analogy can follow along with this. At the top, we have transportation vehicles. Under that, perhaps boats, planes, and automobiles. Under automobiles we have cars, trucks, vans, and so forth and so on, down to any one specific car. So classes and subclasses are nothing new. What's new is simply thinking about representing those things to mindless machines that we call computers. So let's see how you would do that.

From a coding perspective, the easiest way to do inheritance is by creating subclasses within a class. The class defines things that apply to all instances of that class. Each subclass defines things that are relevant only to the subclass without replacing anything that's coming from the generic "parent" class.

# Creating the base (main) class

Subclasses inherit all the attributes and methods of some higher-level main class, or parent class, which is usually referred to as the *base class*. This class is just any class, no different from what you've seen in this chapter so far. We'll use a Members class again, but we'll whittle it down to some bare essentials that have nothing to do with subclasses, so you don't have all the extra irrelevant code to dig through. Here is the basic class:

```python
import datetime as dt
# Class is used for all kinds of people.
import datetime as dt


# Base class is used for all kinds of Members.
class Member:
    """ The Member class attributes and methods are for everyone """
    # By default, a new account expires in one year (365 days)
    expiry_days = 365

    # Initialize a member object.
    def __init__(self, firstname, lastname):
        # Attributes (instance variables) for everybody.
        self.firstname = firstname
        self.lastname = lastname
        # Calculate expiry date from today's date.
        self.expiry_date = dt.date.today() + dt.timedelta(days=self.expiry_days)
```

By default, new accounts expire in one year. So this class first sets a class variable name expiry_days to 365 to be used in later code to calculate the expiration date from today's date. As you'll see later, we used a class variable to define that, because we can give it a new value from a subclass.

To keep the code example simple and uncluttered, this version of the Member class accepts only two parameters, firstname and lastname.

Figure 6-15 shows an example of testing the code with a hypothetical member named Joe. Printing Joe's firstname, lastname, and expiry_date shows what you would expect the class to do when passing the firstname Joe and the lastname Anybody. When you run the code, the expiry_date should be one year from whatever date it us when you run the code.

Now suppose our real intent is to make two different kinds of users, Admins and Users. Both types of users will have the attributes that the Member class offers. So by defining those types of users as subclasses of Member, they will automatically get the same attributes (and methods, if any).

```
import datetime as dt
# Class is used for all kinds of people.
import datetime as dt

# Base class is used for all kinds of Members.
class Member:
    """ The Member class attributes and methods are for everyone """
    # By default, a new account expires in one year (365 days)
    expiry_days = 365

    # Initialize a member object.
    def __init__(self, firstname, lastname):
        # Attributes (instance variables) for everybody.
        self.firstname = firstname
        self.lastname = lastname
        # Calculate expiry date from today's date.
        self.expiry_date = dt.date.today() + dt.timedelta(days=self.expiry_days)

# Outside the class now.
Joe = Member('Joe', 'Anybody')
print(Joe.firstname)
print(Joe.lastname)
print(Joe.expiry_date)

Joe
Anybody
2019-12-08
```

**FIGURE 6-15:**
A simplified
Member class.

# Defining a subclass

To define a subclass, make sure you get the cursor below the base class, and back to no indentation, because the subclass isn't a part of, or contained within, the base class. To define a subclass, use this syntax:

```
class subclassname(mainclassname):
```

Replace *subclassname* with whatever you want to name this subclass. Replace *mainclassname* with the name of the base class, as defined at the top of the base class. For example, to make a subclass of Member named Admin, use:

```
class Admin(Person):
```

To create another subclass named User, add this code:

```
class User(Person):
```

If you leave the classes empty, you won't be able to test because you'll get an error message telling you the class is empty. But you can put the word pass as the first command in each one. This is your way of telling Python "Yes I know these classes are empty, but let it pass, don't throw an error message"). You can put a comment above each one to remind you of what each one is for, as in the following:

```
# Subclass for Admins.
class Admin(Member):
    pass
```

```
# Subclass for Users.
class User(Member):
    pass
```

When you use the subclasses, you don't have to make any direct reference to the Member class. The Admins and Users will both inherit all the Member stuff automatically. So, for example, to create an Admin named Annie, you'd use this syntax:

```
Ann = Admin('Annie', 'Angst')
```

To create a User, do the same thing with the User class and a name for the user. For example:

```
Uli = User('Uli', 'Ungula')
```

To see if this code works, you can do the same thing you did for Member Joe. After you create the two accounts, use print() statements to see what's in them. Figure 6-16 shows the results of creating the two users. Ann is an Admin, and Uli us a User, but both of them automatically get all the attributes (attributes) assigned to members. (The Member class is directly above the code shown in the image. I left that out because it hasn't changed).

```
# Subclass for Admins.
class Admin(Member):
    pass

# Subclass for Users.
class User(Member):
    pass

Ann = Admin('Annie', 'Angst')
print(Ann.firstname)
print(Ann.lastname)
print(Ann.expiry_date)
print()
Uli = User('Uli', 'Ungula')
print(Uli.firstname)
print(Uli.lastname)
print(Uli.expiry_date)

Annie
Angst
2019-12-03

Uli
Ungula
2019-12-03
```

**FIGURE 6-16:** Creating and testing a Person subclass.

So what you've learned here is that the subclass accepts all the different parameters that the base class accepts and assigns them to attributes, same as the Person class. But so far Admin and User are just members with no unique characteristics. In real life, there will probably be some differences between these two types of users. In the next sections you learn different ways to make these differences happen.

# Overriding a default value from a subclass

One of the simplest things you can do with a subclass is give an attribute that has a default value in the base class some other value. For example, in the `Member` class we created a variable named `expiry_days` to be used later in the class to calculate an expiration date. But suppose you want `Admin` accounts to never expire (or to expire after some ridiculous duration so there's still some date there). All you have to do is set the new `expiry_date` in the `Admin` class (and you can remove the `pass` line since the class won't be empty anymore). Here's how this may look in your `Admin` subclass:

```
# Subclass for Admins.
class Admin(Member):
    # Admin accounts don't expire for 100 years.
    expiry_days = 365.2422 * 100
```

Whatever value you pass will override the default set near the top of the `Member` class, and will be used to calculate the `Admin`'s expiration date.

# Adding extra parameters from a subclass

Sometimes, members of a subclass have some parameter value that other members don't. In that case, you may want to pass a parameter from the subclass that doesn't even exist in the base class. Doing so is a little more complicated than just changing a default value, but it's a fairly common technique so you should be aware of it. Let's work through an example.

For starters, your subclass will need its own `def __init__` line that contains everything that's in the base class's `__init__`, plus any extra stuff you want to pass. For example, let's say admins have some secret code and you want to pass that from the `Admin` subclass. You still have to pass the first and last name, so your `def __init__` line in the `Admin` subclass will look like this:

```
def __init__(self, firstname, lastname, secret_code):
```

The indentation level will be the same as the lines above it.

Next, any parameters that belong to the base class, `Member`, need to be passed up there using this rather odd-looking syntax:

```
super().__init__(param1, param2,...)
```

Replace *param1*, *param2*, and so forth with the names of parameters you want to send to the base class. This should be everything that's already in the `Member` parameters excluding self. In this example, Member expects only firstname and lastname. So the code for this example will be:

```
super().__init__(firstname, lastname)
```

Whatever is left over you can assign to the subclass object using the standard syntax:

```
self.parametername = parametername
```

Replace *parametername* with the name of the parameter that you didn't send up to Member. In this case, that would be the secret_code parameter. So the code would be:

```
self.secret_code = secret_code
```

Figure 6-17 shows an example in which we created an Admin user named Ann and passed PRESTO as her secret code. Printing all her attributes shows that she does indeed have the right expiration date still, and a secret code. As you can see, we also created a regular User named Uli. Uli's data isn't impacted at all by the changes to Admin.

```
# Subclass for Admins.
class Admin(Member):
    # Admin accounts don't expire for 100 years.
    expiry_days = 365.2422 * 100
    # Subclass parameters
    def __init__(self, firstname, lastname, secret_code):
        # Pass Member parameters on up to Member class.
        super().__init__(firstname, lastname)
        # Assign the remaining parameter to this object.
        self.secret_code = secret_code


# Subclass for Users.
class User(Member):
    pass

Ann = Admin('Annie', 'Angst', 'PRESTO')
print(Ann.firstname, Ann.lastname, Ann.expiry_date, Ann.secret_code)

print()
Uli = User('Uli', 'Ungula')
print(Uli.firstname, Uli.lastname, Uli.expiry_date)

Annie Angst 2118-12-03 PRESTO

Uli Ungula 2019-12-03
```

**FIGURE 6-17:**
The Admin subclass has a new secret_code parameter.

There is one little loose end remaining, which has to do with the fact that a User doesn't have a secret code. So if you tried to print the .secret_code for a person who has a User account rather than an Admin account, you'd get an error message. One way to deal with this is to just remember that Users don't have secret codes and never try to access one.

As an alternative, you can give `Users` a secret code that's just an empty string. So when you try to print or display it, you get nothing, but you don't get an error message either. To use this method, just add this to the main `Member` class:

```
# Default secret code is nothing
self.secret_code = ""
```

So even though you don't do anything with `secret_code` in the `User` subclass, you don't have to worry about throwing an error when you try to access the secret code for a `User`. The `User` will have a secret code, but it will just be an empty string. Figure 6-18 shows all the code with both subclasses, and also an attempt to print `Uli.secret_code`, which just displays nothing without throwing an error message.

```python
import datetime as dt

# Base class is used for all kinds of Members.
class Member:
    """ The Member class properties and methods are for everyone """
    # By default, a new account expires in one year (365 days)
    expiry_days = 365

    # Initialize a member object.
    def __init__(self, firstname, lastname):
        # Properties (instance variables) for everybody.
        self.firstname = firstname
        self.lastname = lastname
        # Calculate expiry date from today's date.
        self.expiry_date = dt.date.today() + dt.timedelta(days=self.expiry_days)
        # Default secret code is nothing
        self.secret_code = ''

    # Method in the base class
    def showexpiry(self):
        return f"{self.firstname} {self.lastname} expires on {self.expiry_date}"

# Subclass for Admins.
class Admin(Member):
    # Admin accounts don't expire for 100 years.
    expiry_days = 365.2422 * 100

    # Subclass parameters
    def __init__(self, firstname, lastname, secret_code):
        # Pass Member parameters on up to Member class.
        super().__init__(firstname, lastname)
        # Assign the remaining parameter to this object.
        self.secret_code = secret_code

# Subclass for Users.
class User(Member):
    pass

Ann = Admin('Annie', 'Angst', 'PRESTO')
print(Ann.firstname, Ann.lastname, Ann.expiry_date, Ann.secret_code)
print() # Add a blank line to output.

Uli = User('Uli', 'Ungula')
print(Uli.firstname, Uli.lastname, Uli.expiry_date, Uli.secret_code)
```
```
Annie Angst 2118-12-08 PRESTO

Uli Ungula 2019-12-08
```

**FIGURE 6-18:** The complete Admin and User subclasses.

We left the `User` subclass with `pass` as its only statement. In real life, you would probably come up with more default values or parameters for your other subclasses. But the syntax and code is exactly the same for all subclasses, so we won't dwell on that one. The skills you've learned in this section will work for all your classes and subclasses.

# Calling a base class method

Methods in the base class work the same for subclasses as they do for the base class. To try it out, add a new method called showexpire(self) to the bottom of the base class, as follows:

```
class Member:
    """ The Member class attributes and methods are for everyone """
    # By default, a new account expires in one year (365 days)
    expiry_days = 365

    # Initialize a member object.
    def __init__(self, firstname, lastname):
        # Attributes (instance variables) for everybody.
        self.firstname = firstname
        self.lastname = lastname
        # Calculate expiry date from today's date.
        self.expiry_date = dt.date.today() + dt.timedelta(days=self.expiry_days)
        # Default secret code is nothing
        self.secret_code = ''

    # Method in the base class
    def showexpiry(self):
        return  f"{self.firstname} {self.lastname} expires on {self.
    expiry_date}"
```

The showexpiry() method, when called, returns a formatted string containing the user's first and last name and expiration date. Leaving the subclasses untouched and executing the code displays the names and expiry dates of Ann and Uli:

```
Ann = Admin('Annie', 'Angst', 'PRESTO')
print(Ann.showexpiry())


Uli = User('Uli', 'Ungula')
print(Uli.showexpiry())
```

Here is that output, although your dates will differ based on the date that you ran the code:

```
Annie Angst expires on 2118-12-04
Uli Ungula expires on 2019-12-04
```

# Using the same name twice

The one loose end you may be wondering about is what happens when you use the same name more than once? Python will always opt for the most specific one, the one that's tied to the subclass. It will only use the more generic method from the base class if there is nothing in the subclass that has that method name.

To illustrate, here's some code that whittles the Member class down to just a couple of attributes and methods, to get any irrelevant code out of the way. Comments in the code describe what's going on in the code:

```python
class Member:
    """ The Member class attributes and methods """
    # Initialize a member object.
    def __init__(self, firstname, lastname):
        # Attributes (instance variables) for everybody.
        self.firstname = firstname
        self.lastname = lastname

    # Method in the base class
    def get_status(self):
        return f"{self.firstname} is a Member."

# Subclass for Administrators
class Admin(Member):
    def get_status(self):
        return f"{self.firstname} is an Admin."

# Subclass for regular Users
class User(Member):
    def get_status(self):
        return f"{self.firstname} is a regular User."
```

The Member class, and both the Admin and User classes have a method named get_status(), which shows the member's first name and status. Figure 6-19 shows the result of running that code with an Admin, a User, and a Member who is neither an Admin nor a User. As you can see, the get_status called in each case is the get_status() that's associated with the user's subclass (or base class in the case of the person who is a Member, neither an Admin or User).

Python has a built-in help() method that you can use with any class to get more information about that class. For example, at the bottom of the code in Figure 6-19, add this line:

```python
help(Admin)
```

When you run the code again, you'll see some information about that Admin class, as you can see in Figure 6-20.

```
: class Member:
      """ The Member class attributes and methods are for everyone """
      # Initialize a member object.
      def __init__(self, firstname, lastname):
          # Attributes (instance variables) for everybody.
          self.firstname = firstname
          self.lastname = lastname

      # Method in the main class
      def get_status(self):
          return  f"{self.firstname} is a Member."

  # Subclass for Administrators
  class Admin(Member):
      def get_status(self):
          return  f"{self.firstname} is an Admin."

  # Subclass for regular Users
  class User(Member):
      def get_status(self):
          return  f"{self.firstname} is a regular User."

  # Create an admin
  Ann = Admin('Annie', 'Angst')
  print(Ann.get_status())

  #Create a user
  Uli = User('Uli', 'Ungula')
  print(Uli.get_status())

  # Create a member (neither Admin or User)
  Manny = Member("Mindy", "Membo")
  print(Manny.get_status())

  Annie is an Admin.
  Uli is a regular User.
  Mindy is a Member.
```

**FIGURE 6-19:** Three methods with the same name, get_status().

```
help(Admin)

Help on class Admin in module __main__:

class Admin(Member)
 |  Admin(firstname, lastname)
 |
 |  The Member class attributes and methods are for everyone
 |
 |  Method resolution order:
 |      Admin
 |      Member
 |      builtins.object
 |
 |  Methods defined here:
 |
 |  get_status(self)
 |
 |  ----------------------------------------------------------------
 |  Methods inherited from Member:
 |
 |  __init__(self, firstname, lastname)
 |      Initialize self.  See help(type(self)) for accurate signature.
 |
 |  ----------------------------------------------------------------
 |  Data descriptors inherited from Member:
 |
 |  __dict__
 |      dictionary for instance variables (if defined)
 |
 |  __weakref__
 |      list of weak references to the object (if defined)
```

**FIGURE 6-20:** Output from help(Admin).

You don't really need to worry about all the details of that figure right now, so don't worry if it's a little intimidating. For now, the most important thing is the section titled Method Resolution Order, which looks like this:

```
Method resolution order:
    Admin
    Member
    builtins.object
```

What the method resolution order tells you is that if a class (and its subclasses) all have methods with the same name (like get_status), then a call to get_status() from an Admin user will cause Python to look in Admin for that method and to use that one, if it exists. If no get_status() method was defined in the Admin subclass, then it looks in the Member class and uses that one, if found. If neither of those had a get_status method, it looks in builtins.object, which is a reference to certain built_in methods that all classes and subclasses share.

So the bottom line is, if you do store your data in hierarchies of classes and subclasses, and you call a method on a subclass, it will use that subclass method if it exists. If not, it will use the base class method, if it exists. If that also doesn't exist, it will try the built-in methods. And if all else fails, it will throw an error because it can't find the method your code is trying to call. Usually the main reason for this type of error is that you simply misspelled the method name in your code, so Python can't find it.

An example of a built-in method is __dict__. The dict is short for *dictionary*, and those are double-underscores surrounding the abbreviation. Referring back to Figure 6-20, executing the command

```
print(Admin.__dict__)
```

. . . doesn't cause an error, even though we've never defined a method named __dict__. That's because there is a built-in method with that name, and when called with print(), it shows a dictionary of methods (both yours and built-in ones) for that object. It's not really something you have to get too involved with this early in the learning curve. Just be aware that if you try to call a method that doesn't exist at any of those three levels, such as this:

```
print(Admin.snookums())
```

. . . you get an error that looks something like this:

```
---> print(Admin.snookums())

AttributeError: type object 'Admin' has no attribute 'snookums'
```

This is telling you that Python has no idea what snookums() is about, so it can only throw an error. In real life, this kind of error is usually caused simply by misspelling the method name in your code.

Classes (and to some extent, subclasses) are pretty heavily used in the Python world, and what you've learned here should make it relatively easy to write your own classes, as well as to understand classes written by others. There is on more "core" Python concept you'll want to learn about before we finish this book, and that's how Python handles errors, and things you can do in your own code to better handle errors.

IN THIS CHAPTER

» **Understanding exceptions**

» **Handling errors gracefully**

» **Keeping your app from crashing**

» **Using** `try ... except ... else ... finally`

» **Raising your own exceptions**

Chapter **7**

# Sidestepping Errors

We all want our programs to run perfectly all the time. But sometimes there are situations out there in the real world that won't let that happen. This is no fault of yours or your program's. It's usually something the person using the program did wrong. Error handling is all about trying to anticipate what those problems may be, and then "catching" the error and informing the user of the problem so they can fix it.

It's important to keep in mind the techniques here aren't for fixing bugs in your code. Those kinds of errors you have to fix yourself. We're talking strictly about errors in the environment in which the program is running, over which you have no control. *Handling* the error is simply a way of replacing the tech-speak error message that Python normally displays, which is meaningless to most people, with a message that tells them in plain English what's wrong and, ideally, how to fix it.

Again, the user will be fixing *the environment in which the program* is running . . . they won't be fixing your code.

## Understanding Exceptions

In Python (and all other programing languages) the term *exception* refers to an error that isn't due to a programming error. Rather it's an error out in the real world that prevents the program from running properly. As simple example, let's have your Python app open a file. The syntax for that is easy. The code is just

```
name = open(filename)
```

Replace *name* with a name of your own choosing, same as any variable name. Replace *filename* with the name of the file. If the file is in the same folder as the code, you don't need to specify a path to the folder because the current folder is assumed.

Figure 7-1 shows an example. We used VS Code for this example so that you can see the contents of the folder in which we worked. The folder contains a file named showfilecontents.py, which is the file that contains the Python code we wrote. The other file is named people.csv.

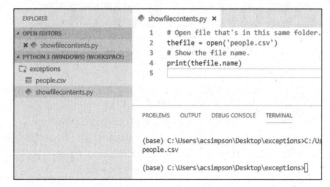

FIGURE 7-1:
The showfile
contents.py
and people.csv
files in a folder
in VS Code.

The showcontents.py file is the only one that contains code. The people.csv file contains data, information about people. Its content doesn't really matter much right now; what you're learning here will work in any external file. But just so you know, Figure 7-2 shows the contents of that file in Excel (top) so it's easy for you to read, and in a text editor (bottom), which is how it actually looks to Python and other languages.

The Python code is just two lines (excluding the comments), as follows:

```
# Open file that's in this same folder.
thefile = open('people.csv')
# Show the file name.
print(thefile.name)
```

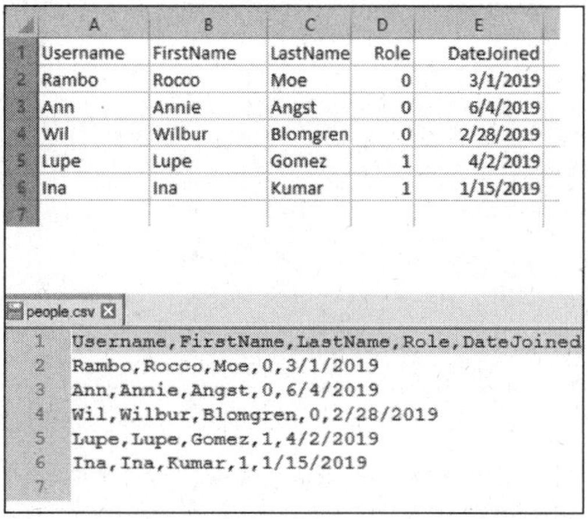

**FIGURE 7-2:**
The contents of the people.csv file in Excel (top) and a text editor (bottom).

So it's simple. The first line of code opens the file named people.csv. The second line of code shows the filename (people.csv) on the screen. Running that simple showfilecontents.py app (by right-clicking its name in VS Code and choosing Run Python File in Terminal) shows people.csv on the screen — assuming there is a file named people.csv in the folder to open. This assumption is where exception handling comes in.

Suppose that for reasons beyond your control, the file named people.csv isn't there because some person or some automated procedure failed to put it there, or because someone accidentally misspelled the filename. It's easy to accidentally type, say, .cvs rather than .csv for the filename, as in Figure 7-3. If that's the case, running the app *raises an exception* (which in English means "displays an error message"), as you can see in the terminal in that same image. The exception reads

```
Traceback (most recent call last):
  File "c:/ Users/ acsimpson/ Desktop/ exceptions/ showfilecontents.py", line 2,
    in <module>
    thefile = open('people.csv')
FileNotFoundError: [Errno 2] No such file or directory: 'people.csv'
```

The Traceback is a reference to the fact that if there were multiple exceptions, they'd all be listed with the most recent being listed first. In this case, there is just one exception. The File part tells you where the exception occurred, in line 2 of the file named showfilecontents.py. The part that reads

```
thefile = open('people.csv')
```

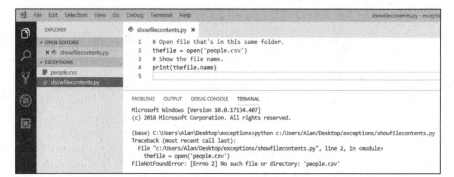

FIGURE 7-3:
The showfile
contents.py
raises an
exception.

. . . shows you the exact line of code that caused the error. And finally the exception itself is described like this:

```
FileNotFoundError: [Errno 2] No such file or directory: 'people.csv'
```

The generic name for this type of error is FileNotFoundError. Many exceptions also have a number associated with them, but that tends to vary depending on the operating system environment, so it's not typically used for handling errors. In this case, the main error is FileNotFoundError, and the fact that's its ERRNO 2 where I'm sitting right now doesn't really matter much.

TECHNICAL
STUFF

Some people use the phrase *throw an exception* rather than *raise an exception*. But they're just two different ways to describe the same thing. There's no difference between *raising* and *throwing* an exception.

The last part tells you *exactly* what went wrong No such file or directory: 'people.csv.' In other words, Python can't do the open('people.csv') business, because there is no file named people.csv in the current folder with that name.

You could correct this problem by changing the code, but .csv is a common file extension for files that contain comma-separated values. It would make more sense to change the name of people.cvs to people.csv so it matches what the program is looking for and the .csv extension is well known.

You also can't have the Python app rename the file, because you don't know whether other files in that folder have the kind of data the Python app is looking for. It's up to a human to create the people.csv file, to make sure it's named correctly, and to make sure it contains the type of information the Python program it looking for.

# Handling Errors Gracefully

The best way to handle this kind of error is to *not* show what Python normally shows for this error. Instead, it would be best to replace that with something the person that's using the app is more likely to understand. To do that, you can code a *try . . . except block* using this basic syntax:

```
try:
    The things you want the code to do
except Exception:
    What to do if it can't do what you want it to do
```

Here's how we can rewrite the showfilecontents.py code to handle the missing (or misspelled) file error:

```
try:
    # Open file and shows its name.
    thefile = open('people.csv')
    print(thefile.name)
except Exception:
    print("Sorry, I don't see a file named people.csv here")
```

Because we know that if the file the app is supposed to open may be missing, we start with try: and then attempt to open the file under that. If the file opens, great, the print() statement runs and shows the filename. But if trying to open the file raises an exception, the program doesn't "bomb" and display a generic error message. Instead it shows a message that's better for the average computer user, as shown in Figure 7-4.

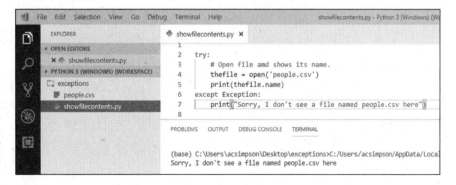

**FIGURE 7-4:** showfile contents.py catches the error and displays something nice.

# Being Specific about Exceptions

The preceding syntax handled the "file not found" error gracefully. But it could be more graceful. For example, if you rename people.cvs to people.csv and run the app again, you see the filename on the screen. No error.

Now suppose you add another line of code under the print statement, something along these lines:

```
try:
    # Open file and shows its name.
    thefile = open('people.csv')
    print(thefile.name)
    print(thefile.wookems())
except Exception:
    print("Sorry, I don't see a file named people.csv here")
```

Running this code displays the following:

```
people.csv
Sorry, I don't see a file named people.csv here
```

It must have found the file in order to print the filename (which it does). But then it says it can't find the file. So what gives?

The problem is in the line except Exception: What that says is "if *any* exception is raised in this try block, do the code under the except line." Hmmm, this is not good because the error is actually caused by the line that reads

```
    print(thefile.wookems())
```

This line raises an exception because there is no property named wookems() in Python.

To clean this up, you want to replace Exception: with the specific exception you want it to catch. But how do you know what that specific exception is? Easy. The exception that gets raised with no exceptions handing is:

```
FileNotFoundError: [Errno 2] No such file or directory: 'people.csv'
```

That very first word is the name of the exception that you can use in place of the generic Exception name, like this:

```
try:
    # Open file and shows its name.
    thefile = open('people.csv')
    print(thefile.name)
    print(thefile.wookems())
except FileNotFoundError:
    print("Sorry, I don't see a file named people.csv here")
```

Granted, that doesn't do anything to help with the bad method name. But the bad method name isn't really an exception, it's a programming error that needs to be corrected in the code by replacing .wookems() with whatever method name you really want to use. But at least the error message you see isn't the misleading Sorry, I don't see a file named people.csv here error. This code just works, and so the regular error — object has no attribute 'wookems' — shows instead, as in Figure 7-5.

**FIGURE 7-5:**
The correct error message shown.

Again, if you're thinking about handling the .wookems error, that's not an exception for which you'd write an exception handler. Exceptions occur when something *outside* the program upon which the program depends isn't available. Programming errors, like nonexistent method names, are errors inside the program and have to be corrected inside the program by the programmer who writes the code.

# Keeping Your App from Crashing

You can stack up except: statements in a try block to handle different errors. Just be aware that when the exception occurs, it looks at each one starting at the top. If it finds a handler that matches the exception, it raises that one. If some exception occurred that you didn't handle, then you get the standard Python error message. But there's a way around that too.

If you want to avoid all Python error messages, you can just make the last one `except Exception:` so that it catches any exception that hasn't already be caught by any preceding `except:` in the code. For example, here we just have two handlers, one for `FileNotFound`, and one for everything else:

I know you haven't learned about `open` and `readline` and `close`, but don't worry about that. All we care about here is the exception handling, which is the `try:` and `except:` portions of the code — for now.

```python
try:
    # Open file and shows its name.
    thefile = open('people.csv')
    # Print a couple blank lines then the first line from the file.
    print('\n\n', thefile.readline())
    # Close the file.
    thefile.closed()

except FileNotFoundError:
    print("Sorry, I don't see a file named people.csv here")
except Exception:
    print("Sorry, something else went wrong")
```

Running this code produces the following output:

```
Username,FirstName,LastName,Role,DateJoined
Sorry, something else went wrong
```

The first line shows the first line of text from the `people.csv` file. The second line is the output from the second `except:` statement, which reads `Sorry, something else went wrong`. This message is vague and doesn't really help you find the problem.

Rather than just print some generic message for an unknown exception, you can capture the error message in a variable and then display the contents of that variable to see the message. As usual, you can name that variable anything you like, though a lot of people use *e* or *err* as an abbreviation for *error*.

For example, consider the following rewrite of the preceding code. The generic handler, `except Exception` now has an `as e` at the end, which means "whatever exception gets caught here, put the error message in a variable named e." Then the next line uses `print(e)` to display whatever is in that e variable:

```python
try:
    # Open file and shows its name.
    thefile = open('people.csv')
```

```
    # Print a couple blank lines then the first line from the file.
    print('\n\n', thefile.readline())
    thefile.wigwam()

except FileNotFoundError:
   print("Sorry, I don't see a file named people.csv here")
   except Exception as e:
   print(e)
```

Running this code displays the following:

```
Username,FirstName,LastName,Role,DateJoined
'_io.TextIOWrapper' object has no attribute 'wigwam'
```

The first line with Username, Firstname and so forth is just the first line of text from the people.csv file. There's no error in the code, and that file is there, so that all went well. The second line is this:

```
'_io.TextIOWrapper' object has no attribute 'wigwam'
```

This is certainly not plain English. But it's better than "Something else went wrong." At least the part that reads object has no attribute 'wigwam' lets you know that the problem has something to do with the word *wigwam*. So you still handled the error gracefully, and the app didn't "crash." And you at least got some information about the error that should be helpful to you, even though it may not be so helpful to people who are using the app with no knowledge of its inner workings.

# Adding an else to the Mix

If you look at code written by professional Python programmers, they usually don't have a whole lot of code under the try:. This is because you want your catch: blocks to catch certain possible errors and top processing with an error message should the error occur. Otherwise, you want it to just continue on with the rest of the code (which may also contain situations that generate other types of exceptions).

A more elegant way to deal with the problem uses this syntax:

```
try:
    The thing that might cause an exception
```

```
catch (a common exception):
    Explain the problem
catch Exception as e:
    Show the generic error message
else:
    Continue on here only if no exceptions raised
So the logic with this flow is
Try to open the file...
    If the file isn't there, tell them and stop.
    If the file isn't there, show error and stop
Otherwise...
    Go on with the rest of the code.
```

By limiting the `try:` to the one thing that's most likely to raise an exception, we can stop the code dead in its tracks before it tries to go any further. But if no exception is raised, then it continues on normally, below the `else`, where the previous exception handlers don't matter anymore. Here is all the code with comments explaining what's going on:

```python
try:
    # Open the file name people.csv
    thefile = open('people.csv')
# Watch for common error and stop program if it happens.
except FileNotFoundError:
    print("Sorry, I don't see a file named people.csv here")
# Catch any unexpected error and stop program if one happens.
except Exception as err:
    print(err)
# Otherwise, if nothing bad has happened by now, just keep going.
else:
    # File must be open by now if we got here.
    print('\n') # Print a blank line.
    # Print each line from the file.
    for one_line in thefile:
        print(one_line)
    thefile.close()
    print("Success!")
```

WARNING

As always with Python, indentations matter a lot. Make sure you indent your own code as shown in this chapter or your code may not work right.

Figure 7-6 also shows all the code and the results of running that code in VS Code.

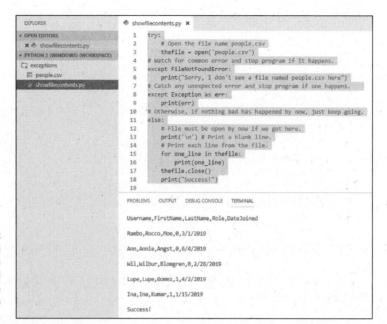

```
1   try:
2       # Open the file name people.csv
3       thefile = open('people.csv')
4   # Watch for common error and stop program if it happens.
5   except FileNotFoundError:
6       print("Sorry, I don't see a file named people.csv here")
7   # Catch any unexpected error and stop program if one happens.
8   except Exception as err:
9       print(err)
10  # Otherwise, if nothing bad has happened by now, just keep going.
11  else:
12      # File must be open by now if we got here.
13      print('\n') # Print a blank line.
14      # Print each line from the file.
15      for one_line in thefile:
16          print(one_line)
17      thefile.close()
18      print("Success!")
19
```

```
PROBLEMS    OUTPUT    DEBUG CONSOLE    TERMINAL

Username,FirstName,LastName,Role,DateJoined

Rambo,Rocco,Moe,0,3/1/2019

Ann,Annie,Angst,0,6/4/2019

Wil,Wilbur,Blomgren,0,2/28/2019

Lupe,Lupe,Gomez,1,4/2/2019

Ina,Ina,Kumar,1,1/15/2019

Success!
```

**FIGURE 7-6:**
Code with
try, exception
handlers, and
an else for when
there are no
exceptions.

# Using try . . . except . . . else . . . finally

If you look at the complete syntax for Python exception handling, you'll see there is one more option at the end, like this:

```
try:
    try to do this
except:
    if x happens, stop here
except Exception as e:
    if something else bad happens, stop here
else:
    if no exceptions, continue on normally here
finally:
    do this code no matter what happened above
```

The `finally:` block, if included, is the code that runs whether an exception occurs or not. This pattern tends to be used in more complex apps, such as those in which a new chunk of code that's dependent on the availability of some external resource is called after some series of events is carried out. If the resource is available, the code plays out, but if the resource isn't available, some other code executes.

To illustrate, here is some code that expects to find an external resource named people.csv to be available to the code.

```python
print('Do this first')
try:
    open('people.csv')
except FileNotFoundError:
    print('Cannot find file named people.csv')
except Exception as e:
    print('e')
else:
    print('Show this if no exception.')
finally:
    print('This is in the finally block')
print("This is outside the try...except...else...finally")
```

When you run this code with a file named people.csv in the folder, you get this output:

```
Do this first
Show this if no exception.
This is in the finally block
This is outside the try...except...else...finally
```

None of the exception-reporting code executed because the open( ) statement was able to open the file named people.csv.

Run this same code without a file named people.csv in the same folder, you get the following result. This time the code reports that it cannot fine a file named people.csv. But the app doesn't "crash". Rather, it just keeps on executing the rest of the code.

```
Do this first
Cannot find file named people.csv
This is in the finally block
This is outside the try...except...else...finally
```

What these examples show you is that you can control exactly what happens in some small part of a program that's vulnerable to user errors or other "outside" exceptions, while still allowing other code to run normally.

# Raising Your Own Errors

Python has lots of built-in exceptions for recognizing and identifying errors, as you'll see while writing and testing code, especially when you're first learning. However, you aren't limited to those. If your app has some vulnerability that isn't covered by the built-in exceptions, you can invent your own.

For a detailed list of all the different exceptions that Python can catch, take a look at `https://docs.python.org/3/library/exceptions.html` in the Python.org documentation.

The general syntax for raising your own error is:

```
raise error
```

Replace *error* with the wording of the known error that you want to raise (such as `FileNotFoundError`). Or, if the error isn't covered by one of those built-in errors, you can just raise `Exception` and that will execute whatever is under `catch Exception:` in your code.

As a working example, let's say you want two conditions to be met for the program to run successfully:

>> The `people.csv` file must exist so you can open it.

>> The `people.csv` file must contain more than one row of data (the first row is just column names, not data, but if it has only column headings we want to consider it empty.

Here is an example of how you may handle that situation, just looking at the exception handling part:

```
try:
    # Open the file (no error check for this example).
    thefile = open('people.csv')
    # Count the number of lines in file.
    line_count = len(thefile.readlines())
    # If there is fewer than 2 lines, raise exception.
    if line_count < 2:
        raise Exception
# Handles missing file error.
except FileNotFoundError:
        print('\nThere is no people.csv file here')
```

```
# Handles all other exceptions
except Exception as e:
        # Show the error.
        print('\n\nFailed: The error was ' + str(e))
        # Close the file.
        thefile.close()
```

So let's step through it. The first lines try to open the people.csv file:

```
try:
    # Open the file (no error check for this example).
    thefile = open('people.csv')
```

We know that if the people.csv file doesn't exist, execution will jump to this exception handler, which tells the user the file isn't there:

```
except FileNotFoundError:
        print('\nThere is no people.csv file here')
```

Assuming that didn't happen and the file is now open, this next line counts how many lines are in the file:

```
line_count = len(thefile.readlines())
```

If the file is empty, the line count will be 0. If the file contains only column headings, like this:

```
Username,FirstName,LastName,DateJoined
```

. . . then the length will be 1. We want the rest of the code to run only if the length of the file is 2 or more. So if the line count is less than 2 the code can raise an exception. You may not know what that exception is, so you tell it to raise a generic exception, like this:

```
if line_count < 2:
    raise Exception
```

The exception handler in the code for general exceptions looks like this:

```
# Handles all other exceptions
except Exception as e:
        # Show the error.
        print('\n\nFailed: The error was ' + str(e))
```

```
        # Close the file.
        thefile.close()
```

The e grabs the actual exception, and then the next `print` statement shows what that was. So, let's say you run that code and `people.csv` is empty or incomplete. The output will be:

```
Failed: The error was
```

Notice there is no explanation of the error. That's because error that Python can recognize on its own was found. You could raise a known exception instead. For example, rather than raising a general `Exception`, you can raise a `File NotFoundError`, like this:

```
if line_count < 2:
    raise FileNotFoundError
```

But if you do that, the `FileNotFoundError` handler is called and displays `There is no people.csv file`, which isn't really true in this case, and it's not the cause of the problem. There is a `people.csv` file; it just doesn't have any data to loop through. What you need is your own custom exception and handler for that exception.

All exceptions in Python are actually objects, instances of the built-in class named `Errors` in Python. To create your own exception, you first have to import the `Errors` class to use as a base class (much like the `Member` class was a base class for different types of users). Then, under that, you define your own error as a subclass of that. This code goes up at the top of the file so it's executed before any other code tries to use the custom exception:

```
# define Python user-defined exceptions
class Error(Exception):
    """Base class for other exceptions"""
    pass

# Your custom error (inherits from Error)
class EmptyFileError(Error):
    pass
```

As before, the word `pass` in each class just tells Python "I know this class has no code in it, and that's okay here. You don't need to raise an exception to tell me that."

Now that there exists an exception called `EmptyFileError`, you can raise *that* exception when the file has insufficient content. Then write a handler to handle that exception. Here's that code:

```python
    # If there is fewer than 2 lines, raise exception.
    if line_count < 2:
        raise EmptyFileError
# Handles my custom error for too few rows.
except EmptyFileError:
        print("\nYour people.csv file doesn't have enough stuff.")
```

Figure 7-7 shows all the code.

```python
1   # Base class for defining your own user-defined exceptions.
2   class Error(Exception):
3       """Base class for other exceptions"""
4       pass
5
6   # Now define your exception as a subclass of Error.
7   class EmptyFileError(Error):
8       pass
9
10  try:
11      # Open the file (no error check for this example).
12      thefile = open('people.csv')
13      # Count the number of lines in file.
14      line_count = len(thefile.readlines())
15      # If there is fewer than 2 lines, raise exception.
16      if line_count < 2:
17          raise EmptyFileError
18
19  # Handles missing file error.
20  except FileNotFoundError:
21          print('\nThere is no people.csv file here')
22
23  # Handles my custom error for too few rows.
24  except EmptyFileError:
25          print("\nYour people.csv file doesn't have enough stuff.")
26
27  # Handles all other exceptions
28  except Exception as e:
29          # Show the error.
30          print('\n\nFailed: The error was ' + str(e))
31          # Close the file.
32          thefile.close()
33  else:
34      # This code runs only if no exceptions above.
35      print() # Print a blank line.
36
37      # File must be open by now if we got here, show content.
38      for one_line in thefile:
39          print(one_line)
40      thefile.close()
41      print("Success!")
```

**FIGURE 7-7:**
Custom
EmptyFileError
added for
exception
handling.

So here is how things will play out when the code runs. If there is no `people.csv` file at all, this error shows:

```
There is no people.csv file here.
```

If there is a `people.csv` file but it's empty or contains only column headings, this is all the program shows:

```
Your people.csv file doesn't have enough stuff.
```

Assuming neither error happened, then the code under the `else:` runs and shows whatever is in the file on the screen.

So as you can see, exception handling lets you plan ahead for errors caused by vulnerabilities in your code. We're not taking about bugs in your code or coding errors here. We're generally talking about outside resources that the program needs to run correctly.

When those outside resources are missing or insufficient, you don't have to let the program just "crash" and display any nerd-o-rama error message on the screen to baffle your users. Instead, you can catch the exception and show them some text that tells them exactly what's wrong, which will, in turn, help them fix that problem and run the program again, successfully this time. That's what exception handling is all about.

# 3
# Working with Python Libraries

# Contents at a Glance

# Chapter **1**

# Working with External Files

Pretty much everything that's stored in your computer, be it a document, program, movie, photograph . . . whatever, is stored in a file. Most files are organized info *folders* (also called *directories*). On a Mac you can use Finder to browse around through folders and files. In Windows you use File Explorer or Windows Explorer (but not Internet Explorer) to browse around through folders and files.

Python offers many tools for creating, reading from, and writing to many different kinds of files. In this chapter, you learn all the most important skills for working with files using Python code.

## Understanding Text and Binary Files

There are basically two types of files:

» **Text files:** Text files contain plain text characters. When you open these in a text editor, they show human-readable content. The text may not be in a language you know or understand, but you will see mostly normal characters that you can type at any keyboard.

>> **Binary files:** A binary file stores information in bytes that aren't quite so humanly readable. We don't recommend you do this, but if you open the binary file in a text editor, what you see may resemble Figure 1-1.

FIGURE 1-1:
How a binary files looks in a program for editing text files.

If you do ever open a binary file in a text editor and see this gobbledygook, don't panic. Just close the file or program and choose **No** if asked to save it. The file will be fine, so long as you don't save it.

WARNING

Figure 1-2 lists examples of different kinds of text and binary files, some of which you may have worked with in the past. There are other files types, of course, but these are among the most widely used.

**Text File**

- **Plain Text**: .txt, .csv
- **Source Code**: .py, .html, .css. .js
- **Data**: .json, .xml

**Binary File**

- **Executable**: .exe, .dmg, .bin
- **Images**: .jpg, .png, .gif, .tiff, .ico
- **Video**: .mp4, .m4v, .mp4, .mov
- **Audio**: .aif, .mp3, .mpa, wav
- **Compressed**: .zip, .deb, .tar.gz
- **Font**: .woff, .otf, .ttf
- **Document**: .pdf, .docx, .xlsx

FIGURE 1-2:
Common text and binary files.

As with any Python code, you can use a Jupyter notebook, VS Code, or virtually any coding editor to write your Python code. In this chapter, we use VS Code simply because its Explorer bar (on the left, when it's open) displays the contents of the folder in which you're currently working.

# Opening and Closing Files

To open a file from within a Python app, use the syntax:

```
open(filename.ext[,mode])
```

Replace *filename.ext* with the filename of the file you want to open. If the file is not in the same directory as the Python code, you need to specify a path to the file. Use forward slashes, even if you're working in Windows. For example, if the file you want to open is foo.txt on your desktop, and your user account name is Alan, you'd use the path C:/Users/Alan/Desktop/foo.txt rather than the more common Windows syntax with backslashes like C:\Users\Alan\Desktop\foo.txt.

The [,mode] is optional (as indicated by the square brackets). Use it to specify what kind of access you want your app to have, using the following single-character abbreviations:

>> **r: (Read):** Allows Python to open the file but not make any changes. This is the default if you don't specify a mode. If the file doesn't exist, Python raises a FileNotFoundError exception.

>> **r+: (Read/Write):** Allows Python to read and write to the file.

>> **a: (Append):** Opens the file and allows Python to add new content to the end of the file but not to change existing content. If the file doesn't exist, this mode creates the file.

>> **w: (Write):** Opens the file and allows Python to make changes to the file. Creates the file if it doesn't exist.

>> **x: (Create):** Creates the file if it doesn't already exist. If the file does exist, it raises a FileExistsError exception.

For more information on exceptions, see Book 2, Chapter 7.

You can also specify what type of file you're opening (or creating). If you already specified one of the above modes, just add this as another letter. If you use just one of the letters below on its own, the file opens in Read mode.

>> **t: (Text):** Open as a text file, read and write text.

>> **b: (Binary):** Open as a binary file, read and write bytes.

There are basically two ways to use the open method. With one syntax you assign a variable name to the file, and use this variable name in later code to refer to the file. That syntax is:

```
var = open(filename.ext[,mode])
```

Replace *var* with a name of your choosing (though it's very common in Python to use just the letter f as the name). Although this method does work, it's not ideal because, after it's opened, the file remains open until you specifically close it using the close() method. Forgetting to close files can cause the problem of having too many files open at the same time, which can corrupt the contents of a file or cause your app to raise and exception and crash.

After the file is open, there are a few ways to access its content, as we discuss a little later in this chapter. For now, we simply copy everything that's in the file to a variable named *filecontents* in Python, and then we display this content using a simple print() function. So to open quotes.txt, read in all its content, and display that content on the screen, use this code:

```
f = open('quotes.txt')
filecontents = f.read()
print(filecontents)
```

With this method, the file remains open until you specifically close it using the file variable name and the .close() method, like this:

```
f.close()
```

It's important for your apps to close any files it no longer needs open. Failure to do so allows open file handlers to accumulate, which can eventually cause the app to throw an exception and crash, perhaps even corrupting some of the open files along the way.

Getting back to the act of actually opening the file, though: another way to do this is by using a *context manager* or by using *contextual coding*. This method starts with the word *with*. You still assign a variable name. But you do so near the end of the line. The very last thing on the line is a colon which marks the beginning of the *with* block. All indented code below that is assumed to be relevant to the context of the open file (like code indented inside a loop). At the end of this you don't need to specifically close the file; Python does it automatically:

```
# ---------------- Contextual syntax
with open('quotes.txt') as f:
    filecontents = f.read()
    print(filecontents)


# The unindented line below is outside the with... block;
print('File is closed: ', f.closed)
```

The following code shows a single app that opens quotes.txt, reads and displays its content, and then closes the file. With the first method you have to specifically use .close() to close the file. With the second, the file closes automatically, so no .close() is required:

```
# - Basic syntax to open, read, and display file contents.
f = open('quotes.txt')
filecontents = f.read()
print(filecontents)
# Returns True if the file is closed, otherwise alse.
print('File is closed: ', f.closed)

# Closes the file.
f.close() #Close the file.
print() # Print a blank line.

# ---------------- Contextual syntax
with open('quotes.txt') as f:
    filecontents = f.read()
    print(filecontents)


# The unindented line below is outside the with... block;
print('File is closed: ', f.closed)
```

The output of this app is as follows. At the end of the first output, .closed is False because it's tested before the close() actually closes the file. At the end of the second output, .closed is True, without executing a .close(), because leaving the code that's indented under the with: line closes the file automatically.

```
I've had a perfectly wonderful evening, but this wasn't it.
Groucho Marx
The difference between stupidity and genius is that genius has its limits.
Albert Einstein
```

```
We are all here on earth to help others; what on earth the others are here for,
    I have no idea.
W. H. Auden
Ending a sentence with a preposition is something up with I will not put.
Winston Churchill


File is closed:  False
```

```
I've had a perfectly wonderful evening, but this wasn't it.
Groucho Marx
The difference between stupidity and genius is that genius has its limits.
Albert Einstein
We are all here on earth to help others; what on earth the others are here for,
    I have no idea.
W. H. Auden
Ending a sentence with a preposition is something up with I will not put.
Winston Churchill


File is closed:  True
```

For the rest of this chapter we stick with the contextual syntax because it's generally the preferred and recommended syntax, and a good habit to acquire right from the start.

The previous example works fine because quotes.txt is a really simple text file that contains only ASCII characters — the kinds of letters, numbers, and punctuation marks that you can type from a standard keyboard for the English language.

```python
with open('happy_pickle.jpg') as f:
    filecontents = f.read()
    print(filecontents)
```

Attempting to run this code results in the following error:

```
UnicodeDecodeError: 'charmap' codec can't decode byte 0x90 in position 40:
    character maps to <undefined>
```

This isn't the most helpful message in the world. Suppose you try to open names.txt, which (one would assume) is a text file like quotes.txt, using this code:

```python
with open('names.txt') as f:
    filecontents = f.read()
    print(filecontents)
```

You run this code, and again you get a strange error message, like this:

```
UnicodeDecodeError: 'charmap' codec can't decode byte 0x81 in position 45:
    character maps to <undefined>
```

So what the heck is going on here?

The first problem is caused by the fact that the file is a .jpg, a graphic image, which means it's a binary file, not a text file. So to open this one, you need a b in the mode. Or use rb, which means *read binary*, like this:

```
with open('happy_pickle.jpg', 'rb') as f:
    filecontents = f.read()
    print(filecontents)
```

Running this code doesn't generate an error. But what it does show doesn't look anything like the actual picture. The output from this code is a lot of stuff that looks something like this:

```
\x07~}\xba\xe7\xd2\x8c\x00\x0e|\xbd\xa8\x121+\xca\xf7\xae\xa5\x9e^\x8d\x89
\x7f\xde\xb4f>\x98\xc7\xfc\xcf46d\xcf\x1c\xd0\xa6\x98m$\xb6(U\x8c\xa6\x83
\x19\x17\xa6>\xe6\x94\x96|g\'4\xab\xdd\xb8\xc8=\xa9[\x8b\xcc`\x0e8\xa3
\xb0;\xc6\xe6\xbb(I.\xa3\xda\x91\xb8\xbd\xf2\x97\xdf\xc1\xf4\xefI\xcdy
\x97d\x1e`;\xf64\x94\xd7\x03
```

If we open happy_pickle.jpg in a graphics app or in VS Code, it looks nothing like that gibberish. Instead, it looks like Figure 1-3.

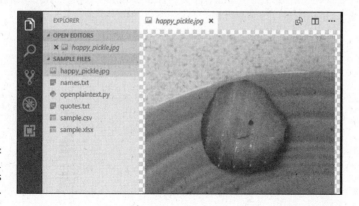

FIGURE 1-3:
How happy_
pickle.jpg is
supposed to look.

So why does it look so messed up in Python? That's because `print()` just shows the raw bytes that make up the file. It has no choice because it's not a graphics app. This is not a problem or issue, just not a good way to work with a .jpg file right now.

The problem with `names.txt` is something different. That file is a text file (.txt) just like `quotes.txt`. But if you open it and look at its content, as in Figure 1-4, you'll notice it has a lot of unusual characters in it characters that you don't normally see in ASCII, the day-to-day numbers, letters, and punctuation marks you see on your keyboard.

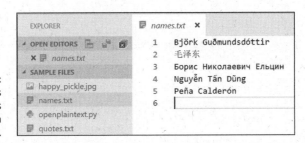

**FIGURE 1-4:**
Names.txt is text, but with lots of non-English characters.

This `names.txt` file is indeed a text file, but all those fancy-looking characters in there tell you it's not a simple ASCII text file. More likely it's a UTF-8 file, which is basically a text file that uses more than just the standard ASCII text characters. To get this file to open, you have to tell Python to "expect" UTF-8 characters by using `encoding='utf-8'` in the `open()` statement, as in Figure 1-5.

Figure 1-5 shows the results of opening `names.txt` as a text file for reading with the addition of the `encoding =`. The output from Python accurately matches what's in the `names.txt` file.

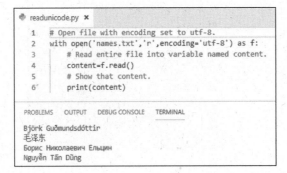

**FIGURE 1-5:**
Contents of names.txt displayed.

**TECHNICAL STUFF**

Not all terminal windows in VS Code show Unicode characters correctly, and these may be replaced with generic question mark symbols on your screen. But don't worry about it, in real life you won't care about output in the Terminal window. Here, all that matters is that you're able to open the file without raising an exception.

When it comes to opening files, there are three things you need to be aware of:

» If it's a plain text file (ASCII) it's sufficient to use r or nothing as the mode.

» If it's a binary file, you have to specify b in the mode.

» If it's a text file with fancy characters, you most likely need to open it as a text file but with encoding set to utf-8 in the open() statement.

## WHAT IS UTF-8?

UTF-8 is short for Unicode Transformation Format, 8-bit, and is a standardized way for representing letters and numbers on computers. The original ASCII set of characters, which contains mostly uppercase and lowercase letters, numbers, and punctuation marks, worked okay in the early days of computing. But when you start bringing other languages into the mix, these characters are just not enough. Many different standards for dealing with other languages have been proposed and accepted over the years since. Of those, UTF-8 has steadily grown in use whereas most others declined. Today, UTF-8 is pretty much the standard for all things Internet, and so it's a good choice if you're ever faced with having to choose a character set for some project.

If you're looking for more history or technical info on UTF-8, take a look at these web pages:

• https://www.w3.org/International/questions/qa-what-is-encoding

• https://pythonconverstheuniverse.wordpress.com/2010/05/30/unicode-beginners-introduction-for-dummies-made-simple/

• https://www.joelonsoftware.com/2003/10/08/the-absolute-minimum-every-software-developer-absolutely-positively-must-know-about-unicode-and-character-sets-no-excuses/

If you really get stuck trying to open a file that's supposed to be UTF-8 but isn't cooperating, Google *convert file to utf-8 encoding*. Then look for a web page or app that will work with your operating system to make the conversion.

# Reading a File's Contents

Earlier in this chapter, you saw how you can read all of an open file's contents using .read(). But that's not the only way to do it. You actually have three choices:

>> **read([*size*]):** Reads in the entire file if you leave the parentheses empty. If you specify a size inside the parentheses, it reads that many characters (for a text file) or that many bytes (for a binary file).

>> **readline():** Reads one line of content from a text file (the line ends wherever there's a newline character).

>> **readlines():** Reads all the lines of a text file into a list.

**TECHNICAL STUFF**

People don't type binary files, so any newline characters that happen to be in there would be arbitrary. Therefore, readline() and readlines() are useful only for text files.

Both the read() and readline() methods read in the entire file at once. The only real difference is that read reads it in as one big chunk of data, whereas readlines() reads it in one line at a time and stores each line as an item in a list. For example, the following code opens quotes.txt, reads in all the content, and then displays it

```
with open('quotes.txt') as f:
# Read in entire file
    content = f.read()
    print(content)
```

The content variable ends up storing a copy of everything that's in the CSV file. Printing this variable shows the contents. It's broken into multiple lines exactly as the original file is because the newline character at the end of each line in the file also starts a new line on the screen when printing the content.

Here is the same code using readlines() rather than read:

```
with open('quotes.txt') as f:
    content = f.readlines()
    print(content)
```

The output from this code is

```
["I've had a perfectly wonderful evening, but this wasn't it.\n", 'Groucho
    Marx\n', 'The difference between stupidity and genius is that genius has its
    limits.\n', 'Albert Einstein\n', 'We are all here on earth to help others;
```

```
what on earth the others are here for, I have no idea.\n', 'W. H. Auden\n',
 'Ending a sentence with a preposition is something up with I will not put.\n',
 'Winston Churchill\n']
```

The square brackets surrounding the output tell you that it's a list. Each item in the list is surrounded by quotation marks and separated by commas. The \n at the end of each item is the newline character that ends the line in the file.

Unlike `readlines()` (plural), `readline()` reads just one line from the file. The line extends from the beginning of the file to just after the first newline character. Executing another `readline()` reads the next line in the file, and so forth. For example, suppose you run this code:

```
with open('quotes.txt') as f:
    content = f.readline()
    print(content)
```

The output is

```
I've had a perfectly wonderful evening, but this wasn't it.
```

Executing another `readline()` after this would read the next line. As you may guess, when it comes to `readline()` and `readlines()`, you're likely to want to use some loops to access all the data in a way where you have some more control.

# Looping through a File

You can loop through a file using either readlines() or readline(). The readlines() method always reads in the file as a whole. Which means if the file is very large, you may run out of memory (RAM) before the file has been read in. But if you know the size of the file and it's relative small (maybe a few hundred rows of data or less), readlines() is a speedy way to get all the data. Those data will be in a list. So you will then loop through the list rather than a file. You can also loop through binary files, but they don't have lines of text like text files do. So those you read in "chunks" as you'll see at the end of this ection.

## Looping with readlines()

When you read a file with `readlines()`, you read the entire file in one fell swoop as a list. So you don't really loop through the file one row at a time. Rather, you loop through the list of items that readlines() stores in memory. The code to do so looks like this:

```
with open('quotes.txt') as f:
    # Reads in all lines first, then loops through.
    for one_line in f.readlines():
        print(one_line)
```

If you run this code, the output will be double-spaced because each list item ends with a newline, and then print always adds its own newline with each pass through the loop. If you want to retain the single spacing, add end='' to the print statement (make sure you use two single or double quotation marks with nothing in between after the =). Here's an example:

```
with open('quotes.txt') as f:
    # Reads in all lines first, then loops through.
    for one_line in f.readlines():
        print(one_line, end='')
```

The output from this code is:

```
I've had a perfectly wonderful evening, but this wasn't it.
Groucho Marx
The difference between stupidity and genius is that genius has its limits.
Albert Einstein
We are all here on earth to help others; what on earth the others are here for,
    I have no idea.
W. H. Auden
Ending a sentence with a preposition is something up with I will not put.
Winston Churchill
```

Let's say you're pretty good with this, except that if the line to be printed is a name, you want to indent the name by a space and put an extra blank line beneath it. How could you do that? Well, Python has a built-in enumerate() function that, when used with a list, counts the number of passes through the loop, starting at zero. So instead of the for: loop shown in the previous example, you write it as for one_line in enumerate(f.readlines()):. With each pass through the loop one_line[0] contains the number of that line, whereas one_line[1] contains its content . . . the text of the line. With each pass through the loop, you can see whether the counter is an even number (that number % 2 will be zero for even numbers, because % returns the remainder after division). So you could write the code this way:

```
with open('quotes.txt') as f:
    # Reads in all lines first, then loops through.
    # Count each line starting at zero.
```

```
for one_line in enumerate(f.readlines()):
    # If counter is even number, print with no extra newline
    if one_line[0] % 2 == 0:
        print(one_line[1], end='')
    # Otherwise print a couple spaces and an extra newline.
    else:
        print('   ' + one_line[1])
```

The output from this will be as follows:

```
I've had a perfectly wonderful evening, but this wasn't it.
  Groucho Marx

The difference between stupidity and genius is that genius has its limits.
  Albert Einstein

We are all here on earth to help others; what on earth the others are here for,
   I have no idea.
  W. H. Auden

Ending a sentence with a preposition is something up with I will not put.
  Winston Churchill
```

# Looping with readline()

If you aren't too sure about the size of the file you're reading, or the amount of RAM in the computer running your app, using readlines() to read in an entire file can be risky. Because if there isn't enough memory to hold the entire file, the app will crash when it runs out of memory. To play it safe, you can loop through the file one line at a time so only one line of content from the file is in memory at any given time. To use this method you can open the file, read one line and put it in a variable. Then loop through the file *as long as* (while) the variable isn't empty. Because each line in the file contains some text, the variable won't be empty until after the very last line is read. Here is the code for this approach to looping:

```
with open('quotes.txt') as f:
    one_line = f.readline()
    while one_line:
        print(one_line, end='')
        one_line = f.readline()
```

For larger files this would be the way to go because at no point are you reading in the entire file. The only danger there is forgetting to do the .readline() inside the loop to advance to the next pointer. Failure to do this creates in infinite loop that prints the first line over and over again. If you ever find yourself in this situation, pressing Ctrl+C in the terminal window where the code us running will stop the loop.

So what about if you want to do a thing like in readlines() where you indent and print an extra blank line after peoples' names? In this example, you really can't use enumerate with the while loop. But you could set up a simple counter yourself, starting at 1 if you like, and increment it by 1 with each pass through the loop. Indent and do the extra space on even-numbered lines like this:

```python
# Store a number to use as a loop counter.
counter = 1
# Open the file.
with open('quotes.txt') as f:
    # Read one line from the file.
    one_line = f.readline()
    # As long as there are lines to read...
    while one_line:
        # If the counter is an even number, print a couple spaces.
        if counter % 2 == 0:
            print('   ' + one_line)
        # Otherwise print with no newline at the end.
        else:
            print(one_line,end='')
        # Increment the counter
        counter += 1
        # Read the next line.
        one_line = f.readline()
```

The output from this loop is the same as for the second readlines() loop in which each author's name is indented and followed by an extra blank line caused by using print() without the end=''.

## Appending versus overwriting files

Any time you work with files it's important to understand the difference between *write* and *append*. If a file contains information already, and you open it in write mode, then write more to it, your new content will actually overwrite (replace) whatever is already in the file. There is no undo for this. So if the content of the file is important, you want to make sure you don't make that mistake. To add content to a file, open the file in append (a) mode, then use .write to write to a file.

As a working example, suppose you want to add the name Peña Calderón to the names.txt file used in the previous section. This name, as well as the names that are already in this file, use special characters beyond the English alphabet, which tells you to make sure you set the encoding to UTF-8. Also, if you want each name in the file on a separate line, you should add a \n (newline) to the end of whatever name you're adding. So your code should look like this:

```
# New name to add with \n to mark end of line.
new_name = 'Peña Calderón\n'
# Open names.txt in append mode with encoding.
with open('names.txt', 'a', encoding='utf-8') as f:
    f.write(new_name)
```

To verify that it worked, start a new block of code, with no indents, so names. txt file closes automatically. Then open this same file in read (r) mode and view its contents. Figure 1-6 shows all the code to add the new name and the code to display the names.txt file after adding this name.

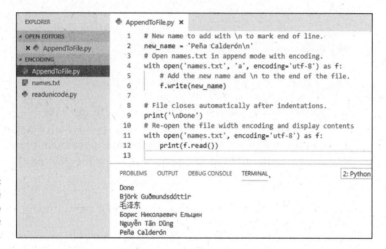

**FIGURE 1-6:**
A new name appended to the end of the names.txt file.

**TIP**

Typing special characters like ñ and ó usually involves holding down the Alt key and typing 3 or 4 numeric digit; for example, Alt+164 for ñ or Alt+0243 for ó. Exactly how you do this depends on the operating system and editor you're using. But as a rule you can google a phrase like *type tilde n on Windows* or *type accented o on Mac* and so on to find out exactly what you need to do to type a special character.

## Using tell() to determine the pointer location

Whenever you loop through a file, its contents are read top-to-bottom, left-to-right. Python maintains an invisible pointer to keep track of where it is in the file. When you're reading a text file with readline(), this is always the character position of the next line in the file.

If all you've done so far is open the file, the character position will be zero, the very start of the file. Each time you execute a readline(), the pointer advances to the start of the next row. Here is some code to illustrate; its output is below the code:

```
with open('names.txt', encoding='utf-8') as f:
    # Read first line to get started.
    print(f.tell())
    one_line = f.readline()
    # Keep reading one line at a time until there are no more.
    while one_line:
        print(one_line[:-1], f.tell())
        one_line = f.readline()
```

```
0
Björk Guðmundsdóttir 25
毛泽东 36
Борис Николаевич Ельцин 82
Nguyễn Tấn Dũng 104
Peña Calderón 121
```

The first zero is the position of the pointer right after the file is opened. The 25 at the end of the next line is the position of the pointer after reading this first line. The 36 at the end of the next line is the pointer position at the end of the second line, and so forth, until the 121 at the end, when the pointer is at the very end of the file.

If you try to do this with readlines() you get a very different result. Here is the code:

```
with open('names.txt', encoding='utf-8') as f:
    print(f.tell())
    # Reads in all lines first, then loops through.
    for one_line in f.readlines():
        print(one_line[:-1],f.tell())
```

Here is the output:

```
0
Björk Guðmundsdóttir 121
毛泽东 121
Борис Николаевич Ельцин 121
Nguyễn Tấn Dũng 121
Peña Calderón 121
```

The pointer starts out at position zero, as expected. But each line shows a 121 at the end. This is because readlines() reads in the entire file when executed, leaving the pointer at the end, position 121. The loop is actually looping through the copy of the file that's in memory; it's no longer reading through the file.

If you try to use .tell() with the super-simple read() loop shown here:

```
with open('names.txt', encoding='utf-8') as f:
    for one_line in f:
        print(one_line, f.tell())
```

. . . it won't work in Windows. So if for whatever reason you need to keep track of where the pointer is in some external text file you're reading, make sure you use a loop with readline().

## Moving the pointer with seek()

Although the tell() method tells you where the pointer is in an external file, the seek() method allows you to reposition the pointer. The syntax is:

```
file.seek(position[,whence])
```

Replace *file* with the variable name of the open file. Replace *position* to indicate where you want to put the pointer. For example, 0 to move it back to the top of the file. The *whence* is optional and you can use it to indicate to which place in the file the position should be calculated. Your choices are:

>> **0**: Set position relative to the start of the file.

>> **1**: Set position relative to the current pointer position.

>> **2**: Set position relative to the end of the file. Use a negative number for *position*.

If you omit the *whence* value, it defaults to zero.

By far the most common use of seek is to just reset the pointer back to the top of the file for another pass through the file. The syntax for this is simply .seek(0).

# Reading and Copying a Binary File

Suppose you have an app that somehow changes a binary file, and you want to always work with a copy of the original file to play it safe. Binary files can be huge, so rather than opening it all at once and risking running out of memory, you can read it in chunks and write it out in chunks. Binary files have no human-readable content in them. Nor do they have lines of text. So readline() and readlines() aren't a good choice for looping through binary files. But you can use .read() with a specified size to achieve a similar result with binary files.

Figure 1-7 shows a file named binarycopy.py that will make a copy of any binary file. We'll take you through it step-by-step so you can understand how it works.

```
binarycopy.py ×
1   # Specify the file to copy.
2   file_to_copy = 'HealthFoodPieChart.png'
3   # Create new file name with _copy before the extension.
4   name_parts = file_to_copy.split('.')
5   new_file = name_parts[0] + '_copy.' + name_parts[1]
6   # Open the original file as read-only binary.
7   with open(file_to_copy,'rb') as original_file:
8       # Create or open file to copy into.
9       with open(new_file,'wb') as copy_to:
10          # Grab a chunk of original file (4MB).
11          chunk = original_file.read(4096)
12          #Loop through until no more chunks.
13          while len(chunk) > 0:
14              copy_to.write(chunk)
15              # Make sure you read next chunk in this loop.
16              chunk = original_file.read(4096)
17
18  # Close is automatic after loops, show done message.
19  print('Done!')
```

**FIGURE 1-7:**
The binarycopy.
py file copies any
binary file.

The first step is to specify the file you want to copy. We chose happy_pickle.jpg, which, as you can see in the figure, is in the same folder as the binarycopy.py folder:

```
# Specify the file to copy.
file_to_copy = 'happy_pickle.jpg'
```

To make an empty file to copy into, you first need a filename for the file. The following code takes care of that:

```
# Create new file name with _copy before the extension.
name_parts = file_to_copy.split('.')
new_file = name_parts[0] + '_copy.' + name_parts[1]
```

The first line after the copy splits the existing filename in two at the dot, so name_parts[0] contains *happy_pickle* and name_parts[1] contains *png*. Then the new_file variable gets a value consisting of the first part of the name with _copy and a dot attached, and then the last part of the name. So after this line executes, the new_file variable contains *happy_pickle_copy.png*.

In order to make the copy, you can open the original file in `rb` mode (read, binary file). The open the file into which you want to copy the original file in `wb` mode (write, binary). With *write*, Python creates a file of this name if the file doesn't already exist. If the file does exist, then Python opens it with the pointer set at 0, so anything that you write into the file will *replace* (not *add to*) the existing file. In the code you can see that we used `original_file` as the variable name from which to copy, and `copy_to` as the variable name of the file into which you copy data. Indentations, as always, are critical:

```python
# Open the original file as read-only binary.
with open(file_to_copy,'rb') as original_file:
    # Create or open file to copy into.
    with open(new_file,'wb') as copy_to:
```

If you use `.read()` to read in the entire binary file, you run the risk of it being so large that it overwhelms the computer's RAM and crashes the program. To avoid this, we've written this program to read in a modest 4MB (4,096 kilobytes) of data at a time. This 4MB chunk is stored in a variable named `chunk`:

```python
# Grab a chunk of original file (4MB).
chunk = original_file.read(4096)
```

The next line sets up a loop that keeps reading one chunk at a time. The pointer is automatically positioned to the next chunk with each pass through the loop. Eventually, it will hit the end of the file where it can't read anymore. When this happens, `chunk` will be empty, meaning it has a length of 0. So this loop keeps going through the file until it gets to the end:

```python
#Loop through until no more chunks.
while len(chunk) > 0:
```

Within the loop, the first line copies the last-read chunk into the `copy_to` file. The second line reads the next 4MB chunk from the original file. And so it goes until everything from `original_file` has been copied to the new file:

```python
copy_to.write(chunk)
# Make sure you read in the next chunk in this loop.
chunk = original_file.read(4096)
```

All the indentations stop after this line. So when the loop is done, the files close automatically, and the last line just shows the word `Done!`:

```python
print('Done!')
```

Figure 1-8 shows the results of running the code. The terminal pane simply shows `Done!`. But as you can see, there's now a file named `happy_pickle_copy.jpg` in the folder. Opening this file will prove that it is an exact copy of the original file.

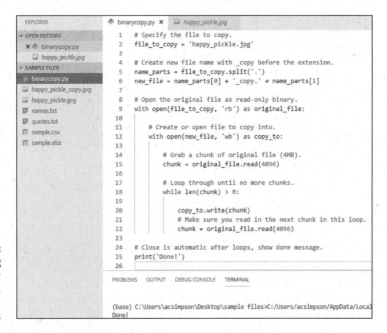

**FIGURE 1-8:**
Running
`binarycopy.py`
added `happy_`
`pickle_copy.`
`jpg` to the folder.

# Conquering CSV Files

CSV (short for comma separated values) is a widely used format for storing and transporting tabular data. *Tabular* means that it can generally be displayed in a table format consisting of rows and columns. In a spreadsheet app like Microsoft Excel, Apple Numbers, or Google Sheets, the tabular format is pretty obvious, as shown in Figure 1-9.

| Full Name | Birth Year | Date Joined | Is Active | Balance |
|---|---|---|---|---|
| Angst, Annie | 1982 | 1/11/2011 | TRUE | $300.00 |
| Bónañas, Barry | 1973 | 2/11/2012 | FALSE | -$123.45 |
| Schadenfreude, Sandy | 2004 | 3/3/2003 | TRUE | $0.00 |
| Weltschmerz, Wanda | 1995 | 4/24/1994 | FALSE | $999,999.99 |
| Malaise, Mindy | 2006 | 5/5/2005 | TRUE | $454.01 |
| O'Possum, Ollie | 1987 | 7/27/1997 | FALSE | -$1,000.00 |
|  |  |  |  |  |
| Pusillanimity, Pamela | 1979 | 8/8/2008 | TRUE | $12,345.67 |

**FIGURE 1-9:**
A CSV file in
Microsoft Excel.

Without the aid of some special program to make the data in the file display in a neat tabular format, each row is just a line in the file. And each unique value is separated by a comma. For instance, opening the file shown in Figure 1-10 in a simple text editor like Notepad or TextEdit shows what's really stored in the file.

```
sample.csv ×
1    Full Name,Birth Year,Date Joined,Is Active,Balance
2    "Angst, Annie",1982,1/11/2011,TRUE,$300.00
3    "Bónañas, Barry",1973,2/11/2012,FALSE,-$123.45
4    "Schadenfreude, Sandy",2004,3/3/2003,TRUE,$0.00
5    "Weltschmerz, Wanda",1995,4/24/1994,FALSE,"$999,999.99"
6    "Malaise, Mindy",2006,5/5/2005,TRUE,$454.01
7    "O'Possum, Ollie",1987,7/27/1997,FALSE,"-$1,000.00"
8    ,,,,
9    "Pusillanimity, Pamela",1979,8/8/2008,TRUE,"$12,345.67"
10
```

**FIGURE 1-10:**
A CSV file in a text editor.

In the text editor, the first row, often called the *header*, contains the column headings, or *field names*, that appear across the first row of the spreadsheet. If you look at the names in the second example, the raw CSV file, you'll notice that they're all enclosed in quotation marks, like this:

```
"Angst, Annie"
```

In real life, they may be single quotation marks, or double, as shown. But either way, they indicate that the stuff *between* the quotation marks is all one thing. In other words, the comma between the last and first name is all part of the name. This comma isn't the start of a new column. So the first two columns on this row one are

```
"Angst, Annie", 1982
```

. . . and not

```
Angst, Annie
```

The same is true in all other rows: The name enclosed in quotation marks (including commas) is just one name, not two separate columns of data.

If any of the strings contains an apostrophe, which is the same character as a single quotation mark, then you have to use double quotation marks around the string. Because if you do it like this:

```
'O'Henry, Harry'
```

The first part of the string looks like `'O'` and then Python won't know what to do with the text after the second single quotation mark. Using double-quotation marks alleviates any confusion because there are no other double quotation marks contained within the name:

"O'Henry, Harry"

Figure 1-10 also contains a few other problems that you may encounter when working with CSV files on your own. For example, the Bónañas, Barry name contains some non-ASCII characters. The second-to-last row just contains a bunch of commas. If in a CSV file a cell is missing its data, you just put the comma that ends this cell with nothing to its left. The Balance column has dollar signs and commas in the numbers, which don't work with the Python `float` data type. We talk about how to deal with all of this in the sections to follow.

Although it would certainly be possible to work with CSV files using just what you've learned so far, it's a lot quicker and easier if you use the `csv` module, which you already have. To use it, just put this near the top of your program:

```
import csv
```

Remember, this doesn't bring in a CSV *file*. It just brings in the pre-written code that makes it easier for you to work with CSV files in your own Python code.

## Opening a CSV file

Opening a CSV file is really no different from opening any other file. Just remember that if the file contains special characters, you need to include the `encoding='utf-8'` to avoid an error message. Optionally, when importing data, you probably don't want to read in the newline character at the end of each row, so you can add `newline=''` to the `open()` statement. Here is how you might comment and code this, except you'd replace `sample.csv` with the path to the CSV file you want to open:

```
# Open CSV file with UTF-8 encoding, don't read in newline characters.
with open('sample.csv', encoding='utf-8', newline='') as f:
```

To loop through a CSV file, you can use the built-in reader function, which reads one row with execution. Again, the syntax is pretty simple, as shown in the following code. Replace f with whatever name you used at the end of your `open` statement (without the colon at the very end).

```
reader = csv.reader(f)
```

Although it's entirely optional, you can also count rows as you go. Just put everything to the right of the = in an enumerate( ), as shown in the following (where we've also added a comment above the code):

```
# Create a CVS row counter and row reader.
reader = enumerate(csv.reader(f))
```

Next, you can set up your loop to read one row at a time. Because you put an enumerator on it, you can use two variable names in your for: the first one (which we'll call i) will keep track of the counter (which starts at zero and increases by 1 with each pass through the loop). The second variable, row, will contain the entire row of data from the CSV file:

```
# Loop through one row at a time, i is counter, row is entire row.
for i, row in reader:
```

You could start with this followed by a print( ) function to print the value of i and row with each pass through the loop, like this:

```
import csv
# Open CSV file with UTF-8 encoding, don't read in newline characters.
with open('sample.csv', encoding='utf-8', newline='') as f:
    # # Create a CVS row counter and row reader.
    reader = enumerate(csv.reader(f))
    # Loop through one row at a time, i is counter, row is entire row.
    for i, row in reader:
        print(i, row)
print('Done')
```

The output from this, using the sample.csv file described earlier as input is as follows:

```
0 ['\ufeffFull Name', 'Birth Year', 'Date Joined', 'Is Active', 'Balance']
1 ['Angst, Annie', '1982', '1/11/2011', 'TRUE', '$300.00']
2 ['Bónañas, Barry', '1973', '2/11/2012', 'FALSE', '-$123.45']
3 ['Schadenfreude, Sandy', '2004', '3/3/2003', 'TRUE', '$0.00']
4 ['Weltschmerz, Wanda', '1995', '4/24/1994', 'FALSE', '$999,999.99']
5 ['Malaise, Mindy', '2006', '5/5/2005', 'TRUE', '$454.01']
6 ["O'Possum, Ollie", '1987', '7/27/1997', 'FALSE', '-$1,000.00']
7 ['', '', '', '', '']
8 ['Pusillanimity, Pamela', '1979', '8/8/2008', 'TRUE', '$12,345.67']
```

Notice how the row of column names is row zero. The weird \ufeff before Full Name in that row is called the Byte Order Mark (BOM) and it's just something Excel sticks in there. Typically you don't care what's in that first row because the real data doesn't start until the next row down. So don't give the BOM a second thought, it's of no value to you, nor is it doing any harm.

Notice how each row is actually a list of five items separated by commas. In your code you can refer to each column by its position. For example, row[0] is the first column in the row (the person's name). Then, row[1] is the birth year, row[2] is date joined, row[3] is whether the person is active, and row[4] is the balance. All the data in the CSV file are strings — even if they don't look like strings. But anything and everything coming from a CSV file is a string because a CSV file is a type of text file, and a text file contains only strings (text), and no integers, dates, Booleans, or floats.

In your app, it's likely that you will want to convert the incoming data to Python data types, so you can work with them more effectively, or perhaps even transfer them to a database. In the next sections, we look at how to do the conversion for each data type.

## Converting strings

Technically, you don't have to convert anything from the CSV file to a string. But you may want to chop it up a bit, or deal with empty strings in some way, so there are some things you can do. First, as we mentioned earlier, we care only about the data here, not that first row. So inside the loop you can start with an if that doesn't do anything if the current row is row zero. Replace the print(i,row) like this:

```
# Row 0 is just column headings, ignore it.
if i > 0:
    full_name = row[0].split(',')
    last_name=full_name[0].strip()
    first_name=full_name[1].strip()
```

This code says "So long as we're not looking at the first row, create a variable named fullname and store in it whatever is in the first column split into two separate values at the comma." After that line executes, full_name[0] contains the person's last name, which we then put into a variable named first_name, and full_name[1] contains the person's first name, which we put into a variable named first_name. But if you run the code that way, it will bomb, because row 7 doesn't have a name, and Python can't split an empty string at a comma (because the empty string contains no comma).

To get around this, you can tell Python to *try* to split the name at the comma, if it can. But if it bombs out when trying, just store and empty string in the full_name, last_name, and first_name variables. Here's that code with some extra comments thrown in to explain all that's going on. Instead of printing i and the whole row, the code just prints the first name and last name (and nothing for the row whose information is missing). You can see the output below the code below.

```python
import csv
# Open CSV file with UTF-8 encoding, don't read in newline characters.
with open('sample.csv', encoding='utf-8', newline='') as f:
    # # Create a CVS row counter and row reader.
    reader = enumerate(csv.reader(f))
    # Loop through one row at a time, i is counter, row is entire row.
    for i, row in reader:
        # Row 0 is just column headings, ignore it.
        if i > 0:
            # Whole name split into two at comma.
            try:
                full_name = row[0].split(',')
                # Last name, strip extra spaces.
                last_name=full_name[0].strip()
                # First name, strip extra spaces.
                first_name=full_name[1].strip()
            except IndexError:
                full_name = last_name = first_name = ""
            print(first_name, last_name)
print('Done!')
```

```
Annie Angst
Barry Bónañas
Sandy Schadenfreude
Wanda Weltschmerz
Mindy Malaise
Ollie O'Possum

Pamela Pusillanimity
Done!
```

# Converting to integers

The second column in each row, `row[1]`, is the birth year. So long as the string contains something that can be converted to a number, you can use the simple built-in `int()` function to convert it to an integer. We do have a problem in row 7 though, which is empty. Python won't automatically convert this to a zero, you have to help it along a bit. Here is the code for that:

```python
# Birth year integer, zero for empty string.
birth_year= int(row[1] or 0)
```

The code looks surprisingly simple, but this is the beauty of Python: It *is* surprisingly simple. This line of code says "create a variable named `birth_year` and put in it the second column value, if you can, or if there is nothing to convert to an integer, then just put in a zero."

# Converting to date

The third column in our CSV file, row[2], is the date joined, and it appears to have a reasonable date in each row (except the row whose data is missing). To convert this to a date, you first need to import the datetime module by adding import datetime as dt up near the top of the program. Then the simple conversion is just:

```
date_joined = dt.datetime.strptime(row[2],"%m/%d/%Y").date()
```

There's a lot going on there, so let us unpack it a bit. First, you create a variable named date_joined. The strptime means "string parse for date time." The [row,2] means the third column (because the first column is always column 0). The "%m/%d/%Y" tells strptime that the string date contains the month, followed by a slash, the day of the month, followed by a slash, and then the four-digit year (uppercase %Y). The .date() at the very end means "just the date; there is no time here to parse."

One small problem. When it gets to the row whose date is missing, this will bomb. So once again we'll use a try ... to do the date, and if it can't come up with a date, then put in the value None, which is Python's word for an empty object.

**REMEMBER**

In Python, datetime is a class, so any date and time you create is actually an object (of the datetime type). You don't use '' for an empty object, '' is for an empty string. Python uses the word None for an empty object.

Here is the code as it stands now with the import up top for the datetime, and try ... except for converting the string date to a Python date:

```
import csv
import datetime as dt
# Open CSV file with UTF-8 encoding, don't read in newline characters.
with open('sample.csv', encoding='utf-8', newline='') as f:
    # # Create a CVS row counter and row reader.
    reader = enumerate(csv.reader(f))
    # Loop through one row at a time, i is counter, row is entire row.
    for i, row in reader:
        # Row 0 is just column headings, ignore it.
        if i > 0:
            # Whole name split into two at comma.
            try:
                full_name = row[0].split(',')
                # Last name, strip extra spaces.
                last_name = full_name[0].strip()
                # First name, strip extra spaces.
                first_name = full_name[1].strip()
```

```
        except IndexError:
            full_name = last_name = first_name = ""
        # Birth year integer, zero for empty string.
        birth_year = int(row[1] or 0)
        # Date_joined is a date.
        try:
            date_joined = dt.datetime.strptime(row[2], "%m/%d/%Y").date()
        except ValueError:
            date_joined = None
        print(first_name, last_name, birth_year, date_joined)
print('Done!')
```

Here is the output from this code, which now prints first_name, last_name, birth_year, and date_joined with each pass through the data rows in the table:

```
Annie Angst 1982 2011-01-11
Barry Bónañas 1973 2012-02-11
Sandy Schadenfreude 2004 2003-03-03
Wanda Weltschmerz 1995 1994-04-24
Mindy Malaise 2006 2005-05-05
Ollie O'Possum 1987 1997-07-27
 0 None
Pamela Pusillanimity 1979 2008-08-08
Done!
```

## Converting to Boolean

The fourth column, row[3] in each row contains TRUE or FALSE. Excel uses all uppercase letters like this, and that is automatically carried over to the CSV file when saving as CSV in Excel. Python uses initial caps, True and False. Python has a simple bool() function for making this conversion. And it won't bomb out when it hits an empty cell . . . it just considers that cell False. So this conversion can be as simple as this:

```
# is_active is a Boolean, automatically False for empty string.
is_active=bool(row[3])
```

## Converting to floats

The fifth column in each row contains the balance, which is a dollar amount. In Python, you want this to be a float. But there's a problem right off the bat. Python floats can't contain a dollar sign ($) or a comma (,). So the first thing you need to do is remove those from the string. Also, you can't have any accidental leading or trailing spaces. These you can easily remove with the `strip()` method. This line creates a variable named `str_balance` (which is still a string), but with the dollar sign, comma, and any trailing leading spaces removed:

```python
# Remove $, commas, leading trailing spaces.
str_balance = (row[4].replace('$','').replace(',','')).strip()
```

You can read this second line as "the new string named balance consists of whatever is in the fifth column after replacing any dollar signs with nothing, and replacing any commas with nothing, and stripping off all leading and trailing spaces." Below that line, you can add a comma and then another line to create a float named `balance` that uses the built-in `float()` method to convert the `str_balance` string into a float. Like `int()`, `float()` has its own built-in exception handler, which, if it can't make sense of the thing it's trying to convert to a float, stores a zero as the value of the float. The code in Figure 1-11 shows everything in place, including a `print()` line that displays the values of all five columns after conversion.

```python
loop_thru_csv.py  ×
1    import csv
2    import datetime as dt
3    # Open CSV file with UTF-8 encoding, don't read in newline characters.
4    with open('sample.csv', encoding='utf-8', newline='') as f:
5        # Create a CVS row counter and row reader.
6        reader = enumerate(csv.reader(f))
7        # Loop through one row at a time, i is counter, row is entire row.
8        for i, row in reader:
9            # Row 0 is just column headings, ignore it.
10           if i > 0:
11               # Whole name split into two at comma.
12               try:
13                   full_name = row[0].split(',')
14                   # Last name, strip extra spaces.
15                   last_name = full_name[0].strip()
16                   # First name, strip extra spaces.
17                   first_name = full_name[1].strip()
18               except IndexError:
19                   full_name = last_name = first_name = ""
20               # Birth year integer, zero for empty string.
21               birth_year = int(row[1] or 0)
22               # Date joined is a date.
23               try:
24                   date_joined = dt.datetime.strptime(row[2], "%m/%d/%Y").date()
25               except ValueError:
26                   date_joined = None
27               # is_active is a Boolean, automatically False for empty string.
28               is_active = bool(row[3])
29               # Remove $, commas, leading and trailing spaces.
30               str_balance = (row[4].replace('$', '').replace(',', '')).strip()
31               # Balance is a float or zero for empty string.
32               balance = float(str_balance or 0)
33               print(first_name, last_name, birth_year, date_joined, is_active, balance)
34   print('Done!')
35
```

```
PROBLEMS   OUTPUT   DEBUG CONSOLE   TERMINAL

C:\Users\Alan\Desktop\csv_files>python c:/Users/Alan/Desktop/csv_files/loop_thru_csv.py
Annie Angst 1982 2011-01-11 True 300.0
Barry Bónañas 1973 2012-02-11 True -123.45
Sandy Schadenfreude 2004 2003-03-03 True 0.0
Wanda Weltschmerz 1995 1994-04-24 True 999999.99
Mindy Malaise 2006 2005-05-05 True 454.01
Ollie O'Possum 1987 1997-07-27 True -1000.0
 0 None False 0.0
Pamela Pusillanimity 1979 2008-08-08 True 12345.67
Done!
```

**FIGURE 1-11:**
Reading a CSV file and converting to Python data types.

## USING REGULAR EXPRESSIONS IN PYTHON

Even though this book assumes you're not already familiar with other programming languages, some readers inevitably will be, and some of those are likely to ask why we didn't use a *regular expression* to remove the dollar sign and comma from the balance instead of the replace() method. The answer to this would be, "Because you're not required to do it that way, and not everyone reading this book is aware that a thing called *regular expressions* is available in most programming languages."

But if you happen to be a person who was thinking of asking this question, the first thing to know is that regular expressions aren't built-in to Python. So if you want to use them, you need to put an import re at the top of your code. In this particular example, which just uses the substitution capabilities of regular expressions, you'd need this near the top of your code:

```
from re import sub.
```

Later in the code, you can remove the

```
str_balance = (row[4].replace('$','').replace(',','')).strip()
```

line completely and replace it with

```
str_balance = (sub(r'[\s\$,]','',row[4])).strip()
```

This line does exactly the same thing as the original line. It removes the dollar sign, commas, and any leading and trailing spaces from the fifth column value.

# From CSV to Objects and Dictionaries

You've seen how you can read in data from any CSV file, and how to convert that data from the default string data type to an appropriate Python data type. Chances are, in addition to all of this, you may want to organize the data into a group of objects, all generated from the same class, or perhaps into a set of dictionaries inside a larger dictionary. All the code you've learned far will be useful, because it's all necessary to get the job done. To reduce the code clutter in these examples, we've taken the various bits of code for converting the data and put them into their own functions. This allows you to convert a data item just using the function name with the value to convert in parentheses, like this: balance(row[4]).

# Importing CSV to Python objects

If you want the data from your CSV file to be organized into a list of objects, write your code as shown here:

```python
import datetime as dt
import csv
# Use these functions to convert any string to appropriate Python data type.
# Get just the first name from full name.
def fname(any):
    try:
        nm = any.split(',')
        return nm[1]
    except IndexError:
        return ''
# Get just the last name from full name.
def lname(any):
    try:
        nm = any.split(',')
        return nm[0]
    except IndexError:
        return ''
# Convert string to integer or zero if no value.
def integer(any):
    return int(any or 0)
# Conver mm/dd/yyyy date to date or None if no valid date.
def date(any):
    try:
        return dt.datetime.strptime(any,"%m/%d/%Y").date()
    except ValueError:
        return None
# Convert any string to Boolean, False if no value.
def boolean(any):
    return bool(any)
# Convert string to float, or to zero if no value.
def floatnum(any):
    s_balance = (any.replace('$','').replace(',','')).strip()
    return float(s_balance or 0)
# Create an empty list of people.
people = []
# Define a class where each person is an object.
class Person:
    def __init__(self, id, first_name, last_name, birth_year, date_joined, is_
    active, balance):
        self.id = id
        self.first_name = first_name
        self.last_name = last_name
        self.birth_year = birth_year
```

```python
        self.date_joined = date_joined
        self.is_active = is_active
        self.balance = balance

# Open CSV file with UTF-8 encoding, don't read in newline characters.
with open('sample.csv', encoding='utf-8', newline='') as f:
    # Set up a csv reader with a counter.
    reader = enumerate(csv.reader(f))
    # Skip the first row, which is column names.
    f.readline()
    # Loop through remaining rows one at a time, i is counter, row is
    entire row.
    for i, row in reader:
        # From each data row in the CSV file, create a Person object with unique
    id and appropriate data types, add to people list.
        people.append(Person(i, fname(row[0]), lname(row[0]), integer(row[1]),
    date(row[2]), boolean(row[3]), floatnum(row[4])))

# When above loop is done, show all objects in the people list.
for p in people:
    print(p.id, p.first_name, p.last_name, p.birth_year, p.date_joined, p.is_
    active, p.balance)
```

Here's how the code works: The first couple of lines are the required `imports`, followed by a number of functions to convert the incoming string data to Python data types. This code is similar to previous examples in this chapter. We just separated the conversion code out into separate functions to compartmentalize everything a bit:

```python
import datetime as dt
import csv
# Use these functions to convert any string to appropriate Python data type.
# Get just the first name from full name.
def fname(any):
    try:
        nm = any.split(',')
        return nm[1]
    except IndexError:
        return ''


# Get just the last name from full name.
def lname(any):
    try:
        nm = any.split(',')
        return nm[0]
    except IndexError:
        return ''
```

```
# Convert string to integer or zero if no value.
def integer(any):
    return int(any or 0)

# Conver mm/dd/yyyy date to date or None if no valid date.
def date(any):
    try:
        return dt.datetime.strptime(any,"%m/%d/%Y").date()
    except ValueError:
        return None

# Convert any string to Boolean, False if no value.
def boolean(any):
    return bool(any)

# Convert string to float, or to zero if no value.
def floatnum(any):
    s_balance = (any.replace('$','').replace(',','')).strip()
    return float(s_balance or 0)
```

This next line creates an empty list named people. This just provides a place to store the objects that the program will create from the CSV file:

```
# Create an empty list of people.
people = []
```

Next, the code defines a class that will be used to generate each Person object from the CSV file:

```
# Define a class where each person is an object.
class Person:
    def __init__(self, id, first_name, last_name, birth_year, date_joined, is_
    active, balance):
        self.id = id
        self.first_name = first_name
        self.last_name = last_name
        self.birth_year = birth_year
        self.date_joined = date_joined
        self.is_active = is_active
        self.balance = balance
```

The actual reading of the CSV file starts in the next lines. Notice how the code opens the sample.csv file with encoding. The newline='' just prevents it from sticking the newline character that's at the end of each row to the last item of data in each row. The reader uses an enumerator to keep a count while reading the rows. The `f.readline()` reads the first row, which is just column heads, so that the `for` that follows starts on the second row. The `i` variable in the `for` loop is just the incrementing counter, and the `row` is the entire row of data from the CSV file:

```
# Open CSV file with UTF-8 encoding, don't read in newline characters.
with open('sample.csv', encoding='utf-8', newline='') as f:
    # Set up a csv reader with a counter.
    reader = enumerate(csv.reader(f))
    # Skip the first row, which is column names.
    f.readline()
    # Loop through remaining rows one at a time, i is counter, row is
    entire row.
    for i, row in reader:
```

With each pass through the loop, this line creates a single `Person` object from the incrementing counter (`i`) and appends the data in the `row`. Notice how we've called upon the functions defined earlier in the code to do the data type conversions. This makes this code more compact and a little easier to read and work with:

```
# From each data row in the CSV file, create a Person object with unique id
    and appropriate data types, add to people list.
people.append(Person(i, fname(row[0]), lname(row[0]), integer(row[1]),
    date(row[2]), boolean(row[3]), floatnum(row[4])))
```

When the loop is complete, the next code simply displays each object on the screen to verify that the code worked correctly:

```
# When above loop is done, show all objects in the people list.
for p in people:
    print(p.id, p.first_name, p.last_name, p.birth_year, p.date_joined,
    p.is_active, p.balance)
```

Figure 1-12 shows the output from running this program. Of course, subsequent code in the program can do anything you need to do with each object; the printing is just there to test and verify that it worked.

## Importing CSV to Python dictionaries

If you prefer to store each row of data from the CSV file in its own dictionary, you can use code that's similar to the preceding code for creating objects. You don't need the class definition code, because you won't be creating objects here. Instead of creating a people list, you can create an empty `people` dictionary to hold all the individual "person" dictionaries, like this:

```
# Create an empty dictionary of people.
people = {}
```

```
34  # Create an empty list of people.
35  people = []
36  # Define a class where each person is an object.
37  class Person:
38      def __init__(self, id, first_name, last_name, birth_year, date_joined, is_active, balance):
39          self.id = id
40          self.first_name = first_name
41          self.last_name = last_name
42          self.birth_year = birth_year
43          self.date_joined = date_joined
44          self.is_active = is_active
45          self.balance = balance
46
47  # Open CSV file with UTF-8 encoding, don't read in newline characters.
48  with open('sample.csv', encoding='utf-8', newline='') as f:
49      # Set up a csv reader with a counter.
50      reader = enumerate(csv.reader(f))
51      # Skip the first row, which is column names.
52      f.readline()
53      # Loop through remaining rows one at a time, i is counter, row is entire row.
54      for i, row in reader:
55          # From each data row in the CSV file, create a Person object with unique id and appropriate data types, add to people list.
56          people.append(Person(i, fname(row[0]), lname(row[0]), integer(row[1]), date(row[2]), boolean(row[3]), floatnum(row[4])))
57
58  # When above loop is done, show all objects in the people list.
59  for p in people:
60      print(p.id, p.first_name, p.last_name, p.birth_year, p.date_joined, p.is_active, p.balance)
61
```

PROBLEMS   OUTPUT   DEBUG CONSOLE   TERMINAL

```
0  Annie Angst 1982 2011-01-11 True 300.0
1  Barry Bónañas 1973 2012-02-11 True -123.45
2  Sandy Schadenfreude 2004 2003-03-03 True 0.0
3  Wanda Weltschmerz 1995 1994-04-24 True 999999.99
4  Mindy Malaise 2006 2005-05-05 True 454.01
5  Ollie O'Possum 1987 1997-07-27 True -1000.0
6  0 None False 0.0
7  Pamela Pusillanimity 1979 2008-08-08 True 12345.67
```

**FIGURE 1-12:**
Reading a CSV file into a list of objects.

As far as the loop goes, again you can use an enumerator (i) to count rows, and you can also use this unique value as the key for each new dictionary you create. The line that starts with newdict= creates a dictionary with the data from one CSV file row, using the built-in Python dict() function. The next line assigns the value of i plus one (to start the first one at one rather than zero) to each newly created dictionary:

```
# Loop through remaining rows one at a time, i is counter, row is entire row.
for i, row in reader:
    # From each data row in the CSV file, create a Person object with unique
    id and appropriate data types, add to people list.
    newdict = dict({'first_name': fname(row[0]), 'last_name': lname(row[0]),
'birth_year': integer(row[1]), \
                    'date_joined' : date(row[2]), 'is_active' : boolean(row[3]),
'balance' : floatnum(row[4])})
    people[i + 1] = newdict
```

To verify that the code ran correctly, you can loop through the dictionaries in the people dictionary and show the *key:value* pair for each item of data in each row. Figure 1-13 shows the result of running that code in VS Code:

```
30   # Convert string to float, or to zero if no value.
31   def floatnum(any):
32       s_balance = (any.replace('$', '').replace(',', '')).strip()
33       return float(s_balance or 0)
34   # Create an empty dictionary of people.
35   people = {}
36   # Open CSV file with UTF-8 encoding, don't read in newline characters.
37   with open('sample.csv', encoding='utf-8', newline='') as f:
38       # Set up a csv reader with a counter.
39       reader = enumerate(csv.reader(f))
40       # Skip the first row, which is column names.
41       f.readline()
42       # Loop through remaining rows one at a time, i is counter, row is entire row.
43       for i, row in reader:
44           # From each data row in the CSV file, create a Person object with unique id and appropriate data types, add to people list.
45           newdict = dict({'first_name': fname(row[0]), 'last_name': lname(row[0]), 'birth_year': integer(row[1]), \
46                    'date_joined' : date(row[2]), 'is_active' : boolean(row[3]), 'balance' : floatnum(row[4])})
47           people[i + 1] = newdict
48
49   # When above loop is done, show all objects in the people list.
50   for person in people.keys():
51       id = person
52       print(id, people[person]['first_name'], \
53                 people[person]['last_name'], \
54                 people[person]['birth_year'], \
55                 people[person]['date_joined'], \
56                 people[person]['is_active'], \
57                 people[person]['balance'])
58
```

PROBLEMS   OUTPUT   DEBUG CONSOLE   TERMINAL

```
(base) C:\Users\acsimpson\OneDrive\AIO Python\csv_files>C:/Users/acsimpson/AppData/Local/Continuum/anaconda3/python.exe "c:/Users/acsimpson/OneDrive/AIC
1  Annie Angst 1982 2011-01-11 True 300.0
2  Barry Bónañas 1973 2012-02-11 True -123.45
3  Sandy Schadenfreude 2004 2003-03-03 True 0.0
4  Wanda Weltschmerz 1995 1994-04-24 True 999999.99
5  Mindy Malaise 2006 2005-05-05 True 454.01
6  Ollie O'Possum 1987 1997-07-27 True -1000.0
7  0 None False 0.0
8  Pamela Pusillanimity 1979 2008-08-08 True 12345.67
```

**FIGURE 1-13:**
Reading a CSV file
into a dictionary
of dictionaries.

Here is all the code that reads the data from the CSV files into the dictionaries:

```python
import datetime as dt
import csv
# Use these functions to convert any string to appropriate Python data type.
# Get just the first name from full name.
def fname(any):
    try:
        nm = any.split(',')
        return nm[1]
    except IndexError:
        return ''
# Get just the last name from full name.
def lname(any):
    try:
        nm = any.split(',')
        return nm[0]
    except IndexError:
        return ''
# Convert string to integer or zero if no value.
def integer(any):
    return int(any or 0)
# Convert mm/dd/yyyy date to date or None if no valid date.
def date(any):
    try:
        return dt.datetime.strptime(any, "%m/%d/%Y").date()
```

```
        except ValueError:
            return None
# Convert any string to Boolean, False if no value.
def boolean(any):
    return bool(any)
# Convert string to float, or to zero if no value.
def floatnum(any):
    s_balance = (any.replace('$', '').replace(',', '')).strip()
    return float(s_balance or 0)
# Create an empty dictionary of people.
people = {}
# Open CSV file with UTF-8 encoding, don't read in newline characters.
with open('sample.csv', encoding='utf-8', newline='') as f:
    # Set up a csv reader with a counter.
    reader = enumerate(csv.reader(f))
    # Skip the first row, which is column names.
    f.readline()
    # Loop through remaining rows one at a time, i is counter, row is
    entire row.
    for i, row in reader:
        # From each data row in the CSV file, create a Person object with
        unique id
        # and appropriate data types, add to people dictionary.
        newdict = dict({'first_name': fname(row[0]), 'last_name': lname(row[0]),
    'birth_year': integer(row[1]), \
                    'date_joined' : date(row[2]), 'is_active' : boolean(row[3]),
    'balance' : floatnum(row[4])})
        people[i + 1] = newdict

# When above loop is done, show all objects in the people list.
for person in people.keys():
    id = person
    print(id, people[person]['first_name'], \
            people[person]['last_name'], \
            people[person]['birth_year'], \
            people[person]['date_joined'], \
            people[person]['is_active'], \
            people[person]['balance'])
```

CSV files are widely used because it's easy to export data from spreadsheets and database tables to this format. Getting data from those files can be tricky at times, but you'll find Python's csv module a big help. It takes care of many of the details, makes it relatively easy to loop through one row at a time, and handles the data however you see fit within your Python app.

Similar to CSV for transporting and storing data in a simple textual format is JSON, which stands for JavaScript Object Notation. You learn all about JSON in the next chapter.

# Chapter **2**

# Juggling JSON Data

J SON (JavaScript Object Notation) is a common marshalling format for object-oriented data. That term, *marshalling format*, generally means a format used to send the data from one computer to another. However, some databases, such as the free Realtime Database at Google's Firebase, actually store the data in JSON format as well. The name *JavaScript* at the front sometimes throws people off a bit, especially when you're using Python, not JavaScript, to write your code. But don't worry about that. The format just got its start in the JavaScript world. It's now a widely known general purpose format used with all kinds of computers and programming languages.

In this chapter you learn exactly what JSON is, as well as how to export and import data to and from JSON. If you find that all the buzzwords surrounding JSON make you uncomfortable, don't worry. We'll get through all the jargon first. As you'll see, JSON data is formatted almost the same way as Python data dictionaries. So there won't be a huge amount of new stuff to learn. Also, you already have the free Python JSON module, which makes it even easier to work with JSON data.

## Organizing JSON Data

JSON data is roughly the equivalent of a data dictionary in Python, which makes JSON files fairly easy to work with. It's probably easiest to understand when it's compared to tabular data. For instance, Figure 2-1 shows some tabular data in an Excel worksheet. Figure 2-2 shows the same data converted to JSON format. Each row of data in the Excel sheet has simply been converted to a dictionary of *key*:*value* pairs in the JSON file. And there are, of course, lots of curly braces to indicate that it's dictionary data.

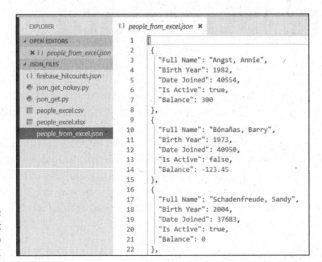

| | A | B | C | D | E |
|---|---|---|---|---|---|
| 1 | Full Name | Birth Year | Date Joined | Is Active | Balance |
| 2 | Angst, Annie | 1982 | 1/11/2011 | TRUE | $300.00 |
| 3 | Bónañas, Barry | 1973 | 2/11/2012 | FALSE | -$123.45 |
| 4 | Schadenfreude, Sandy | 2004 | 3/3/2003 | TRUE | $0.00 |
| 5 | Weltschmerz, Wanda | 1995 | 4/24/1994 | FALSE | $999,999.99 |
| 6 | Malaise, Mindy | 2006 | 5/5/2005 | TRUE | $454.01 |
| 7 | O'Possum, Ollie | 1987 | 7/27/1997 | TRUE | -$1,000.00 |
| 8 | | | | | |
| 9 | Pusillanimity, Pamela | 1979 | 8/8/2008 | TRUE | $12,345.67 |

**FIGURE 2-1:**
Some data
in an Excel
spreadsheet.

**FIGURE 2-2:**
Excel spreadsheet
data converted to
JSON format.

That's one way to do a JSON file. You can also do a *keyed JSON file* where each chunk of data has a single key the uniquely identifies it (no other dictionary in the same file can have the same key). The key can be a number or some text; it doesn't really matter which, so long as it's unique to each item. When you're downloading JSON files created by someone else, it's not unusual for the file to be keyed. For example, on Alan's personal website he uses a free Google Firebase Realtime Database to count hits per page and other information about each page. This Realtime Database stores the data as shown in Figure 2-3. Those weird things that look like *-LAOqOxg6kmP4jhnjQXS* are all keys that the Firebase generates automatically for each item of data, to guarantee uniqueness. The + sign next to each key allows you to expand and collapse the information under each key.

## CONVERTING EXCEL TO JSON

In case you're wondering, to convert that sample Excel spreadsheet to JSON, set your browser to `www.convertcsv.com/csv-to-json.htm` and follow these steps:

1. In Step 1, open the Choose File tab, set the Encoding to UTF-8, click the Browse button, select your Excel file, and click Open.

2. In Step 2, make sure the First Row Is Column Names option is checked and set Skip # of Lines to 1 to skip the column headings row.

3. In Step 5, click the CSV to JSON button.

4. Next to Save Your Result, type a filename then click the Download Result button.

The file should end up in your Downloads folder (or to whatever location you normally download) with a .json extension. It's a plain text file so you can open it with any text editor, or a code editor like VS Code. The converter automatically skips empty rows in Excel files, so your JSON file won't contain any data for empty rows in a spreadsheet. If you often work with Excel, CSV, JSON, and similar types of data, you may want to spend some time exploring the many tools and capabilities of that `http://www.convertcsv.com/` website.

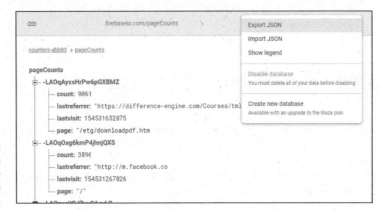

**FIGURE 2-3:**
Some data in a Google Firebase Realtime Database.

As you can see in the image, Firebase also has an Export JSON option that downloads the data to a JSON file to your computer. We did this. Figure 2-4 shows how the data looks in that downloaded file. You can tell that one is a keyed JSON file because each chunk of data is preceded by a unique key, like *-LAOqAyxxHrPw6pGXBMZ* followed by a colon. You can work with both keyed and un-keyed JSON files in Python.

```json
{
    "-LAOqAyxxHrPw6pGXBMZ" : {
        "count" : 9061,
        "lastreferrer" : "https://difference-engine.com/Courses/tml-5-1118/",
        "lastvisit" : 1545316328750,
        "page" : "/etg/downloadpdf.html"
    },
    "-LAOqOxg6kmP4jhnjQXS" : {
        "count" : 3896,
        "lastreferrer" : "http://m.facebook.com",
        "lastvisit" : 1545312678263,
        "page" : "/"
    },
    "-LAOrwciIQJZvuCAcyLO" : {
        "count" : 3342,
        "lastreferrer" : "https://alansimpson.me/",
        "lastvisit" : 1545311601815,
        "page" : "/html_css/index.html"
    },
    "-LAOs2nsVVxbjAwxUXxE" : {
        "count" : 2220,
        "lastreferrer" : "http://alansimpson.me/html_css/codequickies/dropdownmenu.html",
        "lastvisit" : 1545280814480,
        "page" : "/html_css/codequickies/"
    },
    "-LAOwqJsjfuoQx8WISlX" : {
        "count" : 2194,
        "lastreferrer" : "https://alansimpson.me/firebase/hitcounter/",
        "lastvisit" : 1545308609977,
        "page" : "/index.html"
    },
```

**FIGURE 2-4:**
Google Firebase Realtime Database data exported to keyed JSON file.

Some readers may have noticed that the `Date Joined` field in the JSON file doesn't look like a normal *mm/dd/yyyy* date. The `lastvisit` field from the Firebase database is a `datetime`, even though it doesn't look like a date or time. But don't worry about that. You'll learn how to convert those odd-looking serial dates (as they're called) to human readable format later in this chapter.

# Understanding Serialization

When it comes to JSON, the first buzzword you have to learn is *serialization*. Serialization is the process of converting an object (like a Python dictionary) into a stream of bytes (characters) that can be sent across a wire, stored in a file or database, or stored in memory. The main purpose is to save all the information contained within an object in a way that can easily be retrieved on any other computer. The process of converting it back to an object is called *deserialization*. To keep things simple you may just consider using these definitions:

>> **Serialize:** Convert an object to a string.

>> **Deserialize:** Convert a string to an object.

The Python standard library includes a `json` module that helps you work with JSON files. Because it's part of the standard library, you just have to put `import json` near the top of your code to access its capabilities. The four main methods for serializing and deserializing `json` are summarized in Table 2-1.

**TABLE 2-1**

## Python JSON Methods for Serializing and Deserializing JSON Data

| Method | Purpose |
|--------|---------|
| `json.dump()` | Write (serialize) Python data to a JSON file (or stream). |
| `json.dumps()` | Write (serialize) a Python object to a JSON string. |
| `json.load()` | Load (deserialize) JSON from a file or similar object. |
| `json.loads()` | Load (deserialize) JSON data from a string. |

Data types in JSON are somewhat similar to data types in Python, but they're not exactly the same. Table 2-2 lists how data types are converted between the two languages when serializing and deserializing.

**TABLE 2-2**

## Python and JSON Data Conversions

| Python | JSON |
|--------|------|
| dict | object |
| list, tuple | array |
| str | string |
| int and float | number |
| True | true |
| False | false |
| None | null |

# Loading Data from JSON Files

To load data form JSON files, make sure you import `json` near the top of the code. Then you can use a regular file `open()` method to open the file. As with other kinds of files, you can add `encoding = "utf-8"` if you think there are any foreign characters in the data to preserve. You can also use `newline=""` to avoid bringing in the newline character at the end of each row, which isn't really part of the data. It's just a hidden character to end the line when displaying the data on the screen.

To load the JSON data into Python, come up with a variable name to hold the data (we'll use `people`) and then use `json.load()` to load the file contents into the variable, like this:

```python
import json
# This is the Excel data (no keys)
filename = 'people_from_excel.json'
# Open the file (standard file open stuff)
with open(filename, 'r', encoding='utf-8', newline='') as f:
    # Load the whole json file into an object named people
    people = json.load(f)
```

Running this code doesn't display anything on the screen. However, you can explore the `people` object in a number of ways using `print()` un-indented print statements below this last line. For example this

```python
print(people)
```

. . . displays everything that's in the p variable. In the output, you can see it starts and ends with square brackets ([ ]), which tells you that `people` is a list. To verify this, you can run this line of code:

```python
print(type(people))
```

When you do, Python displays `<class 'list'>`, which tells you that the object is an instance of the `list` class. In other words, it's a `list` object, although most people would just call it a list.

```python
<class 'list'>
```

Because it's a list, you can loop through it. Within the loop you can display the type of each item, like this:

```python
for p in people:
    print(type(p))
```

The output from this is:

```python
<class 'dict'>
<class 'dict'>
<class 'dict'>
```

```
<class 'dict'>
<class 'dict'>
<class 'dict'>
<class 'dict'>
```

This's useful information because it tells you that each of the "people" (which we've abbreviated p in that code) in the list is a Python dictionary. So within the loop, you can isolate each value by its key. For example, take a look at this code:

```
for p in people:
    print(p['Full Name'], p['Birth Year'], p['Date Joined'], p['Is Active'],
            p['Balance'])
```

Running this code displays all the data in the JSON file, as in the following. Those data came from the Excel spreadsheet shown back in Figure 2-1.

```
Angst, Annie 1982 40554 True 300
Bónañas, Barry 1973 40950 False -123.45
Schadenfreude, Sandy 2004 37683 True 0
Weltschmerz, Wanda 1995 34448 False 999999.99
Malaise, Mindy 2006 38477 True 454.01
O'Possum, Ollie 1987 35638 True -1000
Pusillanimity, Pamela 1979 39668 True 12345.67
```

## Converting an Excel date to a JSON date

You may be thinking "Hey, waitaminit . . . what's with those 40554, 40950, 37683 numbers in the Date Joined column?" Well, those are serial dates, but you can certainly convert them to Python dates. You'll need to import the xlrd (Excel reader) and datetime modules. Then, to convert that integer in the p['Date Joined'] column to a Python date, use this code:

```
y, m, d, h, i, s = xlrd.xldate_as_tuple(p['Date Joined'],0)
joined = dt.date(y, m, d)
```

To display this date in a familiar format, you can use an f-string like this:

```
print(f"{joined:%m/%d/%Y}")
```

Here is all the code, including the necessary imports at the top of the file:

```
import json, xlrd
import datetime as dt
# This is the Excel data (no keys)
filename = 'people_from_excel.json'
```

```
# Open the file (standard file open stuff)
with open(filename, 'r', encoding='utf-8', newline='') as f:
    # Load the whole json file into an object named people
    people = json.load(f)

# Dictionaries are in a list, loop through and display each dictionary.
for p in people:
    name=p['Full Name']
    byear = p['Birth Year']
    # Excel date pretty tricky, use xlrd module.
    y, m, d, h, i, s = xlrd.xldate_as_tuple(p['Date Joined'],0)
    joined = dt.date(y, m, d)
    balance = '$' + f"{p['Balance']:,.2f}"
    print(f"{name:<22} {byear}   {joined:%m/%d/%Y} {balance:>12}")
```

Here is the output of this code, which, you can see, is fairly neatly formatted and looks more like the original Excel data than the JSON data. If you need to display the data in *dd/mm/yyyy* format just changes the pattern in the last line to %d/%m/%Y.

```
Angst, Annie           1982   01/11/2011      $300.00
Bónañas, Barry         1973   02/11/2012     $-123.45
Schadenfreude, Sandy   2004   03/03/2003        $0.00
Weltschmerz, Wanda     1995   04/24/1994  $999,999.99
Malaise, Mindy         2006   05/05/2005      $454.01
O'Possum, Ollie        1987   07/27/1997   $-1,000.00
Pusillanimity, Pamela  1979   08/08/2008   $12,345.67
```

## Looping through a keyed JSON file

Opening and loading a keyed JSON file is the same as opening a non-keyed file. However, after it's loaded, the data tends to be a single dictionary rather than a list of dictionaries. For example, here is the code to open and load the data we exported from Firebase (the original is shown back in Figure 3-4). This data contains hit counts for pages in a website, including the page name, the number of hits to date, the last referred (the last page that sent someone to that page), and the date and time of the last visit. As you can see, the code for opening and loading the JSON data is basically the same. The JSON data loads to an object we named hits:

```
import json
import datetime as dt
# This is the Firebase JSON data (keyed).
filename = 'firebase_hitcounts.json'
```

```
# Open the file (standard file open stuff).
with open(filename, 'r', encoding='utf-8', newline='') as f:
    # Load the whole json file into an object named people
    hits = json.load(f)

print(type(hits))
```

When you run this code, the last line displays the data type of the `hits` object, into which the JSON data was loaded, as `<class 'dict'>`. This tells you that the `hits` object is one large dictionary rather than a list of individual dictionaries. You can loop through this dictionary using a simple loop like we did for the non-keyed JSON file, like this:

```
for p in hits:
    print(p)
```

The result of this, however, is that you don't see much data. In fact, all you see is the key for each sub-dictionary contained within the larger `hits` dictionary:

```
-LAOqAyxxHrPw6pGXBMZ
-LAOqOxg6kmP4jhnjQXS
-LAOrwciIQJZvuCAcyLO
-LAOs2nsVVxbjAwxUXxE
-LAOwqJsjfuoQx8WIS1X
-LAQ7ShbQPqOANbDmm3O
-LAQrS6av1vØPuJGNm6P
-LI0iPwZ7nu3IUgiQORH
-LI2DFNAxVnT-cxYzWR-
```

This is not an error or a problem. It's just how it works with nested dictionaries. But don't worry, it's pretty easy to get to the data inside each dictionary. You can, for instance, use two looping variables, which we'll call k (for *key*) and v (for *value*), to loop through `hits.items()`, like this:

```
for k, v in hits.items():
    print(k,v)
```

This gives you a different view where you see each key followed by the dictionary for that key enclosed in curly braces (the curly braces tell you that the data inside is in a dictionary). Figure 2-5 shows the output from this.

The values for each sub-dictionary are in the v object of this loop. If you want to access individual items of data, use v followed by a pair of square brackets with the key name (for the field) inside. For example, `v['count']` contains whatever is stored as the `count:` in a given row. Take a look at this code in which we don't even bother with displaying the key:

```
for k, v in hits.items():
    # Store items in variables.
    key = k
    hits = v['count']
    last_visit=v['lastvisit']
    page = v['page']
    came_from=v['lastreferrer']
    print(f"{hits} {last_visit} {page:<28} {came_from}")
```

keyed_json.py ×
1   import json
2   import datetime as dt
3   # This is the Firebase JSON data (keyed).
4   filename = 'firebase_hitcounts.json'
5   # Open the file (standard file open stuff).
6   with open(filename, 'r', encoding='utf-8', newline='') as f:
7       # Load the whole json file into an object named hits.
8       hits = json.load(f)
9
10  for k, v in hits.items():
11      print(k,v)
12

PROBLEMS   OUTPUT   DEBUG CONSOLE   TERMINAL
-LAOqAyxo4rPw6pGXBMZ {'count': 9061, 'lastreferrer': 'https://difference-engine.com/Courses/tml-5-1118/', 'lastvisit': 1545316328750, 'page': '/etg/downloadpdf.html')
-LAOqOxg6kmP4jhnjQX5 {'count': 3896, 'lastreferrer': 'http://m.facebook.com', 'lastvisit': 1545312678263, 'page': '/')
-LAOrwciIQJZvuCAcyLO {'count': 3342, 'lastreferrer': 'https://alansimpson.me/', 'lastvisit': 1545311601815, 'page': '/html_css/index.html'}
-LAOs2nsVxxbjAwdJKxE {'count': 2220, 'lastreferrer': 'http://alansimpson.me/html_css/codequickies/dropdownmenu.html', 'lastvisit': 1545280814480, 'page': '/html_css/co
-LAOxq3sjFxnQoBnI5JX {'count': 2194, 'lastreferrer': 'https://alansimpson.me/firebase/hitcounter/', 'lastvisit': 1545308609977, 'page': '/index.html'}
-LAQ7ShbQRqOANEbOmm3O {'count': 1154, 'lastreferrer': 'http://alansimpson.me/javascript/code_quickies/clickdropdown/', 'lastvisit': 1544974827730, 'page': '/javascript
-LAQr56avlv0PuJGNm6P {'count': 1547, 'lastreferrer': '', 'lastvisit': 1545305365597, 'page': '/how/'}
-LI8iPwJ7nu3JUgiQORH {'count': 1439, 'lastreferrer': 'https://www.youtube.com', 'lastvisit': 1545315903301, 'page': '/datascience/beginner/'}
-LI2DFNAxvnT-CxYzhR- {'count': 1643, 'lastreferrer': '', 'lastvisit': 1545226502089, 'page': '/datascience/cheatsheets/'}

**FIGURE 2-5:**
Output from looping through and displaying keys and values from sub-dictionaries.

The output from this is the data from each dictionary, formatted in a way that's a little easier to read, as shown in Figure 2-6.

```
9061 1545316328750 /etg/downloadpdf.html          https://difference-engine.com/Courses/tml-5-1118/
3896 1545312678263 /                               http://m.facebook.com
3342 1545311601815 /html_css/index.html           https://alansimpson.me/
2220 1545280814480 /html_css/codequickies/         http://alansimpson.me/html_css/codequickies/dropdownmenu.html
2194 1545308609977 /index.html                     https://alansimpson.me/firebase/hitcounter/
1154 1544974827730 /javascript/code_quickies/      https://alansimpson.me/javascript/code_quickies/clickdropdown/
1547 1545305365597 /how/
1439 1545315903301 /datascience/beginner/          https://www.youtube.com/
1643 1545226502089 /datascience/cheatsheets/
```

**FIGURE 2-6:**
Output from showing one value at a time from each dictionary.

You may notice we've run into another weird situation with the `lastvisit` column. The date appears in the format *545316328750* rather than the more familiar *mm/dd/yyyy* format. This time we can't blame Excel because these dates were never in Excel. What you're seeing here is the Firebase timestamp of when the data item was last written to the database. This date is expressed as a UTC date, including the time down to the nanosecond. This's why the number is so long. Obviously, if you need people to be able to understand these dates, you need to translate them to Python dates, as we discuss next.

# Converting firebase timestamps to Python dates

As always, the first thing you need to do when working with dates and times in a Python app is to make sure you've imported the datetime module, which we usually do using the code import datetime as dt, in which the dt is an optional alias (a nickname that easier to type than the full name).

Because we know that the Firebase datetime is UTC-based, we know that we can use the datetime .utcfromtimestamp() method to convert it to Python time. But there is a catch. If you went strictly by the documentation you would expect this to work:

```
last_visit = dt.datetime.utcfromtimestamp(v['lastvisit'])
```

However, in Windows, apparently that nanosecond resolution is a bit much and this code raises an OS Error exception. Fortunately, there's an easy workaround. Dividing that lastvisit number by 1,000 trims off the last few digits, which gets the number into a lower-resolution datetime that Windows can stomach. All we really care about in this application is the date of the last visit; we don't care at all about the time. So you can grab just the date and get past the error by writing the code like this:

```
last_visit = dt.datetime.utcfromtimestamp(v['lastvisit']/1000).date()
```

What you end up with, then, in the last_visit variable is a simple Python date. So you can use a standard f-string to format the date however you like. For example, use this in your f-string to display that date:

```
{last_visit: %m/%d/%Y}
```

The dates will be in *mm/dd/yyyy* format in the output, like this:

```
12/20/2018
12/19/2018
12/17/2018
12/20/2018
11/30/2018
12/16/2018
12/20/2018
12/20/2018
12/19/2018
```

# Loading unkeyed JSON from a Python string

The `load()` method we used in the previous examples loaded the JSON data from a file. However, JSON data is always delivered in a text file, thus you can copy/paste the whole thing into a Python string. Typically you give the whole string a variable name and set it equal to some docstring that starts and ends with triple quotation marks. Put all the JSON data inside the triple quotation marks as in the following code. (To keep the code short, we've included data for only a couple of people, but at least you can see how the data is structured.)

```python
import json
# Here the JSON data is in a big string named json_string.
# It starts and the first triple quotation marks and extends
# down to the last triple quotation marks.
json_string = """
{
"people": [
    {
     "Full Name": "Angst, Annie",
     "Birth Year": 1982,
     "Date Joined": "01/11/2011",
     "Is Active": true,
     "Balance": 300
    },
    {
     "Full Name": "Schadenfreude, Sandy",
     "Birth Year": 2004,
     "Date Joined": "03/03/2003",
     "Is Active": true,
     "Balance": 0
    }
 ]
}
"""
```

Although it may be nice to be able to see all the data from within your code like that, there is one big disadvantage: You can't loop through a string to get to individual items of data. If you want to loop through, you need to load the JSON data from the string into some kind of object. To do this, use `json.loads()` (where the s is short for *from string*), as in the following code. As usual, `peep_data` is just a name we made up to differentiate the loaded JSON data from the data in the string:

```python
# Load JSON data from the big json_string string.
peep_data = json.loads(json_string)
```

Now that you have an object with which to work (peep_data), you can loop through and work with the code one bit at a time, like this:

```
# Now you can loop through the peep_data collection.
for p in peep_data['people']:
    print(p["Full Name"], p["Birth Year"], p["Date Joined"],p['Is
  Active'],p['Balance'])
```

Figure 2-7 shows all the code and the result of running that code in VS Code.

```
1    import json
2    # Here the JSON data is in a big string named json_string,
3    # It starts and the first triple quotation marks and extends
4    # down to the last triple quotation marks.
5    json_string = """
6    {
7    "people": [
8        {
9          "Full Name": "Angst, Annie",
10         "Birth Year": 1982,
11         "Date Joined": "01/11/2011",
12         "Is Active": true,
13         "Balance": 300
14       },
15     {
16         "Full Name": "Schadenfreude, Sandy",
17         "Birth Year": 2004,
18         "Date Joined": "03/03/2003",
19         "Is Active": true,
20         "Balance": 0
21       }
22    ]
23    }
24    """
25    # Load JSON data from the big json_string string.
26    peep_data = json.loads(json_string)
27
28    # Now you can loop through the peep_data collection.
29    for p in peep_data['people']:
30        print(p["Full Name"], p["Birth Year"], p["Date Joined"],p['Is Active'],p['Balance'])
31

PROBLEMS    OUTPUT    DEBUG CONSOLE    TERMINAL

Angst, Annie 1982 01/11/2011 True 300
Schadenfreude, Sandy 2004 03/03/2003 True 0
```

**FIGURE 2-7:** Output from showing one value at a time from each dictionary (see bottom of image).

# Loading keyed JSON from a Python string

Keyed data can also be stored in a Python string. In the following example, we used json_string as the variable name again, but as you can see, the data inside the string is structured a little differently. The first item has a key of 1 and the second item has a key of 2. But again, the code uses json.loads(json_string) to load this date from the string into a JSON object:

```
import json
# Here the JSON data is in a big string named json_string,
# It starts and the first triple quotation marks and extends
```

```
# down to the last triple quotation marks.
json_string = """
  {
  "1": {
    "count": 9061,
    "lastreferrer": "https://difference-engine.com/Courses/tml-5-1118/",
    "lastvisit": "12/20/2018",
    "page": "/etg/downloadpdf.html"
  },
  "2": {
    "count" : 3342,
    "lastreferrer" : "https://alansimpson.me/",
    "lastvisit" : "12/19/2018",
    "page" : "/html_css/index.html"
  }
  }
"""
# Load JSON data from the big json_string string.
hits_data = json.loads(json_string)

# Now you can loop through the hits_data collection.
for k, v in hits_data.items():
    print(f"{k}. {v['count']:>5} - {v['page']}")
```

The loop at the end prints the key, hit count, and page name from each item in the format shown in the following code. Note that this loop uses the two variables named k and v to loop through hits_data.items(), which is the standard syntax for looping through a dictionary of dictionaries:

```
1.  9061 - /etg/downloadpdf.html
2.  3342 - /html_css/index.html
```

## Changing JSON data

When you have JSON data in a data dictionary, you can use standard dictionary procedures (originally presented in Book 2, Chapter 4) to manipulate the data in the dictionary. As you're looping through the data dictionary with *key*, *value* variables, you can change the value of any *key:value* pair using the relatively simple syntax:

```
value['key'] = newdata
```

The *key* and *value* are just the k and v variables from the loop. For example, suppose you're looping through a dictionary created from the Firebase database, which includes a `lastvisit` field shown as a UTC Timestamp number. You want to change this timestamp to a string in a more familiar Python format. Set up a loop as in the following code, in which the first line inside the loop creates a new variable named `pydate` that contains the date as a Python date. Then the second line replaces the content of `v['lastvisit']` with this date in *mm/dd/yy* format:

```
for k, v in hits.items():
    # Convert the Firebase date to a Python date.
    pydate = dt.datetime.utcfromtimestamp(v['lastvisit']/1000).date()
    # In the dictionary, replace the Firebase date with string of Python date.
    v['lastvisit']= f"{pydate:%m/%d/%Y})"
```

When this loop is complete, all the values of the "lastvisit" column will be dates in *mm/dd/yyyy* format rather than the Firebase timestamp format.

## Removing data from a dictionary

To remove data from a dictionary as you're going through the loop, use the syntax `pop('keyname', None)`. Replace `'keyname'` with the name of the column you want to remove. For example, to remove all the `lastreferrer` key names and data from a dictionary created by the Firebase database JSON example, add `v.pop('lastreferrer', None)` to the loop.

Figure 2-8 shows an example where lines 1-8 import Firebase data into a Python object named hits. The line 10 starts a loop that goes through each key (k) and value (v) in the dictionary. Line 12 converts the timestamp to a Python date named `pydate`. Then line 16 replaces the `timestring` that was in the `lastvisit` column with that Python date as a string in *mm/dd/yyyy* format. Line 16, `v.pop('lastreferrer', None)`, removes the whole `lastreferrer` *key:value* pair from each dictionary. The final loop shows what's in the dictionary after making those changes.

Keep in mind that changes you make to the dictionary in Python have no effect on the file or string from which you loaded the JSON data. If you want to create a new JSON string or file, use the `json.dumps()` or `json.dump()` methods discussed next.

```
1    import json
2    import datetime as dt
3    # This is the Firebase JSON data (keyed).
4    filename = 'firebase_hitcounts.json'
5    # Open the file (standard file open stuff).
6    with open(filename, 'r', encoding='utf-8', newline='') as f:
7        # Load the whole json file into an object named hits
8        hits = json.load(f)
9
10   for k, v in hits.items():
11       # Convert the Firebase date to a Python date.
12       pydate = dt.datetime.utcfromtimestamp(v['lastvisit']/1000).date()
13       # In the dictionary, replace the Firebase date with string of Python date.
14       v['lastvisit']= f"{pydate:%m/%d/%Y}"
15       # Remove the entire last referrer column.
16       v.pop('lastreferrer', None)
17
18   # Now look at the lastvisit date in the hits dictionary.
19   for k, v in hits.items():
20       print(k,v)
21
22
```

```
PROBLEMS    OUTPUT    DEBUG CONSOLE    TERMINAL

-LAOqAyxxHrPw6pGXBMZ {'count': 9061, 'lastvisit': '12/20/2018)', 'page': '/etg/downloadpdf.html'}
-LAOqOxg6kmP4jhnjQXS {'count': 3896, 'lastvisit': '12/20/2018)', 'page': '/'}
-LAOrwciIQJZvuCAcyLO {'count': 3342, 'lastvisit': '12/20/2018)', 'page': '/html_css/index.html'}
-LAOs2nsVVxbjAwxUXxE {'count': 2220, 'lastvisit': '12/20/2018)', 'page': '/html_css/codequickies/'}
-LAOwqJsjfuoQxBWIS1X {'count': 2194, 'lastvisit': '12/20/2018)', 'page': '/index.html'}
-LAQ7ShbQPqOANbDmm3O {'count': 1154, 'lastvisit': '12/16/2018)', 'page': '/javascript/code_quickies/'}
-LAQrS6av1v0PuJGNm6P {'count': 1547, 'lastvisit': '12/20/2018)', 'page': '/how/'}
-LT0iPwZ7nu3IUgiQORH {'count': 1439, 'lastvisit': '12/20/2018)', 'page': '/datascience/beginner/'}
-LI2DFNAxVnT-cxYzWR- {'count': 1643, 'lastvisit': '12/19/2018)', 'page': '/datascience/cheatsheets/'}
```

**FIGURE 2-8:**
Changing the value of one key in each dictionary, and removing an entire *key:value* pair from the dictionary.

# Dumping Python Data to JSON

So far we've talked about bringing JSON data from the outside world into your app so Python can use its data. There may be times where you want to go the opposite direction, to take some data that's already in your app in a dictionary format and export it out to JSON to pass to another app, the public at large, or whatever. This is where the json.dump() and json.dumps() methods come into play. The dumps() method creates a JSON string of the data, which is still in memory where you can print() it to see it. For example, the previous code examples imported a Firebase database to a Python dictionary, then looped through that dictionary changing all the timestamps to *mm/dd/yyyy* dates, and also removing all the lastreferrer *key:value* pairs. So let's say you want to create a JSON string of this new dictionary. You could use dumps like this to create a string named new_dict, and you could also print that string to the console. The last two lines of code outside the loop would be:

```
#Looping is done, copy new dictionary to JSON string.
new_dict = json.dumps(hits)
print(new_dict)
```

The new_dict string would show in its native, not-very-readable format, which would look something like this:

```
{"-LAOqAyxxHrPw6pGXBMZ": {"count": 9061, "lastvisit": "12/20/2018)", "page":
            "/etg/downloadpdf.html"}, "-LAOqOxg6kmP4jhnjQXS": {"count": 3896,
            "lastvisit": "12/20/2018)", "page": "/"}, "-LAOrwciIQJZvuCAcyLO":
            {"count": 3342, "lastvisit": "12/20/2018)", "page":
            "/html_css/index.html"}, ... }}
```

Wee replaced some of the data with . . . because you don't need to see all the items to see how unreadable it looks.

Fortunately, the .dumps() method supports an indent= option in which you can specify how you want to indent the JSON data to make it more readable. Two spaces is usually sufficient. For example, add indent=2 to the code above as follows:

```python
#Looping is done, copy new dictionary to JSON string.
new_dict = json.dumps(hits, indent=2)
print(new_dict)
```

The output from this print() shows the JSON data in a much more readable format, as shown here:

```
{
  "-LAOqAyxxHrPw6pGXBMZ": {
    "count": 9061,
    "lastvisit": "12/20/2018)",
    "page": "/etg/downloadpdf.html"
  },
  "-LAOqOxg6kmP4jhnjQXS": {
    "count": 3896,
    "lastvisit": "12/20/2018)",
    "page": "/"
  },
  ...
}
```

If you use foreign or special characters in your data dictionary and you want to preserve them, add ensure_ascii=False to your code as follows:

```python
new_dict = json.dumps(hits, indent=2, ensure_ascii=False)
```

In our example, the key names in each dictionary are already in alphabetical order (count, lastvisit, page), so we wouldn't need to do anything to put them that way. But in your own code, if you want to ensure the keys in each dictionary are in alphabetical order, add sortkeys=True to your .dumps method as follows:

```python
new_dict = json.dumps(hits, indent=2, ensure_ascii=False, sort_keys=True)
```

If you want to output your JSON to a file, use `json.dump()` rather than `json.dumps()`. You can use `ensure_ascii=False` to maintain foreign characters, and `sort_keys = True` to alphabetize key names. You can also include an `indent=` option, although that would make the file larger and typically you want to keep files small to conserve space and minimize download time.

As an example, suppose you want to create a file named `hitcounts_new.json` (or if it already exists, open it to overwrite its content). You want to retain any foreign characters that you write to the file. Here's the code for that; the `'w'` is required to make sure the file opens for writing data into it:

```
with open('hitcounts_new.json', 'w', encoding='utf-8') as out_file:
```

Then, to copy the dictionary named `hits` as JSON into this file, use the name you assigned at the end of the code in the line above. Again, to retain any foreign characters and perhaps to alphabetize the key names in each dictionary, follow that line with this one, making sure this one is indented to be contained within the `with` block:

```
json.dump(hits, out_file, ensure_ascii=False, sort_keys=True)
```

Figure 2-9 shows all the code starting with the data that was exported from Firebase, looping through the dictionary that the import created, changing and removing some content, and then writing the new dictionary out to a new JSON file named `hitcounts_new.json`.

```
1    import json
2    import datetime as dt
3    # This is the Firebase JSON data (keyed).
4    filename = 'firebase_hitcounts.json'
5    # Open the file (standard file open stuff).
6    with open(filename, 'r', encoding='utf-8', newline='') as f:
7        # Load the whole json file into an object named hits.
8        hits = json.load(f)
9
10   # Loop through the new hits data dictionary.
11   for k, v in hits.items():
12       # Convert the Firebase date to a Python date.
13       pydate = dt.datetime.utcfromtimestamp(v['lastvisit']/1000).date()
14       # In the dictionary, replace the Firebase date with string of Python date.
15       v['lastvisit'] = f"{pydate:%m/%d/%Y}"
16       # Remove the entire last referrer column.
17       v.pop('lastreferrer', None)
18
19   # Write the modifed data to a JSON file named hitcounts_new.json.
20   with open('hitcounts_new.json', 'w', encoding='utf-8') as out_file:
21       json.dump(hits, out_file, ensure_ascii=False, sort_keys=True)
22
23   print('Done')
```

**FIGURE 2-9:** Writing modified Firebase data to a new JSON file named hitcounts_ new.json.

Figure 2-10 shows the contents of the `hitcounts_new.json` file after running the app. We didn't indent the JSON because files are really for storing or sharing, not for looking at, but you can still see the `datevisited` values are in the *mm/dd/yyyy* format and the `lastreferrer` *key:value* pair isn't in there, because earlier code removed that *key:value* pair.

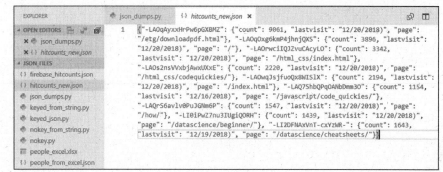

**FIGURE 2-10:**
Writing modified Firebase data to a new JSON file named `hitcounts_new.json`.

JSON is a very widely used format for storing and sharing data. Luckily Python has lots of built-in tools for consuming and creating JSON data. We've covered the most important capabilities here. But don't be shy about searching Google or YouTube for *python json* if you want to explore more.

Chapter **3**

# Interacting with the Internet

s you probably know, the Internet is home to virtually all the world's knowledge. Most of us use the World Wide Web (a.k.a. *the Web*) to find information all the time. We do so using a web browser like Safari, Google Chrome, Firefox, Opera, Internet Explorer, or Edge. To visit a website, you type a URL (uniform resource locator) into your browser's Address bar and press Enter, or you click a link that sends you to the page automatically.

As an alternative to browsing the Web with your web browser, you can access its content *programmatically*. In other words, you can use a programming language like Python to post information to the Web, as well as to access web information. In a sense, you make the Web your personal database of knowledge from which your apps can pluck information at will. In this chapter you learn about the two main modules for access the Web programmatically with Python: urllib and Beautiful Soup.

## How the Web Works

When you open up your web browser and type in a URL or click a link, that action sends a *request* to the Internet. The Internet directs your request to the appropriate web server, which in turn sends a *response* back to your computer. Typically that response is a *web page*, but it can be just about any file. Or it can be an error message if the thing you requested no longer exists at that location. But the important thing is that you the *user* (a human being), and your *user agent* (the program you're using to access the Internet) are on the *client* side of things. The *server*, which is just a computer, not a person, sends back its response, as illustrated in Figure 3-1.

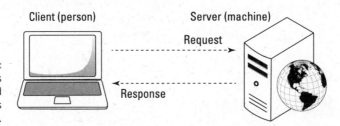

Client (person)   Server (machine)

Request

Response

**FIGURE 3-1:**
The client makes a request, and the server sends back a response.

## Understanding the mysterious URL

The URL is a key part of the whole transaction, because that's how the Internet finds the resource you're seeking. On the Web, all resources use the Hypertext Transfer Protocol (HTTP), and thus their URLs start with `http://` or `https://`. The difference is that `http://` sends stuff across the wire in its raw form, which makes it susceptible to hackers and others who can "sniff out" the traffic. The `https` protocol is *secure* in that the data is *encrypted*, which means it's been converted to a secret code that's not so easy to read. Typically, any site with whom you do business and to whom you transmit sensitive information like passwords and credit card numbers, uses `https` to keep that information secret and secure.

The URL for any website can be relatively simple, such as Alan's URL of `https://AlanSimpson.me`. Or it can be complex to add more information to the request. Figure 3-2 shows parts of a URL, some of which you may have noticed in the past.

Note that the order matters. For example, it's possible for a URL to contain a path to a specific folder or page (starting with a slash right after the domain name). The URL can also contain a query string, which is always last and always starts with a question mark (?). After the question mark comes one or more *name=value* pairs, basically the same syntax you've seen in data dictionaries and JSON. If there are multiple *name=value* pairs, they are separated by ampersands.

**TECHNICAL STUFF**

A # followed by a name after the page name at the end of a URL is called a *fragment*, which indicates a particular place on the target page. Behind the scenes in the code of the page is usually a `<a id="`*name*`"></a>` tag that directs the browser to a spot on the page to which it should jump after it opens the page.

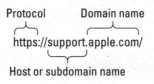

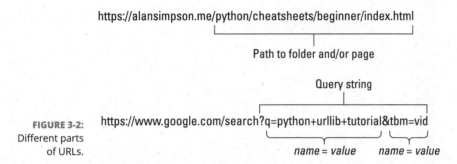

**FIGURE 3-2:**
Different parts
of URLs.

# Exposing the HTTP headers

When you're using the Web, all you really care about is the stuff you see on your screen. At a deeper, somewhat hidden level, the two computers involved in the transaction are communicating with one another through *HTTP headers*. The headers are not normally visible to the human eye, but they are accessible to Python, your web browser, and other programs. You can choose to see the headers if you want, and actually doing so can be very handy when writing code to access the Web. The product we use most often to view the headers is called HTTP Headers, which is a Google Chrome extension. If you have Chrome and want to try it for yourself, use Chrome to browse to `https://www.esolutions.se/`, scroll down to Google Chrome Extensions, click HTTP Headers, and follow the instructions to install the extension. To see the headers involved whenever you've just visited a site, click the HTTP Headers icon in your Chrome toolbar (it looks like a cloud) and you'll see the HTTP header information as in Figure 3-3.

Two of the most important things in the HTTP Headers are right at the top, where you see GET followed by a URL. This tells you that a GET request was sent, meaning that the URL is just a request for information, nothing is being uploaded to the server. The URL after the word GET is the resource that was requested. Another type of response is POST, and that means there's some information you're sending to the server, such as when you *post* something on Facebook, Twitter, or any other site that accepts input from you.

The second line below the GET shows the status of the request. The first part indicates the protocol used. In the example in Figure 3-4, this is HTTP1.1, which just means it's a web request that's following the HTTP version 1.1 rules of communication. The 200 number is the status code, which in this case means "okay, everything went well." Common status codes are listed in Table 3-1.

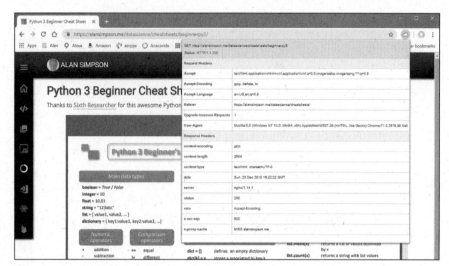

**FIGURE 3-3:**
Inspecting HTTP headers with Google Chrome.

GET https://alansimpson.me/datascience/cheatsheets/beginnerpy3/

Status: HTTP/1.1 200

| Request Headers | |
|---|---|
| Accept | text/html,application/xhtml+xml,application/xml;q=0.9,image/webp,image/apng,*/*;q=0.8 |
| Accept-Encoding | gzip, deflate, br |
| Accept-Language | en-US,en;q=0.9 |
| Referer | https://alansimpson.me/datascience/cheatsheets/ |
| Upgrade-Insecure-Requests | 1 |
| User-Agent | Mozilla/5.0 (Windows NT 10.0; Win64; x64) AppleWebKit/537.36 (KHTML, like Gecko) Ch |
| Response Headers | |

**FIGURE 3-4:**
HTTP headers.

**TABLE 3-1**

## Common HTTP Status Codes

| Code | Meaning | Reason |
|---|---|---|
| 200 | Okay | No problems. |
| 400 | Bad Request | Server is available, but can't make sense of your request, usually because there's something wrong with your URL. |
| 403 | Forbidden | Site has detected you're accessing it programmatically, and doesn't allow that. |
| 404 | Not found | Either the URL is wrong, or the URL is right but the content that was there originally isn't there anymore. |

All of what we've been telling you here matters because it's all related to accessing the Web programmatically with Python, as you'll see next.

# Opening a URL from Python

To access the Web from within a Python program, you need to use aspects of the urllib package. The name *urllib* is short for *URL Library*. This one library actually consists of modules, each of which provides capabilities that are useful for different aspects of accessing the Internet programmatically. Table 3-2 summarizes the packages.

**TABLE 3-2**

### Packages from the Python urllib Library

| Package | Purpose |
| --- | --- |
| request | Use this to open URLs |
| response | Internal code that handles the response that arrived; you don't need to work with that directly |
| error | Handles request exceptions |
| parse | Breaks up the url into smaller chunks |
| robotparser | Analyzes a site's robots.txt file, which grants permissions to bots that are trying to access the site programmatically |

Most of the time you'll likely work with the request module, because that's the one that allows you to open resources from the Internet. The syntax for accessing a simple package from a library is

```
from library import module
```

. . . where `library` is the name of the larger library, and `module` is the name of the specific module. To access the capabilities of the response module of urllib, use this syntax at the top of your code (the comment above the code is optional):

```
# import the request module from urllib library.
from urllib import request
```

To open a web page, use this syntax:

```
variablename = request.urlopen(url)
```

Replace *variablename* with any variable name of your own choosing. Request *url* with the URL of the resource you want to access. You must enclose it in single- or double-quotation marks unless it's stored in a variable. If the URL is already stored in some variable, then just the variable name without quotation marks will work.

When running the code, the result will be an HTTPResponse object.

As an example, here is some code you can run in a Jupyter notebook or any .py file to access a sample HTML page Alan added to his own site just for this purpose:

```
# import the request module from urllib library.
from urllib import request
# URL (address) of the desired page.
sample_url = 'https://AlanSimpson.me/python/sample.html'
# Request the page and put it in a variables named the page.
thepage = request.urlopen(sample_url)
# Put the response code in a variable named status.
status = thepage.code
# What is the data type of the page?
print(type(thepage))
# What is the status code?
print(status)
```

Running this code displays this output:

```
<class 'http.client.HTTPResponse'>
200
```

This is telling you that the variable named thepage contains an http.client. HTTPResponse object . . . which is everything the server sent back in response to the request. The 200 is the status code that's telling you all went well.

# Posting to the Web with Python

Not all attempts to access web resources will go as smoothly as the previous example. For example, type this URL into your browser's Address bar, and press Enter:

```
https://www.google.com/search?q=python web scraping tutorial
```

Google returns a search result of many pages and videos that contain the words *python web scraping tutorial.* If you look at the Address bar, you may notice that the

URL you typed has changed slightly and that blank spaces have all be replaced with %20, as in the following line of code:

```
https://www.google.com/search?q=python%20web%20scraping%20tutorial
```

That %20 is the ASCII code, in hex, for a space, and the browser just does that to avoid sending the actual spaces in the URL. Not a big deal.

So now, let's see what happens if you run the same code as above but with the Google URL rather than the original URL. Here is that code:

```
from urllib import request
# URL (address) of the desired page.
sample_url = ' https://www.google.com/search?q=python%20web%20scraping%20
    tutorial'
# Request the page and put it in a variables named the page.
thepage = request.urlopen(sample_url)
# Put the response code in a variable named status.
status = thepage.code
# What is the data type of the page?
print(type(thepage))
# What is the status code?
print(status)
```

When you run this code, things don't go so smoothly. You may see several error messages, but the most important one is the one that usually reads something like this:

```
HTTPError: HTTP Error 403: Forbidden
```

The "error" isn't with your coding. Rather, it's an HTTP error. Specifically, it's error number 403 for "Forbidden." Basically your code worked. That is, the URL was sent to Google. But Google replied with "Sorry, you can search our site from your browser, but not from Python code like that." Google isn't the only site that does that. Many big sites reject attempts to access their content programmatically, in part to protect their rights to their own content, and in part to have some control over the incoming traffic.

The good news is, sites that don't allow you to post directly using Python or some other programming language often *do* allow you to post content. But you have to do so through their API (application programming interface). You can still use Python as your programming language. You just have to abide by their rules when doing so.

An easy way to find out whether a site has such an API is to simply Google your intention and language. For example, *post to facebook with python* or *post to twitter with python* or something like that. We won't attempt to provide an example here of actually doing such a thing, because they tend to change the rules often and anything we say may be outdated by the time you read this. But a Google search should get you want you need to know. If you get lots of results, focus on the ones that were posted most recently.

# Scraping the Web with Python

Whenever you request a page from the Web, it's delivered to you as a *web page* usually consisting of HTML and *content*. The HTML is markup code that, in conjunction with another language called CSS, tells the browser *how* to display the content in terms of size, position, font, images, and all other such visual, stylistic matters. In our web browser, you don't see that HTML or CSS code. You see only the *content*, which is generally contained within blocks of HTML code in the page.

As a working example we're going to use the relatively simple page shown in Figure 3-5.

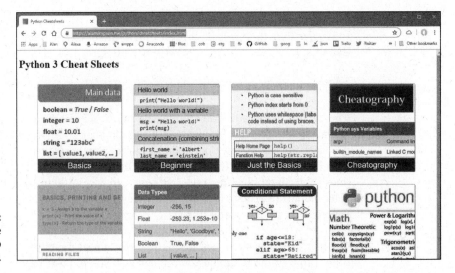

**FIGURE 3-5:**
Sample page used for web scraping.

The code that tells the browser how to display that page's content isn't visible in the browser, unless you view the *source code*. In most browsers, you can do that by pressing the F12 key or by right-clicking an empty spot on the page and choosing View Source or Inspect or some other such option, depending on the brand and version you're using. In most web pages, the real content — the stuff you see in the browser — is between the ‹body› ... ‹/body› tags. Within the body of the page, there may be sections for a header, navigation bar footer, perhaps ads, or whatever. In that particular page, the real "meat" of the content is between ‹article› ... ‹/article› tags. Each card that you see in the browser is defined as a link in ‹a› ... ‹/a› tags.

Figure 3-6 shows some of the HTML code for the page in Figure 3-3. We're only showing code for the first two links in the page, but all the links follow the same structure. And they are all contained within the section denoted by a pair of ‹article› ... ‹/article› tags.

**FIGURE 3-6:**
Some of the code from the sample page for web scraping.

```
<body>
    <h1>Python 3 Cheat Sheets</h1>
    <article>
        <a href="http://www.sixthresearcher.com/python-3-reference-cheat-sheet-for-beginners/">
            <img src="../../datascience/python/basics/basics256.jpg" alt="Python Basics Cheat Sheet">
            <span>Basics</span>
        </a>
        <a href="https://alansimpson.me/datascience/python/beginner/">
            <img src="../../datascience/python/beginner/beginner256.jpg" alt="Python Beginner Cheat Sheet">
            <span>Beginner</span>
        </a>
    </article>
</body>
```

Notice that each link consists of several tags, as summarized here:

» ‹a› ... ‹/a›: The a (sometimes called *anchor*) tags define where the browser should take the user when they click the link. The href= part of the ‹a› tag is the exact URL of the page to which the user should be taken.

» ‹img›: The img tag defines the image that shows for each link. The src= attribute in that tag defines the *source* of the image — in other words, the exact location and filename to show for that link.

» ‹span› ... ‹/span›: At the bottom of the link is some text enclosed in ‹span› ... ‹/span› tags. That text appears at the bottom of each link as white text against a black background.

The term *web scraping* refers to opening a web page, in order to pick its information apart programmatically for use in some other manner. Python has great web scraping capabilities, and this is a hot topic most people want to learn about. So for the first parts of this chapter we'll focus on that, using the sample page we just showed you as our working example.

TECHNICAL STUFF

The term *screen scraping* is also used as a synonym for *web scraping*. Though, as you'll see here, you're not actually scraping content from the computer screen. You're scraping it from the file that gets sent to the browser so that the browser can display the information on your screen.

In the Python code, you'll need to import two modules, both of which come with Anaconda so you should already have them. One of them is the `request` module from urllib (short for URL Library), which allows you to send a request out to the Web for a resource and to read what the Web serves back. The second is called `BeautifulSoup`, from a song in the book *Alice in Wonderland*. That one provides tools for parsing the web page that you've retrieved for specific items of data in which you're interested. So to get started, open up a Jupyter notebook or create a .py file in VS Code and type the first two lines as follows:

```
# Get request module from url library.
from urllib import request
# This one has handy tools for scraping a web page.
from bs4 import BeautifulSoup
```

Next, you need to tell Python where the page of interest is located on the Internet. In this case, the URL is

```
https://alansimpson.me/python/scrape_sample.html
```

You can verify this by typing the URL into the Address bar of your browser and pressing Enter. But to scrape the page, you'll need to put that URL in your Python code. You can give it a short name, like `page_url`, by assigning it to a variable like this:

```
# Sample page for practice.
page_url = 'https://alansimpson.me/python/scrape_sample.html'
```

To get the web page at that location into your Python app, create another variable, which we'll call `rawpage`, and use the `urlopen` method of the `request` module to read in the page. Here is how that code looks:

```
# Open that page.
rawpage = request.urlopen(page_url)
```

To make it relatively easy to parse that page in subsequent code, copy it over a `BeautifulSoup` object. We'll name the object `soup` in our code. You'll also have to tell `BeautifulSoup` how you want the page parsed. You can use `html5lib`, which also comes with Anaconda. So just add these lines:

```
# Make a BeautifulSoup object from the html page.
soup = BeautifulSoup(rawpage, 'html5lib')
```

# Parsing part of a page

Most web pages contain lots of code for content in the header, footer, sidebars, ads, and whatever else is going on in the page. The main content is often just in one section. If you can identify just that section, your parsing code will run more quickly. In this example, in which we created the web page ourselves, we put all the main content between a pair of <article> ... </article> tags. In the following code, we assign that block of code to a variable named content. Later code in the page will parse only that part of the page, which can help improve speed and accuracy.

```
# Isolate the main content block.
content = soup.article
```

# Storing the parsed content

You goal, when scraping a web page, is typically to collect just specific data of interest. In this case, we just want the URL, image source, and text for a number of links. We know there will be more than one line. An easy way to store these, for starters, would be to put them in a list. In this code we create an empty list named links_list for that purpose using this code:

```
# Create an empty list for dictionary items.
links_list = []
```

Next the code needs to loop through each link tag in the page content. Each of those starts and ends with an <a> tag. To tell Python to loop through each link individually, use the find_all method of BeautifulSoup in a loop. In the code below, as we loop through the links, we assign the current link to a variable named link:

```
# Loop through all the links in the article.
for link in content.find_all('a'):
```

Each link's code will look something like this, though each will have a unique URL, image source, and text:

```
<a href="https://alansimpson.me/datascience/python/lists/">
    <img src="../datascience/python/lists/lists256.jpg" alt="Python lists">
    <span>Lists</span>
</a>
```

The three items of data we want are:

>> The link url, which is enclosed in quotation marks after the href= in the <a> tag.

>> The image source, which is enclosed in quotation marks after src= in the img tag.

>> The link text, which is enclosed in <span> ... </span> tags.

The following code teases out each of those components by using the .get() method on BeautifulSoup to isolate something inside the link (that is, in between the <a> and </a> tags that mark the beginning and end of each link). To get the URL portion of the link and put it in a variable named url, we use this code:

```
url = link.get('href')
```

You have to make sure to indent that under the loop so it's executed for each link. To get the image source and put it in a variable named img we used this code:

```
img = link.img.get('src')
```

The text is between <span> ... </span> text near the bottom of the link. To grab that and put it into a variable named text, add this line of code:

```
text = link.span.text
```

You don't have to use .get() for that because the text isn't in an HTML attribute like href= or src=. It's just text between <span> ... </span> tags.

Finally, you need to save all that before going to the next link in the page. An easy way to do that is to append all three items of data to the links_list using this code:

```
links_list.append({'url' : url, 'img': img, 'text': text})
```

That's it for storing all the data for one link with each pass through the loop. There is one other caveat, though. Web browsers are very forgiving of errors in HTML code. So it's possible there will be mistyped code or missing code here and there that could cause the loop to fail. Typically this will be in the form of an attribute error, where Python can't find some attribute. If there's data missing, we prefer that the Python just skip the bad line and then keep going, rather then crash-and-burn leaving us with no data at all. So we should put the whole business of grabbing the parts in a try: block, which, if it fails, allows Python to just skip that one link and move onto the next. The code for that looks like this:

```
# Try to get the href, image url, and text.
try:
    url = link.get('href')
    img = link.img.get('src')
```

```
        text = link.span.text
        links_list.append({'url' : url, 'img': img, 'text': text})
    # If the row is missing anything...
    except AttributeError:
        #... skip it, don't blow up.
        pass
```

Figure 3-7 shows all the code as it stands right now. If you run it like that, you'd end up with the link_list being filled with all the data you scraped. But that doesn't do you much good. Chances are, you're going to want to save it as data to use elsewhere. You can do so by saving the data to a JSON file, a CSV file, or both, whatever is most convenient for you. In the sections that follow we show you how to do both.

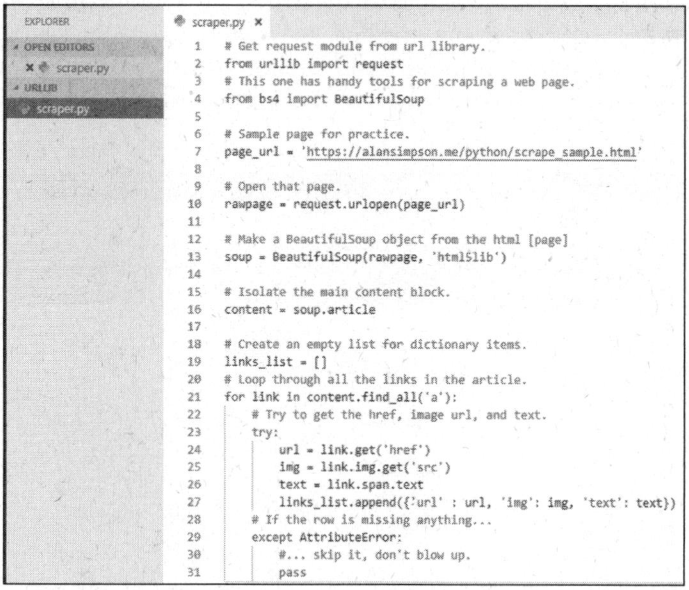

**FIGURE 3-7:**
Web scraping code complete.

## Saving scraped data to a JSON file

To save the scraped data to a JSON file, first import the json module near the top of your code, like this:

```
# If you want to dump data to json file.
import json
```

Then, below the loop (not indented, because you don't want to repeat the code for each pass through the loop), first open a file, for writing, using this code. You can name you file anything you like. We've opted to name ours `links.json`, as you can see in the following code:

```
# Save as a JSON file.
with open('links.json', 'w', encoding='utf-8') as links_file:
```

Then finally, indented under that line, use `json.dump()` to dump the contents of `links_list` to that JSON file. We typically add `ensure_ascii=false` just to preserve any foreign characters, but that is entirely optional:

```
    json.dump(links_list, links_file, ensure_ascii=False)
```

That's it! After you run the code you'll have a file named `links.json` that contains all the scraped data in JSON format. If you open it from VS Code, it will look like one long line, because we didn't add any line breaks or spaces to indent. But when you see it as one long line, you can copy/paste the whole thing to a site like `jsonformatter.org`, which will display the data in a more readable format without changing the content of the file, as in Figure 3-8.

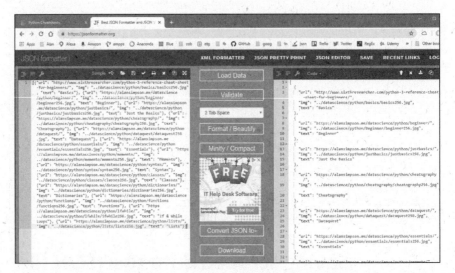

**FIGURE 3-8:** Web scraped data in a JSON file.

## Saving scraped data to a CSV file

If, for whatever reason, you prefer to go straight to a CSV file with our scraped data, start by importing the `csv` module near the top of your code, like this:

```
# If you want to save to CSV.
import csv
```

Then, down below and outside of the loop that creates `links_list`, open in write mode a file with the filename of your choosing. In the following code we named ours `links.csv`. We also used `newline=''` to avoid putting in an extra newline at the end of each row.

```
# Save it to a CSV.
with open('links.csv', 'w', newline='') as csv_out:
```

Indented below that `open`, create a `csv` writer that targets the file based on the name you assigned at the end of the `with . . .` line:

```
csv_writer = csv.writer(csv_out)
```

The first row of a CSV typically contains field names (or column headings, as they're also called). So the next step is to add that row to the table, using whatever names you want to apply to headings, like this:

```
# Create the header row
csv_writer.writerow(['url','img','text'])
```

Then you can write all the data from `link_list` to the CSV file by looping through `link_list` and writing the three items of data, separated by commas, to new rows. Here is that code:

```
for row in links_list:
    csv_writer.writerow([str(row['url']),str(row['img']),str(row['text'])])
```

Running the code produces a file named `links.csv`. If you open that file in Excel or another spreadsheet app, you'll see that the data is neatly organized into a table with columns labeled `url`, `img`, and `text`, as in Figure 3-9.

| | A | B | C |
|---|---|---|---|
| 1 | url | img | text |
| 2 | http://www.sixthresearcher.com/python-3-reference-cheat-sheet | ../datascience/python/basics/basics256.jpg | Basics |
| 3 | https://alansimpson.me/datascience/python/beginner/ | ../datascience/python/beginner/beginner256.jpg | Beginner |
| 4 | https://alansimpson.me/datascience/python/justbasics/ | ../datascience/python/justbasics/justbasics256.jpg | Just the Basics |
| 5 | https://alansimpson.me/datascience/python/cheatography/ | ../datascience/python/cheatography/cheatography256.jpg | Cheatography |
| 6 | https://alansimpson.me/datascience/python/dataquest/ | ../datascience/python/dataquest/dataquest256.jpg | Dataquest |
| 7 | https://alansimpson.me/datascience/python/essentials/ | ../datascience/python/essentials/essentials256.jpg | Essentials |
| 8 | https://alansimpson.me/datascience/python/memento/ | ../datascience/python/memento/memento256.jpg | Memento |
| 9 | https://alansimpson.me/datascience/python/syntax/ | ../datascience/python/syntax/syntax256.jpg | Syntax |
| 10 | https://alansimpson.me/datascience/python/classes/ | ../datascience/python/classes/classes256.jpg | Classes |
| 11 | https://alansimpson.me/datascience/python/dictionaries/ | ../datascience/python/dictionaries/dictionaries256.jpg | Dictionaries |
| 12 | https://alansimpson.me/datascience/python/functions/ | ../datascience/python/functions/functions256.jpg | Functions |
| 13 | https://alansimpson.me/datascience/python/ifwhile/ | ../datascience/python/ifwhile/ifwhile256.jpg | If & While Loops |
| 14 | https://alansimpson.me/datascience/python/lists/ | ../datascience/python/lists/lists256.jpg | Lists |

**FIGURE 3-9:** Web scraped data in Excel.

Figure 3-10 shows all the code for scraping both to JSON and CSV. We removed some comments from the top of the code to get it to all fit in one screenshot. But we just wanted to make sure you can see it all on one place. Seeing all the code in the proper order like that should help you debug your own code, if need be.

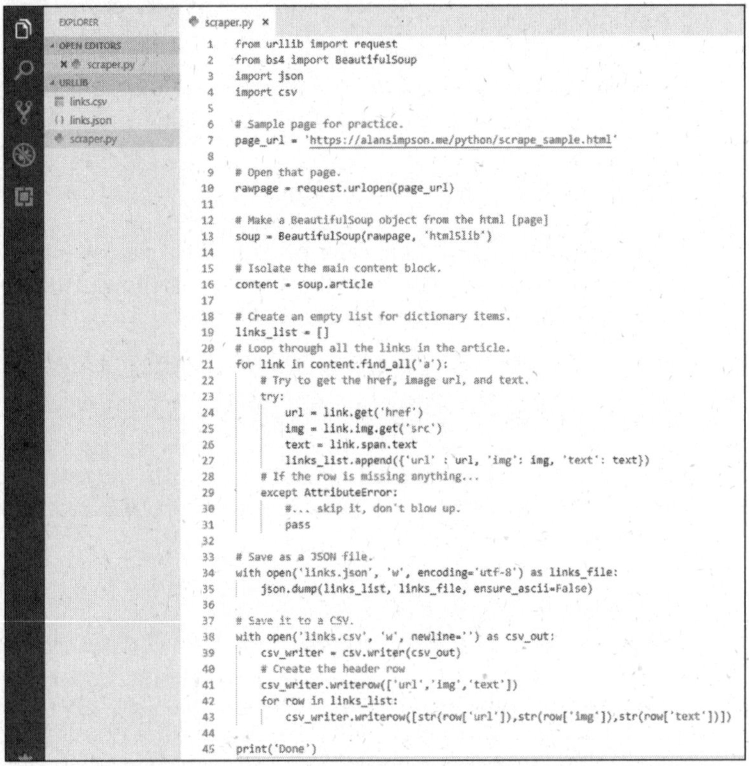

**FIGURE 3-10:**
The entire
scraper.py
program.

Accessing the Web programmatically opens whole new worlds of possibilities for acquiring and organizing knowledge. In fact, there is a whole field of study, called data science, that's all about just that. There are many specialized tools available too, that go far beyond what you've learned here. These you'll learn about in Book 5 of this book.

But before launching into the more advanced and specialized applications of Python, there is just one more fundamental concept we need to discuss. Throughout these first chapters you've used many different kinds of libraries and modules and such. In the next chapter you learn just how far-reaching that is, and how to look for, and find, what you need when you need it.

# Chapter **4**

# Libraries, Packages, and Modules

For the most part, all the chapters leading up to this one have focused on the core Python language, the elements of the language you'll need no matter how you intend to use Python in the future. But as you've seen, many programs start by importing one or more modules. Each module is essentially a collection of pre-written code that you can use in your own code without having to reinvent that wheel. The granddaddy of all this pre-written specialized code is called the Python standard library.

## Understanding the Python Standard Library

The Python standard library is basically all the stuff you get when you get the Python languages. That includes all the Python data types like string, integer, float, and Boolean. Every instance of those data types is actually an instance of a class defined in the standard library. For this reason, the terms *type*, *instance*, and *object* are often used interchangeably. An integer is a whole number; it's also a data type in Python. But it exists because the standard library contains a class for integers, and every integer you create is actually an instance of that class and hence an object (because classes are the templates for things called objects).

The `type()` function in Python usually identifies the type of a piece of data. For example, run these two lines of code at a Python prompt, in a Jupyter notebook or a .py file:

```
x = 3
print(type(x))
```

The output is:

```
<class 'int'>
```

This is telling you that x is an integer, and also that it's an instance of the `int` class from the standard library. Running this code:

```
x = 'howdy'
print(type(x))
```

Produces this output:

```
<class 'str'>
```

That is, x contains data that's the string data type, created by the Python `str` class. The same thing works for a float (a numeric value with a decimal point, like 3.14) and for Booleans (`True` or `False`).

## Using the dir() function

The Python standard library offers a `dir()` method that displays a list of all the attributes associated with a type. For example, in the previous example the result `<class 'str'>` tells you that the data is the `str` data type. So you know that's a type, and thus in instance of a class called `str` (short for *string*). Entering this command:

```
dir(str)
```

Displays something like this:

```
['__add__', '__class__', '__contains__', '__delattr__', '__dir__', '__doc__',
    '__eq__', '__format__', '__ge__', '__getattribute__', '__getitem__',
    '__getnewargs__', '__gt__', '__hash__', '__init__','__init_subclass__',
    '__iter__', '__le__', '__len__', '__lt__', '__mod__', '__mul__', '__ne__',
    '__new__', '__reduce__', '__reduce_ex__', '__repr__', '__rmod__', '__rmul__',
    '__setattr__', '__sizeof__', '__str__', '__subclasshook__', 'capitalize',
    'casefold', 'center', 'count', 'encode', 'endswith', 'expandtabs', 'find',
```

```
'format', 'format_map', 'index', 'isalnum', 'isalpha', 'isascii',
'isdecimal', 'isdigit', 'isidentifier', 'islower', 'isnumeric',
'isprintable', 'isspace', 'istitle', 'isupper', 'join', 'ljust', 'lower',
'lstrip', 'maketrans', 'partition', 'replace', 'rfind', 'rindex', 'rjust',
'rpartition', 'rsplit', 'rstrip', 'split', 'splitlines', 'startswith',
'strip', 'swapcase', 'title', 'translate', 'upper', 'zfill']
```

The dunder named items (the names surrounded by double-underlines) usually represent something that's built into Python and that plays some role in the language that you don't necessarily access directly. These are often referred to as *special variables* or *magic methods*. For example, there's an __add__ method that's actually invoked by using the + (addition) operator to add two numbers or join together two strings.

The regular functions don't have the double underscores and are typically followed by parentheses. For example, take a look at these lines of code:

```
x = "Howdy"
print(type(x), x.isalpha(), x.upper())
```

The output from that code is:

```
<class 'str'> True HOWDY
```

The first part, <class 'str'> tells you that x contains a string. As such, you can use any of the attributes shown in the output of dir(str) on it. For example, the True is the output from x.isalpha() because x does contain alphabetic characters. The HOWDY is the output of x.upper(), which converts the string to all uppercase letters.

Beginners often wonder what good seeing a bunch of names like 'capitalize', 'casefold', 'center', 'count', 'encode', 'endswith', 'expandtabs', 'find', 'format', and so forth does for you when you don't know what the names mean or how to use them. Well, they don't really help you much if you don't pursue it any further. You can get some more detailed information by using help() rather than dir.

## Using the help() function

The Python prompt also offers a help() function with the syntax:

```
help(object)
```

To use it, replace *object* with the object type with which you're seeking help. For example, to get help with `str` objects (strings, which come from the `str` class) enter this command at the Python prompt:

```
help(str)
```

The output will be more substantial information about the topic in the parentheses. For example, where `dir(str)` lists the names of attributes of that type, `help(dir)` provides more detail about each item. For example, whereas `dir(str)` tells you that there's a thing called `capitalize` in the `str` class, `help` tells you a bit more about it, as follows:

```
capitalize(self, /)
  Return a capitalized version of the string.
  More specifically, make the first character have upper case and the rest lower
    case.
```

The word `self` there just means that whatever word you pass to `capitalize` is what gets capitalized. The / at the end marks the end of positional-only parameters, meaning that you can't use keywords with parameters after that like you can when defining your own functions. What usually works best for most people is a more in-depth explanation and one or more examples. For those, Google or a similar search engine is usually your best bet. Start the search with the word *Python* (so it knows what the search is in reference too) followed by the exact word with which your seeking assistance. For example, searching Google for

```
python capitalize
```

. . . provides links to lots of different resources for learning about the `capitalize` attribute of the `str` object, including examples of its use.

TIP

If you get tired of pressing any key to get past More . . . at the end of every page in help, just press Ctrl+C. This gets you back to the Python prompt.

Of course, a really good (albeit technical) resource for the Python standard library is the standard library documentation itself. This is always available at https://docs.python.org/ usually under the link Library Reference. But even that wording may change, so if in doubt, just google *python standard library*. Just be forewarned that it is huge and very technical. So don't expect to memorize or even understand it all right off the bat. Use it as an ongoing resource to learn about things that interest you as your knowledge of Python develops.

The documentation that appears at docs.python.org will generally be for the current stable version. Links to older versions, and to any newer versions that may be in the works when you visit, are available from links at the left side of the page.

## Exploring built-in functions

Both dir() and help() are examples of Python built-in functions. These are functions that are always available to you in Python, in any app you're creating as well as at the Python command prompt. These built-in functions are also a part of the standard library. In fact, if you google *Python built-in functions*, some of the search results will point directly to the Python documentation. Clicking that link will open that section of the standard library documentation and displays a table of all the built-in functions, as in Figure 4-1. On that page, you can click the name of any function to learn more about it.

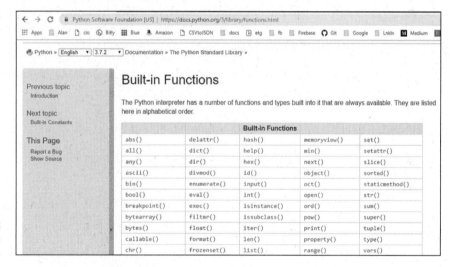

**FIGURE 4-1:**
Python's built-in functions.

# Exploring Python Packages

The Python language supports *modular programming*, where the idea is that there's no need for every individual programmer to reinvent everything herself. Even the largest projects can be broken down into smaller, more manageable components or modules. And in fact, a large project may actually require some components that already exist out there in the world somewhere, because somebody already needed the functionality and spent the time to create, test, and debug it.

Any large project, whether you're working alone or as a team member, can simplified and streamlined if some components can use tried-and-true code that's already been written, tested, debugged, and deemed reliable by members of the Python programming community. The *packages* you hear about in relation to Python are exactly that kind of code — code that's been developed and nurtured, is trustworthy, and generic enough that it can be used as a component of some large project that you're working on.

There are literally thousands of packages available for Python. A good resource for finding packages is PyPi, a clever name that's easy to remember and short for *Python Package Index*. You can check it out at any time using any browser and the URL `https://pypi.org/`. There is also a program named pip, another clever name, which stands for *Pip Installs Packages*. It's commonly referred to as a *package manager* because you can also use it to explore, update, and remove existing packages.

To use pip, you have to get to your operating system's command prompt, which is Terminal on a Mac, or `cmd.exe` or Powershell in Windows. If you're using VS Code, the simplest way to get there is to open VS Code and choose View⇨Terminal from its menu bar.

If you already have pip, typing this command at a command prompt will tell you which version of pip is currently installed:

```
pip --version
```

The result will likely look something like this (but with your version's numbers and names):

```
pip 18.1 from C:\Users\...\AppData\Local\Continuum\anaconda3\lib\site-packages\
    pip (python 3.7)
```

To see what packages you already have installed, enter this at the operating system command prompt:

```
pip list
```

Most people are surprised at how many packages they already have installed. It's a very lengthy list, and you have to scroll up and down quite a bit to see all the names. However, one of the advantages of installing Python with Anaconda is that you get lots of great packages in the mix. And you don't have to rely on `pip list` to find their names. Instead, just open Anaconda Navigator and click Environments in the left column. You'll see a list of all your installed packages, along with a brief description and version number for each, as shown in the example in Figure 4-2.

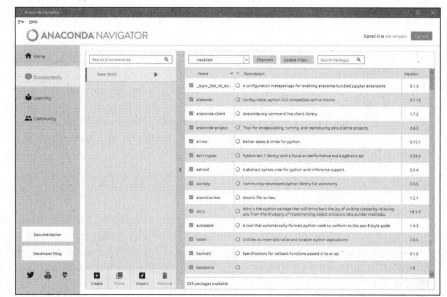

**FIGURE 4-2:**
Installed
packages as
viewed in
Anaconda.

**TIP**

See Book 1 for more information on installing and using Anaconda.

Although it's perfectly okay to use pip to install any packages that you don't already have, the one disadvantage is that those packages may not show up in Anaconda Navigator's list of installed packages. To get around that, any time you see an instruction to *pip* something to install it, you can try replacing the word *pip* with the word *conda* (short for Anaconda). This adds the package to your collection, so it will show up both when you do `pip list` and when you look at the list in Anaconda Navigator.

# Importing Python Modules

You'll hear the word *module* used in conjunction with Python all the time. If you think of the standard library as an actual physical library, and a package as being, perhaps, one book in that library, then you can think of a module as being one chapter in one book. In other words, a package may contain many modules, and a library may contain many packages. The module is a big part of what makes Python a modular language, because code is grouped together according to function. So in the one hand, you don't have to import everything including the kitchen sink to use *some* code. By the same token, if you need to use several related things, such as functions for working with dates and times, you don't have to import them all one at a time. Typically, importing just the whole module will get you what you need. For example, to work with dates and times, you don't have to import every Python module out there. Nor do you need to import every possible little function and object one at a time. You just import the whole module, like datetime, to get lots of handy things for working with dates and times.

There are actually a few ways to import functionality from modules. One of the most common is to simply import the whole module. To do that, you just follow the import command with the name of the module you want to import. For example, this imports the entire math module, which has lots of functions and stuff for doing math:

```
import math
```

After you import a module, the dir() and help() functions work on that too. For example, if you tried doing dir(math) or help(math) before import math, you'd get an error. That's because that math package isn't part of the standard library. However, if you do import math first, and then help(math), then it all works.

There may be times where you don't really need the whole kit-and-caboodle. In those cases, you can import just what you need using a syntax like this:

```
from math import pi
```

In this example, you're just importing one thing (pi), so you're not bringing in unnecessary stuff. The second example is also handy because in your code you can refer to pi as just pi, you don't have to use math.pi. Here is some stuff you can try at the Python prompt, such as in a VS Code Terminal window, to see for yourself:

Enter the command print(pi) and press Enter. Most likely you'll get an error that reads:

```
NameError: name 'pi' is not defined
```

In other words, pi isn't part of the standard library that's always available to your Python code. To use it, you have to import the math module. There are two ways to do that. You can import the whole thing by typing this at the Python prompt:

```
import math
```

But if you do that and then enter

```
print(pi)
```

. . . you'll get the same error again, even though you imported the math package. The reason for that is when you import an entire module and you want to use a part of it, you have to precede the part you want to use with the name of the module and a dot. For example, if you enter this command:

```
print(math.pi)
```

. . . you get the correct answer:

```
3.141592653589793
```

Be aware that when you import just part of a module, the `help()` and `dir()` functions for the whole module won't work. For example, if you've only executed `from math import pi` in your code and you attempt to execute a `dir(math)` or `help(math)` function, it won't work, because Python doesn't have the entire module at its disposal. It only has at its disposal that which you imported, `pi` in this example.

Usually `help()` and `dir()` are just things you use at the Python prompt for a quick lookup. They're not the kinds of things you're likely to use when actually writing an app. So using `from` rather than `import` is actually more efficient because you're only bringing in what you need. As an added bonus, you don't have to precede the function name with the module name and a dot. For example, when you import only `pi` from the `math` module, like this:

```
from math import pi
```

Then you can refer to `pi` in your code is simply `pi`, not `math.pi`. In other words, if you execute this function:

```
print(pi)
```

. . . you'll get the right answer:

```
3.141592653589793
```

This is because Python now "knows" of `pi` as being the thing named `pi` from the `math` module; you don't have to specifically tell it to use `math.pi`.

You can also import multiple items from a package by listing their names, separated by commas, at the end of the `from` . . . command. For example, suppose you need `pi` and square roots in your app. You could import just those into your app using this syntax:

```
from math import pi, sqrt
```

Once again, because you used the `from` syntax for the import, you can refer to `pi` and `sqrt()` in your code by name without the leading module name. For example, after executing that `from` statement, this code:

```
print(sqrt(pi))
```

. . . displays

```
1.7724538509055159
```

. . . which, as you may have guessed, is the square root of the number pi.

You may also notice people importing a module like this:

```
from math import *
```

The asterisk is short for "everything." So in essence, that command is exactly the same as `import math`, which also imports the entire `math` module. But this is a subtle difference: When you do `from math import *` you associate the name of everything in the `math` module with that module. So you can use those names without the `math.` prefix. In other words, after you execute this:

```
from math import *
```

. . . you can do a command like `print(pi)` and it will work, even without using `print(math.pi)`. Although it does seem like a smart and convenient thing to do, we should point out that many programmers think that sort of thing isn't very Pythonic. If you're importing lots of modules and using lots of different pieces of each, avoiding module names in code can make it harder for other programmers to read and make sense of that code. So although in a *Zen of Python* sense it may be frowned upon, technically it works and is an option for you.

# Making Your Own Modules

For all the hoopla about modules, a module is actually a pretty simple thing. In fact, it's just a file with a .py extension that contains Python code. That's it. So any time you write Python code and save it in a .py file, you've basically created a module. That's not to say you always have to use that code as a module. It can certainly be treated as a standalone app. But if you *wanted* to create your own module, with just code that you need often in your own work, you could certainly do so. We explain the whole process in this section.

A module is also just a file with a .py filename extension. The name of the module is the same as the filename (without the .py). Like any .py file, the module contains Python code. As a working example, let's suppose you want to have three functions to simplify formatting dates and currency values. You can make up any name you like for each function. For our working example, we'll use these three names:

- » **to_date(*any_str*)**: Lets you pass in any string (*any_str*) date in *mm/dd/yy* or *mm/dd/yyyy* format and sends back a Python datetime.date that you can use for date calculations.

- » **mdy(*any_date*)**: Lets you pass in any Python date or datetime, and returns a string date formatted in *mm/dd/yyyy* format for display on the screen.

- » **to_curr(*any_num, len*)**: Lets you pass in any Python float or integer number and returns a string with a leading dollar sign, commas in thousands places, and two digits for the pennies. The *len* is an optional number for length. If provided, the return value will be padded on the left with spaces to match the length specified

So here is all the code for that:

```python
# Contains custom functions for dates and currency values.
import datetime as dt

def to_date(any_str):
    """ Convert mm/dd/yy or mm/dd/yyyy string to datetime.date, or None if
    invalid date. """
    try:
        if len(any_str) == 10:
            the_date = dt.datetime.strptime(any_str,'%m/%d/%Y').date()
        else:
            the_date = dt.datetime.strptime(any_str,'%m/%d/%y').date()
    except (ValueError, TypeError):
        the_date = None
    return the_date

def mdy(any_date):
    """ Returns a string date in mm/dd/yyyy format. Pass in Python date or
    string date in mm/dd/yyyy format """
    if type(any_date) == str:
        any_date = to_date(anydate)
    # Make sure its a dateime being forwarded
    if isinstance(any_date,dt.date):
        s_date = f"{any_date:'%m/%d/%Y'}"
    else:
        s_date = "Invalid date"
    return s_date
```

```
def to_curr(anynum, len=0):
    """ Returns a number as a string with $ and commas. Length is optional """
    s = "Invalid amount"
    try:
        x = float(anynum)
    except ValueError:
        x= None
    if isinstance(x,float):
        s = '$' + f"{x:,.2f}"
        if len > 0:
            s=s.rjust(len)
    return s
```

You can create the same file yourself and name it myfunctions.py if you want to follow along. Notice that the file contains only functions. So if you run it, it won't do anything on the screen because there is no code in there that calls any of those functions.

To use those functions in any Python app or program you write, first make sure you copy that myfunc.py file to the same folder as the rest of the Python code that you're writing. Then, when you create a new page, you can import myfunc as a module just as you would any other module created by somebody else. Just use

```
import myfunc
```

You will have to use the module name in front of any of the functions that you call from that module. So if you want to make the code a little more readable, you can use this instead:

```
import myfunc as my
```

With that as your opening line, you can refer to any function in your custom module with my. as the prefix. For example, my.to_date() to call the to_date function. Here is a page that imports the module and then tests out all three functions using that my syntax:

```
# Import all the code from myfunc.py as my.
import myfunc as my

# Need dates in this code
from datetime import datetime as dt

# Some simple test data.
```

```
string_date="12/31/2019"
# Convert string date to datetime.date
print(my.to_date(string_date))

today = dt.today()
# Show today's date in mm/dd/yyyy format.
print(my.mdy(today))

dollar_amt=12345.678
# Show this big number in currency format.
print(my.to_curr(dollar_amt))
```

When you run this code, assuming it's all typed correctly with no errors, the output should look like this:

```
2019-12-31
'12/27/2018'
$12,345.68
```

We also mentioned earlier that you can skip using the prefix if you import items by name. In this case, that means you could call to_date() and mdy() and to_curr() without using the my. prefix. The first line of code would need to be

```
from myfunc import to_date, mdy, to_curr
```

The rest of the code would be the same as in the previous example, except you can leave off the my. prefixes as in the following code:

```
# Import all the code from myfunc.py by name.
from myfunc import to_date, mdy, to_curr

# Need dates in this code
from datetime import datetime as dt

# Some simple test data.

string_date="12/31/2019"
# Convert string date to datetime.date
print(to_date(string_date))

today = dt.today()
# Show today's date in mm/dd/yyyy format.
print(mdy(today))

dollar_amt=12345.678
# Show this big number in currency format.
print(to_curr(dollar_amt))
```

So that's it for Python libraries, packages, and modules. The whole business can be pretty confusing because people tend to use the terms interchangeably. And that's because they all represent code written by others that you're allowed to use in any Python code you write yourself. The only real difference is in size. A library may contain several packages. A package may contain several modules. The modules themselves will usually contain functions, classes, or some other pre-written chunks of code that you're free to use.

In the books and chapters to follow, you'll see lots of modules and classes because it's those things that make Python so modular and so applicable to many different types of work and study. But keep in mind that the core principles of the Python language that you've learned in these first three books apply everywhere, whether you're doing data science or AI or robotics. You'll just be using that core language to work with code that others have already written for that one specialized area.

# 4

# Using Artificial Intelligence in Python

# Contents at a Glance

# Chapter **1**

# Exploring Artificial Intelligence

Artificial intelligence (AI) has been a much-maligned set of words over the past few years. The popular news media tends to take any small advance in AI out of context and proclaims "smart computers are here!" A simple example will suffice to show this point.

In 2017, Facebook engineers programmed two programs to value certain objects more than others (balls, blocks, and such) and then had the two programs, thorough a rules set and a language like English, negotiate with each other to maximize the acquisition of objects that the programs valued. The programs did not have a "language syntax checker" and because of the way the programs learned (a machine learning technique), the communication between the programs soon became syntactically incorrect English (a good example is when a program wanted something, it would say "I want" and the program logic decided that if one "I want" is good, then saying many "I want I want I want" should be better).

Of course, the news media reported this as a new language (it wasn't) and later, when the programs were shut down (because the experiment was finished, a normal thing to do), some pundit decided that the Facebook engineers had shut the programs down right before they had become sentient. Needless to say, this wasn't the case. Interestingly enough, all these programs are available to download for free, so we better hope that everybody shuts them down before they become sentient.

This chapter introduces you to the concept of AI and describes its limitations. We explore different AI techniques and then give a bit of history to put the current AI revolution in context.

**REMEMBER**

From Dictionary.com, "Artificial intelligence is the theory and development of computer systems able to perform tasks that normally require human intelligence, such as visual perception, speech recognition, decision-making, and translation between languages."

# AI Is a Collection of Techniques

The point of this chapter is to demystify AI and to start to understand just how useful and cool these new AI techniques are. Note that we said "AI techniques" and not just "AI." General "AI," in the sense of how intelligent a person is, does not exist, but we do have a bunch of different algorithms, statistical techniques, and tools that can do some pretty impressive "humanlike" things, such as learning and adapting to the environment.

In this chapter, we show you three of these AI techniques. These are

>> Neural networks

>> Machine learning

>> A TensorFlow classifier with Python

After this, you will become sentient. Oh wait, if you have bought this book, you are already over that threshold. Then, on to Python and AI.

Next, we briefly describe each of the major AI techniques and programs that we go through in the next three chapters.

## Neural networks

Just by the name *neural networks*, you know we're going to be talking about brain cells. Human brains have billions of neurons (approximately 80 billion by some counts) and have roughly 10 times the amount of glial cells (which help neurons communicate and play a role in neuron placement). A real key to understanding how the brain works is connections. Each neuron has many connections with other neurons (up to 200,000 connections for some neurons in the brain), so it is not just the neurons that make people intelligent, it's how they are connected.

# ARTIFICIAL INTELLIGENCE IS THE TECHNOLOGY OF THE FUTURE . . . AND ALWAYS WILL BE . . .

*"What magical trick makes us intelligent? The trick is that there is no trick. The power of intelligence stems from our vast diversity, not from any single, perfect principle."*

—MARVIN MINSKY, THE SOCIETY OF MIND (1987)

John Shovic: I had the honor of having lunch and spending an afternoon with Dr. Minsky in 1983 in Pocatello, Idaho. I was working as a VLSI (very large scale integrated circuit) design engineer at American Micro Systems, a company located in Pocatello, and I had just started my Ph.D. work part-time at the University of Idaho. My first AI class was under my belt, and I was beside myself that Dr. Marvin Minsky from the AI Lab at MIT was coming to Pocatello. I made a few phone calls and managed to get him to meet with two of us who had been in the AI class, for lunch and then an afternoon meeting. Looking back, I am amazed that he would take this kind of time for us, but that was the kind of guy he was.

It was like we were Rolling Stones fans and Mick Jagger was coming to town to spend time with us. Honestly, much as I would like to spend an afternoon with Mick Jagger, I would rather have Dr. Minsky.

I had just finished his book, Artificial Intelligence, and I was bursting with questions about his work. He was very interested in what we had learned from our AI class at the University of Idaho and he was quite complimentary about Dr. John Dickinson, the professor of the AI course, and his choice of subjects. I had a lot of enthusiasm about the topic and was thinking that I might make a career of it. Of all we talked about, I remember one thing clearly. He said (and this is paraphrased), "I started in AI about 20 years ago and I was convinced then that 20 years later we would have true AI. I now think we are still about 20 years off from having true AI."

Well, I remember thinking about that day 20 years later, in 2003, and realizing we still weren't there. At that point, I started wondering whether AI is the technology of the future and always will be. Here I am in 2019, another 16 years later, and we still don't have general AI. But one thing has changed in those 16 years. We now have a bunch of AI techniques, learning and searching techniques, that can do some pretty impressive things and may someday lead to that general AI that Dr. Minsky was talking about. Who knows? It may even take less than 20 years!

**REMEMBER**

Elephants have over 270 billion neurons, but they aren't nearly as densely connected as human neurons. Robert Metcalf, the founder of 3Com and an entrepreneur professor at the University of Texas, famously said (referring to Ethernet) that "the value of a telecommunications network is proportional to the square of the number of connected users of the system." With that squared value of connections coming in, we make up for those missing 200 or so billion elephant neurons by having ours much more densely connected.

However, is it any surprise that elephants have good memories and a complex social system?

AI researchers thought (and were right) that if we could reverse engineer neurons and their connections then we could use this information to construct computer models that could be used to make smarter programs. However, the limitations of the first popular model (Preceptrons) quickly led to general disappointment and the first "AI Winter" (see sidebar).

Over the past 30 years, however, much more information has gone into the development of neural networks and now they are quite useful in a number of ways, including convolutional neural networks and deep learning architectures.

## THE AI WINTER

The term AI Winter was first discussed at the 1984 meeting of the American Association of Artificial Intelligence. Our friend from another sidebar, Dr. Marvin Minsky, warned the business community that enthusiasm for AI had spiraled out of control in the 1980s and that disappointment would certainly follow. Three years after he said that, the multi-billion dollar AI business collapsed. An *AI Winter* refers to the moment that investment and research dollars dry up. In economic terms, this is called a bubble, much like the dot-com bubble in 1999, the real estate bubble that collapsed in 2007, and the Dutch tulip bulb market bubble in Holland in 1637. Overhype leads to over-expectations, which lead to inevitable disappointment.

This happened in the 2000s again (partially because of the dot-com bubble) and researchers went to great lengths to avoid using the AI term in their proposals and papers. It seems to me that we are again approaching such a bubble, but none of us are anywhere near smart enough to know when winter is coming (pardon this, *Game of Thrones* fans). One of the big differences is that a number of AI techniques have moved into the mainstream (read consumer), such as Amazon Alexa and Google Home. So there's no doubt that some of the current exuberance and investment in AI is irrational, but we have gotten a lot of good tools out of it this time that we can continue to use even when the bubble pops.

Neural networks are good models for how brains learn and classify data. Given that, it is no surprise that neural networks show up in machine learning and other AI techniques.

A neural network consists of the following parts:

>> The input layer of neurons

>> An arbitrary amount of hidden layers of neurons

>> An output layer of neurons connecting to the world

>> A set of weights and biases between each neuron level

>> A choice of activation function for each hidden layer of neurons

When you set up a network of neurons (and you do define the architecture and layout — creating an arbitrary network of connections has turned into what we call "evolutionary computing" — see sidebar) one of the most important choices you make is the activation function (sometimes known as the *threshold* for the neuron to fire). This activation function is one of the key things you define when you build your Python models of neurons in the next chapter.

## Machine learning

*Learning* is the classic example of what it means to be human. We learn. We adapt.

Today, our AI researchers have brought quasi–human–level learning to computers in specific tasks, such as image recognition or sound processing ("Alexa, find me a new brain"), and there is hope to get to a level of similar learning in other tasks, like driving a car.

**TECHNICAL STUFF**

## DEEP LEARNING

Deep learning has a pretty loose definition. The deep refers to the use of a number of layers of different learning to produce the desired result. It also generally uses neural networks at one level or another, or sometimes even multiple layers of networks.

The general idea is that one layer feeds the output to the next layer and so on. Each layer transforms the data into more abstract information. An example of this might be a picture of blocks being broken down by pixels, analyzed by a neural network and the resulting x, y coordinates of objects are passed down to another layer in the deep learning stack to do more processing for color.

Machine learning isn't fully automated. You can't say, "Computer, read this book" and expect it understand what it is reading. Currently using machine learning techniques require large amounts of human–classified and –selected data, data analysis, and training.

There are many different techniques used for machine learning. Some of these are

>> Statistical analysis

>> Neural networks

>> Decision trees

>> Evolutionary algorithms

Neural networks have many uses both in classification and in machine learning. *Machine learning* really refers to the different ways of using these techniques expert systems that ruled AI in the 1980s. In the late 1980s, John wrote his Ph.D. dissertation on how to build a deeply pipelined machine to speed up the evaluation of expert systems. Hardware acceleration of machine learning is an active area of research today.

In the following chapter, we show you how to use Python to build machines that demonstrate all the important tasks of machine learning.

## AI IN SMARTPHONES

The current AI revolution is making its way into the handhelds. Both Samsung and Apple are racing to add these features to their phones. As of the writing of this book, the Samsung product requires processing off the phone and in the cloud. The A12 chip in the latest Apple smartphones is pretty impressive. It features a four core CPU (central processing units) and a six core GPU (graphics processing unit — a specialized CPU for AI and graphics techniques). It is a processor chip that is dedicated for AI applications, such as facial ID-recognition software. It also has a specialized neural network for a variety of applications.

The AI is capable of performing over 5 trillion operations per second. Take that, Animojis in your text messages.

Samsung is touting that they will have an even more advanced AI chip in their upcoming phones.

# TensorFlow — A framework for deep learning

TensorFlow is an open-source, multi-machine set of API (application programming interfaces) used for building, learning, and doing research on deep learning. It hides a lot of the complexity of deep learning behind the curtain and makes the technology more accessible.

## EVOLUTIONARY COMPUTING

Evolutionary computing is a set of computational algorithms and heuristics (a fancy word for rules of thumb) for global optimization that are inspired by biological evolution. It is derived from machine learning techniques but it differs in that evolutionary computing is generally used to solve problems whose solution is not known (*machine learning programs are taught what they are looking for*) by the programmer beforehand.

By using evolutionary computing algorithms, you can find exuberant but guided solutions to problems in a design space. It has been used to create solutions as diverse as better spacecraft antennas and improved bus routing. It uses very computationally intensive algorithms to search a problem space for solutions. It's very computationally intensive because you have a "population" of solutions that you have look at to see what is doing well and then select the new ones to move to the next generation. Survival of the fittest, in a real sense.

All these population evaluations are difficult for computers to process, which is why so many of the evolution algorithms really require massive parallel computing.

I had a student in my graduate Advanced Robotics class at the University of Idaho use evolutionary computing to allow a robot named Baxter to pick out red or yellow blocks from one box and move them to another box. He used photos from the robot and evolutionary computing to try to find an algorithm to identify and locate these blocks so Baxter could find them. In the picture you can see the two boxes whose blocks Baxter was to move. He did not succeed using evolutionary computing algorithms to find a solution. Why? Using evolutionary computing techniques to find a solution to an ill-defined and unconstrained problem requires exponentially greater computing

*(continued)*

(continued)

resources, and even these still might not come up with a solution. Smaller, constrained problems are a better match for evolutionary techniques.

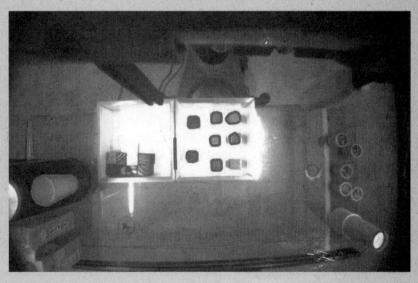

TensorFlow started in 2011 as a proprietary AI environment in the Google Brain group. It has been extensively used within Google and, when it was released to open source, it was embraced by the AI community immediately. Of over 1,500 GitHub source repositories using TensorFlow, only five are from Google. Why is this significant? It shows just how well TensorFlow has been welcomed by the user community. GitHub is a popular website where people place their code for applications and projects in a way that other people can use and learn from them.

TensorFlow gets its name from the way the data is processed. A *tensor* is a multidimensional matrix of data, which is transformed by each of the TensorFlow layers it moves through. TensorFlow is extremely Python-friendly and can be used on many different machines and also in the cloud. TensorFlow is an easy-to-understand-and-use language to get your head into AI applications quickly.

**TIP**

So, TensorFlow is built on matrices. And another name for a matrix is a tensor, which is where the name *TensorFlow* comes from.

# Current Limitations of AI

The key word in all of AI is *understanding*. A machine-learning algorithm has been taught to drive a car, for example, but the resulting program does not "understand" how to drive a car. The emphasis of the AI is to perform an analysis of the data, but the human controlling the data still has interpret the data and see if it fits the problem. Interpretation also goes beyond just the data. Humans often can tell whether the data or a conclusion is true or false, even when they can't really describe just how they know that. AI just accepts it as true.

Considering that we don't even understand a lot of human behavior and abilities ourselves, it is unlikely that anyone will be developing mathematical models of such behavior soon. And we need those models to start getting AI programs to achieve anything approaching human thought processes.

But with all its limitations, AI is very useful for exploring large problem spaces and finding "good" solutions. AI is not anywhere near a human . . . yet.

Now let's go and start using AI in Python!

# Chapter **2**

# Building a Neural Network in Python

N eural networks and various other models of how the brain operates have been around as long as people have been talking about AI. Marvin Minsky, introduced in our last chapter, started mainline interest in modeling neurons with his seminal work in perceptrons in 1969. At the time, there was widespread "irrational exuberance" about how the perceptron was going to make AI practical very quickly. This attracted a good deal of venture capital to the area, but when many of these ventures failed, investment in neural networks dried up. It is like the concept of fashion in science. What's popular, sells.

Fast forward 30 years. There is now renewed interest in neural networks. Better models have been built, but the really important thing is that we now have real, useful, and economical applications based on neural networks. Will this lead to another bubble? Most assuredly, but this time the interest should continue because of the application areas that have been developed.

This chapter introduces you to the concept of neural networks and how to implement them in Python.

# Understanding Neural Networks

These are the six attributes of a neural network:

>> The input layer of neurons

>> An arbitrary amount of hidden layers of neurons

>> An output layer of neurons connecting to the world

>> A set of weights and biases between each neuron level

>> A choice of activation function for each hidden layer of neurons

>> A loss function that will provide "overtraining" of the network

Figure 2-1 shows the architecture of a two-layer neural network. Note the three layers in this "two-layer" neural network: The input layer is typically excluded when you count a neural network's layers. By looking at this diagram, you can see that the neurons on each layer are connected to all the neurons of the next layer. Weights are given for each of the inter-neural connecting lines.

A *neuron*, as the word is used in AI, is a software model of a nervous system cell that behaves more or less like an actual brain neuron. The model uses numbers to make one neuron or another be more important to the results. These numbers are called *weights*.

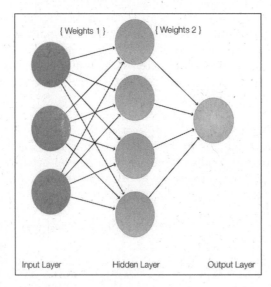

**FIGURE 2-1:**
A two-layer
neural network.

# Layers of neurons

Figure 2-1 shows the input layer, the hidden layer (so called because it is not directly connected to the outside world), and the output layer. This is a very simple network; real networks can be much more complex with multiple more layers. In fact, deep learning gets its name from the fact that you have multiple hidden layers, in a sense increasing the "depth" of the neural network.

Note that you have the layers filter and process information from left to right in a progressive fashion. This is called a *feed-forward input* because the data feeds in only one direction.

So, now that we have a network, how does it learn? The neuron network receives an example and guesses at the answer (by using whatever default weights and biases that they start with). If the answer is wrong, it backtracks and modifies the weights and biases in the neurons and tries to fix the error by changing some values. This is called *backpropagation* and simulates what people do when performing a task using an iterative approach for trial and error.

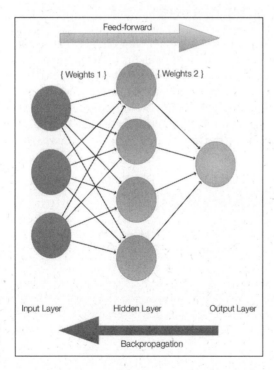

**FIGURE 2-2:**
Feed-forward and
backpropagation.

After you do this process many times, eventually the neural network begins to get better (learns) and provides better answers. Each one of these iterations is called an *epoch*. This name fits pretty well because sometimes it can take days or weeks to provide training to learn complex tasks.

An important point to make at this time is that although it may take days or weeks to train a neural net, after it is trained, we can duplicate it with little effort by copying the topology, weights, and biases of the trained network. When you have a trained neural net, you can use it easily again and again, until you need something different. Then, it is back to training.

Neural networks, as such, do model some types of human learning. However, humans have significantly more complex ways available for hierarchically categorizing objects (such as categorizing horses and pigs as animals) with little effort. Neural networks (and the whole deep learning field) are not very good at transferring knowledge and results from one type of situation to another without retraining.

## Weights and biases

Looking at the network in Figure 2-1, you can see that the output of this neural networks is only dependent on the weights of the interconnection and also something we call the *biases* of the neurons themselves. Although the weights affect the steepness of the activation function curve (more on that later), the bias will shift the entire curve to the right or left. The choices of the weights and biases determines the strength of predictions of the individual neurons. Training the neural network involves using the input data to fine-tune the weights and biases.

**TECHNICAL STUFF**

### BACKPROPAGATION

In the human brain, learning happens because of the addition of new connections (synapses) and the modification of those connections based on external stimuli.

The methods used to propagate from results to previous layers (also called *feedback*) have changed over the years in AI research, and some experts say that what is behind the latest surge of AI applications and the exit from the last "AI Winter" (see Book 4, Chapter 1) is the change of algorithms and techniques used for backpropagation.

Backpropagation is a pretty mathematically complex topic. For a more detailed description of the math and how it is used, check out *Machine Learning For Dummies*, by John Paul Mueller and Luca Massaron (Wiley).

# The activation function

An activation function is an important topic to discuss in building our first neural network. This is a key part of our neuron model. This is the software function that determines whether information passes through or is stopped by the individual neuron. However, you don't just use it as a gate (open or shut), you use it as a function that transforms the input signal to the neuron in some useful way.

There are many types of activation functions available. For our simple neural network, we will use one of the most popular ones — the sigmoid function. A sigmoid function has a characteristic "S" curve, as shown in Figure 2-3.

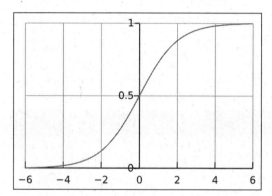

**FIGURE 2-3:**
An example of a sigmoid function.

Remember we talked about neuron bias earlier in this chapter? If you apply a 1.0 value bias to the curve in Figure 2-3, then the whole curve shifts to the right, making the (0,0.5) point move to (1,0.5).

# Loss function

The loss function is the last piece of the puzzle that needs to be explained. The loss function compares the result of our neural network to the desired results. Another way of thinking of this is that the loss function tells us how good our current results are.

This is the information that we are looking for to supply it to our backpropagation channel that will improve our neural network.

I am going to use a function that finds the derivative of the loss function towards our result (the slope of the curve is the first derivative calculus fans) to figure out what to do with our neuron weights. This is a major part of the "learning" activity of the network.

I have now talked about all the parts of our neural network, so let's go build an example.

# Building a Simple Neural Network in Python

For you to build a neural network, you need to decide what you want it to learn. Here we'll choose a pretty simple goal: implement a three-input XOR gate. (That's an eXclusive OR gate.) Table 2-1 shows the function we want to implement in table form (showing our inputs and desired outputs of our neural network shown in Figure 2-1).

**TABLE 2-1: The Truth Table (a Three-Input XOR Gate) for the Neural Network**

| X1 | X2 | X3 | Y1 |
|----|----|----|----|
| 0  | 0  | 0  | 1  |
| 0  | 0  | 1  | 0  |
| 0  | 1  | 0  | 0  |
| 0  | 1  | 1  | 0  |
| 1  | 0  | 0  | 0  |
| 1  | 0  | 1  | 0  |
| 1  | 1  | 0  | 0  |
| 1  | 1  | 1  | 1  |

An Exclusive Or function returns a 1 only if all the inputs are either 0 or 1.

## The neural-net Python code

We will be using the Python library called NumPy, which provides a great set of functions to help us organize our neural network and also simplifies the calculations.

# USES OF XOR FUNCTIONS

**TECHNICAL STUFF**

XOR gates are used in a number of different applications, both in software and in hardware. You can use an XOR gate as part of a one-bit adder that adds one bit to another bit (and provides a carry bit to string them together to make big adders), as well as stringing them together to build a pseudo-random number generator.

The coolest application we know of an XOR gate has to do with coding algorithms and the Reed-Solomon error-correction algorithm. Reed-Solomon algorithms kind of mix up your data by using XOR gates and then adding some additional data (redundant data — kind of a mashup of your data), and then you have a more robust data to transmit long distances (like from Pluto, our former ninth planet), which can have all sorts of events that cause noise in the data, corrupting bits and bytes.

When you receive the data, you use XOR gates again to reconstruct the original data, correcting any errors (up to a point) so you have good data. This allows us to transmit data much further with less power, because with the Reed-Solomon code you become error-tolerant.

Why do we know anything about this? Because John worked with a team on chips for Reed-Solomon codes in the 1980s at the University of Idaho for NASA. Our chips and derivatives ended up on projects like the Hubble Space Telescope and on John's personal favorite, the New Horizons space probe, which visited Pluto and has recently visited Ultima Thule in the Oort Cloud. All the incredible pictures are going through all those little XOR gates.

# NumPy — NUMERICAL PYTHON

**TECHNICAL STUFF**

NumPy is a Python library designed to simplify writing code for matrix mathematics (a matrix is also known as a *tensor*) in linear algebra. NumPy also includes a number of higher mathematical functions that are useful in various types of AI. The start of the development of NumPy goes all the back to 1995 and one of the original Python matrix algebra packages.

It is now the preferred library and is also a part of SciPy and MatPlotLib, two common scientific packages for analysis and visualization of data.

Our Python code using NumPy for the two-layer neural network of Figure 2-2 follows. Using nano (or your favorite text editor), open up a file called "2Layer-NeuralNetwork.py" and enter the following code:

```python
# 2 Layer Neural Network in NumPy


import numpy as np

# X = input of our 3 input XOR gate
# set up the inputs of the neural network (right from the table)
X = np.array(([0,0,0],[0,0,1],[0,1,0], \
    [0,1,1],[1,0,0],[1,0,1],[1,1,0],[1,1,1]), dtype=float)
# y = our output of our neural network
y = np.array(([1], [0],  [0],  [0],  [0], \
    [0],  [0],  [1]), dtype=float)

# what value we want to predict
xPredicted = np.array(([0,0,1]), dtype=float)

X = X/np.amax(X, axis=0) # maximum of X input array
# maximum of xPredicted (our input data for the prediction)
xPredicted = xPredicted/np.amax(xPredicted, axis=0)

# set up our Loss file for graphing

lossFile = open("SumSquaredLossList.csv", "w")

class Neural_Network (object):
  def __init__(self):
    #parameters
    self.inputLayerSize = 3  # X1,X2,X3
    self.outputLayerSize = 1 # Y1
    self.hiddenLayerSize = 4 # Size of the hidden layer

    # build weights of each layer
    # set to random values
    # look at the interconnection diagram to make sense of this
    # 3x4 matrix for input to hidden
    self.W1 = \
          np.random.randn(self.inputLayerSize, self.hiddenLayerSize)
    # 4x1 matrix for hidden layer to output
    self.W2 = \
          np.random.randn(self.hiddenLayerSize, self.outputLayerSize)
```

```python
def feedForward(self, X):
  # feedForward propagation through our network
  # dot product of X (input) and first set of 3x4  weights
  self.z = np.dot(X, self.W1)

  # the activationSigmoid activation function - neural magic
  self.z2 = self.activationSigmoid(self.z)

  # dot product of hidden layer (z2) and second set of 4x1 weights
  self.z3 = np.dot(self.z2, self.W2)

  # final activation function - more neural magic
  o = self.activationSigmoid(self.z3)
  return o

def backwardPropagate(self, X, y, o):
  # backward propagate through the network
  # calculate the error in output
  self.o_error = y - o

  # apply derivative of activationSigmoid to error
  self.o_delta = self.o_error*self.activationSigmoidPrime(o)

  # z2 error: how much our hidden layer weights contributed to output
  # error
  self.z2_error = self.o_delta.dot(self.W2.T)

  # applying derivative of activationSigmoid to z2 error
  self.z2_delta = self.z2_error*self.activationSigmoidPrime(self.z2)

  # adjusting first set (inputLayer --> hiddenLayer) weights
  self.W1 += X.T.dot(self.z2_delta)
  # adjusting second set (hiddenLayer --> outputLayer) weights
  self.W2 += self.z2.T.dot(self.o_delta)

def trainNetwork(self, X, y):
  # feed forward the loop
  o = self.feedForward(X)
  # and then back propagate the values (feedback)
  self.backwardPropagate(X, y, o)


def activationSigmoid(self, s):
  # activation function
  # simple activationSigmoid curve as in the book
  return 1/(1+np.exp(-s))
```

```
    def activationSigmoidPrime(self, s):
      # First derivative of activationSigmoid
      # calculus time!
      return s * (1 - s)


    def saveSumSquaredLossList(self,i,error):
      lossFile.write(str(i)+","+str(error.tolist())+'\n')

    def saveWeights(self):
      # save this in order to reproduce our cool network
      np.savetxt("weightsLayer1.txt", self.W1, fmt="%s")
      np.savetxt("weightsLayer2.txt", self.W2, fmt="%s")

    def predictOutput(self):
      print ("Predicted XOR output data based on trained weights: ")
      print ("Expected (X1-X3): \n" + str(xPredicted))
      print ("Output (Y1): \n" + str(self.feedForward(xPredicted)))

myNeuralNetwork = Neural_Network()
trainingEpochs = 1000
#trainingEpochs = 100000

for i in range(trainingEpochs): # train myNeuralNetwork 1,000 times
  print ("Epoch # " + str(i) + "\n")
  print ("Network Input : \n" + str(X))
  print ("Expected Output of XOR Gate Neural Network: \n" + str(y))
  print ("Actual  Output from XOR Gate Neural Network: \n" + \
         str(myNeuralNetwork.feedForward(X)))
  # mean sum squared loss
  Loss = np.mean(np.square(y - myNeuralNetwork.feedForward(X)))
  myNeuralNetwork.saveSumSquaredLossList(i,Loss)
  print ("Sum Squared Loss: \n" + str(Loss))
  print ("\n")
  myNeuralNetwork.trainNetwork(X, y)

myNeuralNetwork.saveWeights()
myNeuralNetwork.predictOutput()
```

## Breaking down the code

Some of the following code is a little obtuse the first time through, so we will give
you some explanations.

```
# 2 Layer Neural Network in NumPy




import numpy as np
```

If you get an import error when running the preceding code, install the NumPy Python library. To do so on a Raspberry Pi (or an Ubuntu system), type the following in a terminal window:

```
sudo apt-get install python3-numpy
```

Next, we define all eight possibilities of our X1–X3 inputs and the Y1 output from Table 2-1.

```
# X = input of our 3 input XOR gate
# set up the inputs of the neural network (right from the table)
X = np.array(([0,0,0],[0,0,1],[0,1,0], \
    [0,1,1],[1,0,0],[1,0,1],[1,1,0],[1,1,1]), dtype=float)
# y = our output of our neural network
y = np.array(([1], [0],  [0],  [0],  [0], \
    [0],  [0],  [1]), dtype=float)
```

We pick a value to predict (we predict them all, but this is the particular answer we want at the end).

```
# what value we want to predict
xPredicted = np.array(([0,0,1]), dtype=float)

X = X/np.amax(X, axis=0) # maximum of X input array
# maximum of xPredicted (our input data for the prediction)
xPredicted = xPredicted/np.amax(xPredicted, axis=0)
```

Save out our Sum Squared Loss results to a file for use by Excel per epoch.

```
# set up our Loss file for graphing

lossFile = open("SumSquaredLossList.csv", "w")
```

Build the Neural_Network class for our problem. Figure 2-2 shows the network we are building. You can see that each of the layers are represented by a line in the network.

```
class Neural_Network (object):
  def __init__(self):
    #parameters
    self.inputLayerSize = 3  # X1,X2,X3
    self.outputLayerSize = 1 # Y1
    self.hiddenLayerSize = 4 # Size of the hidden layer
```

Set all the network weights to random values to start.

```
# build weights of each layer
# set to random values
# look at the interconnection diagram to make sense of this
# 3x4 matrix for input to hidden
self.W1 = \
        np.random.randn(self.inputLayerSize, self.hiddenLayerSize)
# 4x1 matrix for hidden layer to output
self.W2 = \
        np.random.randn(self.hiddenLayerSize, self.outputLayerSize)
```

Our feedForward function implements the feed-forward path through the neural network. This basically multiplies the matrices containing the weights from each layer to each layer and then applies the sigmoid activation function.

```
def feedForward(self, X):
  # feedForward propagation through our network
  # dot product of X (input) and first set of 3x4  weights
  self.z = np.dot(X, self.W1)

  # the activationSigmoid activation function – neural magic
  self.z2 = self.activationSigmoid(self.z)

  # dot product of hidden layer (z2) and second set of 4x1 weights
  self.z3 = np.dot(self.z2, self.W2)

  # final activation function – more neural magic
  o = self.activationSigmoid(self.z3)
  return o
```

And now we add the backwardPropagate function that implements the real trial-and-error learning that our neural network uses.

```
def backwardPropagate(self, X, y, o):
  # backward propagate through the network
  # calculate the error in output
  self.o_error = y - o

  # apply derivative of activationSigmoid to error
  self.o_delta = self.o_error*self.activationSigmoidPrime(o)

  # z2 error: how much our hidden layer weights contributed to output
  # error
  self.z2_error = self.o_delta.dot(self.W2.T)
```

```
        # applying derivative of activationSigmoid to z2 error
        self.z2_delta = self.z2_error*self.activationSigmoidPrime(self.z2)

        # adjusting first set (inputLayer --> hiddenLayer) weights
        self.W1 += X.T.dot(self.z2_delta)
        # adjusting second set (hiddenLayer --> outputLayer) weights
        self.W2 += self.z2.T.dot(self.o_delta)
```

To train the network for a particular epoch, we call both the `backwardPropagate` and the `feedForward` functions each time we train the network.

```
def trainNetwork(self, X, y):
    # feed forward the loop
    o = self.feedForward(X)
    # and then back propagate the values (feedback)
    self.backwardPropagate(X, y, o)
```

The sigmoid activation function and the first derivative of the sigmoid activation function follows.

```
def activationSigmoid(self, s):
    # activation function
    # simple activationSigmoid curve as in the book
    return 1/(1+np.exp(-s))

def activationSigmoidPrime(self, s):
    # First derivative of activationSigmoid
    # calculus time!
    return s * (1 - s)
```

Next, save the epoch values of the loss function to a file for Excel and the neural weights.

```
def saveSumSquaredLossList(self,i,error):
    lossFile.write(str(i)+","+str(error.tolist())+'\n')

def saveWeights(self):
    # save this in order to reproduce our cool network
    np.savetxt("weightsLayer1.txt", self.W1, fmt="%s")
    np.savetxt("weightsLayer2.txt", self.W2, fmt="%s")
```

Next, we run our neural network to predict the outputs based on the current trained weights.

```
def predictOutput(self):
    print ("Predicted XOR output data based on trained weights: ")
    print ("Expected (X1-X3): \n" + str(xPredicted))
    print ("Output (Y1): \n" + str(self.feedForward(xPredicted)))

myNeuralNetwork = Neural_Network()
trainingEpochs = 1000
#trainingEpochs = 100000
```

The following is the main training loop that goes through all the requested epochs. Change the variable trainingEpochs above to vary the number of epochs you would like to train your network.

```
for i in range(trainingEpochs): # train myNeuralNetwork 1,000 times
    print ("Epoch # " + str(i) + "\n")
    print ("Network Input : \n" + str(X))
    print ("Expected Output of XOR Gate Neural Network: \n" + str(y))
    print ("Actual Output from XOR Gate Neural Network: \n" + \
        str(myNeuralNetwork.feedForward(X)))
    # mean sum squared loss
    Loss = np.mean(np.square(y - myNeuralNetwork.feedForward(X)))
    myNeuralNetwork.saveSumSquaredLossList(i,Loss)
    print ("Sum Squared Loss: \n" + str(Loss))
    print ("\n")
    myNeuralNetwork.trainNetwork(X, y)
```

Save the results of your training for reuse and predict the output of our requested value.

```
myNeuralNetwork.saveWeights()
myNeuralNetwork.predictOutput()
```

## Running the neural-network code

At a command prompt, enter the following command:

```
python3 2LayerNeuralNetworkCode.py
```

You will see the program start stepping through 1,000 epochs of training, printing the results of each epoch, and then finally showing the final input and output. It also creates the following files of interest:

>> **weightsLayer1.txt:** This file contains the final trained weights for input-layer-to-hidden-layer connections (a 4x3 matrix).

>> **weightsLayer2.txt:** This file contains the final trained weights for hidden-layer-to-output-layer connections (a 1x4 matrix).

>> **SumSquaredLossList.csv:** This is a comma-delimited file containing the epoch number and each loss factor at the end of each epoch. We use this to graph the results across all epochs.

Here is the final output of the program for the last epoch (999 since we start at 0).

```
Epoch # 999

Network Input :
[[0. 0. 0.]
 [0. 0. 1.]
 [0. 1. 0.]
 [0. 1. 1.]
 [1. 0. 0.]
 [1. 0. 1.]
 [1. 1. 0.]
 [1. 1. 1.]]
Expected Output of XOR Gate Neural Network:
[[1.]
 [0.]
 [0.]
 [0.]
 [0.]
 [0.]
 [0.]
 [1.]]
Actual Output from XOR Gate Neural Network:
[[0.93419893]
 [0.04425737]
 [0.01636304]
 [0.03906686]
 [0.04377351]
 [0.01744497]
 [0.0391143 ]
 [0.93197489]]
Sum Squared Loss:
0.0020575319565093496


Predicted XOR output data based on trained weights:
Expected (X1-X3):
[0. 0. 1.]
```

```
Output (Y1):
  [0.04422615]
```

At the bottom, you see our expected output is 0. 04422615, which is quite close, but not quite, the expected value of 0. If you compare each of the expected outputs to the actual output from the network, you see they all match pretty closely. And every time you run it the results will be slightly different because you initialize the weights with random numbers at the start of the run.

The goal of a neural-network training is not to get it exactly right — only right within a stated tolerance of the correct result. For example, if we said that any output above 0.9 is a 1 and any output below 0.1 is a 0, then our network would have given perfect results.

The Sum Squared Loss is a measure of all the errors of all the possible inputs.

If we graph the Sum Squared Loss versus the epoch number, we get the graph shown in Figure 2-4. You can see we get better quite quickly and then it tails off. 1,000 epochs are fine for our stated problem.

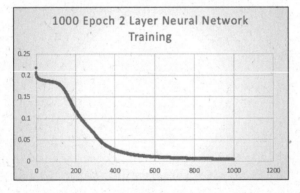

**FIGURE 2-4:** The Loss function during training.

One more experiment. If you increase the number of epochs to 100,000, then the numbers are better still, but our results, according to our accuracy criteria (> 0.9 = 1 and < 0.1 = 0) were good enough in the 1,000 epoch run.

```
Epoch # 99999

Network Input :
[[0. 0. 0.]
 [0. 0. 1.]
 [0. 1. 0.]
 [0. 1. 1.]
```

```
 [1. 0. 0.]
 [1. 0. 1.]
 [1. 1. 0.]
 [1. 1. 1.]]
Expected Output of XOR Gate Neural Network:
[[1.]
 [0.]
 [0.]
 [0.]
 [0.]
 [0.]
 [0.]
 [1.]]
Actual Output from XOR Gate Neural Network:
[[9.85225608e-01]
 [1.41750544e-04]
 [1.51985054e-04]
 [1.14829204e-02]
 [1.17578404e-04]
 [1.14814754e-02]
 [1.14821256e-02]
 [9.78014943e-01]]
Sum Squared Loss:
0.00013715041859631841


Predicted XOR output data based on trained weights:
Expected (X1-X3):
[0. 0. 1.]
Output (Y1):
[0.00014175]
```

# Using TensorFlow for the same neural network

TensorFlow is a Python package that is also designed to support neural networks based on matrices and flow graphs similar to NumPy. It differs from NumPy in one major respect: TensorFlow is designed for use in machine learning and AI applications and so has libraries and functions designed for those applications.

TensorFlow gets its name from the way it processes data. A *tensor* is a multidimensional matrix of data, and this is transformed by each TensorFlow layer it moves through. TensorFlow is extremely Python-friendly and can be used on many different machines and also in the cloud. As you learned in the previous section on neural networks in Python, neural networks are data-flow graphs and are implemented in terms of performing operations matrix of data and then moving the resulting data to another matrix. Because matrices are tensors and the data flows from one to another, you can see where the TensorFlow name comes from.

TensorFlow is one of the best-supported application frameworks with APIs (application programming interfaces) gpt Python, C++, Haskell, Java, Go, Rust, and there's also a third-party package for R called tensorflow.

## Installing the TensorFlow Python library

For Windows, Linux, and Raspberry Pi, check out the official TensorFlow link at https://www.tensorflow.org/install/pip.

TensorFlow is a typical Python3 library and API (applications programming interface). TensorFlow has a lot of dependencies that will be also installed by following the tutorial referenced above.

**TECHNICAL STUFF**

## INTRODUCING TENSORS

You already know from Book 4, Chapter 1 that tensors are multidimensional matrices of data. But an additional discussion will be helpful in getting your head wrapped around the vocabulary of tensors. Neural networks are data-flow graphs and are implemented in terms of performing operations matrix of data and then moving the resulting data to another matrix. Tensor is another name for matricies.

- Scalars: A *scalar* can be thought of as a single piece of data. There is one and only one piece of data associated with a scalar. For example, a value of 5 meters or 5 meters/second are examples of a scalar, as is 45 degrees Fahrenheit or 21 degrees Celsius. You can think of a scalar as a point on a plane.

- Vectors: A *vector* differs from a scalar by the fact that it contains at least two pieces of information. An example of a vector is 5 meters east — this describes a distance and a direction. A vector is a one-dimensional matrix (2x1, for example). You can think of a vector as an arrow located on a plane. It looks like a ray on the plane.

  Plane vectors are the simplest form of tensor. If you look at a 3x1 vector, now you have coordinates for 3D space: *x*, *y*, and *z*.

- Tensors: Vectors are special cases of tensors. A *tensor* is a matrix that can be characterized by magnitude and multiple directions. Scalars can be recognized as individual numbers, vectors as ordered sets of numbers, and tensors by a single or multidimensional array of numbers. Here is a great non-mathematical introduction to tensors: https://www.youtube.com/watch?v=f5liqUk0ZTw.

# Building a Python Neural Network in TensorFlow

For our neural-network example in TensorFlow, we will use the same network that we used to implement an XOR gate with Python. Figure 2-1 shows the two-layer neural network we used; Figure 2-5 shows the new three-layer neural network. Refer to Table 2-1 for the truth table for both networks.

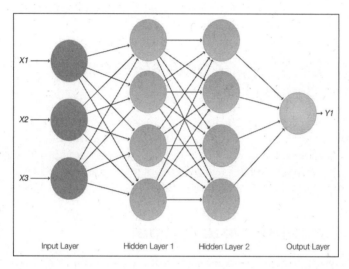

**FIGURE 2-5:** Our TensorFlow three-layer neural network.

TensorFlow is a Python-friendly application framework and collection of functions designed for AI uses, especially with neural networks and machine learning. It uses Python to provide a user-friendly convenient front-end while executing those applications by high performance C++ code.

Keras is an open source neural-network library that enables fast experimentation with neural networks, deep learning, and machine learning. In 2017, Google decided to natively support Keras as the preferred interface for TensorFlow. Keras provides the excellent and intuitive set of abstractions and functions whereas TensorFlow provides the efficient underlying implementation.

The five steps to implementing a neural network in Keras with TensorFlow are

1. Load and format your data.

2. Define your neural network model and layers.

3. Compile the model.

4. Fit and train your model.

5. Evaluate the model.

## Loading your data

This step is pretty trivial in our model but is often the most complex and difficult part of building your entire program. You have to look at your data (whether an XOR gate or a database of factors affecting diabetic heart patients) and figure out how to map your data and the results to get to the information and predictions that you want.

## Defining your neural-network model and layers

Defining your network is one of the primary advantages of Keras over other frameworks. You basically just construct a stack of the neural layers you want your data to flow through. Remember TensorFlow is just that. Your matrices of data flowing through a neural network stack. Here you chose the configuration of your neural layer and activation functions.

## Compiling your model

Next you compile your model which hooks up your Keras layer model with the efficient underlying (what they call the back-end) to run on your hardware. You also choose what you want to use for a loss function.

## Fitting and training your model

This is where the real work of training your network takes place. You will determine how many epochs you want to go through. It also accumulates the history of what is happening through all the epochs, and we will use this to create our graphs.

Our Python code using TensorFlow, NumPy, and Keras for the two-layer neural network of Figure 2-6 follows. Using nano (or your favorite text editor), open up a file called TensorFlowKeras.py and enter the following code:

```
import tensorflow as tf

from tensorflow.keras import layers

from tensorflow.keras.layers import Activation, Dense
```

```
import numpy as np

# X = input of our 3 input XOR gate
# set up the inputs of the neural network (right from the table)
X = np.array(([0,0,0],[0,0,1],[0,1,0],
              [0,1,1],[1,0,0],[1,0,1],[1,1,0],[1,1,1]), dtype=float)
# y = our output of our neural network
y = np.array(([1], [0],  [0],  [0],  [0],
              [0],  [0],  [1]), dtype=float)


model = tf.keras.Sequential()

model.add(Dense(4, input_dim=3, activation='relu',
    use_bias=True))
#model.add(Dense(4,  activation='relu', use_bias=True))
model.add(Dense(1, activation='sigmoid', use_bias=True))

model.compile(loss='mean_squared_error',
        optimizer='adam',
        metrics=['binary_accuracy'])

print (model.get_weights())

history = model.fit(X, y, epochs=2000,
        validation_data = (X, y))


model.summary()


# printing out to file
loss_history = history.history["loss"]
numpy_loss_history = np.array(loss_history)
np.savetxt("loss_history.txt", numpy_loss_history,
        delimiter="\n")

binary_accuracy_history = history.history["binary_accuracy"]
numpy_binary_accuracy = np.array(binary_accuracy_history)
np.savetxt("binary_accuracy.txt", numpy_binary_accuracy, delimiter="\n")


print(np.mean(history.history["binary_accuracy"]))

result = model.predict(X ).round()

print (result)
```

After looking at the code, we will run the neural network and then evaluate the model and results.

# Breaking down the code

The first thing to notice about our code is that it is much simpler than our two-layer model strictly in Python used earlier in this chapter. That's the magic of TensorFlow/Keras. Go back and compare this code to the code for our two-layer network in pure Python. This is much simpler and easier to understand.

First, we import all the libraries you will need to run our example two-layer model. Note that TensorFlow includes Keras by default. And once again we see our friend NumPy as the preferred way of handling matrices.

```
import tensorflow as tf

from tensorflow.keras import layers

from tensorflow.keras.layers import Activation, Dense

import numpy as np
```

Step 1, load and format your data. In this case, we just set up the truth table for our XOR gate in terms of NumPy arrays. This can get much more complex when you have large, diverse, cross-correlated sources of data.

```
# X = input of our 3 input XOR gate
# set up the inputs of the neural network (right from the table)
X = np.array(([0,0,0],[0,0,1],[0,1,0],
            [0,1,1],[1,0,0],[1,0,1],[1,1,0],[1,1,1]), dtype=float)
# y = our output of our neural network
y  = np.array(([1], [0],  [0],  [0],  [0],
            [0],  [0],  [1]), dtype=float)
```

Step 2, define your neural-network model and layers. This is where the real power of Keras shines. It is very simple to add more neural layers, and to change their size and their activation functions. We are also applying a bias to our activation function (relu, in this case, with our friend the sigmoid for the final output layer), which we did not do in our pure Python model.

See the commented model.add statement below? When we go to our three-layer neural-network example, that is all we have to change by uncommenting it.

```
model = tf.keras.Sequential()

model.add(Dense(4, input_dim=3, activation='relu',
    use_bias=True))
#model.add(Dense(4, activation='relu', use_bias=True))
model.add(Dense(1, activation='sigmoid', use_bias=True))
```

Step 3, compile your model. We are using the same loss function that we used in our pure Python implementation, mean_squared_error. New to us is the optimizer, ADAM (a method for stochastic optimization) is a good default optimizer. It provides a method for efficiently descending the gradient applied to the weights of the layers.

One thing to note is what we are asking for in terms of metrics. binary_accuracy means we are comparing our outputs of our network to either a 1 or a 0. You will see values of, say, 0.75, which, since we have eight possible outputs, means that six out of eight are correct. It is exactly what you would expect from the name.

```
model.compile(loss='mean_squared_error',
        optimizer='adam',
        metrics=['binary_accuracy'])
```

Here we print out all the starting weights of our model. Note that they are assigned with a default random method, which you can seed (to do the same run with the same starting weights time after time) or you can change the way they are added.

```
print (model.get_weights())
```

Step 4, fit and train your model. We chose the number of epochs so we would converge to a binary accuracy of 1.0 most of the time. Here we load the NumPy arrays for the input to our network (X) and our expected output of the network (y). The validation_data parameter is used to compare the outputs of your trained network in each epoch and generates val_acc and val_loss for your information in each epoch as stored in the history variable.

```
history = model.fit(X, y, epochs=2000,
        validation_data = (X, y))
```

Here we print a summary of your model so you can make sure it was constructed in the way expected.

```
model.summary()
```

Next, we print out the values from the `history` variable that we would like to graph.

```
# printing out to file
loss_history = history.history["loss"]
numpy_loss_history = np.array(loss_history)
np.savetxt("loss_history.txt", numpy_loss_history,
        delimiter="\n")

binary_accuracy_history = history.history["binary_accuracy"]
numpy_binary_accuracy = np.array(binary_accuracy_history)
np.savetxt("binary_accuracy.txt", numpy_binary_accuracy, delimiter="\n")
```

Step 5, evaluate the model. Here we run the model to predict the outputs from all the inputs of X, using the `round` function to make them either 0 or 1. Note that this replaces the criteria we used in our pure Python model, which was <0.1 = "0" and >0.9 = "1". We also calculated the average of all the `binary_accuracy` values of all the epochs, but the number isn't very useful — except that the closer to 1.0 it is, the faster the model succeeded.

```
print(np.mean(history.history["binary_accuracy"]))

result = model.predict(X ).round()

print (result)
```

Now let's move along to some results.

## Evaluating the model

When you run TensorFlow programs, you may see something like this:

```
/usr/lib/python3.5/importlib/_bootstrap.py:222: RuntimeWarning: compiletime
    version 3.4 of module 'tensorflow.python.framework.fast_tensor_util' does not
    match runtime version 3.5
    return f(*args, **kwds)
/usr/lib/python3.5/importlib/_bootstrap.py:222: RuntimeWarning: builtins.type
    size changed, may indicate binary incompatibility. Expected 432, got 412
    return f(*args, **kwds)
```

This is because of a problem with the way TensorFlow was built for your machine. These warnings can be safely ignored. The good folks over at TensorFlow.org say this issue will be fixed in the next version.

We run the two-layer model by typing **python3 TensorFlowKeras.py** in our terminal window. After watching the epochs march away (you can change this amount of output by setting the Verbose parameter in your model.fit command), we are rewarded with the following:

```
...
Epoch 1999/2000
8/8 [==============================] - 0s 2ms/step - loss: 0.0367 - binary_
   accuracy: 1.0000 - val_loss: 0.0367 - val_binary_accuracy: 1.0000
Epoch 2000/2000
8/8 [==============================] - 0s 2ms/step - loss: 0.0367 - binary_
   accuracy: 1.0000 - val_loss: 0.0367 - val_binary_accuracy: 1.0000

_____
Layer (type)            Output Shape         Param #
=================================================================
dense (Dense)           (None, 4)            16

_____
dense_1 (Dense)         (None, 1)            5
=================================================================
Total params: 21
Trainable params: 21
Non-trainable params: 0
_____

0.8436875
[[1.]
 [0.]
 [0.]
 [0.]
 [0.]
 [0.]
 [0.]
 [1.]]
```

We see that by epoch 2,000 we had achieved the binary accuracy of 1.0, as hoped for, and the results of our model.predict function call at the end matches our truth table. Figure 2-6 shows the results of the loss function and binary accuracy values plotted against the epoch number as the training progressed. Figure 2-2 shows what graphically we are implementing.

A couple of things to note. The loss function is a much smoother linear curve when it succeeds. This has to do with the activation choice (relu) and the optimizer function (ADAM). Another thing to remember is you will get a different curve (somewhat) each time because of the random number initial values in the weights. Seed your random number generator to make it the same each time you run it. This makes it easier to optimize your performance.

# BACKPROPAGATION IN KERAS

With our first neural network in this chapter, we made a big deal about backpropagation and how it was a fundamental part of neural networks. However, now we have moved into Keras/TensorFlow and we haven't said one word about it. The reason for this is that the backpropagation in Keras/TensorFlow is handled automatically. It's done for you. If you want to modify how it is doing it, the easiest way is to modify the optimization parameter in the `module.compile` command (we used ADAM). It is quite a bit of work to dramatically modify the backpropagation algorithm in Keras, but it can be done.

When you run your training for the network, you are using the backpropagation algorithm and optimizing this according to the chosen optimization algorithm and loss function specified when compiling the model.

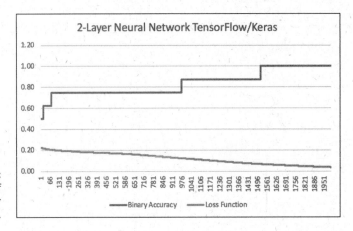

**FIGURE 2-6:** Results of the two-layer training.

Note when the binary accuracy goes to 1.00 (about epoch 1556). That's when your network is fully trained in this case.

## Changing to a three-layer neural network in TensorFlow/Keras

Now let's add another layer to our neural network, as shown in Figure 2-7. Open your TensorFlowKeras.py file in your favorite editor and change the following:

```
model.add(Dense(4, input_dim=3, activation='relu',
    use_bias=True))
#model.add(Dense(4, activation='relu', use_bias=True))
model.add(Dense(1, activation='sigmoid', use_bias=True))
```

Remove the comment character in front of the middle layer, and you now have a three-layer neural network with four neurons per layer. It's that easy. Here is what it should look like now:

```
model.add(Dense(4, input_dim=3, activation='relu',
    use_bias=True))
model.add(Dense(4, activation='relu', use_bias=True))
model.add(Dense(1, activation='sigmoid', use_bias=True))
```

Run the program and you will now have your results from the three-layer neural network, which will look something like this:

```
8/8 [==============================] - 0s 2ms/step - loss: 0.0153 - binary_
    accuracy: 1.0000 - val_loss: 0.0153 - val_binary_accuracy: 1.0000
Epoch 2000/2000
8/8 [==============================] - 0s 2ms/step - loss: 0.0153 - binary_
    accuracy: 1.0000 - val_loss: 0.0153 - val_binary_accuracy: 1.0000

_____
Layer (type)          Output Shape        Param #
===============================================================
dense (Dense)         (None, 4)           16
_____
dense_1 (Dense)       (None, 4)           20
_____
dense_2 (Dense)       (None, 1)           5
===============================================================
Total params: 41
Trainable params: 41
Non-trainable params: 0
_____
0.930375
[[1.]
 [0.]
 [0.]
 [0.]
 [0.]
 [0.]
 [0.]
 [1.]]
```

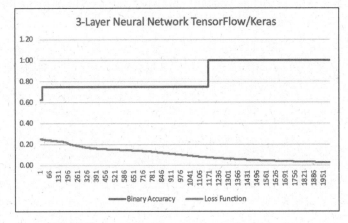

**FIGURE 2-7:**
Results of the three-layer training.

You now can see that you have three layers in your neural network. This is one reason why the TensorFlow/Keras software is so powerful. It's easy to tinker with parameters and make changes.

Notes on our three-layer run: First of all, it converges to a binary accuracy of 1.00 at about epoch 916, much faster than epoch 1556 from our two-layer run. The loss function is less linear than the two-layer run's.

Just for fun and giggles, we changed the number of neurons to 100 per each of the hidden layers. As expected, it converged to a binary accuracy of 1.00 at epoch 78, much faster than the earlier run! Run your own experiments to get a good feel for the way your results will vary with different parameters, layers, and neuron counts.

Believe it or not, you now understand a great deal about how neural networks and machine learning works. Go forth and train those neurons!

Chapter **3**

# Doing Machine Learning in Python

What does it mean to learn something? One definition is "the acquisition and mastery of what is already known about something and the extended clarification of meaning of that knowledge." Another definition is that "learning is a relatively permanent change in a person's knowledge or behavior due to experience."

At the current (and most likely for some time in the future) state of machine learning, it is the second definition that best fits with the current state of AI. Our culture has developed algorithms and programs that can learn things about data and about sensory input and apply that knowledge to new situations. However, our machines do not "understand" anything about what they have learned. They have just accumulated data about their inputs and have transformed that input to some kind of output.

However, even if the machine does not "understand" what it has learned, that does not mean that you cannot do some pretty impressive things using these machine-learning techniques that will be discussed in this chapter.

Maybe these techniques that we are developing now may lead the way to something much more impressive in the future.

What does it mean for a machine to learn something? We're going to use the rough idea that if a machine can take inputs and by some process transform those inputs to some useful outputs, then we can say the machine has learned something. This definition has a wide meaning. In writing a simple program to add two numbers you have taught that machine something. It has learned to add two numbers. We're going to focus in this chapter on machine learning in the sense of the use of algorithms and statistical models that progressively improve their performance on a specific task. If this sounds very much like our neural-network experiments in Chapter 2, you are correct. Machine learning is a lot about neural networks, but it's also about other sophisticated techniques.

# Learning by Looking for Solutions in All the Wrong Places

One of the real problems with machine learning and AI in general is figuring out how the algorithm can find the best solution. The operative word there is *best*. How do we know a given solution is best? It is really a matter of setting goals and achieving them (the solution may not be best but maybe just good enough). Some people have compared the problem of finding the "best" solution to that of a person wandering around on a foggy day trying to find the highest mountain in the area. You climb up a mountain and get to the top and then proclaim, "I am on the highest mountain." Well, you are on the highest mountain you can see, but you can't see through the fog. However, if you define your goal as being on the top of a mountain more than 1,000 feet high, and you are at 1,250 feet, then you have met your goal. This is called a *local maxima*, and it may or may not be the best maxima available.

In this chapter, most of our goal setting (training the machine) will be done with known solutions to a problem: first training our machine and then applying the training to new, similar examples of the problem.

There are three main types of machine-learning algorithms:

>> **Supervised learning:** This type of algorithm builds a model of data that contains both inputs and outputs. The data is known as training data. This is the kind of machine learning we show in this chapter.

>> **Unsupervised learning:** For this type of algorithm, the data contains only the inputs, and the algorithms look for the structures and patterns in the data.

>> **Reinforcement learning:** This area is concerned with software taking actions based on some kind of cumulative reward. These algorithms do not assume

knowledge of an exact mathematical model and are used when exact models are unavailable. This is the most complex area of machine learning, and the one that may bear the most fruit in the future.

With that being said, let's jump into doing machine learning with Python.

# Classifying Clothes with Machine Learning

In this chapter, we use the freely available training Fashion-MNIST (Modified National Institute of Standards and Technology) database that contains 60,000 fashion products from ten categories. It contains data in 28x28 pixel format with 6,000 items in each category. (See Figure 3-1.)

This gives us a really interesting dataset with which to build a TensorFlow/Keras machine-learning application — much more interesting than the standard MNIST machine-learning database that contains only handwritten characters.

**FIGURE 3-1:**
A bit of the
Fashion-MNIST
database.

# Training and Learning with TensorFlow

For this chapter, we are going to once again use TensorFlow/Keras to build some machine-learning examples and look at their results. For more about TensorFlow and Keras, refer to Chapter 2.

Here we use the same five-step approach we used to build layered networks with Keras in Chapter 2. TensorFlow.

1. Load and format your data.

2. Define your neural network model and layers.

3. Compile the model.

4. Fit and train your model.

5. Evaluate the model.

# Setting Up the Software Environment for this Chapter

Most of the action in this chapter is, as usual, in the command line, because you still have to type code and run software. However, we are going to display some graphics on the screen and use MatPlotLib to evaluate what your machine-learning program is doing, so please start a GUI (graphics user interface) if you haven't already. If you are running on a headless Raspberry Pi, either add a keyboard, mouse, and monitor or stop now and bring up VNC (virtual network computer). think of using your computer monitor as a display on a second computer — the Raspberry Pi, in this case. Many links on the web describe how to do this and how to bring up the GUI on your main computer. We are using VNC on a headless Raspberry Pi in this chapter. Feel free to connect a mouse, keyboard, and a monitor directly to the Raspberry Pi if you want. Figure 3-2 shows the GUI running on the Raspberry Pi (it is actually running on VNC on our Mac, but you can't tell from this image).

A great source for tutorials on setting up the software and connecting the Raspberry Pi are located at www.raspberrypi.org.

TIP

If you are missing some of the libraries that we use in this example, then search the web for how to install them on your specific machine. Every setup is a little different. For example, if you're missing seaborn, then search on "installing seaborn python library on [*name of your machine*]." If you do a search on seaborn for the Raspberry Pi, then you will find "sudo pip3 install seaborn."

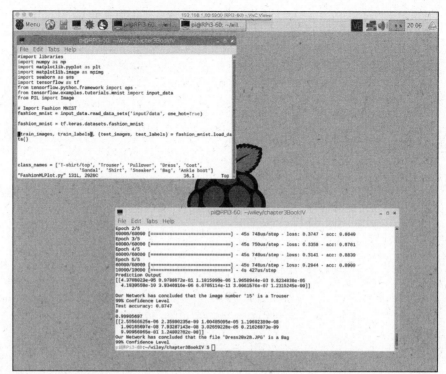

**FIGURE 3-2:**
A full GUI on the
Raspberry Pi.

# Creating a Machine-Learning Network for Detecting Clothes Types

Our main example of machine learning in Python uses a MNIST-format (*MNIST* means that it is a collection of grayscale images with a resolution of 28x28 pixels) Fashion database of 60,000 images classified into ten types of apparel, as follows:

>> 0 T-shirt/top

>> 1 Trouser

>> 2 Pullover

>> 3 Dress

>> 4 Coat

>> 5 Sandal

>> 6 Shirt

>> 7 Sneaker

>> 8 Bag

>> 9 Ankle boot

# Getting the data — The Fashion-MNIST dataset

Turns out this is pretty easy, although it will take a while to first load it to your computer. After you run the program for the first time, it will use the Fashion-MNIST data copied to your computer.

# Training the network

We will train our machine-learning neural network using all 60,000 images of clothes: 6,000 images in each of the ten categories.

# Testing our network

Our trained network will be tested three different ways: 1) a set of 10,000 training photos from the Fashion_MNIST data set; 2) a selected image from the Fashion_MNIST data set; and 3) a photo of a woman's dress.

This first version of the program will run a test on a 10,000 set of files from the Fashion_MNIST database.

Our Python code using TensorFlow, NumPy, and Keras for the Fashion_MNIST network follows. Using nano (or your favorite text editor), open up a file called FMTensorFlow.py and enter the following code:

```
#import libraries
import numpy as np
import matplotlib.pyplot as plt
import matplotlib.image as mpimg
import seaborn as sns
import tensorflow as tf
from tensorflow.python.framework import ops
from tensorflow.examples.tutorials.mnist import input_data
from PIL import Image
```

```
# Import Fashion MNIST
fashion_mnist = input_data.read_data_sets('input/data',
        one_hot=True)

fashion_mnist = tf.keras.datasets.fashion_mnist

(train_images, train_labels), (test_images, test_labels) \
        = fashion_mnist.load_data()




class_names = ['T-shirt/top', 'Trouser',
        'Pullover', 'Dress', 'Coat',
        'Sandal', 'Shirt', 'Sneaker', 'Bag', 'Ankle boot']


train_images = train_images / 255.0

test_images = test_images / 255.0


model = tf.keras.Sequential()


model.add(tf.keras.layers.Flatten(input_shape=(28,28)))
model.add(tf.keras.layers.Dense(128, activation='relu' ))
model.add(tf.keras.layers.Dense(10, activation='softmax' ))


model.compile(optimizer=tf.train.AdamOptimizer(),
                    loss='sparse_categorical_crossentropy',
                            metrics=['accuracy'])


model.fit(train_images, train_labels, epochs=5)

# test with 10,000 images
test_loss, test_acc = model.evaluate(test_images, test_labels)

print('10,000 image Test accuracy:', test_acc)
```

# Breaking down the code

After you've read the description of the Tensform/Keras program in Chapter 2, this code should look much more familiar. In this section, we break it down into our five-step Keras process.

First, we import all the libraries needed to run our example two-layer model. Note that TensorFlow includes Keras by default. And once again we see our friend NumPy as the preferred way of handling matrices.

```
#import libraries
import numpy as np
import matplotlib.pyplot as plt
import matplotlib.image as mpimg
import seaborn as sns
import tensorflow as tf
from tensorflow.python.framework import ops
from tensorflow.examples.tutorials.mnist import input_data
from PIL import Image
```

1. **Load and format your data.**

   This time we are using the built-in data-set reading capability. It knows what this data is because of the `import` statement from `tensorflow.examples.tutorials.mnist` in the preceding code.

   ```
   # Import Fashion MNIST
   fashion_mnist = input_data.read_data_sets('input/data',
           one_hot=True)

   fashion_mnist = tf.keras.datasets.fashion_mnist

   (train_images, train_labels), (test_images, test_labels) \
           = fashion_mnist.load_data()
   ```

   Here we give some descriptive names to the ten classes within the `Fashion_MNIST` data.

   ```
   class_names = ['T-shirt/top', 'Trouser',
           'Pullover', 'Dress', 'Coat',
           'Sandal', 'Shirt', 'Sneaker', 'Bag', 'Ankle boot']
   ```

   Here we change all the images to be scaled from 0.0–1.0 rather than 0–255.

   ```
   train_images = train_images / 255.0

   test_images = test_images / 255.0
   ```

2. **Define your neural-network model and layers.**

   Again, this is where the real power of Keras shines. It is very simple to add more neural layers, and to change their sizes and their activation functions. We are also applying a bias to our activation function (`relu`), in this case with `softmax`, for the final output layer.

```
model = tf.keras.Sequential()


model.add(tf.keras.layers.Flatten(input_shape=(28,28)))
model.add(tf.keras.layers.Dense(128, activation='relu' ))
model.add(tf.keras.layers.Dense(10, activation='softmax' ))
```

3. **Compile your model.**

We are using the loss function sparse_categorical_crossentropy. This function is new to us in this book. It is used when you have assigned a different integer for each clothes category as we have in this example. ADAM (a method for stochastic optimization) is a good default optimizer. It provides a method well suited for problems that are large in terms of data and/or parameters.

```
model.compile(optimizer=tf.train.AdamOptimizer(),
                        loss='sparse_categorical_
    crossentropy',
                                metrics=['accuracy'])
```

**TECHNICAL STUFF**

*Sparse categorical crossentropy* is a loss function used to measure the error between categories across the data set. *Categorical* refers to the fact that the data has more than two categories (binary) in the data set. *Sparse* refers to using a single integer to refer to classes (0–9, in our example). *Entropy* (a measure of disorder) refers to the mix of data between the categories.

4. **Fit and train your model.**

I chose the number of epochs as only 5 due to the time it takes to run the model for our examples. Feel free to increase! Here we load the NumPy arrays for the input to our network (the database train_images).

```
model.fit(train_images, train_labels, epochs=5)
```

5. **Evaluate the model.**

The model.evaluate function is used to compare the outputs of your trained network in each epoch and generates test_acc and test_loss for your information in each epoch as stored in the history variable.

```
# test with 10,000 images
test_loss, test_acc = model.evaluate(test_images,
    test_labels)

print('10,000 image Test accuracy:', test_acc)
```

# Results of the training and evaluation

I ran my program on the Raspberry Pi 3B+. You can safely ignore the code mismatch warnings and the future deprecation announcements at this point.

Here are the results of the program:

```
Epoch 1/5
60000/60000 [==============================] - 44s 726us/step - loss: 0.5009 -
    acc: 0.8244
Epoch 2/5
60000/60000 [==============================] - 42s 703us/step - loss: 0.3751 -
    acc: 0.8652
Epoch 3/5
60000/60000 [==============================] - 42s 703us/step - loss: 0.3359 -
    acc: 0.8767
Epoch 4/5
60000/60000 [==============================] - 42s 701us/step - loss: 0.3124 -
    acc: 0.8839
Epoch 5/5
60000/60000 [==============================] - 42s 703us/step - loss: 0.2960 -
    acc: 0.8915
10000/10000 [==============================] - 4s 404us/step
10,000 image Test accuracy: 0.873
```

Fundamentally, the test results are saying that with our two-layer neural machine-learning network, we are classifying 87 percent of the 10,000-image test database correctly. We upped the number of epochs to 50 and increased this to only 88.7 percent accuracy. Lots of extra computation with little increase in accuracy.

# Testing a single test image

Next is to test a single image (see Figure 3-3) from the Fashion_MNIST database. Add this code to the end of your program and rerun the software:

```python
#run test image from Fashion_MNIST data

img = test_images[15]
img = (np.expand_dims(img,0))
singlePrediction = model.predict(img,steps=1)
print ("Prediction Output")
print(singlePrediction)
print()
NumberElement = singlePrediction.argmax()
Element = np.amax(singlePrediction)
```

```
print ("Our Network has concluded that the image number '15' is a "
        +class_names[NumberElement])
print (str(int(Element*100)) + "% Confidence Level")
```

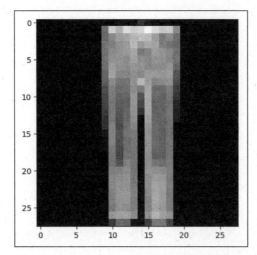

FIGURE 3-3:
Image 15 from
the Fashion-
MNIST test
database.

Here are the results from a five-epoch run:

```
Prediction Output
[[1.2835168e-05 9.9964070e-01 6.2637120e-08 3.4126092e-04 4.4297972e-06
  7.8450663e-10 6.2759432e-07 9.8717527e-12 1.2729484e-08 1.1002166e-09]]

Our Network has concluded that the image number '15' is a Trouser
99% Confidence Level
```

Woohoo! It worked. It correctly identified the picture as a trouser. Remember, however, that we only had an overall accuracy level on the test data of 87 percent.

Next, off to our own picture.

## Testing on external pictures

To accomplish this test, John took a dress from his wife's closet, hung it up on a wall (see Figure 3-4), and took a picture of it with his iPhone.

Next, using Preview on our Mac, we converted it to a resolution of 28 x 28 pixels down from 3024x3024 pixels straight from the phone. (See Figure 3-5.)

**FIGURE 3-4:**
Unidentified dress hanging on a wall.

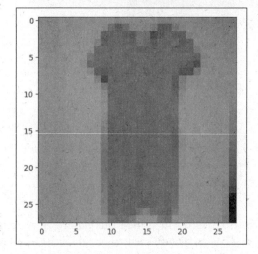

**FIGURE 3-5:**
The dress at 28x28 pixels.

Okay, a few very important comments. First of all, 28x28 pixels does not result in a very clear picture. However, comparing Figure 3-6 to Figure 3-4 from the Fashion-MNIST database, our picture still looks better.

Most of the following code has to do with arranging the data from our JPG picture to fit the format required by TensorFlow. You should be able to use this code to easily add your own pictures for more experiments:

```
# run Our test Image
# read test dress image
imageName = "Dress28x28.JPG"
```

```
testImg = Image.open(imageName)
testImg.load()
data = np.asarray( testImg, dtype="float" )


data = tf.image.rgb_to_grayscale(data)
data = data/255.0


data = tf.transpose(data, perm=[2,0,1])



singlePrediction = model.predict(data,steps=1)
print ("Prediction Output")
print(singlePrediction)
print()
NumberElement = singlePrediction.argmax()
Element = np.amax(singlePrediction)

print ("Our Network has concluded that the file '"
       +imageName+"' is a "+class_names[NumberElement])
print (str(int(Element*100)) + "% Confidence Level")
```

## The results, round 1

We should start out by saying these results did not make us very happy, as you will see shortly. We put the Dress28x28.JPG file in the same directory as our program and ran a five- epoch training run. Here are the results:

```
Prediction Output
[[1.2717753e-06 1.3373902e-08 1.0487850e-06 3.3525557e-11 8.8031484e-09
  7.1847245e-10 1.1177938e-04 8.8322977e-12 9.9988592e-01 3.2957085e-12]]

Our Network has concluded that the file 'Dress28x28.JPG' is a Bag
99% Confidence Level
```

So, our neural network machine learning program, after classifying 60,000 pictures and 6,000 dress pictures, concluded at a 99 percent confidence level . . . *wait for it . . .* that John's wife's dress is a bag.

So the first thing we did next was to increase the training epochs to 50 and to rerun the program. Here are the results from that run:

```
Prediction Output
[[3.4407502e-33 0.0000000e+00 2.5598763e-33 0.0000000e+00 0.0000000e+00
```

```
        0.0000000e+00 2.9322060e-17 0.0000000e+00 1.0000000e+00 1.5202169e-39]]

Our Network has concluded that the file 'Dress28x28.JPG' is a Bag
100% Confidence Level
```

The dress is still a bag, but now our program is 100 percent confident that the dress is a bag. Hmmmm.

This illustrates one of the problems with machine learning. Being 100 percent certain that a picture is of a bag when it is a dress, is still 100 percent wrong.

What is the real problem here? Probably the neural-network configuration is just not good enough to distinguish the dress from a bag. We saw that additional training epochs didn't seem to help at all, so the next thing to try is to increase the number of neurons in our hidden level.

What are other things to try to improve this? It turns out there are many. You can use CNN (convolutional neural networks), data augmentation (increasing the training samples by rotating, shifting, and zooming that pictures) and a variety of other techniques that are beyond the scope of this introduction to machine learning.

We did do one more experiment. We changed the model layers in our program to use the following four-level convolutional-layer model. We just love how easy Keras and TensorFlow makes it to dramatically change the neural network.

CNNs work by scanning images and analyzing them chunk by chunk, say at 5x5 window that moves by a stride length of two pixels each time until it spans the entire message. It's like looking at an image using a microscope; you only see a small part of the picture at any one time, but eventually you see the whole picture. Going to a CNN network on my Raspberry Pi increased the single epoch time to 1.5 hours from a 10 seconds epoch previously.

## The CNN model code

This code has the same structure as the last program. The only significant change is the addition of the new layers for the CNN network:

```
#import libraries
import numpy as np
import matplotlib.pyplot as plt
import matplotlib.image as mpimg
import seaborn as sns
import tensorflow as tf
```

```
from tensorflow.python.framework import ops
from tensorflow.examples.tutorials.mnist import input_data
from PIL import Image

# Import Fashion MNIST
fashion_mnist = input_data.read_data_sets('input/data',
        one_hot=True)

fashion_mnist = tf.keras.datasets.fashion_mnist

(train_images, train_labels), (test_images, test_labels) \
        = fashion_mnist.load_data()




class_names = ['T-shirt/top', 'Trouser',
        'Pullover', 'Dress', 'Coat',
        'Sandal', 'Shirt', 'Sneaker', 'Bag', 'Ankle boot']


train_images = train_images / 255.0


test_images = test_images / 255.0


# Prepare the training images
train_images = train_images.reshape(train_images.shape[0], 28, 28, 1)

# Prepare the test images
test_images = test_images.reshape(test_images.shape[0], 28, 28, 1)


model = tf.keras.Sequential()

input_shape = (28, 28, 1)
model.add(tf.keras.layers.Conv2D(32, kernel_size=(3, 3), activation='relu',
    input_shape=input_shape))
model.add(tf.keras.layers.BatchNormalization())

model.add(tf.keras.layers.Conv2D(32, kernel_size=(3, 3), activation='relu'))
model.add(tf.keras.layers.BatchNormalization())
model.add(tf.keras.layers.MaxPooling2D(pool_size=(2, 2)))
model.add(tf.keras.layers.Dropout(0.25))

model.add(tf.keras.layers.Conv2D(64, kernel_size=(3, 3), activation='relu'))
model.add(tf.keras.layers.BatchNormalization())
model.add(tf.keras.layers.Dropout(0.25))
```

```python
model.add(tf.keras.layers.Conv2D(128, kernel_size=(3, 3), activation='relu'))
model.add(tf.keras.layers.BatchNormalization())
model.add(tf.keras.layers.MaxPooling2D(pool_size=(2, 2)))
model.add(tf.keras.layers.Dropout(0.25))

model.add(tf.keras.layers.Flatten())

model.add(tf.keras.layers.Dense(512, activation='relu'))
model.add(tf.keras.layers.BatchNormalization())
model.add(tf.keras.layers.Dropout(0.5))

model.add(tf.keras.layers.Dense(128, activation='relu'))
model.add(tf.keras.layers.BatchNormalization())
model.add(tf.keras.layers.Dropout(0.5))

model.add(tf.keras.layers.Dense(10, activation='softmax'))

model.compile(optimizer=tf.train.AdamOptimizer(),
                    loss='sparse_categorical_crossentropy',
                          metrics=['accuracy'])


model.fit(train_images, train_labels, epochs=5)

# test with 10,000 images
test_loss, test_acc = model.evaluate(test_images, test_labels)

print('10,000 image Test accuracy:', test_acc)

#run test image from Fashion_MNIST data

img = test_images[15]
img = (np.expand_dims(img,0))
singlePrediction = model.predict(img,steps=1)
print ("Prediction Output")
print(singlePrediction)
print()
NumberElement = singlePrediction.argmax()
Element = np.amax(singlePrediction)

print ("Our Network has concluded that the image number '15' is a "
        +class_names[NumberElement])
print (str(int(Element*100)) + "% Confidence Level")
```

# The results, round 2

This run on the Raspberry Pi 3B+ took about seven hours to complete. The results were as follows:

```
10,000 image Test accuracy: 0.8601
Prediction Output
[[5.9128129e-06 9.9997270e-01 1.5681641e-06 8.1393973e-06 1.5611777e-06
  7.0504888e-07 5.5174642e-06 2.2484977e-07 3.0045830e-06 5.6888598e-07]]

Our Network has concluded that the image number '15' is a Trouser
```

The key number here is the 10,000-image test accuracy. At 86 percent, it was actually lower than our previous, simpler machine-learning neural network (87 percent). Why did this happen? This is probably a case related to "overfitting" the training data. A CNN model such as this can use complex internal models to train (many millions of possibilities) and can lead to *overfitting*, which means the trained network recognizes the training set better but loses the ability to recognize new test data.

TIP

Choosing the machine-learning neural network to work with your data is one of the major decisions you will make in your design. However, understanding activation functions, dropout management, and loss functions will also deeply affect the performance of your machine-learning program. Optimizing all these parameters at once is a difficult task that requires research and experience. Some of this is really rocket science!

# Visualizing with MatPlotLib

Now that we have moved to a GUI-based development environment, we are going to run our base code again and do some analysis of the run using MatPlotLib. We are using a Raspberry Pi for these experiments, but you can use a Mac, PC, or another Linux system and basically do the same thing. If you can install TensorFlow, MatPlotLib, and Python on your computer system, you can do these experiments.

TIP

To install MatPlotLib on your Raspberry Pi, type `pip3 install matplotlib`.

We add the `history` variable to the output of the `model.fit` to collect data. And then we add MatPlotLib commands to graph the loss and the accuracy from our epochs and then to add figure displays for our two individual image tests. Figure 3-6 shows the results of running this program.

Using nano (or your favorite text editor), open up a file called FMTensorFlowPlot.py, and enter the following code:

```
#import libraries
import numpy as np
import matplotlib.pyplot as plt
import matplotlib.image as mpimg
import seaborn as sns
import tensorflow as tf
from tensorflow.python.framework import ops
from tensorflow.examples.tutorials.mnist import input_data
from PIL import Image

# Import Fashion MNIST
fashion_mnist = input_data.read_data_sets('input/data', one_hot=True)


fashion_mnist = tf.keras.datasets.fashion_mnist

(train_images, train_labels), (test_images, test_labels) = fashion_mnist.
    load_data()




class_names = ['T-shirt/top', 'Trouser', 'Pullover', 'Dress', 'Coat',
                     'Sandal', 'Shirt', 'Sneaker', 'Bag', 'Ankle boot']


train_images = train_images / 255.0

test_images = test_images / 255.0


model = tf.keras.Sequential()


model.add(tf.keras.layers.Flatten(input_shape=(28,28)))
model.add(tf.keras.layers.Dense(128, activation='relu' ))
model.add(tf.keras.layers.Dense(10, activation='softmax' ))


model.compile(optimizer=tf.train.AdamOptimizer(),
                    loss='sparse_categorical_crossentropy',
                              metrics=['accuracy'])


history = model.fit(train_images, train_labels, epochs=2)
```

```python
# Get training and test loss histories
training_loss = history.history['loss']
accuracy = history.history['acc']
# Create count of the number of epochs
epoch_count = range(1, len(training_loss) + 1)

# Visualize loss history
plt.figure(0)
plt.plot(epoch_count, training_loss, 'r--')
plt.plot(epoch_count, accuracy, 'b--')
plt.legend(['Training Loss', 'Accuracy'])
plt.xlabel('Epoch')
plt.ylabel('History')
plt.show(block=False);
plt.pause(0.001)

test_loss, test_acc = model.evaluate(test_images, test_labels)

#run test image from Fashion_MNIST data


img = test_images[15]

plt.figure(1)
plt.imshow(img)
plt.show(block=False)
plt.pause(0.001)

img = (np.expand_dims(img,0))
singlePrediction = model.predict(img,steps=1)

print ("Prediction Output")

print(singlePrediction)

print()

NumberElement = singlePrediction.argmax()

Element = np.amax(singlePrediction)


print ("Our Network has concluded that the image number '15' is a "

          +class_names[NumberElement])
```

```
print (str(int(Element*100)) + "% Confidence Level")


print('Test accuracy:', test_acc)

# read test dress image
imageName = "Dress28x28.JPG"


testImg = Image.open(imageName)

plt.figure(2)
plt.imshow(testImg)
plt.show(block=False)
plt.pause(0.001)
testImg.load()
data = np.asarray( testImg, dtype="float" )


data = tf.image.rgb_to_grayscale(data)
data = data/255.0


data = tf.transpose(data, perm=[2,0,1])



singlePrediction = model.predict(data,steps=1)

NumberElement = singlePrediction.argmax()
Element = np.amax(singlePrediction)
print(NumberElement)
print(Element)
print(singlePrediction)

print ("Our Network has concluded that the file '"+imageName+"' is a
    "+class_names[NumberElement])
print (str(int(Element*100)) + "% Confidence Level")

plt.show()
```

The results of running this program is shown in Figure 3-6. The window labeled Figure 0 shows the accuracy data for each of the five epochs of the machine learning training, and you can see the accuracy slowly increases with each epoch. The window labeled Figure 1 shows the test picture used for the first recognition test (it found a pair of trousers, which is correct), and finally, the window labeled Figure 2 shows the dress picture, which is still incorrectly identified as a bag. Harumph.

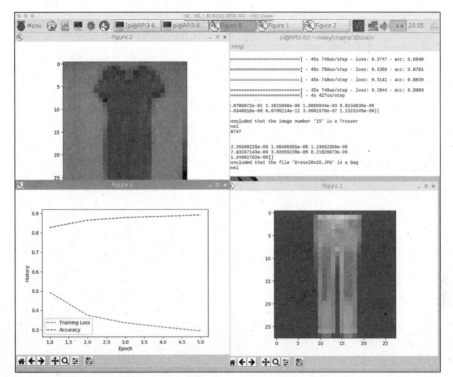

**FIGURE 3-6:**
Our Raspberry Pi GUI with MatPlotLib visualization.

# Learning More Machine Learning

After seeing how useful Python is in building and experimenting with machine learning and neural networks, you can see how powerful it is. Even though you are just beginning to understand the theory behind a lot of the models you have use, you should feel that you now have a tremendous amount of ability to build and experiment with making machines learn.

Next step? We recommend the following books:

>> *Machine Learning for Dummies,* John Paul Mueller and Luca Massaron

>> *Deep Learning with Python,* Francois Chollet

>> And a great beginners overview of the whole AI field: *Artificial Intelligence For Dummies,* John Paul Mueller and Luca Massaron

Next, we explore using Python with some other AI applications.

# Chapter **4**

# Exploring More AI in Python

After reading the previous three chapters, you have learned quite a bit about using some of the basics of artificial intelligence, specifically neural networks and machine learning. There is a lot more to AI than just these two things, though. We could look at advanced searching (not Google searching but rather looking at big problem spaces and trying to figure out solutions to the problem using AI). We could also look at the whole problem of autonomous robotics (which we touch upon in Book 7) but this topic is very complicated.

Instead, in this chapter, we talk about other ways of doing AI software beyond the Raspberry Pi. Remember it took us seven hours to run five epochs of training on our large neural network? Sounds like we could use some bigger iron to accomplish more training in less time. That's what this chapter is about.

## Limitations of the Raspberry Pi and AI

The Raspberry Pi is an inexpensive full-blown computing device. The Raspberry Pi 3B+, which we have used throughout this book, has the following major specifications:

» CPU: Broadcom quad-core 64bit processor @ 1.4GHz

» GPU: Broadcom Videocore-IV

» RAM: 1GB SDRAM

» Networking: Gigabit Ethernet, 802.11b/g/n/ac WiFi

» Storage: SD card

How does this stack up? For a $35 computer, very well. But for a dedicated AI computer, not so much.

The problems are not enough RAM (1GB isn't very much, especially for a Raspberry Pi to do AI) and not a very sophisticated GPU (graphics processing unit). Figure 4-1 shows the Raspberry Pi 3B+ processing chip.

**FIGURE 4-1:** The Raspberry Pi processing chip containing the Videocore-IV.

There are two mitigating circumstances that keep the Raspberry Pi in the running when it comes to doing and experimenting with AI. First of all, you can buy an AI Accelerator that can plug into the USB ports of the Raspberry Pi and secondly, you can use the Raspberry Pi to control processors and AI hardware up on the cloud for all the computationally heavy lifting.

**TECHNICAL STUFF**

# THE BROADCOM VIDEOCORE-IV ON THE RASPBERRY PI 3B+

The Videocore-IV is a low-power mobile graphics processor. It is a two-dimensional DSP (digital signal processor) that is set up as basically a four-GPU core unit. These GPU core units are called *slices* and can be very roughly compared to GPU computer units, such as those used by AMD and Nvidia (which can have 256, 512, or more individual GPU units, far outclassing the Videocore 4 units) to power their GPU cards, which are now proving to be very popular with AI researchers and hobbyists.

This processor is really designed to be used in video encoding and decoding applications and not so much for AI use. However, some researchers have made use of the four slices to accelerate neural-network processing on the Raspberry Pi to achieve up to about three times the performance of the four-core main processor used alone.

One of the main barriers to using the Videocore on the Raspberry Pi for AI type of applications is that the specifications, development tools, and product details have only been available under NDA (non-disclosure agreements), which do not go along with open-source development. However, you can now get full documentation and the complete source code for the Raspberry Pi 3B+ graphics stack under a very nonrestrictive BSD license, which should provide a path forward.

**TIP**

Remember from our previous chapter that the bulk of the computer time in building any kind of machine-learning AI system is for training and that when that training is done, it doesn't take a lot of processing to actually characterize an unknown or new picture. This means you can train on one big machine and then deploy on a simpler computer such as the Raspberry Pi in the application. This doesn't work all the time (especially if you want to keep learning as the program runs) but if it does work, it allows you to deploy sophisticated machine-learning programs on much simpler and less expensive hardware.

Performing AI analysis or training on the small computers that are connected to a network, is called *edge computing* or, phrased a different way, computing on the edge of the network.

# Adding Hardware AI to the Raspberry Pi

It turns out that there have been a number of companies starting to build special-ized AI compute sticks, many of which can be used on the Raspberry Pi. Typically, you will find that there are Python libraries or wrappers, and often TensorFlow Python libraries, that support using these sticks. Two of the most interesting ones are

» **The Intel Modvidius Neural Compute Stick (NCS):** The Movidius NCS stick plugs into the USB port of the Raspberry Pi or other compute and provides hardware support for deep learning based analysis (refer to Chapters 1–3).

For example, you can use the Amazon cloud to perform image analysis, process-ing and classification up in the cloud from your small computer system which moves your computationally expensive task from your Raspberry Pi to the cloud. This does cost money and bandwidth (and latency in your system) to do this. Doing the analysis with your trained deep learning neural network on the edge by using a NCS stick can help and can possibly allow you to disconnect your device running on the edge of the network from the Internet entirely. It runs around 60X faster than doing image analysis on the Raspberry Pi and costs less than $100. Figure 4-2 shows the Movidius Compute Stick.

**FIGURE 4-2:**
The Intel
Movidius Neural
Compute Stick 2.

You can do facial recognition, text analysis, monitoring and maintenance using this NCS stick. Pretty cool!

There is one concept that we need to emphasize here, however. The NCS stick is used to perform analysis and to conduct inferences on data, *but it is not used for training models!* You still need to build and train the models. It has a good interface with Keras and TensorFlow, so this is possible to do in a reasonable fashion.

Think of it as an accelerator for use by your final project when the training is done.

» **The Google Edge TPU accelerator:** The Google Edge TPU (tensor processing unit) has a USB Type-C socket that can be plugged into an Linux-based system to provide accelerated machine learning analysis and inferences. Does the word *tensor* sound familiar? Tensors are matrices like in our neural-network examples in Chapters 2 and 3. Figure 4-3 shows the Google Edge accelerator.

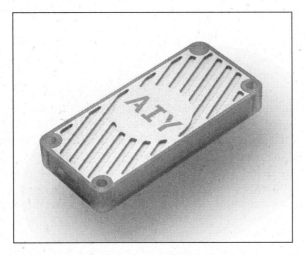

**FIGURE 4-3:**
The Google Edge
TPU accelerator.

Well, it turns out, much like the Intel NCS stick above, this device is all about executing trained machine-learning models. We still train the machine-learning networks using other techniques, and then we execute the model on the stick.

## A FINAL COMMENT ON MACHINE-LEARNING ACCELERATORS

Oh, boy. In the next four years, this type of specialized hardware for running machine-learning models will explode. You will see multiple different architectures and solutions come from Google, Intel, Nvidia, AMD, Qualcomm, and a number of other smaller companies from around the world. Everybody is starting to climb on the AI accelerator hardware bandwagon.

Exploring More AI in Python

# AI in the Cloud

In the tech industry, everyone loves to use buzzwords such as *the cloud*. Often, the use of such language results in arbitrary and nebulous terms that leave consumers (or even sophisticated technical people) unsure what they

When a company says, "your data is in the cloud" or that "you can work in the cloud," this has nothing to do with being white, fluffy, or aboveground. Your "in the cloud" data is on the ground and is stored somewhere in a data center with a bunch of servers that are more similar to your PC or Mac than you may think.

Some people define the cloud as software or services that run on the Internet rather than on your local machine. This is correct to a degree, but nothing really runs on the Internet; it runs on machines that are *connected* to the Internet. Understanding that in-the-cloud software runs on servers and is not "just out there" tends to really quickly demystify the cloud and its functions.

If you have two computers networked together and use the other computer for a data server, you have your own "cloud."

This goes for basic services like storing your data in the cloud, but there is much more than just storage available on the cloud and that is where it gets really interesting.

The advantage of using the cloud is that you can use services and storage unavailable to you on your local network and (in one of the most important game changers of cloud computing) you can ramp your usage up and down depending on your computing needs on a dynamic basis.

Using the cloud requires Internet access. Not necessarily 100 percent of the time (you can fire off a cloud process and then come back to it later), but you do need connections some of the time. This limits the cloud in applications such as self-driving cars that aren't guaranteed to have good Internet access all the time. Interestingly, this "fire and forget" mode is useful for IOT (Internet of Things) devices where you don't want to stay connected to the net all the time for power considerations.

So, how do you use the cloud? That depends on the service and vendor, but in machine-learning applications, the most common way is to set up the Python on a computer that calls cloud-based functions and applications. All cloud vendors provide examples.

What is a great consumer example of cloud usage? The Amazon Echo and Alexa. It listens to you, compresses the speech data, sends it to the Amazon AWS cloud, translates and interprets your data and then sends back a verbal response or commands to make your lights come on.

A number of cloud providers for storage and services exist and more are arriving all the time. The top four cloud providers for AI at the time of this writing are

» Google cloud

» Amazon Web Services

» IBM cloud

» Microsoft Azure

## Google cloud

The Google cloud is probably the most AI-focused cloud provider. You can gain access to TPU (tensor processing units) in the cloud, which, like the Google TPU stick above, can accelerate your AI applications. Much of the Google cloud's functionality reflects the core skill set of the company — that of search.

For example, the Cloud Vision API can detect objects, logos, and landmarks within images. Some excellent students at the University of Idaho are building a Smart City application called ParkMyRide, which uses a Raspberry Pi–based solar-powered camera to take pictures of the street and determines street parking availability by using the Google Cloud Vision API. The software sends a picture of the street to Google and gets back the number of cars found and where they are in the picture. They then supply this information to a smartphone app which displays it graphically. Pretty neat.

Other featured services of the Google cloud are: Video content search applications and speech-to-text/text-to-speech packages (think Google Home — very much like Amazon Alexa). Like Amazon and Microsoft, Google is using its own AI-powered applications to create new services for customers to use.

## Amazon Web Services

Amazon Web Services (AWS) is focused on taking their consumer AI expertise and supplying this expertise to businesses. Many of these cloud services are built on the consumer product versions, so as Alexa improves, for example, the cloud services also improve.

Amazon not only has text and natural language offerings, but also machine-learning visualization/creation tools, vision recognition, and analysis.

# IBM cloud

The IBM cloud has gotten a bad rap over the past few years for being hard to use. One of the big reasons was that there were so many different options on so many different platforms that it was almost impossible to figure out where to start.

In the past couple of years, it has gotten much better. IBM merged its three big divisions (IBM BlueMix cloud services, SoftLayer data services, and the Watson AI group) into one group under the Watson brand. There are still over 170 services available, so it is still hard to get going, but there is much better control and consistency over the process.

Their machine-learning environment is called the Watson Studio and is used to build and train AI models in one integrated environment. They also provide huge searchable knowledge catalogs and have one of the better IOT (Internet of Things) management platforms available.

One of the cool things they have is a service called Watson Personality Insights that predicts personality characteristics, needs, and values through written text. What would Watson Personality make of the authors of this book? We will run the text of the finished book through Watson and report back to you on the Wiley blog.

# Microsoft Azure

Microsoft Azure has an emphasis on developers. They breakdown their AI offerings into three AI categories:

>> AI services

>> AI tools and frameworks

>> AI infrastructures

Similar to Amazon and Google, their AI applications are built on consumer products that Microsoft has produced. Azure also has support for specialized FPGA (field programmable gate arrays — think hardware that can be changed by programming) and has built out the infrastructure to support a wide variety of accelerators. Microsoft is one of the largest, if not the largest, customer of the Intel Movidius chips.

They have products for machine learning, IOT toolkits, and management services, and a full and rich set of data services including databases, support for GPUs and custom silicon AI infrastructure, and a container service that can turn your inside applications into cloud apps.

Microsoft Azure is the one to watch for some pretty spectacular innovations.

# AI on a Graphics Card

Graphics cards (see the Nvidia Graphics chip in Figure 4-4) have been an integral part of the PC experience for decades. People often hunt for the latest and greatest graphics card to make their PCs better gaming machines. One thing becomes obvious after a while: Although CPU speed is important, the quality and architecture of the graphics card makes a bigger difference. Why? Because computing high-resolution graphics is computationally expensive, and the way to solve that is to build graphics cards out of computers that were designed to do graphics to share the burden. Thus was born the GPU (graphics processing unit), a specialized computer core that is designed to work with graphics.

**FIGURE 4-4:**
Nvidia 256 Core GPU chip.

Nvidia and others started building graphics cards that had multiple GPUs on them, which dramatically improved video resolution and frame rates in games. One thing to remember is that graphics algorithms are constructed using data structures called *matrices* (or *tensors*) that are processed in pipelines.

Wait. Tensors? Matrices? This sounds suspiciously like the kind of data structures we use in AI and machine learning. Because of the way machine learning and deep learning are done and implemented, GPUs have proven to be useful and effective.

Deep learning relies on a number of different types of neural networks, (see Chapter 2) and we train and use these networks by using tensors.

Regardless of the type of neural network used, all the techniques rely on performing complex statistical operations. During the training (learning) operations, a multitude of images or data points are fed to the network and then trained with the correct classification or correct answer. You correlate millions of tensors (matrices) to build a model that will get the right result.

To speed up the training, these operations can be done in parallel, which turns out to be a very good use of the GPUs on a graphics board.

An individual GPU core is much simpler than a CPU core as it is designed for a specific, rather than general, purpose. This makes it cheaper to build multicore GPU chips than to build multicore CPU chips.

The proliferation of graphics cards with many GPU cores has made these computers perfect for machine learning applications. The combination of a powerful multicore CPU and many GPUs can dramatically accelerate machine-learning programs. TensorFlow in particular has versions of the software that is designed to work with GPU boards, removing a lot of the complication of using these boards.

To put it in perspective, our Raspberry Pi 3B+ has 4 processor cores and in some sense, 4 GPU cores. One of the latest GPU boards from Nvidia has 3,584 cores. You can do a lot of fast training and executing machine learning networks using these large core count GPU boards.

The GPU-based boards are not the last step in this evolution of specialized computers and hardware to support AI applications. There are starting to be even more specialized chips. At last count, there are over 50 companies working on chips that will accelerate AI functions.

When we discussed the Microsoft Azure cloud offering earlier, we mentioned that Microsoft has built out infrastructure to support AI acceleration hardware in the cloud. This is one of the big reasons to watch what Microsoft is doing.

The future is in more and more specialized hardware, especially as specialized hardware gets easier and easier to deal with from the user software side.

# Where to Go for More AI Fun in Python

If you are interested in furthering your knowledge and abilities in machine learning and AI, check out the following sources for project inspiration. The important thing is to actually build programs and modify other people programs to really learn the technology from experience.

- » "Is Santa Claus Real?," Varun Vohra, https://towardsdatascience.com/is-santa-claus-real-9b7b9839776c

- » "Keras and deep learning on the Raspberry Pi," Adrian Rosebrock, https://www.pyimagesearch.com/2017/12/18/keras-deep-learning-raspberry-pi/

- » "How to easily Detect Objects with Deep Learning on Raspberry Pi," Sarthak Jain, https://medium.com/nanonets/how-to-easily-detect-objects-with-deep-learning-on-raspberrypi-225f29635c74

- » "Building a Cat Detector using Convolutional Neural Network," Venelin Valkov, https://medium.com/@curiousily/tensorflow-for-hackers-part-iii-convolutional-neural-networks-c077618e590b

- » "Real time Image Classifier on Raspberry Pi Using Inception Framework," Bapi Reddy, https://medium.com/@bapireddy/real-time-image-classifier-on-raspberry-pi-using-inception-framework-faccfa150909

# 5

# Doing Data Science with Python

# Contents at a Glance

# Chapter **1**

# The Five Areas of Data Science

ata science impacts our modern lives in far more ways than you may think. When you use Google or Bing or DuckDuckGo, you are using a very sophisticated application of data science. The suggestions for other search terms that come up when you are typing? Those come from data science.

Medical diagnoses and interpretations of images and symptoms are examples of data science. Doctors rely on data science interpretations more and more these days.

As with most of the topics in this book, data science looks intimidating to the uninitiated. Inferences, data graphs, and statistics, oh my! However, just as in our previous chapters on artificial intelligence, if you dig in and look at some examples, you can really get a handle on what data science is and what it isn't.

In this chapter we cover just enough statistics and "asking questions of data" to get you going and get some simple results. The purpose is to introduce you to the use of Python in data science and talk about just enough theory to get you started.

If nothing else, we want to leave you with the process of data science and give you a higher level of understanding of what is behind some of the talking heads on television and the various press releases that come from universities. These people are always citing results that come from big data analysis and are often overstating what they actually mean. An example of this is when one study says coffee is bad for you and the next month a study comes out saying coffee is good for you — and sometimes the studies are based on the same data! Determining what your results mean, beyond simple interpretations, is where the really hard parts of data science and statistics meet and are worthy of a book all their own. At the end of our data science journey, you will know more about the processes involved in answering some of these questions.

There is a mystery to data science, but with just a little knowledge and a little Python, we can penetrate the veil and do some data science.

Python and the myriad tools and libraries available can make data science much more accessible. One thing to remember is that most scientists (including data scientists) are not necessarily experts in computer science. They like to use tools to simplify the coding and to allow them to focus on getting the answers and performing the analysis of the data they want.

# Working with Big, Big Data

The media likes to throw around the notion of "big data" and how people can get insights into consumer (and your) behavior from it. *Big data* is a term used to refer to large and complex datasets that are too large for traditional data processing software (read databases, spread sheets, and traditional statistics packages like SPSS) to handle. The industry talks about big data using three different concepts, called the "Three V's": *volume*, *variety*, and *velocity*.

## Volume

*Volume* refers to how big the dataset is that we are considering. It can be really, really big — almost hard-to-believe big. For example, Facebook has more users than the population of China. There are over 250 *billion* images on Facebook and 2.5 *trillion* posts. That is a lot of data. A really big amount of data.

And what about the upcoming world of IOT (Internet of Things)? Gartner, one of the world's leading analysis companies, estimates 22 billion devices by 2022. That is 22 billion devices producing thousands of pieces of data. Imagine that you are sampling the temperature in your kitchen once a minute for a year. That is over ½ million data points. Add the humidity in to the measurements and now you have 1 million data points. Multiply that by five rooms and a garage, all with temperature and humidity measurements, and your house is producing 6 million pieces of data from just one little IOT device per room. It gets crazy very quickly.

And look at your smartphone. Imagine how many pieces of data it produces in a day. Location, usage, power levels, cellphone connectivity spews out of your phone into databases and your apps and application dashboards like Blynk constantly. Sometimes (as we just recently found out from cellphone companies) location information is being collected and sold even without your consent or opt-in.

Data, data, and more data. Data science is how we make use of this.

## Variety

Note that photos are very different data types from temperature and humidity or location information. Sometimes they go together and sometimes they don't. Photos (as we discovered in Book 4, "Artificial Intelligence and Python") are very sophisticated data structures and are hard to interpret and hard to get machines to classify. Throw audio recordings in on that and you have a rather varied set of data types.

**TECHNICAL STUFF**

Let's talk about voice for a minute. In Book 4, I talked about Alexa being very good at translating voice to text but not so good at assigning meaning to the text. One reason is the lack of context, but another reason is the many different ways that people ask for things, make comments, and so on. Imagine, then, Alexa (and Amazon) keeping track of all the queries and then doing data science on them to find out the sorts of things that people are asking for and the variety of ways they ask for them. That is a lot of data and a lot of information that can be gathered. Not just for nefarious reasons, but to build a system that better services the consumer. It goes both ways.

Data science has a much better chance of identifying patterns if the voice has been translated to text. It is much easier. However, in this translation you do lose a lot of information about tone of voice, emphasis, and so on.

## Velocity

*Velocity* refers to how fast the data is changing and how fast it is being added to the data piles. Facebook users upload about 1 *billion* pictures a day, so in the next couple of years Facebook will have over 1 *trillion* images. Facebook is a high velocity dataset. A low velocity dataset (not changing at all) may be the set of temperature and humidity readings from your house in the last five years. Needless to say, high velocity datasets take different techniques than low velocity datasets.

## THE DIFFERENCE BETWEEN DATA SCIENCE AND DATA ANALYTICS

In a real sense, data analytics is a subset of data science — specifically, steps 3-5 in our data science list. (See "Cooking with Gas: The Five-Step Process of Data Science.") There are a number of people that still like to differentiate between these two types of scientists, but the difference becomes less and less noticeable as time goes on. More and more techniques are being develop to do data analysis on big data (not surprisingly named "big data analytics").

Currently, data science generally refers to the process of working out insights from large datasets of unstructured data. This means using predicative analytics, statistics and machine learning to wade through the mass of data.

Data analytics primarily focuses on using and creating statistical analysis for existing sets of data to achieve insights on that data.

With these somewhat vague descriptions, you can see how the two areas are moving closer and closer together. At the risk of ridicule from my fellow academics, I would definitely call data analytics a subset of data science.

## Managing volume, variety, and velocity

This is a very complex topic. Data scientists have developed many methods for processing data with variations of the three V's. The three V's describe the dataset and give you an idea of the parameters of your particular set of data. The process of gaining insights in data is called *data analytics*. In the next chapters, we focus on gaining knowledge about analytics and on learning how to ask some data analytics questions using Python. After doing data science for a few years, you will be VVVery good at managing these.

# Cooking with Gas: The Five Step Process of Data Science

We generally can break down the process of doing science on data (especially big data) into five steps. I'll finish out this introductory chapter by talking about each of these steps to give us a handle on the flow of the data science process and a feel for the complexity of the tasks. These steps are

1. Capture the data
2. Process the data
3. Analyze the data
4. Communicate the results
5. Maintain the data

## Capturing the data

To have something to do analysis on, you have to capture some data. In any real-world situation, you probably have a number of potential sources of data. Inventory them and decide what to include. Knowing what to include requires you to have carefully defined what your business terms are and what your goals are for the upcoming analysis. Sometimes your goals can be vague in that sometimes, "you just want to see what you can get" out of the data.

If you can, integrate your data sources so it is easy to get to the information you need to find insights and build all those nifty reports you just can't wait to show off to the management.

## Processing the data

In my humble opinion, this is the part of data science that should be easy, but it almost never is. I've seen data scientists spend months massaging their data so they can process and trust the data. You need to identify anomalies and outliers, eliminate duplicates, remove missing entries, and figure out what data is inconsistent. And all this has to be done appropriately so as not to take out data that is important to your upcoming analysis work. It's not easy to do in many cases. If you have house room temperatures that are 170 degrees C, it is easy to see that this data is wrong and inconsistent. (Well, unless your house is burning down.)

Cleaning and processing your data needs to be done carefully or else you will bias and maybe destroy the ability to do good inferences or get good answers down the line. In the real world, expect to spend a lot of time doing this step.

**WARNING**

Oh, and one more cleaning thing to worry about, budding data scientist consumers are giving more and more false and misleading data online. According to Marketing Week in 2015, 60 percent of consumers provide intentionally incorrect information when submitting data online.

We humbly admit to doing this all the time to online marketing forms and even to political pollsters, especially when we sense a political agenda in the questions. Bad boys we are.

Understand that it only takes a very small amount of disproportionate information to dramatically devalue a database. More food for thought.

## Analyzing the data

By the time you have expended all the energy to get to actually looking at the data to see what you can find, you would think that asking the questions should be relatively simple. It is not. Analyzing big datasets for insights and inferences or even asking complex questions is the hardest challenge, one that requires the most human intuition in all of data science. Some questions, like "What is the average money spent on cereal in 2017?" can be easily defined and calculated, even on huge amounts of data. But then you have the really, really useful questions such as, "How can I get more people to buy Sugar Frosted Flakes?" Now, that is the $64,000 question. In a brazen attempt to be more scientific, we will call Sugar Frosted Flakes by the acronym SFF.

A question such as that has layers and layers of complexity behind it. You want a baseline of how much SFF your customers are currently buying. That should be pretty easy. Then you have to define what you mean by *more people*. Do you really mean *more people*, or do you mean *more revenue*? Change the price to $0.01 per box, and you will have lots more people buying SFF. You really want more revenue or more even more specifically, more margin (margin = price – cost). The question is already more complex.

But the real difficult part of the question is just how are we going to motivate people to buy more SFF? And is the answer in our data that we have collected?

That is the hard part of analysis: Making sure we are asking the right question in the right way of the right kind of data.

Analyzing the data requires skill and experience in statistics techniques like linear and logistic regressions and finding correlations between different data types by using a variety of probability algorithms and formulas such as the incredibly coolly named "Naïve Bayes" formulas and concepts. Although a full discussion of these techniques is out of the scope of this book, we go through some examples later.

## Communicating the results

After you have crunched and mangled your data into the format you need and then have analyzed the data to answer your questions, you need to present the results to management or the customer. Most people visualize information better and faster when they see it in a graphical format rather than just in text. There are two major Python packages that data science people us: The language "R" and

MatPlotLib. We use MatPlotLib in displaying our "big data graphics." (If you have read the chapters on AI (Book 4), then you have already experienced MatPlotLib firsthand.)

## Maintaining the data

This is the step in data science that everyone ignores. After you have asked your first round of questions, got your first round of answers many professionals will just basically shut down and walk away to the next project. The problem with that way of thinking is that there is a very reasonable chance that you will have to ask more questions of the same data, sometimes quite far in the future. Is important to archive and document the following information so you can restart the project quickly, or even more likely in the future you will run across a similar set of problems and can quickly dust the models off and get to answers faster.

Take time to preserve:

» The data and sources

» The models you used to modify the data (including any exception data and "data throw-out criteria" you used)

» The queries and results you got from the queries

# Chapter **2**

# Exploring Big Data with Python

I n this chapter we get into some of the tools and processes used by data scientists to format, process, and query their data.

There are a number of Python-based tools and libraries (such as "R") available, but we decided to use NumPy for three reasons. First, it is one of the two most popular tools to use for data science in Python. Second, many AI-oriented projects use NumPy (such as the one in our last chapter). And third, the highly useful Python data science package, Pandas, is built on NumPy.

Pandas is turning out to be a very important package in data science. The way it encapsulates data in a more abstract way makes it easier to manipulate, document, and understand the transformations you make in the base datasets.

Finally, MatPlotLib is a good visualization package for the results of big data. It's very Python-centric, but it suffers from a steep learning curve to get going. However, this has been ameliorated to some degree by new add-on packages, such as "seaborne."

All in all, these are reasonable packages to attack the data science problem and get some results to introduce you to this interesting field.

# Introducing NumPy, Pandas, and MatPlotLib

Anytime you look at the scientific computing and data science communities, three key Python packages keep coming up:

>> NumPy

>> Pandas

>> MatPlotLib

These are discussed in the next few sections.

## NumPy

NumPy adds big data-manipulation tools to Python such as large-array manipulation and high-level mathematical functions for data science. NumPy is best at handling basic numerical computation such as means, averages, and so on. It also excels at the creation and manipulation of multidimensional arrays known as tensors or matrices. In Book 4, we used NumPy extensively in manipulating data and tensors in neural networks and machine learning. It is an exceptional tool for artificial intelligence applications.

**TIP**

There are numerous good tutorials for NumPy on the web. A selection of some of good step-by-step ones are:

>> **NumPy Tutorial Part 1 - Introduction to Arrays** (. `https://www.machine learningplus.com/python/numpy-tutorial-part1-array-python-examples/`): A good introduction to matrices (also known as tensors) and how they fit into NumPy.

>> **NumPy Tutorial** (`https://www.tutorialspoint.com/numpy`): A nice overview of NumPy, where it comes from and how to use it.

>> **NumPy Tutorial: Learn with Example** (`https://www.guru99.com/numpy-tutorial.html`): Less theory, but a bunch of great examples to fill in the practical gaps after looking at the first two tutorials.

Here's a simple example of a NumPy program. This program builds a 2x2 matrix, then performs various matrix-oriented operations on the maxtrix:

```
import numpy as np

x = np.array([[1,2],[3,4]])
```

```
print(np.sum(x))   # Compute sum of all elements; prints "10"
print(np.sum(x, axis=0))   # Compute sum of each column; prints "[4 6]"
print(np.sum(x, axis=1))   # Compute sum of each row; prints "[3 7]"
```

## Pandas

Python is great for munging data and preparing data, but not so great for data analysis and modeling. Pandas fills this gap.

Pandas provides fast, flexible, and expressive data structures to make working with relational or labeled data more intuitive. In our opinion, it is the fundamental building block for doing real-world data analysis in Python. It performs well with tabular type of data (such as SQL tables or Excel spreadsheets) and is really good with time-series data (like, say, temperatures taken on a hourly basis).

Remember our discussion on data massaging? Dealing with missing or bad data? This is one of things that Pandas is designed for and does really well. It also allows for complex hierarchical data structures, which can be accessed using Pandas functions in a very intuitive way. You can merge and join datasets as well as convert many types of data into the ubiquitous Pandas data objects, DataFrames.

Pandas is based on NumPy and shares the speed of that Python library, and it can achieve a large increase of speed over straight Python code involving loops.

**TECHNICAL STUFF**

Pandas DataFrames are a way to store data in rectangular grids that can easily be overviewed. A DataFrame can contain other DataFrames, a one-dimensional series of data, a NumPy tensor (an array — here we go again with similarities to Book 4 on neural networks and machine learning), and dictionaries for tensors and matrices.

Besides data, you can also specify indexes and column names for your DataFrame. This makes for more understandable code for data analysis and manipulation. You can access, delete, and rename your DataFrame components as you bring in more structures and join more related data into your DataFrame structure.

## MatPlotLib

MatPlotLib is a library that adds the missing data visualization functions to Python. It is designed to complement the use of NumPy in data analysis and scientific programs. It provides a Python object-oriented API (applications programming interface) for embedded plots into applications using general-purpose GUI interfaces. For those familiar with MatLab, MatPlotLib provides a procedural version called PyLab.

With MatPlotLib, you can make elaborate and professional-looking graphs, and you can even build "live" graphs that update while your application is running. This can be handy in machine-learning applications and data-analysis applications, where it is good to see the system making progress towards some goal.

# Doing Your First Data Science Project

Time for us to put NumPy and Pandas to work on a simple data science project.

I am going to choose our dataset from the website Kaggle.com. Kaggle, whose tag line is "Your Home for Data Science," is a Google-owned online community of data scientists and users. Kaggle allows users to find datasets, download the data, and use the data under very open licenses, in most cases. Kaggle also supports a robust set of competitions for solving machine-learning problems, often posted by companies that really need the solution.

For this first problem, I want to choose a pretty simple set of data.

## Diamonds are a data scientist's best friend

I chose the "diamonds" database from Kaggle.com because it has a fairly simple structure and only has about 54,000 elements — easy for our Raspberry Pi computer to use. You can download it at `https://www.kaggle.com/shivam2503/diamonds`. Using Kaggle will require you to register and sign in to the community, but does not cost anything to do so.

The metadata (*metadata* is data describing data, hence *meta*data) consists of ten variables, which also can be thought of as column headers. (See Table 2-1.)

**TABLE 2-1**    **Columns in the Diamond Database**

| Column Header | Type of Data | Description |
| --- | --- | --- |
| Index counter | Numeric | |
| carat | Numeric | Carat weight of the diamond |
| cut | Text | Describe cut quality of the diamond. Quality in increasing order Fair, Good, Very Good, Premium, Ideal |
| color | Text | Color of the diamond, with D being the best and J the worst |

| Column Header | Type of Data | Description |
|---|---|---|
| clarity | Text | How obvious inclusions are within the diamond: (in order from best to worst, FL = flawless, I3= level 3 inclusions) FL,IF, VVS1, VVS2, VS1, VS2, SI1, SI2, I1, I2, I3 |
| depth | Numeric | Depth %: The height of a diamond, measured from the culet to the table, divided by its average girdle diameter |
| table | Numeric | Table %: The width of the diamond's table expressed as a percentage of its average diameter |
| price | Numeric | The price of the diamond |
| x | Numeric | Length mm |
| y | Numeric | Width mm |
| x | Numeric | Depth mm |

If you were to use this as a training set for a machine-learning program, you would see a program using NumPy and TensorFlow very similar to the one we show you in Book 4. In this chapter, we are going to show you a set of simple pandas-based data analysis to read our data and ask some questions.

I'm going to use a DataFrame in pandas (a 2D-labeled data structure with columns that can be of different types). The Panels data structure is a 3D container of data. I am sticking with DataFrames in this example because DataFrames makes it easier to visualize 2D data.

**TIP**

If you are installing NumPy and pandas on the Raspberry Pi, use these commands:

```
sudo apt-get install python3-numpy
sudo apt-get install python3-pandas
```

Now it is time for an example.

Using nano (or your favorite text editor), open up a file called FirstDiamonds.py and enter the following code:

```
# Diamonds are a Data Scientist's Best Friend

#import the pandas and numpy library
import numpy as np
import pandas as pd



# read the diamonds CSV file
```

```
# build a DataFrame from the data
df = pd.read_csv('diamonds.csv')


print (df.head(10))
print()

# calculate total value of diamonds
sum = df.price.sum()
print ("Total $ Value of Diamonds: ${:0,.2f}".format( sum))

# calculate mean price of diamonds

mean = df.price.mean()
print ("Mean $ Value of Diamonds: ${:0,.2f}".format(mean))

#  summarize the data
descrip = df.carat.describe()
print()
print (descrip)

descrip = df.describe(include='object')
print()
print (descrip)
```

Making sure you have the diamonds.csv file in your directory, run the following command:

```
python3 FirstDiamonds.py
```

And you should see the following results:

| | Unnamed: 0 | carat | cut | color | clarity | depth | table | price | x |
|---|---|---|---|---|---|---|---|---|---|
| | y | z | | | | | | | |
| 0 | 1 | 0.23 | Ideal | E | SI2 | 61.5 | 55.0 | 326 | 3.95 |
| | 3.98 | 2.43 | | | | | | | |
| 1 | 2 | 0.21 | Premium | E | SI1 | 59.8 | 61.0 | 326 | 3.89 |
| | 3.84 | 2.31 | | | | | | | |
| 2 | 3 | 0.23 | Good | E | VS1 | 56.9 | 65.0 | 327 | 4.05 |
| | 4.07 | 2.31 | | | | | | | |
| 3 | 4 | 0.29 | Premium | I | VS2 | 62.4 | 58.0 | 334 | 4.20 |
| | 4.23 | 2.63 | | | | | | | |
| 4 | 5 | 0.31 | Good | J | SI2 | 63.3 | 58.0 | 335 | 4.34 |
| | 4.35 | 2.75 | | | | | | | |
| 5 | 6 | 0.24 | Very Good | J | VVS2 | 62.8 | 57.0 | 336 | 3.94 |
| | 3.96 | 2.48 | | | | | | | |
| 6 | 7 | 0.24 | Very Good | I | VVS1 | 62.3 | 57.0 | 336 | 3.95 |
| | 3.98 | 2.47 | | | | | | | |

```
7          8  0.26  Very Good  H  SI1  61.9  55.0  337  4.07
     4.11  2.53
8          9  0.22       Fair  E  VS2  65.1  61.0  337  3.87
     3.78  2.49
9         10  0.23  Very Good  H  VS1  59.4  61.0  338  4.00
     4.05  2.39

Total $ Value of Diamonds: $212,135,217.00
Mean $ Value of Diamonds: $3,932.80

count    53940.000000
mean         0.797940
std          0.474011
min          0.200000
25%          0.400000
50%          0.700000
75%          1.040000
max          5.010000
Name: carat, dtype: float64


          cut  color  clarity
count   53940  53940    53940
unique      5      7        8
top     Ideal      G      SI1
freq    21551  11292    13065
```

That's a lot of data for a short piece of code!

# Breaking down the code

```
# Diamonds are a Data Scientist's Best Friend
```

First, we import all the needed libraries:

```
#import the pandas and numpy library
import numpy as np
import pandas as pd
```

Read the `diamonds` file into a pandas DataFrame. Note: We didn't have to format and manipulate the data in this file. This is not the normal situation in real data science. You will often spend a significant amount of time getting your data where you want it to be — sometimes as much time as the entire rest of the project.

```
# read the diamonds CSV file
# build a DataFrame from the data
df = pd.read_csv('diamonds.csv')
```

Just for a sanity check, let's print out the first ten rows in the DataFrame.

```
print (df.head(10))
print()
```

Here we calculate a couple of values from the column named price. Note that we get to use the column as part of the DataFrame object. It's great that you can do this with Python!

```
# calculate total value of diamonds
sum = df.price.sum()
print ("Total $ Value of Diamonds: ${:0,.2f}".format( sum))

# calculate mean price of diamonds

mean = df.price.mean()
print ("Mean $ Value of Diamonds: ${:0,.2f}".format(mean))
```

Now we run the built-in describe function to first describe and summarize the data about carat.

```
#  summarize the data
descrip = df.carat.describe()
print()
print (descrip)
```

This next statement prints out a description for all the nonnumeric columns in our DataFrame: specifically, the cut, color, and clarity columns:

```
descrip = df.describe(include='object')
print()
print (descrip)
```

TIP

To install MatPlotLib on your Raspberry Pi, type pip3 install matplotlib.

# Visualizing the data with MatPlotLib

Now we move to the data visualization of our data with MatPlotLib. In Book 4 we use MatPlotLib to draw some graphs related to the way our machine-learning program improved its accuracy during training. Now we use MatPlotLib to show some interesting things about our dataset.

**WARNING**

For these programs to work, you need to be running them from a terminal window inside the Raspberry Pi GUI. You can use VNC to get a GUI if you are running your Raspberry Pi headless.

One of the really useful things about pandas and MatPlotLib is that the NumPy and DataFrame types are very compatible with the required graphic formats. They are all based on matrices and NumPy arrays.

Our first plot is a scatter plot showing diamond clarity versus diamond carat size.

## Diamond clarity versus carat size

Using nano (or your favorite text editor), open up a file called Plot_Clarity VSCarat.py and enter the following code:

```
# Looking at the Shiny Diamonds

#import the pandas and numpy library
import numpy as np
import pandas as pd
import matplotlib.pyplot as plt


# read the diamonds CSV file
# build a DataFrame from the data
df = pd.read_csv('diamonds.csv')


import matplotlib.pyplot as plt

carat = df.carat
clarity = df.clarity
plt.scatter(clarity, carat)
plt.show()  # or plt.savefig("name.png")
```

Run your program. Now, how is that for ease in plotting? Pandas and MatPlotLib go hand-in-hand.

Remember that diamond clarity is measured by how obvious inclusions (see Figure 2-1) are within the diamond: FL, IF, VVS1, VVS2, VS1, VS2, SI1, SI2, I1, I2, I3 (in order from best to worst: FL = flawless, I3= level 3 inclusions). Note that we had no flawless diamonds in our diamond database.

One would be tempted to make a statement that the largest diamonds are rated as IF. However, remember that you really have no idea how this data was collected and so you really can't draw such general conclusions. All you can say is that "In this dataset, the clarity 'IL' has the largest diamonds."

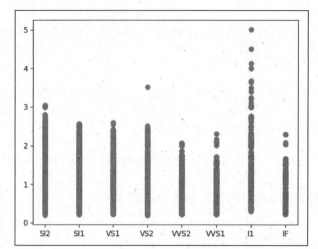

FIGURE 2-1:
Diamond clarity
(horizontal)
versus carat size
(vertical).

## Number of diamonds in each clarity type

Using nano (or your favorite text editor), open up a file called `Plot_Count Clarity.py` and enter the following code:

```python
# Looking at the Shiny Diamonds

#import the pandas and numpy library
import numpy as np
import pandas as pd
import matplotlib.pyplot as plt

# read the diamonds CSV file
# build a DataFrame from the data
df = pd.read_csv('diamonds.csv')


import matplotlib.pyplot as plt

# count the number of each textual type of clarity

clarityindexes = df['clarity'].value_counts().index.tolist()
claritycount= df['clarity'].value_counts().values.tolist()

print(clarityindexes)
print(claritycount)

plt.bar(clarityindexes, claritycount)
plt.show()  # or plt.savefig("name.png")
```

Run your program. The result is shown in Figure 2-2.

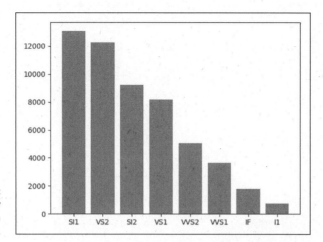

Again, remember that diamond clarity is measured by how obvious inclusions are within the diamond: FL,IF, VVS1, VVS2, VS1, VS2, SI1, SI2, I1, I2, I3 (in order from best to worst: FL = flawless, I3= level 3 inclusions). Note that we had no flawless diamonds in our diamond database.

By this graph, we can see that the medium-quality diamonds SI1,VS2, and SI2 are most represented in our diamond dataset.

## Number of diamonds in each color type

I looked at clarity, now let's look at color type in our pile of diamonds. Using nano (or your favorite text editor), open up a file called Plot_CountColor.py and enter the following code (which generates Figure 2-3):

```
# Looking at the Shiny Diamonds


#import the pandas and numpy library
import numpy as np
import pandas as pd
import matplotlib.pyplot as plt


# read the diamonds CSV file
# build a DataFrame from the data
df = pd.read_csv('diamonds.csv')



import matplotlib.pyplot as plt
```

```
# count the number of each textual type of color

colorindexes = df['color'].value_counts().index.tolist()
colorcount= df['color'].value_counts().values.tolist()

print(colorindexes)
print(colorcount)

plt.bar(colorindexes, colorcount)
plt.show()  # or plt.savefig("name.png")
```

Run your program.

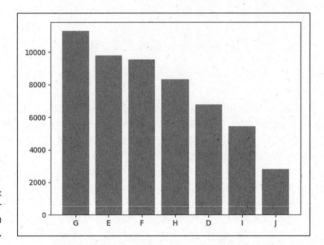

**FIGURE 2-3:**
Diamond color
count in each
type.

The color "G" represents about 25 percent of our sample size. That "G" is almost colorless. The general rule is less color, higher price. The exceptions to this are the pinks and blues, which are outside of this color mapping and sample.

## Using Pandas for finding correlations: Heat plots

The last plot I am going to show you is called a *heat plot*. It is used to graphically show correlations between numeric values inside our database. In this plot we take all the numerical values and create a correlation matrix that shows how closely they correlate with each other. To quickly and easily generate this graph, we use another library for Python and MatPlotLib called seaborn. Seaborn provides an API built on top of MatPlotLib that integrates with pandas DataFrames, which makes it ideal for data science.

**TIP**

If you don't already have seaborn on your Raspberry Pi (and if you have installed MatPlotLib, you probably already do). Run the example Python program `Plot_Heat.py` to find out whether you do. If not, then run the following command:

```
sudo apt-get install python3-seaborn
```

Using nano (or your favorite text editor), open up a file called `Plot_Heat.py` and enter the following code:

```python
# Looking at the Shiny Diamonds

#import the pandas and numpy library
import numpy as np
import pandas as pd

import matplotlib.pyplot as plt
import seaborn as sns

# read the diamonds CSV file
# build a DataFrame from the data
df = pd.read_csv('diamonds.csv')

# drop the index column
df = df.drop('Unnamed: 0', axis=1)

f, ax = plt.subplots(figsize=(10, 8))
corr = df.corr()
print (corr)
sns.heatmap(corr, mask=np.zeros_like(corr, dtype=np.bool),
        cmap=sns.diverging_palette(220, 10, as_cmap=True),
                square=True, ax=ax)

plt.show()
```

Run the program and feast on some real data visualization in Figure 2-4.

The first thing to notice about Figure 2-4 is that the more red the color, the higher the correlation between the two variables. The diagonal stripe from top left to top bottom shows that, for example, carat correlates 100 percent with carat. No surprise there. The $x$, $y$, and $z$ variables quite correlate with each other, which says that as the diamonds in our database increase in one dimension, they increase in the other two dimensions as well.

How about price? As carat and size increases, so does price. This makes sense. Interestingly, depth (The height of a diamond, measured from the culet to the table, divided by its average girdle diameter) does not correlated very strongly at all with price and in fact is somewhat negatively correlated.

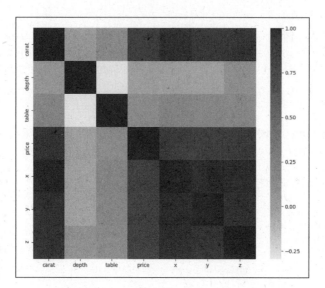

**FIGURE 2-4:**
Correlation
heat chart.

It is amazing the amount of inferences you can draw from this kind of a map. Heat maps are fabulous for spotting general cross-correlations in your data.

It would be interesting to see the correlation between color/clarity and price. Why isn't it on this chart? This is because those columns are textual, and you can do only correlations on numerical values. How could you fix that? By substituting a numerical code (1–8, for example) for each color letter and then re-generating the heat chart again. The same technique can be used on diamond clarity.

# Chapter **3**

# Using Big Data from the Google Cloud

U p to this point, we have been dealing with some relatively small sets of data. Now we are going to use some big data — in some cases, very big data that change every hour!

Sometimes we are working on a powerful enough computer that we can download a large dataset like these, but not every big dataset can be downloaded. For that matter, not all datasets legally can be downloaded. And in the case of the air quality database, you would have download a new version every hour. In cases like those, it's better to leave the data where it is and use the cloud to do the work.

One interesting ramification of doing the heavy lifting in the cloud is that your computer doesn't have to be very big or fast. Just let the cloud do the database and analysis work.

## What Is Big Data?

*Big data* refers to datasets that are too large or complex to be dealt with using traditional data-processing techniques. Data with many cases and many rows offer greater accessibility to sophisticated statistical techniques, and they generally lead to a smaller false discovery rate. As we discuss in Chapter 1 of this minibook, big data is becoming more and more prevalent in our society as the number of computers and sensors are proliferating and creating more and more data at an ever-increasing rate.

In this chapter, we talk about using the cloud to access these large databases using Python and Pandas and then visualizing the results on a Raspberry Pi.

# Understanding the Google Cloud and BigQuery

Well, sometimes to access Big Data, you need to use a BigQuery. It is important to understand that you aren't just storing the data up in the cloud, you are also using the data analysis tools in the cloud. Basically, you are using your computer to command what these computers up in the cloud do with the data.

## The Google Cloud Platform

The Google Cloud Platform is a suite of cloud computing services that run on the same infrastructure as Google end-user products such as Google Search and YouTube. This is a cloud strategy that has been successfully used at Amazon and Microsoft. Using your own data services and products to build a cloud offering really seems to produce a good environment for both the user and the company to benefit from advances and improvements to both products and clouds.

The Google Cloud Platform has over 100 different APIs (application programming interfaces) and data service products available for data science and artificial intelligence uses. The primary service we use in this chapter is the Google API called BigQuery.

## BigQuery from Google

A REST (Representational State Transfer) software system is a set of code that defines a set of communication structures to be used for creating web services, typically using http and https requests to communicate. This provides a large set of interoperability for different computers with different operating systems trying to access the same web service.

BigQuery is based on a RESTful web service (think of contacting web pages with URL addresses that ask specific questions in a standard format and then getting a response back just like a browser gets a webpage) and a number of libraries for Python and other languages hide the complexity of the queries going back and forth.

Abstraction in software systems is key to making big systems work and reasonable to program. For example, although a web browser uses HTML to display web pages, there are layers and layers of software under that, doing things like transmitting IP packets or manipulating bits. These lower layers are different if you are using a wired network or a WiFi network. The cool thing about abstraction here is up at the webpage level, we don't care. We just use it.

BigQuery is a serverless model. This means that BigQuery has about the highest level of abstraction in the cloud community, removing the user's responsibility for worrying about spinning up VMs (bringing a new virtual machines online in the cloud), RAM, numbers of CPUs, and so on. You can scale from one to thousands of CPUs in a matter of seconds, paying only for the resources you actually use. Understand that in this book, Google will let you use the cloud for free, so you won't even have to pay at all during your trial.

BigQuery has a large number of public big-data datasets, such as those from Medicare and NOAA (National Oceanic and Atmospheric Agency). We make use of these datasets in our examples below.

One of the most interesting features of BigQuery is the ability to stream data into BigQuery on the order of millions of rows (data samples) per second, data you can start to analyze almost immediately.

We will be using BigQuery with the Python library pandas. The Python library google.cloud provides a Python library that maps the BigQuery data into our friendly pandas DataFrames familiar from Chapter 2.

# Computer security on the cloud

We would be remiss if we didn't talk just a little bit about maintaining good computer security when using the cloud. Google accomplishes this by using the IAM (identity and access management) paradigm throughout its cloud offerings. This lets administrators authorize who can take what kind of action on specific resources, giving you full control and visibility for simple projects as well as finely grained access extending across an entire enterprise.

We show you how to set up the IAM authentication in the sections that follow.

Medicare is the national health insurance program (single payer) in the United States administered by the Centers for Medicare and Medicade Services (CMS). It provides health insurance for Americans aged 65 and over. It also provides health insurance to younger people with certain disabilities and conditions. In 2017 it provided health insurance to over 58 million individuals.

With 58 million individuals in the system, Medicare is generating a huge amount of big data every year. Google and CMS teamed up to put a large amount of this data on the BigQuery public database so you can take a peek at this data and do some analytics without trying to load it all on your local machine. A home computer, PC or Raspberry Pi, won't hold all the data available.

## Signing up on Google for BigQuery

Go to cloud.google.com and sign up for your free trial. Although Google requires a credit card to prove you are not a robot, they will not charge you even when your trial is over without you manually switching over to a paid account. If you exceed $300 during your trial (which you shouldn't), Google will notify you but will not charge you.

The $300 limit to the trial should be plenty enough to allow you to do a bunch of queries and learning on the BigQuery cloud platform.

# Reading the Medicare Big Data

Now we show you how to set up a project and get your authentication `.json` file to start using BigQuery on your own Python programs.

## Setting up your project and authentication

To access the Google cloud you will need to set up a project and then receive your authentication credentials from Google to be able to use their systems. The following steps will show you how to do this:

1. **Go to** `https://console.developers.google.com/` **and sign in using your account name and password generated earlier.**

2. **Next, click the My First Project button up in the upper-left corner of the screen.**

   It shows you a screen like the one in Figure 3-1.

3. **Click the New Project button on the pop-up screen.**

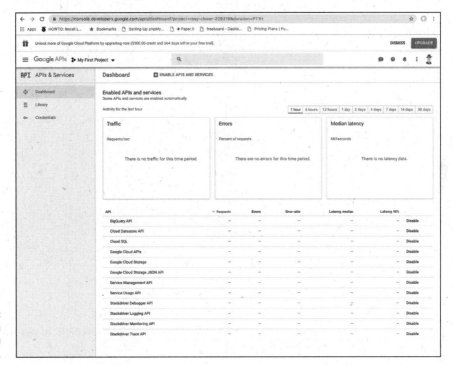

**FIGURE 3-1:**
The Select a Project page on the Google Cloud.

4. **Fill out your project name as** MedicareProject **and click Create.**

5. **Next, select your project,** MedicareProject, **from the upper-left menu button.**

   **REMEMBER**

   Make sure you don't leave this on the default "My Project" selection. Make sure you change it to MedicareProject — otherwise you will be setting up the APIs and authentication for the wrong project. This is an easy mistake to make.

6. **After you have selected** MedicareProject, **click on the "+" button near the top to enable the BigQuery API.**

7. **When the API selection screen comes up, search for** *BigQuery* **and select the BigQuery API. Then click Enable.**

**8.** Now to get our authentication credentials. In the left-hand menu, choose Credentials.

A screen like the one in Figure 3-2 comes up.

**9.** Select the BigQuery API and then click the No, I'm Not Using Them option in the Are You Planning to Use This API with the App Engine or Compute Engine? section.

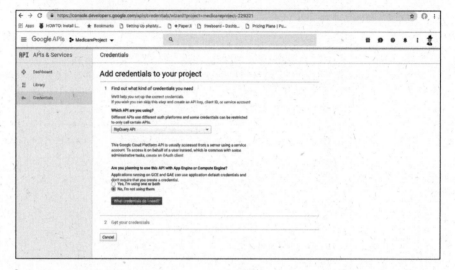

**FIGURE 3-2:**
First credential
screen.

**10.** Click the What Credentials Do I Need? button to get to our last screen, as shown in Figure 3-3.

**11.** Type MedicareProject into the Service Account Name textbox and then select Project⇨Owner in the Role menu.

**12.** Leave the JSON radio button selected and click Continue.

A message appears saying that the service account and key has been created. A file called something similar to "MedicareProject–1223xxxxx413.json" is downloaded to your computer.

**13.** Copy that downloaded file into the directory that you will be building your Python program file in.

Now let's move on to our first example.

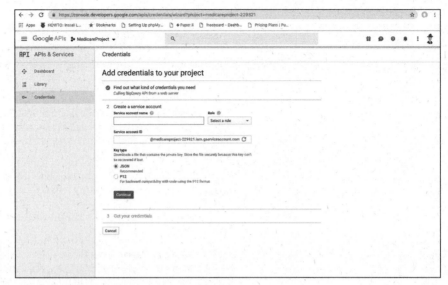

**FIGURE 3-3:**
Second credential
screen.

# The first big-data code

This program reads one of the public data Medicare datasets and grabs some data for analysis. There are several dozen datasets available now and there will be more and more available with time. We start by using the inpatient_charges_2015 dataset. We use a SQL query to select the information from the dataset that we want to look at and eventually analyze. (Check out the nearby sidebar, "Learning SQL," to see where to learn about SQL if you are not already familiar with this ubiquitous query language.)

Table 3-1 shows all the columns in the inpatient_charges_2015 dataset.

**TABLE 3-1** **Columns, Types, and Descriptions of the inpatient_charges_2015 Dataset**

| Column | Type | Description |
| --- | --- | --- |
| provider_id | STRING | The CMS certification number (CCN) of the provider billing for outpatient hospital services. |
| provider_name | STRING | The name of the provider. |
| provider_street_address | STRING | The street address in which the provider is physically located. |
| provider_city | STRING | The city in which the provider is physically located. |

*(continued)*

**TABLE 3-1** *(continued)*

| Column | Type | Description |
|---|---|---|
| provider_state | STRING | The state in which the provider is physically located. |
| provider_zipcode | INTEGER | The zip code in which the provider is physically located. |
| drg_definition | STRING | The code and description identifying the MS-DRG. MS-DRGs are a classification system that groups similar clinical conditions (diagnoses) and the procedures furnished by the hospital during the stay. |
| hospital_referral_region_description | STRING | The hospital referral region (HRR) in which the provider is physically located. |
| total_discharges | INTEGER | The number of discharges billed by the provider for inpatient hospital services. |
| average_covered_charges | FLOAT | The provider's average charge for services covered by Medicare for all discharges in the MS-DRG. These will vary from hospital to hospital because of differences in hospital charge structures. |
| average_total_payments | FLOAT | The average total payments to all providers for the MS-DRG including the MSDRG amount, teaching, disproportionate share, capital, and outlier payments for all cases. Also included 5 in average total payments are co-payment and deductible amounts that the patient is responsible for and any additional payments by third parties for coordination of benefits. |
| average_medicare_payments | FLOAT | The average amount that Medicare pays to the provider for Medicare's share of the MS-DRG. Average Medicare payment amounts include the MS-DRG amount, teaching, disproportionate share, capital, and outlier payments for all cases. Medicare payments *do not* include beneficiary co-payments and deductible amounts nor any additional payments from third parties for coordination of benefits. |

Using nano (or any other text editor) enter the following code into your editor and then save it as MedicareQuery1.py:

```python
import pandas as pd
from google.cloud import bigquery


# set up the query

QUERY = """
        SELECT provider_city, provider_state, drg_definition,
        average_total_payments, average_medicare_payments
        FROM `bigquery-public-data.cms_medicare.inpatient_charges_2015`
        WHERE provider_city = "GREAT FALLS" AND provider_state = "MT"
```

```
        ORDER BY provider_city ASC
        LIMIT 1000
        """


client = bigquery.Client.from_service_account_json(
        'MedicareProject2-122xxxxxf413.json')


query_job = client.query(QUERY)
df = query_job.to_dataframe()

print ("Records Returned: ", df.shape )
print ()
print ("First 3 Records")
print (df.head(3))
```

As soon as you have built this file, replace the `MedicareProject2-122xxxxxf413.json` file with your own authentication filename (which you copied into the program directory earlier).

TIP

If you don't have the google.cloud library installed, type this into your terminal window on the Raspberry Pi:

```
pip3 install google-cloud-bigquery
```

## LEARNING SQL

SQL (Structured Query Language) is a query-oriented language used to interface with databases and to extract information from those databases. Although it was designed for relational database access and management, it has been extended to many other types of databases, including the data being accessed by BigQuery and the Google Cloud.

Here are some excellent tutorials to get your head around how to access data using SQL:

- https://www.w3schools.com/sql/

- http://www.sql-tutorial.net/

- *SQL For Dummies*, Allen G. Taylor

- *SQL All In One For Dummies 3rd Edition*, Allen G. Tayor

- *SQL in 10 Minutes*, Ben Forta

# Breaking down the code

First, we import our libraries. Note the `google.cloud` library and the `bigquery` import:

```
import pandas as pd
from google.cloud import bigquery
```

Next we set up the SQL query used to fetch the data we are looking for into a pandas DataFrame for us to analyze:

```
# set up the query

QUERY = """
        SELECT provider_city, provider_state, drg_definition,
        average_total_payments, average_medicare_payments
        FROM `bigquery-public-data.cms_medicare.inpatient_charges_2015`
        WHERE provider_city = "GREAT FALLS" AND provider_state = "MT"
        ORDER BY provider_city ASC
        LIMIT 1000
        """
```

See the structure of the SQL query? We SELECT the columns that we want that are given in Table 3-1 FROM the database `bigquery-public-data.cms_medicare.inpatient_charges_2015` only WHERE the `provider_city` is GREAT FALLS and the `provider_state` is MT. Finally we tell the system to order the results by ascending alphanumeric order by the `provider_city`. Which, since we only selected one city, is somewhat redundant.

Remember to replace the json filename below with your authentication file. This one won't work.

```
client = bigquery.Client.from_service_account_json(
            'MedicareProject2-122xxxxxef413.json')
```

Now we fire the query off to the BigQuery cloud:

```
query_job = client.query(QUERY)
```

And we translate the results to our good friend the Pandas DataFrame:

```
df = query_job.to_dataframe()
```

Now just a few results to see what we got back:

```
print ("Records Returned: ", df.shape )
print ()
print ("First 3 Records")
print (df.head(3))
```

Run your program using `python3 MedicareQuery1.py` and you should see results as below. Note: If you get an authentication error, then go back and make sure you put the correct authentication file into your directory. And if necessary, repeat the whole generate-an-authentication-file routine again, paying special attention to the project name selection.

```
Records Returned: (112, 5)

First 3 Records
   provider_city provider_state

   drg_ definition  average_total_payments  average_medicare_payments
0   GREAT FALLS          MT  064 - INTRACRANIAL HEMORRHAGE OR CEREBRAL
    INFA...          11997.11                  11080.32
1   GREAT FALLS          MT          039 - EXTRACRANIAL PROCEDURES W/O
    CC/MCC           7082.85                   5954.81
2   GREAT FALLS          MT  065 - INTRACRANIAL HEMORRHAGE OR CEREBRAL
    INFA...          7140.80                   6145.38
Visualizing your Data
```

We found 112 records from Great Falls. You can go back and change the query in your program to select your own city and state.

# A bit of analysis next

Okay, now we have established connection with a pretty big-data type of database. Now let's set up another query. We would like to look for patients with "bone diseases and arthropathies without major complication or comorbidity." This is MS_DRG code 554. This is done through one of the most arcane and complicated coding systems in the world, called ICD-10, which maps virtually any diagnostic condition to a single code.

We are going to search the entire `inpatient_charges_2015` dataset looking for the MS_DRG code 554, which is "Bone Diseases And Arthropathies Without Major Complication Or Comorbidity," or, in other words, people who have issues with their bones, but with no serious issues currently manifesting externally.

# ICD CODES

ICD10 is the well-established method for coding medical professional diagnoses for billing and analysis purposes. The latest version of ICD-10 was finally made mandatory in 2015 with great angst throughout the medical community. It consists of, at its largest expanse, over 155,000 codes, from M79.603 - Pain in Arm, unspecified to S92.4– Fracture of Greater Toe. These codes are somewhat merged into the MS_DRG codes that are used in the Medicare databases we examine here as they are used for hospital admissions. John Shovic had a medical software startup that used ICD 10 codes for ten years, and he got to have a love/hate relationship with these codes.

His favorite ICD-10 codes:

- V97.33XD: Sucked into jet engine, subsequent encounter.

- Z63.1: Problems in relationship with in-laws.

- V95.43XS: Spacecraft collision injuring occupant, sequela.

- R46.1: Bizarre personal appearance.

- Y93.D1 Activity, knitting and crocheting.

The code for this is as follows:

```python
import pandas as pd
from google.cloud import bigquery


# set up the query

QUERY = """
        SELECT provider_city, provider_state, drg_definition,
        average_total_payments, average_medicare_payments
        FROM `bigquery-public-data.cms_medicare.inpatient_charges_2015`
        WHERE drg_definition LIKE  '554 %'
        ORDER BY provider_city ASC
        LIMIT 1000
        """

client = bigquery.Client.from_service_account_json(
            'MedicareProject2-1223283ef413.json')


query_job = client.query(QUERY)
df = query_job.to_dataframe()
```

```
print ("Records Returned: ", df.shape )
print ()
print ("First 3 Records")
print (df.head(3))
```

The only thing different in this program from our previous one is that we added LIKE '554 %', which will match on any DRG that starts with "554."

Running the program gets these results:

```
Records Returned:  (286, 5)

First 3 Records
   provider_city provider_state                              drg_definition
     average_total_payments  average_medicare_payments
0        ABINGTON            PA  554 - BONE DISEASES & ARTHROPATHIES W/O MCC
     5443.67                    3992.93
1           AKRON            OH  554 - BONE DISEASES & ARTHROPATHIES W/O MCC
     5581.00                    4292.47
2          ALBANY            NY  554 - BONE DISEASES & ARTHROPATHIES W/O MCC
     7628.94                    5137.31
```

Now we have some interesting data. Let's do a little analysis. What percent of the total payments for this condition is paid for by Medicare (the remainder paid by the patient)? The code for that will be (let's call it MedicareQuery3.py):

```
import pandas as pd
from google.cloud import bigquery


# set up the query

QUERY = """
        SELECT provider_city, provider_state, drg_definition,
        average_total_payments, average_medicare_payments
        FROM `bigquery-public-data.cms_medicare.inpatient_charges_2015`
        WHERE drg_definition LIKE '554 %'
        ORDER BY provider_city ASC
        LIMIT 1000
        """

client = bigquery.Client.from_service_account_json(
           'MedicareProject2-1223283ef413.json')


query_job = client.query(QUERY)
df = query_job.to_dataframe()
```

```
print ("Records Returned: ", df.shape )
print ()


total_payment = df.average_total_payments.sum()
medicare_payment = df.average_medicare_payments.sum()


percent_paid = ((medicare_payment/total_payment))*100
print ("Medicare pays {:4.2f}% of Total for 554 DRG".format(percent_paid))
print ("Patient pays {:4.2f}% of Total for 554 DRG".format(100-percent_paid))
```

And the results:

```
Records Returned:  (286, 5)


Medicare pays 77.06% of Total for 554 DRG
Patient pays 22.94% of Total for 554 DRG
```

# Payment percent by state

Now in this program we select the unique states in our database (not all states are represented) and iterate over the states to calculate the percent paid by Medicare by state for 554. Let's call this one `MedicareQuery4.py`:

```
import pandas as pd
from google.cloud import bigquery


# set up the query

QUERY = """
        SELECT provider_city, provider_state, drg_definition,
        average_total_payments, average_medicare_payments
        FROM `bigquery-public-data.cms_medicare.inpatient_charges_2015`
        WHERE drg_definition LIKE  '554 %'
        ORDER BY provider_city ASC
        LIMIT 1000
        """

client = bigquery.Client.from_service_account_json(
            'MedicareProject2-1223283ef413.json')


query_job = client.query(QUERY)
df = query_job.to_dataframe()
```

```
print ("Records Returned: ", df.shape )
print ()

# find the unique values of State

states = df.provider_state.unique()
states.sort()

total_payment = df.average_total_payments.sum()
medicare_payment = df.average_medicare_payments.sum()

percent_paid = ((medicare_payment/total_payment))*100
print("Overall:")
print ("Medicare pays {:4.2f}% of Total for 554 DRG".format(percent_paid))
print ("Patient pays {:4.2f}% of Total for 554 DRG".format(100-percent_paid))

print ("Per State:")

# now iterate over states

print(df.head(5))
state_percent = []
for current_state in states:
    state_df = df[df.provider_state == current_state]

    state_total_payment = state_df.average_total_payments.sum()

    state_medicare_payment = state_df.average_medicare_payments.sum()

    state_percent_paid = ((state_medicare_payment/state_total_payment))*100
    state_percent.append(state_percent_paid)

    print ("{:s} Medicare pays {:4.2f}% of Total for 554 DRG".format
    (current_state,state_percent_paid))
```

## And now some visualization

For our last experiment, let's visualize the state-by-state data over a graph using MatPlotLib. (See Figure 3-4.)Moving over to our VNC program to have a GUI on our Raspberry Pi, we add the following code to the end of the preceding Medicare Query4.py code:

```
# we could graph this using MatPlotLib with the two lists
# but we want to use DataFrames for this example

data_array = {'State': states, 'Percent': state_percent}
```

```
df_states = pd.DataFrame.from_dict(data_array)

# Now back in dataframe land
import matplotlib.pyplot as plt
import seaborn as sb

print (df_states)

df_states.plot(kind='bar', x='State', y= 'Percent')
plt.show()
```

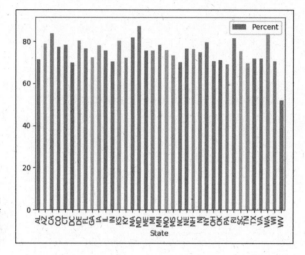

**FIGURE 3-4:**
Bar chart of
Medicare % paid
per state for 554.

Do you already have seaborn on your Raspberry Pi (and if you have installed MatPlotLib, you probably already do)? To find out, run the `MedicareQuery4.py` example Python program. If you don't have seaborne installed, then run the following command:

```
sudo apt-get install python3-seaborn
```

# Looking for the Most Polluted City in the World on an Hourly Basis

Just one more quick example. There is another public database on BigQuery, OpenAQ, which contains air-quality measurements from 47 countries around the world. And this database is updated *hourly*, believe it or not.

Here is some code that picks up the top three worst polluted cities in the world measured by air quality:

```python
import pandas as pd
from google.cloud import bigquery

# sample query from:
QUERY = """
        SELECT location, city, country, value, timestamp
        FROM `bigquery-public-data.openaq.global_air_quality`
        WHERE pollutant = "pm10" AND timestamp > "2017-04-01"
        ORDER BY value DESC
        LIMIT 1000
        """

client = bigquery.Client.from_service_account_json(
                    'MedicareProject2-1223283ef413.json')
query_job = client.query(QUERY)
df = query_job.to_dataframe()

print (df.head(3))
```

Copy this code into a file called PollutedCity.py and run the program.

The current result of running the code (as of the writing of this book) was:

|   | location | city | country | value | timestamp |
|---|----------|------|---------|-------|-----------|
| 0 | Dilovası | Kocaeli | TR | 5243.00 | 2018-01-25 12:00:00+00:00 |
| 1 | Bukhiin urguu | Ulaanbaatar | MN | 1428.00 | 2019-01-21 17:00:00+00:00 |
| 2 | Chaiten Norte | Chaiten Norte | CL | 999.83 | 2018-04-24 11:00:00+00:00 |

It looks like Dilovasi, Kocaeli, Turkey is not a healthy place to be right now. Doing a quick Google search of Dilovasi finds that cancer rates are three times higher than the worldwide average. This striking difference apparently stems from the environmental heavy metal pollution persisting in the area for about 40 years, mainly due to intense industrialization.

I'll definitely be checking this on a daily basis.

# 6

# Talking to Hardware with Python

# Contents at a Glance

Chapter **1**

# Introduction to Physical Computing

We have been talking about how to program in Python for the last several hundred pages in this book. It is now time to use our newly acquired Python skills to start doing things in the real world. We call this *physical computing* — making a computer interact with the world around you!

In our opinion, it is more difficult to learn about the software (Python) than it is about the hardware. That's why this book is mostly focused on learning how to program computers with Python. But now it is time to learn how to make your computers *do* something with Python.

**WARNING**

In this chapter, we hook up various sensors and motors to a Raspberry Pi computer. Although the voltages (3.3V and 5V) used with these computers are not dangerous to people, hooking up things incorrectly can burn out your computer or your sensors. For this reason, follow these two rules assiduously:

» **Rule 1:** Turn *all* the power off before you hook up or change any wires.

» **Rule 2:** Double-check your connections, especially the power connections, power and ground. These are the most important wires to check. See the next chapter on why these are so important!

# Physical Computing Is Fun

One reason that we want to you to learn about physical computing is that little computers doing physical things (typically called *embedded systems*) are everywhere around you. And we mean everywhere. Go up to your kitchen. Look around. Your refrigerator has a computer, maybe two or three if it has a display. Your blender has a computer. Your oven has a computer. Your microwave has a computer. If you use Phillips Hue lights in your house, your light bulbs have a computer. Your car will have upwards of 20 computers in the vehicle.

One more example. How about the lowly toaster? If you have a "Bagel Button" or a display on your toaster, you have a computer in there. Why? Why are there so many computers in your house? Because it is significantly less expensive to build all your gadgets using a computer than it is to design special hardware. Do you know you can buy computers (in bulk) for about $0.15? Computers are everywhere.

Most of these computers are much simpler, slower, and carrying much less RAM (a form of storage) than your average PC. A PC may have about 4–16 or more GB (that's gigabytes, and 1GB equals approximately 1 billion bytes), but the computer running your toaster probably only has about 100 bytes. This is a difference of over 10,000,000 times the amount of RAM. By the way, you can think of one byte as equal to one character in English. In most Asian countries, one character equals two bytes.

So computers are everywhere. But the interesting thing is that all these little computers are doing physical computing. They are sensing and interacting with the environment. The refrigerator computer is checking to see whether it is at the right temperature, and if it is not, it turns on the cooling machinery, paying attention to what it is doing to minimize the amount of electricity it uses. The stove is updating your display on the front panel, monitoring the buttons and dials and controlling the temperature so you get a good lasagna for dinner.

All of these interactions and controllers are called *physical computing*.

# What Is a Raspberry Pi?

In this book, we could use one of these very small computers but the functionality is limited compared to your PC, so we will compromise and use the Raspberry Pi, a $35 computer that has an immense amount of hardware and software available for use (especially in Python). It's more complex than a toaster, but it's much simpler than even the computer used in your TV.

A Raspberry Pi is a popular SBC (single board computer) that has been around since about 2012. It was created by the Raspberry Pi Foundation to teach basic science and engineering in schools around the world. It turned out to be wildly popular and has sold more than 19 million computers around the world. There a are a bunch of other Raspberry Pi models available (from the $5 Raspberry Pi Zero to the new Raspberry Pi 3B+ we will be using in this book).

To demystify some of the technology that we deal with every day, let's talk about the major blocks of hardware on this computer. Remember, your smartphone has computers inside that are very similar in terms of structure to the Raspberry Pi.

Figure 1-1 shows you the major blocks of the computer:

» **GPIO connector:** This is the general purpose input-output pin connector. We will be using this connector a great deal through the rest of this minibook.

» **CPU/GPU:** Central processing unit/graphics (for the screen) processing unit. This block is the brains of the gear and tells everything else what to do. Your Python programs will be run by this block.

» **USB:** These are standard USB (universal serial bus) ports, the same interfaces you find on big computers. There are many devices you can connect to a USB port, just as on your PC. You will plug in your mouse and keyboard into these ports.

» **Ethernet:** Just like the Ethernet interface on your computer. Connects to a network via wires.

» **WiFi:** This block isn't shown on the diagram, but it is very handy to have. With WiFI, you don't have to trail wires all over to talk with the Internet.

» **HDMI Out:** You plug in your monitor or TV into this port.

» **Audio jack:** Sound and composite video (old standard).

» **Other ports:** Three more interesting ports on the board are:

- *Micro USB:* This is your 5V power supply.

- *Camera CSI:* This is for a ribbon cable connection to a Raspberry Pi camera.

- *Display DSI:* This is for high-speed connections to a variety of custom displays — but this is well beyond the scope of our book.

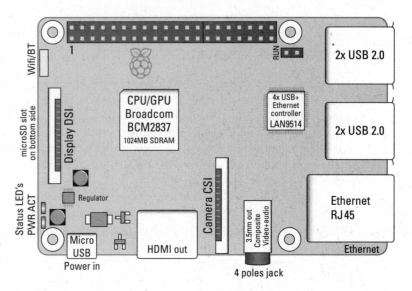

FIGURE 1-1:
The main
components of
the Raspberry
Pi 3B+.

# Making Your Computer Do Things

In order to get our computer to do and sense things apart from the computer screen and keyboard, we need a computer and one of two other things — a sensor or an actuator. A *sensor* is a small piece of electronics that can detect something about the environment (such as temperature or humidity) and an *actuator* is a fancy word for a motor or cable that does things in the real world.

In the remainder of this chapter, we are going to learn about the necessary ingredients of our first physical computing project, turning an LED on and off. This is the physical computing version of "Hello World" that we all do when we are learning software. Blinking LED, here we come!

TIP

Go out now and buy your Raspberry Pi Starter Kit (comes with the power supply, operating system, and a case) and get it set up before continuing. We recommend grabbing a mouse, keyboard, and monitor to do the set-up for beginners, but more advanced users may want to use SSH (Secure SHell) to do a headless setup. Again, the best place to start is with www.raspberrypi.org.

# Using Small Computers to Build Projects That Do and Sense Things

Earlier in this chapter, we talked about computers in the kitchen. All those computers sense the environment (the oven temperature, for example) and most are actually doing something to affect the environment (your blender chopping up ice for a nice Margarita, for example). That pulse, pulse, pulse of your blender is controlled by a computer.

So that we can build projects and learn how to design our own (and believe me, after you get acquainted with the hardware, you are going to be able to design magical things) we need to just jump in and do our first project.

Then, in further chapters, we build more complex things that will be the launching point to your own projects, all programmed in Python!

One last remark before we move on. The software you will be writing in Python is the key to getting all these projects and computers working. Is the hardware or software more important? This is a holy war among engineers, but we really think the software is the more important part, and the easier part to learn for beginners. Now before that statement unleashes a hundred nasty emails, let me humbly acknowledge that none, and we mean none, of this is possible if it wasn't for the hardware and the fine engineers that produce these little miracles. But this is a book on Python!

## WHAT ARE SOME OF THE OTHER SMALL COMPUTERS AVAILABLE?

There are literally hundreds of different types of small computers and boards out there for project building. We chose the Raspberry Pi for this book because of the ease of use for Python and the hundreds of Python libraries available for the Raspberry Pi. It is also the best-supported small computer out there with hundreds of websites (including the fabulous www.raspberrypi.org) to teach you how to set up and use this computer.

In a real sense, there are two general categories of small computer systems out there that are accessible to the beginning user. There are computers that are based on the Linux operating system (Raspbian, the software on the Raspberry Pi, is a form of Linux) and computers that have a much smaller operating system or even no operating system.

Understand that both versions of computers and operating systems are very useful in different applications.

The Raspberry Pi uses Linux. Linux is a multitasking, complex operating system that can run with multiple CPU cores. (Did we mention the Raspberry PI 3B+ has four CPUs on the chip? And for $35 — amazing!) However, don't confuse the complexity of the operating system with the ability to use the computer. The Raspberry Pi operating

*(continued)*

(continued)

system supports a whole Windows-like GUI (Graphical User Interface), just like your PC or Mac. The power of the operating system makes this possible.

Arduinos are small computers that only have a small computer and a limited amount of RAM on board. Interestingly enough, even though they are much smaller and simpler than the Raspberry Pi, the development boards are about the same price. In volume however, the Arduino type of computer is much, much cheaper than a Raspberry Pi. An Arduino has much more input-output pins than a Raspberry Pi and has an onboard ADC (analog digital converter), something that the Raspberry Pi lacks. In a later chapter, we show you how to create a project with an external ADC and the Raspberry Pi. And it involves a flame. You know that will be fun.

Another class of small computers similar to Arduinos (and can be programmed by the same IDE (integrated development environment) that Arduino devices use are the ESP8266 and ESP32 boards from Espressif in China. The small computers have much less RAM than the Raspberry Pi, but they come with built-in WiFi (and sometimes Bluetooth) interfaces that make them useful in building projects you want to connect to the Internet, such as IOT (Internet Of Things) projects.

Both types of computers are fun to play with, but the Raspberry Pi has a much better environment for Python development and learning.

# The Raspberry Pi: A Perfect Platform for Physical Computing in Python

By now you have your Raspberry Pi computer set up and running on your monitor, keyboard, and mouse. If not, go do that now (remember our friend, www. raspberrypi.org) The next few paragraphs are going to be lots more fun with a computer to work with!

The Raspberry Pi is the perfect platform to do physical computing with Python because it has a multiscreen environment, lots of RAM and storage to play with and all the tools to build the projects we want.

We have been talking a lot about the computers in this chapter and not much about Python. Time to change that.

A huge and powerful feature of the Raspberry Pi is the row of GPIO (general purpose input-output) pins along the top of the Raspberry Pi. It is a 40-pin header into which we can plug a large number of sensors and controllers to do amazing things to expand your Raspberry Pi.

## GPIO pins

GPIO pins can be designated (using Python software) as input or output pins and used for many different purposes. There are two 5V power pins, two 3.3V power pins and a number of ground pins that have fixed uses (see the description of what voltages (V) are in the next chapter and the differences between 3.3V and 5V). (See Figure 1-2.)

An GPIO pin output pin "outputs" a 1 or a 0 from the computer to the pin. See next chapter for more on how this is done and what it means. Basically, A "1" is 3.3V and a "0" is 0V. We can think of them just as 1s and 0s. (See Figure 1-2.)

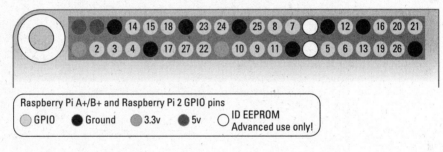

**FIGURE 1-2:** The functions of the Raspberry Pi GPIO pins.

## GPIO libraries

There are a number of GPIO Python libraries that are usable for building projects. The one we use throughout the rest of this book is the gpiozero library that is installed on all Raspberry Pi desktop software releases. The library documentation and installation instructions (if needed) are located on https://gpiozero.readthedocs.io/en/stable/.

Now we are going to jump into the "Hello World" physical computing project with our Raspberry Pi.

# The hardware for "Hello World"

To do this project, we need some hardware. Because we are using Grove connectors (see next chapter) in the rest of the book, let's get the two pieces of Grove hardware that we need for this project:

» **Pi2Grover:** This converts the Raspberry Pi GPIO pin header to Grove connectors (ease of use and can't reverse the power pins!). You can buy this either at shop.switchdoc.com or at Amazon.com. You can get $5.00 off the Pi2Grover board at shop.switchdoc.com by using the discount code PI2DUMMIES at checkout. Lots more on this board in the next chapter. (See Figure 1-3.)

**FIGURE 1-3:**
The Pi2Grover board.

» **Grove blue LED:** A Grove blue LED module including Grove cable. You can buy this on shop.switchdoc.com or on amazon.com. (See Figures 1-4 and 1-5.)

# Assembling the hardware

For a number of you readers, this will be the first time you have ever assembled a physical computer based product. because of this, we'll give you the step-by-step process:

**FIGURE 1-4:**
The Grove
blue LED.

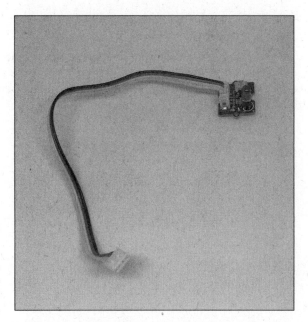

**FIGURE 1-5:**
The Grove
cable (included
with the LED).

1. Identify the Pi2Grover board from Figure 1-3 above.

2. Making sure you align the pins correctly gently press the Pi2Grover Board (Part A) onto the 40 pin GPIO connector on the Raspberry Pi. (See Figure 1-6.)

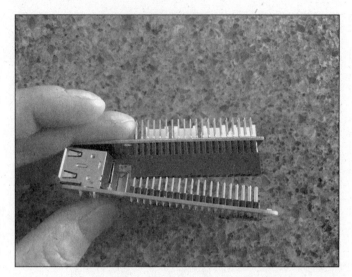

**FIGURE 1-6:**
Aligning the
Pi2Grover
board on the
Raspberry Pi.

3. Gently finish pushing the Pi2Grover (Part A) onto the Raspberry Pi GPIO pins, making sure the pins are aligned. There will be no pins showing on either end and make sure no pins on the Raspberry Pi are bent. (See Figure 1-7.)

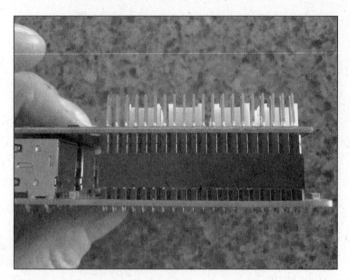

**FIGURE 1-7:**
The installed
Pi2Grover board.

4. Plug one end of the Grove cable into the Grove blue LED board. (See Figure 1-8.)

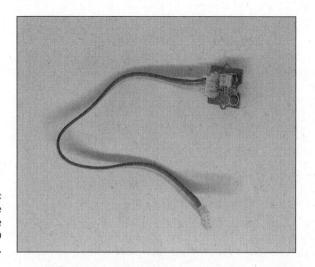

**FIGURE 1-8:**
A Grove cable plugged into the Grove blue LED board.

5. **If your blue LED is not plugged into the Grove blue LED board, then plug in the LED with the flat side aligned with the flat side of the outline on the board as in Figure 1-9.**

Flat Side of LED

**FIGURE 1-9:**
The LED aligned with the outline on the board.

Flat Side of Outline on Board

6. **Plug the other end of the Grove cable into the slot marked D12/D13 on the Pi2Grover board. (See Figure 1-10.)**

You are now finished assembling the hardware. Now it's time for the Python software.

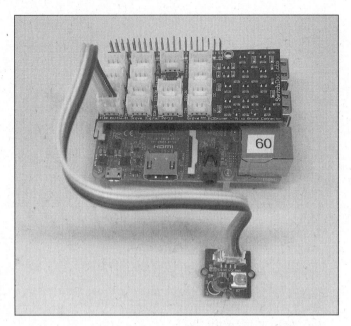

FIGURE 1-10:
The completed
"Hello World"
project.

# Controlling the LED with Python on the Raspberry Pi

Now that we have the hardware all connected, we can apply the power to the Raspberry Pi. If all is well, then you will see your Grove blue LED light up, a blue power LED on the Pi2Grover board, a flashing yellow LED (for a while during bootup) on the Raspberry Pi, and a steady red LED light also on the Raspberry Pi.

**TECHNICAL
STUFF**

The Grove blue LED lights up when we turn the Raspberry Pi power on because the GPIO pins on the Raspberry Pi power up as inputs. Because it is an input and nothing is driving the GPIO pin (the Grove LED wants an output, not an input to control the LED), the GPIO pin just floats (called being in tri-state technically). Because of the circuitry in the Pi2Grover board, the input will float towards a "1" and so the LED will turn on. When you turn your GPIO pin to an output in the code below, the LED will turn off.

To get started, follow these steps:

1. **Go to your keyboard and open up a terminal window.**

**TIP**

If you don't know how to open and use a terminal window and the command line on the Raspberry Pi, go to https://www.raspberrypi.org/documentation/usage/terminal/ for an excellent tutorial.

2. **Enter the following Python code into a file using the nano text editor or an editor of your choice. Save it to the file** HelloWorld.py.

```python
from gpiozero import LED
from time import sleep

blue = LED(12)

while True:
    blue.on()
    print( "LED On")
    sleep(1)
    blue.off()
    print( "LED Off")
    sleep(1)
```

TIP

For an excellent tutorial on using nano, go to https://www.raspberrypi.org/magpi/edit-text/

3. **Now the big moment. Start your program by running this on the command line your terminal window:**

```
sudo python3 HelloWorld.py
```

You will see the LED blink on and off once per second and the following will appear on the screen in the terminal window:

```
LED On
LED Off
LED On
LED Off
LED On
LED Off
LED On
LED Off
LED On
LED Off
LED On
```

TECHNICAL
STUFF

The keyword sudo stands for *super user do*. We use sudo in front of the python3 command in this type of code because some versions of the Raspberry Pi operating system restricts access to certain pins and functions from a regular user. By using sudo, we are running this as a super user. This means it will run no matter how the particular version of the operating system is set up. In the newer versions of the Raspberry Pi OS, you can just type python3 HelloWorld.py and it will work. If it doesn't, go back to sudo python3 HelloWorld.py.

You can stop this program using Ctrl+C (^C, in geek terms).

In the code, the following statement imports the function LED from the Python gpiozero library:

```
from gpiozero import LED
```

This statement imports the function sleep from the Python time library:

```
from time import sleep
```

This assigns an LED on GPIO 12 (remember D12/D13 on the Pi2Grover Board?):

```
blue = LED(12)
```

Now you start the loop that will go on forever:

```
while True:
```

Turn the LED on:

```
    blue.on()
    print( "LED On")
```

Wait for one (1) second to go by:

```
    sleep(1)
```

Turn the LED off:

```
    blue.off()
    print( "LED Off")
    sleep(1)
```

Rinse and repeat.

Wow, you have now entered the world of physical computing. Just wait until you have finished this book. You will be amazed what you can do!

# But Wait, There Is More . . .

Because we have all this hardware set up, how about we do one more interesting project? Let's make this a variable brightness LED by using PWM (pulse width modulation) to vary the brightness of the LED.

**TECHNICAL STUFF**

*Pulse-width modulation (PWM)* is a technique by which you vary the amount of time a signal is at a 1 versus the amount of time the signal is at a 0. Because our LED turns on when it is at a 1 and turns off at a 0, if we vary the time it is at a 1 versus a 0 then we can control the brightness to the human eye. This ratio is called the *duty cycle*. (See Figure 1-11.) 100 percent duty cycle means it is on 100 percent of the time, whereas a duty cycle of 0 percent means it is off all the time. Varying the time the signal is on will change the brightness of the LED.

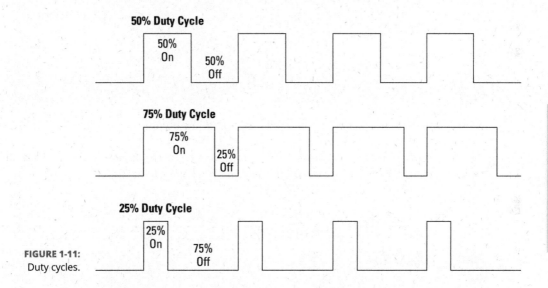

**FIGURE 1-11:** Duty cycles.

Enter this Python code into nano and save it as HelloWorld2.py:

```
from gpiozero import PWMLED
from time import sleep

led = PWMLED(12)

while True:
    led.value = 0   # off
    sleep(1)
    led.value = 0.5 # half brightness
```

```
    sleep(1)
    led.value = 1  # full brightness
    sleep(1)
```

Now run the code:

```
sudo python3 HelloWorld2.py
```

You will see the brightness change every second.

And one more thing, here is how to change your brightness in a continuous fashion:

```
from gpiozero import PWMLED
from signal import pause

led = PWMLED(12)

led.pulse()

pause()
```

With this code, we see a smooth continuous brightening and darkening of the LED.

Boy, you accomplished a lot in this chapter. You have now started to see the possibilities of physical computing. And you have a blue LED!

**TECHNICAL STUFF**

# THE LED CHANGING IS NOT TOTALLY SMOOTH

Turns out that the way the Raspberry Pi Linux operating system works, your program is not the only thing running at the same time. If you want to see everything that is running on your Raspberry Pi, type **ps xaf** at your command-line prompt on your terminal. You will be amazed at what is running on your Rapsberry Pi. Because the operating system on the Raspberry Pi is multitasking, meaning more than one task runs at a time, sometimes your PWM task (as it is being run in software) does not get the CPU quite when it wants and that is why there is just a little bit of jitter in the LED. The Raspberry Pi does have two hardware PWM GPIO pins, which can be used if you aren't using the audio output on the Raspberry Pi. On a Raspberry Pi 3B+ you will barely notice it, but you will on slower Pi versions.

Chapter **2**

# No Soldering! Grove Connectors for Building Things

Okay, okay. We all have been talking about Python for the past several hundred pages. Time to build something! But before we get to that, we need to talk about how to plug things together.

Grove is a modular, standardized connecter prototyping system. Grove takes a building-block approach to assembling electronics. Compared to the jumper or solder-based system, it is easier to connect, experiment, and build, and it simplifies the learning system, but not to the point where it becomes dumbed down. Some of the other prototype systems out there take the level down to building blocks. There is good stuff to be learned that way, but the Grove system allows you to build real systems. However, it requires some learning and expertise to hook things up.

The Grove system consists of a base unit and various modules (with *standardized connectors*).

The base unit, generally a microprocessor, allows for easy connection of any input or output from the Grove modules, and every Grove module typically addresses a single function, from a simple button to a more complex heart-rate sensor.

You don't need a base unit to connect up to Grove modules. You can use a cable (Grove-to-pin-header converter) to run from the pins on the Raspberry Pi or Arduino to the Grove connectors. See some examples of how to do this later in this chapter.

# So What Is a Grove Connector?

Normally, when you're wiring up a board, you have to pay attention. If you plug things in backwards or connect boards incorrectly, you can damage or destroy boards. All it takes is an incorrectly attached wire, and your board is gone forever.

The Grove system, however, works differently. It allows you to connect up boards while taking no chances on hooking up power and ground incorrectly.

A Grove connector is a four-pin standardized size connector used to plug into base units and Grove modules. Figure 2-1 shows the male Grove connector. These standardized connectors (common to all types of Grove connectors) are the key to making this system work. They are keyed so that you cannot plug them in backwards, and the four types of connectors (see "The Four Types of Grove Connectors," later in this chapter) are all designed so that if you plug the wrong type of device into the wrong type of base unit, there is no problem. They aren't destroyed; they just won't work. This is a good thing, a very good thing.

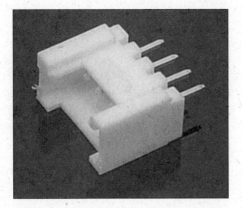

**FIGURE 2-1:**
A Grove
connector.

**WARNING**

The one exception would be if you plugged in a 3.3V I2C Grove module that is non-5V tolerant into a 5V I2C Grove connector you could fry the device. In this book, we avoid such situations by making sure everything we do is 5V!

# Selecting Grove Base Units

A Grove base unit is a controller or shield to which you attach the Grove modules. The base unit provides the processing power, and the modules offer the input sensors and output actuators of your system.

## For the Arduino

We most talk about the Raspberry Pi in this book, but there are other computers out there too! Arduinos are one of the more popular ones. There are a number of good base unit shields available for the Arduino that provide a lot of Grove connectors. Figure 2-2 shows the base unit designed to plug into an Arduino Uno. They are also available for the Arduino Mega, Due, and others.

**FIGURE 2-2:**
The Arduino Uno Grove base board.

Some Arduino boards, such as the Mini Pro LP (see Figure 2-3), have Grove connectors built right into the board so you don't even need a base unit.

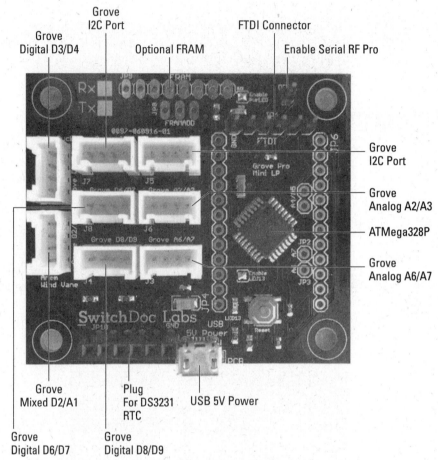

**Grove Digital D3/D4**

**Grove I2C Port**

**Optional FRAM**

**FTDI Connector**

**Enable Serial RF Pro**

**Grove I2C Port**

**Grove Analog A2/A3**

**ATMega328P**

**Grove Analog A6/A7**

**Grove Mixed D2/A1**

**Plug For DS3231 RTC**

**USB 5V Power**

**FIGURE 2-3:**
The Arduino
Mini Pro LB board
with Grove.

**Grove Digital D6/D7**

**Grove Digital D8/D9**

## Raspberry Pi Base Unit — the Pi2Grover

On the Raspberry Pi side, the pickings are much slimmer. The base unit devices available tend to be "too smart" and isolate you from the Raspberry Pi hardware and software. This is a huge problem when you want to connect to hardware using Python. We prefer a solution that is closer to the hardware for learning and flexibility. You can still mask the complexity with software drivers.

The base unit we will be using is the Pi2Grover base unit. It basically is just a level shifter (from the Raspberry Pi 3.3V to 5V for all the Grove sensors), and it does not get in the way of writing drivers in Python. (See Figure 2-4.)

# A TOAST OF WATER TO VOLTAGES

Hmmm. What is the difference between 3.3V and 5V? *V* refers to *voltage*, which is similar to the water pressure in a pipe. The higher the pressure, the more water comes out. With voltage, the higher the voltage, the more current (like water) will come out of the pipe. If the water pressure is too high, it can break the pipe. Similarly, if the voltage is too high, you can break the computer input. Raspberry Pi's are pretty particular about liking only 3.3V on their input lines and can be damaged if you apply higher voltages (like 5V). This is another reason we like to use the Pi2Grover, because it converts and buffers all the lines from the Raspberry Pi back and forth from 3.3V to 5V with no problem.

One more thing about voltages. Voltages are always measured with reference to something, usually called *ground*. This is why grounds are so important to connect and to have a common ground so your voltages running around always know to what they are referenced.

Not having a common ground in a system (thus confusing the voltages!) leads to very flaky behavior. This leads to the Second Law of Shovic, *"You can always trust your mother, but you can never trust your ground."* For those who may be interested in what the First Law of Shovic is, that one is a bit easier to understand. The First Law is *"It works better if you plug it in!"*

**FIGURE 2-4:** The Pi2Grover board at work on the Raspberry Pi.

# The Four Types of Grove Connectors

Now, let's talk about some of the specifics of each of the four types of connectors. First of all, all Grove cables are physically identical and can be interchanged. The differences are in the signal types they provide. Now, note! You will never short out power and ground by plugging in one type of Grove connector in the other. Although you do need to be careful and think about what you are doing, it is a lot less risky than soldering or using jumpers to wire up devices to your Pi or Arduino.

Generically, all the Grove connectors are wired the same: Signal 1, signal 2, power, ground.

Wire colors on standard Grove cables are always the same. (See Figure 2-5.)

>> **Pin 1:** Yellow (for example, SCL on I2C Grove connectors)

>> **Pin 2:** White (for example, SDA on I2C Grove connectors)

>> **Pin 3:** Red (VCC on all Grove connectors)

>> **Pin 4:** Black (GND on all Grove connectors)

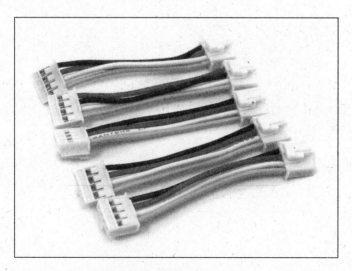

**FIGURE 2-5:**
5cm-long Grove
cables.

# The Four Types of Grove Signals

Now it is time to wax poetic about the different types of signals we use to talk to sensors and devices. It's not hard, but pay attention. By using the wrong connector, you may not fry your board, but your project still may not work correctly!

## Grove digital — All about those 1's and 0's

**TECHNICAL STUFF**

Many sensors only need one or two bits. A *bit* is the basis of all digital computer hardware. It can either be a "1" or a "0". There isn't anything in between. Yes, the bits are represented by voltage levels (see the discussion on Voltage earlier in this chapter), but fundamentally we will treat these bits as only having a "1" or "0" value.

Computers often communicate with each other and with external devices by using digital bits. It turns out that there are two ways of getting information from bits. One is the value ("1" or "0") and the other is timing. Such as how long the bit has a value of "1." The thought of this leads us to the Serial Grove ports we talk about later.

A digital Grove connector consists of the standard four lines coming into the Grove plug. The two signal lines are generically called D0 and D1. Most modules only use D0, but some (like the LED Bar Grove display) use both. Often base units will have the first connector called D0 and the second called D1 and they will be wired D0/D1 and then D1/D2, and so on. See Table 2-1 for a description of each pin of the digital Grove connector.

Examples of Grove digital modules are: Switch modules, the Fan module, and the LED module. In Figure 2-6, you can see what the Grove connector looks like on the schematic for the LED Grove module. They range from the simple to the very complex.

**TABLE 2-1**

### The Grove Digital Connector

| Pin | Name | Description |
|---|---|---|
| Pin 1 - Yellow | D0 | Primary digital input/output |
| Pin 2 - White | D1 | Secondary digital input/output |
| Pin 3- Red | VCC | Power for Grove module (5V or 3.3V) |
| Pin 4 - Black | GND | Ground |

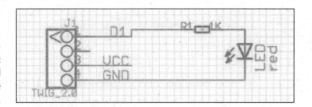

**FIGURE 2-6:**
A simple digital
Grove module
with LED.

# Grove analog: When 1's and 0's aren't enough

A Grove analog connector consists of the standard four lines coming into the Grove plug. The two signal lines are generically called A0 and A1. Most modules only use A0. Often base units will have the first connector called A0 and the second called A1 and they will be wired A0/A1 and then A1/A2, and so on. This simple voltage divider will give you a different analog voltage reading depending on the position of the switch and of course, the voltage present across the green connector on the left side. (See Figure 2-7.) See Table 2-2 for the descriptions of each pin.

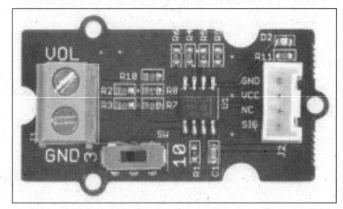

**FIGURE 2-7:**
A Grove analog
simple voltage
divider.

**TABLE 2-2**

### The Grove Analog Connector

| Pin | Name | Description |
|---|---|---|
| Pin 1 - Yellow | A0 | Primary analog input |
| Pin 2 - White | A1 | Secondary analog input |
| Pin 3 - Red | VCC | Power for Grove module (5V or 3.3V) |
| Pin 4 - Black | GND | Ground |

Examples of Grove analog modules are: Potentiometer, voltage divider and a Grove air quality sensor.

# Grove UART (or serial) — Bit by bit transmission

**TECHNICAL STUFF**

Remember when we talked about digital signals? How you can convey information not only in the level of the signal ("1" or "0") but also in how long in terms of time it stays at a "1" or "0". That is the basis of sending a serial signal. For example, 8 single bits sent at a specific speed, such as 0100001, can represent the letter *A*. The speed at which the bit is sent is called a *baud rate*. (*Baud* comes from Emile Baudot, who was an inventor and scientist making great progress in the late 1800s with the telegraph).

The Grove UART module is a specialized version of a Grove digital module that uses the digital level and the timing of the signal to receive and transmit data. It uses both Pin 1 and Pin 2 for the serial input and transmit. The Grove UART (also called a *serial interface*) plug is labeled from the base unit's point of view. In other words, Pin 1 is the RX line (which the base unit uses to receive data, so it is an input) where Pin 2 is the TX line (which the base unit uses to transmit data to the Grove module). See the description of each pin on the UART Grove connector in Table 2-3.

Examples of Grove UART modules are: XBee wireless sockets, 125KHz RFID reader. (See Figure 2-8.)

**TABLE 2-3**   **The Grove UART Serial Connector**

| Pin | Name | Description |
|---|---|---|
| Pin 1 - Yellow | RX | Serial receive (from the base unit's point of view — not the Grove board's) |
| Pin 2 - White | TX | Serial transmit (from the base unit's point of view — not the Grove board's |
| Pin 3 - Red | VCC | Power for Grove module (5V or 3.3V) |
| Pin 4 - Black | GND | Ground |

**FIGURE 2-8:**
A Grove UART
RFID reader.

## ANALOG VERSUS DIGITAL: THE DEBATE CONTINUES

The differences between analog and digital signals are both simple and confusing at the same time. A digital signal has a value of "1" or "0." That's it. Analog voltages are able to take any voltage value, such as 1.2V, or 3.14198V, or any other floating-point value. So with analog, you can have many, many different voltages. Now for the confusing part. We represent a "1" on the devices we are talking about here as a 5V signal and a 0V signal as a "0". And it is even more complicated than that. Typically, any signal above about 2.5V can be considered a "1," and anything less than 0.7V can be considered a "0" if read by a digital port. Okay, okay. Enough about that. Let's just treat signals for this book as digital or analog and leave it at that. Whew!

An analog signal is used when it is important to know what voltage is present at the signal input or output. For example, a value of 1.420V coming from a moisture sensor can indicate a dry plant, whereas a voltage of 3.342V could indicate that the plant has plenty of water. Because the values between 1.420V and 3.342V can indicate how dry the plant is, it is important for us to know what the actual voltage number is. Later, we discuss how to read an analog voltage into a digital computer by converting the analog voltage into a digital number by the use of an ADC (analog-to-digital converter). Then our computer can tell whether the plant is dry or not!

# Grove I2C — Using I2C to make sense of the world

Our favorite devices to plug into little computers are I2C sensors. There are hundreds of types of I2C sensors on the market, and they are generally very inexpensive. There are many types of I2C Grove sensors available just ready to plug and go!

The sensor shown in Figure 2-9 is a SI1145 sunlight I2C sensor. But what, there's more! It not only calculates the visible sunlight strength, it also measures the infrared (IR) and even the ultraviolet (UV) components. This inexpensive sensor can tell you whether you are going to get sunburned as well as if your plants are happy!

You just have to love the things you can do these days with computers.

**FIGURE 2-9:**
The Grove I2C
sunlight sensor.

The actual sensor on the board is the little colored chip marked "U1." It's got a clear top to let the light through to measure.

**WARNING**

Most I2C sensors can be used with both 3.3V and 5V base units, but there are a few that are only 3.3V or 5.0V. You need to check the specifications. It is almost always very obvious as to which voltage they will run at. If you connect a 3.3V I2C sensor to your 5V Grove connector, you will probably destroy the device. See Table 2-4 for the pin descriptions of the Grove connector.

## I2C — THE DANCE OF CLOCK AND DATA

An I2C bus is often used to communicate with chips or sensors that are on the same board or located physically close to the CPU. It stands for standard Inter-IC device bus. I2C was first developed by Phillips (now NXP Semiconductors). To get around hardware licensing issues, sometimes the bus will be called TWI (two wire interface). SMBus, developed by Intel, is a subset of I2C that defines the protocols more strictly.

I2C provides good support for slow, close peripheral devices that only need be addressed occasionally. For example, a temperate measuring device will generally only change very slowly and so is a good candidate for the use of I2C, whereas a camera will generate lots of data quickly and potentially changes often.

I2C uses only two bidirectional open-drain lines, SCL (serial clock) and SDA (serial data). Kind of like two serial data lines next to each other. *Open-drain* means the I2C device can pull a level down to ground ("0"), but cannot pull the line up to VDD ("1"). Hence the name open-drain. You put a resistor on the line to pull it up to a "1" between "0" serial pulses, very much like a dance between SDA and SCL.

I2C devices are addressed by using a 7-bit address (0-127 in decimal) so you can have many devices on the same I2C bus, which is a very cool feature.

The Grove I2C connector has the standard layout. Pin 1 is the SCL signal and Pin 2 is the SDA signal. Power and ground are the same as the other connectors. This is another special version of the Grove digital connector. In fact, often the I2C bus on a controller (such as the ESP8266, Raspberry Pi, and the Arduino) just uses digital I/O pins to implement the I2C bus. The pins on the Raspberry Pi and Arduino are special with hardware support for the I2C bus. The ESP8266 has a purely software I2C interface, which is called "bit banging" for those children of the 90s.

**TABLE 2-4**  **The Grove I2C Connector**

| Pin | Name | Description |
| --- | --- | --- |
| Pin 1 - Yellow | SCL | I2C clock |
| Pin 2 - White | SDA | I2C data |
| Pin 3 - Red | VCC | Power for Grove module (5V or 3.3V) |
| Pin 4 - Black | GND | Ground |

# Using Grove Cables to Get Connected

There are many different lengths of Grove cables available, from 5cm all the way up to 50cm long cables. (See Figure 2-10.) You use these to plug your sensors into the Raspberry Pi. These are easy. They come with a Grove connector on each end and are interchangeable.

Grove cables also come as patch cables (between Grove and pins) and we talk about them next.

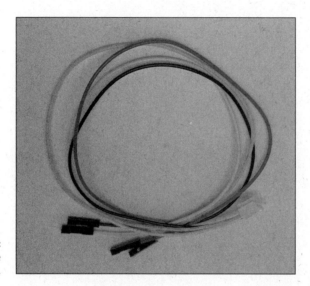

**FIGURE 2-10:**
20cm Grove
cables.

## Grove Patch Cables

There always seems to be some kind of device or sensor that does not have Grove connectors and yet you want to use it in your system. The solution to this is to use a patch cable!

It turns out there are easy ways of converting pin headers to Grove connectors using Grove adaptor cables. There are two types of Grove adaptor cables. One converts the Grove connector to female header pins, as in Figures 2-11 and 2-12.

The second type of Grove adaptor cables are Grove-connector-to-male-header-pins, as shown in Figure 2-13.

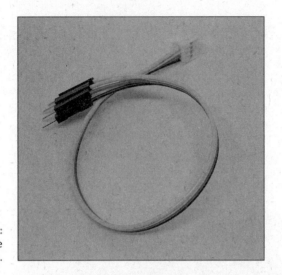

**FIGURE 2-11:**
Grove female
header cables.

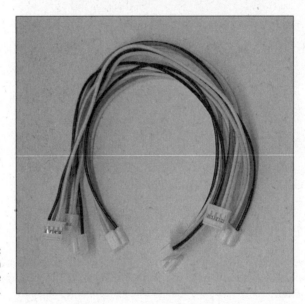

**FIGURE 2-12:**
A close-up of a
Grove female
header cables.

The power of the patch cable is that you can connect to non-Grove sensors.

**WARNING**

Basically, you map the Grove connector to your pin headers. Be careful and make sure you check twice before applying power!

How you map depends on what kind of a sensor you have and what the interface is. Grove connectors support four kinds of interfaces as we talk about earlier in this chapter.

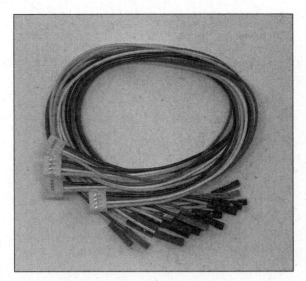

**FIGURE 2-13:**
Grove male
header cables.

## An example of the power of the patch!

SunAirPlus, a solar power controller and data collector, is an example of converting a pin header sensor to use Grove connectors. SunAirPlus has an I2C interface on the pin header that we often want to convert to Grove connectors. We connect the cable in the following way (see Figure 2-14):

Pin 1 – Yellow (SCL)

Pin 2 – White (SDA)

Pin 3 – Red (VDD)

Pin 4 – Black (GND)

Figure 2-15 shows the other end of the adaptor cable plugged into the Pi2Grover adaptor board on the Raspberry Pi.

## Second example: The Adafruit Ultimate GPS

The Adafruit Ultimate GPS connects to a Raspberry Pi/Arduino through a serial interface (UART). To use Grove connectors, we connect the cable in the following way:

Pin 1 – Yellow (TX)

Pin 2 – White (RX)

Pin 3 – Red (VIN)

Pin 4 – Black (GND)

**FIGURE 2-14:**
The SunAirPlus
board with
the Grove
female header
patch cable.

**FIGURE 2-15:**
A Grove adaptor
cable attached to
Pi2Grover.

Note that serial connectors are a bit odd in that you need to connect the RX on the Grove connector to the TX on the sensor and the TX on the Grove connector to the RX on the sensor. (See Figure 2-16.)

It's time to start building!

**FIGURE 2-16:**
A close-up of the Adafruit GPS with a Grove patch cable.

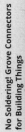

No Soldering! Grove Connectors for Building Things

Chapter **3**

# Sensing the World with Python: The World of I2C

Before we get into how to sense the world in Python, let's go through a few of the hardware issues. You can skip all this and still use Python to talk to these devices, of course, but some background is a good thing to have You can always go back over it later when you have some experience with these devices.

The available sensors for the Raspberry Pi and other small computers number in the thousands. From detecting people in front of your computer (PIR) to detecting a myriad of environmental conditions (temperature/humidity/air quality/and so on), there are many inexpensive ways to have your computer monitor the physical world. As always, the major thing you have to know about these sensors is how you can talk to them with a computer, which is commonly through the *interface*. The interface consists of two things: The *hardware interface*, which contains pins, types, and voltage levels, and the *software interface*, which is usually called a *driver* or an *API (application programming interface)*.

There are four major ways of getting data to your computer from your outside sensors:

» Digital input — GPIO pins programmed to be input lines.

» Digital analog input — Analog values that need to go through an analog-to-digital converter (ADC) to be read by a computer.

>> Digital I2C (pronounced I-squared-C) (Inter-Integrated Circuit) bus

>> Digital SPI (serial peripheral interface)

In this book, we deal with sensors using digital inputs, analog inputs and I2C interfaces. Why not SPI? Just for simplicity. Most SPI parts also have an I2C interface on the chip, and most small computer boards have an I2C interface built into the board.

# Understanding I2C

The first thing to know about I2C is that every device on the I2C bus has an address. For example, the address of the HDC1080 temperature and humidity sensor we use in this chapter has an address of 0x40. What does the "0x" mean in this address? It means that the number that follows is in hexadecimal notation, base 16 instead of base 10 (our normal numbering system).

To understand this interface, let's look at what an I2C bus is. An I2C bus is often used to communicate with chips or sensors that are on the same board or located physically close to the CPU. I2C was first developed by Phillips (now NXP Semiconductors). To get around licensing issues (that have largely gone away), often the bus will be called TWI (Two Wire Interface). SMBus, developed by Intel, is a subset of I2C that defines the protocols more strictly. Modern I2C systems take policies and rules from SMBus, sometimes supporting both with minimal reconfiguration needed. Both the Arduino and the Raspberry Pi support the I2C bus.

I2C provides good support for slow, close peripheral devices that need be addressed only occasionally. For example, a temperature-measuring device will generally only change very slowly and so is a good candidate for the use of I2C, whereas a camera will generate lots of data quickly and potentially changes often.

I2C uses only two bidirectional open-drain lines (*open-drain* means the device can pull a level down to ground, but cannot pull the line up to Vdd. Hence the name *open-drain*. Thus a requirement of I2C bus is that both lines are pulled up to Vdd. This is an important area and not properly pulling up the lines is the first and most common mistake you make when you first use an I2C bus. The Pi2Grover board we use in this book contains 10K Ohm pullup resistors so you should not have to worry about this. The two lines are SDA (serial data line) and the SCL (serial clock line). There are two types of devices you can connect to an I2C bus: Master devices and Slave devices. Typically, you have one Master device (The Raspberry Pi, in our case) and multiple Slave devices, each with their individual 7-bit address. (See Figure 3-1.)

When used on the Raspberry Pi, the Raspberry Pi acts as the Master and all other devices are connected as Slaves.

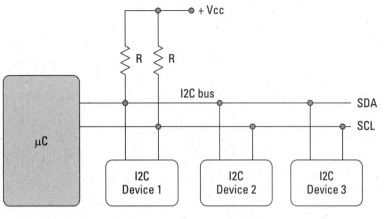

FIGURE 3-1:
The I2C bus.

Multiple devices on common I2C bus

The I2C protocol uses three types of messages:

>> Digital single message where a master writes data to a slave

>> Digital single message where a master reads data from a slave

>> Digital combined messages, where a master issues at least two reads and/or writes to one or more slaves

Lucky for us, most of the complexity of dealing with the I2C bus is hidden by Python drivers and libraries.

## Exploring I2C on the Raspberry Pi

TIP

The first thing you want to do on your Raspberry Pi is to learn a bit about the terminal window, command line, and text editors. If you haven't done that yet, refer to Chapter 1 of this minibook.

To use the I2C bus on the Raspberry Pi, you need to make sure that it is enabled in the operating system. Here is a good tutorial from Adafrui9t on how to do just that: `https://learn.adafruit.com/adafruits-raspberry-pi-lesson-4-gpio-setup/configuring-i2c`.

Did you do it right? The easy way to check for this is to type the following command in your terminal window:

```
I2cdetect -y 1
```

If it returns:

```
-bash: i2cdetect: command not found
```

Then you have not enabled your I2C bus. Repeat the tutorial to fix this.

On the other hand, if it returns:

```
     0  1  2  3  4  5  6  7  8  9  a  b  c  d  e  f
00:          -- -- -- -- -- -- -- -- -- -- -- -- --
10: -- -- -- -- -- -- -- -- -- -- -- -- -- -- -- --
20: -- -- -- -- -- -- -- -- -- -- -- -- -- -- -- --
30: -- -- -- -- -- -- -- -- -- -- -- -- -- -- -- --
40: -- -- -- -- -- -- -- -- -- -- -- -- -- -- -- --
50: -- -- -- -- -- -- -- -- -- -- -- -- -- -- -- --
60: -- -- -- -- -- -- -- -- -- -- -- -- -- -- -- --
70: -- -- -- -- -- -- -- --
```

Then you have been successful! Note that all dashes mean there are no sensors on the I2C bus. In our next section, we are going to add a simple one.

Now, let's talk about how to communicate with I2C devices in Python.

## Talking to I2C devices with Python

In order to talk to an I2C device, you should have one on the bus. A good one to start with is the HDC1080 temperature and humidity sensor. (See Figure 3-2.) You can get one of these inexpensive sensors on store.switchdoc.com or on amazon.com.

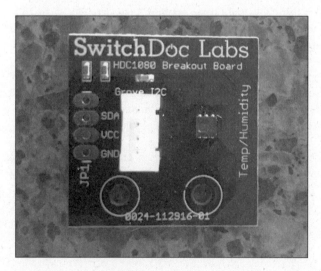

FIGURE 3-2:
HDC1080
temperature and
humidity sensor.

**TECHNICAL
STUFF**

# THE TEXAS INSTRUMENTS HDC1080 TEMPERATURE AND HUMIDITY SENSOR

This is a pretty amazing device considering how inexpensive it is. The HDC1080 is a HDC1000 compatible temperature and humidity sensor. It is located at I2C address 0x40.

The Grove temperature and humidity sensor (HDC1080) utilizes the HDC1080 sensor from Texas Instruments. It is a digital humidity sensor with integrated temperature sensor that provides excellent measurement accuracy at very low power. The device measures humidity based on a novel capacitive sensor. The humidity and temperature sensors are factory calibrated. The innovative WLCSP (wafer level chip scale package) simplifies board design with the use of an ultra-compact package. The HDC1080 is functional within the full –40°C to +125°C temperature range, and 0–100 percent RH range. The accuracy of the chip is +/– 3 percent relative humidity and +/– 0.2C for the temperature.

Note: If you buy one on Amazon, you will need a female-to-Grove patch cable, as discussed in Chapter 2 of this minibook. The SwitchDoc Labs HDC1080 already comes with a Grove connector. You will also need the Pi2Grover Raspberry Pi-to-Grove converter that was described in Chapters 1 and 2 of this minbook, which is also available on store.switchdoc.com or on amazon.com.

Now let's install the HDC1080 I2C sensor on our Raspberry Pi. Follow these steps:

1. **Shut down your Raspberry Pi. When the yellow LED has stopped blinking, unplug the power from your Raspberry Pi.**

   **REMEMBER**

   Never plug anything into or pull anything out a Raspberry Pi without shutting the computer down. Exceptions to this are USB ports, audio cables, and Ethernet cables, which are designed to support "hot-plugging." The rest of the Raspberry Pi is not.

2. **Plug a Grove cable into the HDC1080. (See Figure 3-3.)**

   **REMEMBER**

   We are using the SwitchDoc Labs HDC1080; if you are using an Amazon device, refer to Chapter 2 of this minibook for the use of a Grove patch cable.

   **TIP**

   Always shut down your Raspberry Pi by first typing `sudo halt` on the command line (or by selecting Shutdown from the GUI menu). Wait until the yellow LED on the Raspberry Pi stops blinking before removing the power cord. This ensures that the SDCard on the Raspberry Pi has been prepared for shutdown and you won't corrupt it. Just unplugging your Raspberry Pi may not corrupt the card, but unplugging it without shutting it down increases the likelihood of corruption. Corrupting your SDCard may not be fatal, but repairing it is a long, technical, irritating process.

**FIGURE 3-3:**
HDC1080 with
the Grove cable
plugged in.

3.  **Plug the other end of the Grove cable into one of the Grove connectors marked I2C on the Pi2Grover that plugged on top of your Raspberry Pi. (See Figure 3-4.)**

    Note: The I2C is a bus, which means you can use any of the four I2C connectors.

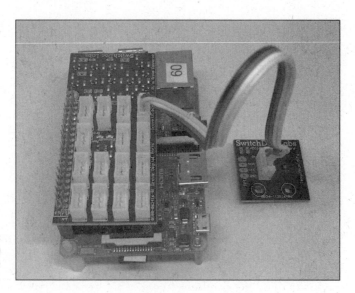

**FIGURE 3-4:**
The HDC1080
hooked up to the
Raspberry Pi.

4. **Power up the Raspberry Pi and open a terminal window.**

5. **Type into the terminal** `sudo i2cdetect -y 1` **and you will be rewarded with this:**

```
     0  1  2  3  4  5  6  7  8  9  a  b  c  d  e  f
00:          -- -- -- -- -- -- -- -- -- -- -- -- --
10: -- -- -- -- -- -- -- -- -- -- -- -- -- -- -- --
20: -- -- -- -- -- -- -- -- -- -- -- -- -- -- -- --
30: -- -- -- -- -- -- -- -- -- -- -- -- -- -- -- --
40: 40 -- -- -- -- -- -- -- -- -- -- -- -- -- -- --
50: -- -- -- -- -- -- -- -- -- -- -- -- -- -- -- --
60: -- -- -- -- -- -- -- -- -- -- -- -- -- -- -- --
70: -- -- -- -- -- -- --
```

Remember the 0x40 address of the HDC1080? There it is in the output above.

Now we are ready to proceed to use Python to read the temperature and humidity from this sensor.

# Reading temperature and humidity from an I2C device using Python

The use of Python libraries are key to being productive in writing Python applications. We will be using the SDL_Pi_HDC1080_Python3, available on github.com.

To read the temperature and humidity, follow these steps:

1. **First, create a directory in your main directory:**

```
cd
mkdir I2CTemperature
cd I2CTemperature
```

Now you are in the I2CTemperature directory.

2. **Before looking at the Python code for reading your temperature, install the library on our Raspberry Pi. You do this by "cloning" the library located at github.com by using the following command in your terminal window:**

```
git clone https://github.com/switchdoclabs/SDL_Pi_HDC1080_Python3.git
```

Here `git clone` clones the git repository located at the address and copies it to your Raspberry Pi. If you enter `ls` in the terminal window, you will see the following output:

```
pi@RPi3-60:~/I2CTemperature $ ls
SDL_Pi_HDC1080_Python3
pi@RPi3-60:~/I2CTemperature $
```

3. **Using nano (or your favorite text editor), open up a file called** `temperature Test.py` **and enter the following code:**

```python
import sys

sys.path.append('./SDL_Pi_HDC1080_Python3')

import time
import SDL_Pi_HDC1080



# Main Program
print
print ("")
print ("Read Temperature and Humidity from HDC1080 using I2C bus ")
print ("")

hdc1080 = SDL_Pi_HDC1080.SDL_Pi_HDC1080()


while True:

        print ("-------------------")
        print ("Temperature = %3.1f C" % hdc1080.readTemperature())
        print ("Humidity = %3.1f %%" % hdc1080.readHumidity())
        print ("-------------------")

        time.sleep(3.0)
```

**TECHNICAL STUFF**

# GITHUB, A REPOSITORY FOR GOOD THINGS

Github.com is a web-based hosting service for version control using Git, a well-known system for providing source control for software. It is mostly used for computer code. It provides access control and collaboration features such as bug tracking, feature requests, task management, and other services for every project.

As of June 2018, GitHub reports having over 28 million users and 57 million repositories making it the largest host of source code in the world.

In 2018, GitHub was acquired by Microsoft, Inc., which pledged to allow github.com to operate as an independent division. So far, so good.

4. **Run the code by typing:**

```
sudo python3 temperatureTest.py
```

You should see the following output, with new temperature and humidity readings every three seconds:

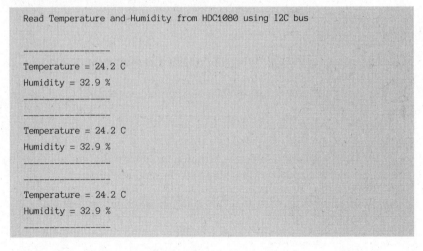

```
Read Temperature and Humidity from HDC1080 using I2C bus


------------------
Temperature = 24.2 C
Humidity = 32.9 %
------------------


------------------
Temperature = 24.2 C
Humidity = 32.9 %
------------------


------------------
Temperature = 24.2 C
Humidity = 32.9 %
------------------
```

You are now reading environmental data from an I2C device. Your Raspberry Pi is connected to the real world.

**TIP**

Try this experiment. Blow on the HDC1080 sensor board and watch the humidity go up! You will see something like this:

```
------------------
Temperature = 24.2 C
Humidity = 32.9 %
------------------

------------------
Temperature = 24.1 C
Humidity = 33.6 %
------------------

------------------
Temperature = 24.1 C
Humidity = 33.9 %
------------------

------------------
Temperature = 24.1 C
Humidity = 36.3 %
------------------

------------------
Temperature = 24.1 C
Humidity = 36.5 %
------------------
------------------
```

## Breaking down the program

The first line imports the Python `sys` library:

```
import sys
```

The next line tells Python to search the `SDL_Pi_HDC1080_Python3` **directory below** our current directory so it can find our library:

```
sys.path.append('./SDL_Pi_HDC1080_Python3')
```

More imports:

```
import time
import SDL_Pi_HDC1080
```

This statement instantiates the hdc1080 object and initializes it:

```
# Main Program
print
print ("")
```

```
print ("Read Temperature and Humidity from HDC1080 using I2C bus ")
print ("")


hdc1080 = SDL_Pi_HDC1080.SDL_Pi_HDC1080()
```

These statements read the temperature and humidity and print them out to the terminal window. Note: You see that all the complexity of using an I2C device is hidden by use of the HDC1080 library:

```
while True:
        print ("------------------")
        print ("Temperature = %3.1f C" % hdc1080.readTemperature())
        print ("Humidity = %3.1f %%" % hdc1080.readHumidity())
```

Sleep for three seconds and then repeat:

```
        print ("------------------")

        time.sleep(3.0)
```

Now that you have this program, you could add all sorts of things to it, such as turning on a red LED if it gets too hot, or turning on a blue LED if it gets to cold.

**TIP**

You could even tweet your temperature and humidity by using the `https://python-twitter.readthedocs.io` Python library.

**TECHNICAL STUFF**

# LOOKING AT AN I2C DRIVER

I2C devices have an address (like 0x40 the address of our HDC1080) and they also have registers. You can think of these as numbered pointers for which to write commands and read data. The HDC1080 has eight different registers with different hex addresses, as shown in the figure below.

| Pointer | Name | Reset value | Description |
|---------|------|-------------|-------------|
| 0x00 | Temperature | 0x0000 | Temperature measurement output |
| 0x01 | Humidity | 0x0000 | Relative Humidity measurement output |
| 0x02 | Configuration | 0x1000 | HDC1080 configuration and status |
| 0xFB | Serial ID | device dependent | First 2 bytes of the serial ID of the part |
| 0xFC | Serial ID | device dependent | Mid 2 bytes of the serial ID of the part |
| 0xFD | Serial ID | device dependent | Last byte bit of the serial ID of the part |
| 0xFE | Manufacturer ID | 0x5449 | ID of Texas Instruments |
| 0xFF | Device ID | 0x1050 | ID of the device |

*(continued)*

(continued)

An I2C driver basically reads and writes from these addresses to control the HDC1080 and to read the temperature and humidity data. The figure below shows the format of the temperature register located at pointer address 0x00.

| Name | Bits | | Description |
| --- | --- | --- | --- |
| TEMPERATURE | [15:02] | Temperature | Temperature measurement (read only) |
| | [01:00] | Reserved | Reserved, always 0 (read only) |

From the SDL_Pi_HDC1080 Python library, let's take a look at the Python code to actually read that I2C register:

```
def readTemperature(self):

    s = [HDC1080_TEMPERATURE_REGISTER] # temp
    s2 = bytearray( s )
    HDC1080_fw.write( s2 )
    time.sleep(0.0625)  # From the data sheet

#read 2 byte temperature data
    data = HDC1080_fr.read(2)

    buf = array.array('B', data)


    # Convert the data
    temp = (buf[0] * 256) + buf[1]
    cTemp = (temp / 65536.0) * 165.0 - 40
    return cTemp
```

This looks a lot more intimidating than it actually is. Breaking it down, we first define the function:

```
def readTemperature(self):
```

The we format the pointer address (0x00 in this case) into a byte array:

```
    s = [HDC1080_TEMPERATURE_REGISTER] # temp
    s2 = bytearray( s )
```

We set up the read from the pointer register:

```
    HDC1080_fw.write( s2 )
```

We delays 6.24ms, as required by the data sheet:

```
time.sleep(0.0625)   # From the data sheet
```

We read two bytes:

```
#read 2 byte temperature data
data = HDC1080_fr.read(2)
```

And place the two bytes into a byte array:

```
buf = array.array('B', data)
```

Then we convert the data bytes using the formula in the data sheet:

```
# Convert the data
temp = (buf[0] * 256) + buf[1]
cTemp = (temp / 65536.0) * 165.0 - 40
```

And send the temperature back to the calling program:

```
return cTemp
```

There are many different low-level drivers and programs out there to read and write from I2C devices on the Raspberry Pi. This is an example of one of the most common methods. Other methods include Adafruit_i2c, SMBUS, PyComms, Quick2Wire, and others. We typically use the SMBUS library, but once in a while you will run into a device that requires some non-SMBUS functionality to get it to work.

# A Fun Experiment for Measuring Oxygen and a Flame

In this more complex experiment, we take an Grove oxygen sensor and place it under a more or less sealed glass jar with a lit candle. The idea is to measure the oxygen in the glass jar and watch the level go down as the candle consumes the oxygen. After a quick search on the Internet, we expect it to drop about 30 percent before the flame is extinguished. That would be from 21 percent oxygen to about 14.7 percent oxygen.

We are storing the information in a CSV file (comma delimited file) to graph later by using MatPlotLib. You could also easily read this data into an Excel spreadsheet and graph it using Excel.

TECHNICAL
STUFF

MatPlotLib is a Python library for making publication quality plots using methods similar to MATLIB. You can output formats such as PDF, Postscript, SVG, and PNG.

Then we lit the candle and watched the data on the browser window connected to the Raspberry Pi.

What we need to do this experiment:

>> **Analog-to-digital converter:** This converts the analog output of the oxygen sensor to digital data for the Raspberry Pi.

>> **Grove oxygen sensor:** This sensor measures the percentage of oxygen in the air and converts it to an analog value (0 – 5V).

>> **A candle:** The candle will consume the oxygen in the bowl. You can use any candle as long as it fits under the bowl.

>> **A large glass bowl:** The bowl will cover and seal the candle to measure the oxygen.

## Analog-to-digital converters (ADC)

An analog-to-digital converter takes an analog signal (see the difference between an analog and digital signal in Chapter 2 of this minibook) and converts it to a digital signal (16 bits, in this case) for a computer to read.

When you have the digital number in the computer, you can scale it back to volts by multiplying it by (5.0/65535.0) to produce a floating point number representing volts.

No question about it. The lack of an analog-to-digital converter is a real knock on the Raspberry Pi.

The Grove analog-to-digital converter we use in this experiment is a Grove four-channel, 16-bit analog-to-digital converter available on store.switchdoc. com and also on Amazon.com. (See Figure 3-5.)

There are other Grove ADC modules available from Seeedstudio.com, but we wanted to use a 16-bit ADC converter for greater accuracy and the fact it has four channels instead of just one channel.

**FIGURE 3-5:**
The Grove
four-channel,
16-bit ADC.

# The Grove oxygen sensor

The Grove gas sensor ($O_2$) is a sensor to test the oxygen concentration in the air. (See Figure 3-6.) It detects the current oxygen concentration and outputs voltage values proportional to the concentration of oxygen. You can interpret these numbers by referring to the oxygen concentration linear characteristic graph.

This sensor value only reflects the approximate trend of oxygen gas concentration in a permissible error range, it does not represent the exact oxygen gas concentration. The detection of certain components in the air usually requires a more precise and costly instrument, which cannot be done with a single gas sensor. This sensor also requires about a 30-minute warm-up time.

**FIGURE 3-6:**
The Grove
oxygen sensor.

# Hooking up the oxygen experiment

By now, you have quite a bit of experience hooking up Grove devices to the Raspberry Pi. Follow these steps to set up the oxygen sensor:

1. **Disconnect the power from the Raspberry Pi.**

2. **Plug a Grove cable into the Grove oxygen sensor and then into the Grove connector marked A1 on the Grove four-channel, 16-bit ADC board.**

3. **Plug another Grove cable into the Grove connector marked I2C on the Grove four-channel, 16-bit ADC board. Plug the other end of that Grove cable into one of the connectors marked I2C on the Pi2Grover board plugged into the Raspberry Pi. (See Figure 3-7.)**

4. **Apply the power to the Raspberry Pi.**

**FIGURE 3-7:**
The complete
Raspberry Pi/
ADC/oxygen
sensor hookup.

5. **Run the command** `i2cdetect -y 1` **inside a terminal window. You should see this output:**

```
     0  1  2  3  4  5  6  7  8  9  a  b  c  d  e  f
00:             -- -- -- -- -- -- -- -- -- -- -- --
10: -- -- -- -- -- -- -- -- -- -- -- -- -- -- -- --
```

```
20: -- -- -- -- -- -- -- -- -- -- -- -- -- -- -- --
30: -- -- -- -- -- -- -- -- -- -- -- -- -- -- -- --
40: -- -- -- -- -- -- -- -- 48 -- -- -- -- -- -- --
50: -- -- -- -- -- -- -- -- -- -- -- -- -- -- -- --
60: -- -- -- -- -- -- -- -- -- -- -- -- -- -- -- --
70: -- -- -- -- -- -- -- --
```

Address 0x48 is the Grove four-channel, 16-bit ADC board. If you don't see this, go back and check your wiring.

Now you will test the setup by running a simple Python program.

First make a new directory for the program:

```
cd
mkdir oxygenProject
cd oxygenProject
git clone https://github.com/switchdoclabs/SDL_Pi_Grove4Ch16BitADC
```

Then enter the following code into a file called senseOxygen.py in your terminal window using nano:

```python
import time, sys

sys.path.append('./SDL_Pi_Grove4Ch16BitADC/SDL_Adafruit_ADS1x15')

import SDL_Adafruit_ADS1x15

ADS1115 = 0x01    # 16-bit ADC

# Select the gain
gain = 6144  # +/- 6.144V

# Select the sample rate
sps = 250  # 250 samples per second

# Initialize the ADC using the default mode (use default I2C address)
adc = SDL_Adafruit_ADS1x15.ADS1x15(ic=ADS1115)
dataFile = open("oxygenData.csv",'w')

totalSeconds = 0
while (1):

    # Read oxygen channel  in single-ended mode using the settings above
```

```
print ("----------------------")
voltsCh1 = adc.readADCSingleEnded(1, gain, sps) / 1000
rawCh1 = adc.readRaw(1, gain, sps)


# O2 Sensor
sensorVoltage = voltsCh1 *(5.0/6.144)
AMP  = 121
K_O2  = 7.43
sensorVoltage = sensorVoltage/AMP*10000.0
Value_O2 = sensorVoltage/K_O2 - 1.05


print ("Channel 1 =%.6fV raw=0x%4X O2 Percent=%.2f" % (voltsCh1, rawCh1,
Value_O2 ))
print ("----------------------")

dataFile.write("%d,%.2f\n" % (totalSeconds, Value_O2))
totalSeconds = totalSeconds + 1
dataFile.flush()
time.sleep(1.0)
```

**WARNING**

When you are done using the oxygen sensor, make sure you put it back in the included capped container and seal the top. Humidity will destroy the sensor over time. (We have destroyed these sensors in the past.)

When you run the program, here are the results:

```
----------------------

Channel 1 =2.436375V raw=0x32C2 O2 Percent= 22.05
----------------------


----------------------

Channel 1 =2.436375V raw=0x32C2 O2 Percent= 22.05
----------------------


----------------------

Channel 1 =2.436375V raw=0x32C1 O2 Percent= 22.05
----------------------


----------------------

Channel 1 =2.436375V raw=0x32C2 O2 Percent= 22.05
----------------------


----------------------

Channel 1 =2.436187V raw=0x32C1 O2 Percent= 22.05
----------------------
```

# Breaking down the code

In these statements, we set the parameters for the ADC module:

```
import time,  sys

sys.path.append('./SDL_Pi_Grove4Ch16BitADC/SDL_Adafruit_ADS1x15')

import SDL_Adafruit_ADS1x15

Normal Imports.  Notice the path goes to the subdirectory in the your directory.

ADS1115 = 0x01        # 16-bit ADC

# Select the gain
gain = 6144  # +/- 6.144V

# Select the sample rate
sps = 250  # 250 samples per second
```

Then we open the text file to store our data that you can graph later with Excel or other method:

```
# Initialize the ADC using the default mode (use default I2C address)
adc = SDL_Adafruit_ADS1x15.ADS1x15(ic=ADS1115)

dataFile = open("oxygenData.csv",'w')
```

Read the data from the ADC. Volts and Raw data (Raw data just for information):

```
totalSeconds = 0
while (1):

    # Read oxygen channel  in single-ended mode using the settings above

        print ("--------------------")
        voltsCh1 = adc.readADCSingleEnded(1, gain, sps) / 1000
        rawCh1 = adc.readRaw(1, gain, sps)
```

This is from the specification of the O2 sensor on how to calculate O2 percentage from the voltage from the ADC:

```
# O2 Sensor
sensorVoltage = voltsCh1 *(5.0/6.144)
AMP  = 121
K_O2  = 7.43
sensorVoltage = sensorVoltage/AMP*10000.0
Value_O2 = sensorVoltage/K_O2 - 1.05
```

Here you write the data out to the file:

```
print ("Channel 1 =%.6fV raw=0x%4X O2 Percent=%.2f" % (voltsCh1, rawCh1,
Value_O2 ))
    print ("---------------------")

    dataFile.write("%d,%.2f\n" % (totalSeconds, Value_O2))
```

We flush the file to make sure the last value is written to the file. You will eventually terminate this program with a Ctrl–C:

```
totalSeconds = totalSeconds + 1
dataFile.flush()
```

Now that you have all the software built, take your candle put it under the bowl with the oxygen sensor, start your program, and light the candle. (See Figure 3-8.) After a while, the flame will go out. Stop your program with a Ctrl-C and look at and graph your data. (See Figure 3-9.)

```
time.sleep(1.0)
```

**FIGURE 3-8:** The Start of Our O2 Experiment.

Looking at the numbers, we determined that we started with about 21 percent oxygen and the candle went out at about 15.8 percent oxygen, a reduction of about 25 percent. This is lower than the expected 30 percent reduction of oxygen levels.

The difference? We would guess a combination of sensor accuracy and candle type. One more thing to note: Look at the graph right after the candle went out. You can see that the seal wasn't perfect as the oxygen started to creep up.

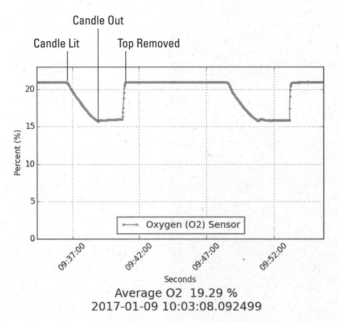

**FIGURE 3-9:**
The graph of the data from our O2 experiment.

Average O2  19.29 %
2017-01-09 10:03:08.092499

# Building a Dashboard on Your Phone Using Blynk and Python

When you drive a car, all the information about how fast you are going, how much fuel remains, and other car information is on your dashboard. We're going to show you how construct a simple dashboard so you can view your project data on your smartphone. To illustrate how to do this, we'll use the free app Blynk (free for small dashboards; they charge you a bit for more energy to build more controls). This app is available on the various app stores for both Android and iPhones. We'll use the iPhone to show the usage, but it is pretty much identical for Android phones.

## HDC1080 temperature and humidity sensor redux

Earlier in this chapter, you built a temperature and humidity sensing project using a Raspberry Pi. Grab that project now and let's write some more software for it to connect it up to Blynk and display our values on the unit. Here Figure 3-10 shows us what our dashboard will look like.

## OTHER DASHBOARDS

Blynk is hardly the only Internet dashboard out there. You can also check out:

- Freeboard
- XOBXOB
- Adafruit IO
- ThinkSpeak
- IBM Cloud
- Initialstate

All of them have different strengths and weaknesses. All of them have some sort of free option that varies on a regular basis.

# How to add the Blynk dashboard

First, we show you how to set up the Blynk app. This is done on an iPhone, but it is very similar to using it on an Android phone. And the Python is identical in both cases!

1. **Install the Blynk app on your mobile phone. (See Figure 3-11.)**

**FIGURE 3-11:**
Blynk in the
Appstore.

2. **Open the Blynk app and create an account. (See Figure 3-12.)**

   You need to supply an account and an email address, but they won't charge you anything for this.

3. **Click the button to scan a QR (see Figure 3-13).**

4. **Scan the QR code shown in Figure 3-14.**

5. **You will now see the MyTemperature app on your screen. (See Figure 3-15.)**

**FIGURE 3-12:**
Creating a
Blynk account.

**FIGURE 3-13:**
Click for QR.

**FIGURE 3-14:**
The QR for generating your myTemperature app in Blynk.

**FIGURE 3-15:**
The MyTemperature app.

6. **Click the middle of the project to select the project. Then click the indicated button to go to project settings.**

    Note: Now copy and paste the authentication token (AUTH TOKEN) into an email to yourself or into some other secure document, as we will be putting this in the Python temperatureTest.py program file in the next section. Figure 3-16 shows the initial screen of the Blynk app. Figure 3-17 shows the authentication code. You now have your myTemperature app loaded.

You have completed the Blynk myTemperature app installation. Now let's modify the software to support the Blynk app.

Settings

**FIGURE 3-16:**
The initial screen
of the Blynk app.

**FIGURE 3-17:**
The authentication
token in the
MyTemperature
app project
settings.

# The modified temperatureTest.py software for the Blynk app

To modify the software to support the Blynk app, follow these steps:

**1.** **Create a directory in your main directory by entering the following:**

```
cd
mkdir myTemperature
cd myTemperature
```

Now you are in the myTemperature directory.

**2.** **Before looking at the Python code for reading and then "Blynking" your temperature, install the library on the Raspberry Pi. You do this by "cloning" the library located up at github.com by using the following command in your terminal window:**

```
git clone https://github.com/switchdoclabs/SDL_Pi_HDC1080_Python3.git
```

**3.** **Enter the code below into a file named myTemperature.py using nano or your favorite editor.**

```python
#!/usr/bin/env python3

#imports

import sys

sys.path.append('./SDL_Pi_HDC1080_Python3')

import time
import SDL_Pi_HDC1080

import requests
import json


BLYNK_URL = 'http://blynk-cloud.com/'
BLYNK_AUTH = 'xxxx'

# Main Program
print
print ("")
```

```python
print ("Read Temperature and Humidity from HDC1080 using I2C bus and send
    to Blynk ")
print ("")

hdc1080 = SDL_Pi_HDC1080.SDL_Pi_HDC1080()

def blynkUpdate(temperature, humidity):
    print ("Updating Blynk")

    try:

        put_header={"Content-Type": "application/json"}
        val = temperature
        put_body = json.dumps(["{0:0.1f}".format(val)])
        r = requests.put(BLYNK_URL+BLYNK_AUTH+'/update/V0', data=put_body,
headers=put_header)


        put_header={"Content-Type": "application/json"}
        val = humidity
        put_body = json.dumps(["{0:0.1f}".format(val)])
        r = requests.put(BLYNK_URL+BLYNK_AUTH+'/update/V1', data=put_body,
headers=put_header)

        put_header={"Content-Type": "application/json"}
        val = time.strftime("%Y-%m-%d %H:%M:%S")
        put_body = json.dumps([val])
        r = requests.put(BLYNK_URL+BLYNK_AUTH+'/update/V2', data=put_body,
headers=put_header)

        return 1

    except Exception as e:
            print ("exception in updateBlynk")
            print (e)
            return 0

while True:

        temperature =  hdc1080.readTemperature()
        humidity = hdc1080.readHumidity()

        print ("------------------")
        print ("Temperature = %3.1f C" % hdc1080.readTemperature())
```

```
     print ("Humidity = %3.1f %%" % hdc1080.readHumidity())
     print ("--------------------")



     blynkUpdate(temperature, humidity)


     time.sleep(3.0)
```

This code updates your Blynk app every three seconds.

**WARNING**

If you update your Blynk app more than once a second, you may be discon-
nected from the server. Try to keep your request sends to less than ten values
per second to be a good Blynk citizen.

**4.** **The last thing you need to do before you run the code is to replace the
'xxxx' with your Blynk authorization code, which will look something
like this: 445730794c1c4c8ea7852a31555f44444.**

Before:

```
BLYNK_AUTH = 'xxxx'
```

After:

```
BLYNK_AUTH = '445730794c1c4c8ea7852a31555f44444'
```

Note: You must use the authorization code you received by email (or by cutting
and pasting from the app) otherwise, you will not connect to your app. The
example code shown here will not work.

## Breaking down the code

This code is very similar to the HDC1080 code from earlier in this chapter with the
exception of the blynkUpdate code.

```
def blynkUpdate(temperature, humidity):
    print ("Updating Blynk")
    try:
```

Why do we have a 'try' here? Because sometimes the requests library will throw
an error if the Internet is being funky.

Next, we set up the required http header for the requests library:

```
    put_header={"Content-Type": "application/json"}
```

## THE REQUESTS LIBRARY

The python requests library is one of most useful libraries for communicating across the Internet using `http` requests.

It is designed to be used by humans to interact with `http` requests without exposing the complexity of the requests. Very Pythonic.

The requests library allows you to send HTTP/1.1 requests using Python. It also allows you to access the response data of the requests using Python.

The following code sets the number of digits to the right of the decimal point to 1 so we won't have long numbers of relatively meaningless digits because of the accuracy of the HDC1080:

```
val = temperature
put_body = json.dumps(["{0:0.1f}".format(val)])
```

The following code does the actual transfer of the data to the Blynk server in the form of an `http` request:

```
r = requests.put(BLYNK_URL+BLYNK_AUTH+'/update/V0', data=put_body,
headers=put_header)
```

Here we print out any exception to the terminal screen. This also helps you figure out if you have set the Blynk authentication code incorrectly:

```
except Exception as e:
            print ("exception in updateBlynk")
            print (e)
            return 0
```

Next, let's run the program:

```
Sudo python3 myTemperature.py
```

You will see this type of output on your terminal screen:

```
---------------------
Temperature = 22.6 C
Humidity = 36.8 %
---------------------
```

```
Updating Blynk
---------------------
Temperature = 22.5 C
Humidity = 36.8 %
---------------------
Updating Blynk
```

Hit the Run key at the top-right of your Blynk app on the phone, and then watch your data start to come in. If you don't get data in a few seconds, check your authentication code and make sure you have started your app by hitting the Start button in the upper-right corner of the app.

Your results should look like Figure 3-18.

**FIGURE 3-18:**
The MyTempera-
ture app's
Live view.

Note that the Live display on the graph can look a little funky, but your other displays will start filling in and looking really good.

# Where to Go from Here

In this chapter, you have learned a lot about how to connect to the real world Python on your Raspberry Pi. We suggest these other interesting things to do, building upon your new expertise:

>> Add more I2C sensors to your Raspberry Pi. There are hundreds of them.

>> Try adding some digital sensors to your Pi, like PIR detectors to detect warm bodies like humans in front of your Pi.

>> Add an I2C compass and accelerometer to your Pi.

>> Build larger and more complex dashboards and show off your project with your friend (yes, you can do this by sharing your authentication code with your friends).

>> Add a motor to make things move. Oh wait, we are doing that in the next chapter!

# Chapter **4**

# Making Things Move with Python

**M**aking things move around with Python is undeniably cool. With motors, physical computing goes to a whole new level.

Robots, microwaves, refrigerators, and electric cars all use electric motors to move around, blow air, pump coolant, and take you 60mph wherever you want to go. Electric motors are everywhere!

At its simplest, an electric motor is a machine that converts electrical energy into mechanical energy. In this chapter, we talk about DC (direct current) motors. Direct current is a single fixed voltage, like 9V or 5V or 3.3V. Alternating current (AC), on the other hand, is what you get out of your house outlets.

Interestingly, electric motors consume more than half of the electric energy produced in the United States.

# Exploring Electric Motors

An electric motor is all about magnetism. All motors use magnets to create motion. All magnets have a north and a south pole. North to north and south to south repel each other whereas north and south attract. Clever people have figured out how to use this fact to create motion. We are all familiar with permanent magnets, like the ones you use to hang things on the front of your refrigerator. However, you can also create magnets by running a current around a coiled wire, which creates a magnetic field. By periodically reversing the current through this electromagnet, you can create force, which then becomes motion. There are many ways to build motors, but this is the fundamental basis of all of them.

In this chapter, we are going to talk about three common types of motors used in small projects and robots. They are:

>> Small DC motors

>> Servo motors

>> Stepper motors

## Small DC motors

A DC motor has two wires, power and ground. When you supply power (putting 5V on the power line, for example), the motor will start spinning. Reverse the power and ground wires, and the motor will spin in the opposite direction. You control the speed of a DC motor by using pulse width modulation (PWM), a technique that we saw in Chapter 1 of this minibook for controlling the brightness of an LED. If the power is cycled at 50 percent (half on/half off) then the motor will spin at one-half the speed. These DC motors are inexpensive and great for driving wheels. Sometimes you will put an "encoder" on the motor shaft so you read into a computer how far the shaft has turned, giving the computer some feedback that can be useful.

Use a DC motor anytime you want something to be spun at a RPM (revolutions per minute), such as a fan or a car wheel. (See Figure 4-1.)

**FIGURE 4-1:**
A DC motor on a
small robot.

## Servo motors

*Servo motors* are a generally a combination of three things: a DC motor, a simple control circuit, and a gearing set. Sometimes you will find a potentiometer (which is a variable resistor) that will give position feedback like the "encoder" in the DC motor discussed earlier. The servo motor is commanded to go to a specific position by using our friend PWM again. However, in this case, a specific pulse wave will hold the motor in a specific position and will resist a load or a force trying to move the motor. The maximum amount of force that the servo motor can exert against an external force or load is called the *torque rating* of that servo motor. Servos are continuously powered and generally only have about a 180-degree range of motion.

A classic place you find servo motors is in model RC airplanes and in some types of robot arms. When you want to move an object and hold it at a specific position, a servo motor is often the answer.

Use a servo motor for fast, high torque and for pretty accurate rotation to a specific position with a limited range of degrees. Good uses include rudder control on an RC boat or flaps on an RC airplane as well as robotic arms.

## Stepper motors

A *stepper motor* is kind of like a servo motor that uses a different way to move the shaft. Whereas a servo motor uses a DC motor, a stepper motor uses multiple-toothed electromagnets surrounding a central-toothed shaft.

Stepper motors use an external controller (you will use the Raspberry Pi to do this) that will sequence the electromagnets surrounding that central shaft to make the central shaft turn in "steps," hence the name *stepper* motor. The design of a stepper motor provides a steady holding torque even when not powered up. Contrast that to the servo motor, which has to be powered up to supply torque. As long as the load is within the limits of the servo motor torque, then there are no positional errors.

Stepper motors are for slow, precise rotation. They are superior to servo motors in those types of applications. 3D printers are a great example of the use of stepper motors. Stepper motors also don't require a feedback system to determine where they are positioned as servo motors do. (See Figure 4-2.)

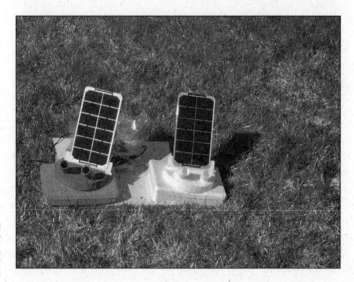

**FIGURE 4-2:**
Sun-tracking solar panels using a stepper motor.

# Controlling Motors with a Computer

Now we get to have some fun with Python in controlling motors. Next up, we go through all three types of motors and show you how to control them with Python. You will learn how to control motors both through GPIO (general purpose input-output) pins and through an I2C controller.

## Python and DC Motors

There are lots of different ways of driving DC motors from a Raspberry Pi. There are dozens of robot controllers and motor controller boards that will work for this project. The one we will be using is an I2C controlled board (tying in with our projects from the last chapter), which gives us control over two motors, their individual direction and their individual speed. Pretty cool.

Here is the parts list:

>> **Pi2Grover Grove interface board:** Try store.switchdoc.com or Amazon.com.

>> **Grove I2C motor drive:** Available at www.seeedstudio.com or Amazon.com (comes with a Grove cable).

>> **Two small DC motors:** Try https://www.adafruit.com/product/711 or Amazon.com.

For more on the Pi2Grover board, refer to Chapters 1–3 of this minibook. Let's spend some time on the Grove I2C motor drive because it has a rather unique way of doing things.

## Grove I2C motor drive

The Grove I2C motor drive (see Figure 4-3) is capable of driving two motors at the same time, all controlled by our old friend, the I2C bus from the Raspberry Pi.

**FIGURE 4-3:**
The Grove I2C
motor drive.

It can drive up to 2A for each motor, but we are using motors a lot smaller than that. It can optionally handle 6V to 15V motors, but again, we are using small motors, so we will just use the Raspberry Pi power supply. If you are using bigger motors or want to use an external power supply, this board can do that for you.

The reason we are using this board is that it uses an I2C interface to control the motors, which gets us up and running quickly.

Figure 4-4 shows what is on the I2C motor drive board.

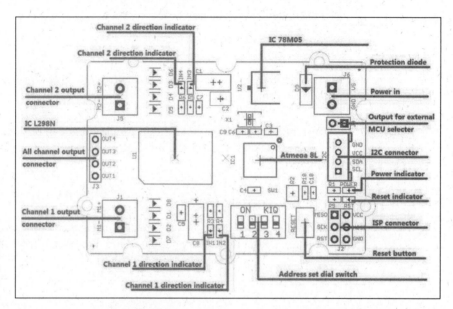

There are a couple of interesting things about this diagram: First of all, there is another computer on this board! It is an Atmega 8L and is another small computer that actually emulates and I2C interface, processes commands coming in from your Raspberry Pi and then controls the motors. Yet another example of how even boards for little computers have little computers on them. Computers are everywhere! You can see the two motor connections on the left side of the board and also what the LEDs mean in the middle of the board.

You can also find the software for the onboard computer on the Grove I2C motor drive on the www.seeedstudio.com product page. You could change the programming if you want or at least understand how you can make a little computer look like an I2C device.

Let's wire it up and start our engines! Turn off the power on your Raspberry Pi before you hook this up:

1. **Loosen the set of two screw terminals on the end of the and insert the bare end of the wires on the motors (see Figure 4-5) into the holes and tighten the screws. (See Figure 4-6.)**

**FIGURE 4-5:**
The Adafruit
DC motor.

**FIGURE 4-6:**
The wires in the
I2C motor drive
screw terminals.

Note that it really doesn't matter which color goes in which hole with a DC motor. It will just rotate in the opposite direction. Just match them both as in Figure 4-6. We added some length to the wires, but that is optional. Figure 4-7 shows the installed motor on your Grove I2C motor drive board.

2. Plug a Grove cable into the Grove connector on the Grove I2 motor drive board and then into an I2C Grove connector on the Pi2Grover board.

**WARNING**

Make sure you have the jumper in place on the board as indicated in Figure 4-4 (called "Output for external MCU selector" in the diagram). It comes that way in the package, but make sure it is still in place. The board won't operate as wired if you don't have that jumper installed.

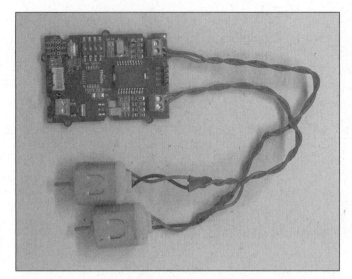

FIGURE 4-7:
Motors
installed on the
motor drive.

TIP

If your board and motor don't respond after hookup, try hitting the Reset button on the board. Figure 4-8 shows the assembled motor and board.

FIGURE 4-8:
The DC
motor setup.

Now, let's power the Raspberry Pi up and start writing some Python! After power-up, you should see all five LEDs shining on the Grove I2C motor drive board. If not, shut the Pi down again and check your wiring.

## Python DC motor software

DC motors are often used for robot wheels, and so the words *forward* and *backward* should start to give you some ideas for later in the book when we are building a robot car.

The software we are going to use for the Python DC motor experiment should have a familiar feel because it is very similar to the I2C software we dealt with in Chapters 2 and 3.

The use of Python libraries are key to being productive in writing Python applications. We will be using the SDL_Pi_HDC1080_Python3 available on Github.com.

To set up the software, follow these steps:

**1.** **Create a directory in your main directory by entering:**

```
cd
mkdir dcMotor
cd dcMotor
```

Now you are in the dcMotor directory.

**2.** **Before looking at the Python code for running your motors, install the library on the Raspberry Pi. You do this by "cloning" the library located up at github.com by using the following command in your terminal window:**

```
git clone https://github.com/switchdoclabs/SDL_Pi_GroveI2CMotorDrive.git
```

The git clone clones the git repository located at the address and copies it to your Raspberry Pi. If you enter ls in the terminal window, you will see the following output:

```
pi@RPi3-60:~/dcMotor $ ls
SDL_Pi_GroveI2CMotorDrive
pi@RPi3-60:~/I2CTemperature $
```

Making Things Move with Python

3. **Using nano (or your favorite text editor), open up a file called** `dcmotorTest.py` **and enter the following code:**

```python
import sys
sys.path.append("./SDL_Pi_GroveI2CMotorDrive")


import SDL_Pi_GroveI2CMotorDrive
import time

#"0b1010" defines the output polarity
#"10" means the M+ is "positive" while the M- is "negative"

MOTOR_FORWARD =  0b1010
MOTOR_BACKWARD =  0b0101


try:

    m= SDL_Pi_GroveI2CMotorDrive.motor_drive()

    #FORWARD
    print("Forward")
      #defines the speed of motor 1 and motor 2;)
    m.MotorSpeedSetAB(100,100)
      m.MotorDirectionSet(MOTOR_FORWARD)
    time.sleep(2)

    #BACK
    print("Back")
    m.MotorSpeedSetAB(100,100)
    #0b0101  Rotating in the opposite direction
      m.MotorDirectionSet(MOTOR_BACKWARD)
    time.sleep(2)

    #STOP
    print("Stop")
    m.MotorSpeedSetAB(0,0)
    time.sleep(1)

    #Increase speed
    for i in range (100):
        print("Speed:",i)
        m.MotorSpeedSetAB(i,i)
        time.sleep(.02)
```

```
        print("Stop")
        m.MotorSpeedSetAB(0,0)

except IOError:
        print("Unable to find the I2C motor drive")
        print("Hit Reset Button on I2C Motor Drive and Try Again")
```

This program runs both motors forward at full speed (100), then backwards at full speed, stops the motors, and then runs them backward at a slow speed ramping up to full speed, and then stops the motors entirely.

The key aspects of this software are calls to the SDL_Pi_GroveI2CMotorDrive library. The library supports the following functions:

>> MotorSpeedSetAB( *MotorSpeedA*, *MotorSpeedB*): Motor speed for the A motor (M1) and the B motor (M2). Range 0–100.

>> MotorDirectionSet(*Direction*): Forward or backward —constants set in the program. MOTOR_FORWARD = 0b1010, MOTOR_BACKWARD = 0b0101

One interesting piece of the SDL_Pi_GroveI2CMotorDrive library is that it uses one of the many I2C libraries available, smbus. In the library, you send the command to the I2C board as a block write consisting of the I2C address, a command byte, and then the arguments. Here is the call for setting the motor direction:

```
#Set motor direction
def MotorDirectionSet(self,Direction):
        bus.write_i2c_block_data(self.I2CMotorDriveAdd, self.DirectionSet,
[Direction,0])
        time.sleep(.02)
```

Time to run the DC motors now. Type this into your terminal window:

```
sudo python3 testMotor.py
```

You will be rewarded by seeing the LEDs change and seeing your motors go through a sequence that you have programmed in Python. You should be able to make your own sequences very easily from this example. Now on to a Servo motor.

**TIP**

All these motors take power from the Raspberry Pi when running, so disconnect the DC motors when you are ready to move to the next section. Shut down the Pi first!

# Python and running a servo motor

Servo motors are a different beast than a DC motor. A servo motor has a DC motor inside, but it also has a controller circuit that allows us to position the DC motor to a specific position and then hold the motor there. A great use of a servo motor is on a robot arm where you want to arm to go to a specific position and wait there for further orders.

You control servo motors by using PWM (pulse width modulation). Although you can buy boards that will do PWM (and support bigger servo motors!) under control of your computer, for this small servo we will be using the built-in PWM capability of the GPIO (general purpose input-output) pins of the Raspberry Pi.

Here is the parts list:

>> **Pi2Grover Grove interface board:** Look for it at store.switchdoc.com or amazon.com.

>> **SG90 micro servo motor:** Try finding it on ebay.com or amazon.com. These are inexpensive so you may end up buying two or more for under $10.

>> **A package of Grove male patch cables:** Grove-connector-to-male-pin cables: Available at store.switchdoc.com or amazon.com.

The Pi2Grover has been described before in Chapters 1, 2, and 3 of this minibook.

The SG90 micro servo motor (see Figure 4-9) is a small, inexpensive servo motor available from many sources. It has an operating voltage of 3.0V – 7.0V with about a current draw of about 40mA (40 milliamps – a milliamp is 1/1000th of an amp of current) at maximum so the 5V on the Raspberry Pi is good to operate this servo. It can turn about 90 degrees in each direction, for a total of 180 degrees. There are three control wires on most servo motors and the SG90 is no exception. The three wires are:

>> Yellow – PWM control signal

>> Red – Power (5V, in our case)

>> Brown – Ground

The Grove-male-pin-to-Grove-connector patch cables (see Figure 4-10) are used to make a connection between the three pins on the servo to a Grove connector, and then you can plug it into your Raspberry Pi.

**FIGURE 4-9:**
The SG90 micro servo with wires.

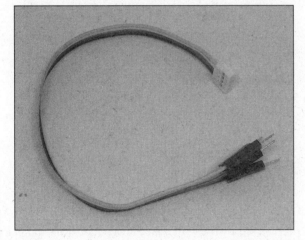

**FIGURE 4-10:**
Grove male-pin-to Grove-connector patch cable.

**TECHNICAL STUFF**

# HOW MUCH CURRENT CAN THE RASPBERRY PI SUPPLY TO THE 5V PINS?

Unfortunately, there isn't a simple answer to this question, because it depends on what you have connected to the Raspberry Pi 3 and what kind of a USB power supply you are using. 250mA is a pretty good number for a rule of thumb, but if you have a beefy 5V USB power supply (say 2.5A) you can go a lot higher, up to 1000mA or more. The Raspberry Pi 3 has a 2.5A fuse on the 5V power supply. It is a resettable fuse so if you pop it, just let it cool down and it will work again. Very good if you make a mistake.

Now let's connect the wires and make a servo motor rock!

1. **Shut down your Raspberry Pi and remove power.**

2. **Plug the Grove patch cable into your SB90 servo motor following this wire chart in Table 4-1. (See Figure 4-11.)**

**TABLE 4-1**

## Servo Motor to Patch Cable Wiring

| SG90 Servo | Grove Patch Cable | Function |
|---|---|---|
| Yellow Wire | Yellow Wire | PWM Signal |
| Red Wire | Red Wire | Power |
| Brown Wire | Black wire | Ground |

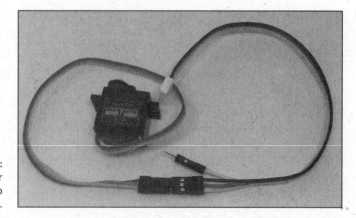

**FIGURE 4-11:**
Servo motor
correctly wired to
patch cable.

**WARNING**

Check your wiring carefully. You can damage your Pi and motor if you reverse these wires.

3. **Plug the end of the Grove cable in the Pi2Grover Grove connector marked D4/D5.**

4. **Put a piece of electrical tape or blue tape over the white exposed pin on the Grove patch cable to keep it from shorting anything out. Also put one of the supplied rocker arms on the servo motor gear so we can see more easily its range of motion. (See Figure 4-12.)**

Now let's look at the Python software.

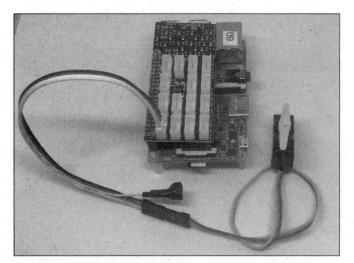

**FIGURE 4-12:**
Fully connected Pi
and servo motor.

## Python servo software

We are not going to use a higher-level servo library (and there are many available for the Raspberry Pi in Python); instead, we are going to show you how to control a servo motor directly by using GPIO and the PWM function of the RPi GPIO built-in library. Okay, okay. We *are* using a library (RPi.GPIO), but we're not adding layers of API (application programming interface) calls like we normally would do. We're getting down and dirty with the GPIO pins. To do so, follow these steps:

**1.** **Create a directory in your main directory by entering:**

```
cd
mkdir Servo
cd Servo
```

**2.** **Using nano (or your favorite text editor), open up a file called servoTest.py and enter the following Python code:**

```
import RPi.GPIO as GPIO
import time


GPIO.setmode(GPIO.BCM)
ServoPin = 4

GPIO.setup(ServoPin, GPIO.OUT)

p = GPIO.PWM(ServoPin, 50)
```

```
    p.start(7.5)

    try:
        while True:
            p.ChangeDutyCycle(7.5)   # turn towards 90 degree
            print ("90 degrees")
            time.sleep(1) # sleep 1 second
            print ("0 degrees")
            p.ChangeDutyCycle(2.5)   # turn towards 0 degree
            time.sleep(1) # sleep 1 second
            print ("180 degrees")
            p.ChangeDutyCycle(12.5) # turn towards 180 degree
            time.sleep(1) # sleep 1 second


    except KeyboardInterrupt:
        p.stop()
        GPIO.cleanup()
```

## Breaking down the code

This is where we set the pin number to the D4/5 Grove connector on the Pi2Grover board:

```
import RPi.GPIO as GPIO
import time


GPIO.setmode(GPIO.BCM)
ServoPin = 4
```

Next, we set the GPIO pin to "Output":

```
GPIO.setup(ServoPin, GPIO.OUT)
```

This command sets an object p to the ServoPin (4) and at a frequency of 50Hz. 50Hz is a good number for this type of servo motor:

```
p = GPIO.PWM(ServoPin, 50)
```

The following line starts the servo motor at 7.5 percent duty cycle. Remember how PWM works on a servo? It goes from one end of the servo turn to the by going from according to the duty cycle. The 7.5 and the number 2.5 and 12.5 are determined by the servo type. We just looked at the numbers and empirically determined these numbers for the SG90 servo. They are similar for most small servos:

```
p.start(7.5)
```

Now we move the servo through its entire range:

```
try:
    while True:
        p.ChangeDutyCycle(7.5)  # turn towards 90 degree
        print ("90 degrees")
        time.sleep(1) # sleep 1 second
        print ("0 degrees")
        p.ChangeDutyCycle(2.5)  # turn towards 0 degree
        time.sleep(1) # sleep 1 second
        print ("180 degrees")
        p.ChangeDutyCycle(12.5) # turn towards 180 degree
        time.sleep(1) # sleep 1 second
```

Notice how we put the entire body of this program in try: except: clause? We did this so when your control-c out of the program, the program will shut down the servo motor and do some cleanup on the GPIO (release all pins back to the operating system). This is generally a good thing to do when you are dealing with GPIO pins directly.

```
except KeyboardInterrupt:
    p.stop()
    GPIO.cleanup()
```

Now it is time to run the program. Type the following into a terminal window:

```
sudo python3 servoTest.py
```

You should be rewarded by your screen printing out the following liens and your servo happily obeying your programmed orders. Change things out and try different angles and sequences. You can't hurt the servo by trying things.

```
90 degrees
0 degrees
180 degrees
90 degrees
0 degrees
180 degrees
90 degrees
0 degrees
```

Now we have a servo motor working on our Raspberry Pi. Remember at the beginning when we told you a servo motor can move an robot arm, a flap on an RC airplane or a rudder on an RC boat? Watching the servo motor go thorough its programmed sequence should spark your thoughts of what to do with a servo motor. You can see why you use a DC motor for wheels and a servo to do things in a non-rotating manner.

Experiment and build your own magical projects! Now we will step right down the line to our last major motor, a stepper motor.

## Python and making a stepper motor step

Stepper motors are yet a different beast than DC motors or servo motors. They are used for accurate positioning of items with a digital interface. You can accurately position things with a servo motor too, but it requires more electronics and definitely needs what is called positional feedback.

A stepper motor gets around this by accurately moving from one "step" to another under command of software. The motor is constructed to use two motor coils to advance the motor one step by sending a specific sequence to the motors. You will be implementing this "stepping" sequence in the Python software controlling the stepper motor.

A stepper motor typically has two coils used to move the motor from one step to another (see Figure 4-13).

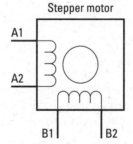

**FIGURE 4-13:** A diagram of a stepper motor.

Table 4-2 shows the sequence for stepping the stepper motor forward one step, and Table 4-3 shows the stepping sequence for moving the motor backward one step. This pattern of steps will be very obvious in our Python software.

TABLE 4-2

## Forward Stepping the Stepper

| Coil_A_1 (Pin 12) | Coil_A_2 (Pin 20) | Coil_B_1 (Pin 13) | Coil_B_2 (Pin 21) |
| --- | --- | --- | --- |
| 1 | 0 | 1 | 0 |
| 0 | 1 | 1 | 0 |
| 0 | 1 | 0 | 1 |
| 1 | 0 | 0 | 1 |

TABLE 4-3

## Backward Stepping the Stepper

| Coil_A_1 (Pin 12) | Coil_A_2 (Pin 20) | Coil_B_1 (Pin 13) | Coil_B_2 (Pin 21) |
| --- | --- | --- | --- |
| 1 | 0 | 0 | 1 |
| 0 | 1 | 0 | 1 |
| 0 | 1 | 1 | 0 |
| 1 | 0 | 1 | 0 |

In Figure 4-14, this digital sequence is graphically portrayed from a logic analyzer connected to the Raspberry Pi GPIO pins used to drive the stepper motor.

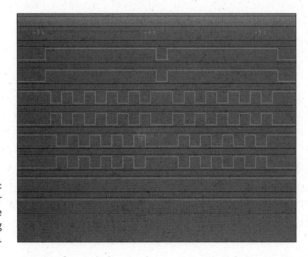

FIGURE 4-14:
Logic analyzer showing the motor stepping sequence.

Well, now you know all you need to know about stepper motors to build your first project.

# FEEDBACK: WHAT A USEFUL THING!

Feedback occurs when you route the output of a system back into the inputs of a system as a loop. Sounds complicated? It can be, but the basics are simple. Say you publish and article and ask for comments. People supply comments (hopefully nice ones) and you change the article based on some of those comments. That is feedback!

You use feedback in electrical circuits to achieve a better and more accurate positioning of a servo motor, for example. By reading an encoder on the shaft of the servo (an encoder gives you an electrical signal proportional to the position of the shaft), your software can tweak the PWM duty cycle to get to a more accurate position depending on the feedback.

There are two types of feedback: negative and positive feedback. In our example above, we think of positive feedback as being good comments or at least constructive criticism on our article, whereas negative feedback is just comments telling us how bad the article is.

However, in electronics, you tend to like negative feedback and not like positive feedback, at least in general. Negative feedback is what we use to get closer to the position on the shaft we want to be at, for example. Positive feedback tends to make differences get larger. Ever hear a speaker wail when you put a microphone too close the speaker? That's positive feedback.

Here is the parts list:

>> **Pi2Grover Grove interface board:** Try store.switchdoc.com or amazon.com.

>> **28BYJ-48 ULN2003 5 V stepper motor:** Look for these at eBay.com or `https://amzn.to/2BuNDV1`. These are inexpensive, so you may end up buying five for $12. Make sure you get the ones with the driver boards (such as the ones at the preceding Amazon.com link).

>> **A package of Grove female patch cables, Grove-connector-to-female-pins:** Available at store.switchdoc.com or amazon.com.

The Pi2Grover has been described before in Chapters 1, 2, and 3 of this minibook.

The 28BYJ-48 stepper motor is a 5V stepper motor that has 5.625 x 1/64 degrees per step (approximately 0.822 degrees per step) and comes with a driver board with a ULN2003 motor drive chip, and the best of all, four LEDs that show what you are doing with the motor from your software. (See Figure 4-15.)

**FIGURE 4-15:**
The 28BYJ-48 stepper motor and UNL2003 driver board.

The female–Grove patch cables are used to connect the stepper motor drive board to the Raspberry Pi. (See Figure 4-16.)

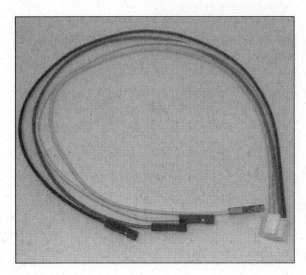

**FIGURE 4-16:**
A Grove-connector-to-female-pin-header patch cable.

Time to build your stepper motor project! Just follow these steps:

1. **Shut down your Raspberry Pi and remove power.**

2. **Take a Grove female patch cord and connect it to the UNL2003 driver board, as in the wire chart in Table 4-4.**

   Note we put a wire tie on the cable to keep things neat and tidy.

### First Grove Female Patch Cord to UNL2003 Driver Board

| Grove Patch Cable | UNL2003 Driver Board | Function |
|---|---|---|
| Yellow Wire | IN1 | Coil A_1 |
| White Wire | IN2 | Coil B_1 |
| Red Wire | + | Power |
| Black wire | – | Ground |

Look very carefully at your red and black wire on the Grove patch cord to make sure it is plugged in, as shown in Figure 4-17.

**FIGURE 4-17:** Close-up of power connections on the UNL2003 driver board.

3. **Take a second Grove female patch cord and connect it as in the wire chart in Table 4-5.**

**TABLE 4-5**

## Second Grove Female Patch Cord to UNL2003 Driver Board

| Grove Patch Cable | UNL2003 Driver Board | Function |
|---|---|---|
| Yellow Wire | IN3 | Coil A_2 |
| White Wire | IN4 | Coil B_3 |
| Red Wire | No Connect | |
| Black wire | No Connect | |

Use a wire tie or a piece of tape to keep the unused red and black wires up and out of the way, as shown in Figure 4-18.

**FIGURE 4-18:**
Second Grove patch cable attached.

Now, check all your connections again and make sure it looks like those in Figure 4-19.

4. **Plug your 28BYJ-4 stepper motor cable into the UNL2003 driver board connector. It is keyed and only goes in one way. (See Figure 4-20.)**

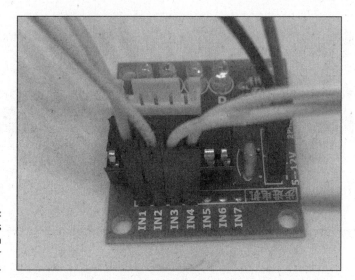

FIGURE 4-19:
All patch wires
installed on
UNL2003 driver
board.

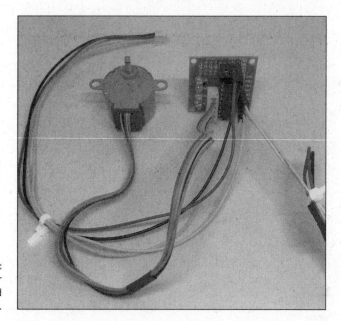

FIGURE 4-20:
Stepper motor
and driver board
connected.

5. **Plug the first Grove patch cable (the one that has all four wires connected to the UNL2003 driver board) into the Pi2Grover Grove connector marked D12/13 and the second Grove patch cable (the one that only has the yellow and white wires connected) into the Pi2Grove Grove connector marked D20/21.**

   Wiring is now complete. The full wired system is shown in Figure 4-21.

6. **Put a cardboard arrow on your stepper motor shaft so you can really see it move. (See Figure 4-22.)**

## Python stepper software

Similar to what we did with the servo motor, we are not going to use a higher level stepper library (and there are many available for the Raspberry Pi in Python — not all work with all stepper motors!), and instead we are going to show you how to control a stepper motor directly by using GPIO pins. Just follow these steps:

1. **Create a directory in your main directory by entering:**

```
cd
mkdir Stepper
cd Servo
```

2. **Using nano (or your favorite text editor), open up a file called** stepperTest.py **and enter the following Python code:**

```python
import sys

import RPi.GPIO as GPIO
import time

GPIO.setmode(GPIO.BCM)
GPIO.setwarnings(False)
coil_A_1_pin = 12
coil_B_1_pin = 13
coil_A_2_pin = 20
coil_B_2_pin = 21

GPIO.setup(coil_A_1_pin, GPIO.OUT)
GPIO.setup(coil_A_2_pin, GPIO.OUT)
GPIO.setup(coil_B_1_pin, GPIO.OUT)
GPIO.setup(coil_B_2_pin, GPIO.OUT)


def forward(delay, steps):
    for i in range(0, steps):
        setStep(1, 0, 1, 0)
        time.sleep(delay)
        setStep(0, 1, 1, 0)
        time.sleep(delay)
        setStep(0, 1, 0, 1)
        time.sleep(delay)
        setStep(1, 0, 0, 1)
        time.sleep(delay)
```

```
def backwards(delay, steps):
    for i in range(0, steps):
        setStep(1, 0, 0, 1)
        time.sleep(delay)
        setStep(0, 1, 0, 1)
        time.sleep(delay)
        setStep(0, 1, 1, 0)
        time.sleep(delay)
        setStep(1, 0, 1, 0)
        time.sleep(delay)


def setStep(w1, w2, w3, w4):
    GPIO.output(coil_A_1_pin, w1)
    GPIO.output(coil_A_2_pin, w2)
    GPIO.output(coil_B_1_pin, w3)
    GPIO.output(coil_B_2_pin, w4)


while True:

    try:

        # Delay between steps (milliseconds)
        delay = 10
        # How many Steps forward
        steps = 50
        forward(int(delay) / 1000.0, int(steps))
        # How many Steps backwards
        steps = 50
        backwards(int(delay) / 1000.0, int(steps))

    except KeyboardInterrupt:
        # shut off all coils
        setStep(0,0,0,0)
        sys.exit()
```

## Breaking down the code

The `stepperTest.py` code is pretty simple. We turn GPIO outputs to 1 and 0, according to the stepper motor sequences shown in Tables 4-2 and 4-3. You can see the exact sequences in the code in the forward and backwards functions.

Now let's run the code and start stepping away. We make sure we shut off all the outputs when you hit Ctrl-C to stop the program.

Time to run! Power up your Pi and open a terminal window. Note that all four of the LEDs turn on when you power up, but these will be turned off when you run your Python program. (See Figure 4-23.)

FIGURE 4-23:
The Raspberry Pi running the stepper motor.

You will see the stepper motor turn 50 steps to the left and then 50 steps to the right. Try changing those variables in the program above to move your stepper motor to other positions. Do you see how these motors can be used in 3D printers and robots to accurately position printing heads, bed height, and robot arms?

# 7

# Building Robots with Python

# Contents at a Glance

# Chapter **1**

# Introduction to Robotics

Robots. That's a name that has been bandied about for a hundred years. It comes from a Czech word, *robota*, which means "involuntary labor." It was first used in the 1920 play "R.U.R. – Rossum's Universal Robots" by Karel Capek, but it was really Capek's brother Josef who coined the word. Did you know there was a robot in Frank Baum's land of Oz in 1907? He didn't call it a robot, but it's definitely a robot.

Robots are everywhere in today's modern world. Your house is filled with them. How is that possible? To understand what we are talking about, you need to understand the definition of *robot* more in computer-science terms than in Hollywood's.

## A Robot Is Not Always like a Human

Two things to know about robots:

» Robots have only two features, a computer and an actuator.

» Robots are dumb; they are not people.

Robots have computers of some kind; think of it as the machine's brain. These brains can vary from IBM's Watson to a small eight-bit processor with a few thousand bytes of RAM. (You will see this with Baxter the Coffee-Making

Robot — yes, Baxter has a computer inside, about 16 of them, to be clear. But more on that in a moment.) The computers don't even have to be in the robot itself. You can have a network connection to the computer controlling the robot.

So, what is an actuator? It is something that physically affects the world outside. Under this definition, an sophisticated IOT (Internet of Things) device connected to a sensor and a database is not really a robot, whereas a computer controlling a toaster (that pops up the toasted bread) is a robot. As with any definition, you can argue corner cases all day. But this is a good working definition that shows just how varied the "body type" of a robot can be.

# Not Every Robot Has Arms or Wheels

The classic conception of a robot tends to be something that looks at least vaguely human. The amazing robots that help us assemble cars in factories, for example, have giant arms that pick up car doors, weld metal, place windshields, and do many other assembly line tasks. Smaller arms are all over manufacturing lines helping to produce small goods as well as large ones.

One of the relatively new categories of robots is called *Cobots* (*cooperative robots*). These are robots that are designed to work closely alongside humans in manufacturing lines. Robots in car lines will hurt you if you get in their way. Cobots will stop if they encounter you when moving. These robots can work right next to people, doing tasks to make the people more efficient. Baxter the Coffee-Making Robot is an example of a Cobot.

Robots don't always have arms (remember our toaster?). Robots can look like microwaves. They can look like cars (yes, self-driving cars, but also like your current car). Modern-day cars are filled with computers doing robotic things. For example, there is a computer that measures you pushing down the gas pedal and then adjusts the fuel-and-air mixture to get you just the increase that you are looking for. It's a drive-by-wire system, just like airplanes. No cables physically connect your pedal to a mechanical gas pump or valve. In the new 2019 BMW X3s, there is a button you can push to change the way your car behaves from "Comfort" mode to "Sport" mode. It changes the way the wheel feels (and how much feedback you get from the road), the way your gas pedal responds, and even the way the suspension reacts to road conditions. (See Figure 1-1.) In a modern car, there are over 20 computers doing all sorts of things all over the vehicle and talking to each other constantly.

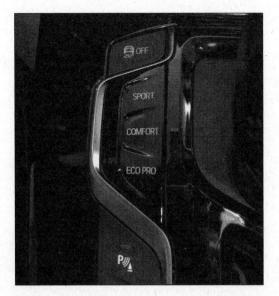

**FIGURE 1-1:**
Inputs for the
BWM Robot
Driving System.

People think of robots as being in assembly lines or those fabulous robotic dogs made by Boston Dynamic. We'll choose a few other types of examples of robots. All three of the following examples are robots under our definition.

# The Wilkinson Bread-Making Robot

Wilkinson Baking is located in Walla Walla, Washington (www.wilkinsonbaking. com). They have invented a robotic bread-making system that may actually bring bread-baking back to the local stores and away from giant bread plants. (See Figure 1-2.)

This type of disruption has happened before. Remember how you used to have to send film away to big plants to get it developed? Then suddenly, machines (yes, robots) came out that allowed mom-and-pop stores to get back into the film-development and picture-printing business. Yes, the proliferation of digital cameras took most of that business way, but you can see the point.

Wilkinson has developed quite a bread-making robot that should be practical for locally mass-producing bread. By the way, one of the claims they make is that their bread only requires one-sixth of the fossil fuel needed to get the product to the consumer.

Introduction to
Robotics

**FIGURE 1-2:**
A robot
making bread.

## Baxter the Coffee-Making Robot

Baxter is a general-purpose Cobot. Manufactured by Rethink Robotics, he is a fairly old Cobot, introduced in 2011, but he is good for helping students to learn robotics because of his really fabulous set of sensors and cameras (one in each arm!) and his two arms, each with a different attachment (a gripper on the left and a suction cup on the right). This allows some very sophisticated projects to be done with the robot. (See Figure 1-3.)

Baxter has around 16 different computers inside: A main computer (actually a Dell PC, believe it or not) strapped in his torso and individual computers controlling all the joints, cameras, and sensors into both arms. Interestingly enough, Baxter's brain for the coffee-making program (all in Python, by the way) is located across the room and is connected to Baxter by a network connection. It uses a distributed ROS (robot operating system) to be controlled and provide information and images to the user and the controlling computer. Take a look at this video: https://youtu.be/zVL8760H768

Three students were called upon to teach Baxter to make coffee in their senior robotics class, and after three months and thousands of lines of code, they succeeded. The team had to use computer vision techniques to recognize when the coffee was done, connect Baxter up to the Amazon AWS Cloud so they could use Alexa ("Alexa, tell Baxter the Robot to make coffee"), and use a variety of pick-and-place code to select a Keurig cup and to deliver a full cup of coffee to the customer's table.

Interestingly, now that he can do this, Baxter appears much smarter, but Rule #2 still applies ("Robots are dumb"). He can make coffee, but he can't make toaster strudel. Yet. Next semester.

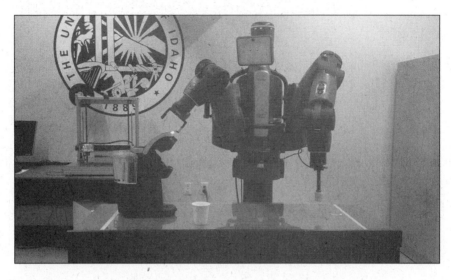

**FIGURE 1-3:** Baxter making coffee.

## The Griffin Bluetooth-enabled toaster

You really didn't think we were going to finish these examples of robots without using a toaster did you? The Griffin Bluetooth-enabled toaster was presented at CES (Consumer Electronic Show) as part of suite of connected kitchen appliances. It allows you to program (by app) your desired level of toasty crispness, and it can send your phone a notification when your toast is done. This is great, but on the other hand, it needs about three minutes to make toast. Also, it looks like it hasn't yet gone into production, which is a great disappointment to John personally, because he wants a connected toaster.

Here is a link to a YouTube video for the toaster: `https://www.youtube.com/watch?v=Z7h8-f-k8C8`.

Before we leave the world of robot toasters, one more toaster: Toasteroid, funded by a Kickstarter campaign takes robotic toast to a whole new level. (See Figure 1-4.) It can print messages on your toast! From a smartphone! Funded in 2016 (but sadly still not available), the company claims a retail price of $85, which tells you how inexpensive a lot of this robotic technology has become.

**FIGURE 1-4:**
The Toasteroid
Internet-
connected
toaster.

Enough examples. Let's now move into to what makes a robot and how we program them in Python!

# Understanding the Main Parts of a Robot

You can break all the robots in generally four types of components:

>> Computers

>> Motors and actuators

>> Communications

>> Sensors

## Computers

Computers are totally ubiquitous in robotics. You have a computer controlling the cameras, another computer controlling each joint in the arms, and another computer interpreting the images coming in from the cameras and reading the sensors monitoring the environment around the robot.

These computers are mostly small computers called *embedded systems*. They may only have one purpose (such as monitoring the amount of current being used for a motor) or they may be coordinating an entire arm, telling the other computers what to do.

The higher-level computers in the system are used for planning and receiving orders from other robots (or the assembly line itself) and people. And, yes, most of these higher-level computers are programmed in Python.

## Motors and actuators

Motors and actuators are what differentiate robots from computers. These motors are all sorts of types and sizes (Refer to Book 5 for an introduction to motors). *Actuator* is a term with a definition that's a bit broader than *motor*'s. For example, an actuator could be memory wire, which is a type of metal that can be heated up to perform an action and later, when it cools down, it goes back to its original size. It is kind of like muscle fiber, and it has a lot of uses in the robotic industry. As we did in Book 5, you will be making motors move using Python in the following chapters.

## Communications

Robots need to communicate. Not just verbally or even onscreen but in digital format that other computers and robots understand to coordinate actions and react to the environment. And robots use communications to offload complex tasks (such as, for example, computer vision interpretation) to other computers, sometimes even up in the cloud. And yes, many of these communication devices (BlueTooth, TCP/IP networks, WiFi) use computers inside the communication devices.

## Sensors

We'll admit it. We love sensors. We are always on the lookout for the latest and greatest sensors. Electricity, temperature, humidity, electronic gyroscopes, pressure, touch sensors, people sensors, cameras, and image-processing sensors are becoming more inexpensive and pervasive every day. And many of these sensors and functions are programmed using Python for data processing and hardware drivers.

Unfortunately, in modern robotics and embedded systems, these components all end up somewhat mixed together. A motor in a robot will have a computer, communications, and sensors all together.

# Programming Robots

Robots are programmed in many different types of languages. Some robots can be programmed by moving the arm to a specific set of locations and other robots are programmed in more traditional ways. We have found that programming by moving the arms will kind of get you in the ballpark and provide a structure for your programming to implement a particular function.

The most popular programming language in the world for programming robots at a high level (above the motor drives and such things) is Python. Hands down. Baxter is programmed via an API (application programming interface) provided for Python. Python is used to call many robotic functions and image processing as well as to provide the movement planning and coordination between robots. Although many robot manufacturers will have their own proprietary software, almost all of them will provide a method for working with Python.

# Chapter **2**

# Building Your First Python Robot

I n this chapter, we open up a robot to take a look inside, and we show you how to talk to all the parts with Python. We tell you how to program a robot after you build it. Why build the robot first? For two reasons: First, a kit-based robot is inexpensive compared to buying a prebuilt one. Second, by building a robot you get to know how a robot works and how you can use Python to control it.

We have chosen a robot that is based on our friend the Raspberry Pi. You can get robots that are based on many other computers, including the Arduino, but with those smaller computers, you can't do the kind of processing or artificial intelligence that you can on the Raspberry Pi.

After all, this is *Python All-In-One For Dummies.* Wouldn't you like to be able to use some of the tools you learned earlier in this book?

## Introducing the Mars Rover PiCar-B

When we were deciding which robot to build in this book, we looked at and assembled four different small robot cars. All of them were similarly priced, and each of them had some drawbacks. However, after careful consideration, we chose to use the Adeept PiCar-B. (See Figure 2-1.) We did this for several reasons:

>> The assembly manual was clear with lots of pictures and diagrams.

>> The supplied software was compatible with Python 3 (and the Stretch version of the Raspberry Pi operating system).

>> The PiCar-B required no soldering.

>> It had a reasonable price and good availability.

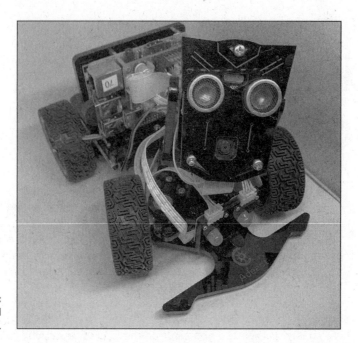

**FIGURE 2-1:**
The assembled
PiCar-B robot.

**TIP**

A radio control car can be considered a robot too. Why did we choose *this* car? It is because you can easily get inside the software and add more software to make the robot do what you want it to do. Yes, it does have a user interface (see the next chapter) on an additional PC. However, we are far more interested in putting our own Python software inside the robot than we are in playing with the joystick.

## What you need for the build

There are three things you need in order to build the robot used in this chapter, in addition to some basic tools (although the kit comes with Allen wrenches and screw-drivers) and some plastic wire ties to get the wires bundled together after assembly:

» **Raspberry Pi 3B+:** Yes, you could get by with a smaller Raspberry Pi (like the Raspberry Pi Zero), but we recommend you get the fast one so you can do more sophisticated processing onboard the robot. The price you pay for a faster Pi (like the 3B+) is in power consumption and battery life. For our purposes here, it is a good tradeoff.

Among other places, you can buy the Raspberry Pi 3B+ at

- Amazon.com (make sure you buy the 3B+)

- Newark.com

- Adafruit.com

- Shop.switchdoc.com

» **Adeept Raspberry Pi PiCar-B:** The Adeept Raspberry Pi PiCar-B is not quite as available as the Raspberry Pi. When you buy this, make sure you are buying the PiCar-B and *not* the PiCar-A. They add *Mars Rover* to the name of this product in their catalog, so look for the "Adeept Mars Rover PiCar-B."

You can buy the PiCar-B at these places:

- Amazon.com (`https://amzn.to/2B7mtop`)

- eBay.com

- Adeept.com

- Shop.switchdoc.com

» **18650 LiPo batteries:** The PiCar-B requires two 18650 3.7V LiPo 5000mAh batteries. You can also power the robot by turning off the power switch (or removing the batteries) and supplying power for the Raspberry Pi from the micro USB plug, which then powers both the robot and the Raspberry Pi. The power for both the robot and the Raspberry Pi are connected together.

The package we chose had two sets of batteries and an included wall charger. You can buy these kinds of batteries all over the place, including

- Amazon.com (`https://amzn.to/2TgPsx1`)

- Many, many other places.

# Understanding the robot components

Now it is time to look at the components in the PiCar–B. We're not going to focus on the mechanical structure of the robots but rather on each of the active components. We'll also talk about the Python software used to communicate with each device used in the Python system test software later on in this chapter and in our own robotic software in Chapter 3.

We will be giving small Python code snippets to show you how each of the sensors and motors are controlled. For more of the code and description, see the "Running Tests on Your Rover in Python" section, later in this chapter.

## Controller board

This motor controller is designed to interface the Raspberry Pi to the sensors and motors on the PiCar-B. (See Figure 2-2.) The main two chips on the board are a PCA9685, an I2C device used to control up to 16 servo motors (of which three are used, so there's lots of room for expansion) and an L289P, which is used to provide power to the main drive motor. The rest of the board is used to connect up the GPIO (general purpose input-output) pins from the Raspberry Pi to the various sensors and devices. It also has a 5.0V power supply that supplies the Raspberry Pi and motors from the LiPo batteries. (See Figure 2-3.)

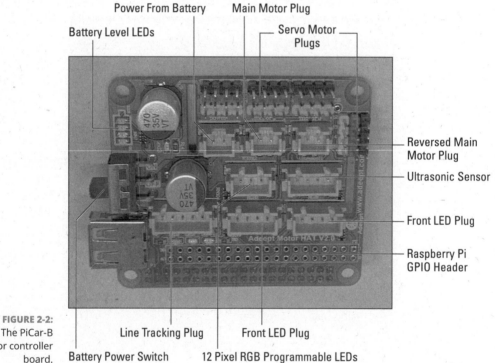

**FIGURE 2-2:** The PiCar-B motor controller board.

Power From Battery    Main Motor Plug

Battery Level LEDs    Servo Motor Plugs

Reversed Main Motor Plug

Ultrasonic Sensor

Front LED Plug

Raspberry Pi GPIO Header

Line Tracking Plug    Front LED Plug

Battery Power Switch    12 Pixel RGB Programmable LEDs

## Servo motors

Servo motors are a generally a combination of three things: a DC motor, a simple control circuit and a gearing set. Sometimes you will find a potentiometer (which is a variable resistor) that will give positional feedback.

You control the position by using pulse width modulation (PWM), a technique that we saw in Chapter 1 for controlling the brightness of an LED.

The SG90 micro servo motor supplied with the robot is a small, inexpensive servo motor available from many sources. (See Figure 2-3.) It has an operating voltage of 3.0V–7.0V with a current draw of about 40mA (40 milliamps; a *milliamp* is 1/1000th of an amp of current) at maximum so the 5V on the Raspberry Pi is good to operate this servo. It can turn about 90 degrees in each direction for a total of 180 degrees. There are three control wires on most servo motors and the SG90 is no exception. The three wires are:

>> **Yellow:** PWM control signal

>> **Red:** Power (5V, in our case)

>> **Brown:** Ground

**FIGURE 2-3:**
The SG90 micro
servo motor.

Servos are continuously powered and generally only have about a 180–270 degree range of motion.

All three of the servo motors are SC-90 9g micro servos.

These servos are controlled from the PCA9685 I2C chip, so it doesn't use any GPIO lines from the Raspberry Pi. It is on the I2C bus of the Raspberry Pi. (See Chapter 3 for more information about the I2C bus.)

To control a servo motor, we just have to set the value to the position we want the servo moved on the appropriate PWM line in the PCA9685:

```
print ("--------------------")
print ("Servo Test - Head Left")
print ("--------------------")
pwm.set_pwm(HEAD_TURN_SERVO, 0, calValues.look_left_max)
time.sleep(1.0)
```

The number we are passing into the servo motor for position (calValues.look_left_max) is empirically determined and is set by looking at the range of the servo motor as you command it to the left and right. See "Calibrating Your Servos," later in this chapter.

## Drive motor

The main drive motor is a DC motor with two wires: power and ground. (See Figure 2-4.) When you supply power (by putting 5V on the power line, for example), the motor will start spinning. Reverse the power and ground wires, and the motor spins in the opposite direction. You control the speed of a DC motor by using pulse width modulation (PWM), a technique for controlling the brightness of an LED (refer to Chapter 1 of this minibook). If the power is cycled at 50 percent (half on/half off) then the motor will spin at one-half the speed. Sometimes you will put an "encoder" on the motor shaft, which allows you to read into a computer how far the shaft has turned, giving the computer some feedback that can be useful.

This motor uses six GPIO lines from the Raspberry Pi to control speed and direction.

The intricacies of controlling this motor are well hidden from the user. Here is the Python code to move the car forward:

```
motor.motor_left(MOTOR_START, forward,left_spd*spd_ad)
motor.motor_right(MOTOR_START,backward,right_spd*spd_ad)
```

TIP

Why are we turning both a left and right motor on when there is only one drive motor in the PiCar-B? The reason is that you can't be sure which way your motor is wired; it may be wired one direction or it may be reversed. (Ours was reversed.) You have two motor plugs on the controller board. If the forward command causes the robot to move backward, you just move the motor to the other motor connection and everything works. Writing the preceding code (using both motor controllers) allows the software to work with either kind of motor.

**FIGURE 2-4:**
The main
drive motor.

## RGB LED

The front of the robot has two single RGB LEDs, one on each side. (See Figure 2-5.) These big LEDs actually have three LEDs inside the housing. The LEDs are red, blue, and green and are individually controlled by GPIO lines (running software PWM code that allows us to mix the R, G and B LEDs).

The RGB LEDs each use three GPIO lines from the Raspberry Pi:

```
print ()
print ("---------------------")
print ("Left Front LED Test – Red ")
print ("---------------------")

led.side_on(led.left_R)
time.sleep(1.0)
led.side_off(led.left_R)
```

You turn the LEDs on individually and can (using other software) actually set the brightness of each LED.

**FIGURE 2-5:**
A single RGB LED.

## Pixel RGB programmable LEDs

There are 12 programmable RGB LEDs on the robot, two sets of three on the bottom of the robot and two sets of three pointing to the rear. (See Figure 2-6.) These 12 LEDs are connected in serial like Christmas lights. And like some Christmas lights, if one goes out, then all the rest of the string goes too. That is because they are controlled by a single serial data stream that is sent through all the lights by the Raspberry Pi. This serial stream is very precisely timed, which requires some pretty special software on the Raspberry Pi to make it work.

The Pixel string uses a single GPIO pin coming from the Raspberry Pi:

```
print ()
print ("--------------------")
print ("12 RGB Pixel LED Test - On ")
print ("--------------------")

rainbowCycle(strip, wait_ms=20, iterations=3)
```

This command cycles a rainbow of colors around all 12 LEDs on the back and bottom of the robot. The driver for these RGB Pixels is very complicated, but we'll provide code to easily control the LEDs and we'll give you some examples of how to use them for other purposes. We really do love these LEDs and use them in many projects.

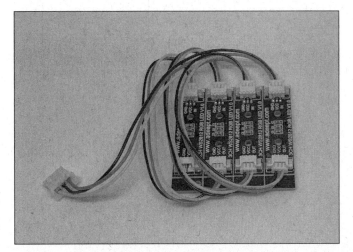

**FIGURE 2-6:**
The 12
programmable
RGB LEDs.

**TECHNICAL STUFF**

# PIXEL RGB STRINGS ON THE RASPBERRY PI

The Raspberry Pi has a complex, multifaceted operating system based on Linux. It is a multitasking preemptive operating system, which means virtually any task (and all user tasks) can be interrupted (meaning stopped) and thus our serial stream to the Pixel LEDs stopped and corrupted to some degree.

The library we are using solves the real-time control problem by using the PWM and DMA hardware on the Raspberry Pi's processor. The PWM (pulse-width modulation) module can generate a signal with a specific duty cycle; for example, to drive a servo or dim an LED. The DMA (direct memory access) module can transfer bytes of memory between parts of the processor without using the CPU. By using DMA to send a specific sequence of bytes to the PWM module, the Pixel data signal can be generated without being interrupted by the Raspberry Pi's operating system.

Because the Arduino type of processors don't really have an operating system, it is pretty easy to generate these signals on an Arduino compared to an Raspberry Pi. Processors like the ESP8266 and the ESP32 do have tasks running in the background (like WiFi) and so require special drivers to compensate for that to avoid data corruption and flickering. Note that although this works well on the Raspberry Pi 3B+, the LEDs do not always work well with the older and smaller Raspberry Pis (A+, 3B, Pi Zero, or Pi Zero W, for example).

## Pi camera

The camera used in the PiCar-B is the classic Raspberry Pi camera, version 2.1. (See Figure 2-7.) It has a Sony 8 megapixel sensor and can support pictures up to 3280 x 2464 at 15 frames per second.

It has good color response and is well supported in Python and with OpenCV (OpenCV is the Open Source Computer Vision package we use later in Chapter 4). The Pi camera talks to the Raspberry Pi via a parallel data ribbon cable directly into the Raspberry Pi board.

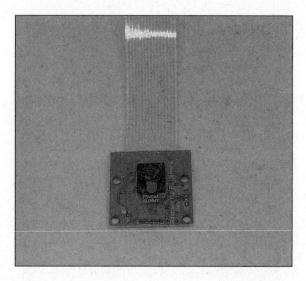

**FIGURE 2-7:** Raspberry Pi camera and cable.

The following code opens up a small window on the GUI of the Raspberry Pi, waits 20 seconds, moves the window and resizes it, waits 2 seconds, moves it again and then closes the window:

```
print ()
print ("--------------------")
print ("Open Video Window")
print ("--------------------")



camera.resolution = (1024, 768)
camera.start_preview(fullscreen=False,window=
(100,100,256,192))
time.sleep(20)
camera.preview.window=(200,200,256,192)
time.sleep(2)
```

```
camera.preview.window=(0,0,512,384)
time.sleep(2)
camera.close()
```

**TIP**

If you are using VNC to see the GUI of the Raspberry Pi (as we are doing), you need to open up the options of the VNC server in the upper-right corner, go into Options, then down into Troubleshooting and click the Enable Direct Capture Mode checkbox. See the "Assembling the Robot" section, later in this chapter.

## Ultrasonic sensor

The ultrasonic detector used in the PiCar-B is a non-contact distance measurement module that works at 40KHz. (See Figure 2-8.)

When provided a pulse trigger signal with more than 10uS through signal pin, the unit issues 8 cycles of 40kHz cycle level and detects the echo. The pulse width of the echo signal is proportional to the measured distance. Simple, yet effective.

**FIGURE 2-8:**
An ultrasonic distance sensor.

The formula used is: Distance = Echo signal high time * Sound speed (340M/S)/2.

In the following code, the call to `ultra.checkdisk()` calls the software that sets the transmit GPIO bit and then waits for the returning echo, marking the time received. It then calculates the time of transit and reports the distance in meters, which we convert to centimeters.

```
print ()
print ("-------------------")
print ("Ultrasonic Distance Test")
print ("-------------------")
```

**Building Your First Python Robot**

```
        average_dist = 0.0
        for i in range(0,10):
            distance = ultra.checkdist()
            average_dist = average_distance + distance
            print ("Distance = {:6.3f}cm ".format( distance*100))
            time.sleep(1.0)

        average_distance = average_distance / 10

    print ("average_dist={:6.3f}cm".format(average_dist*100))
```

# Assembling the Robot

The PiCar-B comes with an assembly manual complete with blow out pictures of how things go together. (See Figure 2-9.)

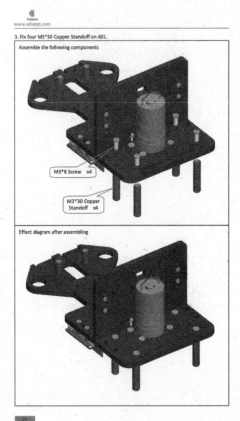

**FIGURE 2-9:**
An example of
the assembly
manual diagrams.

It took us about four hours to put the robot together and get to the point to begin testing.

*Note:* Do not go beyond Chapter 2 in the PiCar-B assembly manual. Chapter 3 starts installing all the Adeept software on the Raspberry Pi and you will want to test the robot using the software in this book to better understand the parts of the robot before continuing.

So, go build your robot and then meet us back here to start testing your new robot. Calibrating your servos is the first step! Then we run a full system test. Figure 2-10 shows the assembled robot.

**FIGURE 2-10:**
The assembled
PiCar-B showing
wiring.

**TIP**

Here are a few helpful tips for building the robot:

>> There is a power switch on the left side of the motor drive board (viewed from the front of the robot). It is not mentioned in the manual. It shuts off the power from the batteries.

>> Make sure you use the longer of the supplied ribbon cables for the Pi camera. The short one will not quite reach. Change it before you install the camera into the robot.

>> Route the wires as shown in Figure 2-10 so the motors won't bind. Use some plastic wire ties to hold things in place, allowing for room for the servos and housing to turn. There is a wire wrap included that will fit some of the wires.

>> Pay close attention to the orientation of the plastic parts and servos during assembly. Almost all of them have an asymmetrical top and bottom and need to be oriented correctly to be assembled.

>> Don't drop tiny screws in the carpet. They're hard to find for sure!

## Calibrating your servos

Now that you have assembled the robot, it is time to start testing things. The first thing to do is to calibrate your servo motors. Why do they need calibration? Because although the instructions have you leave the servos centered during assembly, they will not necessarily be completely in the right place.

The `calibrateServo.py` program runs each of the three servos from one end to the other. By watching the motors as they turn, you can write down the max, min, and center of each servo from the display on the terminal window. Then you place these values in the `calValues.py` program for the rest of the programs to access. The values in the `calValues.py` are right for our robot and will probably be pretty close for yours, but you should run the program to be sure.

The `calibrateServo` code is as follows:

```
#!/usr/bin/python3

# calibrate servos
```

```python
import time

import Adafruit_PCA9685

import calValues

#import the settings for servos


pwm = Adafruit_PCA9685.PCA9685()
pwm.set_pwm_freq(60)


#servo mapping
# pmw 0 head tilt
HEAD_TILT_SERVO = 0
# pwm 1 head turn
HEAD_TURN_SERVO = 1
# pwm 2 wheels turn
WHEELS_TURN_SERVO = 2


if __name__ == '__main__':

    print("---------------------")
    print("calibrate wheel turn")
    print("---------------------")

    for i in range(calValues.turn_right_max,
            calValues.turn_left_max,10):
        pwm.set_pwm(WHEELS_TURN_SERVO,0, i)
        print("servoValue = ", i)
        time.sleep(0.5)


    print("---------------------")
    print("calibrate head turn")
    print("---------------------")

    for i in range(calValues.look_right_max,
            calValues.look_left_max,10):
        pwm.set_pwm(HEAD_TURN_SERVO,0, i)
        print("servoValue = ", i)
        time.sleep(0.5)


    print("---------------------")
    print("calibrate head up/down")
    print("---------------------")
```

```
    for i in range(calValues.look_up_max,
        calValues.look_down_max,10):
    pwm.set_pwm(HEAD_TILT_SERVO,0, i)
    print("servoValue = ", i)
    time.sleep(0.5)
The code is pretty straight forward, but let me talk about one of the servo
    program loops.
    for i in range(calValues.look_right_max,
        calValues.look_left_max,10):
    pwm.set_pwm(HEAD_TURN_SERVO,0, i)
    print("servoValue = ", i)
    time.sleep(0.5)
```

This loop steps through the servo range as given in `calValues.py` from the right to the left, turning the head in steps of 10. This gives you a pretty good idea where the right, left, and center should be (taking into account the robot frame too!) and you can add those values to `calValues.py`.

The `calValues.py` file holds the calibration values for the servo motors. You replace the values in this program with your own values from `calibrate Servos.py`:

```
# Servo calibration values

# head
look_up_max     = 150
look_down_max   = 420
look_tilt_middle = 330

# head turn
look_right_max    = 200
look_left_max     = 450
look_turn_middle = 310

# wheels
turn_right_max   = 180
turn_left_max    = 460
turn_middle      = 320

# turn_speed
look_turn_speed  = 5

# motor speed

left_spd   = 100        #Speed of the car
right_spd  = 100        #Speed of the car
```

# Running tests on your rover in Python

Okay, now you have the PiCar-B assembled, time to run some tests. If you have installed the Adeept software on your Raspberry Pi, you have to disable the auto startup of their software.

To do so, change the following line in the ~/.config/autostart/car.desktop file:

```
Exec=sudo python3 /home/Adeept_PiCar-B/server/server.py
```

To

```
#Exec=sudo python3 /home/Adeept_PiCar-B/server/server.py
```

And then reboot your pi with: `sudo reboot`.

Of course, we told you not to install the software, but if you got too excited and did then you need to do the above or else you will have conflicts in the software.

Here is a video of what the following Python test software does on the PiCar-B robot: `https://youtu.be/UvxRBJ-tFw8`.

That is what you will be running very shortly.

# Installing software for the CarPi-B Python test

First of all, go to this book's support page on `www.dummies.com` (refer to the Introduction) and download the software for Book 7, Chapter 2.

Go into the Testing directory and then complete these instructions, which are necessary to get the 12 programmable RGB LEDs to work on the Raspberry Pi:

1.  **Install some developer libraries, which allow us to compile the software. This is installed using the normal Raspberry Pi installer, as follows:**

    ```
    sudo apt-get install build-essential python3-dev git scons swig
    ```

2.  **Download the neopixel code from github using the `clone` command, which copies all the source code to your local computer:**

    ```
    git clone https://github.com/jgarff/rpi_ws281x.git
    ```

3. **Change to that directory and run scons to compile the software:**

```
cd rpi_ws281x
scons
```

4. **Change to the python directory and install the Python module from there:**

```
cd python
```

5. **Install the Python 3 library file using:**

```
sudo python3 setup.py install
```

## The PiCar-B Python test code

The file is approximately 370 lines long, so we don't provide a full listing here. The important parts of this file have been discussed along with the individual components and sensors above. There are a number of other libraries and files in the Testing directory.

If you haven't already, go to this book's support page at www.dummies.com (refer to the Introduction) and download the software for Book 7, Chapter 2.

Run the test software by typing:

```
sudo python3 PiCar-B-Test.py
```

You should immediately see your car start doing the testing sequence, as shown at https://youtu.be/UvxRBJ-tFw8.

## Pi camera video testing

To prepare for this test, you must be running in a GUI on your Raspberry Pi. If you are using VNC to display the GUI on another computer, you must do enable a VNC option. Open up the options of the VNC server in the upper-right corner, go into Options, then down into Troubleshooting and click the Enable Direct Capture Mode checkbox. (See Figure 2-11.)

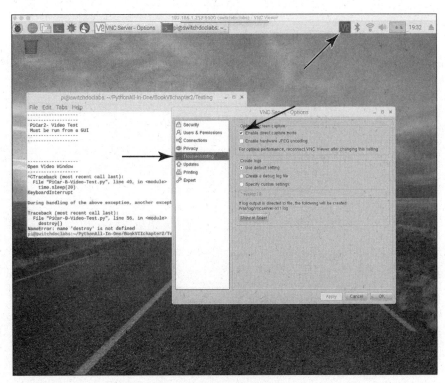

FIGURE 2-11:
Setting the VNC
viewer option.

This test software (PiCar-B-Video-Test.py) follows:

```
#!/usr/bin/python3
DEBUG = True
VIDEOTEST = True
# runs through a video tests for the PiCar-B

import RPi.GPIO as GPIO
import motor
import ultra
import socket
import time
import threading
import turn
import led
import os
import picamera
from picamera.array import PiRGBArray
import cv2
```

```
import calValues


if __name__ == '__main__':

    camera = picamera.PiCamera()                    #Camera initialization
    camera.resolution = (640, 480)
    camera.framerate = 7
    rawCapture = PiRGBArray(camera, size=(640, 480))


    try:

        print ("---------------------")
        print ("---------------------")
        print (" PiCar2- Video Test")
        print (" Must be run from a GUI")
        print ("---------------------")
        print ("---------------------")
        print ()
        print ()

        if (VIDEOTEST):

            print ()
            print ("---------------------")
            print ("Open Video Window")
            print ("---------------------")



            camera.resolution = (1024, 768)
            camera.start_preview(fullscreen=False,
                    window=(100,100,256,192))
            time.sleep(20)
            camera.preview.window=(200,200,256,192)
            time.sleep(2)
            camera.preview.window=(0,0,512,384)
            time.sleep(2)
            camera.close()
    except KeyboardInterrupt:
        destroy()
```

This code opens up a small window on the GUI of the Raspberry Pi, waits 20 seconds, moves the window and resizes it, waits 2 seconds, moves it again, and then closes the window.

Now you are done building and testing your robot. Next, we are going to add some Python brains and have some fun with the robot.

# Chapter **3**

# Programming Your Robot Rover in Python

O kay, let's review where you are now. You have a basic understanding of robots and (more importantly) of the major components of robots and how they work. You understand that these components can be controlled with Python and that they can work together to accomplish robotic tasks. That's really a lot of information. Next, we show you how to string these things together to make a very, very simple "robotic brain" to make our robot move by itself. This won't quite be a fully self-driving car, but after doing this you will have some sense of how those cars are programmed.

## Building a Simple High-Level Python Interface

Let's first make a short Python wrapping function that allows us to build much more complicated programs while hiding the complexity of the robot hardware.

Our high-level interface is a python class file called RobotInterface.py. The code length is beyond what we want to show in this book, so let us describe a couple of functions and then document the rest.

# The motorForward function

The `motorForward` function is typical of the motor functions located within the `RobotInterface` class:

```
def motorForward(self, speed, delay):
    motor.motor_left(self.MOTOR_START, self.forward,speed)
    motor.motor_right(self.MOTOR_START, self.backward,speed)
    time.sleep(delay)
    motor.motor_left(self.MOTOR_STOP, self.forward,speed)
    motor.motor_right(self.MOTOR_STOP, self.backward,speed)
```

This function drives the robot forward for the number of seconds passed into the function in the `delay` argument. This means that when you call this function, you must use an actual number in the `delay` argument.

It basically starts the motors running forward, waits a delay and then shuts them off.

# The wheelsLeft function

```
def wheelsLeft(self):
    pwm.set_pwm(self.WHEELS_TURN_SERVO, 0,
        calValues.turn_left_max)
    time.sleep(0.05)
```

The `wheelsLeft` function sets the `WHEELS_TURN_SERVO` to the leftmost position of the wheels and then delays 50ms. Why the delay? You will see these delays scattered through the `RobotInterface` class file. These are to keep multiple servo commands back-to-back from exceeding the current capacity of the power supply. By delaying the next servo command 50ms, the high current transient caused by the moving the first servo has a chance to die away before the next servo command is executed.

# The wheelsPercent function

This function allows the user to set the servo to a percent of the total range of the servo motor. It goes from the full left (0) to full right (100) for the wheels; 50 would be approximately in the middle. It may differ a little from the middle if you have an asymmetric range of motion of your servo. If you do, then use the `wheelsMiddle()` function to center your wheels.

This code calculates the total range of motion of the servo motor and then multiplies it by the percentage requested. It then sets the servo motor to the requested range:

```
def wheelsPercent(self,percent):
    adder = (calValues.turn_left_max -
        calValues.turn_right_max)*(percent/100.0)
    pwm.set_pwm(self.WHEELS_TURN_SERVO, 0,
        int(calValues.turn_right_max + adder))
    time.sleep(0.05)
```

# Making a Single Move with Python

First of all, go to this book's support page at www.dummies.com (refer to the Introduction) and download the software for Book 7, Chapter 3.

In the following code, we move the robot a short distance ahead with a motor Forward command and then back to its original position with a motorBackward() command. Hopefully, you're starting to see the magic of this approach.

The "Single Move" code:

```
#!/usr/bin/python3
# Robot Interface Test

import RobotInterface
import time

RI = RobotInterface.RobotInterface()

print ("Short Move Test")

RI.wheelsMiddle()

RI.motorForward(100,1.0)
time.sleep(1.0)
RI.motorBackward(100,1.0)
```

First, we import the RobotInterface class library and also the time library (for sleep()). Note the simplicity of this. The complexity underlying robot interface libraries are hidden by this class:

```
import RobotInterface
import time
```

Then we initialize the RobotInterface module and assign the module to the variable RI:

```
RI = RobotInterface.RobotInterface()

print ("Short Move Test")
```

We center the wheels with the wheelsMiddle() function command:

```
RI.wheelsMiddle()
```

Now comes the good part. We drive the robot forward for one second, pause a second, and then run it backwards for one second to the robot's original position:

```
RI.motorForward(100,1.0)
time.sleep(1.0)
RI.motorBackward(100,1.0)
```

Pretty simple, right? Call the file singleMove.py.

Here is a video of what you should see when you run this code on your robot in a terminal window: https://youtu.be/UT0PG7z2ccE.

The job isn't finished until when? Oh yes, when the documentation is finished. Off to document the RobotInterface class functions.

# Functions of the RobotInterface Class

In this section, we document the functions of the RobotInterface class. We show you the Robot Interface Test program, and then it is off to the races in building robot software! The RobotInterface class is derived from both original software by the author and also from internal drivers from the PiCar-B Adeept software.

## Front LED functions

The following functions control the two LEDs on the front of the robot.

### set_Front_LED_On()

This function sets the front LED to On:

```
set_Front_LED_On(colorLED)
```

Remember that these two front LEDs are tricolor with red, green, and blue LEDs, each of which is individually controllable. The parameter, colorLED, controls the side of the robot to turn on and the color to turn on. You set the color and select the side by using the following constants from the RobotInterface class:

```
RobotInterface.left_R
RobotInterface.left_G
RobotInterface.left_B

RobotInterface.right_R
RobotInterface.right_G
RobotInterface.right_B
```

For example, RobotInterface.left_R turns on the red LED on the Robot Left side. *Robot Left* refers to the left side of the robot as viewed from the rear of the robot. You can make multiple calls to this program to turn on all three of the LEDs. Turning on an already on LED does not hurt anything and is ignored.

A more sophisticated driver could be written driving the LEDs GPIOs with PWM (pulse-width modulation) allowing even greater color mixing. Note that unless you are using hardware PWM pins on the Raspberry Pi, you will see flickering of the LEDs when using this technique because of the Raspberry Pi multitasking operating system. You could, however, write drivers for the PCA9685 servo driver board (on the PiCar-B) that currently drives the servo motors to fix the flickering problem.

## set_Front_LED_Off()

This function sets the Front LED to Off:

```
set_Front_LED_Off(colorLED)
```

Remember that these two front LEDs are tricolor with red, green, and blue LEDs, each of which is individually controllable.

The parameter, colorLED, controls the side of the robot to turn on and the color to turn on. You set the color and select the side by using the following constants from the RobotInterface class:

```
RobotInterface.left_R
RobotInterface.left_G
RobotInterface.left_B

RobotInterface.right_R
RobotInterface.right_G
RobotInterface.right_B
```

For example, `RobotInterface.left_R` turns on the red LED on the Robot Left side. *Robot Left* refers to the left side of the robot as viewed from the rear of the robot. You can make multiple calls to this program to turn on all three of the LEDs. Turning on an already on LED does not hurt anything and is ignored.

# Pixel strip functions

There are 12 LEDs on the robot strung together as a single 12 LED strip. These RGB LEDs are called Pixels and are controlled by a single serial line that runs through all 12 of the LEDs. They are controlled by a fairly sophisticated and touchy serial sequence of precisely timed pulses from the Raspberry Pi. The Raspberry Pi (again because of the operating system) cannot generate these pulses accurately enough using Python and GPIO signals. Therefore a complex driver using the DMA (direct memory access) interface on the Raspberry Pi has been created by a "jgarff" (rpi_ws281x — very clever coding) and we are using that driver to generate those signals. Our `RobotInterface` software hides all this complexity from the user.

## rainbowCycle()

This call starts a rainbow cycle that uses all 12 of the Pixel LEDs and runs through many colors:

```
rainbowCycle(wait_ms = 20, iterations = 3)
```

The parameter `wait_ms` sets the delay (in milliseconds) between each color change. It defaults to 20ms. `Interations` sets the number of full color cycles to perform before returning, and it defaults to 3.

## colorWipe()

This function sets all 12 Pixel LEDs to the same color:

```
colorWipe(color)
```

For example, `colorWipe(color(0,0,0))` sets all the Pixels to `Off`. This is a handy way to set all 12 pixels to the same color. The parameter, `color`, specifies the color to be used using the `color()` function. (See the `color()` function later in this chapter.)

## theaterChaseRainbow()

This function starts a 40-second-long pattern of chasing LEDs on all 12 of the LEDs:

```
theaterChaseRainbow(wait_ms = 50)
```

The `wait_ms` parameter sets the delay between each of the movements in milliseconds. It defaults to 50 milliseconds.

## setPixelColor()

This function sets an individual pixel (numbered from 0 through 11) to a specific color. Brightness affects all the pixels and uses the last brightness value set:

```
setPixelColor(pixel, color, brightness)
```

The `pixel` parameter sets the specific pixel to set. Pixels are numbered 0–11.

The `color` parameter specifies the color to be used using the `color()` function.

The `brightness` parameter sets the brightness (0–255) for *all* the pixel string.

## Color()

This function is a helper function that converts the R, G and B values into a single 24 bit integer used by the internal Pixel driver:

```
Color(red, green, blue, white = 0)
```

The parameters `red`, `green`, and `blue` are integers and range from 0 (off) to 255 (fully on). The `white=0` parameter is for RGBW Pixel LEDs. The Pixels on the robot are RGB LEDs.

## allLEDSOff()

This function turns all the LEDs on the robot off, both the front two LEDs and the 12 LED Pixel string:

```
allLEDSOff()
```

# Ultrasonic distance sensor function

The ultrasonic distance sensor functions by sending out a pulse of high frequency sound and then counting the time before it bounces back to the receiver. Because we know the speed of sound, we can calculate the distance in front of the sensor. It's not a perfect method (we would rather be using a laser!), but it is pretty good, and it makes for a good starting distance sensor.

### fetchUltraDistance()

This function does an immediate measurement from the ultrasonic distance sensor in the head of the robot and returns the distance in centimeters (cm):

```
fetchUltraDistance()
```

# Main motor functions

The main motor on our robot is what drives the back wheels and makes our robot move. The motor functions are used to tell how fast and how long to run the main motor.

### motorForward()

This function drives the robot forward at speed for the delay number of seconds before the shutting off the motors:

```
motorForward(speed, delay)
```

The parameter speed sets the duty cycle of the PWM GPIO pin driving the interface for the motor. It goes from 0 (off) to 100 (fast).

The parameter delay tells the driver how long to run the motor in seconds.

### motorBackward()

This function drives the robot backwards at speed for the delay number of seconds before the shutting off the motors:

```
motorBackward(speed, delay)
```

The parameter speed sets the duty cycle of the PWM GPIO pin driving the interface for the motor. It goes from 0 (off) to 100 (fast).

The parameter delay tells the driver how long to run the motor in seconds.

### stopMotor()

This function immediately stops the main motor:

```
stopMotor()
```

This is really only useful if, for example, you were driving the motor in another thread. You can think of a thread as another program running at the same time as your main program. This is a sophisticated programming technique that has some huge benefits to writing robot code.

# Servo functions

This group of functions control the three servos on the robot: head-turning, head-tilting, and front wheels.

## headTurnLeft()

This function turns the robot head all the way to the left:

```
headTurnLeft()
```

"All the way to the left" is defined in the calValues.py file. Refer to Chapter 2 in this minibook for information on the calibration values and how to set them using the calibrateServos.py program.

## headTurnRight()

This function turns the robot head all the way to the right:

```
headTurnRight()
```

"All the way to the right" is defined in the calValues.py file. Refer to Chapter 2 in this minibook for information on the calibration values and how to set them using the calibrateServos.py program.

## headTurnMiddle()

This function turns the robot head towards the front:

```
headTurnMiddle()
```

"The middle" is defined in the calValues.py file. Refer to Chapter 2 in this minibook for information on the calibration values and how to set them using the calibrateServos.py program.

### headTurnPercent()

This function turns the head from 0 (all the way to the left) to 100 (all the way to the right):

```
headTurnPercent(percent)
```

This is useful for more precisely aiming the head. Again, "all the way to the left" and "all the way to the right" " are defined in the calValues.py file. Refer to Chapter 2 of this minibook for information on the calibration values and how to set them using the calibrateServos.py program.

The parameter percent has values 0–100 and represents the linear percent from left to right. Note that the value 50 may not be quite in the middle because your servos may not be set exactly in the middle of their range.

### headTiltDown()

This function tilts the robot head all the way down:

```
headTiltDown()
```

"All the way down" is defined in the calValues.py file. Refer to Chapter 2 of this minibook for information on the calibration values and how to set them using the calibrateServos.py program.

### headTiltUp()

This function tilts the robot head all the way up:

```
headTiltUp()
```

"All the way up" is defined in the calValues.py file. Refer to Chapter 2 of this minibook for information on the calibration values and how to set them using the calibrateServos.py program.

### headTiltMiddle()

This function tilts the robot head towards the front:

```
headTiltMiddle()
```

"The middle" is defined in the calValues.py file. Refer to Chapter 2 of this minibook for information on the calibration values and how to set them using the calibrateServos.py program.

## headTiltPercent()

This function turns the head from 0 (all the way down) to 100 (all the way to the up):

```
headTiltPercent(percent)
```

This is useful for more precisely aiming the head. Again, "all the way down and "all the way up"" are defined in the calValues.py file. Refer to Chapter 2 of this minibook for information on the calibration values and how to set them using the calibrateServos.py program.

The parameter percent has values 0–100 and represents the linear percent from down to up. Note that the value 50 may not be quite in the middle because your servos may not be set exactly in the middle of their range as set by the servo calibration process and because of the way your robot was physically built.

## wheelsLeft()

This function turns the robot front wheels all the way to the left:

```
wheelsLeft()
```

"All the way to the left" is defined in the calValues.py file. Refer to Chapter 2 of this minibook for information on the calibration values and how to set them using the calibrateServos.py program.

## wheelsRight()

This function turns the robot front wheels all the way to the right:

```
wheelsRight()
```

"All the way to the right" is defined in the calValues.py file. Refer to Chapter 2 of this minibook for information on the calibration values and how to set them using the calibrateServos.py program.

## wheelsMiddle()

This function turns the robot front wheels to the middle:

```
wheelsMiddle()
```

"Middle" is defined in the calValues.py file. Refer to Chapter 2 of this minibook for information on the calibration values and how to set them using the calibrateServos.py program.

### wheelsPercent()

This function turns the head from 0 (all the way to the left) to 100 (all the way to the right):

```
wheelsPercent(percent)
```

This is useful for more precisely setting the direction of the robot front wheels. Again, "all the way to the left and "all the way to the right"" are defined in the calValues.py file. Refer to Chapter 2 in this minibook for information on the calibration values and how to set them using the calibrateServos.py program.

The parameter percent has values 0–100 and represents the linear percent from down to up. Note that the value 50 may not be quite in the middle because of how your servos may not be set exactly in the middle of their range as set by the servo calibration process and how your robot was physically built.

## General servo function

We have included general functions to control all the servos at once. Calling this function moves all servos to the center position.

### centerAllServos()

This function puts all the servos on the robot to the center of their ranges as defined in the calValues.py file:

```
centerAllServos()
```

## The Python Robot Interface Test

Now that we have defined our robot API (applications programming interface), let's run the system test using the RobotInterface Python class. This program is useful for two reasons. First, it tests all our functions in the RobotInterface class. Second, it shows how to use each of the functions in a Python program.

The code for RITest.py:

```
#!/usr/bin/python3
# Robot Interface Test

import RobotInterface
```

```python
import time


RI = RobotInterface.RobotInterface()

print ("Robot Interface Test")

print ("LED tests")
RI.set_Front_LED_On(RI.left_R)
time.sleep(0.1)
RI.set_Front_LED_On(RI.left_G)
time.sleep(0.1)
RI.set_Front_LED_On(RI.left_B)
time.sleep(1.0)
RI.set_Front_LED_On(RI.right_R)
time.sleep(0.1)
RI.set_Front_LED_On(RI.right_G)
time.sleep(0.1)
RI.set_Front_LED_On(RI.right_B)
time.sleep(1.0)

RI.set_Front_LED_Off(RI.left_R)
time.sleep(0.1)
RI.set_Front_LED_Off(RI.left_G)
time.sleep(0.1)
RI.set_Front_LED_Off(RI.left_B)
time.sleep(1.0)
RI.set_Front_LED_Off(RI.right_R)
time.sleep(0.1)
RI.set_Front_LED_Off(RI.right_G)
time.sleep(0.1)
RI.set_Front_LED_Off(RI.right_B)
time.sleep(1.0)

RI.rainbowCycle(20, 1)
time.sleep(0.5)

# Runs for 40 seconds
#RI.theaterChaseRainbow(50)
#time.sleep(0.5)

print ("RI.Color(0,0,0)=", RI.Color(0,0,0))
RI.colorWipe(RI.Color(0,0,0))
time.sleep(1.0)

for pixel in range (0,12):
    RI.setPixelColor(pixel,RI.Color(100,200,50),50)
    time.sleep(0.5)
```

```
print ("Servo Tests")
RI.headTurnLeft()
time.sleep(1.0)
RI.headTurnRight()
time.sleep(1.0)
RI.headTurnMiddle()
time.sleep(1.0)

RI.headTiltDown()
time.sleep(1.0)
RI.headTiltUp()
time.sleep(1.0)
RI.headTiltMiddle()
time.sleep(1.0)

RI.wheelsLeft()
time.sleep(1.0)
RI.wheelsRight()
time.sleep(1.0)
RI.wheelsMiddle()
time.sleep(1.0)

print("servo scan tests")
for percent in range (0,100):
    RI.headTurnPercent(percent)
for percent in range (0,100):
    RI.headTiltPercent(percent)
for percent in range (0,100):
    RI.wheelsPercent(percent)


print("motor test")
RI.motorForward(100,1.0)
time.sleep(1.0)
RI.motorBackward(100,1.0)

print("ultrasonic test")

print ("distance in cm=", RI.fetchUltraDistance())

print("general function test")

RI.allLEDSOff()
RI.centerAllServos()
```

*Note:* We have commented out the test code for `RI.theaterChaseRainbow()` because it runs for 40 seconds.

# ROS: THE ROBOT OPERATING SYSTEM

We have written a fairly simple interface class for the PiCar-B robot. This allows us to control the robot from a Python program. If we had more room in this book (actually another whole book could be written about the use of ROS for a robot like ours), we would connect up our robot to the ROS (Robot Operating System). ROS is a system specifically designed for controlling robots in a distributed system. Even though it is called the *Robot Operating System*, it really isn't an operating system.

ROS is what is called *middleware*. Middleware is software that is designed to manage the complexity of writing software in a complex and heterogenous (meaning lots of different types of robots and sensors) environment. ROS allows us to treat very different robots in a very similar manner.

ROS operates using what is called a publish-subscribe system. It works like a newspaper. A newspaper publishes stories, but only the people that subscribe to the newspaper see those stories. You might have a subscriber that only wants a subscription to the comics. Or the front page.

ROS works like that. A robot like ours may publish the current value of the ultrasonic sensor or the current camera image (or even a video stream) and other computers or robots on the network could subscribe to the video stream and see what your robot is seeing. And your robot could subscribe to other sensors (such as a temperate sensor located in the middle of the room) or even look at what the other robots are seeing. The power of this technique is that now you can make your robot part of an ecosystem consisting of computers, sensors, and even people making use of your data and contributing information to your robot.

We could build a ROS interface on our robot and then we could control it remotely and feed sensor data to other computers.

In many ways, ROS really rocks. Find out more about ROS at http://www.ros.org/.

Run the program by typing `sudo python3 RITest.py` into a terminal window. Note that you *have* to use `sudo` because the Pixel LEDs require root permission (granted by `sudo`) to correctly run.

```
Robot Interface Test
LED tests
RI.Color(0,0,0)= 0
Servo Tests
servo scan tests
motor test
```

```
ultrasonic test
distance in cm= 16.87312126159668
general function test
```

Here's a link to the video of the `RobotInterface` class test: `https://youtu.be/1vi-UGao0oI`

# Coordinating Motor Movements with Sensors

The ability to modify and coordinate motor movements with sensor movements is key to movement in the environment. Sensors give information to be acted upon as well as feedback from our motions. Think of the act of catching a baseball with a glove. Your sensors? Eyes and the sense of touch. Your eyes see the ball and then move your hand and arm to intercept the ball. That's coordinating your movement with a sensor. The feedback? Knowing you have caught the ball in your mitt by the feeling of it hitting your gloved hands. Of course, you are also updating your internal learning system to become better at catching the ball.

PiCar-B has two sensors that read information from the outside world. The ultrasonic sensor can detect what is in front of the robot while the camera can photograph the world, and then the robot can analyze what it is seeing. The first thing to remember, however, is that robot vision is hard. Very hard. We touch upon using the camera images for analysis in the next chapter of this book. Chapter 4 talks about using artificial intelligence in robots, and we will be building an example of how to do this using machine learning.

For our example, we will focus on the simpler sensor, the ultrasonic distance sensor.

Here is an example of code that will move the robot forward or backwards depending on the distance from the object in front of the robot. Here is the Python code for `simpleFeedback.py`:

```
#!/usr/bin/python3
# Robot Interface Test

import RobotInterface
import time

DEBUG = True
```

```
RI = RobotInterface.RobotInterface()

print ("Simple Feedback Test")

RI.centerAllServos()
RI.allLEDSOff()

# Ignore distances greater than one meter
DISTANCE_TO_IGNORE = 1000.0
# Close to 10cm with short moves
DISTANCE_TO_MOVE_TO = 10.0
# How many times before the robot gives up
REPEAT_MOVE = 10

def bothFrontLEDSOn(color):
    RI.allLEDSOff()
    if (color == "RED"):
        RI.set_Front_LED_On(RI.right_R)
        RI.set_Front_LED_On(RI.left_R)
        return
    if (color == "GREEN"):
        RI.set_Front_LED_On(RI.right_G)
        RI.set_Front_LED_On(RI.left_G)
        return
    if (color == "BLUE"):
        RI.set_Front_LED_On(RI.right_B)
        RI.set_Front_LED_On(RI.left_B)
        return

try:
    Quit = False
    moveCount = 0
    bothFrontLEDSOn("BLUE")
    while (Quit == False):
        current_distance = RI.fetchUltraDistance()
        if (current_distance >= DISTANCE_TO_IGNORE):
            bothFrontLEDSOn("BLUE")
            if (DEBUG):
                print("distance too far ={:6.2f}cm"
                        .format(current_distance))
        else:
            if (current_distance <= 10.0):
                # reset moveCount
                # the Robot is close enough
```

```
                bothFrontLEDSOn("GREEN")
                moveCount = 0
                if (DEBUG):
                    print("distance close enough ={:.6.2f}cm"
                            .format(current_distance))

                time.sleep(5.0)
                # back up and do it again
                RI.motorBackward(100,1.0)
            else:
                if (DEBUG):
                    print("moving forward ={:.6.2f}cm"
                            .format(current_distance))
                # Short step forward
                bothFrontLEDSOn("RED")
                RI.motorForward(90,0.50)
                moveCount = moveCount + 1


            # Now check for stopping our program
            time.sleep(1.0)
            if (moveCount > REPEAT_MOVE):
                Quit = True


except KeyboardInterrupt:
    print("program interrupted")

print ("program finished")
```

This is a great example of the use of feedback in robotics. The robot first checks to see if it is less than one meter (1000cm) from the wall. If it is, it slowly starts to advance towards the wall in short little steps. When it is closer than 10cm to the wall, it stops, then waits five seconds and backs up to do it again.

It also gives up if it takes more than 10 moves to get to the wall, if somehow we have moved further than 1000cm away from the wall, or if the user has hit Ctrl-C to interrupt the program.

Note how we use the LEDs to give feedback to surrounding people as to what the robot is doing. This sort of visual feedback is an important part of making human–robot interaction more efficient, understandable, and safer.

The main structure of the program is contained within a Python while loop. As long as we haven't interrupted the program (or one of the other quit criteria hasn't been satisfied) our little robot will keep working until the battery goes dead.

Copy the code into `simpleFeedback.py` and give it a try by executing `sudo python3 simpleFeedback.py`. Here are the printed results:

```
Simple Feedback Test
moving forward = 55.67cm
moving forward = 44.48cm
moving forward = 34.22cm
moving forward = 26.50cm
moving forward = 17.53cm
distance close enough = 9.67cm
moving forward = 66.64cm
moving forward = 54.25cm
moving forward = 43.55cm
moving forward = 36.27cm
moving forward = 28.44cm
moving forward = 21.08cm
moving forward = 13.55cm
distance close enough = 6.30cm
moving forward = 64.51cm
moving forward = 52.89cm
moving forward = 43.75cm
moving forward = 33.95cm
moving forward = 26.79cm
^Cprogram interrupted
program finished
```

And you can see the feedback video here: `https://youtu.be/mzZIMxch5k4`.

Play with this code. Try different things and different constants to get different results.

# Making a Python Brain for Our Robot

Now we are going to create a simple self-driving car. In a sense, we are going to apply the results above to create an autonomous vehicle that is not very smart but illustrates the use of feedback in decision-making.

This Python brain we are writing is nothing more than a combination of our code for sensing the wall (from earlier in this chapter) and for generating a random walk based on the information. After running the code for a while, we saw where the robot would get stuck and added code to detect back out of stuck positions.

*Note:* Make sure you have fully charged up batteries to run this code. When the batteries dip a bit your motor speed dramatically decreases. How to fix this? Use bigger batteries.

The "Robot Brain" code:

```python
#!/usr/bin/python3
# Robot Brsin

import RobotInterface
import time

from random import randint

DEBUG = True

RI = RobotInterface.RobotInterface()

print ("Simple Robot Brain")

RI.centerAllServos()
RI.allLEDSOff()

# Close to 20cm
CLOSE_DISTANCE = 20.0
# How many times before the robot gives up
REPEAT_TURN = 10


def bothFrontLEDSOn(color):
    RI.allLEDSOff()
    if (color == "RED"):
        RI.set_Front_LED_On(RI.right_R)
        RI.set_Front_LED_On(RI.left_R)
        return
    if (color == "GREEN"):
        RI.set_Front_LED_On(RI.right_G)
        RI.set_Front_LED_On(RI.left_G)
        return
    if (color == "BLUE"):
        RI.set_Front_LED_On(RI.right_B)
        RI.set_Front_LED_On(RI.left_B)
        return

STUCKBAND = 2.0
# check for stuck car by distance not changing
def checkForStuckCar(cd,p1,p2):
```

```python
        if (abs(p1-cd) < STUCKBAND):
            if (abs(p2-cd) < STUCKBAND):
                return True
        return False


try:
    Quit = False
    turnCount = 0
    bothFrontLEDSOn("BLUE")

    previous2distance = 0
    previous1distance = 0

    while (Quit == False):
        current_distance = RI.fetchUltraDistance()
        if (current_distance >= CLOSE_DISTANCE ):
            bothFrontLEDSOn("BLUE")
            if (DEBUG):
                print("Continue straight ={:6.2f}cm"
                        .format(current_distance))
            if (current_distance > 300):
                # verify distance
                current_distance = RI.fetchUltraDistance()
                if (current_distance > 300):
                    # move faster
                    RI.motorForward(90,1.0)
            else:
                RI.motorForward(90,0.50)
            turnCount = 0

        else:
            if (DEBUG):
                print("distance close enough so turn ={:6.2f}cm"
                        .format(current_distance))
            bothFrontLEDSOn("RED")
            # now determine which way to turn
            # turn = 0 turn left
            # turn = 1 turn right
            turn = randint(0,1)

            if (turn == 0): # turn left
                # we turn the wheels right since
                # we are backing up
                RI.wheelsRight()
            else:
```

```python
            # turn right

                # we turn the wheels left since
                # we are backing up
                RI.wheelsLeft()

        time.sleep(0.5)
        RI.motorBackward(100,1.00)
        time.sleep(0.5)
        RI.wheelsMiddle()
        turnCount = turnCount+1
        print("Turn Count =", turnCount)

    # check for stuck car
    if (checkForStuckCar(current_distance,
        previous1distance, previous2distance)):
        # we are stuck.  Try back up and try Random turn
        bothFrontLEDSOn("RED")
        if (DEBUG):
            print("Stuck - Recovering ={:6.2f}cm"
                    .format(current_distance))
        RI.wheelsMiddle()
        RI.motorBackward(100,1.00)

        # now determine which way to turn
        # turn = 0 turn left
        # turn = 1 turn right
        turn = randint(0,1)


        if (turn == 0): # turn left
            # we turn the wheels right since
            # we are backing up
            RI.wheelsRight()
        else:
            # turn right

            # we turn the wheels left since
            # we are backing up
            RI.wheelsLeft()
        time.sleep(0.5)
        RI.motorBackward(100,2.00)
        time.sleep(0.5)
        RI.wheelsMiddle()


    # load state for distances
    previous2distance = previous1distance
    previous1distance = current_distance
```

```
            # Now check for stopping our program
            time.sleep(0.1)
            if (turnCount > REPEAT_TURN-1):
                bothFrontLEDSOn("RED")
                if (DEBUG):
                    print("too many turns in a row")
                Quit = True


except KeyboardInterrupt:
    print("program interrupted")


print ("program finished")
```

This seems to be a much more complex program than our ultrasonic sensor program earlier in this chapter, but it is really not.

We took the same structure of the program (the while loop) and added several features.

First, we added a clause to speed up the car when we were far away from an obstacle (over 300cm):

```
        if (current_distance >= CLOSE_DISTANCE ):
            bothFrontLEDSOn("BLUE")
            if (DEBUG):
                print("Continue straight ={:6.2f}cm"
                        .format(current_distance))
            if (current_distance > 300):
                # verify distance
                current_distance = RI.fetchUltraDistance()
                if (current_distance > 300):
                    # move faster
                    RI.motorForward(90,1.0)
            else:
                RI.motorForward(90,0.50)
            turnCount = 0
```

We continued to move in short little hops as the robot gets closer to the wall. When the robot gets within about 10cm of the wall, the robot decides to turn its front wheels in a random direction and backs up to try a new direction:

```
        if (DEBUG):
            print("distance close enough so turn ={:6.2f}cm"
                    .format(current_distance))
        bothFrontLEDSOn("RED")
        # now determine which way to turn
        # turn = 0 turn left
```

```
# turn = 1 turn right
turn = randint(0,1)


if (turn == 0): # turn left
    # we turn the wheels right since
    # we are backing up
    RI.wheelsRight()
else:
    # turn right

    # we turn the wheels left since
    # we are backing up
    RI.wheelsLeft()

time.sleep(0.5)
RI.motorBackward(100,1.00)
time.sleep(0.5)
RI.wheelsMiddle()
turnCount = turnCount+1
print("Turn Count =", turnCount)
```

We ran the robot for quite a while with just this logic, and we would see it get stuck if part of the robot was blocked, but the ultrasonic sensor was still picking up greater than 10cm distance.

To fix this, we added a running record of the past two ultrasonic distance readings, and if you had three readings +/- 2.0cm, then the robot would decide it was stuck and back up, turn randomly, and proceed again to wandering. Worked like a champ:

```
if (checkForStuckCar(current_distance,
    previous1distance, previous2distance)):
    # we are stuck.  Try back up and try Random turn
    bothFrontLEDSOn("RED")
    if (DEBUG):
        print("Stuck - Recovering ={:6.2f}cm"
            .format(current_distance))
    RI.wheelsMiddle()
    RI.motorBackward(100,1.00)

    # now determine which way to turn
    # turn = 0 turn left
    # turn = 1 turn right
    turn = randint(0,1)
```

```
        if (turn == 0): # turn left
            # we turn the wheels right since
            # we are backing up
            RI.wheelsRight()
        else:
            # turn right

            # we turn the wheels left since
            # we are backing up
            RI.wheelsLeft()
        time.sleep(0.5)
        RI.motorBackward(100,2.00)
        time.sleep(0.5)
        RI.wheelsMiddle()
```

We set the robot down in a room that has furniture and a complex set of walls and let it loose. Here are the results from the console:

```
Simple Robot Brain
Continue straight =115.44cm
Continue straight =108.21cm
Continue straight =101.67cm
Continue straight = 95.67cm
Continue straight = 88.13cm
Continue straight = 79.85cm
Continue straight = 70.58cm
Continue straight = 63.89cm
Continue straight = 54.36cm
Continue straight = 44.65cm
Continue straight = 36.88cm
Continue straight = 28.32cm
Continue straight = 21.10cm
distance close enough so turn = 11.33cm
Turn Count = 1
Continue straight = 33.75cm
Continue straight = 25.12cm
distance close enough so turn = 18.20cm
Turn Count = 1
Continue straight = 40.51cm
Continue straight = 33.45cm
Continue straight = 24.73cm
distance close enough so turn = 14.83cm
Turn Count = 1
Continue straight = 35.72cm
Continue straight = 26.13cm
distance close enough so turn = 18.56cm
```

```
Turn Count = 1
Continue straight = 43.63cm
Continue straight = 37.74cm
Continue straight = 27.33cm
Continue straight = 84.01cm
```

You can see the robot drive towards a wall and then turn several times to find a way out and then continue on. in the video here: `https://youtu.be/U7_FJzRbsRw`.

# A Better Robot Brain Architecture

If you look at the *robotBrain.py* software from an software architectural perspective, one thing jumps out. The main part of the program is a single `while` loop that polls the sensor (the ultrasonic sensor) and then does one thing at a time (moves, turns, and so on) and then polls it again. This leads to the somewhat jerky behavior of the robot (move a little, sense, move a little, sense, and so on). Although this is the simplest architecture we could use for our example, there are better, albeit more complicated, ways of doing this that are beyond the scope of our project today.

These better architectures are based on what are called *threads*. You can think of threads as separate programs that run at the same time and communicate to each other by using things called *semaphores* and *data queues*. Semaphores and data queues are simply methods by which a thread can communicate with other threads in a safe manner. Because both threads are running at the same time, you have to be careful how they talk and exchange information. This is not complicated, if you follow the rules.

A better architecture for our robot brain would be like this:

>> **Motor thread:** This thread controls the motors. It makes them run on command and can stop the motors anytime.

>> **Sensor thread:** This thread reads the ultrasonic sensor (and any other sensors you may have) periodically so you always have the current distance available.

>> **Head thread:** This thread controls the head servos using commands from the Command thread.

>> **Command thread:** This is the brains of software. It takes current information from the Sensor thread and sends commands to the motors and head to their respective thread.

This architecture leads to a much smoother operation of the robot. You can have the motors running while you are taking sensor values and sending commands simultaneously. This is the architecture that is used in the Adeept software `server.py` file included with the PiCar-B.

## Overview of the Included Adeept Software

The Adeept software supplied with the robot (see Figure 3-1) is primarily a client/ server model in which the client is a control panel on another computer and the server runs on the Raspberry Pi on PiCar-B. The control panel allows you to control the robot remotely and has a lot of interesting features, such as object tracking using OpenCV and a radarlike ultrasonic mapping capability. You can also see the video coming from the robot and use that to navigate manually.

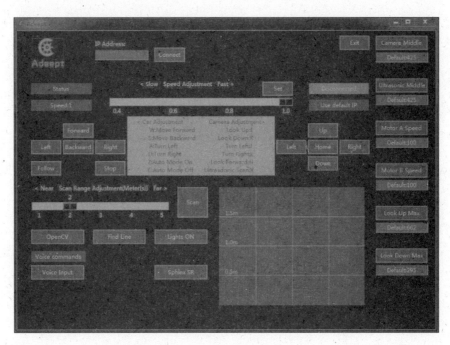

**FIGURE 3-1:**
Adeept remote
control software.

It is pretty complicated to install, however, so pay close attention to the instructions.

The software is definitely fun to use, but it does not require any real programming. The software is all open source, so you can look inside to see how they are doing things. Especially check out `server.py` under the server directory and look at the way they use threading to get smooth motion out of the robot.

## Where to Go from Here?

You now have a small robot that can display quite complex behavior based on the ultrasonic sensor built in. You can add a lot to this robot in terms of adding sensors to the Raspberry Pi. (How about a laser distance finder? Bumper sensors? Light conditions?) Refer back to Book 6 and combine some of the motors and sensors you used there with this robot. Because we choose the PiCar-B, you can plug the Pi2Grover on top of the motor controller so you can use all the Grove devices you have accumulated.

The sky is the limit!

# Chapter **4**

# Using Artificial Intelligence in Robotics

*"Artificial Intelligence (AI) is the theory and development of computer systems able to perform tasks that normally require human intelligence, such as visual perception, speech recognition, decision-making, and translation between languages."*

—DICTIONARY.COM

So, AI is meant to replace people? Well, not really. Modern AI looks to enhance machine intelligence at certain tasks that are normally done by people. Even saying the words "machine intelligence" is somewhat of a misnomer because it is hard to claim that machines have intelligence at all, at least as we think of it in people.

Instead of the philosophical debate, let's focus on how to use some modern AI techniques in a real robot example.

**REMEMBER** For a better overview of AI and some of the philosophy involved, check out Book 4.

So, what AI technique can we use in our robotic car? Turns out there is a Pi camera on the car, and computer vision is really hard, so let's do something with that.

TIP

Making robots see is easy, but making them understand what they are seeing is exceptionally hard. If you want to study up on computer vision using Python, check out *Computer Vision Projects with OpenCV and Python 3* by Matthew Rever.

# This Chapter's Project: Going to the Dogs

In this chapter, we show you how to build a machine-learning neural network and train it to recognize cats versus dogs. (This is a skill all robots should have.)

We will train the network using a 1,000-image subset of the 25,000 element database of pictures of cats and dogs from the Kaggle cats and dog database using TensorFlow.

TensorFlow is a Python package that is also designed to support neural networks based on matrices and flow graphs. It is similar to NumPy, but it differs in one major respect: TensorFlow is designed for use in machine learning and AI applications, and so it has libraries and functions designed for those applications.

TIP

If you need to, refer back to Book 4 as it has extensive information and examples about using TensorFlow in Python and on the Raspberry Pi.

# Setting Up the Project

For the Windows, Linux, and the Raspberry Pi check out this official TensorFlow link: `https://www.tensorflow.org/install/pip`. Download TensorFlow and install according to the directions.

Download the truncated list of the Cats and Dogs database here: `https://github.com/switchdoclabs/CatsAndDogsTruncatedData`. It is about 65mb and is included with our software at dummies.com.

TIP

For more experimentation, download the full Cats and Dogs dataset from this link: `https://www.kaggle.com/c/dogs-vs-cats-redux-kernels-edition/data`. Another source of the full data is: `https://www.microsoft.com/en-us/download/details.aspx?id=54765`.

Unzip the main folder and then unzip the `test.zip` and the `train.zip` subfolders. Test contains test images that have not been classified, and `train` contains our training data that we will use to train our neural network.

Run the following command in your program directory to download the data:

```
git clone https://github.com/switchdoclabs/CatsAndDogsTruncatedData.git
```

Now that we have our data ready, let's go train that network.

# Machine Learning Using TensorFlow

Our goal in this section is to fully train our machine learning neural network on the difference between cats and dogs, validate the test data and then save the trained neural network so we can actually use it on our robot. Then the real fun will begin!

**TIP**

When you run the following program, if you see `ImportError: No module named 'seaborn'`, type `sudo pip3 install seaborn`.

We starting using a pretty simple two-layer neural network for our cats and dogs machine learning network. There are many more complex networks available and may give better results, but we were hoping this would be good enough for our needs.

There is also the option of using a much larger dataset (our training dataset has 1,000 cats and 1,000 dogs but over 25,000 images are available in the full dataset).

Using a simple two-layer neural network on the cats and dog dataset did not really work very well because we achieved only about a 51 percent detection rate (50 percent is as good as just guessing randomly) so we needed to go to a more complex neural network that works better on complex images.

You can use CNN (convolutional neural networks) in place of simple neural networks, data augmentation (increasing the training samples by rotating, shifting, and zooming that pictures) and a variety of other techniques that are beyond the scope of this book. We are going to use a pretty standard six-layer CNN instead of our simple neural network.

We changed the model layers in our program to use the following six-level convolutional layer model. You just have to love how easy Keras and TensorFlow makes it to dramatically change the neural network.

## CONVOLUTIONAL NEURAL NETWORKS

CNNs work by scanning images and analyzing them chunk by chunk, say at a 5x5 window that moves by a stride length of two pixels each time until it spans the entire message. It's like looking at an image using a microscope; you see only a small part of the picture at any one time, but eventually you see the whole picture. Every time we loop through the data is called an *epoch*.

Going to a CNN network on a Raspberry Pi increased the single epoch time to 1,000 seconds from the 10-seconds epoch we had on the simple two-layer network. And it has a CPU utilization of 352 percent, which means it is using 3.5 cores on the Raspberry Pi, a machine that only has a total of 4. This amounts to a pretty high utilization of the Raspberry Pi 3B+. The little board is using almost 3.8W up from about 1.5W normally.

You can see the complexity of our new network by looking at the `model.summary()` results:

```
Layer (type)                    Output Shape            Param #
=================================================================
conv2d (Conv2D)                 (None, 150, 150, 32)    896

max_pooling2d (MaxPooling2D)    (None, 75, 75, 32)      0

conv2d_1 (Conv2D)               (None, 75, 75, 32)      9248

max_pooling2d_1 (MaxPooling2     (None, 37, 37, 32)      0

conv2d_2 (Conv2D)               (None, 37, 37, 64)      18496

max_pooling2d_2 (MaxPooling2     (None, 18, 18, 64)      0

dropout (Dropout)               (None, 18, 18, 64)      0

flatten (Flatten)               (None, 20736)           0

dense (Dense)                   (None, 64)              1327168

dropout_1 (Dropout)             (None, 64)              0

dense_1 (Dense)                 (None, 2)               130
=================================================================
Total params: 1,355,938
Trainable params: 1,355,938
Non-trainable params: 0
```

# The code

```
#import libraries
import numpy as np
import matplotlib.pyplot as plt
import matplotlib.image as mpimg
import seaborn as sns
import tensorflow as tf
from tensorflow.python.framework import ops
from tensorflow.examples.tutorials.mnist import input_data
from PIL import Image
from tensorflow.keras.preprocessing.image import ImageDataGenerator

from tensorflow.keras.layers import *

# load data

img_width = 150
img_height = 150
train_data_dir = 'data/train'
valid_data_dir = 'data/validation'

datagen = ImageDataGenerator(rescale = 1./255)

train_generator = datagen.flow_from_directory(
                directory=train_data_dir,
                target_size=(img_width,img_height),
                classes=['dogs','cats'],
                class_mode='binary',
                batch_size=16)

validation_generator = datagen.flow_from_directory(directory=valid_data_dir,
                target_size=(img_width,img_height),
                classes=['dogs','cats'],
                class_mode='binary',
                batch_size=32)

# build model


model = tf.keras.Sequential()



model.add(Conv2D(32, (3, 3), input_shape=(150, 150, 3), padding='same',
    activation='relu'))
```

```
model.add(MaxPooling2D(pool_size=(2, 2)))

model.add(Conv2D(32, (3, 3), padding='same', activation='relu'))
model.add(MaxPooling2D(pool_size=(2, 2)))

model.add(Conv2D(64, (3, 3), activation='relu', padding='same'))
model.add(MaxPooling2D(pool_size=(2, 2)))

model.add(Dropout(0.25))
model.add(Flatten())
model.add(Dense(64, activation='relu'))
model.add(Dropout(0.5))
model.add(Dense(2, activation='softmax'))

model.compile(optimizer=tf.train.AdamOptimizer(),
                        loss='sparse_categorical_crossentropy',
                        metrics=['accuracy'])

print (model.summary())

# train model

print('starting training....')
history = model.fit_generator(generator=train_generator,
        steps_per_epoch=2048 // 16,epochs=20,
        validation_data=validation_generator,validation_steps=832//16)

print('training finished!!')


# save coefficients

model.save("CatsVersusDogs.trained")

# Get training and test loss histories
training_loss = history.history['loss']
accuracy = history.history['acc']
# Create count of the number of epochs
epoch_count = range(1, len(training_loss) + 1)

# Visualize loss history
plt.figure(0)
plt.plot(epoch_count, training_loss, 'r--')
plt.plot(epoch_count, accuracy, 'b--')
plt.legend(['Training Loss', 'Accuracy'])
plt.xlabel('Epoch')
plt.ylabel('History')
plt.grid(True)
plt.show(block=True);
```

Save the code into a file called CatsVersusDogs.py.

## Examining the code

The code has 93 lines. It's pretty amazing what we can do with so few lines of code.

**TIP**

If you want to learn more about neural networks and machine learning, refer back to Book 4.

First, we import all the libraries:

```
#import libraries
import numpy as np
import matplotlib.pyplot as plt
import matplotlib.image as mpimg
import seaborn as sns
import tensorflow as tf
from tensorflow.python.framework import ops
from tensorflow.examples.tutorials.mnist import input_data
from PIL import Image
from tensorflow.keras.preprocessing.image import ImageDataGenerator

from tensorflow.keras.layers import *
```

Next, we massage the data into tensors (matrices) for training through our neural network. The cat and dog images are stored under separate directories under data:

```
# load data

img_width = 150
img_height = 150
train_data_dir = 'data/train'
valid_data_dir = 'data/validation'

datagen = ImageDataGenerator(rescale = 1./255)

train_generator = datagen.flow_from_directory(
              directory=train_data_dir,
              target_size=(img_width,img_height),
              classes=['dogs','cats'],
              class_mode='binary',
              batch_size=16)
```

```
validation_generator = datagen.flow_from_directory(directory=valid_data_dir,
            target_size=(img_width,img_height),
            classes=['dogs','cats'],
            class_mode='binary',
            batch_size=32)
```

Now we build the neural network that forms the basis of the machine-learning model. It is a six-layer neural network:

```
# build model


model = tf.keras.Sequential()
```

The first layer is a 2D convolutional neural network that starts to extract features from the photograph. We are using the RELU (rectified linear unit) as the neuron activation function. This is quite common:

```
model.add(Conv2D(32, (3, 3), input_shape=(150, 150, 3), padding='same',
    activation='relu'))
```

This next layer, MaxPooling2D, simplifies the features found in the previous layer:

```
model.add(MaxPooling2D(pool_size=(2, 2)))
```

Next, another two layers of convolutional neural networks are added, each followed by a pooling layer:

```
model.add(Conv2D(32, (3, 3), padding='same', activation='relu'))
model.add(MaxPooling2D(pool_size=(2, 2)))

model.add(Conv2D(64, (3, 3), activation='relu', padding='same'))
model.add(MaxPooling2D(pool_size=(2, 2)))
```

One of the problems with neural networks is called "overfitting" — when the machine matches the data too closely such that the network won't match any new, slightly different pictures. Dropout layers help here by randomly setting input units to zero. We are removing 25 percent of the input units in this layer:

```
model.add(Dropout(0.25))
```

Now we flatten the data into a one-dimensional array and then use a final densely connected 64-neuron layer:

```
model.add(Flatten())
model.add(Dense(64, activation='relu'))
```

Next, drop out another 50 percent of the input units to help with overfitting:

```
model.add(Dropout(0.5))
```

And finally, our output layer "Cat or Dog":

```
model.add(Dense(2, activation='softmax'))

model.compile(optimizer=tf.train.AdamOptimizer(),
                        loss='sparse_categorical_crossentropy',
                        metrics=['accuracy'])

print (model.summary())

# train model
```

This training on 1,000 pictures takes about five hours on a Raspberry Pi 3B+:

```
print('starting training....')
history = model.fit_generator(generator=train_generator,
        steps_per_epoch=2048 // 16,epochs=20,
        validation_data=validation_generator,validation_steps=832//16)

print('training finished!!')
```

This next line of code saves the coefficients for use later. This saves five hours per run!

```
# save coefficients

model.save("CatsVersusDogs.trained")
```

Finally, we generate a graph using MatPlotLib that shows how the accuracy improves with each epoch:

```
# Get training and test loss histories
training_loss = history.history['loss']
accuracy = history.history['acc']
```

```
# Create count of the number of epochs
epoch_count = range(1, len(training_loss) + 1)

# Visualize loss history
plt.figure(0)
plt.plot(epoch_count, training_loss, 'r--')
plt.plot(epoch_count, accuracy, 'b--')
plt.legend(['Training Loss', 'Accuracy'])
plt.xlabel('Epoch')
plt.ylabel('History')
plt.grid(True)
plt.show(block=True);
```

## The results

**WARNING**

Install the h5py library before running this program. Otherwise the save statement will not work.

```
sudo apt-get install python-h5py
```

Showtime! Run the following command in your terminal window:

```
python3 CatsVersusDogs.py
```

It takes about five hours on a Raspberry Pi 3B+ to generate 20 epochs of training and save the results into our CatsVersusDogs.training file. A snapshot of the last epoch is as follows:

```
Epoch 20/20
128/128 [==============================] - 894s 7s/step - loss: 0.0996 - acc:
    0.9609 - val_loss: 1.1069 - val_acc: 0.7356
training finished!!
```

**TIP**

You can safely ignore warnings from TensorFlow, such as:

```
/usr/lib/python3.5/importlib/_bootstrap.py:222: RuntimeWarning: compiletime
    version 3.4 of module 'tensorflow.python.framework.fast_tensor_util' does not
    match runtime version 3.5
    return f(*args, **kwds)
/usr/lib/python3.5/importlib/_bootstrap.py:222: RuntimeWarning: builtins.type
    size changed, may indicate binary incompatibility. Expected 432, got 412
    return f(*args, **kwds)
```

This will be fixed in an upcoming version.

After the five-hour-long training, we achieved an accuracy of 96 percent! Pretty good. Figure 4-1 shows how the accuracy improved during training.

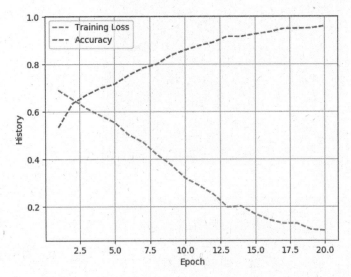

**FIGURE 4-1:**
Cats and dogs recognition accuracy per epoch.

By the shape of the curve, we might have been able to get a little better by running more epochs, but this is good enough for our example.

# Testing the Trained Network

Time to do a test on an external cat/dog image.

We're going to use the trained data from our neural network training session above to do a couple of predictions on new pictures to the neural network.

We chose the cat picture (see Figure 4-2) because it is a low-contrast picture, whereas the dog is pretty much a standard dog picture (see Figure 4-3).

**FIGURE 4-2:**
Panther the
Cat on salmon.

**FIGURE 4-3:**
Winston the Dog.

## The code

```
#import libraries
import numpy as np
import tensorflow as tf
from tensorflow.python.framework import ops
from PIL import Image
```

```
print("import complete")
# load model

img_width = 150
img_height = 150

class_names = ["Dog", "Cat"]

model = tf.keras.models.load_model(
    "CatsVersusDogs.trained",compile=True)
print (model.summary())

# do cat single image
imageName = "Cat150x150.jpeg"
testImg = Image.open(imageName)
testImg.load()
data = np.asarray( testImg, dtype="float" )

data = np.expand_dims(data, axis=0)
singlePrediction = model.predict(data, steps=1)

NumberElement = singlePrediction.argmax()
Element = np.amax(singlePrediction)
print(NumberElement)
print(Element)
print(singlePrediction)

print ("Our Network has concluded that the file '"
    +imageName+"' is a "+class_names[NumberElement])
print (str(int(Element*100)) + "% Confidence Level")

# do dog single image
imageName = "Dog150x150.JPG"
testImg = Image.open(imageName)
testImg.load()
data = np.asarray( testImg, dtype="float" )

data = np.expand_dims(data, axis=0)
singlePrediction = model.predict(data, steps=1)

NumberElement = singlePrediction.argmax()
Element = np.amax(singlePrediction)
print(NumberElement)
print(Element)
print(singlePrediction)

print ("Our Network has concluded that the file '"
    +imageName+"' is a "+class_names[NumberElement])
print (str(int(Element*100)) + "% Confidence Level")
```

# Explaining the code

This code uses the training that we generated by training with the cats and dogs dataset earlier in this chapter.

First, we import our libraries:

```
#import libraries
import numpy as np
import tensorflow as tf
from tensorflow.python.framework import ops
from PIL import Image

print("import complete")
# load model

img_width = 150
img_height = 150
```

We set up the class name array so we have classification names for our images:

```
class_names = ["Dog", "Cat"]
```

Here is the place where we load the training data that we generated earlier for the neural network machine learning model:

```
model = tf.keras.models.load_model(
        "CatsVersusDogs.trained",compile=True)
print (model.summary())
```

Now, we test a single cat image:

```
# do cat single image
imageName = "Cat150x150.jpeg"
testImg = Image.open(imageName)
testImg.load()
```

Convert to a NumPy tensor:

```
data = np.asarray( testImg, dtype="float" )
```

Expand the dimension, since this function looks for an array of images:

```
data = np.expand_dims(data, axis=0)
```

Now, we do the predication based on our image:

```
singlePrediction = model.predict(data, steps=1)
```

We print out the raw data:

```
NumberElement = singlePrediction.argmax()
Element = np.amax(singlePrediction)
print(NumberElement)
print(Element)
```

```
print(singlePrediction)
```

Interpret the prediction:

```
print ("Our Network has concluded that the file '"
        +imageName+"' is a "+class_names[NumberElement])
print (str(int(Element*100)) + "% Confidence Level")
```

Next, we do the same with a single dog image:

```
# do dog single image
imageName = "Dog150x150.JPG"
testImg = Image.open(imageName)
testImg.load()
data = np.asarray( testImg, dtype="float" )

data = np.expand_dims(data, axis=0)
singlePrediction = model.predict(data, steps=1)

NumberElement = singlePrediction.argmax()
Element = np.amax(singlePrediction)
print(NumberElement)
print(Element)
print(singlePrediction)

print ("Our Network has concluded that the file '"
        +imageName+"' is a "+class_names[NumberElement])
print (str(int(Element*100)) + "% Confidence Level")
```

## The results

Save the code into singleTestImage.py and run using sudo python3 singleTest
Image.py.

Here are the results:

```
import complete
WARNING:tensorflow:No training configuration found in save file: the model
    was *not* compiled. Compile it manually.

_____
Layer (type)                 Output Shape              Param #
=================================================================
conv2d (Conv2D)              (None, 150, 150, 32)      896
_____
max_pooling2d (MaxPooling2D) (None, 75, 75, 32)        0
_____
conv2d_1 (Conv2D)            (None, 75, 75, 32)        9248
_____
max_pooling2d_1 (MaxPooling2 (None, 37, 37, 32)        0
_____
conv2d_2 (Conv2D)            (None, 37, 37, 64)        18496
_____
max_pooling2d_2 (MaxPooling2 (None, 18, 18, 64)        0
_____
dropout (Dropout)            (None, 18, 18, 64)        0
_____
flatten (Flatten)            (None, 20736)             0
_____
dense (Dense)                (None, 64)                1327168
_____
dropout_1 (Dropout)          (None, 64)                0
_____
dense_1 (Dense)              (None, 2)                 130
=================================================================
Total params: 1,355,938
Trainable params: 1,355,938
Non-trainable params: 0
_____
None
1
1.0
[[ 0.  1.]]
Our Network has concluded that the file 'Cat150x150.jpeg' is a Cat
100% Confidence Level
0
1.0
[[ 1.  0.]]
Our Network has concluded that the file 'Dog150x150.JPG' is a Dog
100% Confidence Level
```

Well, this network worked very well. It identified both the cat and dog as their respective species. See the 100 percent confidence intervals? It is actually like

99.99 percent or something like that and is just rounded to 100 percent by the formatting.

Now that we have the trained model and have tested it with some real images, it is time to put it into our robot and use the Pi camera for some dog and cat investigation.

WARNING

A real limitation of the way we built this neural network is that it really is only looking at images of cats and dogs and determining whether the image is a cat or dog. However, the network classifies *everything* as either a cat or dog. If we were to build a more comprehensive network, we would have to train it to differentiate between a cat, a dog, or a dress, for example. (See Figure 4-4.) We ran one more test of the network using the much maligned dress picture from Book 4.

FIGURE 4-4:
A picture
of a dress?

And, as expected, the network got it wrong:

```
Our Network has concluded that the file 'Dress150x150.JPG' is a Cat
```

There is a lot more to the practice of teaching a machine to learn in a general manner.

TIP

If you get an error such as: undefined symbol: cblas_sgemm from your import numpy, try running your program with sudo.

# Taking Cats and Dogs to Our Robot

Time to add a new experience to last chapter's robot. We are going to install the trained cats and dogs neural network on the PiCar-B robot and use the onboard LEDs to display whether the onboard Pi camera is looking at a cat or a dog.

As mentioned earlier, our neural network classifies just about everything as a cat or a dog. So, what we are going to do is trigger the neural network classification when the ultrasonic sensor changes, such as when a dog or cat may walk in front of the robot.

Our test setup, because John's cat would not cooperate, is shown in Figure 4-5. It has the robot staring at the screen (triggering the ultrasonic sensor) showing a PowerPoint presentation of various cats and dogs.

**FIGURE 4-5:**
Robot vision neural network test setup.

## The code

```
#!/usr/bin/python3
#using a neural network with the Robot

#import libraries
import numpy as np
import tensorflow as tf
```

```
from tensorflow.python.framework import ops
from PIL import Image


import RobotInterface
import time
import picamera


print("import complete")
RI = RobotInterface.RobotInterface()

# load neural network model

img_width = 150
img_height = 150


class_names = ["Dog", "Cat"]
model = tf.keras.models.load_model("CatsVersusDogs.trained",compile=True)



RI.centerAllServos()
RI.allLEDSOff()

# Ignore distances greater than one meter
DISTANCE_TO_IGNORE = 1000.0
# How many times before the robot gives up
DETECT_DISTANCE = 60

def bothFrontLEDSOn(color):
    RI.allLEDSOff()
    if (color == "RED"):
        RI.set_Front_LED_On(RI.right_R)
        RI.set_Front_LED_On(RI.left_R)
        return
    if (color == "GREEN"):
        RI.set_Front_LED_On(RI.right_G)
        RI.set_Front_LED_On(RI.left_G)
        return
    if (color == "BLUE"):
        RI.set_Front_LED_On(RI.right_B)
        RI.set_Front_LED_On(RI.left_B)
        return
```

```python
def checkImageForCat(testImg):

    # check dog single image
    data = np.asarray( testImg, dtype="float" )

    data = np.expand_dims(data, axis=0)
    singlePrediction = model.predict(data, steps=1)

    print ("single Prediction =", singlePrediction)
    NumberElement = singlePrediction.argmax()
    Element = np.amax(singlePrediction)

    print ("Our Network has concluded that the file '"
        +imageName+"' is a "+class_names[NumberElement])

    return class_names[NumberElement]

try:
    print("starting sensing")
    Quit = False
    trigger_count = 0
    bothFrontLEDSOn("RED")

    #RI.headTiltPercent(70)
    camera = picamera.PiCamera()
    camera.resolution = (1024, 1024)
    camera.start_preview(fullscreen=False,
        window=(150,150,100,100))
    # Camera warm-up time
    time.sleep(2)

    while (Quit == False):

        current_distance = RI.fetchUltraDistance()
        print ("current_distance = ", current_distance)
        if (current_distance < DETECT_DISTANCE):
            trigger_count = trigger_count + 1
            print("classifying image")


            camera.capture('FrontView.jpg')
            imageName = "FrontView.jpg"
            testImg = Image.open(imageName)
            new_image = testImg.resize((150, 150))
            new_image.save("FrontView150x150.jpg")
```

```
            if (checkImageForCat(new_image) == "Cat"):
                bothFrontLEDSOn("GREEN")
            else:
                bothFrontLEDSOn("BLUE")


            time.sleep(2.0)
            bothFrontLEDSOn("RED")
            time.sleep(7.0)

except KeyboardInterrupt:
        print("program interrupted")


print ("program finished")
```

## How it works

Most of the preceding code is pretty straightforward and similar to the robot brain software earlier in the chapter. One part does deserve to be talked about, however, and that is our classifier function:

```
def checkImageForCat(testImg):

    # check dog single image
    data = np.asarray( testImg, dtype="float" )

    data = np.expand_dims(data, axis=0)
    singlePrediction = model.predict(data, steps=1)

    print ("single Prediction =", singlePrediction)
    NumberElement = singlePrediction.argmax()
    Element = np.amax(singlePrediction)

    print ("Our Network has concluded that the file '"
        +imageName+"' is a "+class_names[NumberElement])

    return class_names[NumberElement]
```

This function takes the incoming test vision (taken from the Pi camera and then resized into an 150 x 150 pixel image — the format required by our neural network).

## The results

Save the program into a file called robotVision.py and run the program — sudo python3 robotVision.py — to get your machine to start looking for cats. You really should run this program on the Raspberry Pi GUI so you can see the small camera preview on the screen.

Here is some results from our test setup in Figure 4-5:

```
current_distance =  20.05481719970703
classifying image
single Prediction = [[ 0.  1.]]
Our Network has concluded that the file 'FrontView.jpg' is a Cat
100.00% Confidence Level
current_distance =  20.038604736328125
classifying image
single Prediction = [[ 1.  0.]]
Our Network has concluded that the file 'FrontView.jpg' is a Dog
100.00% Confidence Level
current_distance =  19.977807998657227
```

Overall, the results were pretty good. We found variations in recognition due to lighting, which wasn't a big surprise. However, the network consistently identified one picture as a dog that was actually a cat. (See Figure 4-6.)

We suspect it is the folded ears, but one of the really hard things about figuring out what is wrong with a neural network machine learning model like this is there is no way to really know how the machine made its decision. Looking at the network you can look at 1.3 *million* parameters and weights and you can't tell where it is going wrong. After a while, you get a feel for what works and what doesn't in machine learning, but as for figuring out what this network is doing exactly wrong, you are just out of luck.

**FIGURE 4-6:**
The cat who is apparently a dog.

We have a nefarious plan here for a variant of this neural network in the future. We're going to use it on a new project, the Raspberry Pi based MouseAir, that will launch toy mice when the camera spots a cat but not when it spots a dog. You can see the Pi camera at the top-right corner of the Figure 4-7. That should definitely be fun.

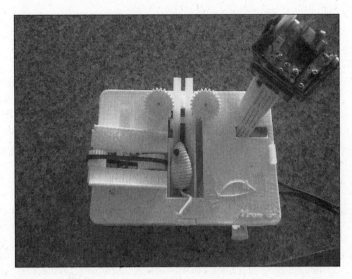

**FIGURE 4-7:**
MouseAir, an AI
mouse-launching
cat toy.

# Other Things You Can Do with AI Techniques and the Robot

As part of an advanced Python brain on the PiCar-B, there are a number of things you could do with neural networks and other AI techniques. Here are a few examples:

## Cat/Not Cat

Retrain our Cat/Dog network to focus only on cats; it lumps everything else into the "Not Cat" category. You can kind of do that with the current network because this training set tends to somewhat classify anything that doesn't look like a cat as a dog. It doesn't do that all the time though. Remember the dress picture in Figure 4-4 (classified as a cat by our network)?

## Santa/Not Santa

Take the streaming video from our Raspberry Pi and grab a frame once in a while and check with a neural network (trained on Santa images) to determine whether Santa is here for Christmas. Impossible! No, wait. It's been done in a very cool series of articles here: https://www.pyimagesearch.com/2017/12/18/keras-deep-learning-raspberry-pi/.

## Follow the ball

You can program the Raspberry Pi using a library called OpenCV (Open-Source Computer Vision) to detect a ball in your camera stream and give you the image coordinates. Then you can drive towards it. You can swivel the head and change the tilt to look for it too. A version of this project is part of the Adeept software included with the PiCar-B. You can see the source code inside of server.py under the server directory.

## Using Alexa to control your robot

You can use the power of the Amazon Alexa program to order your robot to do things. If you'd like to see how to connect up your Raspberry Pi to Alexa to do just that kind of project, check out the ebook *Voice Time: Connecting Your Raspberry Pi to the Amazon Alexa* by John Shovic.

# AI and the Future of Robotics

In our opinion, artificial intelligence is the future of robotics. As the hardware becomes less and less expensive and the software techniques more easily accessible, there will be more and more uses for robots, not only manufacturing but also in the home and on the road.

We expect to see new AI in many new consumer products in the coming years. The only question we have is "How long before we have AI in my toaster?" We'll buy one when they come out.

# Index

## Special Characters

## Numbers

# D

# W

# About the Author

**John Shovic** has been working with software and electronics since he talked his school into letting him use their IBM 1130 computer for the whole summer of 1973. That really launched him into his lifelong love affair with software. Dr. Shovic has founded multiple companies: Advance Hardware Architectures; TriGeo Network Security; Blue Water Technologies; InstiComm, LLC; and bankCDA. He has also served as a professor of computer science at Eastern Washington University, Washington State University, and the University of Idaho. Dr. Shovic has given over 70 invited talks and has published over 50 papers on a variety of topics on Arduinos, Raspberry Pis, iBeacons, HIPAA, GLB, computer security, computer forensics, embedded systems, and others. Currently John is proud to be serving as a computer science faculty member, specializing in robotics and artificial intelligence, at the University of Idaho, Coeur d'Alene, Idaho, and is surrounded by a bunch of students that are as excited about technology and computers as he is.

**Alan Simpson** is the author of over 100 computer books on database, programming, and web development. His books have been published throughout the world in over a dozen languages, and have sold millions of copies. Alan left the writing world a few years ago to get out of the ivory tower and into the real working world, first as a developer, and now as a manager, of the Apps and DBA team in his county government's IT department. Alan has been called a "master communicator" throughout his extensive career, and his online courses and YouTube videos continue to get rave reviews from his many students and followers.

# Author's Acknowledgments

**John Shovic:** I would like thank the wonderful staff at Wiley and give full credit to my co-author, Alan. Thanks to my literary agent Carol Jelen for encouraging me to pursue writing this book. I would like to specifically thank the University of Idaho for their support and suggestions, especially to Dr. Bob Rinker and Dean Larry Stauffer. Great people, great university. Also, no book like this would be complete without my thanking my fabulous students, especially Amanda, Adrian, and Doug, who inspire me every day and who had to listen to the chapters of this book as I wrote them. And of course, my cat Panther, who spent most of this book curled up on my lap.

**Alan Simpson:** Many thanks to Steve Hayes and everyone else at Wiley for offering me this great opportunity. Thanks to Christopher Morris, my intrepid editor. Thanks to my literary agents Carol Jelen and Margot Maley Hutchinson of Waterside Productions. And thanks to my wife Susan for her patience while I was working at all kinds of crazy hours.

# Dedication

**John Shovic:** To my wife, Laurie. She has supported me in so many ways including making sure my socks match in the morning. Thank you!

**Alan Simpson:** To Susan, Ashley, and Alec.

## Publisher's Acknowledgments

**Executive Editor:** Steve Hayes
**Project Editor:** Christopher Morris
**Copy Editor:** Christopher Morris

**Technical Editor:** Russ Mullen
**Production Editor:** Vasanth Koilraj
**Cover Image:** © matejmo/iStock.com

# PERSONAL ENRICHMENT

**Staying Sharp**
9781119187790
USA $26.00
CAN $31.99
UK £19.99

**Facebook**
9781119179030
USA $21.99
CAN $25.99
UK £16.99

**Guitar**
9781119293354
USA $24.99
CAN $29.99
UK £17.99

**Investing**
9781119293347
USA $22.99
CAN $27.99
UK £16.99

**Beekeeping**
9781119310068
USA $22.99
CAN $27.99
UK £16.99

**Digital Photography**
9781119235606
USA $24.99
CAN $29.99
UK £17.99

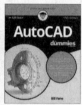

**Meditation**
9781119251163
USA $24.99
CAN $29.99
UK £17.99

**Pregnancy**
9781119235491
USA $26.99
CAN $31.99
UK £19.99

**Samsung Galaxy S7**
9781119279952
USA $24.99
CAN $29.99
UK £17.99

**iPhone**
9781119283133
USA $24.99
CAN $29.99
UK £17.99

**Crocheting**
9781119287117
USA $24.99
CAN $29.99
UK £16.99

**Nutrition**
9781119130246
USA $22.99
CAN $27.99
UK £16.99

# PROFESSIONAL DEVELOPMENT

**Windows 10**
9781119311041
USA $24.99
CAN $29.99
UK £17.99

**AutoCAD**
9781119255796
USA $39.99
CAN $47.99
UK £27.99

**Excel 2016**
9781119293439
USA $26.99
CAN $31.99
UK £19.99

**QuickBooks 2017**
9781119281467
USA $26.99
CAN $31.99
UK £19.99

**macOS Sierra**
9781119280651
USA $29.99
CAN $35.99
UK £21.99

**LinkedIn**
9781119251132
USA $24.99
CAN $29.99
UK £17.99

**Windows 10**
9781119310563
USA $34.00
CAN $41.99
UK £24.99

**SharePoint 2016**
9781119181705
USA $29.99
CAN $35.99
UK £21.99

**Fundamental Analysis**
9781119263593
USA $26.99
CAN $31.99
UK £19.99

**Networking**
9781119257769
USA $29.99
CAN $35.99
UK £21.99

**Office 2016**
9781119293477
USA $26.99
CAN $31.99
UK £19.99

**Office 365**
9781119265313
USA $24.99
CAN $29.99
UK £17.99

**Salesforce.com**
9781119239314
USA $29.99
CAN $35.99
UK £21.99

**Coding**
9781119293323
USA $29.99
CAN $35.99
UK £21.99

**dummies**
A Wiley Brand